"Bernard of Clairvaux has not been well served by his admirers. From the time of Geoffrey of Auxerre and his first biographers, his rich and complex career has been plundered by image-makers with a view to advancing their own agenda. The panegyrists of the seventeenth century, studied in this volume, were no exception. They sought to make the saint a mouthpiece for their own well-intentioned priorities and, in the process, created an image of Bernard that would feed the prejudices of later generations. *A Saint in the Sun* makes available a selection of these largely inaccessible texts and provides a wealth of contextualizing detail. This masterly study will serve to make clear this important phase in the history of the reception of Bernard's writing. David Bell is to be congratulated for throwing light on this neglected area of scholarly research."

> —Michael Casey, OCSO
> Tarrawarra Abbey, Australia

"Bernard of Clairvaux, spiritual and doctrinal councilor of popes, prelates, and princes, vanished in scholastic theological debate to be remembered during the late Middle Ages for his Marian devotion and battles with the devil. *A Saint in the Sun* reveals the Bernard of eloquent and erudite seventeenth-century French preachers. Their Bernard was neither theologian nor mystic but austere penitent and ardent defender of authority. Those who read *A Saint in the Sun* in tandem with James France's *The Medieval Images of Saint Bernard of Clairvaux* may well be alerted by this chameleon of passing ages against narrowly viewing bygone saints and heroes in the light of the preoccupations of their own age."

> —Dr. E. Rozanne Elder
> Professor Emerita
> University of Michigan

"This volume is vintage David Bell. It brims with verve and erudition. With its informed introductions and rich explanatory notes, Bell's collection of *grand-siècle* representations of Bernard of Clairvaux offers valuable insights for anybody interested in the fate of the medieval Cistercian through the ages or the religious landscape of Early Modern France."

    —Mette Birkedal Bruun
       Professor of Church History
       University of Copenhagen

CISTERCIAN STUDIES SERIES: NUMBER TWO HUNDRED SEVENTY-ONE

A Saint in the Sun

Praising Saint Bernard in the France of Louis XIV

David N. Bell

Cistercian Publications
www.cistercianpublications.org

LITURGICAL PRESS
Collegeville, Minnesota
www.litpress.org

A Cistercian Publications title published by Liturgical Press

Cistercian Publications
Editorial Offices
161 Grosvenor Street
Athens, Ohio 54701
www.cistercianpublications.org

Scripture texts, prefaces, introductions, footnotes, and cross references used in this work are translated by the author.

© 2017 by Order of Saint Benedict, Collegeville, Minnesota. All rights reserved. No part of this book may be reproduced in any form, by print, microfilm, microfiche, mechanical recording, photocopying, translation, or any other means, known or yet unknown, for any purpose except brief quotations in reviews, without the previous written permission of Liturgical Press, Saint John's Abbey, PO Box 7500, Collegeville, Minnesota 56321-7500. Printed in the United States of America.

Library of Congress Cataloging-in-Publication Data

Names: Bell, David N., 1943– editor, translator.
Title: A saint in the sun : praising Saint Bernard in the France of Louis XIV / David N. Bell.
Other titles: Saint Bernard in the France of Louis XIV
Description: Collegeville, Minnesota : Cistercian Publications, 2017. | Series: Cistercian studies ; 271 | Includes bibliographical references and index.
Identifiers: LCCN 2016051053 (print) | LCCN 2017011163 (ebook) | ISBN 9780879071714 (ebook) | ISBN 9780879072711 (paperback)
Subjects: LCSH: Bernard, of Clairvaux, Saint, 1090 or 1091-1153—Appreciation. | Bernard, of Clairvaux, Saint, 1090 or 1091-1153—Sermons—Translations into English. | Eulogies—France—Translations into English. | Eulogies—France—History and criticism. | Orators—France—Biography. | Christian saints—France—Biography. | France—Religion—17th century—Sources. | France—Politics and government—17th century—Religious aspects. | BISAC: RELIGION / Monasticism. | RELIGION / Religion, Politics & State. | RELIGION / Christianity / Saints & Sainthood.
Classification: LCC BX4700.B5 (ebook) | LCC BX4700.B5 S19 2017 (print) | DDC 271/.1202—dc23
LC record available at https://lccn.loc.gov/2016051053

Contents

List of Abbreviations vii

Preface xi

1 The Background 1

2 The Quietist Controversy 26

3 Sermons and Panegyrics 51

4 Paving the Way: Divisions and Subdivisions in Jacques Biroat 33

5 Moving Forward: Commonplaces and Curiosities in Jean-François Senault, Bernard Planchette, Claude Texier, and Jean-Louis de Fromentières 109

6 The Bernard of the Strict Observance: Armand-Jean de Rancé 147

7 Bernard Returns to Metz: Jacques-Bénigne Bossuet 185

8 Touching, Moving, Converting: The Unction of François Fénelon 236

9 Bernard in Battle: The Anti-Quietist Polemic of Charles de La Rue 271

10 The Flames Die Down: The Revised Panegyric of Charles de La Rue 320

11 Bernard the Mystic: Henri-Marie Boudon 354

12 Panegyrical Plagiarism? Claude Lion, François Ogier, and Esprit Fléchier 397

13 Last of the Fathers and the Angel of the Lord: Antoine Anselme and Louis-Bénigne Bourru 446

14 Bernard the Second Samuel: The Psychological Acuity of Jean-Baptiste Massillon   485

15 Conclusion: The Saint in the Sun   530

Appendix 1: Technical Terms   539

Appendix 2: Personalities   549

Bibliography   568

Index of Names and Places   574

Abbreviations

Albert / Court = Antoine Albert and Jean-François de Court. *Dictionnaire portatif des prédicateurs François*. Lyon: Pierre Bruyset Ponthus, 1757; repr. Geneva: Slatkine Reprints, 1970.

Apol = Athenagoras of Athens, *Apology*.

Bell, *Many Mansions* = David N. Bell. *Many Mansions. An Introduction to the Development and Diversity of Medieval Theology West and East*. Cistercian Studies 146. Kalamazoo and Spencer: Cistercian Publications, 1996.

CF = Cistercian Fathers series (Cistercian Publications).

CCCM = Corpus Christianorum, Continuatio Mediaevalis. Turnhout: Brepols Publishers.

CS = Cistercian Studies series (Cistercian Publications).

DBF = *Dictionnaire de biographie française*. Paris: Letouzey et Ané, 1933–.

Denzinger = Heinrich Denzinger. *Enchiridion symbolorum definitionum et declarationum de rebus fidei et morum. Compendium of Creeds, Definitions and Declarations on Matters of Faith and Morals. Latin – English*. Edited by Peter Hünermann. 43rd ed. San Francisco: Ignatius Press, 2012.

DHGE = *Dictionnaire d'histoire et de géographie ecclésiastiques*. Paris: Letouzey et Ané, 1912–.

DLF XVII = *Dictionnaire des lettres françaises. Le XVIIe siècle*. Edited by Patrick Dandrey. Paris: Fayard, 1951; repr. with revisions 1996.

DLF XVIII = *Dictionnaire des lettres françaises. Le XVIIIe siècle*. Edited by François Moureau. Paris: Fayard, 1960; repr. with revisions 1995.

DS = *Dictionnaire de spiritualité*. Paris: G. Beauchesne, 1937–1995.

DTC = *Dictionnaire de théologie catholique*. Paris: Letouzey et Ané, 1903–1972.

François = Jean François. *Bibliothèque générale des écrivains de l'Ordre de Saint Benoît*. Bouillon: Aux dépens de la Société Typographique, 1777–1778; repr. Louvain-Héverlé: Éditions de la Bibliothèque S. J., 1961.

Hurel = Augustin-Jean Hurel. *Les orateurs sacrés à la cour de Louis XIV*. 2nd ed. Paris: Didier et Cie, 1872.

Janauschek = Leopold Janauschek. *Bibliographia Bernardina*. Vienna: A. Hölder, 1891; repr. Hildesheim: G. Olms, 1959.

Le Maistre = [Antoine Le Maistre]. *La Vie de S. Bernard premier abbé de Clairvaux, et Père d'Église. Divisée en six livres*. Paris: A. Vitré et la veuve Martin Durand, 1648.

Maury = Jean Sifrein Maury. *Essai sur l'éloquence de la chaire, par le cardinal Jean Sifrein Maury. Édition publiée sur les manuscrits autographes de l'auteur*. Paris: A. Pigoreau, [1810].

PG = Patrologia Cursus Completus, Series Græca.

PL = Patrologia Cursus Completus, Series Latina.

RB = Rule of Saint Benedict.

SBOp = Sancti Bernardi Opera. Edited by Jean Leclercq, C. Hugh Talbot, Henri M. Rochais. Rome: Editiones Cistercienses, 1957–1977.

SCh = Sources chrétiennes.

Tréverret = Armand-Germain de Tréverret. *Du Panégyrique des Saints au XVIIe siècle*. Paris: Ernest Thorin, 1868.

Williams, Saint Bernard = Watkin W. Williams. *Saint Bernard of Clairvaux*. Manchester: Manchester University Press, 1935; repr. 1953.

Williams, Studies = Watkin W. Williams. *Studies in St. Bernard of Clairvaux*. London: SPCK; New York and Toronto: Macmillan, 1927.

Bernard's works

Csi   *De consideratione*. SBOp 3:379–493.

Dil   *De diligendo Deo*. SBOp 3:109–54.

Div   *Sermones de diversis*. SBOp 6/1:57–106.

Ep   *Epistolae*. SBOp 7–8.

Hum   *Liber de gradibus humilitatis et superbiæ*. SBOp 3:13–59.

Miss   *Homiliae super "Missus est" in Laudibus Virginis Matris*. SBOp 4:3–58.

OS   *Sermo in festivitate omnium sanctorum*. SBOp 5:327–70.

SC   *Sermo super Cantica canticorum*. SBOp 1–2.

Scriptural references are always to the Vulgate (including the enumeration of the Psalms), and all translations of the Vulgate text are my own. The panegyrists regularly quote their sources in Latin. All such quotations have been translated and appear in square brackets.

Preface

This collection of translations, summaries, and studies of seventeenth- and early eighteenth-century panegyrics on Saint Bernard began in a very limited way, with a translation of a single conference by Armand-Jean de Rancé. But then, having translated that, I thought it might be interesting to translate the very different discourse of Rancé's close friend, Jacques-Bénigne Bossuet, generally considered to be one of the greatest, if not the greatest, of the seventeenth-century French pulpit orators. Neither Rancé nor Bossuet, however, spoke of Bernard the mystic—it was always Bernard the ascetic, the great penitent, the defender of the church, the scourge of heretics—and so I decided to translate the remarkable panegyric of Henri-Marie Boudon, who, alone of the panegyrists, deals at length with Bernard's mystical experiences. This then led to a translation of Charles de La Rue's fiery polemic against Quietism, in which Bernard goes to battle against the so-called false mystics, Madame Guyon and Fénelon, but since this had been set beside La Rue's revised version of the same panegyric, I translated that as well.

And so one sermon led to another, and, since only one of the panegyrics—that of Bossuet—had ever been translated into English (and that only in an abridged version[1]), I decided to translate or, if full translation was not warranted, to summarize the great majority of the panegyrics on Bernard that had been preached in the France of Louis XIV. The Bernard they portray is not, for the most part, the popular Bernard of today—as I

---

[1] See chap. 7 (Bossuet), n. 30.

have said, Bernard the mystic tended to be carefully avoided—but those who are interested in how the abbot of Clairvaux was viewed and used (perhaps sometimes abused) in the France of the Sun King now have the primary material at their disposal in English.

Given that all the panegyrists used the same basic source—the *Vita prima S. Bernardi* in the editions of Horstius or Mabillon, or its French adaptation in Antoine Le Maistre's *Vie de S. Bernard* (matters to be considered in detail in chapter 1)—it is inevitable that a number of well-known scenarios from Bernard's life appear again and again, and that the same *dramatis personae* play their roles on the panegyrical stage.[2] This does not mean, however, that the panegyrics are all the same, any more than two buildings designed by two different architects will be the same because both are using the same basic materials. Jacques Biroat's approach, for example, is as different from that of Bossuet as Bossuet's is from Massillon's, and one of the pleasures I found in reading and translating these discourses was the way in which one could hear so clearly the individual voices of their authors.

Some of the panegyrics were easier to translate than others—I found those of Fénelon and Massillon the most difficult—and one must always bear in mind that the meaning of a particular word in seventeenth-century French and modern French may not be quite the same. *Sentiments*, for example, are not quite sentiments, and *crimes* tend to be sins, not crimes. There are many other such words, and there are also a number of important technical terms that appear again and again and that are listed and defined in appendix 1. All the translations, as distinct from the summaries, are complete translations—they are not abridged or paraphrased—and everything the writers wrote or the preachers preached has been translated. I have tried, as best I can, to render the stately French into stately

---

[2] See appendix 2, "Personalities."

English, but I fear that I cannot possibly have done justice to the fire of Charles de La Rue's first panegyric on Bernard, or the *onction* of Fénelon, or the tidal wave of words with which Massillon sweeps his listeners away.

The task of translation was made infinitely easier by the fact that with only two exceptions, every one of the editions needed was readily available on the internet, digitalized mainly by Google. The only exceptions were Bernard Velat's edition of Bossuet[3] and the excellent edition by Henri Chérot of La Rue's anti-Quietist attack on the ideas of Miguel de Molinos, Madame Guyon, and Fénelon.[4] It is perfectly possible, of course, that both may now be available. But for me, being stationed in Newfoundland, the old days of long and expensive travel to distant locations, and the hours spent in libraries, pencil in hand, are a thing of the past.

The panegyrists could obviously expect certain things of their audiences that we cannot, in general, expect nowadays. If, for example, they were preaching to a congregation of Feuillants—reformed Cistercians stricter in their observances than even the Strict Observance—they could expect their audience to be intimately familiar with Scripture, some parts more than others, equally familiar with the story of Bernard's life, and fairly familiar not only with Bernard's own writings but also with the writings of at least the four Doctors of the Latin Church: Augustine, Gregory the Great, Jerome, and Ambrose. Few readers today will share the same familiarity, and it has therefore been necessary to add numerous footnotes to indicate what is going on and how the argument is being developed. Sometimes these footnotes are necessarily copious.

Furthermore, in order to appreciate the content of the panegyrics—what is not included as well as what is—and the intentions of the preacher, it is essential to have some acquaintance with the nature of society in *le grand siècle*, the

---

[3] See chap. 7 (Bossuet), nn. 4 and 30.
[4] See chap. 9 (La Rue 1), n. 9.

attitude of the church to human sin and human frailty, the fear in so many quarters of mysticism and mystical experiences, and the popularity, importance, and structure of sermons in seventeenth-century France. These matters are discussed in the first three chapters, and they are essential reading if one wishes to come to any appreciation of what the preachers were trying to do. If this seems much to ask, readers should remember Luke 21:19, possess their souls in patience, and remember that when Madame de Sévigné and her friends went to one of the great Parisian churches to hear Bossuet or Bourdaloue, the preacher commonly preached for an hour and a quarter or an hour and a half. It was not an instant age, and the preacher would take his time in touching, moving, and converting the hearts of his audience. Some of the greatest preachers of the age are represented in these pages, though whether they still have the power to touch, move, and convert is a question that can be answered only by those who have the patience to read them.

It seems to me appropriate that the concluding chapter of this volume was written in the delightful cloister of the former Cistercian abbey of Fontaine-Vive, also known as Grosbot, near Charras in the southwest of France, a cloister that had been extensively rebuilt at just the time that many of these panegyrics were being delivered and that has since been superbly restored by Jonathan Clowes and Ann Evans, the present owners of the abbey. To them I offer my thanks for their generous hospitality. Much of the seventeenth-century work was completed by Jean de La Font, abbot of Grosbot from 1641 to his death on March 21, 1673, and his able prior, Dom François Pasquet,[5] and if there is anything of value in the pages that follow, it may surely be attributed to their benign influence.

---

[5] See Adolphe Mondon, *Notes historiques sur la Baronnie de Marthon en Angoumois* (Angoulême: G. Chasseignac, 1895–1897), 250–55.

1

The Background

The sun rose—that is to say, the future Louis XIV was born—at about a quarter past eleven in the morning of Sunday, September 5, 1638, in the splendid château of Saint-Germain-en-Laye, about twenty kilometers west of the center of Paris. The area is now one of the city's most exclusive and affluent suburbs. From an astrological point of view, the young Louis was therefore born under the sign of the Virgin, which means that, on the one hand, he should have been intelligent, devout, methodical, industrious, good at organizing, and open to reason, but, on the other, narrow-minded, hypocritical, interfering, suspicious, too censorious, and utterly convinced of the rightness of his own opinions. All things considered, it is not a bad summary.

His parents were Louis XIII and Anne of Austria, and since Louis XIII died in 1643 when his son was but five years old, his mother, Anne, served as regent until Louis himself reached his legal majority in 1651. Anne was aided and guided in her regency by Cardinal Mazarin, chief minister of France, who had succeeded to the position on the death of Cardinal Richelieu in 1642. Mazarin's policies were more successful on the international than the national stage, and he played a significant role in bringing an end to the Thirty Years' War with the Peace of Westphalia in 1648. Ten years later he negotiated the League of the Rhine, which was intended to check the ambitions of the Austrian house of Habsburg, and a year later, in 1659, he made peace with Habsburg Spain with the Peace of the Pyrenees. At home, however, he was unpopular with the French public, especially the Parisian public, and this unpopularity led to a violent uprising that began in January 1648. It was known as the Fronde, the French word for the slings used by the Paris mob to smash the windows of Mazarin's associates and supporters. The Fronde rapidly escalated into a civil war and lasted five years—five years of terrible suffering for the French people— until it finally fizzled out in the late summer of 1653. Louis was crowned king on June 7 of the following year, and if he learned anything from the disaster of the Fronde, it was the need for a strong centralized government with the reins of power firmly established in the person of an absolute monarch. When Mazarin died in 1661, that absolute monarch was Louis XIV, and so he remained until his death on September 1, 1715.

His reign was dominated by battle, war, and conquest carried out, for the most part, under a series of exceptionally talented commanders, and Louis himself was an effective, though overconfident, military leader. Unfortunately, wars cost money, and his ambitious and expansionist policies were economically disastrous for France. On the other hand, it was in the course of his long reign of more than seventy-two years that we see the true birth of *la gloire*, that rarefied yet real idea that still remains so important a part of the French mentality. Louis was an intelligent king, diligent, industrious, and unflagging in the exercise of his kingship, though in his old age he became ever more despotic and out of touch with public opinion. He was also, as is well known, a dedicated and discerning promoter of literature and the arts, and it was during his reign that France—and, indeed, all Europe—was illuminated by some of the greatest lights ever to grace the cultural stage.

In music there was the Couperin family, especially Louis and his nephew François, there was Jean-Philippe Rameau, there was Marc-Antoine Charpentier (a superb composer), and there was Jean-Baptiste Lully, who came to a sad and curious end. He was born in 1632, had attracted the attention of the young Louis, and by March 1653 had been appointed royal composer, where his contributions to the court ballets (a favorite form of entertainment) made him indispensable. He was the director of the *Petits Violons*, Louis's personal violin orchestra, but in later years he lost the royal favor: Lully was bisexual, and Louis did not approve of his homosexual encounters. Then, in 1687, when Lully was conducting his *Te Deum* to celebrate the king's recovery from a certain surgery, he struck his foot with the long baton with which he was beating time and drew blood. The performance, it seems, was not up to standard, and Lully was not pleased. The wound became infected, the infection turned to gangrene, and the gangrene brought about his death on March 22. He was buried in the basilica of Notre-Dame-des-Victoires in Paris, where his tomb, surmounted by a marble bust, may still be seen.

Lully had collaborated with Molière, and Molière was but one of the great names that graced the world of literature in the days of the Sun King. Others were Corneille, Racine, Boileau-Despréaux, La Fontaine, La Rochefoucauld, Girardon, Malherbe, Guez de Balzac, Descartes, Pascal, La Bruyère, Madame de Sévigné, Madame de La Fayette, a host of *mémorialistes*, including the best of them, Saint-Simon, and some of the greatest preachers ever to mount the steps of the pulpit. Some of them will appear in the pages of this book. It was an astonishing flowering of art and culture, and Louis's support for the arts was reflected not only in the realms of music and literature but also in architecture and landscape gardening (witness Versailles), sculpture, painting, building technology, and the decorative arts in general.

It was also the age of the *salons*, whose influence on French literature and society was immense. They were held in private houses, often weekly, presided over by the mistress of the house, and attended by many of the most notable literary and philosophical figures of the day. There were also *salons* attended only by the highest aristocracy, and others that catered to the most important financiers of the times. The intellectual *salons* appreciated purity, elegance, and beauty of language (low-class and barbarous words were to be avoided), polite manners, intelligence, and wit, and the subjects of conversation might include literature, religion, philosophy, art, politics, and, naturally, the most up-to-date gossip and talk of the town. The prototype of the *salon* was that held in the town house of Catherine de Vivonne, marquise de Rambouillet—the *Hôtel de Rambouillet*—who presided over her *salon* for more than thirty years. Most of the great conversationalists of the day attended at one time or another, and there is a story of the young Bossuet, then sixteen years old and a student at the Collège de Navarre, being asked to preach a sermon to the *literati* gathered at the *Hôtel*. The topic would be chosen for him and he was not permitted to consult any books. Having been given the topic and having pondered it for a few moments, the precocious teenager delivered a sermon that apparently won unqualified approval.[1] But as Ella Sanders has said, "this feat was too much of the nature of a drawing-room performance to be creditable, and its celebrity might have aroused all the latent vanity of youth."[2] It may be regarded, however, as good practice for one who would become the greatest preacher of his age, though Bossuet's panegyric on Saint Bernard does not reveal him at his best.

The century of the Sun King, *le grand siècle*, was also a century dominated by religion and the sense of sin. Religious literature enjoyed huge popularity, and we are told by Henri-Jean Martin that between 1598 and 1643 a third of all books printed in Paris were concerned with religion,[3] and that be-

---

[1] This well-known story appears in most biographies of Bossuet but has its beginnings in Tallemant des Réaux: see *Les Historiettes de Tallemant des Réaux*, ed. Georges Mongrédien (Paris: Garnier, 1931–1934), 3:38.

[2] Ella K. Sanders, *Jacques Bénigne Bossuet: A Study* (London: SPCK, 1921), 13.

[3] Henri-Jean Martin, *Print, Power, and People in 17th-Century France*, trans. David Gerard (Metuchen and London: Scarecrow Press, 1993), 73.

tween 1666 and 1700 this proportion had risen to over forty percent.[4] Much of this literature was devotional—it dealt with what we would now call spirituality, though that term was avoided at the time[5]—and it was not the warm, fuzzy, self-help type of spirituality so common today. Popular works offered arguments that could be both subtle and profound, and what they required might be demanding. Such works were generally in French (though any educated man and a lesser number of educated women had little or no difficulty with Latin), and there was an astonishing range of material.

Apart from the Bible and the great names of the patristic and medieval period (the *Imitation of Christ* was hugely popular), Capuchin and (especially) Jesuit authors produced vast amounts of devotional literature, virtually all of it calling for *pénitence*, which, in French, may mean "repentance," "penitence," or "penance," or, frequently, all three at the same time.[6] Hagiography was likewise popular, and the lives of saints, almost saints, miracle workers, and those considered in their time to have been just plain good delighted the publishers with their sales. Books on the life and miracles of the Virgin Mary were guaranteed to sell, although, as Martin has said, "many of the books about her were abysmal in their puerility."[7]

Collections of sermons were, it seems, somewhat less popular. Many of them were bought by parish priests, who did not always find themselves especially inspired and needed something to mine for good source material, but the literate public preferred to hear the great preachers rather than read them. This is understandable. It is one thing to read (for example) Martin Luther King's "I have a dream" speech from August 28, 1963; it is quite another thing to hear it. Senault, Bossuet, Mascaron, Fléchier, Massillon, and so many others

---

[4] Martin, *Print, Power, and People*, 529.
[5] See appendix 1, s.v. *spiritualité* / spirituality.
[6] See appendix 1, s.v. *pénitence* / penitence.
[7] Martin, *Print, Power, and People*, 99.

could draw huge audiences, and if their pulpit oratory emphasized, incessantly, the faults and vices of their listeners, and if, continually, they called on them to repent, their congregations were eager to be touched, moved, and converted.[8] In many, perhaps most cases, their conversion may not have lasted very long, and the tears that flowed so copiously (for it was an emotional and lachrymose age) would not take too long to dry. Yet in other cases, it lasted their whole lives. Armand-Jean le Bouthillier de Rancé left a life of luxury and pleasure to reform La Trappe and establish the Cistercian Strict Observance. Louise de La Vallière, the most moral of Louis XIV's mistresses, was converted by Bossuet, made a dramatic and public act of repentance, and ended her days as an exemplary Carmelite nun, Sister Louise de la Miséricorde, in the Carmelite convent on the Faubourg Saint-Jacques in Paris. In 1671 she had published her *Refléxions sur la miséricorde de Dieu,* which went through many editions and was translated into English and published in 1674 as *The Penitent Lady: or Reflections on the Mercy of God.*

The mercy of God was essential for a society soaked in sin, and to the matter of sin we must now turn our attention. The distinction between mortal and venial sin had been clearly established by Saint Thomas Aquinas and was (and is) standard catholic teaching. The difference is straightforward. Mortal sin refers to an act so grievous that it cuts one off entirely from the grace of God, and if one dies entirely cut off from the grace of God, the only place one can go is hell. A venial sin is anything less than this: however serious it may be, a little bit of grace may still trickle through, death is followed by the cleansing pains of purgatory, and the soul eventually takes its place in heaven. We need not here enter into the question of indulgences or the distinction between guilt and punishment. If those who have committed mortal sin wish to go to heaven, they must confess that sin and receive absolution before they

---

[8] *To touch, move,* and *convert* are all technical terms of French pulpit oratory, and we shall examine them in some detail in chap. 3.

die. This is not incumbent on those who have committed venial sins. In other words, the only way in which a Catholic can go to hell is if he or she dies in a state of unconfessed mortal sin. So what is a mortal sin?

For a sin to be so serious as to cut the sinner off entirely from the grace of God it must meet three conditions. First, it must involve what the church calls "a grave matter." Nowadays, grave matters are indeed grave, and might involve (for Roman Catholics) abortion, adultery, atheism, blasphemy, euthanasia, incest, or rape. These are but examples, and other "grave matters" are subject to interpretation. Second, it must be committed with full knowledge of both the nature of the sin and its gravity. And third, it must be committed with the total consent of one's will. In other words, one cannot commit a mortal sin accidentally, and a sinful act committed when one is under duress or fear or, in general, when one is not in control of oneself, cannot be considered mortal. It may be very serious, but it does not cut one off entirely from the grace of God. For an act to be a mortal sin, you have to know exactly what you are doing and do it deliberately, with one hundred percent of your will. In today's world, it is not all that easy to commit mortal sin.

This was not the case in the seventeenth and eighteenth centuries. Indeed, it was not the case until after the Second Vatican Council. As John McManners has said, during *le grand siècle* and after, "most sins were mortal; a venial sin would be something like speaking an idle, frivolous word, or stealing something of no consequence like an apple or a pin."[9] And as far as one can gather, most parish priests judged an act as mortally sinful or venially sinful simply by the action itself, taking little account of the motives behind it or the psychological state of the sinner. To seventeenth-century French Catholics,

---

[9] John McManners, *Church and Society in Eighteenth-Century France* (Oxford: Clarendon Press, 1998), 2:246. The comment is no less true of the seventeenth century.

hell was an ever-present reality, and the need for regular confession absolute.

But let us now venture within the confessional and put ourselves in the place of the priest. We will suppose that he is dedicated and intelligent, and that in his confessional there appears a penitent who has either committed a sin or is contemplating committing an act that might be a sin. If it is a sin, how serious is it? And if it is about to be committed, is it a sin at all? The priest may consult an authority such as Jean Pontas. The three volumes of his *Dictionnaire de cas de conscience, ou décisions des plus considérables difficultez touchant la Morale et le Discipline Ecclésiastique*, beginning with *Abandon* "Abandonment" and ending with *Yvresse* "Drunkenness," were extremely popular with the clergy.[10] But then, having noted the opinions of his authorities, our priest may arrive at two conflicting opinions, one that says that the action is probably sinful (or that the sin is probably mortal), the other that says that it is probably not (or that the sin is probably venial). What is he to do? According to what, at the time, was known as Probabilism, the priest may give the penitent the benefit of the doubt. That is to say, even though his external authorities (extrinsic opinions) and internal logic (intrinsic opinions) suggest that of the two opinions it is more likely that the action is indeed sinful (or mortally sinful), the priest may choose the *less* probable opinion and declare the action permissible. That this could be taken too far is obvious. If we go so far as to say that there is a one percent probability of an action's being permissible and a ninety-nine percent probability of its being sinful, and yet choose the former alternative, we end up with what was termed, with justice, Laxism, in which it was much more difficult to be sinful than good. Laxism, we might add, was condemned by Pope Alexander VII in 1665 and 1666, and again by Pope Innocent XI in 1679.

---

[10] An *Abrégé* was published, and there was a considerable number of similar handbooks.

There were, of course, those who had no time for this view at all. In their opinion, if a priest had examined the question, either extrinsically, intrinsically, or both, and come to two conflicting opinions, then he should follow not the opinion that was less or more probable, but the opinion that was safer, more cautious, or more prudent, and that was more in accord with established morality. Putting it in four words: If in doubt, don't! Since the Latin word for safer, more cautious, or more prudent is *tutior*, this system came to be known as Tutiorism or, more obviously, as Rigorism, the rigorous approach to human sin.

Sin, however, whether treated more benignly or more rigorously, was omnipresent, and since sin demands repentance (assuming, that is, that one does not wish to spend eternity in the fires of hell) it is only logical that the spirituality of the times would be a spirituality of *pénitence,* which, as we have seen, may mean repentance, penance, penitence, or a mixture of all three. The business of a monk, said Rancé, is "to weep for our own sins and for the sins of all others,"[11] but in the view of the spiritual guides of seventeenth-century France, that was the business of all Christians. What is the essential key to the Christian path? It is surely the imitation of Christ. The principle appears clearly in Saint Paul[12] and was developed by the fathers of the church, both Eastern and Western. "Why are you proud?" asks Saint Augustine. "For your sake God was made low. Perhaps you would be ashamed to imitate a lowly man; then at least imitate the lowly God!"[13] For Augustine, the imitation of the sinless Christ was the counterbalance to

---

[11] Armand-Jean de Rancé, *De la sainteté et des devoirs de la vie monastique* (Paris: F. Muguet, 1683), 1:394. See also David N. Bell, *Understanding Rancé. The Spirituality of the Abbot of La Trappe in Context,* CS 205 (Kalamazoo, MI: Cistercian Publications, 2005), 88.

[12] E.g., 1 Thess 1:6; Eph 5:1-2.

[13] Augustine of Hippo, *In evangelium Johannis, tractatus* XXV.16; PL 35:1604: *Deus propter te humilis factus est. Puderet te fortasse imitari humilem hominem, saltem imitare humilem Deum.*

the imitation of the sinful Adam. By the Middle Ages, the idea was standard and unquestioned, and Thomas Aquinas (as usual) put the matter in a nutshell: *Perfectio religionis maxime consistit in imitatione Christi*, "The perfection of religion consists primarily in the imitation of Christ."[14]

Such was the principle that the seventeenth-century theologians inherited, but the question we must ask is who was the Christ we should imitate? Was he the loving Christ of the gospel of John? Was he the righteous Christ of Saint Paul? Was he the humble Christ of Augustine (and Bernard)? He was indeed, but he was, above all, Christ the Great Penitent, an idea somewhat alien to twenty-first-century Christian theology. But what does this mean? What has the pure and sinless Son of God to be penitent about? He cannot repent of sins that he did not commit, nor return to a purity that he always possessed. Indeed not. So it is not his sins for which he is penitent, but ours. Jean-Jacques Olier (1608–1657), the founder of the Society of Saint-Sulpice (the Sulpicians), explains the matter thus:

> Let us respectfully consider Jesus Christ doing penance for our sins. Let us honor in him the holy spirit of penitence, which was the driving-force of his whole life and which, afterwards, filled the hearts of all the penitents in the church. Thus, in honor of and in union with Jesus Christ Our Lord, penitent before God for my sins and for the sins of the whole world, I state my intention to do penance all the days of my life, and to regard myself in all things as a poor and miserable sinner, an utterly unworthy penitent.[15]

This view was shared by all the theologians and preachers of the time, and Jacques Biroat, the first of the panegyrists we shall consider, asks the same question of Bernard. How can we

---

[14] Thomas Aquinas, *Summa theologica* 2/2, qu. 186, art. 5.

[15] Jean-Jacques Olier, *Introduction à la vie et aux vertus chrétiennes. Pietas seminarii*, ed. François Amiot (Paris: Le Rameau, 1954), 23 and 73.

explain the fact that he and the other saints, though innocent, do penance as if they were guilty? There are three reasons, he says:

First, they do it to expiate past sins, even though those sins might have been trifling in themselves. Second, they do it to ward off the dangers of those sins they might commit. And finally, they do it to imitate Christ, and to bear in their mortified bodies something similar to his crucified body. It is through these three principles that the gospel moved the heart of Bernard to the love of penance and repentance.[16]

Seventeenth-century French spirituality is therefore penitential spirituality, a spirituality that imitates the Great Penitent and that is precisely in accord with John the Baptist's instructions in Matthew 3:2 and Jesus' own instructions in Matthew 4:17: *Poenitentiam agite*! "Do penance! For the Kingdom of Heaven is at hand!"

Of the two ways of looking at human sin and human frailty, Probabilism, with its more benign approach, was particularly associated with the Jesuits. Rigorism, with its much more hard-line attitudes, was more closely associated with the Jansenists, those followers (to varying degrees) of the ideas put forth by Cornelius Jansen, the Flemish bishop of Ypres, in his *Augustinus*, published in 1640. He was a staunch follower of Saint Augustine and followed the latter in his view of the total depravity of the human race as a consequence of the sin of Adam: every baby born into this world is wholly corrupted with Original Sin and Original Guilt and grows up, if it grows up at all, to be a totally corrupt and totally guilty adult. It follows, therefore, that since each one of us is totally corrupt (not just very corrupt, but totally—one hundred percent—corrupt), there is not one of us who can do a single good action, any more than a totally dark room can give out a single gleam of light. And since no human being can do a single good action, no human being can ever merit, earn, or deserve grace,

---

[16] See below, chap. 4 (Biroat), §8.

and without grace, our only destination can be the everlasting pains of hell. Without grace, then, we are doomed, and since we can never deserve grace, the only ones not doomed are those to whom God, for his own reasons (unknown to us), decides to give grace. In other words, there are some souls who are predestined to receive grace and thus have the possibility of salvation, and there are other souls (certainly the majority, in Augustine's view) who are not predestined to receive it and who will therefore end up in eternal torment. Without grace, there is nowhere else for them to go.[17]

It is perfectly understandable, then, that the Jansenists were accused of being crypto-Calvinists, for it was Calvin who was primarily responsible for establishing the depressing doctrine of Double Predestination. Single Predestination maintains that God actively predestines some to receive his grace and leaves the rest to their own devices, but since (as Augustine said) "of our own power, we can only fall,"[18] those not so predestined will go to hell. Double Predestination, on the other hand, maintains that God actively predestines some people for eternal life in heaven and actively predestines the rest for eternal torment in hell. The end result for most of us will be the same, but there is a difference between watching someone who cannot swim drown in a lake and actively pushing that person under the water and holding him down. Neither scenario, however, says much for the character of God, and Calvinism met with fierce resistance.

The Jansenists were not, in fact, Calvinists and vigorously defended themselves against the accusations, but they shared with the Calvinists a stern and intractable morality. If, after all, you were convinced (rightly or wrongly) that you were one of the elect, the predestined chosen, you were not going to jeopardize your chances of heaven by sinning, and it was

---

[17] We need not here enter into the theological debate as to whether grace was resistible or irresistible.

[18] Augustine of Hippo, Enarr in Ps 129.1; PL 37:1696.

inevitable that Jansenism would be associated with a rigorist attitude to human error. This moral austerity or austere morality was attractive to many who did not accept the essential doctrines of Jansenism, and it can easily be heard in the voices of the preachers we shall meet in these pages. There cannot be the least doubt that Bernard of Clairvaux shared this rigorist approach, and the Bernard who appears in their sermons (if we may be permitted the anachronism) was no Jesuit probabilist. The Jesuits loathed the Jansenists, and vice versa, and did all that they could to bring about their downfall. The whole complicated story, deeply enmeshed in some rather unsavory politics, is not here our concern, but five propositions from Jansen's *Augustinus* were condemned by Pope Innocent X in 1653. Sixty years later, in the bull *Unigenitus*, Pope Clement XI condemned a hundred and one propositions from a book by the Jansenist Pasquier Quesnel (at that time the chief spokesman for the Jansenist cause) as "false, deceptive, evil-sounding, offensive to devout ears, scandalous, pernicious, rash, injurious to the Church and her practices, insulting not only to the Church but to the civil powers, seditious, impious, blasphemous, suspect of heresy, and tasting of heresy itself," and so on.[19] It must be said that His Holiness does not leave us in doubt.

Calvinists in France, and French Protestants in general, had been guaranteed a certain amount of religious and political freedom by the Edict of Nantes, issued on April 13, 1598, by Henry IV, a king with Protestant sympathies. He had been baptized Catholic but was brought up as a Protestant by his mother, the queen of Navarre, and when his cousin, Henry III of France, died childless in 1589, he inherited the French throne. His inheritance, however, was no more than nominal, and for some years he had to fight for his kingdom. He also found it politic to renounce his former Calvinism and accept Roman Catholicism—"Paris," he is supposed to have said, "is well worth a

---

[19] Denzinger, no. 2502.

Mass"[20]—and this he did in July 1593. His conversion earned him the approval and allegiance of almost all his subjects but alienated him from the French Protestants (the Huguenots) and from his former ally, Queen Elizabeth I of England. He was crowned in the cathedral of Chartres on February 27, 1594.

The Edict of Nantes was intended to bring to an end the French Wars of Religion, which are usually said to have begun with the Massacre of Vassy (or Wassy) on March 1, 1562. It was on that day that sixty-three unarmed Huguenots were slaughtered by troops of the duke of Guise, and more than a hundred wounded. The massacre precipitated more than three decades of almost uninterrupted internecine strife, with hideous atrocities on both sides, until the Edict of Nantes brought hostilities to an end, though local problems and revolts continued into the early eighteenth century. The Edict was aimed at achieving civil unity in the country, not religious unity (it reaffirmed Catholicism as the established religion of France), but Protestants were granted liberty of conscience and freedom from persecution, the right to private worship anywhere and to public worship in certain specific locations (but not in Paris or anywhere within five leagues of Paris), the right to work in any public office, and the right to bring grievances directly to the king.[21] It was a wise and remarkable gesture of toleration, though fervent Protestants objected to it because it did not go far enough, and fervent Catholics because it recognized what they regarded as a heretic and schismatic sect and created a state within a state. Henry himself was assassinated by a fanatical Catholic, François Ravaillac, on May 14, 1610 (who paid for his crime by being executed in a manner that, even by the standards of the times, was horrific and barbarous), and was succeeded by his nine-year-old son, Louis XIII.

---

[20] "Paris vaut bien une Messe," though whether Henry ever actually said this is disputed. It may have been attributed to him by his contemporaries.

[21] The text of the Edict is readily available on the internet.

Under the centralizing endeavors of Louis XIV and his ministers, the articles of the Edict of Nantes were gradually watered down, and persecution, open and covert, of Protestants began anew. From 1681 the king's dragoons were sent out into Protestant areas and billeted in Protestant homes, where they were permitted, indeed encouraged, to loot, plunder, molest, abuse, intimidate, and maltreat the men and women of the household until they abjured their Protestantism and returned to the Catholic fold. Such were the *dragonnades* (from the French word for a dragoon), and such was their effect that by 1685 Louis could maintain that since the majority of Protestants had now been converted to Catholicism, the Edict of Nantes was irrelevant and could be revoked. Revoked it was, and the Revocation of the Edict of Nantes (more accurately, the Edict of Fontainebleau) was issued by Louis in October 1685. It was welcomed by Rancé, abbot of La Trappe,[22] and by virtually every French bishop. "Let us pour out our hearts," said Bossuet of Meaux, "for the piety of Louis! You have affirmed the faith, you have exterminated the heretics: it is a work worthy of your reign, and its proper character. Thanks to you, heresy is no more. God alone can have worked this marvel!"[23] Many of the Jansenists, on the other hand, were strongly opposed to the revocation.

Its impact on the Huguenots was disastrous. Persecution intensified, and Protestant ministers were given two weeks to leave the country unless they converted to Catholicism. All other Protestants were forbidden to leave, though this did not prevent thousands of them from fleeing France at the risk of

---

[22] See Alban J. Krailsheimer, "L'Abbé de Rancé et les Protestants: autour de la Révocation de l'Édit de Nantes (1685)," *Collectanea Cisterciensia* 48 (1986): 297–310; and Yves Krumenacker, "Le Camus, Barillon, Rancé: trois artisans de la réforme catholique face à la révocation de l'Édit de Nantes," in *Homo Religiosus: autour de Jean Delumeau* (Paris: Fayard, 1997), 386–92.

[23] *Bossuet: Oraisons funèbres, Panégyriques*, ed. Bernard Velat, Bibliothèque de la Pléiade, 33 (Paris: Gallimard, 1951), 206.

their lives and seeking asylum in Britain, Prussia, Switzerland, the Dutch Republic, and elsewhere. Many of these fugitives were skilled craftsmen and artisans, and with them they took their skills in (for example) cabinetmaking, watchmaking, and the working of silk, silver, jewelry, and glass. It was a colossal loss to France and a colossal gain to the countries that welcomed the fleeing exiles. And it did Louis no good, for the Protestant nations bordering France became even more hostile to him and his regime.

To those who had no time for Protestants or Protestant ideas—the "adversaries" of Bossuet,[24] the "monstrous sects" of Fénelon and Massillon[25]—Bernard of Clairvaux was a godsend. He had no time for the followers of people like Arnold of Brescia or Peter of Bruys or Henry of Toulouse[26]—preachers who certainly anticipated some of the essential features of the Protestant Reformation—and he had no doubt as to what should be done with them: "Therefore, dearly beloved, persecute them [*persequimini*] and seize them, and do not stop until they have utterly perished [*penitus depereant*] and disappeared from all your domains, for it is unsafe to sleep near snakes."[27] He may have loved these proto-Protestants in the depths of his God-given charity, but he did not like them. He did not like Jews or Muslims either, and although, like others of his time, he strongly objected to massacring Jews,[28] he remained, as David Berger has said, "an equally strong spokesman for anti-Jewish stereotypes and prejudices."[29] "Bernard himself," Berger continues, "was not led to violence by his prejudices, but the hatred which he preached was fanning the flames of violence in

---

[24] See below, chap. 7 (Bossuet), §1.
[25] See below, chap. 8 (Fénelon), §30, and chap. 14 (Massillon), §56.
[26] See under their names in appendix 2.
[27] Bernard, Ep 242; SBOp 8:128.
[28] The standard proof-text was Ps 58:12: "Do not kill them . . . ."
[29] David Berger, "The Attitude of St. Bernard of Clairvaux Toward the Jews," *Proceedings of the American Academy for Jewish Research* 40 (1972): 89–108, here 107.

lesser men. The great Christian protector of twelfth-century Jewry sowed seeds which would claim the life of many a Jewish martyr."[30] As to Muslims, although Bernard tells us that he does not mean that pagans are to be slaughtered if there is some other way of preventing them from attacking or oppressing the faithful, "It seems better now that they be killed."[31]

Bernard, in any case, was a popular figure in *le grand siècle*. He had become, in the words of Simon Icard, *effigie du Catholicisme classique*, "an icon of classical Catholicism."[32] He had been the moving force behind those monastic reforms that led to the Feuillants, the Cistercians of the Strict Observance, and the austere nuns of Port-Royal; he was beloved by those Catholic reformers who sought to look back beyond the advent of scholasticism to what they considered a "purer" form of theology and spirituality; he stood as a bulwark, a "wall of bronze,"[33] against all those who sought to introduce "novelties"[34] into the substance of the faith (especially Quietism); he was a French

---

[30] Berger, "Attitude," 108.

[31] Bernard, *In laude novae militiae* 3.4; SBOp 3:217. The verb is *occido*, "to cut down, slay, kill, put to death." See further Eoin de Bhaldraithe, "Jean Leclercq's Attitude Toward War," in *The Joy of Learning and the Love of God: Studies in Honor of Jean Leclercq*, ed. E. Rozanne Elder, CS 160 (Kalamazoo, MI: Cistercian Publications, 1995), 217–37. This is a strange paper, but not without value.

[32] Simon Icard, "Saint Bernard, effigie du catholicisme classique, Étude du frontispiece de *La Vie de saint Bernard* d'Antoine Le Maistre (1648) d'après Philippe de Champaigne," *Cîteaux—Commentarii cistercienses* 62 (2011): 321–37. See also Marie-Élisabeth Henneau, "Bernard de Clairvaux: Du Classicisme aux lumières: destin d'une œuvre, image d'un homme," in *Vies et légendes de saint Bernard de Clairvaux. Création, diffusion, réception (XIIe–XXe siècles). Actes des Rencontres de Dijon, 7–8 juin 1991*, ed. Patrick Arabeyre, Jacques Berlioz, and Philippe Poirier (Brecht and Saint-Nicolas-lès-Cîteaux: "Présence cistercienne"; *Cîteaux—Commentarii cistercienses*, 1993), 291–305.

[33] This expression, which derives from Jer 1:18, is used by Rancé, Fénelon, and Massillon to describe Bernard.

[34] See appendix 1, s.v. *nouveautés*/novelties.

saint who, in 1653, had been declared by Louis XIV protector of the throne of France; from 1641 his complete works were available in sound editions; and his life, by William of Saint-Thierry and others, was easily available in both Latin and French. He was also popular among many Jansenists and semi-Jansenists who appealed to him as a saint who stood firmly in the footsteps of Augustine of Hippo, who was dedicated to the purity of doctrine and rigorous in his approach to sin, who showed clearly how the church might be reformed from within, and how the absolutism of Louis XIV, and his desire to control both church and state, was contrary to the law of God. As we shall see in a moment, the author of the most popular translation of Bernard's life into French was a fervent Jansenist.

Works by and attributed to Bernard appeared from the very earliest days of printing,[35] the earliest being the pseudonymous *Epistola de gubernatione rei familiaris* (actually by Bernardus Silvestris) printed at Augsburg by Günther Zainer about 1468–1470.[36] Of the genuine works, the *De consideratione* was available from 1474, the sermons *De tempore*, *De sanctis*, and *De diversis* from 1475, the sermons on the Song of Songs from 1481, and so on. Collections of works, again both genuine and pseudonymous, also appeared from an early date (the most significant being that published in 1508[37]), but by far the most important was the new edition by Jacob Merlo Horstius published in Cologne in 1641.[38] Horstius was born in 1597 in the northern part of the province of Limburg in the Netherlands but eventually made his way to Cologne, where he was the parish priest of the church of Our Lady *in Pasculo*. His edition

---

[35] The repertorium of Janauschek retains its value but must now be supplemented by the British Library *Incunabula Short Title Catalogue* (= ISTC), available online at www.bl.uk.

[36] ISTC no. ib00375800.

[37] Janauschek, no. 350; Adriaan H. Bredero, *Bernard of Clairvaux: Between Cult and History* (Grand Rapids: W. B. Eerdmans, 1996), 164–65.

[38] Janauschek, no. 1002.

was vastly superior to any that had preceded it, and it formed the basis for all subsequent editions until the twentieth century. There were, of course, areas for improvement, and Horstius himself was aware of this. After the publication of the 1641 collection, he intended to work on a second and better edition, but death forestalled him in 1644. It would be another quarter of a century before the improved edition appeared, and that was the work of the great Maurist Jean Mabillon.

Mabillon was born on November 23, 1632, in a tiny house (it can still be seen) in the tiny village of Saint-Pierremont in the northeast of France, not far from the Belgian border. His early studies were at the Collège des Bons Enfants in Reims where, in due course, he became a seminarian. In 1653 he left the seminary to take monastic vows at the abbey of Saint-Remi in Reims but was eventually transferred to Saint-Germain-des-Prés in Paris, where he spent the rest of his life. There he died on December 27, 1707, and there he is buried. It was at Saint-Germain (a center of monastic studies with a superb library) that he began work on a new and more accurate edition of Horstius's *opera omnia sancti Bernardi*. This, as Adriaan Bredero has said, "formed part of the ambitious project undertaken by the congregation of Saint-Maur to promote the writings of Christian authors from the early centuries and the Middle Ages,"[39] and work had already begun on the new edition by Dom Claude Chantelou, one of Mabillon's confrères at Saint-Germain. He had compared Horstius's edition with whatever manuscripts of Bernard's works he had at his own disposal and had found so many variant readings that he felt a new edition was essential. Mabillon collaborated with him in this, and when Chantelou died in 1664, it was Mabillon who brought the task to completion.[40] The new edition was

---

[39] Bredero, *Bernard of Clairvaux*, 167–68.

[40] By the time of his death, Chantelou had published the sermons *De tempore* and *De sanctis* and the life of Saint Malachy: see Janauschek, no. 1125.

published in six volumes at Paris in 1667 as *S. Bernardi Abbatis Primi Clarevallensis, et Ecclesiae Doctoris, Opera Omnia*,[41] and on the title page we are told that it is based on the work of John (*sic*) Merlo Horstius, which has been revised and corrected by various other manuscripts by Dom John Mabillon, a Benedictine monk of the Congregation of Saint-Maur. Mabillon realized, however, that even this revised edition was not wholly satisfactory and continued to work on the project for a further twenty-three years until the definitive edition was published in 1690.[42] This is the version that was reproduced in volumes 182 to 185 of the Migne Patrology and was the standard text for all Bernardine studies until the publication of the new edition by Dom Jean Leclercq, C. H. Talbot, and H. M. Rochais, in eight volumes between 1957 and 1977.[43]

So much for Bernard's works. What, then, of the *Vita prima*, the life of the saint compiled by William of Saint-Thierry, Arnold of Bonneval, and Geoffrey of Auxerre? The complicated history of its creation and development is not here our concern,[44] but we do need to draw attention to the fact that the *Vita* is to be found in two forms, a longer and a shorter, generally cited as Redaction A and Redaction B. Redaction A was the earlier of the two, and material had begun to be collected for it as early as 1145 while Bernard was still alive. It seems most probable that Geoffrey of Auxerre, who at that time was Bernard's secretary and companion, had asked Rainald, a former abbot of Foigny (where Bernard excommunicated the flies),

---

[41] Janauschek, no. 1154.

[42] Janauschek, no. 1306.

[43] *Sancti Bernardi Opera*, ed. Jean Leclercq, C. Hugh Talbot, Henri M. Rochais (Rome: Editiones Cistercienses, 1957–1977).

[44] This is not the place for a comprehensive bibliography on this question, but the work of Adriaan Bredero, "Études sur la *Vita prima* de saint Bernard," *Analecta Cisterciensia* 17 (1961): 3–72, 215–60; and 18 (1962): 3–59, and his *Bernard of Clairvaux, passim*, remain fundamental. What follows here is based on his studies.

to compose a Life, but if Rainald began the work, he did not complete it, and the details are unclear. What is clear is that two years later Geoffrey approached William of Saint-Thierry, now a monk of Signy, and asked him to undertake the task. This William did, but by the time of his death not long afterward, there still remained work to be done. Geoffrey then approached Arnold of Bonneval, a Benedictine abbot from the diocese of Chartres, who composed what is now Book Two of the *Vita*, and Geoffrey himself composed the remaining three books.

Thus things stood until Pope Alexander III called a council at Tours in 1163. All the writing that had been done before this had been associated, in one way or another, with a desire for Bernard's canonization, and a council at Tours seemed an ideal place to move the process forward. As it happened, this did not occur, and Bernard would not join the saints until 1174. Meanwhile, new guidelines were being established for the process of canonization, and to accord with these changes in procedure, Geoffrey found it necessary to revise the *Vita* he had in hand. He made certain improvements in style and corrected a few errors (not always correctly), but his revision mainly involved the elimination or abridgement of a considerable number of passages. It is this shorter, revised version of the *Vita prima*, prepared by Geoffrey at Clairvaux, that is known as Redaction B.

The earliest printed text of the *Vita prima* appeared in the first volume of the *Sanctuarium seu vitae sanctorum* prepared by the Italian humanist Bonino Mombrizio (Boninus Mombritius in Latin) and published at Milan in about 1477.[45] It follows Redaction B, which was by far the most common version to be found in both Italy and France. Adriaan Bredero tells us

---

[45] Fols. 96^r–140^v, more readily available in *Boninus Mombritius. Sanctuarium seu vitae sanctorum. Novam hanc editionem curaverunt duo monachi Solesmenses* (Paris: A. Fontemoing, 1910), 1:175–250 (available online). Bredero, *Bernard of Clairvaux*, 163, gives the date as about 1480, but more recent research suggests about 1477.

that the only other printed edition of the *Vita* to appear before Horstius's edition of 1641 is to be found in the four-volume *De probatis sanctorum historiis* of the German Carthusian Lorenz Sauer (Laurentius Surius) published at Cologne between 1570 and 1575.[46] It follows the longer Redaction A, which was the most widely disseminated in Germany and Austria.

Then, in 1641, the *Vita* appeared at the very beginning of Horstius's edition, but in a form that combined both redactions. French manuscripts of the work, as we have said, usually followed the shorter Redaction B, but when Horstius examined Surius's text he was immediately aware of a large number of differences, too many and too important simply to be ignored. So what he did was to use Redaction B as his base text and add, in square brackets, the variants to be found in Redaction A. He did not always do this consistently, and he did not always do it accurately, but it was, at the very least, the first attempt to distinguish between the two redactions. So what of Mabillon?

Mabillon was less interested in the *Vita prima* than he was in Bernard's own writings, and in his edition the *Vita* appears not as an introduction, but as an appendix. Nor did he spend much time hunting for manuscripts that might have clarified the relationship between the two redactions, though he did examine those that he had to hand at Saint-Germain-des-Prés. They all came from French monasteries and all followed Redaction B. There were, however, some differences from Horstius's version, so in his edition of 1667 Mabillon reproduced Horstius's text, square brackets and all, and added marginal notes where he had found variant readings in the manuscripts he had himself consulted. This was essentially the same text that also appeared in the definitive edition of 1690, but when it was reproduced in volume 185 of the Migne Patrology, there was further confusion. Mabillon's marginal notes were now included in the text itself, and also enclosed in square brackets, so that the poor scholar working from this text is by no means

---

[46] Bredero, *Bernard of Clairvaux*, 163–64.

certain who added what and when. What happened after Horstius and Mabillon is not here our concern,[47] but it must be noted that the recent edition of Redaction A published in the series Corpus Christianorum, Continuatio Mediaevalis in 2011 is, alas, disappointing. Every one of the panegyrists represented in these pages could, in theory, have used Horstius's edition, many of them could have used the 1667 edition of Mabillon, and some might have had access to the 1690 edition. In the following pages I have merely cited the edition in volume 185 of the Migne Patrology, partly because it is freely and easily available on the internet, and partly because it reflects the text read and used by the preachers and Antoine Le Maistre, whom we shall meet in a moment. I have also added references to the English translation of the *Vita prima* by Hilary Costello that appeared in 2015.[48] This translation is not without flaws, but it is the only complete translation at present available in English.

What, then, of French translations of the *Vita prima*? The earliest appears to have been made by Guillaume Flameng, a monk of Clairvaux, whose *La Vie de Monseigneur sainct Bernard devost chapelain de la Vierge Marie et premier abbé de Clereuaulx* in seven books was printed at Paris and Troyes sometime between 1501 and 1513.[49] Far more important and far more popular, however, was the translation by the Jansenist Antoine Le Maistre (or Lemaistre), *La Vie de S. Bernard premier abbé de Clairvaux, et Père d'Église. Divisée en six livres*, published for the first time in 1648[50] at Paris by "A. Vitré et la veuve Martin

---

[47] See Bredero, *Bernard of Clairvaux*, 169–73.

[48] *The First Life of Bernard of Clairvaux by William of Saint-Thierry, Arnold of Bonneval, and Geoffrey of Auxerre*, trans. Hilary Costello, CF 76 (Collegeville, MN: Cistercian Publications, 2015).

[49] Janauschek, nos. 428–29. Neither edition has a date, but Janauschek's "1520?" is somewhat too late. Abbreviated translations had been printed earlier: see Bredero, *Bernard of Clairvaux*, 162 n. 52.

[50] Bredero, *Bernard of Clairvaux*, 177–78, gives the year as 1647, but although this date is recorded elsewhere, no copy of a 1647 edition appears to exist: see Janauschek, nos. 1039 and 1041.

Durand," and reissued numerous times thereafter. The author appears on the title page not under his real name but as "le sieur Lamy." Le Maistre was born in 1608, the son of Isaac Le Maistre, a king's counselor, and Catherine Arnauld. Catherine was a member of the celebrated Arnauld family, all of whom were Jansenists or Jansenist sympathizers, and most of whom had close ties with the abbey of Port-Royal-des-Champs. Le Maistre could count among his close relatives several nuns, two abbesses of Port-Royal, and at least one bishop. He himself became rapidly known as an effective lawyer at the tribunal of Paris, but during the Fronde he was persuaded by Jean du Vergier de Hauranne, *abbé* of Saint-Cyran (who was primarily responsible for introducing Jansenism into France), to give up his legal practice and retire to Port-Royal, where Saint-Cyran became his spiritual director. He was not quite thirty. There he was joined by a number of others, including several of his brothers, and they became the Solitaires—*les Solitaires*—of Port Royal-des-Champs under the direction of Saint-Cyran. It was here, at the request of Saint-Cyran, that Le Maistre produced his *Vie de S. Bernard*. He died on November 4, 1658, still a comparatively young man.

The first three books of his *Vie* contain an abridged translation of the whole of the *Vita prima*, while the last three books (as Le Maistre tells us on the title page) "are taken from his works and present to us his spirit and his way of life."[51] They begin with a chapter on Bernard's "great love for God," and it is here, and in the unpaginated Introduction "To the Reader" of just over twenty-five pages, that Le Maistre's Jansenist principles may most clearly be seen. Almost all, perhaps all (I am not quite sure of Biroat) of the panegyrists represented here made use of Le Maistre's translation, some more than others (Antoine Anselme refers to it directly[52]), and most of them

---

[51] "les trois derniers sont tirez de ses Ouvrages, & representent son esprit & sa conduitte."

[52] See below, chap. 13 (Anselme and Bourru), n. 14.

clearly mined his introduction for useful material. How much they used Le Maistre and how much they used the editions of Horstius and Mabillon is often impossible to say, since the same information frequently appears in both French and Latin, but there is not the slightest doubt that the *Vita prima* is the foundation for their work.

The Bernard who appears in that work is almost always Bernard the penitent, Bernard the ascetic, Bernard the victor over temptation, Bernard the defender of the legitimate papacy, Bernard the peacemaker, Bernard the scourge of heresy and heretics, and Bernard the fearless and outspoken critic of misconduct and immorality. He is rarely Bernard the miracle worker and hardly ever the Bernard so beloved today: Bernard the mystic. In fact, of the sixteen panegyrists who appear in these pages, only one—Henri-Marie Boudon, archdeacon of Évreux—is prepared to deal with Bernard's mysticism and mystical experiences. All the others either studiously avoid it or mention the matter only in passing. The explanation for this cannot simply be found in the fact that the *Vita prima* says little on the question, for as we have seen, sound editions of all of Bernard's works were readily available. All a reader need do is to glance at the *De diligendo Deo* or a few sermons from the commentary on the Song of Songs to find the Bernard of, for example, Watkin Williams' *The Mysticism of S. Bernard of Clairvaux* (1931) or Étienne Gilson's *Le théologie mystique de saint Bernard* (1947) or Michael Casey's *Athirst for God* (1986). Why did the panegyrists not do so? Or, if they did, why were they so reticent to speak of what they found? The answer is complex and demands a chapter to itself.

2

The Quietist Controversy

The reason the panegyrists generally avoided the question of Bernard's mystical experiences was not that there was no interest in mysticism in the France of the Sun King, but because there was too much of it. One could find, in fact, a whole variety of mysticisms, like so many exotic orchids,[1] but the essen-

---

[1] The only comprehensive account of seventeenth-century French spirituality and mysticism is to be found in the marvelously rich (but quirky and idiosyncratic) pages of Henri Bremond's *Histoire du sentiment religieux en France depuis les guerres de religion jusqu'à nos jours* (Paris: Bloud & Gay, 1916–1933 [eleven vols.]). Much of the material presented there cannot be found elsewhere. The first three volumes were translated into English as *A Literary History of Religious Thought in France from the Wars of Religion down to Our Own Times*, trans. K. L. Montgomery (London: SPCK, 1928–1936). Much briefer summaries may be found in Pierre Pourrat, *Christian Spirituality. Later Developments. Part II: from Jansenism to Modern Times*, trans. Donald Attwater (Westminster, MD: Newman Press, 1955), chaps. 1–12, pp. 1–307, and Louis Cognet, *Post-Reformation Spirituality*, trans. P. Hepburne Scott (New York: Hawthorne Books, 1959), especially chaps. 3–5, pp. 56–141. Cognet offers a very sound and readable summary; Pourrat offers more detail with a good commentary, provided one can sidestep his conservative Tridentine Catholicism. But for the pure joy of reading, in English, a wonderfully entertaining account of Quietism that yet penetrates to the heart of the matter, one cannot do better than to read Ronald A. Knox, *Enthusiasm. A Chapter in the History of Religion, with Special Reference to the XVII and XVIII Centuries* (Oxford: Clarendon Press, 1950), chaps. 11–16, pp. 231–388. On the term *spiritualité*, see appendix 1, s.v. *spiritualité* / spirituality. See further Bernard Plongeron,

tial problems, theological, ecclesiastical, and political, lay with Quietism. Unless we understand what the Quietists taught and what they were said to have taught, we cannot understand the aversion to discussing Bernard's mysticism on the part of the panegyrists, we cannot understand the antagonism between Bossuet and Fénelon, and we cannot understand the fire of Charles de La Rue's anti-Quietist polemic, which masquerades as a panegyric in praise of Saint Bernard.

We must begin with Miguel de Molinos, born in 1628 in the northeast of Spain. He studied for the priesthood, was ordained in Valencia and then sent to Rome, where he became well known as a spiritual director and where he made powerful friends in the Curia. In 1675 he published his *Spiritual Guide* (*Guía spiritual*) with the usual approval of the ecclesiastical authorities, and the book proved extremely popular, being translated into Dutch, English, French, German, Italian, and Latin. In the *Guide* Molinos distinguishes meditation from contemplation and then divides contemplation into two forms: acquired or active contemplation and infused or passive contemplation. What are we talking about here? Meditation is discursive, that is to say, it uses the mind and the imagination. Guigo II of La Chartreuse provides a clear explanation: "Reading [*lectio*] is an attentive examination of the Scriptures [made] with the directed attention of the spirit. Meditation [*meditatio*] is the studious action of the mind, seeking out the understanding of a hidden truth under the direction of one's own reason. Reading, as it were, puts food whole into one's mouth. Meditation chews it up and breaks it into pieces."[2]

"Lumières contre épopée mystique: les 'lectures' de saint Bernard du XVIIe au XIXe siècles," in *Vies et légendes de saint Bernard de Clairvaux*, ed. Patrick Arabeyre, Jacques Berlioz, and Philippe Poirier (Brecht and Cîteaux: *Cîteaux—Commentarii Cistercienses*, 1993), 306–27.

[2] Guigo II of La Chartreuse, *Scala claustralium* ii–iii; SCh 163:84–86. Molinos himself cites the *Scala* as one of his authorities, attributing it, as was usual at the time, to Saint Bernard: see Denzinger, no. 2223.

If reading remains on the outside of the subject, says Guigo, meditation enters within, climbs higher, and by using all the powers of one's own intellect, penetrates to the heart of the matter. This is precisely the usage of Molinos.

Contemplation is a different matter entirely. If meditation demands the use of our reason, intellect, and imagination, contemplation involves their annihilation, in the literal sense of being reduced to nothing (*nihil* in Latin). This, according to Molinos, is the true *via interna*, the interior way,[3] and in its simplicity it does away completely with the old threefold path of purgation, illumination, and union, "which is the greatest absurdity to be spoken of in mystical [theology], for there is but one single way, the interior way."[4] Rather than being used, the mind is quietened down and opened up to God, and one's entire human will is placed in submission to the divine will. If temptations and untoward thoughts should arise, they are not to be attacked or cast out or countered by the cultivation of the opposite virtues, but rather ignored or disregarded, something that Molinos calls "negative resistance" (*resistencia negativa*). Under the guidance of a wise spiritual director, anyone can experience this interior contemplative unity, though unless God himself intervenes it will always be acquired and imperfect. But if God does intervene, then we have perfect contemplation, which is passive and infused, and entirely the gift of God. In this state, one's human will has become completely God's will, one is totally abandoned in God, and afterward one's existence continues "as if one were a lifeless body [*corpus exanime*]."[5] By doing nothing, says Molinos, "the soul annihilates itself and returns to its beginning and its origin, which is the essence of God. In this [essence] it remains transformed and divinized, and God then remains in himself, for then there are no longer

---

[3] Denzinger, no. 2201.
[4] Denzinger, no. 2226.
[5] Denzinger, no. 2202.

two things united, but only one, and in this way God lives and reigns in us and the soul annihilates itself in operative being."[6]

This infused and total annihilation of one's human will has certain ineluctable logical consequences. First, if one wills nothing at all, this must include one's own salvation. A soul thus annihilated "ought not to think of reward or punishment or Paradise or hell or death or eternity."[7] There is, after all, no "you" to do the willing. "When a soul has achieved mystical death, it cannot will anything other than what God wills, for it no longer has a will, since God has taken it away from it."[8]

Second, since one is now nothing more than a musical instrument on which God plays,[9] the tune that emerges is not one's own but God's. Thus, what may appear sinful in the eyes of others cannot be sinful for you, since you have no part in it. "When doubts arise as to whether what one is doing is right or not, there is no need to reflect [on the matter],"[10] and "through acquired contemplation one arrives at the state of no longer committing any sins, either mortal or venial."[11] God may allow the devil to tempt one, and even to move one's members against their will, but the acts that result from this, "though sinful in themselves, are not in this case sins because there is no consent in them."[12]

Third, one must obviously not ask God for anything nor thank him for anything one may receive, for both asking and thanking are acts of the human will.[13] Since you are now "divinized," what happens is God's doing, and, in essence, no

---

[6] Denzinger, no. 2205.
[7] Denzinger, nos. 2207, 2212.
[8] Denzinger, no. 2261.
[9] I have borrowed the analogy from the second-century Apologist Athenagoras of Athens, Apol 7.
[10] Denzinger, no. 2211.
[11] Denzinger, no. 2257.
[12] Denzinger, no. 2241.
[13] See Denzinger, no. 2215.

business of yours. It follows, therefore, that petitionary prayer is no more than ignorance, for true prayer consists in "remaining in the presence of God in order to adore, love, and serve him, but without effecting any acts [of your own will]."[14] This includes the Lord's Prayer, for interior souls find themselves unable to recite it.[15]

Fourth, since one's own human will has now been subsumed in God, it is not fitting for one to perform works, even virtuous works, by one's own choice and activity; otherwise one would not be mystically dead. Such virtuous works include "acts of love for the blessed Virgin, the saints, or the humanity of Christ, for since they are objects of the senses, so too is love towards them."[16] And as for "the voluntary cross of mortifications, this is a heavy and useless burden which is to be given up,"[17] and for interior souls, there is obviously no place for the sacrament of penance.[18]

In short, a soul that has achieved the perfection of contemplation—a state that, according to Molinos, can be *continuus*, "continuous," "unbroken," "uninterrupted"[19]—has no desires of its own, not even a desire to be saved, and has achieved a state of sinlessness where what would be sins in others are not sins for that soul. And for such a soul, prayer, acts of devotion, good works, mortification of the senses, and the sacrament of penance have no place at all.

It is hardly surprising that Molinos found himself before the tribunal of the Holy Office (the Inquisition), and despite his reputation as a spiritual director and despite his powerful friends in the Curia, he was condemned for heresy. On September 3, 1687, he was obliged to retract his errors publicly and

---

[14] Denzinger, no. 2221.
[15] See Denzinger, no. 2234.
[16] Denzinger, no. 2235.
[17] Denzinger, no. 2238.
[18] See Denzinger, nos. 2259–60.
[19] Denzinger, no. 2262.

condemned to imprisonment in the papal prison, the Castel Sant'Angelo in Rome, for the rest of his days. He died in prison on December 29, 1696. After his public retraction in 1687, Pope Innocent XI condemned sixty-eight propositions of Molinos taken from his letters, from witnesses at his trial, and from the Memorandum he himself presented to the Holy Office. It is possible, therefore, that not all of the propositions represent exactly what Molinos said, but they certainly represent what he was thought to have said, which is what is of importance here.

We must now travel back in time almost half a century to Monday, April 13, 1648, when Jeanne-Marie Bouvier de La Mothe was born at Montargis, about seventy miles south of Paris. She was a sickly child, and her parents neglected her education; in its place they instilled a deep and fervent piety. She had wanted to become a nun, but her parents had other ideas, and, at the age of fifteen, she was forced into an arranged marriage with Jacques Guyon, sieur du Chesnoy, who was wealthy, an invalid, and twenty-two years her senior. The marriage was unhappy from the start, and was made even worse by the abuse that the young girl suffered at the hands of her husband's mother. It is not surprising that she took refuge in religion, spending long periods in intensive prayer and apparently experiencing mystical raptures. After twelve years of marriage and five children, Jacques Guyon died, and in 1676 his wife found herself a wealthy widow, twenty-eight years old, in a comfortable house in Montargis.

Five years earlier, in June or July 1671, Madame Guyon had first met François Lacombe, a Barnabite friar five years older than she, and the meeting proved spiritually enriching for both of them. The Barnabites had been founded in Milan by three Italian noblemen in 1530, and Father Lacombe was superior of the Barnabite house in Thonon in Savoy, south of Geneva. In 1680 Madame Guyon had a further mystical experience in which she felt herself summoned to Geneva; as a result she had contacted the bishop of the diocese, Jean d'Arenthon d'Alex, who suggested she use her considerable wealth to set up a house for "New Catholics"—i.e., converts to Catholicism—at Gex in Savoy as part of a wider plan for the conversion of Protestants in the area. The project was not a success, for Madame Guyon clashed with the sisters who were looking after the house, and tensions were so great that the bishop sent Father Lacombe to intervene. At this time he, officially, became Madame Guyon's spiritual director, though who directed whom in the relationship is a moot point. Father Lacombe may well have been more influenced by Madame Guyon's ideas than she was influenced by his.

It is clear that by this time Madame Guyon had developed her own interior spirituality, a spirituality that, like that of Molinos, involved opening oneself up to God and annihilating one's human will in the divine will. We shall say more on this in a moment. But her unorthodox mystical ideas and the difficult situation in Gex led Jean d'Arenthon to expel both Madame Guyon and Father Lacombe, who were now inseparable, from his diocese. The two then began a five-year journey that would take them from France to Italy and back again to France, and it was inevitable that rumors circulated about the nature of their relationship.

During this period, in January 1685, while Madame Guyon was in Grenoble, she published her *Moyen court et trés-facile de faire oraison*, "A Short and Very Easy Method of Prayer," which contained ideas that disturbed Étienne Le Camus, the bishop of Grenoble. Nor was the bishop happy with Madame Guyon giving informal spiritual instruction in her house and on her own authority spreading teachings dangerous to the faith. As far as the bishop was concerned, the content of Apostolic Tradition was defined by the church; it was not defined by private personal revelations supposedly coming directly from God. He therefore asked her to leave Grenoble, as she did, and she rejoined Father Lacombe, who was then at Vercelli, in the north of Italy.

In July of the next year, 1686, the two returned to Paris, where Madame Guyon continued to teach and offer spiritual direction, but their timing could not have been more unfortunate. By this time Miguel de Molinos was already in the hands of the Holy Office, and Louis XIV did not care for Quietists or any ideas that smacked of Quietism. Direct communications from God could too easily challenge the authority of the king, and too many revolutionary millenarian movements had had their bases in mystical revelations. On his orders, therefore, Father Lacombe was arrested and imprisoned in the Bastille, and the world knew him no more. In 1688 he was transferred to a prison on the island of Oléron, in 1689 to the fortress at Lourdes, and in 1698 to the castle of Vincennes. Nowhere was he treated well, and after fourteen years in Vincennes he lost his reason and was sent to the asylum of Charenton, where he died in 1715.

Madame Guyon was arrested at the end of January 1688 (by which time Pope Innocent XI had condemned the sixty-eight propositions attributed to Molinos) and confined to the convent of the Visitation on the rue Saint-Antoine in Paris. There she spent the next seven months, before being released through the intervention of Madame de Maintenon, second wife of Louis XIV, who also arranged for her to teach at the prestigious boarding school for young noblewomen at Saint-Cyr that Louis had founded in 1684 at Madame de Maintenon's request. There she continued to teach her doctrines on the interior way, passive prayer, and total submission to God's will—doctrines that, in just a few years, resulted in her removal from Saint-Cyr.

Shortly after her release from the convent of the Visitation Madame Guyon met François de Salignac de La Mothe-Fénelon, who became her most influential supporter. Fénelon, who himself had the soul of a mystic, considered the mystical experiences of Madame Guyon to be authentic and was impressed with her teaching on passive prayer and pure love (of which more in a moment), though he did not agree with all that she taught. From the time of their first meeting they were regular correspondents, and through Fénelon's connections at Court, Madame Guyon's teachings permeated a number of influential religious circles and were looked on favorably by Madame de Maintenon herself. Then, in 1693, certain of Madame Guyon's students at Saint-Cyr claimed that they had experienced exalted mystical states and that, having achieved union with God, they were no longer bound by conventional morality but were free to follow their own will, which, by definition, was that of God. When news of this development came to the ears of Paul Godet des Marais, bishop of Chartres (Saint-Cyr lay within his diocese), he was naturally alarmed and contacted Madame de Maintenon to express his concerns and warn her of the dangers of Madame Guyon's teachings. Nor was the situation helped by the fact that by this time Fénelon's own writings were showing distinct signs of Quietist ideas. Madame de Maintenon then sought the advice of a number of bishops and priests, all of whom expressed doubts about Madame Guyon's teachings, and it was then decided to consult the bishop of Meaux, Jacques-Bénigne Bossuet, a prelate of undisputed authority and unquestioned orthodoxy. Bossuet had no desire to undertake the inquiry, being busy with other matters, but royal pressure left him little alternative. Madame Guyon agreed to the choice of arbiter and in October 1693 provided Bossuet with copies of her writings, including her autobiography.

Bossuet undertook his commission with his customary thoroughness and spent three months examining the documents, as well as studying the works of such great mystics as Teresa of Jesus, John of the Cross, and Francis de Sales. That was necessary, for Bossuet, unlike Fénelon, disliked and distrusted mysticism and had not immersed himself in their writings. Bossuet and Madame Guyon met face-to-face for the first time on January 30, 1694, in Paris at the house of one of Bossuet's friends, and once they got down to business, if I may quote E. E. Reynolds, "Mme. Guyon found that she had to face a very thorough criticism of her notions and method. For the first and probably only time in her life, she met someone who could talk her down; in fact, she complained afterwards that she could not get a word in; the experience was so disconcerting that she took to her bed."[20]

Bossuet found her sincere and well intentioned but muddled in her thinking, and he was in no doubt that, even if her ideas could be defended, they could too easily be misinterpreted. The events at Saint-Cyr, which had led to her dismissal, had shown that. He was also in no doubt that some of her ideas were just plain wrong. When Bossuet had been suggested as the arbiter in the case, Madame Guyon had agreed to accept his judgment, but when she saw the way the wind was blowing, she requested a further inquiry, preferably conducted by a layman. Madame de Maintenon, who was deeply involved in the whole process, agreed to the inquiry but—reasonably—suggested that it should be conducted by a small commission of ecclesiastics, and, after some negotiation, three well-known churchmen were appointed to the commission. One of them was Bossuet; the other two were Louis-Antoine de Noailles, then bishop of Châlons-sur-Marne, and Louis Tronson, the superior of the Society of Saint-Sulpice. All three were friends of Fénelon, and Fénelon wrote to the committee defending Madame Guyon's notion of "pure love" while recognizing that certain other of her ideas were, one might say, idiosyncratic. Madame de Maintenon, on the other hand, supplied the committee with material decidedly antagonistic to Madame Guyon, for Madame de Maintenon wanted no further harm done to the reputation of her school at Saint-Cyr. The inquiry took eight months, and the committee finally met at Issy, near Paris, in February 1695 to make a final decision. Issy was the summer residence of the Society of Saint-Sulpice, and Louis Tronson was old and plagued by rheumatism. By this date, Fénelon had just been nominated archbishop of Cambrai (a nomination approved by Madame de Maintenon), and in consequence of his new and elevated standing, the three

---

[20] Ernest E. Reynolds, *Bossuet* (Garden City, NY: Doubleday, 1963), 221.

members of the committee invited him to attend the concluding conference at Issy. This he did, and the committee drew up a list of thirty-four "Articles on the States of Prayer" that called attention to erroneous ideas in the writings of Madame Guyon. But before we examine these articles, let us outline briefly what it was that Madame Guyon was teaching. Her writings are voluminous, to say the least, but her essential ideas are set forth in her *Short and Very Easy Method of Prayer*, which we mentioned above.[21]

She begins by emphasizing the simplicity of her approach. Her method is indeed short and very easy, and it is open to all. All are called to prayer, all are capable of prayer, just as all are called to salvation. And what is prayer? "Prayer is nothing but the application of the heart to God, and the internal exercise of love."[22] Discursive meditation, on the other hand—meditation that depends on the intellect and reason—is not something to which all are called, nor something of which all are capable; so meditative prayer is not the sort of prayer that God asks of us, and it is not the sort of prayer that the author of the book recommends. Not everyone is gifted with brains, but everyone has a heart, and prayer is simply the giving of one's heart to God. Furthermore, since "prayer alone can give you [the experience of] the presence of God, and give it to you continually,"[23] you must learn the sort of prayer that may be exercised at all times, whatever your state in life and whatever you happen to be doing. But since prayer that comes from one's head can have but one object at a time, continual or unceasing prayer must be the prayer of the heart, which is not interrupted by

---

[21] See further Nancy C. James, *The Spiritual Teachings of Madame Guyon, Including Translations into English from Her Writings* (Lewiston: Edwin Mellen Press, 2007).

[22] Jeanne-Marie Bouvier de La Mothe-Guyon, *Moien court & très-facile de faire oraison. Que tous peuvent pratiquer très-aisément, & arriver par la dans peu de tems à une haute perfection. Nouvelle édition* (n.p., n.d.), 9.

[23] Guyon, *Moien court*, 11.

the exercise of reason. The only things that can interrupt it, in fact, are disordered or unregulated affections.

The normal ways of introducing a soul to prayer are meditation and meditative reading (*lecture méditée*), but, as we said above, not everyone is capable of this. But "those who do not know how to read are not excluded from prayer on this account,"[24] for the great book that teaches all things is Jesus Christ himself. How, then, should they pray? They should first make an act of adoration and abasement before God and then gather themselves together inwardly and experience the presence of God directly, firmly believing that he dwells within them and controlling their thoughts and senses as best they can. This is the first degree of prayer.

"The second degree is called by some Contemplation, the Prayer of Faith, and of Stillness (*repos*); others give it the name of the Prayer of Simplicity."[25] Madame Guyon prefers this last designation, and here we begin to move into dangerous territory. In this second stage, recollection[26] becomes much easier, and one begins to be aware of the sweetness of the presence of God. Nevertheless, one should not enter this stage of prayer seeking such sweetness: one should enter it "with courage, and with a pure and disinterested love [*un amour pur, & sans interêts*], so that one seeks nothing whatever from God save to please him and do his will."[27] A servant who does his duty only for hope of reward does not deserve a reward, and we should not go to prayer to enjoy spiritual delights, but to experience whatever God wills us to experience, whether it be periods of spiritual drought or spiritual abundance. It is all up to God.

The next stage is to begin the abandonment and giving up (*l'abandon et la donation*) of our whole self to God. By this we become resigned in all things and accept all that happens as

---

[24] Guyon, *Moien court*, 16.
[25] Guyon, *Moien court*, 19.
[26] See appendix 1, s.v. *recueillement* / recollection.
[27] Guyon, *Moien court*, 20.

from God himself: "Abandonment is a stripping off of every care we may have for ourselves to leave ourselves completely at the disposal of God."[28] If God wishes us to suffer (and suffering is the way of the cross), then we must abandon ourselves to that suffering, and in this state of abandonment, Jesus Christ "often gives revelations of his own states in a very specific way."[29] What states? "Illumination or darkness, fruitfulness or barrenness, strength or weakness, sweetness or bitterness, temptations, distractions, pain, weariness, or doubt,"[30] and not one of these should hold us back from pursuing our course. It follows, too, that in this state we cannot wish for anything for ourselves, for our human will has been subsumed in that of God. "These are souls for God alone," she says in her autobiography, "who have no more interest in themselves or for themselves: all is for God, with no care or concern for their own salvation, perfection, eternity, life, or death. All that is nothing to them: their business is to let Divine Justice eat its fill of them."[31]

Furthermore, this abandonment "is a short and certain way of acquiring virtue, for if God is the source of every virtue, to possess God is to possess every virtue."[32] Abandoned souls, one might say, are passively, not actively, virtuous, because whatever they do that is virtuous is actually being done by God. All that is required is a pure and disinterested love, as Saint Augustine says—"Love, and do what you will"[33]—"for when we really love, we cannot wish to do anything that might

---

[28] Guyon, *Moien court*, 22.

[29] Guyon, *Moien court*, 26.

[30] Guyon, *Moien court*, 26.

[31] *La Vie de Madame J. M. B. de La Mothe-Guyon, écrite par elle-même, qui contient toutes les expériences de la vie intérieure*. Nouvelle édition (Paris: Libraires Associés, 1790), 2:243. The verb is *se rassasier*, "to eat one's fill, to gorge oneself with something." It is a powerful image.

[32] Guyon, *Moien court*, 27.

[33] Augustine of Hippo, *In epistulam Johannis ad Parthos*, tract. 7.8; PL 35:2033.

displease the Beloved."[34] Austerities and mortifications, therefore, are to be avoided. All they do is draw undue attention to the senses they are trying to control, and the more one mortifies one's senses, the further one withdraws from God! The only way to control the senses is not to attack them outwardly but to separate oneself from them inwardly. Once we possess God in pure love, God will do all that needs to be done, and since our will is now God's will, all we need do is follow our inward inspiration, and then, without any specific thought of mortifications, God will have us do whatever mortifications may be necessary.

The more we love and adhere to God, the more God takes us over. Indeed, "we must state it as a matter of the greatest importance that one must put an end to one's own actions and exertions so that God alone may act."[35] At this stage, all a soul needs is its quietude (*repos*), "for it is now that, during the whole day, the presence of God (which is the great effect of prayer, or, rather, the continuation of prayer) begins to be infused, almost continually."[36] This infused state of God's presence must inevitably have consequences for the sacrament of confession, for any soul that has achieved this condition need only open itself up to God to have all its faults and sins revealed. Active self-reflection is ineffective in this matter; passive resignation to the Divine Light reveals all. And not only does this passivity reveal all, but because one knows that one is totally in the presence of God, one feels not regret or contrition for one's sins, but only a sensation of love and tranquilvjity. More than that, "the soul will be astonished that it will forget its faults and have difficulty remembering them. But this, for two reasons, must not cause it any unease. The first reason is that this forgetfulness is a sign that we are purified from the fault and that at this stage it is better to forget everything that

---

[34] Guyon, *Moien court*, 28.
[35] Guyon, *Moien court*, 34.
[36] Guyon, *Moien court*, 37.

concerns us so as to remember only God. The second reason is that when we must confess, God will not fail to reveal to the soul its greatest faults," and this he will do far more effectively than anything we can do ourselves.[37]

It is clear, she continues, that by this stage the soul will find petitionary prayer more and more difficult. If you are utterly abandoned in pure love to the will of God, what can there be to ask for? Do not be surprised or concerned about your defects and failings: the more these are revealed to you, the more you must abandon yourself to God and rely on his infinite strength. Do not struggle directly with distractions and temptations, for this will only make them worse: "you should simply avert your eyes from them and draw closer and closer to God."[38] Be like a little child confronted with a monster. He does not fight it; he can hardly bear to look at it but shrinks back to his mother's breast where he knows he will find safety. Let God do the work!

We are now approaching the highest level of prayer, which is the total annihilation of oneself in God: "There are but these two truths: the All and the Nothing. Everything else is a lie. We can honor the All of God only by our own annihilation [*anéantissement*], and we are no sooner annihilated than God, who never suffers a void [in nature] without filling it, fills us with himself."[39] This is Divine Union, which cannot be achieved by discursive prayer or active contemplation, but only by the repose of one's human will, by absolute passivity in pure and disinterested love. In this state the soul does nothing, being no more than an instrument in the hands of God, who does everything. Is the path that leads to this end difficult? It is not. Is it dangerous? It is not. Is it open to all? It is:

> There is no one who does not know that God is the Supreme Good, that eternal blessedness consists of

---

[37] Guyon, *Moien court*, 42.
[38] Guyon, *Moien court*, 46.
[39] Guyon, *Moien court*, 49.

union with God, that the saints are more or less great as this union is more or less perfect, and that this union cannot be achieved in the soul by any activity of its own, for God communicates himself to the soul only to the extent that its capacity for passivity is great, noble, and extensive. One cannot be united to God without passivity and simplicity, and since this union is blessedness itself, the way that leads us to it in this passivity cannot be evil. On the contrary, it is the best way of all, and there is no risk in treading it. This way is not dangerous. If it were, would Jesus Christ have made it the most perfect and the most necessary of all ways? Everyone can tread this path, and just as everyone is called to blessedness, so too everyone is called to the enjoyment of God, both in this life and in the next, since our blessedness consists in the joyful possession [*jouissance*] of God.[40]

Such, briefly, is the essence of Madame Guyon's teaching in her *Short and Very Easy Method of Prayer*, and it is a short and very easy task to see why it would be of deep concern to any conservative churchman. It begins innocently enough with the nature of prayer, but once we get into disinterested love, resignation, abandonment, and total passivity, there are statements with regard to virtue, virtuous action, confession, sin, mortifications, temptations, and so on that were certainly at odds with the traditional teaching of the day.[41] Let us see, then, what Bossuet and his colleagues at Issy had to say on the matter. The content of the thirty-four articles[42] may be summarized under four headings.

---

[40] Guyon, *Moien court*, 76–77.
[41] See further Nancy C. James, *The Conflict Over the Heresy of "Pure Love" in Seventeenth-Century France. The Tumult over the Mysticism of Madame Guyon* (Lewiston: Edwin Mellen Press, 2008).
[42] For the text of the articles, see *Œuvres de Bossuet, évêque de Meaux, revues sur les manuscrits originaux, et les éditions les plus correctes*

First of all, there is always a place for the three theological virtues of faith, hope, and charity, just as there is always a place for acts of faith, acts of hope, and acts of charity (I). Likewise, there is always a place for an explicit faith in God as Father, Son, and Holy Spirit (II), in Jesus Christ as the God-Man and mediator (III), and in such things as his cross and resurrection and "all those things seen only by faith." To exclude these from the act of contemplation is dangerous (XXIV). Just as there is always a place for the three theological virtues, so there is always a place for the virtues and virtuous acts in general. It is God's will that all Christians should ask expressly for the remission of their sins, grace that they may no longer commit them, perseverance in good, increase in virtue, and everything else necessary for eternal salvation (VI, XV). Mortifications, too, are appropriate for every Christian condition and are often necessary, and to avoid them on the pretext that one has achieved perfection is openly condemned by Saint Paul (XVIII). Furthermore, all these virtuous acts are united in charity, for it is charity that animates all the virtues and commands their exercise, just as Saint Paul says in 1 Corinthians 13:7: "Charity bears all things, believes all things, hopes all things, endures all things" (XIII). In short, if anyone suggests that the state of perfection excludes virtuous acts, that person is in error, and what he or she says is contrary to the tradition of all the saints (XIX).

Second, just as hope always remains, so, too, does the hope of our salvation, and "every Christian in every condition, though not at every moment, is obliged to will, desire, and request explicitly his or her eternal salvation, as something willed by God and what he wills that we will for his glory" (V). No Christian, therefore, may be indifferent to the question of his or her salvation or to those things associated with it. There is indeed a "holy Christian indifference," but it involves

---

(Versailles: J. A. Lebel, 1817), 27:12–24. In the following paragraphs, Roman numerals in parentheses refer to the numbers of the articles.

being indifferent to the things of this life (save for sin) and being indifferent as to whether God, in his wisdom, decides to grant us spiritual consolations[43] or, conversely, periods of spiritual drought. That is entirely up to God (IX). On this point, Madame Guyon is quite correct. No Christian soul, however, may acquiesce to its own apparent damnation, but, with Saint Francis de Sales, it must rest assured that God will not abandon it (XXXI). Abandonment, in other words, is *not* abandoning the hope of reward or the fear of punishment. As with holy Christian indifference, there is a holy Christian abandonment, and that involves a soul's "laying aside all its uneasiness in God, entrusting to his goodness the hope of one's salvation, and, as Saint Augustine, following Saint Cyprian, teaches us, giving all to him: *Ut totum detur Deo* ['that all may be given to God']"[44] (XXXII).

Third, as to Madame Guyon's interpretation of the "unceasing prayer" of Saint Paul:[45] "Unceasing prayer does not consist in an unceasing and unique act that one imagines [takes place] without any interruption and that ought never to repeat itself. It is rather an unceasing and habitual intention and preparation to do nothing that is displeasing to God and to do everything that pleases him" (XIX). There are, of course, extraordinary states of prayer, such as the prayer of the simple presence of God or the prayer of quiet, which may be found described in such spiritual guides (*spirituels*) as Saint Francis de Sales, but these extraordinary prayers are not incompatible with virtuous acts, and they are not essential for Christian perfection—"Without these extraordinary prayers one can become a very great saint and achieve Christian perfection" (XXII)—and to limit the idea of such perfection and the purification of the soul to

---

[43] See appendix 1, s.v. *consolations* / consolations.

[44] Augustine of Hippo, *Enchiridion* 32; PL 40:248, reading *Ut totum Deo detur*. The phrase occurs nowhere in Cyprian, though it does appear in John Cassian and Peter Lombard.

[45] 1 Thess 5:17.

these extraordinary states is an obvious error (XXIII). Passive prayer does not mean that one does nothing but wait for God to inspire one to do something. True Christian submission to his will, that submission that every Christian (even those who are perfect) owes to God, is to make full use of that natural and supernatural illumination one receives from him and from the rules of Christian prudence, always presupposing that God directs everything by his Providence and that he is the author of all good counsel (XXV–XXVI). Furthermore, although Saint Francis de Sales and the other *spirituels* testify to these extraordinary graces, they also make it clear that, first, they are very rare and are granted to very few, and, second, that their authenticity is to be evaluated by bishops, ecclesiastical superiors, and learned ecclesiastics, who will judge them not by the experiences themselves, but by the immutable rules of Scripture and Tradition (XXVIII).

Fourth, it is Scripture and Tradition that are the guides to the Christian life, and the Tradition of the Church is the Apostolic Tradition, handed down from Christ to his apostles, and from his apostles to the successors of the apostles, the bishops of the church. This tradition, or these traditions, have behind them the authority of the Council of Trent, and they are the only traditions recognized by the church. Any so-called secret apostolic traditions[46] are no more than snares for the faithful and a way of introducing into the Christian faith all manner of wicked doctrines (XX).

In summary, (i) whatever the state of one's soul, there is always a place for the virtues and the performance of virtuous acts, (ii) there is no time when one should be indifferent to one's salvation or punishment, and no time when one should not hope for the one and fear the other, (iii) extraordinary states of prayer certainly occur, but they are unquestionably rare and

---

[46] *Les prétendues traditions apostoliques secrètes*: i.e., the teaching of Madame Guyon, which was supposedly received by direct revelation from God.

come but rarely to very few people, and they never preclude the performance of virtuous acts. Nor are they necessary indications of Christian perfection, and (iv) there is no place in the church for secret personal revelations purporting to come directly from God and masquerading as apostolic traditions.

When the articles were signed, Madame Guyon was staying with the nuns of the convent of the Visitation at Meaux. There she submitted formally to their content and undertook not to write, teach, act as a spiritual director, or circulate her books, and this, essentially, is the end of her story. After her submission she returned secretly to Paris, but at the end of 1695, on the king's orders, she was arrested and imprisoned in the castle of Vincennes (Madame de Maintenon almost certainly had a hand in this). From there she was removed to a convent in Vaugirard (now part of Paris) and then to the Bastille, where she remained until March 21, 1703. She was then released and entrusted to the care of her son, who lived near Blois (on the banks of the Loire, between Orléans and Tours), and there, under his watchful eye, she lived on for another fourteen years. She died on June 9, 1717, at the age of sixty-nine, and her numerous works, in various translations, found a wide audience not among Catholics but among Protestants, especially those Protestants who espoused the principles of the Radical Reformation, in the Netherlands, Germany, England, and, later, North America. They found her teachings on an experience of God unmediated by either the church or the sacraments and open to all much to their taste.

From the time of her submission to the articles of Issy, Madame Guyon withdrew from public life and took no further part in the Quietist controversy, but just as she withdrew, so the controversy erupted again and became yet more heated with the battle between Bossuet and Fénelon. It was a battle that did no good to either party, a battle that certainly revealed Bossuet in a bad light, and a battle that did grave damage to the church. The details need not concern us, but at its core lay Fénelon's recognition that although a considerable number of

Madam Guyon's ideas were contrary to the traditional teaching of the church, her central notion of a pure and disinterested love for God was not only Christian but could be supported by a plethora of recognized authorities going back to the period of the early church. He, of course, could not have known the eighth-century female Muslim mystic, Rabi'a al-'Adawiyya, who famously prayed, "Oh my Lord! If I worship you from fear of Hell, burn me in Hell. And if I worship you in hope of Paradise, exclude me from there. But if I worship you for your own sake, do not withhold from me your everlasting beauty!"[47] That, however, is the heart of the matter.

After the conference at Issy, Bossuet had prepared his own rejoinder to Madame Guyon's *Short and Very Easy Method*. It was a long, solid, and polemical volume, divided into ten books, with the title *Instruction sur les états d'oraison, où sont exposées les erreurs des faux mystiques de nos jours* ("Instruction on the States of Prayer, in which the Errors of the False Mystics of Our Days are Exposed"). It was also a book that was much to the taste of the times, and it would enjoy considerable success. In July 1696, Bossuet sent a copy of the manuscript to Fénelon, who condemned it without having read it, and Fénelon himself was busy with his own work defending the essential principles of Madame Guyon's Quietism. This would be the famous (or infamous, depending on whose side you were on) *Explication des maximes des saints sur la vie intérieure* ("An Explanation of the Sayings of the Saints on the Interior Life"), which was rushed into print by one of Fénelon's friends at the very end of January 1697. Bossuet's *Instruction* was published two months later.

Fénelon was, of course, much better educated than Madame Guyon, and a far better theologian. He was therefore able to rectify, as it were, some of her statements in order to bring them closer to the traditional teachings of the church. He

---

[47] Farid-uddin 'Attar, ed. Reynold A. Nicholson, *The Tadhkiratu'l-Awliya of Muhammad ibn Ibrahim Faridu'd-Din 'Attar* (London: Luzac & Co., 1907), 1:73.

could demonstrate, for example, that although pure love was indeed a totally disinterested love, the virtue of hope nevertheless remained. He could demonstrate that the practice of confession was not incompatible with the state of pure love. He could show that both Saint Augustine and Saint Thomas Aquinas taught that if pure love is to be found in the heart, this necessarily implies the existence of all the other virtues, but that this principle is not incompatible with the actual practice of the virtues. And so on. Fénelon's arguments are far more subtle than those of Madame Guyon, and the authorities he quotes to support his arguments—Augustine, for example, or Anselm, Aquinas, Cardinal Bona, Clement of Alexandria, Francis de Sales (a particular favorite), Gregory of Nazianzus, John Cassian, John Chrysostom, John of the Cross—were irreproachable in their orthodoxy. But the *Explication* had been written too quickly, and despite Fénelon's subtle arguments, there were still to be found statements too close to the condemned ideas of Madame Guyon. Nor had the ecclesiastical authorities examined the text so carefully as they should, and complaints and criticisms followed immediately after its too hasty publication.

The archbishop of Paris, Louis-Antoine de Noailles, admitted that his examination of the book had been too cursory and decided that it should be reexamined, but Fénelon would not agree to this. It was, perhaps, an unwise decision, for it not only antagonized the archbishop of Paris, but it also antagonized the king. At this time, Fénelon was preceptor to Louis's grandson, the duke of Burgundy, and Louis had no desire for his grandson to be tutored by a crypto-Quietist. Thus, on August 1, 1697, Fénelon was ordered to withdraw to his diocese of Cambrai, and there he would spend the rest of his life. Two days after his banishment he wrote to a friend, the duke de Beauvilliers, expressing his feelings on the matter; the letter was printed; Bossuet published a reply; this was the beginning of two years of bitter pamphlet warfare between two great churchmen who had once been fast friends.

We need not follow the intricacies of what Ronald Knox has called the Battle of the Olympians,[48] which all too soon became entangled in ecclesiastical politics and intrigues in Rome, but the result was inevitable. However ably Fénelon defended himself, there was no way he could win. On March 12, 1699, under pressure from Louis XIV, Pope Innocent XII issued the Apostolic Brief *Cum alias ad apostolatus,* which condemned twenty-three articles from Fénelon's *Explication,* and in his own *Mandement* of April 9, Fénelon formally informed the people of his diocese that he had submitted to the pope's decision. What are the essential points of the pope's Brief? They can be subsumed under four headings.

First, it condemns the idea that there is a habitual state of pure love or holy indifference in which is neither fear of punishment nor desire for reward, and in which every self-interested motive of fear or hope is lost. In this state, we no longer seek salvation out of our own personal interest, but "we will it with our whole will as the glory and good pleasure of God, as the thing that he wills and that he wills us to will for his sake."[49]

Second, it condemns the idea the soul can experience such extreme trials, sufferings, and difficulties that it can become invincibly (*invincibiliter*) convinced that God has justly rejected it (for God cannot act unjustly), and that in this state the soul may willingly make a sacrifice of its eternal happiness to God. Such an idea is incompatible with the principle of Christian hope, which, as Saint Paul says, always remains.[50]

Third, it condemns the idea that, in the state of absolute passivity, "all the separate virtues are exercised without thinking that they might be virtues," and that "holy mystics have excluded from the state of transformed souls the practice of the virtues."[51]

---

[48] Knox, *Enthusiasm,* chap. 14.
[49] Denzinger, no. 2356.
[50] See chap. 9 (La Rue), §29.
[51] Denzinger, nos. 2368 and 2371.

And fourth, it condemns the idea that in confession a soul that has been transformed by and into pure love must detest its sins and seek their remission "not for one's own personal purification and liberation, but as the thing that God wills, and wills us to will for his glory."[52]

It must be observed that some of the condemned articles are taken out of context and that Fénelon could have defended what he wrote, not least with regard to the continuance of hope, the practice of the virtues, and the question of confession. We might also suggest that had he not written the book so quickly and had it not been published so hastily, he might have modified some of the statements and made them less objectionable and have polished his language to make it more theologically precise. Now, however, it was too late. The teaching of Molinos had been condemned, the teaching of Madame Guyon had been condemned, and the much more subtle teaching of Fénelon had also been condemned.

They were not the only ones. In Italy the brothers Simone and Antonio Maria Leoni had been condemned for Quietist errors on September 4, 1687, and on December 17 of the same year, after a sensational trial, Cardinal Pier Matteo Petrucci was obliged to make a public retraction of fifty-four Quietist propositions extracted from his works by the Holy Office.[53] Dozens of books had been placed on the *Index*, and, as Pierre Pourrat says, spiritual writers were filled with panic: "Surely, they said, mysticism was a dangerous matter. Molinos and others had, under the pretext of extraordinary prayer, succumbed to shocking immoralities. Was it not safer to walk in the common ways of asceticism and carefully to avoid that mystical path so full of peril? Such was the reasoning of many spiritual authors."[54]

---

[52] Denzinger, no. 2370.

[53] See Henry C. Lea, "Molinos and the Italian Mystics," *American Historical Review* 11 (1906): 243–62.

[54] Pourrat, *Christian Spirituality. Later Developments. Part II*, 261–62.

It was certainly the reasoning of almost all the panegyrists presented in these pages. Bernard of Clairvaux may indeed have been a great mystic, but to discuss his mysticism was far too dangerous and could lead one all too easily into theological and spiritual quicksands. With the exception of Henri-Marie Boudon, the Bernard of the panegyrists is the ascetic Bernard of the cloister and the active Bernard who comes forth from his cloister in his staunch defense of the church. In the hands of Charles de La Rue he becomes the anti-mystic, or, more accurately, the anti-Quietist, but La Rue's fiery denunciation of Quietism clearly shows that it was never one unified system. Some of the ideas he attacks come from Molinos, some from Madame Guyon, and some from Fénelon, for Quietism represented an amorphous amalgamation of ideas, all proceeding, more or less logically, from the notion of the absolute passivity of the soul in God. It is not hard to see its attraction. Madame Guyon's method of prayer was indeed "short and very easy," and people like short and very easy methods. I do myself. Who now bothers to learn multiplication or long division when a calculator will do it for you? Furthermore, the concept of "pure love," as Fénelon made clear, had a long and honorable history in Christian spirituality, and there are few clearer or more concise discussions of its nature and the stages that lead to it than Bernard's *De diligendo Deo*. But the church has always looked on mysticism with a wary eye, for it can too easily lead to challenges to ecclesiastical authority, to the principle of the intermediary priesthood, and to the sacraments as channels of grace. Whether or not Madame Guyon's system works—and that is a matter beyond our consideration in these pages—one can understand why Bossuet and his colleagues were so opposed to it, and why this "new spirituality" (*la nouvelle spiritualité*) and the teachings of these "false mystics" (*faux mystiques*) caused them so much anxiety. And what was true of Bossuet and his colleagues was also true of almost all those who wrote panegyrics in praise of Saint Bernard. To the nature of those panegyrics, and to the great importance of sermons in seventeenth-century France, we must now turn our attention.

3

Sermons and Panegyrics

In the France of Louis XIV, religion, like life in general, was public rather than private. That is to say, what one did, one generally did in company, and one's religious observances were not just to be carried out but seen to be carried out. Personal privacy, as we know it today, had not yet been invented. If one reads the duc de Saint-Simon's account of the daily regimen of Louis himself, it is clear that from waking and dressing in the morning to undressing and retiring at night, there was virtually no time of the day when the king was unobserved.[1] It was all part of a public display of power. Going to church, therefore, and listening to the sermons of some of the greatest orators of the time, was not something one did just for personal pleasure, but something one did as a statement of one's position in society. Furthermore, the sanctity of the church and pulpit, together with the nature of their calling, allowed the preachers to criticize an autocratic society that did not take kindly to criticism. Sermons, as Gerald Cragg has said, "were one of the few means of moulding public opinion; they were almost the only vehicle of criticism in matters of high public concern."[2] They served as a source of public instruction and

---

[1] See [Louis de Rouvroy] Duke of Saint-Simon, *Memoirs of Louis XIV and His Court and of the Regency*, vol. 11, chap. 78, readily available at gutenberg.org.
[2] Gerald R. Cragg, *The Church and the Age of Reason 1648–1789*, The Pelican History of the Church, 4 (Harmondsworth, UK: Penguin Books,

51

as "a rhetorical instrument implicitly sustaining (and sometimes subverting) the social and political order, and a mode of discourse reflecting religious mentalities."[3] They were also part of literary culture in a literary age.

It is understandable, therefore, that congregations were large. Many went to see and be seen, many went to hear what was going on (and what should not be going on) in the world around them, many went to be edified or "touched" (an important word we shall discuss in a moment) by the words of the preacher, connoisseurs of oratory went to judge the rhetorical brilliance and delivery of the sermon, and the common people went, as Voltaire said, for much the same reason they went to public executions: because they could get in free. It was one of their few forms of entertainment.

All had plenty of choice. Sermons were preached on all Sundays and important feast days, as well as at weddings, funerals, the taking of monastic vows, and a large variety of civic and national functions. There were also the important Lenten and Advent series (*stations* in French), the former being either the *Grand carême* ("Great Lent"), with sermons being delivered on the Sundays and weekdays of the whole Lenten period, and the *Petit carême* ("Small Lent"), which comprised the Sunday sermons only. Those selected to preach the Lenten and Advent series were well paid for their services, and those selected to preach the Lenten and Advent series before the

---

1970), 35. For a discussion of the usefulness of studying seventeenth-century French sermons, see Peter Bayley, *French Pulpit Oratory 1598–1650. A Study in Themes and Styles, with a Descriptive Catalogue of Printed Texts* (Cambridge: Cambridge University Press, 1980), chap. 1 (3–16). None of the panegyrists who appear in this present study is listed in Bayley's "Descriptive Catalogue."

[3] Joris Van Eijnatten, "Reaching Audiences: Sermons and Oratory in Europe, 1660–1800," in *The Cambridge History of Christianity, Volume VII: Enlightenment, Reawakening and Revolution 1660–1815*, ed. Stewart J. Brown and Timothy Tackett (Cambridge: Cambridge University Press, 2006), 138.

royal Court at Versailles might well end up with a bishopric. Antoine Furetière called them "prédicateurs épiscopants,"[4] which defies neat translation. Other sermons of major importance were funeral orations for well-known figures, especially those associated with the royal house, the annual panegyric on Saint Louis delivered before the *Académie française*, and the sermon on Saint Augustine preached before the Assembly of the Clergy at its decennial meetings. Sermons were preached in the morning, afternoon, and sometimes evening, and, for a regular Sunday Mass, most sermon guidelines followed the recommendations of the Council of Trent that suggested a length of fifteen to thirty minutes. More important sermons for more significant occasions would naturally be longer, and sermons of about an hour were far from uncommon. Louis Bourdaloue had a reputation for excessive length, not wholly justified, and is, I think, the only preacher in history to have a chamber pot named after him. A *bourdaloue* was such a receptacle designed for women so that they could relieve themselves beneath their skirts if the sermon proved too great a strain on their capacity. They were small and often came with a case and a cover or lid. If a lady needed to use one, her maid would bring it to her and, after use, would put on the cover, take away the pot and dispose of the contents.[5] Whether and how often this was necessary we do not know, but chamber pots of this nature would have proved invaluable on, say, a long journey in a closed and ill-sprung coach (they were known as coach-pots in England) or during a long play at the theater. But unless there were medical problems or an unwise consumption of too much liquid before attending church, most men and women would have been able to last through the service without too much discomfort. My own estimate for a

---

[4] See W. Pierre Jacoebee, "The Classical Sermon and the French Literary Tradition," *Australian Journal of French Studies* 19 (1982): 230. See also McManners, *Church and Society*, 2:59–60.

[5] Illustrations of examples may be found on the internet.

long sermon by Bourdaloue is just over an hour and a half, but there was an old joke that the Holy Spirit himself had limited the sermon to a maximum of one hour, for do we not read in chapter 10:19 of the gospel according to Saint Matthew that "in that hour it shall be given you what to speak"?[6] Most of the panegyrics presented or translated here would have taken, I think, between about an hour and a quarter and an hour and a half to deliver, though the precise time would naturally depend on the speed at which the preacher spoke. Armand-Jean de Rancé's conference on Bernard would have taken about an hour, which was about average for his conferences.

The basic form of the sermon was simple: introduction, substance, and conclusion. In the introduction or exordium the preacher would normally outline the major divisions or points of his discourse—invariably two or three—and briefly present the general course of his argument. He would conclude the exordium with a prayer for the inspiration of the Holy Spirit and an invocation to the Virgin Mary in the words of the *Ave Maria*, something for which (as we shall see) Bossuet provides a reason.[7] The exordium, in fact, was rather like the overture to an opera, and the whole sermon, as a literary production, was just as much bound by rules as a piece of music. The preacher would then begin the substance of his discourse by returning to the first point or heading, and his delivery had to be in accordance with well-defined rules of structure, expression, intonation, and gesture. At the end of his exposition, he would deliver his conclusion, in which he would summarize the main points of his discourse and apply them directly, and often unsparingly, to the audience before him.

As to its structure, the seventeenth-century sermon was deeply influenced by the principles of late medieval scholas-

---

[6] See Jules Candel, *Les Prédicateurs français dans la première moitié du XVIIIe siècle* (Paris: A. Picard, 1904), 439. See also McManners, *Church and Society*, 2:64–65, and Bayley, *French Pulpit Oratory*, 16.

[7] See chap. 7 (Bossuet), §§1–3.

ticism, which found its epitome in the multitudinous divisions and subdivisions of the great *Summa theologica* of Saint Thomas Aquinas. The texts, as Joris Van Eijnatten has said, "were carefully divided into divisions and subdivisions, generals and particulars, and numerous heads, points, doctrines, uses and improvements,"[8] and it cannot be denied that this can be somewhat tedious to the modern ear. Jacques Biroat's panegyric on Saint Bernard, translated in chapter 4, provides us with an excellent example of this, but Biroat was criticized for adhering too slavishly to this rigid scheme. In preachers like Bossuet and Massillon, "the rules are obeyed, but in the spirit of the master, not of the slave; structure and progress are apparent, but not obtrusive,"[9] and Bossuet always retained a degree of freedom. He was, one might say, always guided by the rules but never bound by them. In a charming analogy, Denis O'Mahony likens the seventeenth-century sermon to a formal French garden of the period, "with its straight bordered alleys, its beds of geometrical design—where nothing is wanting but the picturesque and the unexpected."[10] True, he is speaking specifically of Bourdaloue, but the description, in varying degrees, is common to all.

As to style, every sermon by any preacher worthy of the name was deeply influenced by the principles of rhetoric, and rhetoric occupied an important place in the formal curriculum of all secondary education.[11] Both lawyers and clergy studied

---

[8] Van Eijnatten, "Reaching Audiences," 139. See further Bayley, *French Pulpit Oratory*, 101–11.

[9] Edwin C. Dargan, *A History of Preaching*, Vol. II: *From the Close of the Reformation Period to the End of the Nineteenth Century 1572–1900* (New York: Armstrong, 1912; repr. New York: B. Franklin, 1968), 88.

[10] *Panegyrics of the Saints, from the French of Bossuet and Bourdaloue*, ed. Denis O'Mahony (London: Kegan Paul, Trench, Trubner & Co., 1924), ix.

[11] See Jacoebee, "The Classical Sermon," 240 n. 15. For a detailed and excellent study of rhetoric in the schools and in the church, see Bayley, *French Pulpit Oratory*, chaps. 2–3, pp. 17–71.

it assiduously, and there was a large variety of textbooks from which it might be learned. Rhetoric defined the rules that governed any spoken composition that was intended to influence the judgment or the feelings of those who heard it, and, accordingly, the textbooks dealt with such matters as linguistic beauty, forcefulness of style, arrangement of topics, and mode of delivery. Putting it another way, rhetoric was the art and science of persuasion, and there was always a problem that, in the technical study of rhetoric, the emphasis on persuasion might obscure an emphasis on truth. Long ago, Plato had discussed precisely this problem in the *Gorgias*, and in the *Phaedrus* had set out the essential principles of rhetoric. Aristotle, too, had criticized those who sought to sway the members of an audience by appealing to their emotions rather than changing their minds by a persuasive presentation of the truth. Book learning alone, of course, could not achieve this. The orator had to be a gifted orator, having both a natural gift of expression or speech and the ability to gauge an audience. He also had to be an acute psychologist, for if (as Plato defined it) "oratory is the art of enchanting the mind,"[12] the orator must be aware of the multitudinous differences among human minds and be able to judge just which type of speech or appeal will be effective with which type of person. Plato likened him to a physician, who has to hand not only the necessary medical supplies but also skill in diagnosis, knowing rapidly and accurately the nature of the problem and the remedy that needed to be applied.[13] Of the great French preachers, Massillon was perhaps the most astute psychologist, combining with a beautiful, measured, and persuasive delivery a thorough appreciation and understanding of his audience. Fléchier, on the other hand, despite the popularity of his sermons, tended to apply the rules of rhetoric too stringently, and, as Edwin Dargan has said, his

---

[12] Plato, *Phaedrus* 271c.
[13] See *Phaedrus* 272b.

sermons were "too evidently studied with their carefully balanced periods and set phrases."[14] This we shall see to be true.

The basis for all the sermons is Scripture, and its use is, if we may use the word, indiscriminate. Almost any biblical verse might be used to support a line of reasoning, prove a point, or embellish a theme,[15] and preachers regularly translated the Vulgate to suit their own purposes. Scripture, in fact, is quoted, misquoted, applied, and misapplied, but the great advantage of Scripture is that if one knows what it says (and the preachers knew it intimately), and if one is prepared to accept a little forced logic, there is something in Scripture to substantiate and reinforce virtually any argument. Quotation from other sources is much less common. In Bossuet's and Rancé's panegyrics on Saint Bernard, for example, the only authorities cited are Augustine of Hippo, Gregory the Great, and Fastred of Clairvaux, and the *Vita prima*, which, as we saw in the first chapter, was the standard and unquestioned source for all those seventeenth-century orators who preached on Bernard. Citation from Bernard's own works is surprisingly rare. Fénelon adds Tertullian and Saint John Chrysostom (Bossuet would have approved of both), and Biroat adds Gregory of Nazianzus and Maximus of Turin, but unlike the preachers of an earlier age, there is no overt display of patristic erudition in any of these great orators. Henri-Marie Boudon, archdeacon of Évreaux, stands out as an exception. In his remarkable and, indeed, unique panegyric, apart from Scripture and the *Vita prima*, he introduces the names of no fewer than twenty-one authorities: *ps.*-Albertus Magnus, Ambrose of Milan, Augustine and *ps.*-Augustine, Cardinal Baronius, Bede, Bonaventure and *ps.*-Bonaventure, *ps.*-Dionysius the Areopagite, François de Sales, Gilbert of Hoyland, Gregory the Great, Jerome, Richard of Saint-Victor, Rupert of Deutz, Teresa of Ávila, Tertullian, Theodoret of Cyrrhus, Thomas Aquinas, William of Saint-Thierry

---

[14] Dargan, *History of Preaching*, 2:108.
[15] See Van Eijnatten, "Reaching Audiences," 139.

(referred to, as usual, as "the historian of [Bernard's] life"), and Zeno of Verona. But this is decidedly unusual. We shall say more on sources in our final chapter.

It is doubtful nowadays that many would appreciate the formality and length of a sermon of, say, Bossuet or Bourdaloue, and we would certainly raise our eyebrows at the actions of the preacher. As we said above, a fine delivery involved structure, expression, intonation, and gesture, and the gestures of the preacher might conceivably cause us just as much astonishment as they did British travelers to France in the seventeenth century. They were clearly not accustomed to this style of preaching and sometimes commented upon it. One of them, Sir John Lauder, heard a learned Jesuit preach, "affecting strange gestures in his delivery more beseeming a Comedian than a pulpit man,"[16] and John Locke speaks of a friar preaching in the cathedral at Carcassonne "with great action."[17] The English naturalist and physician Martin Lister approved neither the delivery nor the language of a preacher he heard delivering a Lenten sermon in 1698: "I was strangely surprised at the Vehemency of his Action," he wrote, "which to me appeared altogether Comical, and like the Actors upon the Stage, which I had seen a few days before: Besides his Expressions seemed to be in too Familiar a Style: I always took a Sermon to the People to require a grave and ornate kind of Eloquence, and not *Verba Quotidiana*, with a certain dignity of Action."[18]

On the other hand, even in staid and conservative England the actions of the preacher played an important role. In 1749 John Wesley published a little pamphlet of twelve pages entitled *Directions concerning Pronunciation and Gesture*,[19] in which

---

[16] John Lough, *France Observed in the Seventeenth Century by British Travellers* (Stocksfield, UK, and Boston: Oriel Press, 1985), 212, with modernized spelling.

[17] Lough, *France Observed*, 215.

[18] Lough, *France Observed*, 215.

[19] John Wesley, *Directions concerning Pronunciation and Gesture* (Bristol: F. Farley, 1749). See also n. 37 below.

he explained how one should speak, how one should vary one's voice, and how one should act. One's gestures, he tells us, should be free from affectation, and there should be "nothing in all the Dispositions and Movements of your Body, to offend the Eyes of the Spectators."[20] You should not hold your head too high, nor "clownishly thrust forward."[21] When you speak of heaven you should raise your eyes; if you speak of disgraceful things, you should cast them down. You must not bite your lips, shrug your shoulders, lean on your elbow, clap your hands, or thump the pulpit. But when you speak of your own faculties, you should gently lay your right hand on your breast, and your eyes, mouth, and hands should all move in concert. Only seldom should you stretch out your arms sideways, and "your hands are not to be in perpetual Motion: This the Ancients call'd, The Babbling of the Hands."[22] From the comments of the travelers, however, it seems that the practice in seventeenth-century France was rather more dramatic and (as Lister said) vehement.

It is obvious from all this that the sermon could become no more than a spectacle, in which the message was subordinated to the way in which it was delivered. In fact, despite the frequent condemnations of the theater that echoed from the pulpits,[23] the sermon itself could become a form of theater. Indeed, some missionary sermons were theater, "replete with banners, processions, choruses and dramatic action performed in front of imposing stage designs."[24] According to Jean de La Bruyère, Christian preaching had become a show, a spectacle, "one sort of amusement among a thousand others,"[25] and in Lent, when the theaters were closed, attending a good Lenten sermon, rhetorically brilliant and beautifully delivered, could be a very

---

[20] Wesley, *Directions*, 9.
[21] Wesley, *Directions*, 10.
[22] Wesley, *Directions*, 10.
[23] See, for example, chap. 14 (Massillon), §62 and n. 192.
[24] Van Eijnatten, "Reaching Audiences," 132.
[25] Quoted in Dargan, *History of Preaching*, 2:248.

enjoyable alternative. And just as in the theater play would be compared with play, so too in the churches, especially the churches of Paris, sermon would be compared with sermon and preacher with preacher. Who was better? Who was more stylish? Who touched one more? During one Lent, Madame de Sévigné wrote to her cousin, Bussy-Rabutin, telling him that "We are presently engaged in judging some fine sermons [*juger des beaux sermons*]," and complaining that her favorite preacher, Louis Bourdaloue, was preaching in a church that, for her, was not easily accessible.[26] The preachers themselves were, of course, well aware of the motives of those who went to hear them, and both Bourdaloue himself and, forty years later, Massillon criticized their congregations for being more concerned with how a sermon was delivered than with the message they were trying to convey.[27]

The subject of the sermons was invariably morality. Christian doctrine was rarely discussed. Why should it be? The Catholic Church in the France of Biroat, Bossuet, Fléchier, and the others knew exactly where it stood and knew exactly what it believed. There might be disagreements on the details of those beliefs—Jansenists and Jesuits might disagree on the role of grace, for example—but neither would or could deny its necessity, and the beliefs themselves were well known, solidly established, firmly believed, and unquestioningly accepted. In the first half of the fifth century, Vincent, abbot of the monastery of Lérins (on the island of Saint-Honorat on the French Riviera), discussed the question of whether there can be progress (*profectus*) in the church. If the canon of Scripture is perfect and wholly sufficient for salvation, and if, in interpreting that Scripture, "we, in the Church Catholic, take the greatest care to hold that which has been believed

---

[26] See Jacoebee, "The Classical Sermon," 228.
[27] See Jacoebee, "The Classical Sermon," 230–31. See also chap. 12 below, nn. 89–90 (Ogier) and nn. 129–30 (Fléchier).

everywhere, always, and by all,"[28] what possible room can there be for progress? There *is* room, he answers, but only if progress means advancement and not change. Progress implies growth and development within a thing itself; change implies the transformation of that thing into something else. With the course of time, he says, the facts of the faith are "to be carefully tended, refined, and polished. They are not to be changed, mutilated, or lessened. They may certainly gain clarity, light, and distinctness, but they must also retain their completeness, integrity, and characteristic nature."[29] This was also the view of the Catholic Church in seventeenth-century France. So far as that church was concerned, what it believed was what had been believed everywhere, always, and by all, and those unfortunates who disputed this and belonged to *la religion prétendue réformée*—that is to say, Protestantism—could only look forward to an eternity of torment, gnashing of teeth, and the worm that dieth not. Bossuet, in his brilliant *Histoire des variations des églises protestantes* ("History of the Variations of the Protestant Churches"), published in 1688, had already made the case that any variation in religion is always a sign of error, and that the lack of continuity in Protestant doctrine and the subordination of ecclesiastical authority to individual judgment stood in sharp contrast to the solid, static, majestic, immutable stronghold of Catholic truth. There was no place, then, for doctrinal discussion in Catholic sermons of the seventeenth century, but there was plenty of room for moral exhortation.

The preachers' discourses contained forceful and moving descriptions of the world as it was, with all its faults, sin, and corruption. The faults, sin, and corruption were not generally described in detail—it was not the preachers' business to play to the prurient interests of their audience—but their indirect descriptions were intended to bring about a change,

---

[28] *The Commonitorium of Vincentius of Lerins*, ed. Reginald S. Moxon (Cambridge: Cambridge University Press, 1915), 10 (II.3).

[29] *The Commonitorium*, 88–89, 93 (XXIII.28, 30).

hopefully a lasting change, of heart and conscience in their audience. What they were seeking was *conversion* (the same word in French and English), and the conversion they were seeking was what, in Latin, was termed *conversatio morum*,[30] an ongoing transformation in one's way of living. It required a shift in values, a change in direction, a renunciation of sin and all that leads to sin, and, ideally, a complete surrender of one's own will to the will of God. This is, of course, asking a great deal, and it is asking a great deal more to maintain it. It is easy to go on a diet in January after the splendid excesses of Christmas; it is not easy to maintain that diet in February and March. The preachers, naturally, were perfectly aware of this, and if they could not bring about a permanent change of heart, they could at least hope to sow the seeds. What they condemned in their sermons, therefore, were pride, vanity, lust, and sin—the things of this world—and what they emphasized was penance and penitence, "a sincere repentance for one's sins accompanied by the resolution to follow the commands of one's religion more faithfully."[31] How were they to achieve this end? Fénelon tells us in his *Dialogues sur l'éloquence*, a work that was not published until 1718, three years after his death.[32]

In the first of the three *Dialogues* he tells us what we already know: that the purpose of true eloquence, especially eloquence in a sermon, is emphatically not display or entertainment. It is, rather, to instruct the intelligence and improve the morals of the hearers. This is what preaching is all about. Then, in the

---

[30] The term appears in chapter 58.17 of the Rule of Saint Benedict: a Benedictine (and Cistercian) monk or nun vows stability, conversion of life, and obedience. The principle, however, obviously applies to all Christians. The seventeenth-century preachers were not asking their congregations to take monastic vows.

[31] Jacoebee, "The Classical Sermon," 235.

[32] *Dialogues sur l'éloquence en général, et sur celle de la chaire en particulier, Par feu Messire François de Salignac de La Mothe Fénelon . . . avec les Réflexions sur la Poésie françoise. Par le P. Du Cerceau* (Amsterdam: J. F. Bernard, 1718).

second *Dialogue*, Fénelon explains that in order to achieve this goal, the preacher must *prouver, peindre*, and *toucher*, "prove, paint, and touch."[33] That is to say, he must appeal to the reason with proof or demonstration that what he is saying is true, he must appeal to the imagination by conjuring up pictures in the minds of his hearers, and he must appeal to the feelings and emotions with words and gestures that touch or move the heart. Every preacher regarded the third point—*toucher*—as essential, and as Joris Van Eijnatten has said, "A sermon failing to appeal to the emotions was considered barren."[34] It was, in any case, an emotional age. Tears flowed more freely than they do with us, and sentiment was often mistaken for conviction. There is no doubt that a sermon by, say, Bourdaloue could be effective, that he could truly touch the hearts of those who heard him, and there is also no doubt that his audience wished to be touched and wished to be converted. They wanted preaching that stirred the soul, showed them their faults, rebuked them for their errors, brought tears to their eyes, and offered them hope. And what was true of the audiences in the churches of Paris was also true of the king and his court at Versailles. Louis XIV, wrote Edwin Dargan,

> not merely took pleasure in orations marked by imagination, passion, and elegance, as a good many monarchs have done, but he wanted earnest and kindling appeals to the conscience—real preaching. His preachers saw that he listened attentively, that his feelings could be touched, his conscience could sometimes be reached. They were constantly hoping to make him a better man, and through him to exert a powerful influence for good upon the court and the nation.[35]

---

[33] See the first two pages of the unpaginated Preface to the *Dialogues*.
[34] Van Eijnatten, "Reaching Audiences," 136.
[35] Dargan, *History of Preaching*, 2:86.

Thus, when Bossuet confronted Louis with his matrimonial infidelity with Madame de Montespan, or appealed to him to take better note of the sufferings of the people, Louis was ready to listen.[36] He may not have listened for very long, and the flames of his passion for Madame de Montespan might soon have burned up any resolve he might have had to do something about it, but at least he was ready to listen.

How a sermon should be judged was clearly set out in the popular work by Cardinal Jean-Sifrein Maury, *Essai sur l'éloquence de la chaire*, which ran to thirteen French editions between 1777 and 1851.[37] Maury, of course, was writing many years after the death of the last of the preachers mentioned in this book, but the principles he sets forth were the principles that Madame de Sévigné and her friends were using when they set out on their regular rounds of sermon-tasting. Maury himself had an eventful life. He was born in 1746 to an impoverished family, and was educated and took holy orders at the seminary in Avignon. His rise to fame began with the huge success of his panegyric on Saint Louis, delivered to the *Académie française* in 1772, and he then preached to great acclaim in the churches of Paris as well as before Louis XVI. We should add, however, that his mode of life and his, let us say, relaxed morality did not always accord with the subject of his sermons. He was elected to the *Académie* in 1785 and was then caught up in the turmoil of the French Revolution. As a member of the National Constituent Assembly, he staunchly opposed the alienation of the property of the clergy, and did so with great courage. His life was more than once in peril, but he was able to turn aside the threats with his ready wit. Late in 1791, however,

---

[36] See Ian Dunlop, *Louis XIV* (London: Chatto & Windus, 1999), 196.
[37] An abridged English translation was made by John Neal Lake and published in 1833: *The Principles of Eloquence Adapted to the Pulpit and the Bar by the Abbé Maury. To Which are added Mr. Wesley's Directions concerning Pronunciation and Gesture* (New York: B. Waugh & T. Mason, 1833).

he found it politic to leave France, first for Koblenz and then for Rome, and Pope Pius VI recognized his efforts on behalf of the French clergy (and the French monarchy) by appointing him archbishop of Nicaea *in partibus infidelium*, and then, in 1794, cardinal. When Rome was occupied by Republican forces in 1798, Maury fled to Venice and then to St. Petersburg, but returned to Rome the next year as the ambassador of Louis XVIII, who was then exiled in what is now Latvia. It was not long, however, before Maury saw the way the winds were blowing, ingratiated himself with Napoleon, and returned to Paris in 1806 when he accepted from the emperor the see of Paris, though he never referred to himself as anything other than archbishop-elect. In April 1814, Napoleon was forced to abdicate and was exiled to the island of Elba, and Louis XVIII found himself back on the throne. Maury was then expelled from France and returned to Rome, where he was imprisoned for six months in the Castel Sant'Angelo for disobeying the pope. Friends obtained his release and his reconciliation with Pope Pius VII, but his time in prison had destroyed his health, and he died on May 10, 1817. He was found dead by his servants, holding his rosary.

In his *Essai sur l'éloquence de la chaire*, the cardinal deals with everything one needs to know when it comes to judging a sermon. He has chapters on the overall plan of the homily, how it should develop, the structure of the exordium, the choice of subjects, the difference between sermons and panegyrics, the need for ardor (*chaleur*) in the delivery, the use of metaphor, the proper choice of words, the use of Scripture and the fathers of the church, citations from profane authors, the need for *onction* (which Lake translates as *pathos*), and so on. *Onction*, "unction," is of particular importance, and it will appear a number of times in these pages. Hugh Blair, professor of rhetoric and belles lettres at the University of Edinburgh in the second half of the eighteenth century, defined it as "the affecting, penetrating, interesting manner, flowing from a strong sensibility of heart in the Preacher to the importance of those truths which he delivers, and an earnest desire that they may make full impression on the hearts of his hearers."[38] Not everyone, says Cardinal Maury, is able to lay hold of an ingenious idea, but "everyone has a soul that can be affected by a weighty sentiment; and the listeners are never more universally attentive than in those moments of emotion when a preacher opens up all hearts by becoming *pathétique*,"[39] that is to say, when a preacher opens up all hearts by moving or touching them. "But," he continues, "guard yourselves against that superficial sensibility that stops with the accents of the voice without penetrating to the depths of the soul. Everything that does not come from the heart, everything that comes only from the mouth[40] of a public speaker, will die away in the ear of the listener."[41] True *onction*, however, is the true language of the heart, and "this happy gift of touching and moving is undoubtedly the greatest triumph of Christian eloquence."[42] Henry Crawford, we might add, would have been in complete agreement. "A thoroughly good sermon," he said to Edmund Bertram,

> thoroughly well delivered, is a capital gratification. I can never hear such a one without the greatest admiration and respect, and more than half a mind to take orders and preach myself. There is something in the eloquence of the pulpit, when it is really eloquence, which is entitled to the highest praise and honour. The preacher who can touch and affect such an heterogeneous mass of hearers, on subjects limited, and long worn threadbare in all common hands; who can say anything new or striking, anything that rouses the

---

[38] Hugh Blair, *Lectures on Rhetoric and Belles Lettres* (Basil: J. J. Tourneisen, 1788), 2:277.

[39] Maury, 2:231.

[40] Literally "throat" (*gosier*).

[41] Maury, 2:232.

[42] Maury, 2:231.

attention without offending the taste, or wearing out the feelings of his hearers, is a man whom one could not, in his public capacity, honour enough.[43]

It is generally agreed that the two greatest preachers of seventeenth-century France were Bossuet and Bourdaloue. In the past, Bourdaloue tended to be put first, and Madame de Sévigné would certainly have agreed. So would the Anglican cleric Gilbert Burnet (1643–1715), later bishop of Salisbury, who visited France in 1683 and heard Bourdaloue preach in the church of Saint Paul-Saint Louis on the rue Saint-Antoine (Burnet was fluent in French). He was favorably impressed: "There I saw P. Bourdaloue, esteemed one of the greatest preachers of the age, and one of the honours of his [Jesuit] order. He was a man of sweet temper, not at all violent against Protestants: On the contrary, he believed good men among them might be saved, which was a pitch of charity that I had never observed in any of the learned of that Communion."[44] Nowadays, however, the tendency is to give the crown to Bossuet,[45] whose sermons riveted his audience and who combined powerful and effective rhetoric with imagination, clarity, and a brilliant delivery. There is an unequaled majesty in Bossuet's orations—the best of all is probably the great funeral oration for Louis II, prince de Condé (called *le grand Condé*)—and he combined easily and effectively all three of the principles set out by Fénelon: he proved, he painted, he touched, and he did so to great effect. Bourdaloue did not have the same sublimity, and he adhered more stringently to the old scholastic divisions and subdivisions. Some found his sermons to be too argumentative and, indeed, rather too prolix, and he appealed more to the reason than to the emotions. His sermons are nothing if not logical.

---

[43] Jane Austen, *Mansfield Park* (1814), chap. 34.
[44] Lough, *France Observed*, 210.
[45] Maury played an important part in this: see his chapter "On Bossuet," whom he calls "the French Demosthenes" (Maury, 1:59–61).

But until his death he was generally regarded as the greatest preacher of his time and was commonly referred to as "the king of preachers and the preacher of kings."

In the second rank were men like the Oratorian Jules Mascaron, later bishop of Tulle and then of Agen; Valentin-Esprit Fléchier, later bishop of Nîmes; and Jean-Baptiste Massillon, also an Oratorian who became bishop of Clermont-Ferrand. Some would include Fénelon here, but not many of his sermons have been preserved. Happily we do have his panegyric on Saint Bernard and will discuss it in detail in its proper place. Fléchier and Massillon (my personal favorite) we shall meet again. After these come many others whose work in the pulpit, though eminently commendable, lacked the depth or the style of those who were clearly their superiors in oratory and eloquence. More than fifty are discussed in the *abbé* Augustin-Jean Hurel's *Les Orateurs sacrés à la cour de Louis XIV*.

So far we have been speaking of sermons in general, but we must now say something of panegyrics. The relationship between the two is the relationship of the general to particular. Just as all greyhounds are dogs but not all dogs are greyhounds, all panegyrics are sermons but not all sermons are panegyrics. A panegyric of a saint is not a biographical study—indeed, the paucity of reliable information about many early saints would make this virtually impossible—but a celebration of his or her sanctity and an examination of the ways in which we may be instructed and enlightened by his or her example. In 1868 Armand-Germain de Tréverret published a study of seventeenth-century panegyrics on the saints[46]—it was actually his thesis presented to the Faculty of Letters at Paris for the *Agrégé des classes supérieures*—that throws interesting light on how these panegyrics were regarded in the second half of the nineteenth century. The author was born in Paris on December 1, 1836, and went on to become professor of rhetoric

---

[46] Armand-Germain de Tréverret, *Du Panégyrique des Saints au XVIIe siècle* (Paris: Ernest Thorin, 1868).

Sermons and Panegyrics 69

at the Lycée d'Agen from 1858 to 1869, and then professor of foreign literature (primarily German) in the Faculty of Letters at Bordeaux. He was a member of numerous learned societies and a *chevalier* of the Legion of Honour. He taught at Bordeaux until 1898, but I have not been able to trace the date of his death, which, in any case, is not relevant to this present study.[47]

Tréverret disparages the panegyrics that were produced in the early years of the seventeenth century, for they were "infected by a pretentious and declamatory style, by *recherché* ideas, and by empty and bizarre comparisons."[48] In his view, a panegyric has to contain as much solid, historical fact as possible—he is insistent on this—and only then should the preacher enter upon a clear and telling moral or theological exposition. Thus, he criticizes the Oratorian Jean-François Senault (ca. 1601–1672) for not providing the listener or reader with sufficient information about the saints he praises—this is especially true in the panegyrics on Saint Louis, Saint Teresa, and Saint Francis de Sales—and even his moral expositions are always formal and academic. They have "nulle onction, nul accent pathétique," he tells us, and they possess a coldness that never warms up.[49] How different is Bossuet—clearly Tréverret's favorite—who, even if reliable information about the saint he is celebrating is lacking, and even if miracles are given the same weight as historical fact, can overcome these difficulties with the excellence of his moral exposition and his effective exhortations.[50] He lavishes especial praise on Bossuet's

---

[47] See Jules Andrieu, *Bibliographie générale de l'Agenais et des parties du Condomois & du Bazadais incorporées dans le département de Lot-et-Garonne* (Paris: A. Picard; Agen: J. Michel et Médan, 1887), 2:347.

[48] Tréverret, *Du Panégyrique des Saints*, 17.

[49] Tréverret, *Du Panégyrique des Saints*, 20.

[50] Chap. 4 (pp. 37–58) of Tréverret's work is devoted to an examination of Bossuet's conception of the nature of a panegyric. Chap. 6 (pp. 68–95) deals with the "details of composition and style in the panegyrics of Bossuet."

panegyrics on Saint Paul and Saint Bernard—they get a chapter to themselves[51]—and he tells us that the panegyric on Saint Bernard is "very well regarded today," i.e., in 1868. It is perhaps understandable, he says, that Bossuet found the panegyric of Bernard so much to his taste, given that he, like Bernard, fought ceaselessly for the church he loved. But even here Tréverret is not quite satisfied with the amount of historical information. The panegyric is "full of magnificence and poetry, of theological and moral instruction; more abundant than the others in historical details, but yet incomplete in this matter since the greatest deeds of the saint are still left in shadow."[52]

Bourdaloue does not fare nearly so well, primarily because of his failure to balance reason with the imagination, as, in Tréverret's view, is essential in a panegyric: "For Bourdaloue, the imagination is only the very humble and much effaced servant of reason, and, in consequence, he brings to the panegyric what he brings to his sermons and even to his funeral orations: an exclusive desire to enlighten the mind and to lay down the sure rules of belief and morality."[53] We may say of him, "with a mixture of admiration and reproach, 'O *ratio*! O severe reason! O analysis! O everlasting proofs!'"[54] And when we read his funeral oration on the Great Condé, delivered in the church of the Jesuit *maison professe* in Paris on April 26, 1687, "we seem to see a skilful anatomist dissecting, with cold deliberation, the bowels of a lion."[55] We see just the same approach in his panegyrics, which, says Tréverret, "are as sensible, as instructive, as full of the Christian spirit as his sermons. None other but he could have composed such masterpieces. But Bourdaloue, despite his conscientious study of the facts, does not know how

---

[51] Chap. 5 (pp. 59–67), most of which is concerned with the panegyric on Saint Bernard.
[52] Tréverret, *Du Panégyrique des Saints*, 63.
[53] Tréverret, *Du Panégyrique des Saints*, 97.
[54] Tréverret, *Du Panégyrique des Saints*, 97.
[55] Tréverret, *Du Panégyrique des Saints*, 97.

to give us that particular pleasure which the title of 'panegyric' promises our heart and our imagination."[56] As we shall see in a moment, Tréverret had high esteem for Fénelon, and Fénelon's suggestion that an effective preacher must "prove, paint, and touch" is not to be found in Bourdaloue. There is far too much proving, and far too little painting and touching. Bourdaloue, however, did not deliver a panegyric on Saint Bernard—or, if he did, it has not survived—and Bourdaloue, therefore, is not here our concern.

Fléchier did deliver such a panegyric, but Fléchier does not fare well under Tréverret's cold and critical gaze.[57] What he has to say we shall see in chapter twelve. In Tréverret's view, the panegyrics of Charles de La Rue are something of an improvement on those of Fléchier, for La Rue presents the lives of his saints not so much as a portrait but as a sort of biography, solidly based on historical facts. This, we may remember, is always of first importance for Tréverret, and he criticizes La Rue for not always providing as many facts as he should. In some cases, of course, there is a conspicuous dearth of any historical facts at all, and La Rue (together with the other panegyrists) will fill the void with moral reflections and exhortations. La Rue's panegyric on Saint Agnes is a good example, for what little is known of her is almost entirely legendary, and even the legends contradict one another. La Rue's important anti-Quietist panegyric on Bernard is not, however, discussed by Tréverret, for the text was not available until 1901, more than three decades after the publication of Tréverret's study.

Further than this we need not go, and Tréverret's assessments of the various panegyrists will be discussed in their proper place. In this volume we shall summarize or translate in full panegyrics on Bernard by sixteen preachers. Some will certainly be better known than others. The earliest is Jacques Biroat, who died in 1666; the latest is Jean-Baptiste

---

[56] Tréverret, *Du Panégyrique des Saints*, 121.
[57] Chap. 8 (pp. 122–57) is devoted to Fléchier.

Massillon, who lived from 1663 to 1742. They comprise parish priests, members of religious orders, and high-ranking ecclesiastics, and many of them preached before Louis XIV and his court at Versailles. The best known today are probably Bossuet, bishop of Meaux; his friend Armand-Jean de Rancé, abbot of La Trappe; Fénelon, archbishop of Cambrai, whose Quietistic ideas were abhorrent to both Bossuet and Rancé; Esprit Fléchier, bishop of Nîmes; Jean-François Senault, fourth superior-general of the Oratory; Jean-Louis de Fromentières, bishop of Aire; and Jean-Baptiste Massillon, bishop of Clermont. Less well known, perhaps, are Jacques Biroat; the *abbé* François Ogier; the Maurist Bernard Planchette; the Jesuit provincial of Aquitaine Claude Texier; Charles de La Rue, another Jesuit; Henri-Marie Boudon, archdeacon of Évreux; the Oratorians Claude Lion and Louis-Bénigne Bourru, *curé* of Grury; and Antoine Anselme, *abbé* of Saint-Sever in Gascony. Brief biographies of all of them will be found in the relevant chapters, and we shall begin with a presentation and translation of the panegyric on Saint Bernard by Jacques Biroat.

4

Paving the Way

Divisions and Subdivisions in Jacques Biroat

INTRODUCTION

According to Antoine Albert and Jean-François de Court,[1] Jacques Biroat was a native of Bordeaux, but we do not know the date of his birth. Since he died in about 1666 after a full and productive life, we may presume that he came into this world sometime in the last quarter of the sixteenth century. He was a doctor of theology of the Sorbonne and, according to Albert and Court and all the other encyclopedists, had originally been a Jesuit, but left the Society to join the Order of Cluny, in which Order he was appointed prior of Beussan. This view is challenged by Dom Jean François, who maintains that Biroat remained a Jesuit,[2] but as Cluniac prior of Beussan he appears on the title page of his collected panegyrics.[3] He may also have been steward (*chambrier*) of the Cluniac priory of Coincy.[4] Whatever his affiliation, his sermons and panegyrics were held in high esteem—he was a royal counselor and

---

[1] Antoine Albert and Jean-François de Court, *Dictionnaire portatif des prédicateurs françois* (Lyon: Pierre Bruyset Ponthus, 1757; repr. Geneva: Slatkine Reprints, 1970), 35–36.

[2] François, 1:127–28.

[3] See n. 8 below.

[4] See Louis Bertrand, *Histoire des Séminaires de Bordeaux et de Bazas. Tome troisième*. Séminaires de Bazas (Bordeaux: Feret et fils, 1894), 231, §3.

prédicateur du roi—but few were published during his lifetime. It was after his death that Nicolas Blampignon (ca. 1640–1710), *chefcier curé* of the church of Saint-Merry in Paris, himself a distinguished preacher,[5] published very many more, including the panegyric on Saint Bernard.[6] Albert and Court criticize the sermons for being somewhat old-fashioned but praise their erudition and theological solidity. But (they say) if we may admire the abundance of Biroat's ideas and the subtle way in which he divides up his compositions,

> it also seems that these divisions and subdivisions are too studied and too numerous, for all his discourses are divided into three parts, and each part is then subdivided into a further three sections. This is contrary to true eloquence, which requires some subjects to be given broader treatment than others. Few preachers have left a greater number of panegyrics than M. Biroat. He composed seventy-four of them, all of which appear in the three volumes of the *Panégyriques* [published between 1667 and 1669], save for two which are to be found in his sermons on different subjects [published in 1671].[7]

Albert and Court are right. The interminable threefold divisions in the panegyric on Saint Bernard can prove tiresome, but at least you know where you are. In the published text they are regularly numbered 1., 2., 3., but one could also number them as 1., 1.a, 1.a.i, and so on. But the content of Biroat's panegyric is fairly typical of what early seventeenth-century preachers were composing, and it provides us with a sound basis from

---

[5] We know a great deal about Nicolas Blampignon, *curé* of Saint-Merry for forty years (he died in office), thanks to the researches of the *abbé* Constant Baloche: see his *Église Saint-Merry de Paris. Histoire de la paroisse et de la collégiale 700–1910* (Paris: H. Oudin), 1:378–431.

[6] For a complete list of Biroat's works, see Bertrand, *Histoire*, 229–32.

[7] Albert and Court, *Dictionnaire portatif*, 36.

which we can assess the work of other panegyrists on Saint Bernard. It is a good place from which to start, and to appreciate it fully we need a complete translation, warts and all. The panegyric was published in the third volume of Blampignon's edition,[8] but when it was preached we do not know. It was certainly delivered, like all the panegyrics on Bernard, on his feast day, August 20, but I can find no clue in the text of the sermon to indicate a year. We may, however, make reasonable suggestions as to where and to whom it was preached.

In §2 Biroat tells his audience that since today is the feast day of Saint Bernard, it is also the day on which "*les Religieux* of Saint Bernard ought especially to pay their respects to him, since he is their Father."[9] The French masculine plural may indicate just male religious or, inclusively, male and female, and it is clear from Biroat's comment in §35 that he is delivering his discourse in some Bernardine house: "This holy house in which I have the honor of speaking [today] visibly displays the greatness of its Father's spirit and sanctity!"[10] And since, in the *Approbations* at the beginning of Blampignon's edition, we are told that the panegyrics were preached "in the principal churches of the City of Paris," by far the most likely location is the church of the Feuillants on the rue Saint-Honoré, where, in due course, Ogier, Fléchier, Charles de La Rue, and probably Antoine Anselme would also preach their panegyrics.[11] We cannot, however, state this as a certainty. Whether there were Feuillantines (or

---

[8] Jacques Biroat, *Panégyriques des Saints, preschez par M. Iaques Biroat, Docteur en Théologie, Prieur de Beussan de l'Ordre de Cluny, Conseiller & Prédicateur du Roy. Par les soins de M. N. Blampignon, Prestre, Bachelier en Théologie, Chefcier Curé de S. Merry. Nouvelle edition. Tome troisième* (Paris: Edme Couterot, 1671), 170–98.

[9] Biroat, *Panégyriques*, 171.

[10] Biroat, *Panégyriques*, 195.

[11] The Feuillants' monastery, with its church dedicated to Saint Bernard, lay close to the Tuileries gardens and the Louvre and was founded in 1587. The buildings lay behind the present nos. 229–235 of the rue Saint-Honoré and were completely demolished between

Feuillantes) in his audience we do not know. The female branch of the congregation had two houses, one founded in 1588 at Montesquieu-Volvestre in the southwest of France (which later moved to Toulouse) and the other, founded in 1622, on the Faubourg (now rue) Saint-Jacques in Paris. Their name is preserved today by the rue des Feuillantines, created in 1850. Their convent was less than four kilometers from the church of the Feuillants. But it is also clear that Biroat's congregation did not consist entirely of religious. He tells his audience that not all of them need to practice "the fullness of the Gospel *comme les Religieux*, with all its rigors and continual mortification," but that each one of them, whatever their position in life, should ask themselves what they might learn from their example.[12]

Biroat makes no great display of his sources. Apart from the Bible (especially Saint Paul), he cites Augustine (who is not, in fact, Augustine), Gregory the Great, Gregory of Nazianzus, Maximus of Turin, and, apparently, *ps.*-Bonaventure, whom he thinks is Bernard. There is also a passing reference to Paulinus of Nola and to the legend of the Forty Martyrs of Sebaste. Of Bernard's own works, there are citations of or references to the sermons on the Song of Songs, the sermons *De laudibus Virginis matris*, the *De diligendo Deo*, a few letters, and the *De consideratione*. It is rare that the quotations are quite accurate, but the panegyrists have no hesitation in adapting texts to their own purposes.

Who is Biroat's Bernard? He is, above all, a model of penance and penitence,[13] a model of humility, and a model of asceticism and austerity, who, in following the way of the cross, has died to the world and all worldly things. He is a man whose love for God and the Gospel is manifested in his deeds and a man whose life is, in essence, an imitation of his Lord

---

1804 and 1831. All that remains today is a small section of the walls of the apse behind the present no. 229.

[12] Biroat, *Panégyriques*, 197.

[13] *Pénitence*: see appendix 1, s.v. *pénitence* / penitence.

and Savior, Jesus Christ, who, for the seventeenth-century *spirituels*, was the Great Penitent.[14] He is a man who has no fear in reproving, when necessary, the great and mighty (even the pope himself), and neither has he any fear when he goes into battle on behalf of a church torn asunder by schism and beleaguered by enemies. Like virtually all the panegyrists, Biroat mentions Bernard's signal role in putting an end to the papal schism between Innocent II and Anacletus, and in defeating heresy and heretics, the invariable culprits being Peter Abelard, Gilbert de la Porrée (Biroat refers to him as Gilbert Porrette), and Henry of Toulouse. It is rare indeed to find a preacher who does not mention these three, and their accounts of Bernard's victories must all be taken with several grains of salt. The business of the panegyrists is to present a panegyric, not to provide a balanced historical account. History, however, there is—at least, history of a sort. Armand-Germain de Tréverret would have approved.[15] Biroat is happy to mention names—Henry I of England, Louis VII of France (though he means Louis VI), Roger of Sicily, Duke William X of Aquitaine, and so on—and places, such as the Councils of Sens, Reims, and Étampes. And after having taken Bernard out of the cloister for all these notable deeds, he ends by bringing him back again, to reform the Benedictine Order, bring about the astonishing growth of the Cistercians, and lay down principles that can only be of advantage to all those other orders that would follow him. He mentions Bernard's many miracles but provides no specific examples, and of Bernard the mystic there is no trace whatever. But as we have seen in chapter 2, that should not surprise us.

The form of the sermon is much as it should be: the exordium, ending with the *Ave Maria*, the main exposition with its (too many) divisions, sub-divisions, and sub-sub-divisions, and the final exhortation to his audience. He obviously does not expect them to do all that Bernard did—how could they?—

---

[14] This matter is discussed in chap. 1.
[15] See chap. 3, though Tréverret does not mention Biroat.

but they can do what they should do, and what they should do is set out in the last two paragraphs of his panegyric. I estimate the time of delivery to have been about an hour and a half, which is about average for the panegyrics we are introducing. Biroat's discourse certainly has order, perhaps too much of it; I cannot say that it has *onction*, but that is a matter for the reader to decide. Let us therefore turn to the panegyric and see what Biroat has to say in his own words.

THE PANEGYRIC
PANEGYRIC ON SAINT BERNARD

Collabora Evangelio secundum virtutem Dei. (2 Tim 1:8)
"Work for the Gospel according to the strength that God gives you."[16]

1. One of the beautiful ways in which Saint Paul praises the Gospel, of which he was the preacher and the apostle, is that it announces the glory of God: *Collabora Evangelio secundum virtutem Dei* ["Work with the Gospel according to the power of God"]. He invites us to do this for three main reasons:[17] first, because [the Gospel] represents the greatness of the glory of God; second, because it instructs us in some of the notable things that Jesus Christ did for Christians; third, because it is destined to be the foundation of this Church that Jesus, by preaching it in his words and by demonstrating its truth through his deeds as Redeemer, has brought into being for his glory: *Collabora Evangelio secundum virtutem Dei* ["Work with the Gospel according to the power of God"].

---

[16] This is Biroat's version (170). A literal translation is "Work with the Gospel according to the power of God." The panegyrists frequently provide a French version of their Latin text that accords more with what they intend to say in their discourse.

[17] This is the first of Biroat's innumerable—some would say interminable—threefold divisions, for which, as we have seen, he was criticized by Albert and Court.

2. But do not think that the glory of the Gospel stops with Jesus, its author and source: it spills over into his saints whose business it was to broadcast it and to act as its ministers.[18] Indeed, we may truly say that there is nothing they could do better than to cooperate in this ministry, first, in the way in which they work together to preserve the truth [of the Gospel], and second, in the way in which they labor for its glory. It is as [a model] for this glorious undertaking that I want to set before you Saint Bernard on this day when the Church honors him,[19] and when the monks and nuns[20] of Saint Bernard ought especially to pay their respects to him, since he is their Father. I do not think that there is anything that redounds more to his glory than to say that he worked excellently for the Gospel, and that he carried out faithfully the commission he had received from it: *Collabora Evangelio*.

3. [Bernard] had a special devotion to the Virgin, and it was with her help that he was able to do all the wonderful things he did and that he received so many graces from God to sustain him in what he had to do in his ministry. We implore her to help us in speaking of these things, and, with the angel, we greet her in saying to her, *Ave*.[21]

4. We may begin our discourse by taking it for granted that the greatness of the praise and glory of Saint Bernard should have its roots in the benefits and fruits he brought about for the sake of the Gospel. He bore witness to the Gospel of Jesus in

---

[18] Lit. "who were its dispensers and ministers" (171): Biroat is echoing 1 Cor 4:1: *ministros Christi, et dispensatores mysteriorum Dei*, "ministers of Christ and dispensers of the mysteries of God."

[19] August 20, but we have no idea of the year.

[20] *Les Religieux* (171), which makes it impossible to tell whether Biroat is addressing a congregation of only male religious, or male and female religious. I have discussed the question of Biroat's congregation in the introduction to the panegyric.

[21] As was customary, Biroat ends his exordium by invoking the help and intercession of the Virgin and repeating the *Ave Maria*. I discussed the matter in chap. 3.

three ways: in what he did for himself, for the Church of Jesus, and then for the monastic state. (1)[22] He put into practice in himself all that the Gospel demanded. (2) He preserved its holiness amid all the dangers that beset the Church. (3) Finally, he carried its glory into the monastic estate. He achieved the first in his private life, the second in his public life, and the third in both his private and public lives. These are the three ways in which he bore witness to the Gospel, and the three parts of my sermon.

[FIRST POINT][23]

5. The first way in which the saints should use the Gospel is working with its virtues[24] so as to make themselves saints. Before preaching it to others, they must practice it themselves. It is a seed of holiness that can bear much good fruit, but its first workings must be reflected in the person in whom it is to be found: *Collabora Evangelio*. It is on these trustworthy terms that Saint Bernard received the grace of the Gospel as a Christian by baptism and as a monk by vocation, and we may say of him what Saint Gregory said of saints in general: that his life was a demonstration[25] of the Gospel, and that he carried out its demands to the highest point of perfection that any human power could achieve: *secundum virtutem Evangelii*.

---

[22] The paragraph numbers of this translation are my own, but all the other numbers (in parentheses) appear in the printed text.

[23] *I. Point* in the left margin of page 172.

[24] *Vertus* in the plural: see appendix 1, s.v. *vertu* / virtue. The meaning here is "powers." The virtues of the Gospel are what the Gospel can do, for in Biroat's panegyric the Gospel is not something passively preached, but a living entity with which we are required to collaborate. See also appendix 1, s.v. *Providence* / Providence.

[25] *Explication* (172), which would normally be translated as *explanation*. It can also mean "justification" or "clarification," but *demonstration* seems best here. A saint is someone who in his or her life demonstrates what the Gospel teaches and shows what it can do. I assume that Saint Gregory is Gregory the Great, but I have not been able to trace Biroat's exact source here.

6. Now the Gospel of Jesus possesses three principal qualities that it takes from its author whose character it bears: it is strict, it is humble, it is gentle. You see here the fruit of that precious seed [sown] in the heart of a saint: he is strict with himself, humble before God, gentle and meek[26] with regard to his neighbor. But when you find these three qualities joined with certain other factors that serve to reinforce their propensities—when the rigor of penitence[27] is joined with humility in one's conduct, humility with fame or renown, gentleness with the steadfastness and freedom of the Gospel—we may say that their fruits are doubled and that they work miracles. But we will not wait to see Saint Bernard in the pulpit or at [Church] councils to witness how he preached and upheld the Gospel: we will venture into the solitude of Clairvaux to see there how he worked for the truth of the Gospel by making three alliances: (1) of penitence with innocence, (2) of humility with fame, (3) of gentleness with openness and firmness.

7. (1)[28] Although the law of the Gospel is one of grace and sweetness, we must state that it is rigorous with regard to the senses, for it also sets out laws of mortification and penance,[29] which contain something of thorns and the cross. What Saint Maximinus[30] says is true: the whole life of a Christian who practises the Gospel is a sort of cross, *Tota vita Christiana, si secundum Evangelium vivat, crux est atque martyrium* ["The whole life of a Christian, if it is lived according to the Gospel, is a cross and a

---

[26] *Débonnaire*, which does not mean debonair. Biroat equates it with the Latin *mitis*, "meek" (see n. 54 below).

[27] *Pénitence*, which, in French, can mean penitence, repentance, or penance, or all three at the same time. See appendix 1, s.v. *pénitence* / penitence.

[28] Biroat now deals with the alliance of penitence / penance with innocence. His discussion of the second alliance—that of humility with fame or renown—begins at §12 below, and of the third—of gentleness with openness (or outspokenness) or firmness—at §15.

[29] See n. 27 above.

[30] For Maximinus, read Maximus [of Turin].

martyrdom"].[31] But when these rigorous practices go hand in hand with moral innocence and purity of life, which, it would seem, should dispense a saint from these demanding laws, then we see the very acme of the Gospel. There is nothing odd about someone who has committed many grave sins subjecting his body to the austerities of penance—that is something wholly just—but when an innocent man torments himself as if he were a sinner, and when both, in their different conditions, undergo the same afflictions, that indeed is something quite extraordinary in religion![32] Sometimes, when innocence is seen side by side with penitence in some saints, it is said that they undergo this hardship for the sins of others. Again, when we see a Saint John the Baptist, sanctified from his mother's womb to do penance in a desert, it is said that he wished to provide an example of austerity and mortification. But it is hard to justify such rigorous conduct in the lives of other saints.

8. Yet it is exactly these two contrary demands that the Gospel brought about in Bernard! It made him as pure as an angel, but it made him suffer as a martyr! He himself is innocent, but he does penance as if he were guilty! How can we explain this? There are three main reasons that the saints, though innocent themselves, should do penance. They do it to expiate past sins, even though those sins might have been trifling in themselves. They do it to ward off the dangers of those sins they might commit. And finally, they do it to imitate Christ, and to bear in their mortified bodies something similar to his crucified body. It is through these three principles that the Gospel moved the heart of Bernard to the love of penance and repentance.[33]

---

[31] Biroat, *Panégyriques*, 173, quoting Maximus of Turin, *Hom* 83 *de sanctis martyribus*; PL 57:430B, reading *Tota igitur vita Christiani hominis* for *Tota vita Christiana*. Exactly the same sentence appears in ps.-Augustine, S 207.3 *in natali sancti Laurentii*; PL 39:2129.

[32] *Dans la Religion* (173). *Religion* is a word of wide meaning—see appendix 1, s.v. *religion* / religion—but here it means the Christian religion in general.

[33] Biroat will now discuss these three principles one by one.

9. (1) It is true that he had never committed any grave sins and, with regard to his body, he had preserved its purity together with his virginity, but for a saint who loves God, the least shadow of sin demands the strictest vengeance. That is why he undertook the monastic way of life,[34] which he saw as being the penitential way of life. He himself wrote to Pope Honorius II saying that he prayed to God in the monastery to which his sins had forced him to withdraw,[35] and [once there], in this spirit of penitence, he was not content with the usual austerities of monastic life: he invented new ones to satisfy his zeal and expiate the least trace of his sins.

10. (2) He is in no great danger of offending God: apart from the fact that he is under a special protection of his Providence,[36] he has sought refuge in the harbor of the religious life from storms that could destroy him. But for a saint who fears sin, the least shadow of danger causes great alarm and [leads him] to take unfailing precautions. He would say with Saint Paul, *Castigo corpus meum et in servitutem redigo* (1 Cor 9:27), "I chastise this body of mine, however pure and innocent it may be, to prevent it from becoming culpable."[37] But he did not practice this precautionary penitence only in the monastery: [he also practiced it] in the world. One day, he felt the memory of a beautiful woman he had seen in passing ignite fires in his heart dangerous to his innocence. What will the Gospel do when thus attacked? It demands that he throw himself into an icy

---

[34] *L'état de la Religion* (174). *Religion* here means the religious or monastic life. See n. 32 above.

[35] Biroat, *Panégyriques*, 174, is echoing Bernard, Ep 13–14; SBOp 7:62–63; to Pope Honorius II.

[36] The concept of Providence and its directing power was of major importance for French theologians and preachers of the period. See appendix 1, s.v. *Providence* / Providence.

[37] What Saint Paul actually says is "I chastise my body and bring it into subjection."

pond to put out the flames and forestall the danger.[38] This was so that Jesus could restage the spectacle that had occurred long ago when the tyrant [Licinius] had forty martyrs thrown into an icy pond in order to quench the faith of the Gospel.[39] There was, however, a difference: the martyrs were thrown into [the pond] by the executioners, but here Bernard afflicts himself! Angels held crowns over the heads of these dying martyrs. I picture in my mind Bernard's guardian angel,[40] holding a crown of roses and lilies, to show the innocence of his purity and the rigors of his penitence.

11. (3) The main reason for this rigorous [demand of the] Gospel is Jesus himself, who, in bringing the Gospel to [Bernard], led him to say what he said so often: *Nolo vivere sine vulnere, cum te videam vulneratum.*[41] "Ha![42] my Savior, I do not

---

[38] Biroat, *Panégyriques*, 175, referring to *Vita prima* 1.3.6 (William of Saint-Thierry); PL 185:230 BC; CF 76:9. It is a favorite story among the panegyrists.

[39] Biroat is referring to the story of the Forty Martyrs of Sebaste, forty Roman soldiers of the XII Legion *Fulminata* who were martyred on the orders of the Roman emperor Licinius I (d. 325) for their adherence to Christianity. They were stripped naked, bound, and exposed on a frozen pond near Sebaste (Sivas in modern Turkey) on a night of bitter cold so that they would slowly freeze to death. The earliest account of their martyrdom appears in the fourth century in a homily of Basil of Caesarea, but the story became well known in both East and West.

[40] There was a great deal of interest in guardian angels in the seventeenth and eighteenth centuries—an interest that spread into the nineteenth and that gave rise to a considerable literature. Both Biroat himself and Claude Lion preached panegyrics on guardian angels, Bossuet preached a sermon on them, and Henri-Marie Boudon wrote a great deal about them.

[41] Biroat, *Panégyriques*, 176. So far as I know, there is no record of Bernard saying this at all, much less often. It appears to be from Part I, chap. 2 of *ps.*-Bonaventure, *Stimulus amoris* (*Stimulus Divini Amoris Sancti Bonaventurae, viris ecclesiasticis dicatur* [Turin: Canfari, 1836], 21), which reads, *Nolo enim, Domine, sine vulnere vivere, quia te video vulneratum.*

[42] Ha! is Biroat's favorite exclamation, and by the end of panegyric he has Ha'd no less than sixteen times.

want to live without suffering pain when I see you wounded. I see the Gospel and you as two models that I should imitate, and I see in myself a copy of you. This Gospel is engraved on your body with the graving tool of the cross, it is written in the color of your blood, and it must therefore pass from you to me with similar effect." Is it surprising, then, that he treats his body so severely, that he mortifies his senses until they cease to function, that he fasts until his digestion is so ruined that he can take no solid food?[43] Ha! If he could not die all at once as did Jesus and the martyrs, he would die slowly, little by little, giving up his life bit by bit. It is this that allows us to transfer to his penitent lips those qualities that the bride gives to the lips of the Bridegroom: *Labia eius lilia distillantia myrrham* ["His lips are lilies dropping myrrh" (Song 5:13)]: This mortified mouth is like lilies that, drop by drop, secrete myrrh to expiate sins, to ward off corruption, and to imitate the myrrh of Jesus and his cross. These are the lilies mixed with myrrh that show the union of his purity with the penitence that the Gospel brings into his body, while, on the other hand, he has joined in his spirit the sense of his humility with a life of the most illustrious deeds.[44]

12. (2) This is the second quality of the Gospel of the Savior, a quality that comes from the humiliations of its author and Master. It humbles human beings under God for the sake of his glory, but when we find this humility joined with that fame that should normally be its enemy, it must be said that this is one of the most notable ways in which its truth works and one of the most illustrious miracles of grace: *Magna virtus est humilitas honorata* ["Honored humility is a great virtue"],[45] says

---

[43] See *Vita prima* 1.4.22 (William of Saint-Thierry); PL 185:239C–40B; CF 76:25–26.

[44] Biroat will now discuss the second of the three alliances set out in §6 above: that of humility with fame or renown.

[45] Biroat, *Panégyriques*, 177, quoting Bernard, Miss 4.9; SBOp 4:55, which actually reads *Magna prorsus et rara virtus, humilitas honorata*, "A great and rare virtue indeed [is] honored humility."

Saint Bernard, who knew well the secret of this profitable alliance. Oh, what a great virtue we see in this honored humility! There is nothing unusual in seeing ordinary people, who do not have the necessary qualities to practice this virtue, acting humbly: they are already humbled by their condition, and the virtue of acting humbly is not difficult for them. But to see a saint abasing himself in the midst of his greatness, humbling himself while crowned with crowns, ha! the Gospel has to put forth all its power to work this miracle, and that is why [Bernard] adds, *Magna et rara virtus est, ut licet magna opereris, magnum te esse nescias* ["It is a great and rare virtue when you do great things but do not know you are great"].[46] It is as rare a virtue as it is great to do great things and not to know that they are great,[47] to appear famous in everyone's eyes and to be unaware of this fame, to do deeds that are regarded with astonishment and to count them as nothing. It is as if he said that humility acts in two ways, both of which make it worthy of admiration: it acts as a veil to escape what it sees as its own renown, and it acts as a mirror that receives light only to give it back by faithfully reflecting it. Thus this virtue receives glory only to give it back to the God from whom it comes. This is why Saint Bernard, when he is describing humility in general, has made a panegyric of his own [humility]! He practices what he teaches. We have only to look at his writings on the one hand and his life on the other to say that there was never a man who appeared at one and the same time more renowned yet more humble.

---

[46] Biroat, *Panégyriques*, 177, quoting (more or less) Bernard, SC 13.3.3; SBOp 1:70, which reads *Magna et rara virtus profecto est, ut magna licet operantem, magnum te nescias*, "Great and rare is the virtue of those who, doing great things, are unaware of their own greatness."

[47] This is what Biroat says, but is not quite what Bernard says. The rare virtue is to do great things and be unaware of your *own* greatness, not of the greatness of the things you do, though the two are obviously related.

13. The glory and fame that surrounded him was made up of four rays or came from four sources: (1) His reputation and esteem in the eyes of everyone, since ordinary people, the great in the land, kings, bishops, popes, and [Church] councils all respected him and acted in accordance with his advice. (2) The rewards he was offered, for many bishoprics were laid before him, such as those of Reims and Milan.[48] (3) His natural and acquired qualities, which made him the most cultivated man of his time and the most knowledgeable and eloquent man of the Church. (4) His supernatural gifts, such as his virtues, his miracles, and all the wonderful things he did for his Church and his religious profession.

14. So great, in fact, was the luster of his fame that it might have been dangerous and capable of jeopardizing any other humility but his. But what did Bernard's humility do? It made his sentiments the same as those of the prophet [David] when he says to God, *Ab altitudine diei timebo* ["I fear the noonday light" (Ps 55:4)]: "I do not fear the power of my enemies: I fear the great light of the [worldly] glory I see surrounding me." He therefore has recourse to the pall and veil [of his humility] to keep this light from his eyes and reflect it from himself [back to God]. Does there not seem to be a battle here between God's liberality and the saint's humility? God works to make him famous; he works to become more humble! God kindles the fire; his humility douses every flame and eclipses the sun with its veil! If anyone testified to the esteem in which he was held, he concealed his reputation by the mean idea he had of himself and by the respect he wanted to pay to others. He writes to a prelate[49] that he is not what people think him to be and that they take him for somebody else: *Non sum talis*

---

[48] Biroat, *Panégyriques*, 178. According to the *Vita prima* 2.4.26 (Arnold of Bonneval); PL 185:283B; CF 76:106, Bernard was offered the sees of Langres, Châlons-sur-Marne, Genoa, Milan, and Reims.

[49] Guy (or Guigues) de Chastel / Guigo de Castro, fifth Prior of La Grande Chartreuse.

qualis putor ["I am not what I am thought to be"].[50] He falls at the feet of bishops and asks for their blessing; if he is offered some high position he protests that he does not deserve it; he honors such [high positions] in the person of those priests who possess them, but he renounces them himself; if anyone praises him for his intelligence or learning, he tells them they are mistaken; if he performs miracles, he attributes them to God alone; and finally, if anyone should address him in a letter as "the venerable first abbot of Clairvaux," he replies "What are you saying? You are praising a sinner, you are exalting a poor wretch!"[51] Ha! How radiant you are, Gospel of Jesus, yet how sombre! What glory you gain for Bernard, but what shadows you give him to hide it! We may say that the Gospel of this saint is like the pillar of cloud and of fire that led the Israelites.[52] It is a pillar of light and fire by night: the more Bernard humbles and hides himself, the more God glorifies him in the eyes of the people. It is a pillar of cloud by day: the more God glorifies this saint, the more he humbles and hides himself. It is indeed a pillar of light and fire in the eyes of those who see him, shining with so many virtues and miracles, but in his own eyes it is a pillar of cloud, for it covers up this light. He is little affected by this renown, which he covers with darkness, but he makes an alliance between his humility and this fame, just as he does between his gentleness and his outspokenness and forthrightness.[53]

---

[50] Biroat, *Panégyriques*, 179, quoting Bernard, Ep 11.10; SBOp 7:60, to Guigo of La Grande Chartreuse, with the additional *vel dicor*: "I am not what I am thought or said to be."

[51] Biroat, *Panégyriques*, 179, quoting Bernard, Ep 265; SBOp 8:174, to Peter the Venerable: *Quid facis, O bone vir? Laudas peccatorem, miserum beatificas!* "What are you doing, O you good man? You are praising a sinner, you are numbering a poor wretch among the blessed!"

[52] See Exod 13:21.

[53] Biroat will now discuss the third of the alliances set out in §6 above: that of gentleness or sweetness with firmness, openness, or outspokenness.

15. (3) It must be said from the start that acting with gentleness and meekness possesses a wonderful quality that comes from the works and words of Jesus himself: *Discite a me quia mitis sum et humilis corde* (Matt 11:29): "Learn from me, for I am meek[54] and humble of heart." And this is to show, as Saint Bernard tells us, that gentleness is a result of humility just as haughtiness is a real proof of pride. It is true that this virtue is worthy of a Christian even on its own, but when it is combined with steadfastness of heart and courageous openness in all one's dealings then it is truly the third miracle of the virtue [of humility]. What saint ever possessed gentleness of heart to a greater degree than Saint Bernard? He was gentle by temperament and had a most tender heart, but the grace of Jesus mingled with his natural inclinations and his own development and prepared this seed of balm, which spilled over into his manners, his writings, and his way of life. He deserved, therefore, to be called a "Honey-Sweet Doctor,"[55] for he breathed only gentleness and meekness.

16. And yet, on the other hand, where could one ever find a doctor more resolute and firm, one who spoke more firmly and forthrightly than this saint, one who had more courage than he in bringing his reproofs to the throne of kings and

---

[54] *Débonnaire*: see n. 26 above.

[55] Biroat, *Panégyriques*, 180, uses the French *Docteur emmiellé* for the Latin *Doctor Mellifluus*. Mabillon refers to Bernard by this title, though he did not invent it. It appears, for example, in a sermon on Bernard by the Belgian theologian Josse van Clichtove, who died in 1543. For a full account of the origin and significance of the title, see Henri de Lubac, trans. Edward M. Macierowski, *Medieval Exegesis. Volume 2. The Four Senses of Scripture* (Grand Rapids: W. B. Eerdmans, and Edinburgh: T. & T. Clark, 2000), 162–78. See also Simon Icard, "Saint Bernard, effigie du catholicisme classique," *Cîteaux—Commentarii cistercienses* 62 (2011): 321–37, here 328–33. The title does not mean that Bernard was a Doctor of the Church in Biroat's time: he was not. The title was given him by Pope Paul VIII in 1830. In the seventeenth century, a *docteur* was a scholar or savant or learned teacher.

the tribunals of judges? We may accurately say of him what was said long ago of Saint Paulinus: that he had such power that he would act as a prince among princes and as a master among kings.[56] It is this that we are now going to witness in what he did in public for the Church and in his dealings with the princes of his time, whether secular or ecclesiastic. But we need only look at his actions and his letters to see that if there was no one more humble and more gentle, there was also no one more resolute and more courageous!

17. He writes to [Henry], archbishop of Sens. At the beginning of his letter there is nothing but sweetness, but he then goes on to express his outspoken opinions on the abuses and disorders that were being committed at the time.[57] He writes to the Sovereign Pontiff [Eugenius III].[58] What could be gentler and more respectful? He calls him the successor of the apostles and gives him the most august titles[59]—but he does not hesitate to remind him of his duties in no uncertain words. He writes to Conrad [of Zeringen], duke of Burgundy, to dissuade him from making war.[60] He writes to the count of Geneva, whom he treats with all submission and respect and

---

[56] Paulinus of Nola (353/5–431) belonged to a noble and wealthy family with a large estate in Aquitaine. He married, settled on the family estate, underwent some sort of spiritual conversion, and was baptized. On Christmas Day in 393 or 394, he was ordained a priest and some years later consecrated bishop of Nola in southern Italy. He was still married, but he and his wife were both living a monastic life. In the second reading for his feast day (June 22) he is referred to as "first among the princes of his people" (echoing Ps 112:8).

[57] Bernard, Ep 182; SBOp 8:2, to Henry of Sens. See appendix 2, s.v. Henry of Sens.

[58] There are numerous letters from Bernard to Eugenius, but as is clear from the next sentences, Biroat is referring to the five books *On Consideration*. See appendix 2, s.v. Eugenius III.

[59] Bernard, Csi 2.8.15; SBOp 3:423: "You are the prince of the bishops, you are the successor of the apostles, in primacy you are Abel," and so on.

[60] Bernard, Ep 97; SBOp 7:247–48, to Duke Conrad.

to whom he attributes all honorable qualities. But he then joins outspokenness to gentleness and tells [the count] that God will take vengeance on him for his wrathful actions and espouse the cause of the poor and the orphans whom [the count] is immolating in his fury.[61]

18. Ha! What is it that makes this division or this blending [of sweetness and severity] possible? It is the grace of the Gospel! *Vox Domini intercidentis flammam ignis* ["The voice of the Lord divides the flame of fire" (Ps 28:7)]: The voice of God distinguishes between the fire of his charity[62] and his zeal, depending on what he sees needs to be done. When [Bernard] considers only his own interests, he is gentle, but when it comes to the interests of God and his Church, he is courageous and fearless. If it is only Bernard who is attacked, he acts as a simple monk: he is a lamb. But if his Master is attacked, he takes on the fire of a lion! Ha! He speaks as an apostle with the apostles: *Verbum Dei non est alligatum* ["The word of God is not bound" (2 Tim 2:9)]. It is the powerful love[63] of the Gospel that makes him act in this way. No, the word of God is not bound by any fear of human intimidation, nor by any worldly hopes. It acts with a sovereign freedom in all that it does. No, I [Bernard][64] shall not just protect the Gospel, I shall practice

---

[61] I know of no letter of Bernard to any count of Geneva. The letter to Conrad of Zeringen was intended to dissuade him from going to war against Amadeus I, count of Geneva, but (so far as I know) we have no letter to Amadeus himself. It is just possible that Biroat has got his history wrong and is referring to the destruction of Vitry by Louis VII in his conflict with Theobald II, count of Champagne: see appendix 2, s.v. Louis VII the Young.

[62] *Sa charité*. On the distinction between charity and love—*charité* and *amour*—see appendix 1, s.v. *charité*/charity.

[63] *Amour*: see n. 62 above.

[64] That the "I" is Bernard and not Biroat is clear from the fact that this sentence summarizes the First Point of Biroat's discourse and introduces the Second Point, which shows precisely how Bernard

it in myself so as to sanctify myself, and I shall uphold it amid the disorders [that trouble] the Church!

[SECOND POINT][65]

19. For it is not enough, great saint, for you to put the Gospel into practice only in yourself: you find you must leave your solitude and take [the Gospel] out into the world. You must use it in the necessary defense of the Church: *Collabora Evangelio* ["Work with the Gospel!"]. Work for it and with it, and through your works double the power it has for the Church. For although all the saints in general should work with the Gospel to defend this Bride of Jesus, we must nevertheless say that there are some extraordinary saints whom God raises up from time to time especially for this important task, and to whom he gives the commission and necessary qualities for this ministry. It is in this second group that Saint Bernard occupies a first rank and, in these latter times, we can call him the Defender of the Church and the Holy Minister of the Gospel.

20. The Church has three perfections given to her by the Gospel, and each of these can be attacked by a different enemy: its unity, its truth, and its holiness. (1) The unity of the Church is attacked by schisms, (2) its truth by heretics, (3) its holiness by vices and moral corruption. Let us see how all three of these monsters reared themselves up against the Church in the time of Saint Bernard, and how he vanquished them by the strength and grace of the Gospel.

21. (1) Saint Paul represents the Church as the mystical Body of Jesus whose unity consists in the union of its members one with another, and principally in the union they have with their visible Head on Earth, the Sovereign Pontiff in Rome, and through this [union] they receive the guidance and direction

---

upheld the sanctity of the Gospel in the face of all the dangers that beset the church in his time.

[65] *II. Point* in the left margin of page 182.

of Jesus, who is the invisible Sovereign Head of this family. It follows, therefore, that any schism that separates Christians from this visible Head destroys the unity of the Church and inflicts a dangerous wound on this mystical and holy body. To show how grave is this sin, Saint Bernard likens it to a sword that cuts open the side of Jesus: *Latus Domini gloriosi crudeliter confodit non velle Papam* [sic], and gives the reason: *dividit nempe Ecclesiam pro qua illud est in cruce divisum*: He divides the Church for whom the holy side [of Christ] was divided on the cross.[66]

22. Jesus has two bodies: the physical one he received from his mother, and the mystical one, which is his Church. Ha! When you cause divisions in his mystical body, so you open up the wounds in his physical body! It was in this way that Peter Leon,[67] who was called Anacletus, rent asunder the union of the Church in the see of Saint Peter after the election of Innocent II.[68] This Anacletus laid claim to this dignity, and ascended the throne of Saint Peter by a series of unjust measures. He then strove openly to keep himself there by his crimes and thus divided both the Church and the whole population of Rome.

---

[66] Biroat, *Panégyriques*, 183, [mis-]quoting Bernard, Ep 126.6; SBOp 7:313; to the bishops of Aquitaine, against Gerard, bishop of Angoulême. What Bernard actually writes is *Latus denuo Domini gloriae crudeliter confodere non veretur. Dividit nempe Ecclesiam, pro qua illud est in cruce divisum*, "He is not afraid to cruelly stab once again the side of the Lord of Glory. He divides the Church for whom [the side of Christ] on the cross was divided." The words *non velle Papam* do not appear. If it is not an error, we would have to translate the sentence as something like "Not to want the pope cruelly stabs the side of the Lord of glory."

[67] His name was actually Pietro Pierleoni. Biroat's Pierre Léon follows the Latin form *Petrus Leonis*, which appears in the *Vita prima*. See appendix 2, s.v. Anacletus II.

[68] Honorius II died during the night of February 13/14, 1130, and both Innocent and Anacletus were elected on February 14. Both elections were, in fact, irregular, but Biroat is obviously not going to say that, even if he knows it.

He drew to his party a large number of princes and lured to him a large part of the Church. Whom will God oppose to this notorious sinner? Whose arms will he use to subdue this monster? It is Bernard whom he chooses for his plans, and he commissions him to maintain the Gospel and defend the Church: *Collabora Evangelio*. I need only say that the whole of the French Church, assembled under King Louis VII[69] at the Council of Étampes [in 1130], left the decision in this matter to the judgment of Bernard, and once he had pronounced in favor of Innocent, it was Innocent who, from then on, was held to be the legitimate pontiff. To the extent that, on this occasion, his mouth was the organ of the Holy Spirit, so his voice was a conclave in itself. Such was the effect of his authority.

23. Let us follow him now where his zeal took him. He sought out the king of England [at Chartres] and persuaded him to recognize his authority.[70] He drew to him a bishop of Guyenne who had previously favored the party of Leon. Persuaded by [the bishop] of Angoulême, he went to meet Duke William [X], who was a powerful and stubborn supporter of this party, and when he found that his prayers had no effect, he converts him, holding the Holy Sacrament in his hand. He casts down the duke at his feet to bring him into subjection to the Sovereign Pontiff of the Church.[71] Then, since it was not enough to have won over France, England, and Germany, he crosses the Alps a second time so that Innocent might also possess Italy. He made the people of Milan obedient to him not just by the power of his prayers but also by the effectiveness of his miracles.[72] He took the battle as far as the lands of Roger

---

[69] Biroat, *Panégyriques*, 184, has the wrong Louis. The Council was convoked by Louis VI le Gros, not by Louis VII le Jeune. See appendix 2, s.v. Louis VI the Fat.

[70] See *Vita prima* 2.1.4 (Arnold of Bonneval); PL 185:271AB; CF 76:82–83. The king was Henry I. See appendix 2, s.v. Henry I.

[71] See appendix 2, s.v. William (Guillaume) X, duke of Aquitaine.

[72] See *Vita prima* 2.2.9–3.16 (Arnold of Bonneval); PL 185:273D–78A; CF 76:87–96.

[II] of Sicily,[73] and once he had restored Innocent to the see of Rome, from which, until Leon's unhappy death,[74] he had previously been banished by the ambition of his adversary and the efforts of his followers, we see the remnants of the schism smothered by the work of Bernard. We may therefore compare him to balm: *Sicut odor balsami*.[75] This liquor is extremely sweet and perfumed and has the virtue of healing wounds, but it is itself produced from wounds made on the tree from which it comes, for incisions are made in its bark. You have here an image of Bernard's charity: it is a balm because of the sweetness and perfume that are spread everywhere by his glorious reputation. It heals the wounds of the Church and reunites the parties that the schism had divided. But it comes from the wounds in this victorious tree, for it is by his mortifications, his prayers, and his tears that it works these marvels, and [as well as] defending the unity of the Church against schism, it also [defends] its truth against heretics.

24. (2) This[76] is one of the most important qualities that the Gospel gives and promises to the Church, and that is why Saint Paul calls it the pillar of truth: *Columna et firmamentum veritatis* ["the pillar and foundation of truth" (1 Tim 3:15)]. The [Church] Fathers explain this in two ways: passively and actively. Passively, because [the Church] is supported by the truth of the Gospel that Jesus taught; actively, because she herself is the organ of the truth of the Gospel, and she requires her children to believe. Thus, we are told by Saint Augustine

---

[73] Bernard met Roger at his camp just behind Salerno: see *Vita prima* 2.7.43–44 (Arnold of Bonneval); PL 185:293B–94B; CF 76:126–28; and appendix 2, s.v. Roger II of Sicily.

[74] On January 25, 1138.

[75] Biroat, *Panégyriques*, 185. This is from one of the antiphons from the Common of the Saints: *Sancti tui, Domine, florebunt sicut lilium, alleluia; et sicut odor balsami erunt ante te, alleluia*, "Your saints, O Lord, will flourish as lilies, alleluia; and they will be before you as the odor of balm. Alleluia."

[76] I.e., truth, the second of the three perfections listed in §20 above.

that the Church participates in the truth of Jesus, who is the First Truth: *Ex ore veritatis agnosco Christum verum; ex ore veritatis agnosco Ecclesiae Pastorem vivum* ["From the mouth of Truth I acknowledge the true Christ; from the mouth of Truth I acknowledge the living Shepherd of the Church"].[77]

25. So what do these heresies do? They attack the truth of the Church in themselves and, by reflection, the truth of Jesus. And by refusing to believe the Gospel, they make it a liar, just as Saint John says in his letter: *Qui non credit Filio, mendacem facit eum* ["Whoever does not believe the Son makes him a liar" (1 John 5:10)]. But of all the heresies that attacked this truth and sought to make the Gospel of Jesus a liar, the worst were those heresies that arose in France in the time of Saint Bernard, whether because their authors—Peter Abelard, Gilbert Porrette,[78] and Henry of Toulouse—were some of the greatest enemies of the Church and some of the most able men of their generation or because not being content with denying the truth of the Gospel, they removed its very foundations in their desire to destroy the mysteries of the Faith by [exposing them to] the light of human reason and by making philosophy the arbiter and ruler of religion. This is why Saint Bernard, when speaking of one of these [heresies], wrote to Pope Innocent saying that a new Gospel is being created and a new faith propounded: *Nove proponitur fides*.[79]

26. Oh Providence of God,[80] where are you? Where is your concern for the Gospel of your Son? How can you bear it when

---

[77] *Pace* Biroat, *Panégyriques*, 186, this is certainly not Augustine (or ps.-Augustine, for that matter) and appears nowhere in the Patrologia Latina or any of the standard databases. The only part that is from Augustine is the phrase *ex ore veritatis*, which occurs twice in his works.

[78] I.e., Gilbert de la Porrée or Gilbert of Poitiers. Abelard, Gilbert, and Henry of Toulouse all appear under their names in appendix 2.

[79] Biroat, *Panégyriques*, 186, quoting Bernard, Ep 189.2; SBOp 8:13, to Pope Innocent II.

[80] See n. 36 above.

a heresy that arises from the human mind destroys its truth with its own falsehood? And so God calls forth Saint Bernard for the second time to fight against these three monsters and prepares him for battle by providing him with two excellent qualities: learning and the power of miracles. How strange this is! Only on the rarest occasions do we find God making this alliance! He gave to the apostles the power of miracles, but the apostles were not learned. The doctors of the Church, [on the other hand], were learned, but could not perform miracles. There was hardly anyone but Saint Bernard who possessed both of these qualities: in his head was the light of knowledge, and in his hands were miracles, so as to triumph effectively over heresies both by the reasoning and by the grace of the Gospel.

27. It is with these weapons that he went to battle with Peter Abelard at the Council of Sens [in 1141]. He fought him effectively by the use of reason, but he also had [the advantage of] certain miraculous workings of grace. For this man, who had one of the most acute and intelligent minds of his century and who had never lacked a response to any question put to him, states that he had felt such an indescribable sense of astonishment that he had been brought to tears.[81] Ha! It is the Gospel of Jesus that acts as the rod of Moses in creating light and darkness. It instructs the apostles, and it enlightens the ignorant, but when it wills, it blinds the learned and the most enlightened in the world.

28. It was with this victorious Gospel that [Bernard] set out to confound Gilbert Porrette at the Council of Reims [in 1148], where Pope Eugenius was to be found, and as with [Abelard], he compelled him to submit himself to the judgment of the Church. Finally, he came to Languedoc, where heresy had caused infinite harm, and then went to all the other places

---

[81] Biroat, like all the panegyrists, exaggerates here. But their business was not to give a balanced account of any of the controversies in which Bernard played a part.

in the area that had been infected by its poison.[82] He thus deserves the same glorious praise that was given to Saint Augustine, namely, that he was the Master of Heretics, and that in his day he found no error that he did not destroy. We may say, therefore, that he preserved the unity of the Church against schisms, its truth against heretics, and its holiness against moral corruption.

29. (3) [Holiness] is the last of the perfections of that Church that Saint Paul calls the Bride of Christ: [the Church] that he sanctified with his own blood and to whom he gave the Gospel so as to show forth her holiness, not only as an ornament of her beauty but also as a proof of her truth. But there is nothing that defaces this ornament or destroys this adornment more effectively than the vice of Christians and moral corruption. Saint Bernard says so very clearly in [his commentary on] the Song of Songs where he has the Church complain that her children are fighting against her and causing her to lose her beauty.[83] This is why he fights against the vices of Christians, for this can be the most dangerous persecution faced by the Church. She has been attacked by the cruelty of tyrants and then by the errors of heretics. She has overcome these former enemies by the long suffering of the martyrs and the latter by the wisdom of the saints. But a third enemy arises in the wake of these two others, which [Bernard] calls the malice of darkness.[84] All the tyrants could attack the Church, but they

---

[82] The poison, that is, which had been spread by Henry of Toulouse, mentioned by Biroat in §25 above. See appendix 2, s.v. Henry of Toulouse.

[83] See especially Bernard, SC 24–26; SBOp 1:151–81, and n. 85 below.

[84] *La malice des ténèbres* (188). The phrase *malitia / malignitas tenebrarum* is not to be found in Bernard, and Biroat is almost certainly referring to Bernard's SC 33.8.15; SBOp 1:243: *En tempora ista, libera quidem, Deo miserante, ab utraque illa malitia, sed plane faeda, a negotio perambulante in tenebris* (Ps 90:6), "The times in which we live are, by God's mercy, free from this twofold malice, but clearly polluted by 'the pestilence that walks in darkness.'" See n. 85 immediately below.

could not destroy her. All the heretics wanted to overthrow her, but her foundation remained unshakeable. It is only these wicked Christians, of whom there are so many, who tear her apart and overthrow her by their corrupt morals: *Iam latere prae abundantia non potest, prae impietate velum non quaerit*: "Vice is so widespread that it cannot be hidden; it is so sure of itself that it seeks no veil."[85] Ha! Nothing could move Bernard more to convince him that the whole Church is there before his eyes and his zeal, saying to him *Collabora Evangelio*! Ha! Bernard will indeed work with the Gospel to banish moral corruption so as to restore to [the Church] that first holiness that was given to her by the blood of the martyrs. He had received from God a wonderful anointing to preach the Gospel and a gentleness that, flowing from his words, drew even the most obdurate to the holiness of Christianity.

30. We may compare his eloquence to that of the virtuous woman Jael.[86] When the captain of the army of the enemies of God's people comes to rest in her house, she gives him milk to drink and then takes a nail and drives it through his temple, and by this one death triumphs over the whole army. This is just what Bernard's eloquence does! It is like the milk

---

[85] Biroat, *Panégyriques*, 189, but neither text nor translation is quite what it should be. Biroat is sort of quoting Bernard, SC 33.8.15; SBOp 1:243, which actually reads *Iam latere prae abundantia non valet, et prae impudentia non quaerit*. Bernard has just cited Luke 12:1, "Beware the leaven of the Pharisees, which is hypocrisy," and continues "if that can be called hypocrisy that is so widespread that it cannot be hidden, and so shameless that it does not try to be!" He goes on to describe the "stinking corruption" (*putida tabes*) that permeates the whole body of the church, and his denunciation is savage.

[86] This is Jael, the wife of Heber the Kenite, who killed Sisera in order to give the Israelites victory over King Jabin: see Judges 4:17-24. These Old Testament women could be formidable adversaries. Likening Bernard's eloquence to a tent peg being driven through somebody's skull might not be a wholly pleasing analogy to the modern reader.

that softens up the sinner and gently insinuates itself into the heart, but at the same time, he takes in his mouth the iron of the Gospel and with it pierces the sinner's temple and drives from his head all the vices and everything contrary to the purity of the Gospel. It is with this iron that the saint goes forth to battle with sin wherever it appears, and to restore holiness to every part of the Church.

31. It is not enough, therefore, just to preach the Gospel to the common people: he writes to the great in the land, he instructs bishops, he rebukes kings for their vices, and, by revealing dreadful sins, he [condemns] the abuses being perpetrated in the Court of Rome. He is not even afraid to address himself to the head of the Church and tell him, in all humility, what the Church requires of him if she is to be sanctified in her most eminent part. Witness the book *On Consideration*, which he wrote to Pope Eugenius III, who had once been his disciple at Clairvaux[87] but who had ascended even as far as the throne of Saint Peter. He spoke out to the whole world and called all to their duty—so much so that we may say of him what the prophet Jeremiah said of the power of God in nature: *Fulgura in pluviam facit, et educit ventum de thesauris suis* ["He makes lightning with rain, and brings forth the wind from his treasuries" (Jer 10:13)]. In him we see a happy combination of lightning flashes with dew, of the sword of the Gospel with the sweetness of grace; uniting them together, he made the wind of the Holy Spirit blow into the hearts of those who heard him with such force that they had no choice but to turn again to God. In this way he restored holiness, he defended the Church, and, finally, he worked for the good of the monastic way of life.[88]

---

[87] The future pope had met Bernard in Italy, fallen under his spell, and entered Clairvaux as a monk in 1138. See appendix 2, s.v. Eugenius III.

[88] *De la Religion*: see n. 34 above.

[THIRD POINT][89]

32. This is the last of the services the saint rendered to the Gospel and the last way in which he worked to uphold its truth. It is the last of the areas in which he put forth his power. The reason for this last concern may be seen in a beautiful thought of Saint Gregory of Nazianzus, who calls this state *Plenitudo Evangelii*, the Fullness of the Gospel.[90] There are three reasons for this. First, because it is in this state that one undertakes one of the most difficult yet most important demands of the Gospel: fighting against the passions and chastising the flesh. Second, because it is [in this state] that the Gospel finds its entire perfection, something that derives from two moral virtues that give it its whole glory: one practices it, and one preaches it: a life of action [combined with] a life of words. Third, because it is in this state that one prepares oneself to preach the Gospel effectively, and we can say that just as God's Providence gave to his Church apostles to found it, through all those many centuries when the fury of tyrants reigned, so too it has provided Christians with preachers to guide them. It was through this learned holiness that Bernard preserved the purity of the Church; it was on this basis that he established the bases of all the care he took for the monastic profession of which he was part, just as the stars principally illumine the heavens of which they are part. This he achieved in three ways: by reforming it, by founding it, and by guiding it. Thus, (1) he reformed the Order of Saint Benedict, (2) he founded his own order,[91] and (3) he worked to share his precepts with those who would establish other orders in the Church.

---

[89] *III. Point* in the left margin of page 190.

[90] Biroat, *Panégyriques*, 190–91. I have not traced this in the Greek text of Gregory, but I admit that I have not hunted assiduously. The Latin expression occurs nowhere in the Patrologia Latina nor any of the standard databases. Greek databases are regrettably lacking.

[91] This is not, of course, correct, but Bernard was sometimes called the "Second Founder" of the Cistercian Order, and under the *Ancien*

33. (1) We will begin this last part of our discourse with the noteworthy observation that there is a remarkable rapport between the Providence that God preserves in the way of life of religious and [the Providence] he puts into practice in the establishment and way of life of the Church. The Church needs two types of apostles: one group to establish it, and the other to reform it when its first beauty has been marred by laxity in discipline. Similarly, for the religious life, there is a first group of apostles and a second. The first apostles of the monastic life are those who found it; the second are those who reform it. The first apostle of the monastic life is the incomparable Saint Benedict, the great patriarch of the monastic way in the West, but we can say that Saint Bernard is the second apostle, whom God raised up to reform it. What a dreadful thing! It shows all too well the weakness of the human spirit that lets itself grow lax in those matters that are most holy! This first order, which had filled the Church with saints, which had given the Church so many pontiffs, so many martyrs for the faith, so many patriarchs, so many bishops, so many preachers, relaxed its first fervor and fell into disorders that touched [the hearts of] those saints who remained. But do not think from this that the Providence of God had abandoned [the order] or that he had forgotten the blood and tears of so many holy monks and nuns. No. He raises up a second apostle to reform it and restore to it its first spirit.[92] This is just what Saint Bernard did in [two] different places: first at Cîteaux, where he established and then

---

Régime Cistercians and sort-of-Cistercians (including Feuillants) were regularly referred to as *Bernardins* (male) or *Bernardines* (female). See n. 95 below.

[92] *Premier esprit* (192). In 1653, a dozen years or so before Biroat's death, Julien Paris, abbot of the Cistercian abbey of Foucarmont, had published the first edition of his *Du premier esprit de l'ordre de Cîteaux*, a book that had a profound influence on Rancé. What was the *premier esprit* of the order? Nothing less than that strict and unswerving fidelity to the Rule of Saint Benedict that Rancé would demand at La Trappe. See further Bell, *Understanding Rancé*, 128–33.

began to revive the spirit of Saint Benedict and this first Gospel; second, at Cluny, where he points out to the monks the laxity that had crept into the order and the need for reform. He offers to help them in this task for the sake of Saint Benedict, as we may see from the fine letter he writes to the abbots of the order who had assembled at Soissons for precisely this purpose. He says at the beginning that his desire is to cooperate with them and work with them to achieve their goal,[93] which is why Peter [the Venerable], abbot of Cluny, sought out Saint Bernard in his monastery and begged him to use his influence and his power for this reform.[94]

34. Have you ever seen a stately temple that the passage of time or some other misfortune has left half ruined? It stands in some secluded spot, its stones scattered here and there. But then one gathers up the ruins, reassembles the stones, and builds a new temple that has something of the majesty of the old. And to what may we compare the great Order of Saint Benedict in the time of Saint Bernard? To a half-ruined temple, of which we may say what Jeremiah said of the temple in Jerusalem: *Dispersi sunt lapides sanctuarii in capite omnium platearum* ["The stones of the sanctuary are scattered at the top of every street" (Lam 4:1)]. The stones of the sanctuary are strewn about in different places as a result of the disorders of the times and laxity in monastic discipline. What does Saint Bernard do? He gathers up the ruins, he restores the stones to what they first were, he rekindles its first spirit, and, in reforming this whole order, he [re]founds it as a new order to his own glory and honor, [an order] that bears his name[95] and that possesses, as its own distinctive character, the particular spirit of this saint.

---

[93] Biroat, *Panégyriques*, 193, referring to Bernard, Ep 21; SBOp 7:239-41, to the abbots assembled at Soissons.

[94] Peter came to visit Bernard at Clairvaux in 1149. See further appendix 2, s.v. Peter the Venerable.

[95] See n. 91 above.

34. (2) The saints, in their charity, seek to perpetuate their services by giving to their zeal three qualities that I see in God himself: they are infinity, immensity, and eternity. Christians, likewise, should seek to give to their services these three excellent things, thus: by wishing to render to God infinite service, by wishing to spread his word and his honor everywhere, and by wishing always to live in such a way as to make their zeal eternal. Bernard possessed all three desires in that charity that he took as his motto in all that he did: *Modus amandi Deum, est amare sine modo* ["The measure of loving God is to love him without measure"].[96] His desires, therefore, were infinite, immense, and eternal, but he had three limitations that resisted his desires and made them less far-reaching than he would have liked. How did he manifest the immensity of love? He devised ways to compensate for these limitations. Since he could not be infinite himself, he would be infinite by means of his [monastic] children. Since he could not be everywhere himself, he would be everywhere through his order and the monasteries he built throughout the world. Since he himself could not live forever, he would live forever through his continuing [monastic] family and the eternity of his children. And surely his desires were fulfilled! For even during his own lifetime he saw a great number of religious who made up his family, and through them he built a hundred and sixty monasteries in various parts of the world[97]—monasteries that he founded so well that they promise an eternity to his family.

---

[96] Biroat, *Panégyriques*, 194. This is a paraphrase of the first two sentences of Bernard's *De diligendo Deo* 1.1; SBOp 3:119: *Vultis ergo a me audire quare et quo modo diligendus sit Deus. Et ego: Causa diligendi Deum, Deus est: modus, sine modo diligere*: "So you wish to hear from me why and in what measure God should be loved. And I [reply]: God is the reason for loving God, and the measure is to love him without measure."

[97] Biroat, *Panégyriques*, 194, is following the *Vita prima* 5.2.15 (Geoffrey of Auxerre): PL 185:360C; CF 76:248 (*amplius quam centum sexaginta*) and 5.3.20; 363A; 253 (*centum sexaginta*). The figure is also to

35. (3) On the other hand, at the same time he is providing guidance for all the other orders that are part of the Church or that will be one day.[98] How is this so? Because Bernard's spirit and the guidance of the Church can offer direction to all religious orders in the way they govern themselves, and, moreover, he himself has left a visible impression of his spirit in three ways: (1) by his example, (2) in his writings, (3) through his children. Ha! This holy house in which I have the honor of speaking visibly displays the greatness of its Father's spirit and sanctity! And it is from his example, from his writings, and from his children that the Church collects the light of his spirit and applies it to all the other religious orders so that they might pattern themselves on this idea. But here, at the end of my discourse, I will restrain myself from firing us up further in these matters, and I will simply repeat the words of my text, *Collabora Evangelio*, so as to show that each one of us should work on his or her part for the effectiveness and glory of the Gospel.

[CONCLUSION][99]

36. (1) Saint Bernard worked with the Gospel for his own sanctification and practiced it in himself. We have received the same Gospel as Saint Bernard, but do we practice it with the same dedication and the same ardor? We have it under the same terms—*Collabora*—but do we work with the grace it gives us to make ourselves saints? Do not think it enough just to believe the Gospel in spirit or in theory! Its light must descend into your heart and pass from theory into practice! What use is it to know that penitence, humility, and meekness find favor with God if

---

be found in Le Maistre's *Vie de S Bernard*. This was and is the usual number given for daughterhouses of Clairvaux founded during Bernard's lifetime. It is approximately correct.

[98] Biroat changes to the present tense here.

[99] *Conclusion* in the right margin of page 195.

you do not do what is necessary to acquire these virtues—and what is necessary is set out before you in detail in the Gospel! Ha! Far from imitating Saint Bernard, who united in his own body such great innocence with such extreme rigor, you continue in your sins,[100] and you live your lives with as much assurance as if you were pure as angels! Saint Bernard fled from all human interaction lest the least fault should soil his soul; yet we make it our goal to seek out all such interaction so as to have the freedom to offend God and soil our souls with countless shameful impurities. I do not say this only of Christians, but even of pagans who live according to the light of human reason alone. Ha! great saint, how unknown are your gentleness and humility in our own century! How many Christians do we see who display the pride and haughtiness of demons rather than the submissiveness and meekness of Jesus Christ? *Discite a me quia mitis sum et humilis corde* ["Learn from me, for I am meek and humble of heart" (Matt 11:29)]. We might change this and, with respect to most of our Christians, say with the devil, *Discite a me quia immitis sum et superbus corde*: "Learn from me how one should be proud and cruel."[101] Ha! For one humble and kind-hearted Saint Bernard, how many Christians are there who are proud and haughty?

37. (2) This saint upheld the Gospel in the defense of the Church. We are not all called to such great tasks, but we can still work with [the Gospel] in defending its unity, truth, and holiness. (1) How can Christians defend the unity of the Church? By their unswerving attachment to the throne of Saint Peter and by their obedience in submitting their spirit to the articles of the faith and the decisions of the Church. Ah! But how many Catholics are there now who have a thousand doubts about these decisions? Believe me, there are those who, incredibly, are in sympathy with this spirit of schism, but this is to open great wounds that separate the limbs from the head, it is to

---

[100] *Crimes* (196): see appendix 1, s.v. *crimes* / sins.
[101] Lit. "Learn from me, for I am harsh and proud of heart."

sharpen the sword that wounds the bride of Jesus Christ.[102] It is tendencies like these that shake the other foundations of the Faith. (2) How can we uphold the truth of the Church if we doubt its power, or substitute for the form and rule of our Faith our own capricious ideas or what our own reason leads us to believe? And (3) How can we Christians fulfill the great responsibility we have to defend the holiness of the Church if we make a disastrous alliance of our bodies with sin and if the devil reigns in our hearts? Ha! Let us imitate the example and zeal of Saint Bernard and say to ourselves, *Collabora Evangelio* ["Work with the Gospel"]! Let us make a strong resolution this very day to preserve the unity, truth, and holiness of the Church so as to be her true children!

38. (3) Finally, Saint Bernard carried the glory of the Gospel into the religious life, and what we should learn from this is how we may find in the perfection of the religious life a stimulus to amend our own. You are not called upon to practice the fullness of the Gospel[103] as monks or nuns, with all its rigors and continual mortification, but each one of you, whatever your position in life, should ask yourself what you might learn from their example. You should ponder what it is that makes these religious, themselves so innocent, mortify themselves day and night to preserve the grace [of the Gospel], for by so doing we will learn what we must do to obtain its mercy: *Collabora Evangelio*! Ha![104] we should make our soul a holy and secret solitude where we can meet God as a familiar friend;[105] this should be our religious profession in which we should make Jesus Christ our Superior[106] and strive continually for his

---

[102] See §21 above.
[103] See n. 12 and §32 above.
[104] This, happily, is the last of Biroat's *Ha*'s.
[105] *Traiter familièrement avec Dieu* (198).
[106] Superior in the monastic sense: Christ becomes our abbot to whom (as is stated in the Rule of Saint Benedict) we owe absolute obedience.

glory. We should regulate all our actions, words, and thoughts in accordance with his holy will, and thus, having worked, as did Saint Bernard, to bring about the triumph of the Gospel, we may enter with him into that eternal glory to which we hope he will lead us, etc.[107]

---

[107] The "etc." represents the standard concluding doxology: "In the name of the Father and of the Son and of the Holy Spirit . . . ." In Blampignon's edition, all the panegyrics end in this way.

5

Moving Forward

*Commonplaces and Curiosities
in Jean-François Senault, Bernard Planchette,
Claude Texier, and Jean-Louis de Fromentières*

In this chapter we shall move on in time from Jacques Biroat and summarize the panegyrics of four preachers: two Oratorians, one Maurist, and one Jesuit. Biroat lived from the late sixteenth century to 1666, and the lifespans of the four preachers to be considered in this chapter range from the early 1600s to 1687. In other words, we have moved on about twenty years, though we have no idea of the exact year in which any of the panegyrics were preached. Of the four figures, Jean-François Senault certainly enjoyed the highest renown, though his panegyric is disappointing; the Jesuit Claude Texier and Jean-Louis de Fromentières, bishop of Aire, both preached before the royal Court; and Bernard Planchette, the learned Maurist, though far less celebrated, is unique among the panegyrists in introducing us to Saint Bernard as a second Osiris. None of their panegyrics warrants a complete translation, but all of them, for one reason or another, deserve a summary. Let us begin with the panegyric of Jean-François Senault.

Jean-François Senault

Jean-François Senault, the fourth superior-general of the Oratory of Jesus, was esteemed in his day as one of the greatest preachers in France. He was born at Antwerp in 1599 and entered the Oratory, not quite twenty years old, in 1618. There he taught Humanities, but after his ordination to the priesthood in 1627 his superiors decided that his true calling was preaching and instructed him to devote himself to this end. This he did, and after spending a dozen years preparing himself for the task, met with great success, first in the provinces and then in Paris. He delivered no fewer than twenty-seven *stations* for Advent and Lent (two of them to a royal audience at the Louvre), and his renown was so great that up to twenty copyists would cluster round the foot of his pulpit to note down his sermons and sell them.[1] He was no less effective as an organizer, governing the Oratorian house in Orleans and then the seminary of Saint-Magloire in Paris, before moving to the motherhouse of the congregation on the rue Saint-Honoré, where, in 1663, he was appointed superior-general. He died on August 3, 1672.

In his sermons he eschewed the flashy delivery, the *ridicules plaisanteries*,[2] and the displays of erudition common at his time, and based his words austerely on Scripture and the Fathers. His panegyrics, however, cannot be said to be his best work—Albert and Court, writing in the eighteenth century, maintain that in many places "they need to be retouched to conform to present-day taste"[3]—and Tréverret did not like them at all. Senault, he writes, certainly tells us something of the saints he praises, but what he says is insufficient and incomplete.[4] Senault did not regard himself as a historian, and, as we have seen in chapter 3, Tréverret demands a good, solid, historical foundation from his panegyrists. And to com-

---

[1] See DLF XVII, 1174. Senault receives high praise from Hurel, 1:77–94.

[2] Albert / Court, 245.

[3] Albert / Court, 245.

[4] Tréverret, 20. He singles out the panegyrics of Saints Dominic, Louis, Teresa of Ávila, and François de Sales, of which he says "rien de plus incomplet."

pound this problem, he says, "the moral and theological developments, which serve to make up for the huge lacunae in his discourses, weary us with their pretentious elegance. There is no unction, no touching tone. The form they take is always academic and measured; there is a coldness that never warms up; in a word, there is nothing that leaves any trace on the mind or the heart."[5] This is a harsh criticism, no doubt about it, but, regrettably, it is what I see in his panegyric on Saint Bernard.[6] It is elegant, certainly, but it is also rather boring and eminently predictable, and all we need do here is to present to the reader a brief summary.

Senault delivered his discourse to a congregation of *Pères Bernardins*—that is to say, to a congregation of Feuillants—on Bernard's feast day, August 20 of an unknown year, taking as his text 2 Timothy 2:11-12, "A trustworthy saying: if we have died with him, we shall also live with him; if we endure, we will also reign with him." Senault gives the Latin,[7] but not, oddly, a translation. What he is going to say for about the next hour and a half is encapsulated in what he says at the very beginning of his panegyric. These words of Saint Paul,[8] he tells us, may be applied to all the saints, and they are in themselves a promise of God's mercy, for if one has died to sin one can live to grace, and one will share in the glory of Jesus Christ to just the same extent as one has shared in his humiliations and sufferings.

---

[5] Tréverret, 20.

[6] [Jean-François Senault], *Panégyriques des Saints. Par le R. P. Iean François Senault, Prestre de l'Oratoire de Iesus. Second volume* (Paris: Pierre Le Petit, 1657), 363–97 (cited below as Senault).

[7] *Fidelis sermo: si commortui sumus et convivemus; si sustinemus et conregnabimus*. The Vulgate text has the future *sustinebimus* for Senault's *sustinemus*.

[8] Most, though not all, modern scholars are of the opinion that 2 Timothy was not written by Saint Paul, but by one of his followers after Paul's death. But Senault could not have known that.

Yet it seems to me that there are some who seem to have more right to speak in this way than others and who, having been more conformed to the Son of God dying on the Cross, may hope to be more like Jesus Christ living and glorious in Heaven. And we must certainly admit that of all these we do not see one who has a greater right to lay claim to this bliss than Saint Bernard, for his greatest task on earth was to die to himself and live to Jesus Christ Our Lord.[9]

And just as he died to himself so that Christ might live in him, so he imposed silence upon himself so that Christ might speak through his mouth, and lived in holy passivity (*oisiveté*) so that Christ might act in and through him. Such will be the subject and the three divisions of Senault's discourse.

The whole of the first division deals with the way in which Bernard died to the world and to himself. We hear allusions to the usual stories of his withdrawal to Cîteaux, "not as a fugitive but as a conqueror,"[10] drawing with him in his train his friends and brothers, and how, once there, he subjected his body to the strictest asceticism and his senses to the strictest control. The senses, says Senault (quoting Gregory the Great), are like windows through which the soul looks out and concupiscent desire enters in.[11] And so we hear the well-known tales of how Bernard was unaware of his immediate surroundings, and how he took no account of what he was eating or drinking: "He regarded the table as his torment, he went to the refectory only with sorrow, and through a grace that is accorded to few of the saints, he made a penance of what others considered a pleasure."[12]

---

[9] Senault, 364.

[10] Senault, 368.

[11] Senault, 369, quoting Gregory the Great, *Moralia in Job* 21.2.4; PL 76:189C.

[12] Senault, 372, echoing *Vita prima* 1.4.22 (William of Saint-Thierry); PL 185:239D; CF 76:26.

Senault then deals with how Bernard guarded his tongue, imposing upon himself strict silence and speaking only when absolutely necessary. He was dead to himself and the world, and the dead do not speak. Silence goes hand in hand with solitude, and here, too, Bernard is a model. His solitude was a solitude of the heart, and he was never more alone than when he was with others. Senault quotes the *Vita prima*, telling us that "he provided for himself his own solitude of heart, and carrying this solitude with him, he was everywhere alone."[13] There then follows a page in which our preacher dwells on the similarity of solitude to the tomb—the idea of the monastery as a tomb was commonplace at the time—and summarizes his discourse thus far by telling us that "our saint died to the world when he entered the religious life; he died to all his friends when he left them; he died to his hopes when he renounced them; and he died to himself when he buried himself in the cloister."[14] And once in the cloister, he continued his task, living only to see his self-love expire in the fire of charity, the light of his intelligence in the darkness of faith, and the strength of his body in the austerity of penance.

The purpose of all this was that Bernard should live no more, but that Christ should live in him, for as he himself says (following Saint Paul), *Necesse est qui non vivit in se, vivat Christus in illo*: "It is necessary that Christ live in him who does not live in himself."[15] And he achieved this to such an extent that it was Christ who spoke through Bernard's mouth, Christ who worked miracles through Bernard's hands, Christ who guided the church by Bernard's prudence. Senault will now explain how this was so, but the song he sings has old and familiar melodies. We have heard them in Biroat, and we

---

[13] Senault, 375, quoting *Vita prima* 1.4.24 (William of Saint-Thierry); PL 185:241A; CF 76:27.

[14] Senault, 376.

[15] Senault, 378, quoting Bernard, *In Quadragesima* S 6.2; SBOp 4:378, echoing Gal 2:20.

shall hear them again and again in the other panegyrists. We learn of Bernard's deep immersion in Scripture, how he was able to unravel its deepest mysteries, and how he had no fear in rebuking, when necessary, popes and princes. Once again we hear the story of the conversion of Duke William X of Aquitaine (though Senault has not recalled it quite correctly), once again we hear of Bernard at the Council of Étampes (Senault refers to it simply as "the Council") declaring in favor of Innocent II, once again we see Bernard (like Moses before Pharaoh) rebuking Louis VII the Young[16] for challenging the rights of the bishop of Paris. We hear of his letter to Conrad III of Hohenstaufen urging him to restore order in Rome, where the citizens had risen up against Pope Eugenius III,[17] we hear of his letters of rebuke to Suger of Saint-Denis,[18] Ardutio, bishop of Geneva,[19] Henry, archbishop of Sens,[20] and even Pope Innocent II himself, chastising him for not coming to the assistance of the church in Orleans.[21] And once again, inevitably, we hear, in some detail, of his strictures in *De consideratione*, when he praises Eugenius for what he is—the light of the world, the priest of the Most High God, the Vicar of Christ, the Anointed of the Lord, and so on[22]—and then tells him, in no uncertain terms, just what duties and responsibilities these roles entail.

But if Bernard was powerful in what he said, he was no less powerful in what he did, and in the third division of his discourse Senault turns to the saint's miracles. In the greatest saints, he tells us, the gift of miracles was no more than a transient grace, but it remained with Bernard for the whole

---

[16] Senault, 385, errs; the king in question was Louis VI the Fat. See appendix 2, s.v. Louis VI the Fat.

[17] Ep 244; SBOp 8:134–36.

[18] Ep 78; SBOp 7:201–10.

[19] Epp 27–28; SBOp 7:80–82.

[20] Ep 42; SBOp 7:100–31, the letter-treatise *De moribus et officio episcoporum*.

[21] Ep 156; SBOp 7:363.

[22] Senault, 390, quoting Bernard, Csi 4.7.23; SBOp 3:466.

of his life. Yet of all Bernard's miracles, Senault recounts only one, that which took place in Sarlat in the Dordogne, though Senault locates it, incorrectly, in "a town in Germany."[23] This is the miracle, recounted also (and more accurately) by Fénelon, when Bernard promised that everyone who ate of the bread he had blessed would be cured. When the papal legate, Geoffrey of Chartres, queried this promise and suggested that what Bernard meant was that all those who ate the bread *with faith* would be cured, Bernard shook his head: God's work has nothing to do with faith, he said, and all who eat the bread will be cured, believers and unbelievers alike.[24] But that is all we hear of miracles, and Senault now turns to the conclusion of his panegyric by returning to a variant of the text of his discourse: *Si sustinemus et conregnabimus; si commorimur et convivemus*: "If we endure [hardships], we shall also reign with him; if we die with him, we shall also live with him."[25]

Bernard passed the first years of his life in the mortification of all his senses, using them only in ways pleasing to God. He used his eyes only to weep for his sins, his ears only to hear the word of Jesus Christ, and his sense of taste only to mix (like David[26]) ashes with his bread. And as he had killed off his senses, so too he killed off his passions, and, being wholly detached from all earthly things, he had no interest in riches or honor, and no fear of poverty or dishonor. But should this not also apply to us? It should! To die to oneself is the task of all Christians from the very moment of their entry into the church. We renounce all worldly vanities in our baptism, and in that sacrament we express our desire to be buried with Christ.

---

[23] Senault, 394.

[24] Senault, 394–95. See *Vita prima* 3.6.18 (Geoffrey of Auxerre); PL 185:313D–14A; CF 76:164, Williams, *Saint Bernard*, 341, and chap. 8 of this book (Fénelon), §27.

[25] Senault, 394. Senault here reverses the phrases and changes the past *commortui sumus* to the present *commorimur*.

[26] See Ps 101:10.

"What have you done to acquit yourselves of these promises?" Senault asks his audience, "Which passions have you stifled?"[27] Hatred? Pride? Lust? Vain desire? False hope? "But if you wish to live with Saint Bernard, you must also die with him, and if you wish to reign with the Son of God, you must suffer with him on earth."[28] True, it is not for us to aspire to the same heights as Saint Bernard. It is not for us to have authority over kings, bishops, and popes: "But at least control your passions, rule over your senses, and be slaves of Jesus Christ in order to be masters of yourselves; and this glorious servitude will be followed in Heaven by an eternal sovereignty, and may he lead us to that end."[29]

Such, briefly, is Senault's panegyric on Saint Bernard. It is, as we said earlier, nothing if not predictable, and although the language is indeed elegant (as befits Senault's reputation as a preacher), what he tells us so elegantly is conventional material. We have heard most of it before. His sources, too, are limited: Gregory the Great, Tertullian (always a favorite at the time), Augustine, and Ambrose. There is a single line from Seneca.[30] For Bernard's life, Senault has used the *Vita prima* together (probably) with Antoine Le Maistre's *Vie de Saint Bernard*. If he did indeed use Le Maistre's work, the panegyric cannot have been composed before 1648, the date of the first edition of Le Maistre. Of Bernard's own works, he quotes only from the letters, the *De consideratione*, and (rarely) an occasional sermon. There is no mention whatever of Bernard's mysticism, nor is there any mention of Peter Abelard, Gilbert de la Porrée, or Henry of Toulouse, as is certainly unusual. And despite the buildup at the beginning of his third division, Senault recounts only one miracle, and even then he locates it in the wrong

---

[27] Senault, 395.
[28] Senault, 396.
[29] Senault, 397.
[30] Senault, 383, quoting Seneca the Younger, *Agamemnon* 259: *Nec regna socium ferre, nec taedae sciunt.*

place. It is true that Senault was not a historian and had no time for pyrotechnical displays of scholarly erudition, but the fact remains that his panegyric is unimpressive and rather old-fashioned, though its moral teaching, as we would expect, is unimpeachable. Let us see whether a learned Maurist, Bernard Planchette, who had nothing like the reputation of Senault, can do any better.

Bernard Planchette

Planchette was born at Aubignac in the diocese of Reims and made his profession in the Order of the Congregation of Saint-Maur at the abbey of Vendôme on August 15, 1637, when he was about thirty. He lived (says the Cluniac Louis-Mayeul Chaudon) *dans une grande régularité* until his death at Saint-Remi of Reims on April 6, 1680, aged 71.[31] He wrote a life of Saint Benedict, published in 1652, of which the third book contains eulogies of the most esteemed writers of the Benedictine Order. In 1671 he published an account of the miracles said to have occurred as a result of intercession of the Virgin Mary in the abbey of Saint-Pierre-sur-Dive: "this is a translation of the old manuscript by Haymo, abbot of this monastery." And he composed the panegyrics, first published in 1675.[32] But Chaudon's verdict on the panegyrics is that "Ces discours sont très-faibles."[33] *Faible* or weak they may be from the point of view of pulpit oratory—they certainly lack the elegance of

---

[31] [Louis-Mayeul Chaudon], *Dictionnaire historique des auteurs ecclésiastiques: renfermant la Vie des Pères & des Docteurs de l'Église . . . Tome quatrième* (Lyon: La veuve Bessiat, 1767), 56.

[32] See François, 408, who gives the details of his published works.

[33] Chaudon, *Dictionnaire*, 4:56. François, 408, likewise has little time for them, and François's comments are repeated verbatim by René-Prosper Tassin, *Histoire littéraire de la Congrégation de Saint-Maur, Ordre de S. Benoît . . .* (Brussels and Paris: Chez Humbert, 1770), 95. Albert and Court, 211, simply list the contents of the 1675 edition of the panegyrics (Paris: Louis Billaine) and give no critical assessment.

Senault—but the first part of Planchette's panegyric on Saint Bernard has a number of curious and unique features that deserve our attention.[34] It was preached, like that of Senault, to a congregation of Feuillants in one of their churches,[35] but Planchette does not tell us which. Nor have we any indication of the year in which he delivered his discourse.

He takes as his text a variant of Hosea 2:14, which, in the original, is God speaking of Israel and promising that, despite all her iniquities (like Hosea's wife), he still loves her and is still prepared to take her back to himself: *Propter hoc ecce ego lactabo eam et ducam eam in solitudinem et loquar ad cor eius*, "Therefore behold, I will charm[36] her, and I will lead her into the wilderness, and I will speak to her heart." Planchette alters the order of the sentence, adds an *ibi*, and changes the feminine pronouns to masculine so that the text can refer to Bernard: *Ducam eum in solitudinem, et loquar ad cor ejus; et ego ibi lactabo eum*, "I will lead him into the wilderness and I will speak to his heart; and there I will charm him."

In his exordium, Planchette foreshadows Claude Lion and Henri-Marie Boudon in introducing the two miracles of the Lactation[37] and the *Amplexus Bernardi*,[38] and he tells us that it is

---

[34] [Bernard Planchette], *Panégyriques de plusieurs saints, Preschez par le Révérend Père Dom Bernard Planchette, Religieux Bénédictin de la Congrégation de Saint Maur. Seconde partie* (Paris: Jean Couterot and Louis Guerin, 1684), 89–136 (cited below as Planchette).

[35] Planchette, 89: "Prononcé dans une Église de la Congrégation des Révérends Pères Feüillans."

[36] The Douai-Reims version translates *lacto* as "allure." It could also be translated as "entice" or "cajole."

[37] See Léon Dewez and Albert van Iterson, "La Lactation de saint Bernard: légende et iconographie," *Cîteaux in der Nederlanden* 7 (1956): 165–89; and Patrick Arabeyre, "La Lactation de saint Bernard à Châtillon-sur-Seine: données et problèmes," in *Vies et légendes de saint Bernard de Clairvaux* (Brecht and Saint-Nicolas-lès-Cîteaux: Présence cistercienne; *Cîteaux—Commentarii cistercienses*, 1993), 173–97.

[38] The miracle is first mentioned by Herbert of Clairvaux in his *Liber miraculorum/De miraculis*, 2.19; PL 185:1328CD; then by Conrad

from these two wondrous springs—the breast of Mary and the cross of Jesus—that Bernard received the graces that enabled him to do all that he did. And since it is impossible for him to tell the whole story of Bernard in all its detail in what he calls "a short Panegyric,"[39] he will concentrate on three things: first, the divine wisdom that was infused into Bernard in his solitude and that made him so celebrated and renowned. Second, the supreme authority he exercised over the minds and conduct of kings and princes. And last, the profound knowledge he had of sacred and secular laws, which led to his being seen as a guide, mediator, and arbitrator in all manner of disputes, political, ecclesiastical, and monastic: "He is therefore at one and the same time the Disciple, the Master, and the School: the disciple of the forests,[40] the Master of the Princes of the world, and the School of Law."[41] And so, as usual, Planchette asks Mary to intercede with her Son to grant him what he needs to praise Bernard fittingly, "and we greet her with the Angel, [saying] *Ave Maria*."[42]

So far there is nothing unusual, nothing to raise one's eyebrows, but then, in Part One of his sermon, our learned Maurist enters on a long discussion of the ways in which the desert and the wilderness were the teachers not only of Bernard but also

---

of Eberbach, *Exordium Magnum Cisterciense* 2.7 (= *Vita prima* 7.7.10; PL 185:419D–20A). See Franz Posset, "The Crucified Embraces Saint Bernard: The Beginnings of the *Amplexus Bernardi*," *Cistercian Studies Quarterly* 33 (1998): 289–314, the same author's "*Amplexus Bernardi*: The Dissemination of a Cistercian Motif in the Later Middle Ages," *Cîteaux—Commentarii cistercienses* 54 (2003): 251–400, and Anthony N. S. Lane, *Bernard of Clairvaux: Theologian of the Cross*, CS 248 (Collegeville, MN: Cistercian Publications, 2013), 230–32.

[39] Planchette, 91. "Short" is something of an understatement. I estimate a time of delivery for this sermon of not less than an hour and a half.

[40] See n. 43 below.

[41] Planchette, 91.

[42] Planchette, 91.

of many who came before him. Bernard himself tells us that we will find in the woods things we can never find in books, and that stones and trees will teach us more than we can ever learn from masters in the medieval schools.[43] But this was not true only of Bernard. It was also true of the sages of India and Egypt, of the many Greek pupils of the wise centaur Chiron (Planchette names Aesculapius and Hercules), of many of the worthies of the Old Testament, and of certain scions of royal houses who retreated to the desert to separate themselves from the world and find the solace of contemplation. But, says our preacher, "the desert did not serve as a school only for pagan philosophers, the heroes of the Gentiles, and the children of kings." Witness the praise bestowed on the solitude of the woods by "our abbot Guerric"—that is, Guerric of Igny—at the beginning of his fourth sermon: "We should pay attention to the advantage of the desert and the blessed delights of the hermitage, which, from the beginning of grace, were worthy of being dedicated to the contemplative repose of the saints and the instruction of those who listened to the Spirit of God."[44]

It was in this Academy of the Desert that the word of God inspired the great solitaries of old—the Pauls, Antonys, and Hilarions[45]—and, of course, Saint Bernard himself, who was in no way inferior to these great names. Bernard, in fact, was like a second Moses and a second John the Baptist (Planchette is here foreshadowing Massillon and others): he was a voice crying in the wilderness to make straight those ways that had

---

[43] Planchette, 92–93, quoting, in Latin and French, Bernard's Ep 106.2; SBOp 7:266–67, to Henry Murdac: "Believe me, who have experience of this: you will find more in the woods than in books, and stones will teach you what you cannot hear from any master." See also *Vita prima* 1.4.23 (William of Saint-Thierry); PL 185:240CD; CF 76:27.

[44] This is Planchette's adapted and expanded translation (94–95) of Guerric's In adv Dom S 4.1; SCh 166:134. I have rendered Planchette's *repos* (*quies* in Latin) as "contemplative repose."

[45] I.e., Saint Paul the First Hermit, Saint Antony the Great, and Saint Hilarion.

been made crooked by such men as Peter Abelard, and by the contagious corruption that had infected the whole church. He spoke out against the iniquity of the papal schism, against negligence and laxity in the Church and monasticism, and against the wicked violence of kings and princes. And where did he learn these skills? In the same place as did Moses: in the desert, and in the School of the Holy Spirit; Planchette quotes Philo of Alexandria to prove his point.[46] But then, in an extraordinary passage that deserves to be translated in full, Planchette likens Bernard to the Egyptian god Osiris and the way in which, as an infant, he was suckled by his mother Isis:

> Even though we are told by Saint Paul to shun the fables and all the imaginative fictions of the pagan poets,[47] I cannot refrain from telling you here what they dreamed up so charmingly about the education of Osiris, who, for the Egyptians, represented the sun. These men, who were used to dissimulations, delusions, and fantasies, had invented the tale that while Osiris was still a baby, the goddess Isis had nourished him with nothing more than flames. For instead of baring her bosom and offering him her breast, she gave him her finger to suck, and from it came forth those flashes and sparks of fire that would nourish one destined to appear in the assembly of the gods. Allow me, Gentlemen, to adorn my subject, which is holy, with the luster of this fiction, which is entirely pagan, and to say that the Holy Spirit, who is called "the finger of the hand of God" and who is the original source of the light and flame by which the angels and the blessed are nourished in heaven, has done to Saint Bernard what the poets said that Isis did with regard to the sun. It nourished him with fire and flames alone in the desert of Clairvaux: with the fire and flames of

---

[46] Planchette, 97–98, quoting from Philo's *Life of Moses*.
[47] See 1 Tim 1:4; 2 Tim 2:16.

charity,[48] and the splendor of a wisdom that came forth from the dim places of the woods to triumph over the philosophers of Egypt, the fake wise men of the world, tyrants, princes, and kings, [a wisdom] to which the whole world would listen in humble silence, as though to that of a new prophet.[49]

Planchette now leads us back to familiar ground when he emphasizes that Bernard's remarkable wisdom and understanding were combined with an equally remarkable humility. Worldly learning puffs up the human heart (Planchette is echoing 1 Corinthians 8:1), but the learning infused into his disciples by the word of God humbles the human spirit and heart and cures its puffed-up-ness. This is why the Bride says to her companions, "I have drunk my wine with my milk" (Song 5:1), for wine symbolizes learning or knowledge, and milk, which is the food of little children, symbolizes humility. I admit, says Planchette, that it is difficult to make a good drink from mixing wine and milk (he's right: the result is disgusting), but it is even more difficult to combine learning with humility. The learned of this world generally have the highest opinion of their own abilities and want themselves and their ideas known to all. As Persius says, "It's a fine thing to have people point their finger at you and say 'That's him!'"[50] But the humble prefer to live a life hidden from human eyes, and if they wish to be known to the world, it is only to be the object of its insults and contempt. Bernard (as we might expect) was a rarity who combined both vast knowledge and deep humility in one and the same person.

The rest of Planchette's Part One is predictable and, indeed, somewhat repetitive. He elaborates on the way in which

---

[48] See appendix 1, s.v. *charité* / charity.

[49] Planchette, 100–101. His source for the story of Isis and Osiris is the *De praeparatione evangelica* of Eusebius of Caesarea.

[50] Planchette, 104, quoting Persius, Satire I, line 28. It was a well-known line.

Bernard mixed wine and milk and then, as we would expect, contrasts the virtues of the saint with the vices of his audience: "Let us compare now, Gentlemen, our lights with the lights of Saint Bernard, and the ideas we have of them with his. We will discover in ourselves as much ignorance and pride as we have seen, in him, competence and humility."[51] "So let us, my brothers, leave aside these vanities of [worldly] knowledge that puff up and seek to acquire Christian humility, if we wish to gain true knowledge, which is that of the saints."[52] Knowledge, he continues, is like a painting: you cannot paint a picture on nothing; you need a good solid canvas on which to paint it, and the good solid canvas is humility. As Bernard himself said, "the knowledge of the truth can be found only at the height of humility,"[53] and Bernard maintained this profound humility even when he was forced to leave his monastic wilderness, venture forth into the world, and become the master of princes, kings, and the greatest powers in the church. Such is the subject of Part Two of Planchette's panegyric.

Here we are on familiar ground. Planchette dwells on the difficulty of teaching the virtues of penance and humility—humility, that is, of both heart and will. This is especially the case with princes, who become ever more proud and ambitious as they become ever more successful. Only such eminent and respected figures such as the Ambroses, John Chrysostoms, and Gregory the Greats of this world are able to overthrow their pride and quell their ambition. Such a person was Bernard, who could humble kings, princes, and tyrants—a lamb subduing lions—and what is a better example of this than the story we have heard (and will hear so often) of the dramatic conversion of Duke William X of Aquitaine?[54] Planchette tells

---

[51] Planchette, 107.
[52] Planchette, 110.
[53] Planchette, 110, quoting Bernard, Hum 2.3; SBOp 3:18.
[54] Planchette, 115–17. See appendix 2, s.v. William (Guillaume) X, duke of Aquitaine.

the tale, and tells it well, and then (after apologizing for appearing to be more a historian than an orator[55]) goes on to give the further examples of the humbling of Lothair in the investiture controversy[56] and of Louis the Fat in the matter of his persecution of the French bishops.[57] And if teaching humility to the great of the world is difficult, teaching penance is no less so—and no less dangerous. Yet Bernard achieves it, and Planchette gives the examples of the penance of Louis the Young for the massacre at Vitry,[58] and the repentance of his father, Louis the Fat, and of Thibault, count of Champagne.[59]

But Bernard does not limit his strictures to secular princes: he is prepared to rebuke popes, cardinals, and bishops and point out to them, in no uncertain terms, where their duty lies. Planchette then does the same thing with the preachers of his own day, preachers who pander to popular taste by delivering entertaining and worldly sermons, full of over-refined and novel ideas. When the truth serves their purpose, they are happy to proclaim it. But if it does not serve their purpose, that is a different matter. What does Saint Augustine say? "'They love truth when it enlightens them.' But when your servants, O my God, proclaim to them those holy truths that condemn their disordered lives and the impiety of their hearts, they straight-

---

[55] Planchette, 117: "Si je n'apprehendois de paroître trop Historien dans une action d'Orateur . . . ."

[56] Planchette, 117. See appendix 2, s.v. Lothair III of Supplinburg. Planchette provides no details and has but a single sentence referring to Lothair's attempts at "extorting from the pope the investitures of bishops." Rancé and Fénelon also refer to the incident.

[57] Planchette, 117. Planchette is referring to Louis's opposition to the French bishops taking part in the Council of Pisa in 1135: see appendix 2, s.v. Louis VI the Fat.

[58] Planchette, 121, probably based on the account in the unpaginated preface "to the Reader" of Le Maistre's *Vie*. See appendix 2, s.v. Louis VII the Young.

[59] See Williams, *Saint Bernard*, 207–14.

away become their enemies, for 'they hate [the truth] when it rebukes them'!"[60] And so Planchette addresses his audience:

> But you, my brothers, among whom I see a considerable number of preachers, do not let yourselves be blinded by a vain desire for the plaudits of those of debased tastes. Take upon yourselves rather the responsibility of a preacher of the Gospel and fulfill, as Saint Paul says, all the duties of your ministry by preaching a holy doctrine and confirming it by a wholly apostolic life: "Do the work of an evangelist; fulfill your ministry." (2 Tim 4:5)[61]

And just how does one fulfill one's ministry and live an apostolic life? By cultivating humility and penitence, for the spirit of Saint Bernard—a spirit filled to the brim with the idea of penance and penitence[62]—cries out to all in the words of the gospel, "Unless you do penance, you shall all perish together!"[63]

In the third and final part of his panegyric, Planchette turns to Bernard as law-giver and arbiter—that is to say, one who is consulted by all on any matters of major consequence, and one whose pronouncements were seen to overthrow error, reveal lying doctrines for what they were, and proclaim the truth to all. He was a second Solomon, "filled like a river with wisdom,"[64] and the voice of the Holy Spirit at church councils. Planchette mentions the Council of Étampes and Bernard's recognition of Innocent II as the true pontiff. But he was also a law-giver for the monastic order, which by his time had fallen into laxity and indiscipline and was in dire need of reform. Here he becomes a second Ezra (Esdras), who re-establishes the

---

[60] Planchette, 125–26, quoting Augustine, Conf 10.23.34; PL 32:794.
[61] Planchette, 126–27. We may compare the later censures of François Ogier and Esprit Fléchier (see chap. 12).
[62] See appendix 1, s.v. *pénitence* / penitence.
[63] Planchette, 128, quoting Luke 13:3.
[64] Planchette, 129, quoting Sir 47:16.

law, and a second Maccabee—Judas Maccabeus—who repairs the ruins of the temple of God. The monastic order, says our author, was a heavenly school in which one studied the rules of the perfect life, the sound maxims of moral progress laid down by Jesus Christ,

> and the art—so divine and so necessary—of loving God above all things, of suffering transitory pain in order to gain eternal joy and delight, of doing great things and counting them as little, of despising riches and all the gods of the Egyptians to embrace a holy poverty that consists not in possessing nothing, but in possessing things with detachment and, as the apostle says, "as having nothing."[65]

Planchette then quotes the same passage from Bernard's thirteenth sermon on the Song of Songs, as does Biroat: "It is a great and rare virtue when you do great things but are unaware of their greatness, and when your holiness, while obvious to all others, is hidden from yourself."[66]

And so he concludes his panegyric with the usual exhortations. Let us learn from Bernard's example to humble ourselves before all, he says, to abase ourselves to the same degree as we are raised up, to scorn possessions, to uphold righteousness whatever the cost, and so on. As for ministers, they must remember what they are—the light of the world and the salt of the earth[67]—which means they must purify themselves, become truly holy, and (like Saint Paul) glorify Christ in their bodies by their mortifications and penitence.[68] And as for monks and nuns, because of their vocation the demands on them are higher than on ordinary men and women. The

---

[65] Planchette, 132–33, quoting 2 Cor 6:10.
[66] Planchette, 133, quoting Bernard, SC 13.3.3; SBOp 1:70. See chap. 4 (Biroat), n. 46.
[67] See Matt 5:13-14.
[68] See 1 Cor 6:20.

slightest disobedience is enough to stain them (Planchette is quoting Saint Bernard[69]), and to neglect the least observance of their rule is a grave defect. Indeed, there is no part of society, great or low, rich or poor, religious or lay, on which the rules and maxims of Christian morality do not bear, and such rules and maxims are laid out for us in the writings of Saint Bernard. They are like so many heavenly flaming torches that light our way among the shadows that surround us, and it is these teachings that we must follow if we wish to have the honor of being his disciples on earth and the joy of being his companions in heaven.

There are three points of interest in Planchette's panegyric. The first, as we have seen, is what he has to say on the desert as a stimulus for spiritual awakening and his extraordinary use of the tale of Isis suckling Osiris as an allegory of Bernard's being nourished by the Holy Spirit. It is one thing to see Bernard as a second John the Baptist; to see him as a second Osiris is somewhat more startling. The second is the wide range of Planchette's sources. He does not equal Claude Lion or Henri-Marie Boudon, that is true, but the variety of his sources is unusual. Persius represents the classical age (though the line quoted was well known), and then we have Philo, Tertullian, Eusebius of Caesarea, and Augustine. He gives about a dozen direct quotations from the *Vita prima*, a citation from Guerric of Igny, and allusions and/or quotations from seven works of Bernard himself: the sermons on the Song of Songs, the sermons on Psalm 90, the sermons *De diversis*, the letters, the *De consideratione*, the treatise on the errors of Abelard, and the *De gradibus humilitatis et superbiae*.

The third point of interest is that Planchette, like Senault, is unusual in making no mention of Bernard's battles against Gilbert de la Porrée and Henry of Toulouse, and Abelard appears not by name, but as "a Philosopher who preferred his

---

[69] Planchette, 135, quoting Bernard, Div S 17.1; SBOp 6/1:151, reading *minimorum* for Bernard's *minorum*.

own novelties to the teaching of the holy Fathers, and did his utmost to destroy [that teaching] by the empty subterfuges of his learning and the supposed sublimity of his reasoning."[70] On the other hand, Planchette tends not to dwell on historical details—he sees himself as an orator, not a historian[71]—and the only tale he tells at any length is (as we have seen) the story of the conversion of Duke William X of Aquitaine. He makes no mention whatever of Bernard's mysticism or mystical experiences, and there is no reference to any of his miracles.

From the point of view of the head rather than the heart, Planchette's panegyric has more to offer than Senault's, though in my own view he is not a little guilty of peppering his sermon with just those strange and rare ideas that he himself condemns.[72] The introduction of Chiron, Aesculapius, Hercules, Isis, and Osiris are obvious examples, and there is a display of erudition of which Senault would not have approved. When judged by the exacting standards of seventeenth-century French pulpit oratory his discourse is, as Louis-Mayeul Chaudon said, undoubtedly weak,[73] but in his exhortations at the end he does rather better than Senault. And some of his more bizarre analogies hit home, if not for quite the right reason.

We shall therefore move on from the Benedictine congregation of Saint-Maur to the Society of Jesus and introduce Claude Texier, who was far more renowned as a preacher than Planchette—he delivered the Lenten series before Louis XIV and his court in 1661—and whose preaching (says the abbé Hurel) was "simple, methodical, and even didactic."[74]

---

[70] Planchette, 108; Planchette proves his point by referring to Bernard's letter 190 to Innocent II on the errors of Abelard. See appendix 2, s.v. Abelard, Peter.
[71] See n. 55 above.
[72] Planchette, 125: "des idées de choses rares, & curieuses."
[73] See n. 33 above.
[74] Hurel, 1:156.

Claude Texier

Texier was born at La Rochelle on March 20, 1611, and admitted into the Society of Jesus as a novice in 1628. He taught rhetoric and the humanities for some five years before devoting himself to three decades of preaching. He was also rector of the Jesuit colleges in Limoges and Poitiers, superior of the *maisons professes* at Toulouse and Bordeaux, and finally provincial of Aquitaine. He left no fewer than ten octavo volumes of sermons (two of them are *Panégyriques des Saints*), published at Paris between 1673 and 1678, and he died at Bordeaux, aged seventy-seven, on April 24, 1687.[75] According to Albert and Court, Texier's usual method in his sermons was to follow the custom of the preachers of his time, "basing the first part of his discourse on the authority of Scripture, the second on the ideas of the Fathers, and the third on his own reasoning." What this meant was that he had but a single point that he proved in three different ways.[76] We shall see whether this is so.

Truth to tell, there is not a great deal in his panegyric[77] to attract our attention. He takes as his text Psalm 70:7, *Tanquam prodigium factus sum multis*, which he translates, more or less accurately, as "I have appeared as a prodigy in the eyes of many," and begins by distinguishing prodigies of nature from prodigies of grace. The former, such as tidal waves or a moon the color of blood, arouse in us aversion and horror. Prodigies of grace arouse in us admiration and love. Saint Bernard was a prodigy of grace, though he was also a prodigy in another way. How? "I am neither cleric nor monk; neither layman nor ecclesiastic; I am the chimera of my age. *Ego enim quaedam*

---

[75] See Albert / Court, 257–58; Augustin and Alois De Backer, *Bibliothèque des écrivains de la Compagnie de Jésus. Deuxième série* (Liège: L. Grandmont-Donders, 1854), 632; and DS 15:311–13.

[76] Albert / Court, 258. See also Hurel 1:156, n. 1.

[77] [Claude Texier], *Panégyriques des Saints, preschez Par le R. P. Texier de la Compagnie de Jésus. Tome second* (Paris: Estienne Michallet, 1678), 22–41 (cited below as Texier).

chimaera saeculi."⁷⁸ And how is he a prodigy of grace? In (inevitably) three ways: first, as an innocent penitent; second, as an untaught teacher; third, as an active contemplative. Throughout all these three themes there run, as we have seen them run before, the key principles of humility and penitence / penance. And so, as was customary, Texier begs for the help of the Virgin in inspiring his panegyric, not least because Bernard was her favorite, to whom she once accorded the grace "of wetting his lips with her own virginal milk."⁷⁹ Texier is confident, therefore, of her intercession, and he says with the angel *Ave Maria*.

Yet there is very little in this sermon that we have not seen before and will not see again. We find some details of the purity of Bernard's early life taken from the *Vita prima*, including the episode of the icy pool. We find the usual descriptions of his innocence and asceticism, and Innocent II's wonderment at it when he and his entourage visited Clairvaux in 1131.⁸⁰ In which case, what possible reason could there be for such a man to be a penitent? There are, in fact, three reasons. The first is that, with Bernard, the least and most trifling fault was monstrous in his own eyes. Then second was that he wished to imitate his Lord and Savior, Jesus Christ, the Great Penitent, crucified and dying, and say with Saint Paul, "I am nailed to the Cross with Christ" (Gal 2:19). And the third was that through the example of his own penitence he wished to rouse others, including us, to penitence, and, "in imitation of his Savior, to expiate the faults of sinners with his own tears and

---

[78] Texier, 24, quoting Bernard, Ep 250.4 to Bernard, Carthusian prior of Portes; SBOp 8:147: *Ego enim quaedam chimaera mei saeculi, nec clericum gero nec laicum,* "I am a sort of modern chimera: what you see is neither cleric nor layman!" Not surprisingly, this vivid description is quoted by a number of the other panegyrists.

[79] Texier, 24–25. The reference, of course, is to the miracle of the Lactation, which we have already witnessed in Planchette: see n. 37 above.

[80] Texier, 28. See *Vita prima* 2.1.6 (Arnold of Bonneval); PL 185:272AB; CF 76:84–85, and Williams, *Saint Bernard*, 110–11.

his own blood."[81] This, too, we have seen before (and will see again), though that in no way disparages the sentiment.

In his second point Texier turns to the untaught teacher, whose masters were the woods and trees.[82] Bernard was not like Augustine, trained in the Academies of Carthage; not like Jerome, educated in Rome; not like Ambrose, so familiar with the imperial Court; not like Basil the Great or Gregory of Nazianzus or Gregory of Nyssa or John Chrysostom, educated in Athens. No indeed. And Texier echoes his contemporary Planchette by saying what "Philo the Jew" said of Moses, that God spoke to him in the desert and that the burning bush was the pulpit of his school.[83] What sort of teaching was that of Bernard? It was (1) holy and pure, it was (2) vast and all-embracing, and it was (3) sublime, "but more sublime, if I am not wrong, for its spiritual teaching [*la mystique*] than that of the other Doctors of the Church."[84] Here, at last, we have one of those rare references to Bernard's mysticism, but (unlike Boudon's lengthy discussion) it is no more than a mention in passing, a single sentence: "This saint had been introduced into the bedchamber of the Bridegroom, and we see how he pours out in his writings the perfume of this delightful and delectable devotion."[85] And that is all. Texier now leads us back to the broad and safe highway of Bernard's exoteric learning: "Just as he was the last of all the Fathers,[86] so he gathered together in himself the fullness of their

---

[81] Texier, 29. For Christ as the Great Penitent, see chap. 1.

[82] See n. 43 above.

[83] Texier, 31.

[84] Texier, 31. In the seventeenth century, *la mystique* (as a feminine noun) could mean a female mystic, which is obviously not the case here, or (as, for example, in Bossuet) spiritual teaching or the study of spirituality.

[85] Texier, 31, referring to the bridal chamber of the Song of Songs.

[86] On the title *ultimus Patrum* or *ultimus inter Patres*, see the essential discussion by Mabillon in the *Praefatio generalis* to his edition of Bernard's works: Praef Gen 2.23–29; PL 182:26–29 (English translation in *Life and Works of Saint Bernard, Abbot of Clairvaux*, trans./ed. Samuel J. Eales,

spirit. We see in his writings the subtlety of Saint Augustine, the sweetness of Saint Ambrose, the solidity of Saint Gregory [the Great], and the profundity of Saint Jerome."[87]

And how did this untaught teacher demonstrate his prodigious learning? In ways we know very well: in the defeat of Peter Abelard (Texier mentions the Council of Sens), Henry of Toulouse, and Gilbert de la Porrée, though Texier also introduces that "wicked hypocrite" Arnold of Brescia, which is not so common.[88] But he tells us nothing of Arnold's ideas, and he confines himself to quoting Bernard's vituperations in his letter to the bishop of Constance: "he is a man who comes neither eating nor drinking,[89] but hungering and thirsting with the Devil alone for the blood of souls. He is an enemy of Christ, a sower of discord, a manufacturer of schisms, a disturber of the peace, a divider of unity!"[90] Less common, too, is Texier's mention of Bernard's miracles. That is to say, not only *is* he a prodigy or marvel, he *does* prodigies or marvels. Texier introduces two of them, both eucharistic. The first is the healing of a demoniac woman by the expulsion of the demon;[91] the second is the now familiar story of the conversion of Duke William X of Aquitaine.[92]

2nd ed. [London: Burns & Oates Ltd., 1889], 1:20–29). See also the entire panegyric on Bernard as the Last of the Fathers by Antoine Anselme (chap. 13 below).

[87] Texier, 31–32, following the unpaginated preface to Le Maistre's *Vie*.

[88] Texier, 32. Arnold also appears in the panegyrics of Ogier, Fléchier, and Claude-Bénigne Bourru. See appendix 2, s.v. Arnold of Brescia.

[89] Like John the Baptist: see Matt 11:18; Luke 7:33.

[90] Texier, 32, quoting (with abbreviations) Bernard's Ep 195.1–2; SBOp 8:49–50, to the bishop of Constance.

[91] Texier, 35, following *Vita prima* 2.3.14 (Arnold of Bonneval); PL 185:276C–77A; CF 76:93–94.

[92] Texier, 35. See appendix 2, s.v. William (Guillaume) X, duke of Aquitaine.

Moving Forward   133

We then have the healing of the papal schism with a fairly extensive cast of characters,[93] and Bernard's intervention in the affairs of the two Louis, father and son, before the preacher applies all that he has said to his audience. This is the old traditional approach that we saw in Biroat and Senault: a long account of Bernard's life and deeds, followed by a short application to either the preacher's specific audience or to the men and women of his day in general. Massillon does far better. So, says Texier, after glorying in the words and deeds of Bernard, I now turn to the Christians of my own time with a sense of shame and embarrassment: "In truth, they are made up of totally opposing parts: of faith and of paganism! They are semi-Christians and semi-Pagans, Christian chimeras,[94] in that their faith is not sufficiently dynamic to eradicate sin, and sin is not sufficiently strong to destroy and annihilate faith!"[95] But this is not true of Texier's audience, and what he says now makes it clear that he is addressing some congregation of Cistercian nuns or Feuillantines:

> But you, my Ladies, I know that you share in the glorious qualities of your holy Patriarch, and the saint speaks well of you today. For what he says of all his true children who dwell in the sanctity of his cloisters is what Isaiah says: "Behold me and my children, a wonder in Israel from the Lord of Hosts."[96] With Saint Bernard, you unite penitence with innocence, professing no other knowledge than Jesus Christ crucified,

---

[93] On page 36 he mentions the antipope Peter Leon, Roger of Sicily, Lothair III of Supplinburg, Henry I of England, Peter of Pisa, and Duke William X of Aquitaine. All are listed in appendix 2.

[94] *Chréstiens chimériques*, echoing, in a pejorative way, Bernard's description of himself at n. 78 above.

[95] Texier, 38. In other discourses he also lashes out (as does Planchette) at those men and women who come to church to listen to sermons for the wrong reasons: see Hurel, 1:155–56.

[96] Isa 8:18, abbreviated.

having no other school than your oratory, and no other Master than your Bridegroom. Thus do you see that you are learned and enlightened in the knowledge of the saints. Continue, then, in this happy state and remember the teaching of your Father, namely, that not to move forward on the path to God is to go backwards: *non progredi, regredi est* ["Not to go forward is to go backward"[97]]. Pursue your course and redouble your efforts, so that one day you may come whither Saint Bernard has already come, the dwelling-place of everlasting glory.[98]

Such, in summary, is Texier's rather old-fashioned panegyric on Saint Bernard. There are some fine lines in it, to be sure, but as Charles-Yves Cousin d'Avallon has said, "All [Texier's] sermons may be consulted with profit, but they cannot be put forward as models."[99] I must agree. Texier's divisions and subdivisions remind one of Biroat, and his discourse is rather dry, lacking that *onction* so esteemed by his contemporaries. If I may paraphrase Doctor Johnson, his panegyric on Saint Bernard is a good enough sermon, to be sure, but not a sermon to ask a man to.[100] Texier's sources, however, are interesting in that they are as much Greek as Latin: Tertullian, Jerome, Cassiodorus (an uncommon source) on the one hand, and Philo, "the ancient solitaries of the Thebaid,"[101] Gregory of Nyssa,[102] and John

---

[97] Bernard, *In purificatione S. Mariae S* 2.3; SBOp 4:340.

[98] Texier, 40–41, abbreviated.

[99] [Charles-Yves Cousin d'Avallon], *Dictionnaire biographique et bibliographique des prédicateurs et sermonnaires français, par l'abbé de La P****** (Paris: Persan & Lyon: Périsses Frères, 1824), 243.

[100] The great doctor was referring, of course, not to a sermon, but to a dinner: see *Boswell's Life of Johnson, Volume I—Life (1709–1765)*, ed. George B. Hill (New York: Harper & Brothers, 1889), 543–44.

[101] Texier, 26.

[102] Texier, 29 and 39. Gregory of Nyssa was available in Latin translation from 1562.

Chrysostom (all in Latin translation) on the other. His source for Bernard's life is, as with all the panegyrists, the *Vita prima*, almost certainly in the edition of Horstius, together with Le Maistre's *Vie*. He quotes little from Bernard's own works (primarily his letters), and, unlike most of the other panegyrists, makes no mention of his five books *On Consideration* addressed to Eugenius III.[103] According to the abbé Hurel, however, his sermons are sometimes a little overloaded—*quelque peu surchargé*—with quotations from Scripture and the Fathers in both Latin and French.[104] But he does at least mention Bernard's mysticism and two of his miracles, though he clearly has no intention of lingering on such dangerous ground.

We shall end this chapter as we began with an Oratorian, but an Oratorian of the next generation. Senault was born in 1599 and died in 1680; Jean-Louis de Fromentières, bishop of Aire, was born in 1632 and died, only in his fifties, in 1684. It is to his panegyric on Saint Bernard that we now turn.

Jean-Louis de Fromentières

Born in 1632 in Saint-Denis-de-Gastines, a small town in the northwest of France, Jean-Louis de Fromentières began his studies at Le Mans, which lies about seventy kilometers to the southeast. He then went to Paris where, in 1648, he entered the Oratorian seminary of Saint-Magloire, and there, under the direction of Jean-François Senault, he perfected his natural aptitude for preaching. As a preacher he enjoyed a great reputation, and, as *prédicateur du roi*, preached the Advent series before the royal court in 1672 and the Lenten series in 1680. The following year he was appointed bishop of Aire in Aquitaine (now the diocese of Aire and Dax) and administered his see for just over a decade before his death in December

---

[103] He does, however, quote from the *De consideratione* in his panegyric on Saint Michael the Archangel: see Texier, 498–99.

[104] Hurel, 1:156.

1684. During his episcopate he was responsible for bringing many Calvinists into the Catholic fold, and he also succeeded (against strong opposition) in abolishing bullfighting. His sermons, in six duodecimo volumes, were published the year of his death, and again, in four octavos, at Paris in 1689 and 1690. The abbé Hurel praised him for his even, well-proportioned, and elegant delivery—it was never monotonous on the one hand or pretentious on the other—and says, in a sentence that defies easy translation, that in all his discourses there appears a certain balance, "and, if you will, a certain ordinariness, but of gold."[105] We may see this "golden ordinariness" in his panegyric on Bernard. He never shows off, his language is never pretentious, he never seeks empty grandiloquence, but what he says he says beautifully, which is only what we would expect from a *prédicateur du roi* preaching to an audience whose most important member was a member of the royal family. Fromentières addresses her as "Your Majesty" and, perhaps with some hyperbole (characteristic both of himself and his era[106]), praises her as "a princess who edifies the court by her example, who corrects its vices by her zeal, pride by her humility, vanity by her modesty, ungodliness by her piety, callousness by her charity, soft living by her mortifications, and cupidity and an immoderate love of the world by her attachment to God."[107]

Who is this paragon of virtue? Undoubtedly Anne of Austria, wife of Louis XIII and, after the king's death and during the minority of her son, Louis XIV, regent of France. She was a devout Catholic and a fervent supporter of the Counter Reformation, and, in 1621, founded the exquisite church of Val-de-Grâce, which lies not too far south of the great cathedral of Notre-Dame

---

[105] Hurel, 1:132: "Bref, en tout paraît un certain niveau et, si l'on veut, une certaine médiocrité, mais d'or."

[106] See Hurel 1:141.

[107] [Jean-Louis de Fromentières], *Sermons de Messire Jean Loüis de Fromentières, evêque d'Aire, Prédicateur ordinaire de sa Majesté. Tome second* (Paris: J. Couterot & L. Guerin, 1689), 414.

in Paris. Construction eventually began in 1634 (two years after the birth of Fromentières), but the church—an architectural gem—took more than three decades to complete. It is perfectly possible, even probable, that it was here that Fromentières delivered his panegyric, but we cannot be certain of that. There is no clue in the sermon to either place or date. What is clear is that he was preaching to a mixed congregation, and it is equally clear, as we shall see in due course, that the women in his audience included members of some religious order or orders, "brides of Christ."[108] After Anne's death from breast cancer on January 20, 1666, Fromentières preached her funeral oration.

For his panegyric on Bernard,[109] Fromentières takes as his text the description of Jesus given to the risen Jesus himself on the road to Emmaus by Cleopas and the other unnamed disciple, "a man powerful in deed and word before God and all the people."[110] In Fromentière's translation, *deed* and *word* become *deeds* and *words*.[111] And lest anyone in his audience should think it impertinent to apply to Saint Bernard a description of Jesus himself, Fromentières defends himself by appealing to Cardinal Baronius (whom we shall meet again), who cites precisely the same verse from the same gospel in the same circumstances.[112] Fromentières will illustrate these deeds and words in the three divisions of his sermon, and while their style is superb, their content is unexceptional. First, he will

---

[108] Fromentières, 399.

[109] Fromentières, 390–416, reproduced (with the usual typographical errors) in *Collection intégrale et universelle des Orateurs sacrés du premier et du second ordre, Tome huitième,* ed. Jacques-Paul Migne (Paris: J.-P. Migne, 1866), cols. 982–95. All references here are to the 1689 edition.

[110] Luke 24:19, with *vir* for the biblical *vir propheta*.

[111] Fromentières, 390.

[112] See *Caesaris S. R. E. Cardinalis Baronii Annales Ecclesiastici* (Paris and Fribourg: Consociatio S. Pauli, 1880), vol. 19 (1147–1198), 69, §14. Boudon quotes the same passage from Baronius: see chap. 11 (Boudon), §30.

show us Bernard as the example for the cloister, then he will put before us Bernard as the oracle of the church, and finally we shall see Bernard as the censor of the court. And to aid him in his discourse, Fromentières, as was customary, prays for the light of the Holy Spirit through the intercession of the Holy Virgin: *Ave Maria*.

The first part of his discourse reveals a familiar landscape. Bernard dies to the world and, in accordance with the provisions of the gospel (and Gregory the Great[113]), leaves his parents and his family and withdraws into the desert. But not only does he himself leave the world and all its corruption, but he also persuades his friends and family—even his own father—to leave the world. All of them end up within the enclosure of Cîteaux. But more than that, the fire of his zeal persuades yet others to leave the world in order to conquer their passions and mortify their senses. They came from all states and conditions of life—princes, prelates, and ordinary people—and found in Bernard the ideal model for their imitation. Fromentières tells of his fasts and how he so put to death his sense of taste that he could not distinguish between the foods he ate and whatever it was that he drank. The table, which is generally a pleasure for others, was, for him, a torment.[114] He was a model, too, in his solitude, for unlike others, who are now alone, now in a crowd, Bernard's own solitude was always with him in his heart, and Fromentières quotes just the same passage from William of Saint-Thierry as does Jean-François Senault, Fromentières's director at Saint-Magloire: "he provided for himself his own solitude of heart, and carrying this solitude with him, he was everywhere alone."[115] So powerful

---

[113] Fromentières, 394–95, quoting Gregory, *Moralia in Job*, 7.30.41; PL 75:790C: "If anyone wishes to be more truly united to the Parent of All, he must be beyond any thought of friends or relatives."

[114] Fromentières is echoing *Vita prima* 1.4.22 (William of Saint-Thierry); PL 185:239D; CF 76:25. Senault says precisely the same thing.

[115] Fromentières, 398: see n. 13 above.

was the work of the Holy Spirit operating through him that by the end of his life Clairvaux (according to Geoffrey of Auxerre) had a population of seven hundred, and no fewer than a hundred and sixty monasteries recognized Bernard as their master.[116] But that, essentially, is all that Fromentières has to say in the first part of his panegyric, and we have heard it all before. He says it, obviously, in very many more words, but that is its essence, and he now moves on to his second point. Bernard must now leave his beloved cloister to come out into the world and instruct the very highest in the church: "Indeed, Gentlemen, after having been the model for all religious, Saint Bernard now becomes the master of prelates! After having quickened the former by his actions, he strengthened the latter by his teaching. In a word, after having been the example of the cloister, he now becomes the oracle of the Church. This is the subject of my second point."[117]

But his second point, like the first, offers nothing new. Bernard, not himself a bishop, is yet the master of bishops (he is as Moses to Aaron, says Fromentières, inferior in dignity, yet superior in power), and it is he who keeps the Christian world in order through his letters. He establishes canons at church councils, puts an end to schisms through his teaching and his prudence, and confirms his words through his miracles. Think of the Council of Sens, when he put to confusion "a philosopher who was the enemy of our mysteries";[118] think of the Council of Reims, when he was victorious over a prelate who had wrong ideas about the simplicity of God; think of him at Toulouse, casting down an apostate who was intent on destroying the Catholic faith; think of him rebuking a dean of the chapter whose conduct was too worldly; think of him

---

[116] Fromentières, 398–99, following *Vita prima* 5.3.15 (Geoffrey of Auxerre); PL 185:360C; CF 76:248. Biroat, Bourru, and Claude Lion provide much the same information.

[117] Fromentières, 401.

[118] Fromentières, 403.

exhorting a bishop of Geneva to be worthy of the nature of his office; think of him reminding sovereign pontiffs of their duties and responsibilities; and finally, think of him at Sarlat, when he confirmed his words with the miracle of the blessed bread. But nowhere here does Fromentières mention even a single name—not Abelard, Gilbert de la Porrée, Henry of Toulouse, or anybody else—and obviously assumes that his audience will know whom he's talking about. Indeed, from what Fromentières has told us, Bernard appears more powerful in the church than the very vicars of Jesus Christ, though far inferior to them in rank.

Our preacher then goes on to deal at some length—almost two pages—with the origin, course, and resolution of the papal schism, and he concludes by quoting, in Latin, Arnold of Bonneval's account in the *Vita prima*. At the Council of Étampes (Fromentières simply refers to it as "the Council"), Bernard is the voice of the Holy Spirit, and his words had such power that the whole church acknowledged the truth that came from his mouth and unanimously recognized Innocent II as the legitimate pontiff.[119] Is this not a man *potens sermone*, "powerful in word"?

Fromentières now turns to his audience and applies what he has said to them, but his exhortation is fairly predictable. He obviously does not expect them to do the extraordinary things that Bernard did. He does not expect them to have authority over bishops and popes, to direct church councils, and put an end to heresies. So how can they make themselves useful to the church? The answer is, or should be, clear. Bishops should take care to guide the souls entrusted to them appropriately; preachers should preach the word of God faithfully; and "you, every one of you who is listening to me, can [aid the church] by the blind submission you owe to the Gospel."[120] Fromentières then elaborates on these points and bewails the fact that

---

[119] Fromentières, 405, quoting *Vita prima* 2.1.3 (Arnold of Bonneval); PL 185:270D; CF 76:81–82.

[120] Fromentières, 406.

now—in his day and age—there is so much pride, ambition, and disobedience. He then turns to the female religious in his audience and addresses them thus:

> Ah, Ladies! Do you understand how the regular life you should observe in your cloisters is often so important for the Church? Christianity today is threatened by the oppression of its enemies, but its weapons are weak, and what help we are given lacks any real power. Without a miracle, the Church is on the verge of losing its strongest defenses, and to what shall we attribute this dreadful chastisement of Divine Justice? There is not one sinner in the whole Church whose disordered life may not be said to have brought down God's scourge on Mother Church: ecclesiastics by their lukewarmness, worldly people by their debauched lives, but you too, perhaps, by the laxity with which you observe your rule and your constitutions.[121]

And if you are surprised to hear this, he continues, then I call on the great Cardinal Baronius to prove my point! England defended itself from schism and heresy while its monks and nuns maintained their ancient monastic discipline. And why did that great kingdom become lost and heretical? Because of the laxity of its monks and nuns, and their abandonment of their Rule![122] What an awesome responsibility, therefore, is placed on the shoulders of the nuns in his audience: to know that the destiny of the church depends to some extent on how they fulfill their vows! Or, conversely, to understand that what they do may perhaps maintain a kingdom in the true faith!

---

[121] Fromentières, 407.
[122] See *Caesaris S. R. E. Cardinalis Baronii Annales Ecclesiastici* (Paris and Fribourg: Consociatio S. Pauli, 1867), vol. 12 (680761), 189, but Baronius is quoting the Venerable Bede. Fromentières provides the Latin text in the margins of pages 407–8; Migne incorporates it into the text (col. 991).

But Fromentières must be fair. I know, he says, that you are not the only ones to blame for all the problems the church is facing. The sins of princes and those in power also play their part, just as they did in the days of Saint Bernard; and just as Bernard had no hesitation in correcting monks, nuns, and prelates, so too he had no hesitation in rebuking those who wielded civil power. If he was the example of the cloister and the oracle of the church, he was also the terror of the Court, and that will be Fromentières's third and final point.

It is hard enough, says our preacher, to reprove common or garden, run-of-the-mill sinners for their sins. "Who shall reprove his way to his face?" asks the prophet Job (Job 21:31). But if it is difficult to reprove ordinary people, it is almost impossible to reprove kings! If few people have the courage, it seems that no one has the authority. Indeed, Scripture itself implies that only God may accuse a king of being an apostate, and only God may condemn rulers for being ungodly.[123] But the same Scripture also tells us that God may sometimes delegate this power to human beings, as he did to Moses when Moses rebuked Pharaoh: "and it seems, Gentlemen, that God did with Bernard what he did with Moses."[124] So who, then, were the kings and rulers that Bernard rebuked? Fromentières names five. The first is Henry I of England, whom Bernard met at Chartres, and the second is the Holy Roman emperor Lothair III of Supplinburg. In both cases, we are dealing with the resolution of the papal schism. The third and fourth are Louis VI the Fat and Louis VII the Young: the former is reproved for his conduct with regard to the French bishops,[125] the latter for the ghastly massacre in the church at Vitry.[126] Fromentières,

---

[123] See Job 34:18.

[124] Fromentières, 410.

[125] See appendix 2, s.v. Louis VI the Fat, and Bernard, Ep 255; SBOp 8:161–62.

[126] See appendix 2, s.v. Louis VII the Young.

like Massillon,[127] likens Bernard to Saint Ambrose and Louis VII to Theodosius. The fifth is our favorite duke, William X of Aquitaine (Fromentières calls him the *duc de Guienne*), whose dramatic conversion we have witnessed before and will certainly witness again. Who, after all, could resist telling such a good story?

Fromentières now concludes his discourse. He first praises the manifold virtues of Anne of Austria and reminds her how delighted Saint Bernard was to see such virtues in other noble women: "the queens of England and Jerusalem, the sisters of kings of Spain, the duchesses of Lorraine and Brabant."[128] "What joy did he not have when he saw them maintaining the interests of God against unbelievers,[129] [the interests] of the Church against her enemies, and [the interests] of the poor and the oppressed against the rich?"[130]

And would he not have the same joy today if he could see all these virtues, shared then among so many noble women, reunited in the one person of the princess whom Fromentières is addressing?

Yet there is still much disorder in the Court and in the world (Fromentières does not provide prurient detail, though he could be outspoken on this matter[131]), and whose duty is it to fight against this? His answer is the same answer as he gave earlier in his sermon:

---

[127] See chap. 14 (Massillon), §35. Both are dependent on Le Maistre's *Vie*.

[128] In the margins of pages 414–15, Fromentières cites Bernard's letters 116 to Sophia, 120 to Countess Ermengarde of Brittany, 125 to the duchess of Burgundy, and 390 to Sancia, sister of the king of Spain.

[129] *Les libertins*: in Fromentières's time, a *libertine* generally meant a freethinker whose ideas were contrary to those of the church, but it could also mean someone who was dissipated, dissolute, and immoral—or, indeed, all of these in varying proportions.

[130] Fromentières, 414.

[131] See Hurel, 1:133–40.

> Yes, Ladies, if you are zealous for the glory of Jesus Christ, you should compensate for their idleness with your watchfulness, for their gluttony with your fasts, for their dissipation with your withdrawal, for all their pleasures with your mortifications. In this way you may even be doing them a great service, by instilling in them, through your holy life, that terror that your sex and your profession do not allow you to instill in them by your words.[132]

And so Fromentières comes to his final prayer, beseeching Saint Bernard to turn away from us the storm of divine retribution that threatens us, to continue his powerful protection of France, and to obtain for sinners the spirit of penitence and compunction that they so desperately need:

> May our hope, great saint, not be disappointed; through your intercession, sanctify in France all those conditions that once you sanctified by your deeds and your words. Maintain in the cloister that charity[133] that has been renewed there by your example; preserve discipline in the Church of which you were the oracle; and look with as much favor on the court as once you were its terror. By these means we may profit from your example and, one day, follow you into your glory. Amen.[134]

There is no doubt as to the beauty and balance of this sermon, but apart from his appeal to Cardinal Baronius on the vital importance of keeping one's religious vows, Fromentières tells us nothing we do not know. He makes no display of his learning. His only sources, apart from Scripture and a single

---

[132] Fromentières, 415.
[133] See appendix 1, s.v. *charité* / charity.
[134] Fromentières, 415–16.

reference to Philo,[135] are Augustine, Gregory the Great, and the *Annales Ecclesiastici* of Baronius. His source for Bernard's life is, naturally, the *Vita prima*. He records but a single miracle, and of Bernard the spiritual teacher, Bernard the mystic, there is no trace whatever. He cites little more than his letters. But for the golden elegance of its language and as a fine example of Fromentières's chaste style (though there were some in his day who found it too chaste), the panegyric is a pleasure to read.

Who, then, is Bernard of Clairvaux at the end of this chapter? He is a man who, like Saint Paul, no longer lives, for Christ lives in him. He has put to death his senses and his passions—crucified them with his crucified Savior—and has left the corruption of the world for the fecund solitude of the cloister. Planchette's paean in praise of solitude deserves particular mention. Bernard's masters were the woods and trees, and his learning came not from any human teacher but from God himself. Throughout all four panegyrics we see the essential themes of Bernard's humility (all the more remarkable given the high esteem in which he was held) and the need for penance and penitence (all the panegyrists tell of the saint's extraordinary mortifications). And then all four preachers bring Bernard out of his beloved solitude to deal with the problem of the papal schism and the threats posed by the heretical views of Abelard, Gilbert de la Porrée, Henry of Toulouse, and (in Texier) Arnold of Brescia. Given that all four panegyrists are dependent on the *Vita prima* or Le Maistre's *Vie de Saint Bernard* for their information, it is inevitable that the same characters tend to appear again and again. All four follow the somewhat old-fashioned path of telling the story of Bernard and then, at the end, applying it to their audience in the required exhortation.

---

[135] On page 398, Fromentières compares Bernard with Abraham, in whose deeds, according to Philo's *De Abrahamo*, God's commandments could be read long before they were set out in stone by Moses. Bernard, similarly, edified the religious by his actions before he instructed them by his words.

The Bernard they present, however, is an ascetic, a preacher like themselves, a fearless censor of Court and church, the staunch supporter of Pope Innocent II, the courageous conqueror of heretics, the model of penance and penitence, the very image of the Great Penitent, Jesus Christ himself. He is not Bernard the worker of miracles, though miracles are mentioned, and he is certainly not Bernard the mystic. Senault, Texier, and Fromentières all mention the miracle of the blessed bread at Sarlat (though Senault gets the location wrong), and Texier adds a second eucharistic miracle, but that is all. Both Planchette and Texier refer to the story of the miraculous Lactation, when Mary nourishes Bernard with milk from her own breast, and Planchette adds a reference to the *Amplexus Bernardi*. The Bernard of the fourth stage of love in the *De diligendo Deo* is entirely absent, and Bernard as "the saint who had been introduced into the bedchamber of the Bridegroom" appears only in a single sentence in the panegyric of Claude Texier.

All the panegyrists we have met so far heap on Bernard lavish praise, but none of them was a Cistercian. They were Jesuits, Oratorians, or Maurists. It is time now, then, to turn our attention to a Cistercian, and not to just any Cistercian, but to *the* Cistercian of the seventeenth century, Armand-Jean de Rancé, the abbot of La Trappe and founder of the Strict Observance, who was an exact contemporary of the four figures we have discussed in this present chapter. On Bernard's feast day in an unknown year Rancé, as abbot of La Trappe, delivered to his religious "a conference or instruction" on Saint Bernard, who, he says, had more authority for his abstinent monks than did a thousand others.[136] And given the importance of Bernard for Rancé and Rancé for the Cistercian tradition, it seems only proper to present, for the first time, a complete English translation of his discourse.[137]

---

[136] See Bell, *Understanding Rancé*, 133.

[137] I have already presented a summary of the conference in *Understanding Rancé*, 134–36.

6

The Bernard of the Strict Observance

Armand-Jean de Rancé

INTRODUCTION

Of the life of Armand-Jean Le Bouthillier de Rancé we need say little.¹ He was born in Paris on January 9, 1626, and died at La Trappe on October 27, 1700, at the age of seventy-four. As a young man he had studied at the University of Paris, had enjoyed the life of an intelligent, witty, and good-looking man about town, and had frequented the fashionable *salons,* where he made the acquaintance of Marie d'Avaugour de Bretagne, Duchesse de Montbazon, a beautiful, statuesque, and wholly immoral woman at least fourteen years older than he, who became his mistress. He was, it seems, deeply in love with her, and when she died unexpectedly from either measles or scarlet fever in April 1657, he was utterly devastated. Exactly what happened immediately after her death—whether Rancé accidentally stumbled upon her autopsied body, as has been reported²—is not something we need consider here. Suffice it to say that the

---

¹ The standard biography is Alban J. Krailsheimer, *Armand-Jean de Rancé, Abbot of La Trappe. His Influence in the Cloister and the World* (Oxford: Clarendon Press, 1974). For a brief summary of Rancé's life, see Bell, *Understanding Rancé,* xv–xxiii. After Rancé entered La Trappe, he ceased to use the family name Le Bouthillier.

² For a full discussion, see David N. Bell, "Daniel de Larroque, Armand-Jean de Rancé, and the Head of Madame de Montbazon," in *Cîteaux—Commentarii cistercienses* 53 (2002): 305–31.

duchess's death was the final straw that led Rancé to forsake the world he knew so well and to withdraw to the silent solitude of the dilapidated abbey of La Trappe in what were then the wilds of Normandy, a house of which he had been commendatory abbot from his youth. He took the monastic habit at Perseigne on June 13, 1663, endured a shattering year's novitiate, and entered La Trappe as its regular abbot on July 14, 1664. It would be his home for the next thirty-six years and the real driving force behind the rise of the Cistercian Strict Observance.

Unlike so many of the other panegyrists, therefore, Rancé was not a *prédicateur du roi* and was not a celebrated preacher in the pulpits of Paris. He might well have been, had he not left the world for the somber silence of La Trappe, for the young Rancé had been interested in preaching from an early age. In 1643, when he was only sixteen, he wrote to his old tutor, Jean Favier, that not only were his theological studies proceeding apace but that he would like to begin preaching as soon as possible.[3] His public preaching began, in fact, three or four years later, in 1646 or 1647, when he preached at the convent of the Annonciades on the rue de la Couture Sainte-Catherine in Paris. Other sermons followed,[4] including an Easter sermon to the male Discalced Carmelites in their house on the rue de Vaugirard. A great crowd had gathered to hear the twenty-year-old preacher,[5] and if we may believe Dom Pierre Le Nain,

---

[3] *Abbé de Rancé. Correspondance*, ed. Alban J. Krailsheimer (Paris: Les Éditions du Cerf / *Cîteaux—Commentarii Cistercienses*, 1993), 1:65–66 (Letter 431100). "Le plus tôt que je pourrai," he says, "je me mettrai dans la prédication" (66).

[4] See Louis Dubois, *Histoire de l'abbé de Rancé et de sa réforme, composée avec ses écrits, ses lettres, ses règlements et un grand nombre de documents contemporains inédits ou peu connus*, 2nd ed. (Paris: Ambroise Bray, 1869), 1:50–51.

[5] See Armand-François Gervaise, *Jugement critique, mais équitable des vies de feu M. l'abbé de Rancé, réformateur de l'abbaye de la Trappe. Écrites par les Sieurs Marsollier et Maupeou. Divisé en deux parties où l'on voit toutes les fautes qu'ils ont commises contre la vérité de l'Histoire,*

who is not an impartial witness, his sermon was received with universal admiration.[6] According to Dom Gervaise, Rancé's successor as abbot of La Trappe,

> There are few sermons of this type to equal it, whether in his manner of dealing with the mystery, or the soundness of his discourse, or the force of his arguments, or the singular design of his sermon. Moral exhortations are brief and infrequent, but this only goes to show the judgment and prudence of the young preacher. An extended discourse on morality, stern and specific, is fitting only for men of a certain age and certain character, which he did not yet have. In general, he possessed an elevated eloquence that persuaded people, that touched [their hearts], that captured them. His delivery was moving and fervent. In a word, he had all the talents and qualities that go to make a perfect orator. These he preserved to the end of his days, even under the habit of penitence. I have never heard anyone more capable of persuading people to do what he wanted. He had something of the torrent [of words] that, more recently, has been admired in Father Bourdaloue, but his impact was greater than his, and he did not speak so quickly.[7]

The young preacher, we might add, was not unaware of his own abilities. On one occasion, when he met François de Harlay de Champvallon in Paris—a friend who, one day, would be archbishop of the city—Harlay de Champvallon asked Rancé what he was doing that day. "This morning," he replied, "I'll

---

contre le bon sens, contre la vray-semblence, contre l'honneur même de M. de Rancé, et de la Maison de la Trappe ("Londres" [= Troyes or Reims]: Aux dépens de la Compagnie, 1742), 55, and Dubois, *Histoire*, 1:50.

[6] Pierre Le Nain, *La Vie du Révérend Père Dom Armand-Jean Le Boutillier de Rancé, abbé et réformateur de la Maison-Dieu Nôtre-Dame de la Trappe* ([Rouen]: [s.n.], 1715), 1:11.

[7] Gervaise, *Jugement critique*, 55–56.

preach like an angel; this afternoon I'll hunt like a devil."[8] Angels and devils notwithstanding, if he was as skilled in the pulpit as he was in the saddle (he was a superb horseman and adored hunting[9]), his oratorical displays must have been spectacular. But were they effective? Did they touch the heart? Did they have that *onction* that could pierce the armor of a sinful soul? Contrary to what we have just read, Dom Gervaise did not think so.

"I do not believe," he wrote, "that in these early days his preaching produced many conversions in the world. Words that are not underpinned by example make little impression, and the Abbé de Rancé thought more about enjoying himself than becoming a saint."[10] In a lachrymose and sentimental age, they might have moved many to momentary tears, but it is unlikely that there was any lasting spiritual impact. Yet they would certainly have profited his career, for as we have seen, good preaching was recognized as a sure way to ecclesiastical preferment. Fénelon put it accurately: "Young men of no reputation are eager to preach," he said, but "they seek their own glory more than the glory of God, and are more concerned with their own advancement than the salvation of souls."[11]

This was certainly not the case with Rancé as abbot of La Trappe. He obviously brought his preaching skills with him—how could he not?—and according to André Félibien des Avaux, writing to the duchess de Liancourt,

---

[8] Gervaise, *Jugement critique*, 56–57: "Ce matin, prêcher comme un ange; ce soir, chasser comme un diable."

[9] "La chasse," Gervaise tells us, "faisoit encore sa passion dominante" (56).

[10] Gervaise, *Jugement critique*, 56.

[11] François de Pons de Salignac de la Mothe Fénelon, ed. Jean-Edme-August Gosselin, *Œuvres complètes* (Geneva: Slatkine Reprints, 1971), 6:619 (Lettre à M. Dacier sur les occupations de l'Académie). "Ils parlent en orateurs brillans," he continues, "plutôt qu'en ministres de Jésus-Christ" (619).

His words are like a devouring fire that sets aflame all who hear them. You may perhaps remember with what eloquence he expressed himself on worldly things while he was still at Court: this cannot be compared with the force and power with which he speaks of the things of Heaven, of the end of the world, of the blindness of those who prefer the joys of [earthly] life, so short and full of misery, to the delights of eternal joy, of the bliss of the saints, of the blessed state of those who, here below, have a true love for God.[12]

Rancé's sermon for the feast of Saint Bernard is, technically, an "instruction or conference," and the precise nature and purposes of conferences is set out in detail in Rancé's Regulations.[13] The conference on Saint Bernard was obviously delivered on August 20—Bernard's feast day—but in what year is unknown. I suspect that the criticism of mitigations and the attack on those who find the regulations set out by Benedict and the way of life practiced by Bernard to be too hard[14]—that is to say, those anti-Abstinents who would become the Common Observance—indicate the earlier part of Rancé's abbacy rather than the later, but that is all we can say—indeed, that may be more than we can say.

Rancé takes as his text Psalm 4:4, which he translates as "God has made his saint worthy of admiration." It appears as a refrain throughout the entire conference, appearing no less

---

[12] [André Félibien des Avaux], *Description de l'abbaye de la Trappe. Nouvelle Édition* (Paris: J. Le Febvre, 1689), 93–94.

[13] Armand-Jean de Rancé, *Règlemens de l'abbaye de Nôtre-Dame de La Trappe en forme de Constitutions. Avec des reflexions, et la Carte de Visite à N. D. des Clairets* (Paris: F. Delaulne, 1718), 52–59. For an English translation, see *The Regulations of the Abbey of Our Lady of La Trappe in the Form of Constitutions. Printed at Paris, by Estienne Michallet, First Printer of the King, rue S. Jacques, at the Image of St. Paul, 1690, with the privilege of the King*, trans. John Baptist Hasbrouck (Lafayette: Guadalupe Translations, 1999), 35–38.

[14] See §§6–9, 21–22, 31–33, 45–47.

than fifteen times. But in what was Bernard worthy of admiration? Worthy of admiration in the way he kept so scrupulously the prescriptions of the Rule of Saint Benedict, worthy of admiration in what he did for the church and the papacy, and worthy of admiration in the three areas Rancé lists at the end of §19: mortification of the heart, mortification of the senses, and the love of humiliations. Rancé, of course, is speaking to an audience of monks—he is not preaching in a church or cathedral—and his conference is clearly directed at monks. More accurately, it is directed at monks of the Strict Observance, whose business it was to return to the *premier esprit*, the "first spirit," of the Cistercian Order, which had been set out by Julien Paris, abbot of Foucarmont, in the pages of his *Du premier esprit de l'ordre de Cîteaux*, first published in 1653. This was a book that had a profound influence on Rancé and that set forth the essence of the reform.[15] What was the *premier esprit* of the Order? Nothing less than that strict and unswerving fidelity to the Rule of Saint Benedict that Rancé demands in this conference. He makes this clear in the exordium, and once he has finished telling of Bernard's exploits in the world, the theme dominates the rest of his sermon.

Like the other panegyrists, Rancé emphasizes humility, mortification, penance, and penitence, but whereas Biroat and the others link this to the great theme of *imitatio Christi*, Rancé links it to what we might call *imitatio Bernardi et Benedicti*. Bernard is the model monk, the true disciple of Saint Benedict, who exemplified in all that he did all that a monk need do. In some areas, of course, this is not possible: we do not expect the monks of La Trappe to solve the problems of the church and tell the pope what to do. In what, then, should they imitate the chief adornment of their order? In the strictness with which he kept the Rule, in the faithfulness with which he rendered to God everything he had promised him, in his love of withdrawal and

---

[15] See Bell, *Understanding Rancé*, 128–33.

silence, in his fervent charity, in his profound humility, and in his perfect mortification, whether of the spirit or of the senses.

Biroat and the other panegyrists we have considered begin with an account of Bernard's inner life and then tell us what he did in the world. Rancé reverses this. He gets the drama out of the way so that he can concentrate on what is more relevant to the monks of the Strict Observance. But for all that, he provides a considerable amount of information on Bernard's activities *extra claustrum*, though he prefers to mention the protagonists by their titles rather than their names. Innocent II is "the legitimate Pastor" and other such titles, Anacletus is "the Antipope," William X is "the Duke of Aquitaine," and so on. Rancé then goes on to speak of Bernard's defense of the church against the attacks of heretics and schismatics, mentioning by name Peter Abelard, Gilbert de la Porrée, and Henry of Toulouse. His account, however, is brief, and he says nothing of their ideas. He is equally brief in what he tells us of Bernard's miracles. He cast out demons, healed the sick, gave sight to the blind, cured paralytics, and preserved the life of those who were near death, but Rancé gives no specific examples. Bernard certainly did not expect his monks to do the same things.

And so Rancé turns to the heart of his conference, Bernard's life not in the world but in the desert of the monastery: "It is this, my brothers, to which you should pay special attention. It is here that you should study the way he lived and all the circumstances of his life. It is here that you must take him as the model to follow" (§19). He speaks of Bernard's mortification of the heart, by which he means his total detachment from earthly things, and contrasts this with the worldliness and lack of discipline that—alas!—can be seen in most communities of his day. From this he moves to Bernard's mortification of the senses, and, once again, contrasts this with what he sees in the communities around him. Some of them simply contravene all the regulations. Some pick and choose what they will or will not follow. Some alter and weaken the regulations so as to make them more palatable. It is the same with sickness, which is a gift from God to be borne patiently and steadfastly in accordance with his will. But is this the case? It is not. Too many religious respond to sickness in just the same way as those in the world: at the first signs of illness they seek medicines and remedies to cure it. But those who have chosen to withdraw from the world must remember that the monastery is a monk's tomb, and the purpose of withdrawal from the world is to carry the cross of Jesus Christ.

So we come to Bernard's humility, a humility all the more remarkable given his renown in the world. Bernard is the perfect model of humility, and it is the business of Rancé's monks to follow in his footsteps and profit from his example. They must make themselves part of his purposes. They must resolve to follow the Rule of Saint Benedict with all their strength and bind themselves wholly to the maxims it imparts. Oh yes, says Rancé, there are those who say that it asks too much and that we cannot hope to follow in the footsteps of the great Saint Bernard—he is certainly referring to his critics in the Common Observance—but this is simply a reflection of a human nature, which, he says, "desires to be neither subjugated nor constrained" (§46). Let us therefore keep the Rule, let us follow in the footsteps of Bernard, that saint so worthy of admiration, and thus make ourselves worthy of his intercession, finish the course that is set before us, and gain the immortal crown destined for those who truly keep the faith.

Rancé's Bernard, then, is Bernard the monk—more accurately, the ideal monk of the Order of the Strict Observance. Given Rancé's audience, what else could he be? And his discourse is therefore rather different from those we have discussed so far. Yet in one matter his presentation is the same. The Bernard Rancé sets before us is Bernard the humble, Bernard the penitent, Bernard the follower of the Rule of Saint Benedict. He is not the Bernard of mystical rapture, not the Bernard of ecstatic experiences, something that Rancé actively discouraged. As we have seen, he had no time at all for Quietism, a system he denounced as the chimeras of fanatics and absolute impiety,[16] and while he had no choice but to admit that mystical experiences were possible—he had read the great Teresa as well as Saint Bernard—it was not a monk's business to solicit them. What was a monk's business? To live a religious life in community strictly in accordance with the prescriptions of the Rule of Saint Benedict and (in the words of the book of Tobit) "to bless the God of Heaven and bear witness to him in the sight of all who live."[17]

Rancé's sources for his conference are fairly limited. His main source is Scripture, with the Old and New Testaments being more or less evenly divided. Other than Scripture he cites the Rule of Saint Benedict, refers in a general way to two of the Desert Fathers (Paul the First Hermit and one of the Paphnutii), and quotes from a letter of Fastred, abbot of Clairvaux and then of Cîteaux (a letter that Rancé himself had translated and published[18]). Of Bernard's own writings, he refers to two letters, the sermons on the Song of Songs, and one of the sermons for the feast of All Saints. His source for Bernard's life is, as we would expect, the *Vita prima*, for which he may have used either the edition of Horstius or that of Mabillon. Rancé was regular abbot of La Trappe from 1664 to 1695, and Mabillon's edition first appeared in 1667. The 1752 catalogue of the library of La Trappe lists two copies of Mabillon's edition: one is the Paris 1719 edition in two folio volumes, which obviously cannot have been used by Rancé; the other is an earlier edition in ten octavos that may well have been used by the abbot.[19] The catalogue also lists two editions of Horstius's version.[20]

---

[16] *Abbé de Rancé. Correspondance*, 4:412 (Letter 970414).
[17] Tob 12:6: see Bell, *Understanding Rancé*, 227.
[18] See n. 76 below.
[19] See David N. Bell, *The Library of the Abbey of La Trappe. A Study of its History from the Twelfth Century to the French Revolution, with an Annotated Edition of the 1752 Catalogue* (Turnhout: Brepols, 2014), 322 (B.71–72). We cannot be certain of the date of publication of B.72, but it certainly preceded that of B.71.
[20] See Bell, *The Library*, 322 (B.73–74). B.73 is the Lyon 1658 edition in two folios; B.73 is an earlier edition, but we cannot specify the date.

Rancé's panegyric is not quite as long as the others we have considered—I estimate a delivery time of just about an hour, as is fairly standard for Rancé's conferences—and in the pages that follow we are back in the Chapter Room of La Trappe, listening to the Great Reformer telling us just what it means to be true disciples and followers of Saint Bernard.

THE PANEGYRIC
INSTRUCTION OR CONFERENCE
FOR THE FEAST DAY OF SAINT BERNARD[21]

Mirificavit Dominus sanctum suum. (Ps 4:4)

"God has made his saint worthy of admiration."

1. My brothers, I cannot pass by the solemn feast[22] that has just been proclaimed without saying a few words to stir up your faith, to refresh your zeal, rekindle your pious devotion,[23] make your religious way of life[24] more alive, and, finally, to put you in the proper frame of mind to receive the benefits and blessings that you have no doubt been awaiting from such a happy encounter on such a propitious day.

---

[21] [Armand-Jean de Rancé], *Instructions ou Conférences sue les Épîtres et Évangiles des Dimanches et Principales Festes de l'Année, et sur les Vêtures & Professions Religieuses, par le R. Dom Armand Jean, Ancien Abbé de La Trappe, Tome quatrième* (Paris: F. Delaulne, 1720), 259–99, reproduced (with some inaccuracies) in *Collection intégrale et universelle des Orateurs Chrétiens. Deuxième série*, vol. 90 of the entire series (= vol. 23 of the second series), ed. Jacques-Paul Migne (Paris: J.-P. Migne, 1866), cols. 578–93. In Migne's edition, the sermon is entitled "Eighty-second Conference. For the Feast Day of Saint Bernard. Saint Bernard, the Model Monk [*modèle du cénobite*]."

[22] *la solemnité*: a solemnity is one of the highest ranking feast days in the liturgical calendar of the Roman Catholic Church.

[23] *piété*: see appendix 1, s.v. *piété* / piety.

[24] *vôtre religion*: see appendix 1, s.v. *religion* / religion. The word here refers to the way of life of a religious.

2. It is certainly one of the greatest feasts that we can celebrate, this [feast] of Saint Bernard, for if he did not lay the first foundations of our holy Order,[25] we can at least say that he was its principal adornment and its greatest light. No one worked harder than he at establishing it, whether by the holiness of his life, his example, his teaching, his dedication to the monastic path,[26] or the excellent instructions he has left us: [instructions] that contain, in so vital and so telling a way, the most essential duties and virtues of our position [as monks]. We therefore have good reason to apply to him these words that, today, the Church puts in our mouths: *Mirificavit Dominus sanctum suum*.

3. My brothers, I have no fear of saying too much when I tell you that since the time of the apostles and their colleagues[27] none has appeared in the Church of Jesus Christ with more dignity and more renown than this great man. There is no doubt that in all the circumstances of his life, in every place where he was engaged in God's purposes, in every situation in which he wished to fulfill his ministry, he prospered with such blessing and such success that he deserved to be called great. In fact, since no one in his time made a greater contribution than he to the glory of Jesus Christ, there can be no doubt that he also worked for his own glory, since the glory of a servant is to exert himself, devote himself, and give himself wholly, as did he, to the greatness and glory of his Master.

4. Is it not true, my brothers, that this is just what the great Bernard did in all those different circumstances in which divine Providence was pleased to place him?[28] Before the greatest of the earth and before the least, before kings and [ordinary] people, before emperors and sovereign pontiffs, before the

---

[25] That was Saint Benedict and, in 1098, Robert of Molesme.

[26] *sa religion*: see n. 24 above. Rather than repeat "religious way of life," I have paraphrased the word as "dedication to the monastic path." It is cumbersome, but accurate.

[27] Lit., "since the apostles and apostolic men [*les hommes apostoliques*]."

[28] See appendix 1, s.v. *Providence* / Providence.

learned and the simple, among the multitudes in the world as in the heart of his cloister, God made him great everywhere, and he deserves to have the whole Church sing in his praise, *Mirificavit Dominus sanctum suum.*

5. Therefore, my brothers, you cannot have too exalted or too high an opinion [of this man], for [on the one hand,] it is difficult for you to outdo him in what he has done before the whole world and, [on the other,] there is nothing of greater profit to you, nothing more useful, than to hold him up before you with all those rare and excellent qualities that distinguished him from the rest of humanity and that made him the marvel of his age: *totius orbis miraculum* ["the wonder of the whole world"].[29]

6. The reason that those who join monastic congregations do not make all the progress they should is because they do not have the proper esteem or admiration for their founders, because they have no desire to recognize in them the benefits they have received from the open-handedness of God, and because they regard as ordinary men and women those who, by God's Providence, have been born to occupy the highest ranks and preeminent places in his Church.

7. There is an almost infinite multitude of persons of both sexes living under the Rule of Saint Benedict who claim that they have all the esteem and veneration justly due to this great saint. But if they regard him as a man chosen by God to interpret his will and to give to all the monks of the West, in his name and on his behalf, those regulations[30] and holy instructions by which he wants them to live their lives and sanctify themselves, should they not be wholly faithful in observing the

---

[29] If *totius orbis miraculum*, as a description of Bernard, is a quotation, I have not been able to trace it. It is not biblical and does not appear in any of the standard electronic databases. It appears occasionally as a description of other saints—e.g., Saint Nicholas von Flüe (de Rupe), Switzerland's only canonized saint (*Acta SS.* 8:399 [22 March])—but that does not help us here.

[30] Lit. "laws" (*loix*). It is a common usage.

Rule he left them? Should they not have the utmost respect for the prescriptions it contains and the greatest fear of neglecting or omitting the least of its points or practices?[31]

8. It is for this reason, my brothers, that we glory in having Saint Bernard for a father, and that we consider it our true happiness if, at the least, we may speak of ourselves as being numbered among his children. But if this sentiment were truly in the hearts of those who boast of having this advantage, then surely they should take the greatest care to regulate their conduct by the examples and teachings he has left them and to follow him faithfully as their master in all the circumstances of their lives. But, my brothers, are we as conscientious in this as we ought to be? Are we as meticulous[32] as we should be? Or do we not have boundless reasons to pull ourselves together and to reproach ourselves for finding ourselves in paths so contrary to those he has traced for us?

9. There were false sages of old who had their followers, and they found in those who gloried in being their disciples such total compliance that, for them, their words were as oracles. It was enough for them simply to utter a maxim for it to be received as absolute truth. But those who are the disciples of the saints (whose light is as much superior to that of these profane

---

[31] The background to this paragraph (and a number of others in the sermon—§§8–9, 21–22, 31–33, 46–47) is Rancé's attitude to mitigations, which is more complex than is often supposed. See Bell, *Understanding Rancé*, index, 364, s.v. Mitigations, and the long (and polemical) discussion in the last chapter (chap. XXIII, "Des Mitigations") of Rancé's *De la sainteté et des devoirs de la vie monastique*. In general, Rancé had no time whatever for any mitigations, which, in his words, were "a violation of God's law, contempt for his orders, a determined and wholly public resistance to his will, a ministry of iniquity, and, consequently, a state of death" (see Bell, *Understanding Rancé*, 225).

[32] "aussi religieux qu'on le devroit être?" *Religieux* here might also be translated as scrupulous, careful, painstaking, or dedicated to the religious life. See n. 24 above.

people as truth is superior to lies, wisdom to folly, and light to darkness), these, I say, who have the instructions [of the saints] continually before their eyes, who have had presented to them all these great maxims—[*maxims*] that they have proclaimed with an authority and eloquence wholly divine—live as if they had never known them, or as if they had been altogether lost from their memory. Not only do they excuse themselves from observing what [the saints] have taught and practiced with such religious fervor, not only are they pleased to walk in paths that, in the view [of the saints], lead only to ruin, but they have the temerity to treat [the saints] as simple folk, who have spoken with neither experience nor illumination and who have put forth as truth mere fantasies worthy of condemnation by anyone with any wisdom. What audacity, my brothers, what stupidity! Can they doubt that these great saints will one day appear before the Judgment seat of Jesus Christ[33] to reproach them for their disordered lives and their excesses, and that at that terrible moment the weight of their sanctity will overwhelm them?[34]

10. But now, my brothers, you are doubtless getting impatient and are waiting for me to speak of the reasons for the prominence and glory of this great saint and to tell you at some length of the acts and marvels that have made him worthy to be called great—but for that I must refer you to the history of his life.[35] I must pass over a great number of events in silence and content myself with telling you only of those that now come to mind and that seem to me more worthy of notice.

---

[33] *au tribunal de Jésus Christ*, echoing Rom 14:10, *Omnes enim stabimus ante tribunal Christi*, and 2 Cor 5:10, *Omnes enim nos manifestari oportet ante tribunal Christi.*

[34] This is the end of the standard exordium. It is long, but not, as with some panegyrists, overlong, and in it Rancé is primarily concerned with attacking what he regarded as the grave error of mitigations. He now begins the first point of his sermon—with the other panegyrists it is normally the second point—with a discussion of Bernard's major achievements in the world beyond the cloister.

[35] I.e., the *Vita prima* in the edition of either Horstius or Mabillon.

11. The Church was divided by a painful schism that threatened it with almost complete ruin.[36] Everything was in confusion and disorder. The people were unsure which faction to follow, and the situation of their rulers was neither more certain nor more consistent. Each of them followed his own desires and his own interests, whereas this man of God, [Saint Bernard,] having been summoned by the voice of the legitimate pastor [Innocent II] to support his disputed[37] authority, was constrained to come forth from his solitude and leave the repose and holy tranquility to which he had consecrated himself. He appeared in the world as a second Moses to strengthen by his light and his authority those who still supported the cause of God and to set himself up as a wall of bronze[38] against the violence of those who fought against it.

12. You have no doubt read what he accomplished in this great enterprise,[39] but nothing is more worthy of admiration than what he did with [William X], the duke of Aquitaine. He was a man of inflexible obstinacy who, by his pride, malice, audacity, and power, ignited fires everywhere, empowering and enlarging the rebel faction. [Saint Bernard] overthrew him and cast him down at his feet as if he had been struck by lightning, and he changed the fury of this lion (so to speak), of this ravening wolf, into the meekness of an innocent lamb. In a single moment, by a wholly unexpected marvel, he turned a fierce persecutor into a faithful disciple.[40] What a transformation, my brothers! Has there been anything more sudden or more extraordinary since the conversion of the great apostle

---

[36] I.e., the schism in the papacy between Innocent II and the antipope Anacletus. Rancé provides a considerable amount of detail.

[37] Lit. "shaky" (*chancelante*).

[38] *Un mur d'airain*, which is the *murus aereus* of Jer 1:18. Fénelon and Massillon use the same expression.

[39] They would have read it in detail in the *Vita prima* 2.1.1–2.7.48 (Arnold of Bonneval); PL 185:268C–97A; CF 76:79–134.

[40] Rancé is summarizing *Vita prima* 2.6.37–38 (Arnold of Bonneval); PL 185:289C–90D; CF 76:118–21. See appendix 2, s.v. William (Guillaume) X, duke of Aquitaine.

[Paul]?[41] And does this not give us cause to say, to cry aloud, *Mirificavit Dominus sanctum suum*?

13. It was by a wholly similar grace and strength that he preserved in [Henry I], king of England, the fidelity he owed to the Apostolic See and persuaded him to ally himself with the cause of [Innocent II], the legitimate pontiff, against the advice and efforts of those who were trying to mislead him in his religious views and associate him with the interests of the antipope.[42] He worked with a wholly similar blessing with regard to the emperor [Lothair III] and destroyed every possible prejudice he had in his mind against [Innocent] the true pastor.[43] But what is more surprising is that he resisted this emperor, who, wishing (as it were) to buy his devotion to the Holy See and turn to his advantage the state in which the Vicar of Jesus Christ then found himself, demanded that he grant him rights contrary to the sacred canons and the prerogatives of the Church.[44] The saint objected to what appeared to him to be an obvious injustice, and the respect that was due to such great majesty did not stop him from reproving [the emperor]. He checked him, he opened his eyes to what he was doing, and he let him know that his claims were unjust.

14. After he had pacified all of France and all the countries this side of the Alps, he made his way to Italy, and led by this spirit that nothing could resist, he reassured almost all those whom he found to be troubled or uncertain.[45] He led home those who had strayed in the submission they owed to the Apostolic Throne; by the might of his prayers he put to flight the army

---

[41] See Acts 9:3-20.

[42] See *Vita prima* 2.1.4 (Arnold of Bonneval); PL 185:271AB; CF 76:82–83, and appendix 2, s.v. Henry I.

[43] See *Vita prima* 2.1.5 (Arnold of Bonneval); PL 185:271B–72A; CF 76:83–84, and appendix 2, s.v. Lothair III of Supplinburg.

[44] Rancé is referring to the Investiture Controversy: see appendix 2, s.v. Lothair III of Supplinburg.

[45] For the details, see Williams, *Saint Bernard of Clairvaux*, 114–58.

of [Roger II], king of Sicily,[46] and by the power of his reasoning he confounded those who dared dispute with him and oppose the cause he defended. He poured oil on troubled waters, he appeased dissension, and he made the sheep who had lost their way return to the fold of [Innocent] the true Shepherd. In a word, he reestablished the Sovereign Pontiff on his throne, told him of those who had had the audacity and presumption to rise up against him, restored peace to the Church, and delivered it from one of the greatest oppressions it had ever suffered. What power! What authority! But even if we pay but little heed to these great achievements, my brothers, can we not say that God has been pleased to glorify his saint, or, rather, to glorify himself in the person of his servant? *Mirificavit Dominus sanctum suum*!

15. He was no less fortunate nor less favored by God in maintaining the truth of the faith than in preserving the unity of the Church, and we can say that he fought against heresy and schism with the same success. What did he not do to destroy the absurd ideas[47] of [Peter] Abelard, to confute the errors of the bishop of Poitiers, Gilbert de la Porrée, and to stamp out the impieties of Henry and the heretics of the Languedoc?[48] In all these different struggles he appeared as the defender of truth and the shield of the faith.[49] He maintained it by his teaching, by the force of his arguments, by the holiness of his life, and by his steadfast courage. In a word, wherever he happened to be, truth triumphed over lies and falsehood. Everything yielded to the grace that filled him; whatever he did was glorious, and we see in all his actions the fulfillment of these words: *Mirificavit Dominus sanctum suum*.

---

[46] See *Vita prima* 2.7.43–46 (Arnold of Bonneval); PL 185:293B–95C; CF 76:126–31, and Williams, *Saint Bernard of Clairvaux*, 151–53. Rancé is referring to the Battle of Rignano, fought on October 30, 1137: see appendix 2, s.v. Roger II of Sicily.

[47] Lit. "extravagances" (*extravagances*).

[48] See appendix 2, s.v. Henry of Toulouse.

[49] Cf. Eph 6:16: *in omnibus sumentes scutum fidei*.

16. What can we not say of the blessings that accompanied him when he had no choice but to proclaim to people these eternal truths, or of the successes that followed his preaching? He penetrated the hardest hearts and imprinted therein the love of God's law and of his holy name. He made the most rebellious souls malleable. Sinners did not know what it was not to heed his voice, and, by the magnitude of their penitence, they bore witness to the sincerity of their conversion. Nothing [and no one] could resist this apostolic man: wives locked up their husbands and parents their children lest they leave them to follow him. Everything yielded to the power of his words—or, rather, to [the power of the words of] God that came forth from his mouth like a sharp two-edged sword: *Penetrabilior omni gladio ancipiti* ["more piercing than any two-edged sword" (Heb 4:12)]. Nothing, therefore, is more fitting for this man who is so celebrated than this testimony that is so seemly: *Mirificavit Dominus sanctum suum*.

17. God, who wanted men and women to regard [the saint] with that esteem and confidence that would make him more useful for his intentions, forgot nothing that could give him glory and renown. To all the other graces he had granted, he added that of miracles, and this was accorded to him in such measure that he seemed to be the master of both humans and demons. He drove out the latter from the bodies of those who were possessed, and the mere name of Bernard filled them with dread. He restored health to the sick and sight to the blind. He gave to paralytics the strength and freedom of their limbs. He preserved the life of those who were near to losing it, and the whole of his own life was no more than a succession of miraculous acts. He had, in fact, such absolute power over everything here below and commanded nature with such authority that one could say that God had suspended the order that he normally imposed on his day-to-day operations so that nothing would prevent them from obeying the commands or wishes of this great saint. Thus we read in Scripture, *obediente Deo voci hominis* ["the Lord obeying the voice of a man" (Josh

10:14)]. Have we ever seen the like since the earliest days of the Church? And is it not true that he who worked all these marvels deserves to have said of him, *Mirificavit Dominus sanctum suum*?

18. My brothers, I could spend whole days telling you what God has done through the ministry of this great man—what he has done for the conversion of sinners, for the service of the Church, for the sanctification of the world—but that would not be time enough. He was indeed great, but if he was so esteemed among men and women because of all these actions (which deserve to be remembered forever), he was no less great when, driven by the Spirit of God, he established in remote and lonely places holy retreats, hallowed refuges, houses of sorrow in which God was offered a perpetual sacrifice of tears and penitence.[50] [Nor was he any less great] when he enclosed himself therein in order to train his disciples and, by his own example,[51] to teach others the rules by which they ought to lead their lives.

19. It is this, my brothers, to which you should pay special attention. It is here that you should study the way he lived and all the circumstances of his life. It is here that you must take him as the model to follow. And just as he is the object of your admiration in the world, he is also the one you should imitate in the desert.[52] The practices he undertook there with such edification and example should be your own rule of life,

---

[50] Rancé is referring to the dozens of daughterhouses of Clairvaux founded during the lifetime of Bernard. Biroat and a number of the other panegyrists follow Geoffrey of Auxerre in giving the number as a hundred and sixty: see chap. 4 (Biroat), n. 97.

[51] In accordance with the principles set forth in RB 2.11-13, which states that an abbot should teach his disciples even more by his deeds than by his words.

[52] This is the transition point in Rancé's sermon. He has concluded his account of Bernard's admirable achievements "dans le monde" outside the cloister and now turns his attention to his life of austerity and mortification "dans le désert" of the monastery.

and from this [rule] you are not permitted to part company.[53] It is in the strictness with which he kept the Rule to which he had consecrated himself that you should strive to be like him, it is in the faithfulness with which he rendered to God everything he had promised him, it is in the love that he had for withdrawal and silence, it is in his ardent charity, his profound humility, his perfect mortification, whether of the spirit or of the senses, it is in the practice of all the virtues that are the essence, ornament, value, and splendor of your [religious] profession: those virtues, in fact, which, no less than all the other wonderful things [he did in the world and] of which we have already spoken, have made him worthy of this immortal praise: *Mirificavit Dominus sanctum suum*. But among all this multiplicity of gifts, graces, and different characteristics that I could tell you about, my brothers, I will limit myself to three that, to me, seem to be outstanding qualities and from which all the others issue forth as corollaries and necessary consequences: I mean mortification of the heart, [mortification] of the senses, and the love of humiliations.

20. As to mortification of the heart, was there ever anything to parallel what we have seen in this great man? Has there ever been recollection[54] equal to that which showed itself in everything he did? He appeared so shut off from all external things that we might say that his consciousness of them was wholly extinguished. He spent the year of his novitiate without even noticing that there was a window in the place where he was, even though it was the only aperture that let in the light.[55] He alone did not see what struck the eyes of everyone and which

---

[53] See §7 above.

[54] See appendix 1, s.v. *recueillement* / recollection.

[55] Rancé's memory is playing him false here, for this is not quite what we are told by William of Saint-Thierry. Bernard, he says, was continually in and out of the church but thought that there was only one window in the apse, whereas there were actually three (*Vita prima* 1.4.20 [William of Saint-Thierry]; PL 185:238D; CF 76:23 = *Vita*

it was virtually impossible not to notice. What death! What destruction! How deeply he must have entered within himself to refuse to his senses something so obvious! Cannot someone who finds himself in this condition say with the apostle, *Vivo autem, jam non ego*: "I live as if I lived no longer"?[56] He was certainly surrounded with things here below, but they made no more impression on him than if he had neither the right, the power, nor the necessary faculties to use them, and since his soul was continually raised above the earth, it can be said that heaven was his usual habitation.

21. What connection is there, my brothers, between this holy disinterest and the lack of discipline[57] that reigns among the great majority of communities consecrated to solitude and silence? Everything there is in turmoil and change. Those there wish to know everything and learn everything. "The ear," if I may use the words of Scripture, "is never satisfied with what it hears nor the eye with what it sees": *Non saturatur oculus visu, nec auris auditu impletur* (Eccl 1:8). And if one ignores the fact that the senses are the doors through which the passions enter the soul,[58] one takes in every object that appears [to them] indifferently. The house, so to speak, is always open, and even though one refuses nothing to its voracity, one does so in vain, for it is never satisfied.

22. It is this that has weakened, this that has altered all the observances that, from their origin and birth, have contributed so much to the glory of Jesus Christ and the edification of his

---

secunda 4.16; PL 185:479B). The story about the *cella novitiorum* concerned the vaulting.

[56] Gal 2:20, which actually reads "And I live, now not I: [but Christ lives in me]." Rancé's translation, "Je vis comme si je ne vivois plus," is a paraphrase, but that is common with the panegyrists.

[57] *dissipation*, which I have rendered as "lack of discipline." To translate it as "dissolute way of life" is too strong. The ideas expressed in §§21–22 are elaborated in §31–33.

[58] See Gregory the Great, *Moralia in Iob* 21.2.4; PL 76:189C. See also chap. 5, n. 11.

Church. It is this that has pulled away these [observances] from what they were when they were first instituted—or, rather, [pulled them away] from his order and his hand—and that has resulted in so many places that once were fields of infinite abundance becoming unproductive and sterile land, producing only brambles and thorns.

23. We must not imagine, my brothers, that in Saint Bernard this grace was short-lived and transitory.[59] He possessed it at all times, and it appeared wherever he was throughout the whole of his life. Neither his travels nor his responsibilities nor his business, however important they were, were capable of drawing him out from within himself: he preserved this gift, so excellent and rare, in the midst of everything that could taint it, disperse it, or destroy it. We read in the history of his life that for one full day he traveled the length of Lake Geneva, and when, that evening, those who were with him were talking about the countryside through which they had passed and, above all, the grandeur and beauty of the lake, he asked them where was this lake they were talking about.[60] They could not express their amazement at this, for they could not understand how a mortal man, necessarily subject to the laws of nature, could be in a state of detachment[61] that seemed more appropriate to angels than human beings.

24. What were you doing, great saint, while your eyes were shut to created things,[62] while you were unaware and unconscious of them? For you, it was as if they no longer existed, and you were wholly inaccessible to every [impression] they sent to you. There is no doubt that God occupied all the places from which you had expelled them: his infinite majesty filled the

---

[59] Lit. "that this grace was a *disposition passagère.*"

[60] *Vita prima* 3.2.4 (Geoffrey of Auxerre); PL 185:306A; CF 76:150 = *Vita secunda* 16.45; PL 185:496BC.

[61] *Dégagement*: see appendix 1, s.v. *dégagement*/detachment.

[62] The words *pendant que vous vous refusiez aux créatures* are accidentally omitted in Migne's edition of the conference.

whole of your heart, and your only concern was to meditate on those days of old and eternal years spoken of by the prophet [David]: *Cogitavi dies antiquos, et annos æternos in mente habui*, ["I thought on the days of old, and I had in mind the eternal years" (Ps 76:6)]. And in this region of death you rejoiced in the blessed anticipation of the ineffable joys and consolations that await you in the land of the living.[63]

25. It was in this same spirit that [the saint] went to visit [the Carthusian monastery of] la Grande Chartreuse. He was received with all the respect and consideration due to virtue and piety as outstanding as his. All who saw him were edified by his bearing, his humility, and the words of life and blessing that came from his mouth. Only one thing troubled them: the harness of the horse he was riding. It seemed to them too distinctive, too rich, and hardly appropriate for a man of his profession. But when the saint became aware of this, he was no less astonished than the others: the horse had been loaned to him for his journey, and he simply stated that at no time had he noticed its trappings.[64]

26. God gave him the same protection and preserved him in the same detachment to the very end of his life, despite the different activities and occupations in which he found himself. Shortly before his death, one of his friends, a bishop,[65] came to see him at Clairvaux, but while he was talking with the saint,

---

[63] See Pss 26:13; 51:7; 114:9; and 141:6. See also appendix 1, s.v. *consolations* / consolations.

[64] *Vita prima* 3.2.4 (Geoffrey of Auxerre); PL 185:305CD; CF 76:149–50 = *Vita secunda* 16.45; PL 185:496AB. The prior at the time was Guigo de Castro / Guigues du Chastel, the fifth prior, so the episode must have taken place sometime before his death in 1137.

[65] This was Godefroid (or Geoffroy) de La Roche-Vanneau, a cousin of Saint Bernard and bishop of Langres from 1138 to 1161. He had previously been the first abbot of Fontenay and third prior of Clairvaux, and it was to Clairvaux that he retired just a few years before his death on November 8, 1166. See DHGE 20:554–56. His visit to the dying Bernard took place in the winter of 1152–1153.

[Bernard] would often stay [silent] for some time and make no reply to what the bishop was saying. [The latter] expressed his surprise at this, but the saint, rousing himself from [what appeared to be] profound lethargy but was actually sublime meditation,[66] replied, "Alas! I am no longer of this world."[67] It is true, great saint, you were no longer there—or, more accurately, you had never been there. God separated you from it forever from the moment he gave you your second birth [in baptism]. You never had any part in its passions, its business, its concerns, or its pleasures. You belonged with those of whom Jesus Christ said, "They are no longer of the world, any more than I am": *non sunt de mundo, sicut ego non sum de mundo* ["They are not of the world, just as I am not of the world" (John 17:14)]. He preserved you from everything that could do the slightest harm to the innocence you received in the sacred waters of baptism, and this plenitude of graces, which it pleased him to bestow upon you in advance, ensured that these precious vestments, with which you had then been clothed anew, would preserve their whiteness and original purity and protect you from that iniquity that is so general that the great majority of even the most holy souls have not been able to escape it.

27. If a Saint Paul[68] had spoken in this way, or a Saint Paphnutius,[69] or some solitary who had spent his days in the

---

[66] *Méditation sublime*: see appendix 1, s.v. *contemplation* / contemplation.

[67] *Vita prima* 5.2.8 (Geoffrey of Auxerre); PL 185:356A; CF 76:241. "Ne mireris," said Bernard, "ego enim jam non sum de hoc mundo."

[68] Given the context, this is undoubtedly Saint Paul the first hermit, not Saint Paul the apostle. Rancé had certainly read Jerome's *Vita S. Pauli*.

[69] There were a number of solitaries called Paphnutius, and it is sometimes impossible to be sure which one said and did what. Rancé would have known the stories contained in the *Vitas Patrum*, *Historia monachorum in Aegypto*, and *Lausiac History* of Palladius. Paphnutius appears again in Rancé's *De la sainteté et des devoirs de la vie monastique*.

heart of a forsaken solitude, I would not have been surprised. But that a man who had applied himself to so many important matters, who had dealt with them with such concern, attention, and painstaking care, could absent himself so entirely and completely from all created things that, by training, his eyes no longer saw them, his ears no longer heard them, and his mind no longer thought on them, that indeed is a marvel never yet reported, and it only leads us to see in the person of Saint Bernard what today we have good reason to cry aloud: *Mirificavit Dominus sanctum suum.*

28. For Saint Bernard, my brothers, mortification of the spirit was in no way more excellent than mortification of the senses.[70] He rejoiced in afflicting his body with continual macerations, and to this end he made use of long vigils, laborious tasks, severe fasts, and abstinences, and from the first years of his dedication to the cloister he so destroyed his constitution that it seemed that his career would begin and end at the same time, much like a sun that rises and sets on the same day. He himself saw his health decline without the least concern, and this torch, which had been lit to illumine the whole Church, was on the point of extinction. Yet no one ordered him to do anything about it until a higher authority halted the course of his austerities.[71] He had no choice but to submit, and he was placed in the hands of a man who promised to heal him. No doubt you expect that this new physician made use of choice electuaries and rare drugs for this purpose, remedies that were appropriate to the quality of the person and the gravity of his illness. On the contrary. This rustic (for such is the name we

---

[70] Rancé now turns to the physical mortifications described in *Vita prima* 1.4.21–22 (William of Saint-Thierry); PL 185:239C–40B; CF 76:24–26; and elsewhere.

[71] The higher authority was William of Champeaux, bishop of Châlons-sur-Marne from 1114 to his death in 1122 (see DHGE 22:876–77 and DTC 6:1976–77). See *Vita prima* 1.7.32 (William of Saint-Thierry); PL 185:246BC; CF 76:37.

can give him[72]) treated him with so little regard and so much brutality that those who witnessed it were deeply sorry for him. One saw this servant of God, whose preservation was so precious to the whole world, take for his relief what could only increase his afflictions: eating grease instead of butter and drinking olive oil instead of a herbal infusion,[73] as if he lacked both discrimination and taste.

29. Finally, however, God restored him to health independently of human care and attention, but no sooner had he recovered than he once again took up his customary mortifications.[74] To acknowledge the graces he had received from God during his illness, he believed that he owed him nothing less than the sacrifice of the life he had preserved. This, for him, was sufficient cause to pass his days and nights in prayer until his body could no longer sustain it and forced him to suspend [these practices]. His nourishment was no more than a little bread, milk, and herbs cooked without butter. And to all these austerities he added the harshness of a hairshirt. He carried

---

[72] See *Vita prima* 1.7.33 (William of Saint-Thierry); PL 185:246D–47A; CF 76:38: *de quodam homine rusticano et vano, nihil prorsus sciente*, "a boorish and conceited fellow, knowing absolutely nothing."

[73] Mabillon, following Horstius, has *Nam et sanguinem crudum per errorem sibi oblatum pro butyro multis diebus noscitur comedisse; oleum bibisse tanquam aquam* (*Vita prima* 1.7.33 [William of Saint-Thierry]; PL 185:247AB; CF 76:39). Two nineteenth-century biographers of Bernard (Georg Huffer in 1886 and Elphège Vacandard in 1895) both suggested, undoubtedly correctly, that *sanguinem* ("blood") was a misreading by Horstius of *sagimen*, which means fat, grease, or lard. Pace Verdeyen (CCCM 89B:59) and Costello (CF 76: 39) *sartaginem*, *saguimen*, and *sagenam* are all unlikely. Bernard was not eating large fishing nets (*sagena*). Rancé, correctly, translates *sanguis crudus* ("fresh blood") as "la graisse"—grease, fat, lard, or dripping—and the *aqua* or "water" becomes "une tisane." The effects of this medical malpractice on Bernard's "ruined stomach" (*Vita prima* 1.4.22 [William of Saint-Thierry]; PL 185:239D; CF 76:25) would have been disastrous.

[74] The whole of §29 is a summary of *Vita prima* 1.8.38–39 (William of Saint-Thierry); PL 185:249C–50B; CF 76:43–45.

out all the regular duties with such strictness that he found the least exemption unbearable. Judge, my brothers, whether indeed it is with good reason that we say of him, *Mirificavit Dominus sanctum suum*.

30. This attitude never left him. He had it at all times and in all the different occupations in which, by the decree of Providence,[75] he found himself employed. He always regarded his flesh as a deadly enemy and would never make peace with it, not even a truce. He had declared war on it in his youth, and he continued [that war] to the end of his days. When almost wholly incapacitated, this martyr, this victim of penitence, was seen to take—though only with misgivings—a little liquor prepared with a little milk, oil, and honey that was given to him to restore his natural bodily heat, which had virtually disappeared. What a relish, my brothers, what a mixture to give to such a man! But when one of the brothers expressed surprise at the difficulties he was making about using such a common and hackneyed remedy, he said to him these words which deserve to be remembered: *Si scires, o fili, quanta sit obligatio monachi, omnis buccella quam comedis, lacrymis tuis irriganda foret* ["If you knew, my son, how great are our monastic obligations, you would soak every morsel you eat in your tears"].[76] Oh great saint! So great are the obligations of a monk that in order to satisfy them he should indeed soak the bread he eats in the water of his tears.

---

[75] See n. 28 above.

[76] Rancé has taken this story and this saying from the "Ep. CDXCI Fastredi abbatis Claræ-Vallensis tertii ad quemdam ordinis sui abbatem" (PL 182:704D–6C), of which Rancé published a French translation: *Lettre du B. Fastrède, abbé de Cambron, disciple de S. Bernard et depuis 3. abbé de Clairvaux, à un abbé de l'Ordre qui sous prétexte de faiblesse ne mangeoit que des viandes délicates et différentes de la nourriture commune de l'Ordre, traduite en françois par M. A.J.B.D.R., abbé de N.-Dame de la Trape, du mesme Order de Cisteaux* ([Paris?]: [s.n.], [1655?]). It is a very rare quarto pamphlet of seven pages. The text in Migne reads "Fili mi, si monachi obligationem nosses, omnis bucella, quam edis, lacrymis irriganda foret" (PL 182:706B).

31. What an embarrassment, my brothers, and what a condemnation for all such as us, us who have made our profession [to live] a holy and sequestered life! Where can we see in our own conduct the slightest clues that would indicate to us that the qualities of this great servant of God might be ours? He lived in severe want and privation, whereas we live in abundance. His concern was only to crucify his body and walk in strait and narrow ways,[77] and all that we care about is how we can make things pleasant, easy, and comfortable for ourselves. I have to say this, my brothers, I cannot hold myself back: the majority of those consecrated to Jesus Christ under strict and penitential rules find reasons to extricate themselves from too pressing an obligation. Some do this by openly contravening [all the rules]. Others maintain a greater number of regulations and reject only those that they do not know how to bend to their purposes without obvious transgression. Others are even more assiduous, yet there is hardly a single point or single article of the Rule that they do not alter and weaken. Finally there are those who are yet more strict and whose way of life is more consistent with the truth of the Rule. But alas! What a difference there is between what we have just been saying and what these people practice! And every time they wish to compare themselves with this great and unique figure, what reason do they not have to be lost in confusion and, acutely aware of their own misery, to cry aloud the words spoken by the first of their Fathers, [Saint Benedict], in the depths of his humility: *Nobis vero desidiosis et male viventibus rubor confusionis est* ["For us who are lazy and ill-living, (the rules laid down by the Fathers) are a source of shame and confusion"]?[78] The penitence of this incomparable man condemns our laxity and sloth, and covers us with confusion.

32. What relationship is there, my brothers, between what he underwent in his sufferings and what the vast majority of

[77] See Matt 7:14.
[78] RB 73.7.

[present-day] religious undergo in their infirmities? This saint suffered his pains as a guilty man undergoes a punishment to which he believes he has been justly condemned, and he said that which had earlier been said by [Job], the most afflicted and patient of men: *Qui coepit, ipse me conterat, solvat manum [suam, et succidat me? Et haec mihi sit consolatio, ut affligens me dolore, non parcat,] nec contradicam sermonibus sancti,*[79] "Strike me, my God, raise your arm and strike me with all your might. I shall never be so wretched as to [seek to] escape from any thought or action that is contrary to your will."[80]

33. The religious of our day and age—I say the greatest number of them—are uneasy. As soon as it pleases God to visit them [with illness and suffering], they have recourse to remedies: they hunt them out and desire them with just the same ardor and eagerness as the rest of humankind. And instead of responding to God's plan by submitting to it peacefully and steadfastly ([a plan that is] intended only to purify their faith, exercise their virtue, and strengthen their perseverance), they are agitated and troubled: they want their health at any price and are moved neither by the example of this great saint nor by the instructions he gave to all religious when he said that monks have not been instructed in the school of Hippocrates and Galen, who teach the preservation of life, but in that of Jesus Christ, who tells us to lose it.[81] This is a maxim that should be graven on the heart of everyone who has renounced the world in order to carry the cross of Jesus Christ in a life of withdrawal.

---

[79] Job 6:9-10. In the printed text of the sermon, the section in square brackets is represented simply by ellipses: . . .

[80] Rancé has paraphrased this rather cumbersome passage. A literal translation reads, "[Who will grant my request] that he who has begun may crush me, that he may loose his hand and cut me down? And that this may be my comfort: that in afflicting me with sorrow, he does not spare me, nor do I contradict the words of the Holy One."

[81] Bernard SC 30.4–5; SBOp 1:216–17.

34. Our saint was no less great in his love of humiliation (the third virtue we have mentioned[82]) than in his love of seclusion and his love of penance. And since it would be difficult to find a humility more consummate than his, and since Jesus Christ has told us that he will raise up all those who humble themselves for love of him,[83] it cannot be doubted that he was raised to an eminent glory, and, taking into consideration the greatness of his humility, we may say of him, *Mirificavit Dominus sanctum suum*.

35. The nature and greatness of humility are judged by the qualities, the esteem, and the dignity of the person who is humbled. Those who have much of these things renounce, abandon, and sacrifice more when they humble themselves, provided that their humility is sincere and that it comes from the very bottom of their heart. [What happens, then,] if we judge [the humility] of Saint Bernard by this principle? If we take into consideration the rank he occupied among men, if we recall how he filled the whole Church with the glory of his name, [if we remember] his wisdom, his teachings, his mortifications, his miracles, his holiness, and the great number of successes he met with in all aspects of his life, and if we put all these achievements side by side with his ardor in negating and humbling himself before men as well as before God,[84] [what is the result?] We will have no choice but to admit that it would be hard to find any humility to compare with his. But not only does he humble himself; he dishonors and degrades himself! It seems that when it is a question of covering himself with

---

[82] The other two are mortification of the heart and mortification of the senses (see §19). There Rancé speaks of "l'amour des humiliations," in the plural; here of "l'amour de l'humiliation," in the singular.

[83] Matt 23:12; Luke 14:10-11; 18:14.

[84] "pour s'humilier *devant les hommes, aussi-bien que* devant Dieu." The words in italics are incorrectly omitted in Migne's edition of the conference.

embarrassment and ignominy, he cannot get enough if it, and that he would like to bury forever the distinction and eminence above others that God had bestowed upon him.

36. It is in this spirit that he tells all those who praise him that they praise him only because they do not know him, that it is really not he they love and esteem but someone else, for the person they esteem is not, in fact, what he is, but what he is not! Thus, in speaking to [Peter the Venerable], the abbot of Cluny, who had written in fitting terms to a man of his quality and holiness, he exclaims, "What are you doing, my dearest friend? Are you praising a sinner, are you beatifying a worthless wretch? The only thing you can do is to pray to God for me that he may preserve me from falling into illusion and error, something that very nearly happened to me when I received this letter from Your Beatitude concerning my beatification!"[85] And in writing to another of his friends he says that he wishes that those who praise him may be covered with shame and embarrassment, and that he may appear to them so abject and despicable that they may regret having lavished praise on a man who was in no way worthy of it.[86]

37. We cannot pay too much heed to the reply he gave to those who were unable to approve the austerity in which he lived. There were those, he admitted, who could follow a more moderate way of life, but as for him, he was a sinner given up to sin and had need of stronger and more violent remedies for the healing of his evils.[87] But what evils, my brothers, could this man of God punish with such rigor? What is it that could lead him to speak of himself in such a harsh and pitiless

---

[85] Bernard, Ep 265.1 to Peter the Venerable; SBOp 8:174. Rancé's translation is not strictly literal. See also appendix 2, s.v. Peter the Venerable.

[86] Rancé is referring to Bernard's Ep 72; SBOp 7:175–78, to Rainald, abbot of Foigny (especially §3).

[87] See *Vita prima* 1.8.41 (William of Saint-Thierry); PL 185:251BC; CF 76:46–47.

way? It is not enough for him to be a sinner: he is a slave of sin, *venumdatus sub peccato* ["sold under sin"],[88] he who had been favored with such special blessings from his infancy, he to whom these words of the prophet [David] could justly be applied: *Praevenisti eum in benedictionibus dulcedinis* ["You have preceded him with blessings of sweetness" (Ps 20:4)]. What irregularity could [lead him] to take up arms against himself, he who had never known such and who, in all things and at all times, had followed the will of God as the sole rule of his life and conduct?

38. But who is there, my brothers, who would not be filled with admiration at the lengths to which he took his zeal? When he was oppressed by the weight and horror of sins he had never committed, he cried out under the pressure of the spirit that possessed him, "Beat me, Lord, beat me as an unfaithful servant! It may be that the blows I receive from a hand that is so righteous yet so loving will, for me, take the place of the merits [I do not have], and since there is no good to be seen in me that is worthy of reward, may you find in my afflictions and sorrows a reason for showing me your compassion and mercy": *Vapulem, vapulem tanquam servus male operans, si forte flagella computentur in merita, forsitan mihi miserebitur, qui nihil invenerit in me quod remuneret.*[89]

39. What is this? Have you forgotten, great saint, all that Jesus Christ has done for your ministry in his Church? Do you no longer remember that in your time you contributed more

[88] Rom 7:14, which Bernard uses to describe himself in his SC 26.4; SBOp 1:177; and OS S 5.8; SBOp 5:367.

[89] Bernard SC 44.4; SBOp 2:49, which Rancé may be either adapting or [mis]quoting from memory. The actual text reads: *Vapulem sane, vapulem ut male operans; si forte verbera in merita reputentur, fortassis miserebitur flagellato, qui bonum in me non invenit quod remuneret sponsus Ecclesiae,* "Let him beat me, beat me as a bad workman. If the lashes may be counted as merits, then perhaps the Bridegroom of the Church will have mercy on the one he has flogged, even if he finds in me nothing good to reward."

than anyone to the preservation of the glory of his house? That you saved his pontiff from an almost universal conspiracy? That you reestablished him on his throne, from which some would have driven him and sacrilegiously usurped his place? Do you not know that all the powers of the earth have humbled themselves before you? That princes, kings, emperors, prelates, cardinals, and popes have sought your friendship? That they have counted themselves truly fortunate to be among those whom you love? And that one can say of you what was said of the great prophet [Elijah], *Beati sunt qui te viderunt, et in amicitia tua decorati sunt* ["Blessed are those who saw you, and who were honored with your friendship" (Sir 48:11)]? It is true that you have not made fire descend from Heaven like a second Elijah,[90] but you have drawn down rivers of graces which, in the field of the Church, have given birth to an almost countless multitude of people of all ages and both sexes who have made it prosper and who have been its adornment and its sanctification.

40. These are some of the ways in which the whole world has borne witness to you, great saint, and it is this that is hidden from you by your humility, for when you were the light of the world,[91] you saw yourself as a dim lamp that produced only smoke. Finally, you debased yourself to the same degree that your virtue had become renowned, and people will say of you until the end of the ages, *Mirificavit Dominus sanctum suum*.

41. Be on your guard, my brothers, lest the humility of this great saint should be our condemnation, for that is what it will be for all those of our [religious] profession who, with so much ardor and eagerness, seek after honors and superiority and distinction, for which [our saint] had only aversion and condemnation. Such people, who have neither dignity nor merit, often strive to display virtues they do not possess, whereas this man of immortal memory did all that he could

---

[90] See 1 Kgs 18:38.
[91] See John 8:12; 9:5.

to bury his many rare qualities and glittering achievements in everlasting oblivion.

42. To say that Saint Bernard possessed a consummate humility is to say that he possessed all the virtues to an eminent degree. According to the Prophet [Isaiah], the Spirit of God rests on those souls who are humble and peaceful.[92] It is these whom he chooses for his habitation, and it is in them that he establishes his kingdom. Since this Spirit works and acts unceasingly wherever he may be—provided there are no obstacles to prevent him and no opposition to hinder him—we may say that he gave himself to Saint Bernard in his fullness, that he shed his graces in his heart in profusion, that he filled up all those depths, all those abysses that his profound humility had hollowed out. In a word, the Creator made himself the absolute master and took pleasure in adorning and enriching him to recompense him for all the creature comforts[93] that he sacrificed to him.

43. God, whose goodness and wisdom are infinite, imparts to those who love him the gifts appropriate to their condition and situation, and the graces with which he favors them are always those that they need to fulfill their duties. To a monarch he gives magnanimity, prudence, and love of his people. To a prelate, vigilance, knowledge, and charity. To a magistrate, fairness, firmness, and discernment. Thus, by the same Providence, we may say that God gave to this great man the qualities, virtues, and holy disposition that were necessary for him to observe [God's] precepts and counsels. For since his life was divided between the affairs of the world and the Church and the occupations of the cloister, there was hardly anything that did not concern him.

---

[92] Isa 66:2 in the Old Latin version: *Super quem requiscit Spiritus meus, nisi super humilem et quietum?* Bernard quotes the verse in his Miss 1.5; SBOp 4:18, and elsewhere. Bernard himself might have found it in any number of patristic writers from Novatian onward. The most likely source is either Jerome or Augustine.

[93] "toutes les créatures." We might paraphrase this as "all the things of this world," but Rancé is here contrasting *Créateur* with *créatures*.

44. It is this that made Jesus Christ bestow on him the charity and self-denial of the apostles, the faith and steadfastness of his martyrs, the hope of his confessors, and the purity of his virgin brides. It is for this reason that he established him in a freedom that made him superior to all those with whom he had to deal in matters concerning his service and the glory of his Church, and [it is for this, too,] that he placed him in a holy independence that, drawing him forth from the hand of created things, bound him to his [hand] alone. It is for this reason, I say, that he heaped upon him all those graces that could make him regarded in his [religious] profession as a prodigy of saintliness, mortification, and penitence, so that he could say with the apostle, "The world is dead and crucified to me, as I am dead and crucified to the world," *Mihi mundus crucifixus est, et ego mundo* ["The world is crucified to me, and I to the world" (Gal 6:14)]. Does he not deserve this witness that the Church bears of him today: *Mirificavit Dominus sanctum suum*?

45. On this solemn feast, my brothers, the intention of the Church is not only to lead us to offer a eulogy and panegyric to this great saint but also to profit from the example and the instruction that he has given to all monastic observances, and especially to those who have the advantage of serving Jesus Christ under the Rule that he followed and of being counted among his children. Let us make ourselves part of his purposes, my brothers, and let us today make a new resolution to observe this Rule that sanctified him by means of so many acts of mortification and penance. Let us bind ourselves to all the maxims he has taught us as to immutable truths, which, for us, it is essential to observe. Let us never leave, so to speak, the ways that he has canonized, let us consider it inestimable joy to have him at our head, and let us find our glory and our assurance in following this angel[94] whom God has given us to lead us.

---

[94] For Bernard as an angel sent by God, see Louis-Bénigne Bourru's long discussion in chap. 13 below.

46. I am not unaware that there can be found today those who are sufficiently audacious as to attack his conduct, to regard as excessive the holy instructions he has left us, and to attribute to unreasonable fervor that which he has taught us through an abundance of grace, discernment, and wisdom. These people, of no consequence and no experience, dare to extend to this incomparable man the malice of their censures. To cover up their own insignificance and hide their own impenitence, they say that he has carried things to excess and filled his writings with ideas that it is impossible to put into practice.[95] Such thoughts as these, my brothers, merit no response, for it is the voice of a [human] nature that desires to be neither subjugated nor constrained. In short, they are little people measuring themselves against a giant of towering stature and—to use the words of Scripture—they are [like] the thistles that take root in the bottom of valleys and dare to compare themselves with the cedars growing on the summit of Mount Lebanon, which, in their immense height, carry and hide their heads in the highest clouds: *Carduus Libani misit ad cedrum quæ est in Libano* ["A thistle of Lebanon sent to a cedar that is on Lebanon"].[96]

47. Truly, my brothers, what comparison is there between these imprudent critics and him whom they attack with such audacity? He is filled with light, but in these others there is only darkness. He is inspired by God; they are dominated by their cupidity. He finds his fulfillment in the doctrine of the saints; they have not the least smattering of this knowledge. He

---

[95] There was certainly criticism—severe criticism—of Bernard by writers such as Pierre Bayle, but Rancé may well have been thinking of his critics and enemies in what, for convenience, we may refer to as the Common Observance. In §47 he refers to them as *ces hommes relâchez*, "these lax people."

[96] 2 Chr 25:18, which actually reads, *Carduus qui est in Libano misit ad cedrum Libani*, "The thistle that is in Lebanon sent to the cedar of Lebanon."

was the voice, the adornment, and the defense of the Church; these others, in order to remain part of it, occupy very different places. Thus, despite the envy of these lax people, the Church will never cease to sing to his glory these words of blessing: *Mirificavit Dominus sanctum suum.*

48. My brothers, those to whom God has given more appropriate and more religious sentiments should show their gratitude by the care with which they display in what they do that which he has engraved on their inmost heart. In all that they do in their lives, they must take note—if it is possible—of those divine characteristics that molded [the life] of this great saint. They should bear witness, by the fidelity with which they embrace all that he taught and practiced, that his instructions contain nothing that is not holy and pleasing, and that those who observe [these instructions] religiously and lovingly will find in them both their sanctification and their comfort.

49. Such are some of the graces, my brothers, that you should await from the goodness of God, and if there is anything that will enable you to deserve [this goodness], it will be the intervention of this great saint, it will be his intercession. Let us have him look on us with favor by the ardor of our prayers and the sincerity of our intentions. Let us act in such a way that our determination in acquitting ourselves of our duties and fulfilling the promises we have made to Jesus Christ obliges him to beg [God's] mercy [for us], and let us press the case so strongly and earnestly on this blessed day that [God] will at last open his generous hands, that he will pour out upon our souls his abundant blessings from the heights of heaven, [blessings] which, like heavenly dew,[97] will bestow upon them that holy fruitfulness without which they will be condemned to the fire, as will those barren trees that, in the field of the Church, occupy positions of which they are not worthy.

---

[97] See Gen 27:28, 39.

50. I hope, my brothers, that we shall escape this misfortune and that, sustained by the example, instructions, and prayers of this great saint, we shall finish the course happily and win that immortal crown that he has intended for those who have kept the faith and fought [for it][98] in accordance with the instructions and rules he has prescribed for them.

---

[98] See 1 Cor 9:24-25.

7

Bernard Returns to Metz

Jacques-Bénigne Bossuet

INTRODUCTION

It is generally agreed that Jacques-Bénigne Bossuet was the greatest preacher in the France of Louis XIV, especially in his funeral orations. It was not always generally agreed, for there were those in the eighteenth century who thought that the laurels should have been bestowed on Jean-Baptiste Massillon. It was Jean-Siffrein cardinal Maury who, if not entirely responsible, was certainly a driving force behind the elevation of Bossuet to the dignity he surely deserves. "See the French Demosthenes," he cries; "See before you Bossuet! We may praise his oratorical writings in the same way that Quintilian praised the Jupiter of Phidias, when he said that the statue had added something to the religious life of the people."[1] Bossuet, he continues, "was, in Europe, the true creator and the most perfect model of pulpit eloquence," but (adds the cardinal) he also had the wisdom to end his oratorical career in 1687 at the age of sixty with the greatest of his funeral orations, for *le grand Condé*, Louis II de Bourbon, prince de Condé.[2] Madame de Sévigné, on the other hand, preferred Louis Bourdaloue,

---

[1] Maury, 1:61, referring to Quintilian, *Institutio oratoria* 12.10.9. There is a vast literature on Bossuet's preaching and on Bossuet as a preacher.
[2] Maury, 1:61, 74.

but it would be improper for us to enter here into that sermon-judging so vigorously condemned (as we shall see) by François Ogier and Esprit Fléchier. Let us content ourselves, then, with simply saying that Bossuet was undoubtedly one of the greatest preachers ever to grace the pulpit in the reign of the Sun King. No one, I am sure, will disagree with that. He was also one of the greatest, if not the greatest, friend of Armand-Jean de Rancé, abbot of La Trappe.

The standard biographies tell us that Bossuet was born in Dijon on the night of September 27–28, 1627, and we will not discuss certain Burgundian traditions that cast some doubt on this date. The month and year at least are certain. He studied at the Jesuit College—the *Collège des Godrans*—in Dijon, and while he was there his father was appointed as judge to the *parlement* of Metz. Bossuet remained in Dijon in the care of his uncle until he went to the *Collège de Navarre* in Paris to complete his studies. Having done so, and done so with distinction, he left Paris to join his father in Metz, and there, in the cathedral of Metz in 1649, he was ordained deacon. He took his doctoral degree in 1652, was ordained to the priesthood the same year, and at about the same time was appointed archdeacon of Metz.[3]

Metz was (and is) an interesting city. Situated in Lorraine, at the confluence of the Moselle and Seille Rivers, its origins lie far back in the mists of Celtic Gaul, but its strategic position meant that its citizens had often had to fight to maintain their freedom. The fourteenth and fifteenth centuries were especially hard, but one of the most notable confrontations took place in 1153 when there was open war between Stephen, bishop of Metz, and Matthew, duke of Lorraine. The situation became so serious, and bloodshed so imminent, that the archbishop of Trèves, Hillin de Falmagne, went to Clairvaux to beg the aid of Bernard who, at that time, was nearing the end of his life (he died six months later). Bernard responded by immediately

---

[3] See Georges Minois, *Bossuet. Entre Dieu et le Soleil* (Paris: Perrin, 2003), 61–68, for details and dates.

setting off for Metz and, once having arrived, straightaway set to work to reconcile the contending parties. Such was the power of his persuasion and personality that he succeeded in putting a temporary end to the hostilities, but even he was not able to ensure a lasting peace. The dramatic events of 1153 are recounted by Bossuet in his panegyric on Saint Bernard, which was preached in the cathedral of Metz in 1653, the five hundredth anniversary of the deliverance of the city.[4] Bossuet, we might add, considered Bernard (after Saint Augustine) to be one of the greatest Doctors of the Church, and according to his secretary, the abbé François Ledieu, he read and reread his works many times in his battles with the Quietists.[5] Late in his life, in 1689, he preached a second panegyric on the saint to the Bernardines of the Pont-aux-Dames in the diocese of Meaux, but of that discourse we have, alas, no record.[6]

By that date, Metz had been officially French for five years. Before that, it had, in theory, been part of the German Empire, but in practice the city had regarded itself as occupying a virtually independent position between Germany and France. In 1552, however, Henry II of France seized the three bishoprics of Metz, Toul, and Verdun, but it was not until the end of the

---

[4] The date was established by the *abbé* Joseph Lebarq, *Œuvres oratoires de Bossuet. Tome premier: 1648–1655*, ed. Joseph Lebarq (Lille/Paris: Desclée, De Brouwer, 1890), 391, n. 1, and is accepted by Bernard Velat in his edition of *Bossuet: Oraisons funèbres, Panégyriques*, Bibliothèque de la Pléiade, 33 (Paris: Gallimard, 1951), 909. In the *Panégyrique de Saint Bernard par Bossuet. Édition classique accompagnée de remarques et notes littéraires et précédée d'une notice* (Paris: J. Delalain et fils, 1877), 4, A.-M. Lebobe suggested 1656, but this may safely be discounted. His edition, we might add, is not *classique*, the page and a half of the *notice précédée* tells us nothing we do not know, and the *remarques et notes littéraires* are of no consequence.

[5] [François Ledieu], *L'abbé Le Dieu. Mémoires et Journal sur la vie et les ouvrages de Bossuet. I, Mémoires et fragments de l'abbé Le Dieu*, ed. René-François Guettée (Paris: Didier, 1856), 57.

[6] See [Ledieu], *L'abbé Le Dieu*, 57.

Thirty Years' War and the signing of the Treaty of Westphalia in 1648 that the city was formally conceded to France. Bossuet arrived four years later and found a city containing a very mixed population, with an unusually high proportion of Jews and, especially, Protestants, who seem to have formed at least a third of the population.[7] Bossuet refers to them as "our adversaries" at the very beginning of his panegyric.

Bossuet's residence in Metz came to an end in 1656 when he returned to Dijon for three months and then made his way to Paris, where he took up residence at the Doyenné du Louvre.[8] Once in Paris, his skill in preaching came to the ear of the king, and in 1662 he received the royal command to preach the Lenten *station* at the Louvre.[9] He had already preached the series to the Minims in Paris in 1660[10] and to the Carmelites of the Faubourg Saint-Jacques in 1661,[11] but the *station* of 1662 would be before the Sun King himself, Queen Marie-Thérèse, the widowed and exiled Henrietta Maria of England, and all the nobility of the Court.

Bossuet's sermons were well received, but the royal favor was not to last. Early in 1663, Bossuet opposed the king's will with regard to certain matters involving the relationship of the Church in France to the Papal See, and the king was not pleased. Bossuet, therefore, was not called back to preach at Court until the Advent series of 1665,[12] and exactly how he found himself once again in the king's favor is unclear. It might

---

[7] See Ella K. Sanders, *Jacques Bénigne Bossuet: A Study* (London: SPCK, 1921), 55.

[8] See Amable Floquet, *Études sur la vie de Bossuet jusqu'à son entrée en fonctions en qualité de précepteur du Dauphin (1627–1670)* (Paris: Firmin Didot frères, 1855), 2:28.

[9] See the excellent collection of twelve papers (and "éléments bibliographiques" [pp. 231–48]) in *Littératures classiques* 46 (2002), "Bossuet. Le Carême du Louvre (1662)."

[10] Lebarq, *Œuvres oratoires*, 3:213–467.

[11] Lebarq, *Œuvres oratoires*, 3:541–770.

[12] Lebarq, *Œuvres oratoires*, 4:545–616. See Minois, *Bossuet*, 176–78.

have been through the influence of the queen mother, Anne of Austria. Once he was back in favor, however, the king nominated him to be bishop of Condom, a rather neglected (but surprisingly rich[13]) diocese in Gascony, and after various delays he was consecrated as its bishop on September 21, 1670. Bossuet had had every intention of moving to Condom and taking up his duties (he had very strong opinions on the obligations and responsibilities of bishops), but shortly before his consecration he had been appointed, quite unexpectedly, as tutor to the nine-year-old dauphin. This was a coveted position, though there is no evidence that Bossuet had sought it, and the fortunate preceptor might expect to be rewarded with a suitably rich benefice after his tutorial labors were over. But Bossuet could not see how he could dedicate himself fully to the education of the young prince and to the affairs of a distant bishopric, and in October 1671 he resigned the see.

That he was utterly dedicated in his attempt to educate the dauphin cannot be doubted, but, despite an early optimism, he was disappointed. On July 6, 1677, he wrote to his friend the Maréchal de Bellefonds, saying that since Monseigneur (the dauphin) was now growing up, he could not be much longer under Bossuet's care. "There is much to endure," he went on, "with so inattentive a mind: one sees no perceptible encouragement, and one goes on, as Saint Paul says, hoping against hope."[14]

By this time, Bossuet and Rancé, now abbot of La Trappe for some thirteen years, were fast friends. How they first met is unclear, but in 1681 Bossuet wrote to Rancé from Paris saying

---

[13] See Minois, *Bossuet*, 198–99. According to Cardinal Bausset, when Bossuet resigned the bishopric, "il perdoit *quarante mille livres* [£40,000] de rente" (Louis-François de Bausset, *Histoire de Bossuet, Évêque de Meaux, composée sur les manuscrits originaux*, 4th ed. (Paris: De Lebel, 1824), 1:224 [Bausset's emphasis]).

[14] [Jacques-Bénigne Bossuet], *Correspondance de Bossuet*, ed. Charles Urbain and Eugène Levesque (Paris: Hachette, 1909–1925), 2:35 (Letter 156), quoting Rom 4:18.

that he hoped to visit him and spend some time in prayer at the abbey: "I shall make the journey with all possible discretion, and, since I have other reasons to be in Normandy,[15] that will also cover my journey to La Trappe. Only the king need know of it, and he will certainly approve. My heart is full of joy when I think that I will actually accomplish my resolve, and I implore you to agree to it."[16] As it happened, Bossuet's duties in Paris prevented him from realizing his dream until October 1682.

His thankless task of trying to educate the dauphin had come to an end in 1681, and the former bishop of Condom could justly expect a royal appointment to another and more prestigious see. Suitable sees, however, were by no means plentiful. A number of them were traditionally reserved for members of the nobility; Bossuet was not of the nobility, and that was not something Louis was prepared to overlook. Thus, when it was suggested to him that Bossuet be elevated to Beauvais or Lyon or Sens, the suggestions came to nothing. But when the aged and infirm Monseigneur Dominique de Ligny, bishop of Meaux, died on April 27, 1681, the king acted with dispatch. Meaux was (for Louis) if not an ideal, certainly a convenient choice. It was close to the Court, where, said the king, the bishop's presence would always be welcome and desired,[17] and—more important—it was not a see traditionally held by a member of the nobility. Bossuet's appointment as bishop of Meaux was confirmed on November 17, 1681, and he administered the diocese until his death on April 12, 1704.

It is clear that Bossuet had told Rancé of his appointment to Meaux and that Rancé had promised to pray for him.[18]

---

[15] He intended to visit one of his benefices, the priory of Plessis-Grimoult, not far from Caen (see Bossuet, *Correspondance*, 2:241, n. 7).

[16] Bossuet, *Correspondance*, 2:241 (Letter 233).

[17] E. Bellon, *Bossuet, Directeur de conscience* (Paris: Bloud et Barral, 1895), 104.

[18] Bossuet, *Correspondance*, 2:240 (Letter 233): "Your promise that you will pray to God to guide me in what I must do as bishop is a great comfort to me."

Finally, in October 1682, the bishop was able to make the visit to La Trappe for which he had so longed. It would be the first of what seem to have been ten visits,[19] and Bossuet clearly loved the place. He used to say that, after his own diocese, La Trappe was the place that gave him most pleasure.[20] When he was there, he participated in all the offices and lived the austere life of a monk of the abbey. He found particular pleasure, said the *abbé* Ledieu, in the celebration of the divine office: "The chanting of the Psalms, which alone disturbed the silence of this vast solitude, the long pauses at Compline,[21] the sweet sounds, tender yet penetrating, of the *Salve Regina*, aroused in him a sort of religious melancholy."[22]

Nor does there seem any doubt that Rancé enjoyed the visits of Bossuet as much as Bossuet enjoyed visiting the abbey. Each day before Vespers the two of them would walk together around the lakes and in the woods that surrounded the monastery, and Cardinal Bausset tells us that the abbot regarded Bossuet's visits as "true favors of Providence."[23] A year before his death, when he was very ill and thought his end was near, Rancé said to the *abbé* of Saint-André, afterward *grand vicaire* of Meaux, "I would die content if I could see him [Bossuet] just one more time and receive his holy blessing."[24] Rancé died on October 27, 1700,

---

[19] Bausset, *Histoire de Bossuet*, 2:195–96, lists only eight visits, ending in 1696. The *abbé* Serrant, however, on the authority of Dom Gervaise, mentions a later visit, which almost certainly took place in the summer of 1698 (Marie-Léon Serrant, *L'Abbé de Rancé et Bossuet: ou, Le grand moine et le grand évêque du grand siècle* [Paris: C. Douniol, 1903], 494–95). There was also a visit in 1686, not noticed by Bausset: see Bossuet, *Correspondance*, 3:305 and n. 12 (Letter 402), and Serrant, *L'Abbé de Rancé*, 272–73.

[20] Bausset, *Histoire de Bossuet*, 2:196.

[21] This was characteristic of chant at La Trappe: see Dubois, *Histoire de l'abbé de Rancé*, 1:657–64.

[22] Bausset, *Histoire de Bossuet*, 2:196, quoting Ledieu.

[23] Bausset, *Histoire de Bossuet*, 2:197.

[24] Rancé, *Correspondance*, 2:664 (Letter 820627) = Bossuet, *Correspondance*, 2:306–7 (Letter 256).

and Bossuet heard the news from his successor as abbot of La Trappe, Jacques de La Cour, on November 3: "Monsieur de Meaux exhibited great sadness at this news, as at the loss of the best friend he had in the world. And it is true that the illustrious abbot had had a tender love for him and, throughout his whole life, had regarded him with special esteem."[25]

Bossuet's panegyric on Saint Bernard is a young man's work—Bossuet was in his mid-twenties—and although it has some very fine passages, it does not yet have the grandeur of the great orations of his maturity. Nor does it have the balance we might seek, for the exordium is certainly too long, and—if I may put it bluntly—looks to me too much like a young and brilliant theologian showing off. Tréverret, on the other hand, considers the panegyric on Bernard, together with that on Saint Paul, to be excellent specimens of their genre (though they take second place to the best of the funeral orations) and notes that that on Saint Bernard "is very well regarded today"—that is to say, in 1868.[26] Yet he must admit that the sermon is somewhat lacking in those firm historical facts that, for Tréverret, are so important. The panegyric, he says, "is full of magnificence and poetry, of theological and moral instruction; more abundant than the others in historical details, but yet incomplete in this matter since the greatest deeds of the saint are still left in shadow."[27] In all his panegyrics, continues Tréverret, Bossuet remains faithful to the methodical forms of composition adopted by the orators of his day, dividing each discourse into two or three distinct parts. Yet there is nothing dry in his exposition, for what might have been dry and lacking in *onction* is transformed by his profound knowledge of the ways of God and the innermost thoughts of men and women, his remark-

---

[25] Ledieu, *L'Abbé Le Dieu. Mémoires et Journal sur la vie et les ouvrages de Bossuet. II, Journal de l'abbé Le Dieu I*, 161.

[26] Tréverret, 59. The two panegyrics are given a chapter to themselves: chap. V (59–67).

[27] Tréverret, 63.

able imagination, his innumerable echoes of the Bible and the Fathers, and the power with which he presents his ideas.[28] In short, of all the panegyrists of the seventeenth century, there is no doubt that Bossuet is Tréverret's favorite.

Bossuet takes as his text 1 Corinthians 2:2: "I did not judge myself to know anything among you, save Jesus Christ, and him crucified" (his own translation is very slightly different). It is an appropriate text for a sermon in which the dominant themes are penance and penitence—*pénitence*[29]—and an utter contempt for the world and the things of the world. He opens his panegyric by explaining why the French Church has introduced the custom of beginning a homily "by invoking the divine assistance through the intercession of blessed Mary," and this allows him to introduce Bernard as a man with a deep devotion to the Mother of God and the most faithful and chaste of her children. But no sooner does Bernard appear than he disappears, and Bossuet launches into a too long and ferociously theological exordium beginning with a discussion of Jesus as the High Priest of the Epistle to the Hebrews. This leads to an extended and far from simple discussion of God as pure reason and intelligence, the eternal generation of the Son, the nature of creation and how it cannot be other than good and reasonable, the incarnation, the hypostatic union and its consequences (such as *communicatio idiomatum* and how it works), ending with an explanation of Jesus' "theandric activities." The purpose of all this is to show that we need no other source of instruction than the Divine Wisdom—all other wisdom is as nothing compared with this—and that Jesus Christ was himself the incarnation of truth and true doctrine.

Why do we not see this? Why do we not act upon it? Because of our attachment to the world and the senses. But in his crucifixion Jesus epitomizes that mortification and contempt for the world that is essential if we are to be saved. The cross

---

[28] Tréverret, 76–77.
[29] See appendix 1, s.v. *pénitence* / penitence.

itself is the book, written in the blood of Christ, that we must study, and that is just what Bernard did (who now reappears in §15). Bossuet then divides his panegyric into two parts: the first deals with Bernard's Christian life—i.e., the way in which he practiced the life of the Gospel in himself—and the second with his apostolic life: his life of preaching and practicing the Gospel in the world. In this, Bossuet is at one with all the panegyrists we have met so far, with the exception of his friend Rancé, who reverses the order.

In the first part, Bossuet begins by showing how Bernard renounced the world not as a weary old man or overenthusiastic young boy, but at an age when it had everything to offer him. Bossuet's description of youth and its perils are quite splendid and all too accurate. Bernard, he tells us, is a young man in his early twenties with all a young man's optimism, foolishness, and, above all, hope! He has all that anyone could ask: education, intelligence, good looks, good manners, and nobility. But he gives them all up for the cross. Bossuet mentions his early asceticism—the famous icy pool appears in §23—and then passes on to Bernard's life at Cîteaux under the austere guidance of Stephen Harding (there is a veiled criticism of Cluniac monasticism here). He did not notice what was there in front of him, he had no interest in what he ate, he chose a damp and unwholesome place in which to live, and he slept on the bare floor. He was truly dead to the world, and his ascetic and penitential way of life is a rebuke to our own. We must change our own way of life and change it completely, for our salvation, the thing we neglect most, is the most important thing of all.

So much for Bernard the ascetic. It is familiar material. But let us note that nowhere does Bossuet mention him as a mystic or, indeed, spiritual teacher, save for exemplifying in himself the penitential spirituality of seventeenth-century France. We then turn to Bernard's work in the world. Bossuet begins with Bernard's conversion of his own family—his uncle, brothers (he tells the story of Nivard), his sister (a conversion that takes some time), and finally his father. All this is taken from the first book of the *Vita prima* of William of Saint-Thierry, which is Bossuet's source for almost everything he tells us of Bernard's life. He then goes on to mention the community at Clairvaux, united in a "companionship of penitence," but then tells us how Bernard had to leave his abbey to deal with events in the world. Bossuet is unusually brief here: he mentions only the papal schism and refers by name only to "Pierre Léon," i.e., Anacletus, and Duke William X of Aquitaine. He is equally brief in his mention of "signs and wonders" (§44)—they are dismissed in a single sentence—and when he mentions Bernard's letters of censure and rebuke to princes, potentates, bishops, cardinals, and popes, he mentions no names and no specific writings. There then follows a peroration against the Protestants—Metz was the center of Protestantism in the Lorraine—and Bossuet mentions, but only in passing, Bernard's involvement in fighting "suspect doctrine" and in resolving quarrels among princes. But once again, he mentions no names and provides no details: he does not even mention Abelard, and that is most unusual. Almost everyone else does.

We then get a fine elegy in praise of Metz—"Puissante ville de Metz . . . O belle et noble cité!" (§48)—mentioning Bernard's intervention, in the last year of his life, in the war between Stephen, bishop of Metz, and Matthew, duke of Lorraine. Then, as Bernard's life draws to its close, so does Bossuet's panegyric. He concludes with a further call to penance and penitence, and a fervent call for Christians to return to God and take up, once again, the cross of mortification. He ends with a prayer to Bernard that the saint will intercede with God to bring peace to France, for France in 1653 was in a parlous state. Just a week before Bossuet delivered his panegyric the royal troops had seized Villeneuve-sur-Lot, one of the last towns to hold out in the civil war of the Fronde. France, in fact, was involved in one war or another for almost the whole of Bossuet's life.

The sources named or quoted by Bossuet in his panegyric are far from numerous. The New Testament predominates (there are only about four verses from the Old: from Exodus, Job,

1 Samuel, and Proverbs), and it is the Pauline and pseudo-Pauline epistles that take pride of place. The most commonly cited is 1 Corinthians, from which, as we have seen, Bossuet takes his text. Of the gospels, Luke and John both provide about half a dozen citations. Apart from that, there is one echo of Gregory the Great, a vague reminiscence of Aristotle, a single quotation from Augustine's *Confessions*, and a great deal of material from the *Vita prima* of William of Saint-Thierry, Arnold of Bonneval, and Geoffrey of Auxerre (but primarily William), for which Bossuet undoubtedly used Horstius's edition, first published in 1641. The better edition of Mabillon did not appear until 1667, fourteen years after Bossuet preached the panegyric. He may also have consulted Le Maistre's *Vie*, which had appeared five years earlier. There is no quotation at all from any of Bernard's own works, nor any mention of any of his writings by name, and the passage from Bernard's Sermon 30 on the Song of Songs that appears at the end of §28 has been interpolated into the text by some unknown early editor.

Such is the thread of Bossuet's panegyric, but to appreciate in full his arguments, sentiments, and style, we need to read the whole of his sermon. It could not have been delivered in less than an hour and a quarter, but that, as we have seen, is not unusual for a seventeenth-century French sermon, and I have done my best to render Bossuet's splendidly stately French into a reasonably stately English.

PANEGYRIC ON SAINT BERNARD
METZ, AUGUST 20, 1653[30]

*Non enim judicavi me scire aliquid inter vos,
nisi Jesum Christum, et hunc crucifixum.* (1 Cor 2:2)

"I did not think that I knew anything at all among you,
if it is not Jesus Christ, and Jesus Christ crucified."[31]

1. In the last century, our churches in France introduced the devout custom of beginning homilies by invoking divine assistance through the intercession of blessed Mary. Since our adversaries[32] could not bear to see us offering so just an honor to the holy Virgin, and since they condemned it with invectives as scathing as they were rash and unjust, the Church believed that it was well to resist their audacious attempts by recommending this devotion to the faithful all the more strongly as the heresy that opposed it grew more furious. And since we have nothing more worthy of veneration than the preaching of the holy Gospel, it is at that point that [the Church] invites all its children to solicit the prayers of Mary, knowing how beneficial that will be for them.

2. But it seems to me that there is another and more specific reason for this holy ceremony: it is because the duty of preachers is to give birth to Jesus Christ in the souls [of their hearers].

---

[30] I have translated the panegyric from Bernard Velat's edition in his *Bossuet: Oraisons funèbres, Panégyriques*, 287–314 (henceforth cited as Velat), with notes on 908–28, but have compared it throughout with that of Lebarq, *Œuvres oratoires*, 391–421 (henceforth cited as Lebarq). This is the only panegyric on Bernard of which there is an English translation, and that in an abridged form. It is to be found in Denis O'Mahony, *Panegyrics of the Saints from the French of Bossuet and Bourdaloue* (London: Kegan Paul, Trench, Trubner & Co.; and St. Louis, MO: B. Herder Book Co., 1924), 85–109.

[31] This is Bossuet's translation and is sufficiently accurate.

[32] The *adversaires* are the Protestants, who, with Jews, were particularly numerous in Metz. Bossuet will say more on Protestants later in his panegyric.

"My little children," says the apostle [Paul], "for whom I am again in labor until Jesus Christ be formed in you" (Gal 4:19). You see how [Saint Paul] generates and gives birth to Jesus Christ in our souls? In just the same way, there is a certain similarity between preachers of the divine word and the holy Mother of God. This is why the great Saint Gregory was not afraid to give the title of "mothers of Christ" to those called to this glorious ministry.[33] Thus the Church was easily persuaded that you, O most blessed Mary, blessed among all women,[34] you who were predestined from eternity to give birth according to the flesh to the Son of the Most High, would willingly help through your devout intercession those who must now engender Him spiritually in the hearts of all the faithful.

3. But in what preaching should we hope more for your help than in that which these people are awaiting today? We are about to praise the grace and divine mercy in the holiness of the devout Bernard,[35] of that Bernard who was the most faithful and chaste of your children, who, more than any other, has honored your glorious maternity, who has best imitated your angelic purity, who believed that he owed to your care and your maternal love[36] the continual influx of graces that he received from your dear son. Help us, then, by your holy prayers, oh most blessed Mary! Help us to praise this product

---

[33] Gregory the Great, *Homiliae in Evangelium* 3.2; PL 76:1086D: "Whoever, through believing, is a brother or sister of Christ is made his mother by preaching."

[34] Bossuet is echoing Luke 1:28 and the *Ave Maria*.

[35] In the course of the panegyric, Bossuet refers to Bernard as *dévot* (as here), *pieux, admirable, bienheureux, humble, vénérable,* and *zélé*. Of these descriptions, *pieux* is the most common, but since there is no satisfactory English translation (see appendix 1, s.v. *piété* / piety), I have simply rendered it as "pious." *Dévot* "devout" is stronger than "pious," and, according to Velat, "au XVIIe siècle, ce mot *dévot* désignait les personnes qui faisaient profession de piété" (Velat, 910, n. 8).

[36] *Charité maternelle*: see appendix 1, s.v. *charité* / charity.

of your prayers. To this end we cast ourselves at your feet, greeting you and saying to you with the angel, "*Ave!*"[37]

4. Among the various ornaments worn by the high priest of the old Law, that which seems to me to be the most remarkable was the mysterious breastplate on which, according to Scripture, he bore the Urim and Thummim, that is to say, truth and doctrine[38]—or, as other interpreters understand it, light and perfection. I know that this is written to help us see what the qualities of those who minister to sacred things should be, but even though their magnificent vestments seem to make them so exceptional, it is not that which should distinguish them from [ordinary] people. No. The true priestly characteristic, the true ornament of a high priest, is doctrine and truth. And that is what is set before us in this passage.

5. But if we take these thoughts further, if we see the high priest of the Old Testament as a shadow and symbol of Jesus Christ, who is the end of the Law and the high priest of the new covenant,[39] we will find something even more wonderful. Christians, it is this holy high priest, it is this great sacrificer, who truly carries on himself doctrine, perfection, and truth. These are not to be found on precious stones[40] or in graven letters, as was the case with the children of Aaron, but in his blameless actions and in his wholly divine conduct.

6. To grasp this truth (which is essential for understanding our text), bear in mind, if you will, that Jesus Christ, our Master, is the Son of God. You have been too well taught not to know that God did not give birth to him in an ordinary way

---

[37] Luke 1:28.
[38] See Exod 28:30 and Lev 8:8, referring to *doctrina* and *veritas*. The precise nature of the urim and thummin remains uncertain, though Bossuet, together with most modern commentators, thought that they were precious stones (see n. 40 below). Whatever they were, they were undoubtedly used for divination.
[39] Bossuet's exposition is here based on the Epistle to the Hebrews.
[40] See n. 38 above.

and that there was nothing material or corruptible about his generation. "God is spirit,"[41] faithful people, and exists only as reason and intelligence. It follows, therefore, that he gives birth by means of his intelligence and reason, and does so in such a way that the Son of God is the offspring of a very pure knowledge, and yet, in incomprehensible simplicity, his being never ceases to encompass infinity. Since he is the offspring of divine reason and intelligence, he is himself reason and intelligence, which is why Scripture calls him the Word and Wisdom of the Father.[42]

7. Furthermore, since it is impossible for God to act other than by his reason and his wisdom, it follows from this that we read in the holy Scriptures that God has done everything by means of his Word, who is his Son—*Omnia per ipsum facta sunt* ["All things were made by him" (John 1:3)]—because his Word is his reason and his light. This is why the great machine of the world[43] is such a vast work, gleaming in all its parts with wholly admirable order and excellent reason. Its arrangement cannot be other than good, and all its movements are governed by reason, because they come from a very wise idea, and from a very sure knowledge, and from a sovereign reason, which is

---

[41] John 4:24: *Spiritus est Deus*. Bossuet now embarks upon a formidable patristic exposition, beginning with the idea of God as pure *ratio* and *intelligentia* (Origen, whom Bossuet esteemed, refers to God as a *simplex intellectualis natura* [*De principiis* 1.1.6]) and continuing with a discussion of what, in technical terms, are the doctrines of eternal generation, hypostatic union (see n. 49 below), and *communicatio idiomatum* (see n. 47 below). We may perhaps question how much of this was intelligible to his congregation at Metz. The exposition, which lasts for five paragraphs (§§6–10), is that of a young man still fresh from his university studies. The older and more experienced Bossuet would never have done it (see n. 60 below).

[42] See John 1:1; 1 Cor 1:24, 30.

[43] Velat, 911, n. 25, suggests Lucretius as a source for the expression *machina mundi*, but the term appears in a number of patristic and medieval theologians, from Tertullian to Alan of Lille.

the Word and the Son of God, by whom all things were made and by whom they are arranged and governed.

8. But, faithful people, after this divine Word had let his wisdom shine forth in the structure and government of the universe (for as the apostle Saint John says, all things were made by him [John 1:3]), then, moved by inconceivable love for our [human] nature, he showed himself to us in a way that was altogether more familiar and more excellent, in a work that, though it was yet more divine, did not fail to bring goodness even closer to us. How is this? you ask. Ah! You see here the great plan of our good God, and the great comfort of the faithful: as you know, this eternal Word was made man in the fullness of time. He united himself to our nature, he took on humanity in the womb of blessed Mary, and it is this miraculous union that gave us Jesus Christ, God and man, our Master and our Savior.

9. Thus, since the holy humanity of Jesus was united with the divine Word, it was ruled and governed by this same Word. I beg you to pay careful attention to this[44] and understand the reasoning. Just as human reason governs the appetites of the body with which it is united in such a way that even the very lowest part participates in some way in reason, inasmuch as it submits to [reason] and obeys it, so the divine Word governs the humanity with which it has clothed itself, and since it has made [this humanity] its own in such an extraordinary way, it also rules it. It moves and animates it with ineffable care in an indescribable way, so that all the actions of this human nature, which the divine Word has appropriated[45] to itself, are completely filled with this uncreated wisdom, which is the Son of God and is worthy of the eternal Word, with which it is divinely united and by which it is governed in such a singular

---

[44] A necessary plea! See n. 41 above.

[45] "que le Verbe divin s'est appropriée." *Appropriare* is a technical term and may be found used in this sense in Cassian, Thomas of Perseigne, Alan of Lille, Peter of Poitiers, and especially the Victorines.

way. Thus, when the ancient Fathers [of the Church] spoke of the actions of this God-Man, they called them "theandric activities,"[46] that is to say, activities that were a mixture of the divine and the human, activities at one and same time both divine and human: human by their nature, divine by their principle. Moreover, since the God-Word made the holy humanity of Jesus his own, he also regarded the [human] actions as his own,[47] and through them there ran unceasingly an influx of wholly divine grace and wisdom that animated them and raised them beyond anything we can conceive.

10. Given this teaching, it is not difficult for us to apply to it the words of the holy apostle [Paul], which form the basis for this whole discourse.[48] I say, therefore, that since the humanity of Jesus was in such close contact with the divine Word and belonged to it by such an intimate type of union, in the interests of its own glory, it had no choice but to guide it by its wisdom. The result of that was that all the acts of Jesus stemmed from a divine principle and from a foundation of infinite wisdom.[49] Therefore, if we wish to appreciate in what esteem we should hold the things set before us [in the gospels], we have only to consider how the Savior Jesus chose some and scorned others during his life on earth. Since he is the substantial Word of the

---

[46] "opérations théandriques." Bossuet is here translating the Greek expression θεανδρικά ἐνεργεία, an expression that caused the Fathers considerable problems: see the essential information in Geoffrey W. H. Lampe, *A Patristic Greek Lexicon* (Oxford: Clarendon Press, 1978), 615.

[47] Bossuet is echoing the principle of *communicatio idiomatum*, i.e., the theory that while the divine and human natures in Christ always remain distinct, the attributes of one may be predicated of the other because of the hypostatic union (see n. 49 below).

[48] I.e., 1 Cor 2:2, the text for his sermon.

[49] This is a simplified corollary of the doctrine of the hypostatic union, i.e., the union of the divine and human natures in the one Person (*hypostasis*) of the incarnate Christ. See also n. 47 above.

Father, all his actions speak to us, and all his deeds provide us with instruction.

11. It is always said that the best way of teaching is by doing. An action, in fact, has indescribably more life and more impact than the most eloquent words. It is also for this reason that the Son of God, this divine teacher whom God sent us from heaven, chose this lofty way of teaching us by his actions, and since this instruction is all the more persuasive and all the more powerful because it is ruled by the very wisdom of God, we can rest assured that it can lack nothing. Behold the inconceivable goodness of our God! Seeing that we were forced to go to various places to draw from them the beneficent waters of truth (not without great labor and the grave danger of losing our way in so difficult a quest), he has set before us his dear Son, in whom he has gathered together all those truths that are useful for us, as in a holy and mysterious epitome. And, looking with pity on our ignorance and lack of resolve, he arranged his life in such a way that, through it, everything necessary for moral conduct is set forth with the utmost clarity. Thus it is that the apostle Saint Paul assures us that "in Jesus Christ are hidden all the treasures of knowledge and wisdom" (Col 2:3). And this is why, says the same Saint Paul, I do not look for good doctrine either in the titillating[50] writings or uncertain reasonings of philosophers and orators, puffed up with their own eloquence. I study the Savior Jesus alone, and in him I see all things.[51] In this way, faithful people, Jesus is not only our Master; he is also the object of all our knowledge. He is not only the light that guides us to the truth,[52] but he himself is the Truth that our knowledge seeks to know.[53] This is why we are called Christians: not only because we profess that we follow no other master save Jesus Christ, but also because we

---

[50] *écrits curieux*: see appendix 1, s.v. *curiosité* / curiosity.
[51] Bossuet is paraphrasing the ideas of 1 Cor 2.
[52] See John 8:12; 12:46; and elsewhere.
[53] See John 14:6.

glory in knowing nothing other than Jesus Christ. And there is no doubt that if we seek other teachings, we will get nothing from them, for in the Word made man Knowledge itself has spoken to us, and, in order to teach us, Wisdom has done in our presence what needed to be done, and Truth itself has been revealed to our spirit and made visible to our eyes.

12. You see how Jesus Christ, our great high priest,[54] carried on himself doctrine and truth.[55] But more than that, it was on the cross that he fulfilled his duty as the highest of priests. It is there, my brothers, it is there that, despite the fury of his enemies and the shame of his ignominious nakedness, he appeared to us attired in the best possible way in his beautiful adornments of doctrine and truth. Jesus was the book in which God has written our instructions; but it is on the cross that this great book is opened wide, by his stretched-out arms, by his cruel wounds, and by his flesh pierced in so many places. And after such a wonderful lesson, what is left for us to learn?

13. Faithful people, the thing that deludes us, the thing that hinders us from recognizing the highest good (which is the only fruitful knowledge), is the attachment and blind esteem we have for the things of the senses. It is this that forced the Savior Jesus to choose willingly the injuries, the torments, and death. And not only that. Of all injuries, he chose the most painful, of all tortures, the most vile, and of all forms of death, the most excruciating. This he did to make us see how contemptible are the things that deluded mortals call goods, and [to show us] that whatever the extremity of misery, poverty, or sorrow to which we might be reduced, we may always be strong, rich, and happy provided that God dwells within us.

14. These are the truths, Christians, that the great high priest Jesus shows us written on his torn body, and it is this that he cries out to us by the many mouths of his wounds. The cross, therefore, is not only the sanctuary of the high priest and the

---

[54] See n. 39 above.
[55] See n. 38 above.

altar of a victim, but the pulpit of a master and the high-seat of a lawgiver. It is for this reason that after the apostle Saint Paul has said that he knows nothing save Jesus Christ, he straightaway adds "and him crucified" (1 Cor 2:2); for if we are shown these Christian truths in the life of Jesus, we read them with yet greater impact in his death, sealed and confirmed by his blood, in such a way that Jesus crucified, the disgrace of the world, who appeared to worldly philosophers as ignorance and folly,[56] has confounded human arrogance by becoming the culmination of our wisdom!

15. Ah! What progress the admirable Bernard made in this wisdom! He was ever at the foot of the cross, reading, pondering,[57] and studying this great book. This book was his first alphabet in the tender years of his infancy; this same book was all [he needed for] counsel in his wise and venerable old age. He would kiss the sacred letters—I mean these wounds so worthy of love, which, for him, were still wholly fresh and scarlet, stained with the precious blood that is both our price and our drink. He would say with the apostle Saint Paul, let the wise of this world be glorified, some for their knowledge of the stars, others for [what they know of] the elements; these for [their knowledge] of ancient and modern history, those for [what they know] of politics. Let them be praised as much as they like for their useless inquisitiveness.[58] As for me, if God will allow me to know Jesus crucified, my knowledge will be perfect and my desires fulfilled. This is all that Saint Bernard

---

[56] See 1 Cor 1:18-25.
[57] The verb is *contempler,* "to contemplate," but Bossuet is not using it any mystical sense. He had, as we saw in chap. 2, little time for mysticism, and *contempler* simply means to reflect on, muse on, think about, ruminate, or (as I have translated it here) ponder. See further appendix 1, s.v. *contemplation* / contemplation.
[58] Paul himself never says exactly this. What we have here is Bossuet's expansion of 1 Cor 1:20.

knew, and since one preaches only what one knows, he, who knew only the cross, preached only the cross.

16. The knowledge of the cross makes Christians; the preaching of the cross produces apostles. This is why Saint Paul, who glories in knowing nothing save Christ crucified,[59] openly and loudly proclaims that he preaches only Christ crucified. So, too, did the devout Saint Bernard. I will show him to you in his private life and in his little cell studying the cross of Jesus, so that you may revere the virtue of this good and perfect Christian. But after that, I will present him to you in the pulpit and in his ecclesiastical functions, preaching and proclaiming the cross of Jesus, so that you may glorify God who sent us this apostle. You will then see, my brothers, the Christian life and the apostolic life of Saint Bernard, both of them founded on the knowledge of our crucified Master. That is the subject of my discourse. It is simple, I confess, but I will bless this simplicity if, in the cross of Jesus, I can show you the source of the admirable qualities of pious Bernard. That is my hope, by the grace of the Holy Spirit, if you will be humbly attentive to his holy word. Let us then begin, with divine help, and enter upon the first part [of our discourse].[60]

[FIRST POINT]

17. If I have been so fortunate as to have you understand what I have just said to you, you should have noticed that

---

[59] See Gal 6:14.

[60] As Lebarq, 399, n. 1, and Velat, 913, n. 66, rightly say, this introductory exordium has been far too long, and shows all the shortcomings of youth. Even Tréverret, who esteemed the panegyric, observes that in this lengthy exordium, Bossuet is less interested in praising Saint Bernard than in teaching us the great mysteries of the Christian faith (Tréverret, 60). Bossuet now moves on to the first of the two main points of his sermon: Bernard's penitential life, which shows us (i) how we must have utter contempt for the things of the world and of the senses, and (ii) the vital necessity of penitence and penance.

the Savior, hanging on the cross, teaches us contempt for the world in a very powerful and very effective way. For if Jesus crucified is the Son and the delight of the Father, if he is his only and well-beloved [Son] and the sole object in which he takes pleasure;[61] and if, nevertheless, he is (according to our way of judging things) the most forsaken and most wretched of mortals, if he is the greatest in the sight of God and the most contemptible in the sight of men, [what does this show us?]. Who is there who cannot see how mistaken we are in our estimate of good and evil, and that the things that are most highly valued by us and most in demand are, in fact, the least and the lowest? It is this that kindles, in the very depths of the soul, a contempt for the world and its vanities among those who are scholars of the cross of our Savior Jesus, [that cross] on which the pomp and false pleasures of earth were eternally condemned. This is why the apostle Saint Paul, contemplating Jesus on the tree of infamy, says, "Ah! I am crucified with my good Master!"[62] I see him, I see him on the cross, stripped of all the goods we value most, bowed down with the worst of all that afflicts and terrifies us. I, who believe him to be Wisdom itself, hold in esteem what he holds in esteem, and what he despised, I despise. With him I crucify myself, and I reject with all my heart the things that he has rejected: *Christo confixus sum cruci!* ["With Christ I am nailed to the cross" (Gal 2:19)].

18. Such are the sentiments of a true Christian, but how hard this truth appears to our [human] understanding. Who can grasp it, faithful people, if Christ himself does not imprint it on our hearts? Thus it is that he delights in commanding us to do things that our whole being finds repugnant so as to make his strength shine forth in our weakness; to bolster up our courage he has set before us a number of prime [examples of] people in whom his grace has made easy what seems to us impossible.

---

[61] See Matt 3:17 and parallels: "This is my beloved Son, in whom I am well pleased."

[62] A paraphrase of Gal 2:19, quoted immediately below.

But among those illustrious men whose example arouses our hope and puts to shame our cowardice, we must confess that the admirable Bernard holds an exalted position. He was a gentleman of an illustrious line who saw his house in high repute and his near relations in important positions, and his birth, his character, and his wealth all promised good fortune. Yet, at the age of twenty-two,[63] he renounced the world, to the extent of becoming [a saint:] Saint Bernard! Christian people, does this seem to you an insignificant effect of divine omnipotence? If he had done it when he was older, it might perhaps have been the distasteful and troubling things, the worries and anxieties, that arose in the course of his life that might have led him to make this change. And if he had made this resolution in the first flower of his youth, at a time when we hardly know who we are and when our passions have not yet come to life, it would have been no more than a lackluster victory. But to show us the triumph of the cross over the vanities [of the world], God chose Saint Bernard in the most remarkable circumstances that we have ever seen in anyone's history.

19. May I describe to you here, in this place, what a young man of twenty-two is like?[64] [May I tell you] about his ardor?

---

[63] Until recently, it was generally thought (following Vacandard) that Bernard and his companions arrived at Cîteaux in the spring of 1112. In 1987, however, Ferruccio Gastaldelli presented a sound case for the later date of May 1113: see Ferruccio Gastaldelli, "I primi vent'anni di San Bernardo: Problemi e Interpretazioni," *Analecta Cisterciensia* 43 (1987): 116–21 ("La data della nascita di san Bernardo e della sua entrata a Cîteaux"). This accords with Mabillon's text of the *Vita prima*, 1.4.19 (William of Saint-Thierry); PL 185:237BC; CF 76:21–22, which reads *Anno ab incarnatione Domini millesimo centesimo decimo tertio* [= 1113], *a constitutione domus Cisterciensis quindecimo, servus Dei Bernardus annos natus circiter tres et viginti [al. duo et viginti], Cistercium ingressus* . . . . Most modern scholars now prefer 1113 and *tres et viginti* (twenty-three).

[64] Velat, 914, n. 82, tells us that in his description of youth, Bossuet is often dependent on Aristotle, *Rhetoric* 2.12.

His impatience? His impetuous desires? His strength, his vigor, his hot and seething blood, just like a heady wine,[65] leave him no room for balanced judgment or moderation. As he grows older, he begins to form his character, his passions attach themselves to various objects, and whichever one dominates at least restrains the vehemence of the others. But in the green of one's youth there is nothing yet fixed or decided, no one passion dominates the others, and [a young man] is violently tossed around by all his passions. There we find the foolish loves, the superfluous goods, the ambition, and the vain desire to show off that exercise their power without any opposition. Everything is done with thoughtless enthusiasm, and how could any of this age, who take pleasure only in hustle and bustle and disorder, and who hardly ever act in a considered way, accustom themselves to the rule, the solitude, and the discipline [of monastic life]? [As Saint Augustine says], *Et pudet non esse impudentem* ["He is ashamed not to be shameless"]![66]

20. It is true that when we see ourselves sliding into old age, when we can already count the long course of years that have slipped away, when our strength is failing, and when the past has become the greater portion of our life, and when our hold on the world is no more than an uncertain future, ah! then the present touches us but little. But in youth we dream that there is nothing that can still escape us, we feel our vigor whole and present, we think of nothing but the present and direct to it all our thoughts. Tell me, I beg you, if someone believes the present to be so completely his own, when will he devote himself to serious thoughts about the future? And there is more: what likelihood is there that we would abandon the world at an age when [the world] seems to offer us nothing that is not pleasurable? We see everything according to our

---

[65] Bossuet was fond of this comparison and elsewhere uses it of those intoxicated by power, riches, or rank: see Velat, 910, n. 84.

[66] Augustine, Conf 2.9.17; PL 32:682. The quotation appears on page 401 of Lebarq's text, but Velat incorrectly omits it (see Velat, 915, n. 90).

present frame of mind, and it follows that youth, which seems to exist only for joy and pleasure, sees nothing to trouble it. Ah! Everything smiles on it, everything commends it. It has no experience yet of the woes of the world, nor of the setbacks that will [inevitably] happen to it, and it therefore imagines that it will experience nothing distasteful or unfavorable. Feeling itself healthy and vigorous, it does away with fear and sets all its sails to be filled and directed by [the wind of] hope.

21. You know, faithful people, that of all the passions, the most delightful is hope.[67] It supports and nourishes us, it sweetens all the bitterness of life. Indeed, we often forgo the blessings we actually have rather than give up our hopes. But it is in youth, which is so reckless and ill-advised, which is always too presumptuous because it has so little experience, which sees no difficulty in anything, that hope is most fervent and most audacious—so much so that young people, intoxicated with their hopes, believe they already possess whatever they seek, and everything they imagine seems to them to be a reality. Enraptured by a certain sweetness that comes from their boundless aspirations, they imagine that they would suffer infinite loss if they abandoned any of their grandiose designs. This is especially the case with persons of high rank, who, having been brought up with an idea of their own importance, and who always build themselves up on the honor of their house and their ancestors, easily persuade themselves that there is nothing to which they cannot lay claim.

---

[67] On Bossuet's understanding of the nature and importance of hope—both hope as a theological virtue and as a human passion—see the interesting paper by André Lebois, "L'Espérance, passion flatteuse," in *Journées Bossuet. La prédication au XVIIe siècle. Actes du Colloque tenu à Dijon les 2, 3 et 4 décembre 1977 pour le trois cent cinquantième anniversaire de la naissance de Bossuet*, ed. Thérèse Goyet and Jean-Pierre Collinet (Clermont-Ferrand: Les Amis de Bossuet, 1980), 209–16.

22. Picture to yourselves now the young Bernard, brought up as a person of quality, with a natural civility, and a character polished by a fine education, good-looking and charming in his appearance, good tempered, gentle, and agreeable in his manners.[68] Ah! What strong chains to keep him shackled to the earth! Such people are always being urged [to bind themselves to worldly things]. One person flatters them, another praises them, one is intent on goading them on, another inspires them with ambition. I know that [Bernard's] pious mother [Aleth] often taught him contempt for the world,[69] but the truth of the matter is that at this usually imprudent age, [young men] are incapable of taking good advice. The counsel of their friends and their peers, who believe no one is as wise as they, prevails over [the advice] of their parents.

23. Triumph, Lord, triumph over all the attractions of this deceitful world, and show the young Bernard, as you showed Saint Paul,[70] what he must endure in your service! Already you have inspired him with a tender devotion to Mary and a generous love of purity, already he has scorned the most dangerous blandishments [of the world] in circumstances that decency prevents me from describing to this congregation,[71] already your grace has led him to seek wholesome and refreshing

---

[68] On Bernard's character, see Gastaldelli, "I primi vent'anni di San Bernardo," 121–26 ("Il carattere del giovane Bernardo").

[69] See *Vita prima* 1.1.1–2 (William of Saint-Thierry); PL 185:227B–28B; CF 76:3–5. For an admirably detailed account of Aleth, see Gastaldelli, "I primi vent'anni di San Bernardo," 141–48 ("Appunti sulla madre di san Bernardo").

[70] See Acts 9:16: "I will show him how much he must suffer for my name's sake."

[71] Bossuet is referring to the stories that appear in the *Vita prima* 1.3.7 (William of Saint-Thierry); PL 185:230D–31B; CF 76:9–10, which include a naked girl climbing into his bed while he was asleep. See further the very sound discussion in Gastaldelli, "I primi vent'anni di San Bernardo," 126–28 ("Le tentazioni di Bernardo ventenne").

baths among the snows and in icy pools,[72] where his assaulted integrity built itself a rampart against the soft allurements of the world. His glance was wholly modest, as were his eyes, for he had learned from your Gospel and your apostle [Peter][73] that even the eyes may commit adultery. Though he has more than human courage, we see on his face the modesty and reserve of a pure and demure maiden. But now, Lord, go on to complete the great work of your grace in the person of this holy young man.

24. And this indeed is what you see, Christian people, as [Bernard] becomes pensive and thoughtful, so much so that he flees this wide world and falls passionately in love with withdrawal and solitude. There he carefully asks himself these or similar questions: Bernard, what do you seek in this world? Do you see anything here that could satisfy you? What, after all, are these false delights that ignorant mortals pursue so passionately, but a short-lived illusion? As soon as that first excitement that makes them so delightful has settled down a little with the course of time, even those who pursued them most eagerly are often amazed at how hard they worked for nothing! Age and experience clearly show us the vanity of the things we have most desired. And even these pleasures, such as they are, occur but rarely in our lives! What happiness can we feel that is not thwarted by sorrow? And if we were to delete from our days all those we have spent badly—even according to the reckoning of the world—could we actually

---

[72] *Vita prima* 1.3.6 (William of Saint-Thierry); PL 185:230C; CF 76:9: on one occasion Bernard found himself gazing at a woman. Suddenly coming to his senses, he leaped into a nearby pool of freezing water—it came up to his neck—and stayed there until, "having become almost bloodless, he had, through the power of co-operating grace, completely cooled himself down from the fire of carnal concupiscence." This is a common *topos* in hagiographical literature.

[73] Matt 5:28: "But I say to you, that whoever looks on a woman to lust after her has already committed adultery with her in his heart"; and 2 Pet 2:14: "Having eyes full of adultery and unceasing sin."

find enough left in the whole of our life to make up three or four months? But even if we agree with those who foolishly love this world that there is a lot in it to love, how long does this happiness last? It flies away, flies away like a phantom that offers us some sort of contentment while it stays with us but, once it departs, leaves us nothing but trouble.

25. Bernard, Bernard, he said, these salad days of youth cannot last forever. The fatal hour will come when all false hopes will be cut short by an irrevocable sentence. Like a false friend, life will fail us in the very midst of our endeavors. Then all our splendid plans will tumble to earth, and all our thoughts will vanish away. The rich, who, during their lives in this world, enjoyed the illusion of a pleasant dream, imagining themselves to possess all manner of good things, will suddenly wake up on the great day of eternity and will be utterly amazed to find themselves empty-handed. Death, our inescapable enemy, will carry away with him all our pleasures and all our honors into oblivion and nothingness. Alas! We speak only of "passing time." Time is indeed passing, and we are passing with it, and that which passes with respect to me by means of time that runs out enters into that eternity that never passes away, and all is gathered up into the treasury of divine knowledge, which, likewise, never passes. Oh eternal God! How great will be our astonishment when the severe Judge, who rules over that other world to which this one leads us whether we like it or not, will set before us our whole life in a single instant and say to us in a terrible voice, "Fools that you are, you so esteemed passing pleasures that you gave no consideration to that which follows and which shall never pass away!"[74]

26. Make haste, then, says [Bernard] in conclusion, and since our life is always carried away by time, which never ceases to escape us, let us try to attach to it something that will stay with us. Then, returning to his great book, which he continually

---

[74] Bossuet has in mind the parable of the foolish rich man in Luke 12:16-21.

studied with inconceivable pleasure (I mean the cross of Jesus), he slaked his thirst in [Christ's] blood, and with this divine liquor drank down a contempt for the world. I come, he said, I come, oh my Master, to crucify myself with you. I see that your gentle eyes, a single glance from which reduced Saint Peter to tears,[75] no longer give forth their light. I will keep my own forever closed to the world's pomp; their light will be extinguished for vanities. I see your divine lips, from which flowed rivers of eternal life, closed by death; I condemn my own to silence, and I will open them only to confess my sins and your mercy. My heart will be as ice to all idle pleasures, and since I see that no part of your body has been left whole, I will bear in my own, from head to toe, the marks of your sufferings, so that one day I may be clothed completely in the glory of your resurrection. Finally, oh my beloved dead [Savior], I will recklessly throw myself down upon you and wrap myself with you in your winding-sheet. For I learn from the apostle that we are buried with you in holy baptism.[76]

27. In this way (as we may easily gather from his writings) the pious Bernard kindled in himself a contempt for the world. His only dream was to find a place for retreat and penance. But since he desired only strictness and humility, he did not throw himself at one of those famous monasteries whose reputation or wealth made them so renowned throughout the world.[77] At that time, a small number of religious were living at Cîteaux under abbot Stephen [Harding].[78] The austerities practiced there prevented it from attracting many followers, but this did

---

[75] See Luke 22:61-62.

[76] Rom 6:4: "For we are buried together [*consepulti*] with him by baptism into death"; Col 2:12: "Buried with him in baptism."

[77] Bossuet is, of course, thinking of Cluny, and Bernard's strictures on what he saw as the Cluniac way of life.

[78] Stephen Harding, the third abbot, was elected in 1108. Bossuet is here echoing the *Vita prima* 1.3.18 (William of Saint-Thierry); PL 185:236D–37A; CF 76:21.

not lead them into any relaxation. They judged it more fitting to persist in it for the love of God than to change anything at all for the love of men. This abbey, which is now so celebrated, was then unrenowned and little known. But since blessed Bernard lived in the neighborhood, he had some knowledge of the virtues of these holy men, and he embraced their rule and their discipline, delighted to have found among them holiness of life, the most rigorous penitence, and obscurity. Once there, he began to live in such a way that he was soon held in admiration, even by these earthly angels, and as they saw him ever growing [in virtue], he was not long among them (young though he was) before they judged him capable of the formation of others.[79] I will leave aside the more dazzling achievements of this great saint, and in order to put to confusion our own negligence, and to praise the grace of God, I will show you a picture of his penitential life drawn from his own words and writings.[80]

28. He used to say that when a novice entered the monastery, he should leave his body at the gate,[81] and this is certainly what the holy man did himself. His senses were mortified

---

[79] Bossuet is presumably referring to Bernard's appointment as abbot of the new foundation of Clairvaux in 1115.

[80] With all due respect to Bossuet, there is actually very little in the discussion that follows that is drawn from Bernard's own words and writings. His main source is the first book of the *Vita prima*, by William of Saint-Thierry, though he also uses the sections by Arnold of Bonneval and Geoffrey of Auxerre. That Bossuet had read Bernard is not in doubt, but he gives little evidence of it in this panegyric.

[81] *Vita prima* 1.4.20 (William of Saint-Thierry); PL 185:238B; CF 76:23: when men hastened to Clairvaux, eager to enter the monastery and become novices, Bernard would say to them, "If you are in such a hurry for what is inside, leave here, outside, those bodies that you have brought with you from the world." But this, William continues, so terrified the prospective novices that Bernard would explain the matter more gently (*clementius*), saying that what was to be left outside was not their actual bodies, but bodily concupiscence.

to such an extent that he no longer saw what was before his eyes.[82] His long habit of condemning the pleasures of taste had extinguished in him any concern with flavor. He made no choices in what he ate, and whether he drank water or oil was of no concern to him—it was whatever he had to hand. The bread he ate was so coarse[83] that one could see at once that his deepest fear was to give his body any gratification. To those who were afraid of solitude, he represented the horrors of outer darkness and endless gnashing of teeth.[84] If someone found the long and dreadful silence too arduous, he would tell him that if he gave proper attention to the great Judge who would rigorously examine all his words, he would find no difficulty in being silent. He paid little attention to his bodily health and strongly disapproved of the fastidious care that people took of themselves, saying that their disordered desire for life [on earth] was so great that they would make themselves immortal. As for him, he regarded his infirmities as part of his penance. In opposition to the self-indulgence of the world, he usually chose to live in a place where the air was damp and unwholesome, so as to be not so much sick as feeble, and he reckoned a monk to be in good health if he was well enough to sing [the Office] and chant the Psalms.[85] He wanted monks

---

[82] *Vita prima* 1.4.20 (William of Saint-Thierry); PL 185:238D; CF 76:23. After a year in the novitiate he still did not know whether or not the ceiling of the novices' *domus* was vaulted, and despite his regular attendance at church, he thought there was only one window in the sanctuary when there were actually three.

[83] *amer*, literally "bitter." The source is *Vita prima* 1.5.25 and 1.7.36 (William of Saint-Thierry); PL 185:241D–42A and 248B; CF 76:29, 41, describing the bread at Clairvaux, which was what the prophet Isaiah called barley, millet, and vetch (Isa 28:25) and which seemed to be made not so much from bran as from earth.

[84] See Matt 8:12; 13:42, 50; 22:13; 24:51; 25:30; Luke 13:28.

[85] An early editor has added here a passage from Bernard's SC 30.4–5.10; SBOp 1:216–17: "He used to say that Epicurus teaches us to nourish our bodies in the midst of pleasures, and Hippocrates promises that he will keep them in good health. As for me, I am a disciple

to whet their appetites not by food but by fasting, not by tasty dishes but by [manual] labor. He slept on the bare floor, but he used to say that in order to sleep there, he would lure sleep to him by vigils, by the psalmody of the night office, and by daily manual labor,[86] so that in this man even the natural functions were exercised not so much by nature as by his own virtuous strength.[87] Could anyone ever have more just cause to say what the apostle Saint Paul said, "The world is crucified to me, and I am crucified to the world" (Gal 6:14)?

29. Ah! What excellent reflections were made by the admirable Saint Chrysostom on these beautiful words of Saint Paul![88] It was not enough for him, said the holy bishop, to say that the world was dead to him; he had to add that he himself was dead to the world. There is no doubt, continued this wise interpreter, that the apostle thought that living people might not only have feelings for other living people but might also still feel some affection for the dead, since they preserved their memory and at least gave their bodies the honor of a burial. Thus, in order to help us grasp the extreme lengths to which the faithful should go in freeing themselves from worldly pleasures, Saint Paul tells us that it is not enough for Christians to break off whatever dealings they have with the world as the living from the dead—for between [the living and the dead]

---

of Jesus Christ, who teaches me to despise both the former and the latter." But as Lebarq informs us, "there is not a word of this passage in the manuscript" (Lebarq, 407, n. 1; Velat, 919, n. 167).

[86] See *Vita prima* 1.4.21 (William of Saint-Thierry); PL 185:239BC; CF 76:24–25.

[87] "par la vertu." *Vertu*, like *virtus* in Latin, can mean courage, moral strength, valor, quality, bravery, worth, or, indeed, virtue. I have here rendered it as "virtuous strength." See appendix 1, s.v. *vertu*/virtue.

[88] As is clear from the pages of Théodore Delmont's *Bossuet et les saints pères d'après des documents originaux et inédits* (Paris: Putois-Cretté, 1896; repr. Geneva: Slatkine Reprints, 1970), Bossuet esteemed Chrysostom for the clarity and simplicity of his style and for his appeal to the people (see especially Delmont, 148–50). The passage that follows is from Chrysostom's *De compunctione* 2.2; PG 47:412–13.

there may yet remain some trifling association. No. The regard of a Christian for the world should be like that of a corpse for a corpse.

30. Oh, what terrible logic for those of us who are lax and who lack courage,[89] who are Christians only in name! But the great Saint Bernard engraved it deep in his heart. What makes us alive to the world is an attachment to the world; what makes the world alive for us is that certain luster of the things of the senses that we find so charming. Death extinguishes all our attachments; death tarnishes the luster of all things. Look at the most beautiful body in the world: as soon as the soul withdraws from it, then, even though its features may remain much the same, the flower of its beauty fades, and all its lovely charm vanishes away. Thus, since the world held no more lure for Bernard and Bernard had no more inclination for the world, the world was dead to him and he was dead to the world.

31. Christians! What a sacrifice the pious Bernard offered to God by his continual mortifications! His body is a victim consecrated to [God] by charity: by sacrificing it, [charity] preserves it, so as to be able to sacrifice it again and again. What offering could be more acceptable to the Savior Jesus than a soul disgusted with everything but Jesus himself? [A soul] that so delights in Jesus that it is afraid to take pleasure in anything but him? [A soul] that desires always to be afflicted until it possesses him perfectly? For Jesus, the pious Bernard strips himself of all things—and (if I dare say so) for the sake of Jesus, he even strips himself of his good works.

32. Indeed, faithful people, since good works have no merit unless they come from Jesus Christ, they lose their value as soon as we attribute them to ourselves.[90] We must restore them

---

[89] "lâches et efféminés."

[90] Bossuet, a staunch Augustinian, is here reflecting the Augustinian concept of humankind as "one lump of sin" (*una massa peccati*). We have inherited the entirety of Adam's sin and guilt, and since, in consequence, we are wholly corrupt, we cannot possibly do one good

to him who gave them, and this is what the humble Bernard learned at the foot of the cross. How beautiful, how Christian, were these words of the humble Bernard when he was seized with dread at the thought of the terrible Judgment of God: "I know, I know," he said, "that I do not deserve the Kingdom of the Blessed, but Jesus, my Savior, possesses it for two reasons: it belongs to him by nature and by his labors, as his inheritance and as his conquest. This good Master contents himself with the first title and generously yields the second to me."[91] Oh words worthy of a Christian! No, you will not be confounded, oh pious Bernard! For you base your hope on the foundation of the cross.

33. But, oh God, shall we not tremble, miserable sinners that we are, when we hear these words? Bernard, so accomplished in virtue, believes that he has done nothing for heaven, and we, who presume [to rely] on ourselves, we believe we have done much when we have carelessly acquitted ourselves of some trifling duty of superficial devotion! What sorrow! The love of the world reigns in our hearts, and the very word *mortification* fills us with horror. It is in vain that divine justice strikes us and threatens us with yet greater misfortunes; we do not stop running after pleasures, as if it were possible to be happy in both this world and the next. My brothers, what do you think you are doing when you praise the virtues of the great Saint Bernard? In eulogizing him, you are pronouncing your own condemnation!

34. [Bernard], certainly, did not have a body of iron and bronze. He was sensitive to pain and had a delicate constitu-

---

action. As Augustine said, "Of our own power, we can only fall" (En in Ps 129.1; PL 37:1696). It follows, therefore, that if an action is good, it is good only by the grace of God mediated to us through his Son. Bossuet develops the idea further in his sermon on worldly honor: see Lebarq, 3:352–58.

[91] This is a loose translation of Bernard's words as recorded in the *Vita prima* 1.12.57 (William of Saint-Thierry); PL 185:258B; CF 76:59–60. "Par ses travaux," "by his labors," is *merito passionis*, "by virtue of his Passion," in Latin.

tion[92] and thereby teaches us that it is not the body that lets us down, but rather [our lack of] courage and faith. It was God's will that his penitence should begin in his earliest youth and that in feeble old age[93] he should never see it relaxed, and thus, in this one person God condemns [laxity] at every age. You make excuses for yourselves because of all the important things you have to do, but Bernard was overwhelmed with business, not only that of his own order, but of virtually the whole Church! He preached, he wrote, he handled the affairs of popes and bishops, kings and princes. He acted on behalf of both great and small, opening to all the depths of his charity, but in all these various occupations he never made the slightest mitigation in his own austerities, and in this way the self-indulgence of every person at every age was eternally condemned by the example of this holy man.

35. You will say to me, perhaps, that it is not necessary for everyone to live like him. But surely, Christians, at the very least we should look for some sort of similarity between disciples of the same Gospel. If we aim at the same paradise, where Bernard is now in glory, how can there be such an inequality, such a contradiction, between his actions and ours? Can we hope to reach the same goal by taking such contrary paths? To arrive by way of sensual pleasures at [that end] that he believed could be attained only by suffering? If we do not aspire to his eminent perfection, then we should at least imitate something of his penitence. But we give ourselves up completely to the foolish joys of the world; we love dissolute living and good cheer, a life of ease and enjoyment—and after that we still want to be called Christians!

---

[92] See *Vita prima* 1.4.22 (William of Saint-Thierry); PL 185:239D; CF 76:25–26.

[93] "Exaggeration!" says Velat; "Saint Bernard died at sixty-four, well before the age of decrepitude" (Velat, 921, n. 190). But the learned *abbé* has not taken into account Bernard's long and serious illness, and the average age at death in the twelfth century. For the aristocracy this was the early sixties; for the peasantry, considerably less.

36. But how is it that we do not understand that the cross of Jesus should be carved deep in our souls if we wish to be Christians? This is why the apostle tells us that we are dead and that our life is hidden,[94] and that we are buried with Jesus Christ.[95] We hear little of what is meant if, when he speaks to us only of death and burial, we do not realize that the Son of God is not content with asking us to make only a mediocre change. We must change completely, and to bring about this change, Christians, let us not think that it is enough to be diligent in no more than an ordinary way. Yet the matter of our salvation is always the thing we neglect most. Everything else presses upon us and demands our attention, and it is only for our salvation that we are cold and listless. Yet the Savior tells us that the Kingdom of heaven can be taken only by force and that "it is only the violent who bear it away" (Matt 11:12). Oh eternal God! If it must be by force, if it must be by violence, what hope can we have in this blessed inheritance? But I will leave you to think about that, for I myself am too weak and feeble to show you its real importance. To do that I would need some spark of that apostolic zeal that Saint Bernard had, and that we are now going to consider for a while in the second part [of this sermon].[96]

[SECOND POINT]

37. What I have left to say to you of Saint Bernard is so great and admirable that even a series of sermons would be

---

[94] Col 3:3: "For you are dead, and your life is hidden with Christ in God."

[95] See n. 76 above.

[96] Bossuet now turns to Bernard's achievements in the world but provides us with very little detail. His first concern (§§37–41), based almost entirely on Book I (William of Saint-Thierry) of the *Vita prima*, is Bernard's conversion of his family. He then moves on to deal with his missionary journeys, his involvement in the papal schism, and the nature and impact of his preaching.

insufficient to tell you of it in a way that would do it justice. But since I promised you that I would show you this holy man when he was engaged in his public and apostolic life, let us say something of it briefly so that, in your devotion, you will not be disappointed in what you have been happily anticipating. Do you want me to show you how the apostolate of Saint Bernard began? The first light that he shed was upon his own family, when, from his early youth, he would preach the cross of Jesus to his uncles and his brothers, to his friends and his cousins, and to all those who used to frequent his father's house.[97] From that time onward, he would speak to them of eternity with such fervor that he left in their souls a certain something—I know not what—that made it impossible for them to take any pleasure in the world. His good uncle Gaudry,[98] a man of high standing in the neighborhood, was the first disciple of his beloved nephew. His elders and his juniors alike all surrendered themselves to his instruction, and it was God's will that, after resisting for some time, all his brothers came to him, one after another, at the times determined by Providence.[99] Guy, the oldest in the house, left his military profession and the joys of his recent marriage.[100] All of them renounced the responsibili-

---

[97] What follows in the next five sections is derived essentially from the *Vita prima* 1.3.9–18 (William of Saint-Thierry): PL 185:231D–37B; CF 76:11–21, and 1.6.30; 244C–45B; CF 76:34–35 (the story of his sister's conversion).

[98] Gaudry (Galdericus), seigneur of Touillon, a château and domain about five miles north by east of Montbard. He subsequently donated the property of Touillon to the abbey of Fontenay. See Williams, *Saint Bernard*, 10, and DHGE 20:49–50.

[99] Bernard had five brothers—Guy, Gerard, Andrew, Bartholomew, and Nivard—and one sister, Hombeline or Homberge, whom we shall meet again in a moment.

[100] His wife, Elizabeth, we might add, was not at all happy about this, and refused to give her consent. Bernard then warned Guy that if she did not consent, she would soon sicken and die. Sicken she did, and the seriousness of her condition led her to send for Bernard and

ties they either had or to which they aspired in the war,[101] and these brave and princely men, used to command and the noble tumult of armed conflict, disdained neither the baseness nor the silence nor the routine of Cîteaux, occupied as they were in such a holy [enterprise]. They moved on to more glorious battles, where death itself gave them victory.

38. These four brothers[102] bade their last farewell to the world and made their way [to the monastery], accompanied by many other gentlemen[103] whom Bernard, this young fisherman, had caught in the net of Jesus. They had intended to leave Nivard, the youngest, with their good father as a support in his old age and declining days, and when they embraced him, they said, "You will have all our property." But this child, inspired by God, replied to them in this wonderful way: "What? You take Heaven, and leave Earth to me!" In this way, he would complain gently that, as the youngest brother, they were sharing with him too little, and this holy thought made such an impression on his soul that, after spending a short time in the world, he obtained his father's permission to go and take

---

ask his forgiveness. She and Guy then took vows of chastity, and as he became a monk, so she became a nun. See *Vita prima* 1.3.10 (William of Saint-Thierry); PL 185:232C–33A; CF 76:12–14.

[101] I.e., the civil strife between the dukes of Burgundy (whom Bernard's family supported) and the lords of Grancey-le-Château. Bossuet omits the saga of Bernard's brother Gerard at the siege of Grancey (which probably took place late in 1112) and his subsequent conversion: see *Vita prima* 1.3.11–12 (William of Saint-Thierry); PL 185:233A–34C; CF 76:14–16. On Grancey and its siege, see Jacques Berlioz, *Saint Bernard en Bourgogne. Lieux et mémoire* (Dijon: Les Éditions du Bien Public, 1990), 59–64.

[102] Guy, Gerard, Andrew, and Bartholomew.

[103] William of Saint-Thierry says "more than thirty" (*amplius quam triginta*) (*Vita prima* 1.4.19 [William of Saint-Thierry]; PL 185:237C; CF 76:22). Most scholars now speak of thirty (including Bernard).

possession of the same inheritance as his beloved brothers—not indeed to divide it, but to enjoy it together with them.[104]

39. But the pious Bernard had not yet seen his whole family conquered for the Savior. Who remained? He still had a sister, [Hombeline] who, taking advantage of her brothers' piety,[105] lived in luxury and splendor. One day, bedecked with jewels and with a haughty mien, she came to visit them in her magnificent carriage. She had never been able to have the pleasure of seeing [her brothers] until she had agreed (as now she did) that she would follow their good teachings. The venerable Bernard came out to her: "What's this?" he said. "Why do you come to trouble the peace of this monastery and bring the Devil's pomp into the house of God? What shame to bedeck yourself from the patrimony of the poor!" He gave her to understand that she was grievously at fault in adorning corruption in this way, for [corruption] was what he called our body.[106]

40. In fact, Christians, this body is no more than a lump of clay that we decorate with inconsequential adornments because of the soul that lives within it. It is just as if a king were compelled by some untoward circumstance to lodge for a while in a hut. One would try to decorate it in some way so that even there one would see a little gleam of royal splendor. Yet the cottage would still be [a cottage], and the fleeting honor done to it (of which it will soon be stripped), in no way changes its nature. In just the same way, this filth[107] that is our body is clothed with sort of empty glamor because of the soul, which, for a certain time, must inhabit it. Yet filth it remains, which, at the close of its short life, will return to its first sordid state of natural corruption. But surely, to take so much care of such a

---

[104] For the story of Nivard, see *Vita prima* 1.3.17 (William of Saint-Thierry); PL 185:236CD; CF 76:20–21.

[105] Their various conversions had taken them all to Cîteaux, thus leaving her in possession of the entire family fortune.

[106] For the story of Hombeline/Humbelina, see *Vita prima* 1.6.30 (William of Saint-Thierry); PL 185:244C–45B; CF 76:34–35.

[107] Or dung or excrement (*ordure*). The Latin term is *stercus*: see *Vita prima* 1.6.30 (William of Saint-Thierry); PL 185:244D; CF 76:34.

trifling thing, and to neglect for its sake this soul made in the image of God, immortal and divine in its nature, is this not the height of folly? Ah! The sister of pious Bernard is touched to the quick by this thought, and straightaway she hastens to fasting, to withdrawal [from the world], to sackcloth, to the monastery, to penitence. This prideful woman, tamed by the words of Saint Bernard, [henceforth] follows the standard of Jesus with unconquerable resolution.[108]

41. But how can I not tell you about this holy man's greatest happiness [when he achieved] his last conquest within his family? His good father, old Tescelin, who alone remained in the world, came to join his children at Clairvaux![109] O eternal God! What joy! What tears from both father and son! We cannot conceive the steadfast courage with which this good man had lost his children, the honor of his house, and the support of his declining years. When they withdrew [from the world], he saw his [ancestral] name blotted out on earth, but he rejoiced that his holy family would live forever in Heaven. And thus, touched by the Spirit of God, this good old man determined that his whole house would be consecrated to him, and, in his declining years, he becomes a child in Our Lord Jesus Christ under the guidance of his dear son, whom he thereafter regards as his [spiritual] father. Oh you parents, be sure to take the greatest care to raise the children whom God has entrusted to you in the fear of God: you do not know the reward that

---

[108] She became a nun (and eventually first prioress) at the Benedictine house of Jully-les-Nonnains, a dependency of the abbey of Molesme in what is now the *département* of the Yonne.

[109] Tescelin / Tesselin, who may have been in his seventies, earns only a sentence in the *Vita prima* 1.6.30 (William of Saint-Thierry): PL 185:244C; CF 76:34: "his father, too, who had remained at home alone, came and joined his sons, and when he had spent a little time [*aliquantum tempus*] there, died in goodly old age." Watkin Williams puts the *aliquantum tempus* at two to three years: "Manriquez dates his arrival at Clairvaux at 1117; Mabillon at 1119. Meglinger saw the tomb at Clairvaux in which he and his sons Bartholomew and Gerard were interred" (Williams, *Saint Bernard*, 29).

this infinite goodness reserves for you. At the end of his days, pious Tescelin, who had reared his children so well in piety, received from this a plentiful blessing; for by means of his son, he died after a long life with good hope, and, if I dare say so, in the peace and embrace of the Savior. Thus you see how the great Saint Bernard is the apostle of his family.

42. Would you like me to go further and show him to you preaching the cross in his monastery? [Shall I tell you] how many different kinds of people came there, from everywhere in the world, to do penance under his direction? He usually had seven hundred angels,[110] for thus I call those heavenly men who served God with him at Clairvaux, [men who were] so recollected,[111] so mortified, that we are told by the venerable William, abbot of Saint-Thierry, that when he entered the abbey and saw the ordered life, the silence, and self-restraint, he was seized with no less a reverence than if he had approached [one of] our most famous altars.[112] Bernard, who, by his divine preaching had accustomed [his monks] to the sweetness of the cross, had made them live in such a way that they knew no more of the world's news than if they were separated far from it by a measureless ocean. Moreover, so ardent were they in their [spiritual] exercises, so exacting in their penances, so demanding of themselves, that it was easy to see that they thought not of living, but of dying. This companionship of penitence united them to each other as brothers, with Saint Bernard as a good father, and [it united] Saint Bernard with them as with his beloved children. They were in such perfect and heartfelt agreement that nowhere else in the world could

---

[110] See *Vita prima* 5.3.20 (Geoffrey of Auxerre); PL 185:363AB; CF 76:253. See also DHGE 8:616, and 12:1056.

[111] "si recueillis": see appendix 1, s.v. *recueillement* / recollection.

[112] *Vita prima* 1.7.33 (William of Saint-Thierry); PL 185:246CD; CF 76:38. William is actually talking about Bernard's little *cubiculum*, not the abbey in general.

one see a more perfect picture of the early Church, which had but one heart and one soul.[113]

43. What sorrow, then, must this man of God have suffered when he was forced to leave his children, whom he loved so tenderly and deeply in Jesus Christ! But God, who had brought him forth from his mother's womb to renew in his own times the spirit and preaching of the apostles, drew him forth from his solitude for the salvation of those souls whom he wished to save through [Bernard's] ministry. It is here, here, Christians, that he truly appears as an apostle. The apostles traveled throughout the whole world, carrying with them the Gospel of Jesus Christ to the most remote peoples, and what part of the world has not been illumined by the preaching of Bernard? The apostles founded churches, and in the great schism of Pierre Léon,[114] how many rebellious churches, how many dispersed flocks, did Bernard bring back to Catholic unity, thus making himself the second founder of churches? The apostle [Paul] includes among the functions of the apostolate "the care of all churches,"[115] and did not the pious Bernard govern almost all churches by the salutary advice that was asked of him by all parts of the world? It seemed that God did not wish to attach him to any particular church so that he would be the common father of all.

44. Both signs and wonders[116] followed the preaching of the apostles: and what prophecies, what healings, what extraordinary and supernatural events confirmed the preaching of

[113] See Acts 4:32: *cor unum et anima una*.

[114] I.e., Pietro Pierleoni, Anacletus II. See appendix 2, s.v. Anacletus II.

[115] 2 Cor 11:28. It cannot be denied that Bossuet's account of Bernard's apostolic achievements is somewhat tinged with hagiographical exaggeration, but this is, after all, a panegyric, and we must expect a little panegyrical license.

[116] See Acts 7:36; 14:3; Rom 15:19; 2 Cor 12:12. The Latin phrase is always *signa et prodigia* (or vice versa). Miracle stories play a significant role in the various parts of the *Vita prima*, but Bossuet does not

Saint Bernard! Saint Paul glories in that he did not preach with studied eloquence, nor with flattering and pleasing words: the only decoration he gave to his sermons was simplicity and truth.[117] And what could be more solid and penetrating than the simplicity of Bernard, which draws every thought and idea[118] into the service of the faith of Jesus? When the apostles preached Jesus Christ, they were transported with heavenly fervor that could clearly and visibly be seen in the vehemence of their actions. It is this that led the apostle Saint Paul to say that he acted boldly in Our Lord, and that his preaching was accompanied by the evidence of the Spirit.[119] This is just how the zealous Bernard appeared when he preached to the Germans in a language they did not know yet did not leave them unmoved because he spoke to them as a man sent from heaven, jealous for the honor of Jesus.[120]

45. One of the most admirable things about the apostles was how, though so humble in appearance, they exercised a magisterial authority and impartial censorship on morals, using that power for edification, not destruction. This is why the apostle, when forming Timothy for the ministry of the word, says, "Take care that no one scorns you."[121] With regard to the impious, God had imprinted on the countenance of the

---

dwell on them. This single summary sentence is all that he has to say on the matter.

[117] 2 Cor 1:12: "For our glory is this: that our conscience testifies that we have lived in this world—and more abundantly towards you—in simplicity of heart and the sincerity of God, not in carnal wisdom but in the grace of God."

[118] *tout entendement*, which I have rendered as "every thought and idea."

[119] Lebarq, 416, nn. b–c, and Velat, 925, nn. 259–60; compare 1 Thess 2:2 and 1 Cor 2:4, the latter being closer to Bossuet's text.

[120] See *Vita prima* 3.3.7 (Geoffrey of Auxerre); PL 185:307B; CF 76:152–53.

[121] 1 Tim 4:12, which actually reads *Nemo adolescentiam tuam contemnat*, "Let no one despise your youth."

venerable Bernard so terrible a majesty that, in the end, they were forced to bend [to his will]: witness the infuriated prince of Aquitaine[122] and so many others whose anger was often disarmed by his words alone.

46. But what was even more divine about the holy apostles was their charity[123] for those to whom they preached. They were fathers in their guidance, mothers in their tenderness, and nurses in their gentleness. Saint Paul shows all these qualities. [The apostles] would admonish, they would give warning, both in and out of season,[124] sometimes with open-hearted gentleness, sometimes with holy anger, with tears, with reproaches. They made use of a thousand different methods, but it was always the same charity that dominated. With children they spoke as children, with adults as adults.[125] They were Jews to the Jews, Gentiles to the Gentiles, "all things to all people," said the apostle Saint Paul, "in order to gain all" (1 Cor 9:20, 22). Look at the writings of the admirable Bernard: there you will see the same intentions and the same apostolic love. What man was ever more compassionate and tender to the weak, the wretched, and the ignorant? He never scorned the poorest or the most abject. Yet what other man reproved more fearlessly the depraved manners of his age? He spared neither princes, potentates, bishops, cardinals, nor popes.[126] While he respected their rank, so on occasion did he rebuke their person—but [his reproofs were] so justly tempered with love that, without being either indulgent or hot-tempered, he

---

[122] I.e., Duke William X of Aquitaine: see appendix 2, s.v. William (Guillaume) X, duke of Aquitaine. Velat, 925, n. 265, misidentifies him as William IX of Aquitaine.

[123] See appendix 1, s.v. *charité* / charity.

[124] "opportunément, importunément" is a literal translation of *opportune, importune* in 2 Tim 4:2.

[125] Lit. "they stammered [*bégayaient*] with children, they spoke with men."

[126] Unlike many of the other panegyrists, Bossuet gives no specific examples of Bernard's censures.

exhibited all the sweetness of benevolence and all the vigor of a truly Christian freedom.

47. What a splendid example for the [Protestant] reformers of the last centuries![127] If their all too visible arrogance had allowed them to deal with things with similar moderation, they would have censured what was morally wicked without severing their communion [with the Catholic Church], and they would have repressed vice without violating legitimate authority.[128] But to be called the head of a party was too flattering, and urged on by the vain desire to show off, their eloquence ran over into deadly insults, containing nothing but malice and rage. These [reformers] were not forceful, but proud, quick-tempered, and contemptuous, and, as a result, they brought about schism, not reformation.[129] To achieve that would have needed the courage and humility of Bernard. He was revered by all, for he was seen to be impartial and modest, as firm as he was respectful, and it was this that gave him such great authority in the world. If some schism arose, or some suspect doctrine,[130] the bishops would refer everything to the authority of Bernard. If there were quarrels among princes,[131] Bernard was immediately the mediator.

---

[127] The criticisms set out in §47 are elaborated at length in Bossuet's *Histoire des variations des églises protestantes* (arguably his greatest work), first published thirty-five years later at Paris in May 1688.

[128] I.e., the authority of the church, manifested in and through the supreme pontiff.

[129] As Ernest Reynolds points out, "Bossuet acknowledged that there had been need for reforming many things early in the sixteenth century, but these, he contended, were matters of discipline and not matters of doctrine" (Ernest E. Reynolds, *Bossuet* [New York: Doubleday, 1963], 155).

[130] Bossuet is thinking of Bernard's condemnations of people like Abelard, Gilbert de la Porrée, and Henry of Toulouse, but he does not name any of them.

[131] Yet again, Bossuet gives no specific examples.

48. Oh mighty town of Metz, there was a time when you profited greatly from his intervention.[132] Oh beautiful and noble city, long ago you were coveted! The position you occupied was too important, and almost always set you up as someone's prey.[133] You were often reduced to the last degree of misery. But from time to time, God sent you good protectors. Neighboring princes had plotted your ruin; your good citizens had been defeated in a great battle;[134] your enemies were puffed up with their great success, and you were aflame with the desire for vengeance! Everything was leading up to a ruthless war if Hillin, the good archbishop of Trèves,[135] had not looked for a charitable peacemaker. This was the pious Bernard, who, with his strength exhausted by his long austerities and extreme old age,[136] awaited his last hour at Clairvaux. But what weakness could ever diminish the ardor of his charity? He overcame his illness to make his way swiftly within your walls. But he could not overcome the animosity of such grossly overheated passions. Every man seized his weapons with inconceivable rage; the armies were in sight of each other and ready to give

---

[132] As we saw in the Introduction to the panegyric, Bossuet's peroration on Metz (§§48–49) is a key to dating the sermon. The events to which he alludes took place in 1153, and the full account may be read in the *Vita prima* 5.1.3–6 (Geoffrey of Auxerre); PL 185:352B–55A; CF 76:234–39. See also Williams, *Saint Bernard*, 358–59. Unfortunately, the peace brokered by Bernard was not to last.

[133] The city was of such strategic importance that it was fought over almost continually from the sixteenth century to the twentieth. The war to which Bossuet is referring was between Stephen, bishop of Metz, and Matthew, duke of Lorraine.

[134] "Caught in a narrow defile of the Moselle under the heights of Froidmont, in the direction of Pont-à-Mousson, and unable to extricate themselves, more than two thousand of the men of Metz perished, some by the sword, others by drowning, on 28th February, 1153" (Williams, *Saint Bernard*, 358).

[135] On Illin / Illinus / Hillin de Falmagne, archbishop of Trèves / Trier from 1152 to his death in 1169, see DHGE 24:554–59.

[136] See n. 93 above.

battle. But the venerable Bernard was goaded by charity, which never despairs. He spoke, he begged, he entreated them not to shed Christian blood, [which had been redeemed by] the price of the blood of Jesus. They let the iron in their souls be bent; enemies became as brothers; they all detested their blind fury, and, with common accord, they venerated the author of such a great miracle.[137]

49. Oh city [of Metz], so good and faithful! Do you not wish to honor your liberator? But, faithful people, what honor can we bestow on him? Surely, we do not know how to honor the saints if we do not imitate their virtues. Without that, our praises are a burden to them, and we are damaging to ourselves. Faithful people, what do you think we should do when we praise the virtues of the great Saint Bernard?

50. Oh God of our hearts! What indignity! This innocent [man] did penance for so long, and we sinners[138] do not want to do it at all. There was a time when penance occupied a very high place in the Church; I do not now know any corner of the world from which it has not been removed. There was a time when those who scandalized the Church with their riotous living were regarded as heathens and tax collectors;[139] now everyone applauds them. There was a time when one was not admitted to the mysteries of [eucharistic] communion save

---

[137] Bernard then returned to Clairvaux by way of Toul and Gondreville (his journey being accompanied by the usual miracles of healing), and there he died on Thursday, August 20, 1153, at "about the third hour of the day" (*Vita prima* 5.2.13 [Geoffrey of Auxerre]; PL 185:359A; CF 76:245–46).

[138] *Criminels*, which does not here mean "criminals." The word *crimes* for "sins" is a common usage among seventeenth-century French spiritual writers. See appendix 1, s.v. *crimes / sins*.

[139] "comme des Gentils et des publicains." Publicans and sinners are associated together in the Gospels of Matthew, Mark, and Luke, but Bossuet is using *publicain* / publican with its old meaning of tax collector, not with its more recent meaning of tavern-keeper.

after long reparation and clear proof of penitence;[140] now they enter into the very sanctuary. There was a time when those who, through mortal sins,[141] had trampled underfoot the blood of Jesus did not dare to look upon the altars where that [blood] was communicated to the faithful, unless they had previously cleansed themselves by tears, fasting, or almsgiving. They believed that they had to punish themselves for their ingratitude lest God should punish it in his implacable anger. Since they had enjoyed those pleasures that are unlawful, they did not expect to receive mercy unless they now deprived themselves even of those that we are permitted.

51. That was how our fathers lived, at a time when piety flourished in the Church of God. Do you think that, since that time, the flames of hell have lost their unbearable heat because

---

[140] These are actually the principles set forth in Antoine Arnauld's *Traité de la fréquente communion*, first published in 1643—a book that, despite its dense style and superabundant patristic quotations, achieved rapid notoriety. From a theological point of view, Bossuet had no truck with Jansenism; from a sacramental point of view, there is no doubt that he leaned toward the views of Arnauld. Nevertheless, in a superb and hard-hitting passage in his funeral oration for Nicolas Cornet, he makes it quite clear that, as usual, he sought a middle way: "In our days, two dangerous maladies have afflicted the body of the Church. Some doctors have been seized with an unfortunate and misjudged forbearance, a deadly compassion, which has led them to make cushions for the elbows of sinners [see Ezek 13:18], to look for coverlets [to conceal] their passions, to condescend to their vain way of life, and to accommodate to their conceited ignorance. Certain others, no less extreme, have held consciences captive by unjustified restrictions: they cannot bear any sign of weakness, hell is always breathing over their shoulders, and all they do is thunder forth anathemas. The enemy of our salvation makes equal use of both parties: he uses the leniency of the former to make vice attractive, and the severity of the latter to make virtue odious!" (Velat, 55).

[141] It must be remembered that in seventeenth-century France, it was extremely easy to commit mortal sin: we discussed the matter in chap. 1.

our coldness has forced the Church to relax the rigor of its ancient discipline, or because ecclesiastical vigor has weakened? Do you think that this jealous God, who punishes sins so severely,[142] will take this as a reason to treat us less harshly, or that he will treat us more gently because we have added to our iniquities? You see the utter absurdity of this idea! Yet we act as if we believed it, and instead of thinking of penitence, we think only of how to make ourselves rich. This is already a dangerous thought, for as the apostle warned Timothy, "The desire for riches is the root of all evil" (1 Tim 6:10). Furthermore, we also think how we might make ourselves rich in unjust ways: by graft, by usury, by robbery. We do not have a Christian heart, for [our heart] is hard with regard to the misery of the poor. In our charity we are apathetic, but in our hatreds, irreconcilable! In vain are we struck by divine justice, and we do not cease giving ourselves utterly and always to the foolish joys of this world. We do not hear this terrible sentence of the Son of God: "Woe to you who laugh, for you shall weep!" (Luke 6:25). And this: "Laughter is mixed with sorrow, and tears follow close on joy" (Prov 14:13). And this too: "They pass their days with their goods about them, but in an instant they will descend into Hell" (Job 21:13).

52. Return, then, faithful people, let us return to God with all our heart![143] Penance is bitter but for a time; afterward, all its bitterness is turned into inconceivable sweetness. It mortifies disordered desires, it lets us taste celestial pleasures, it gives us good hope, it opens the gates of heaven. When we strive with all our power to appease justice with penance, we can await divine mercy with great consolation.

---

[142] See Exod 20:5: "I am the Lord your God, mighty, jealous, visiting the iniquity of the fathers upon the children as far as the third and fourth generation of those that hate me." The same idea may be found in a number of other places.

[143] See 1 Sam 7:3: "If you return to the Lord with all your heart."

53. Oh pious Bernard! Oh penitent saint, by your holy intercession obtain for us the tears of penitence that gave you such holy joy and, so that [penitence] may be renewed in the world, pray to God to inflame our preachers with that apostolic spirit that animated you! And we ask of you still another favor. Oh you, who so many times disarmed princes preparing for war, you see for how many years our rivers have been dyed with Christian blood, and how it steams up throughout the whole land.[144] Christians, who ought to be children of peace, have become bloodthirsty wolves. Christian brotherhood has been sundered, and the most pitiful thing of all is that the abuse of arms never stops enriching hell. Pray that God may give us peace,[145] and that he may bring repose to this city [of Metz] that was so dear to you so long ago. Or if it be written in the book of his eternal decrees that we cannot see peace in this world, may he bestow it upon us at the last in heaven, through Our Lord Jesus Christ. Amen.

---

[144] The Thirty Years' War, in which France was bloodily involved, lasted from 1618 to 1648; the First and Second Frondes lasted from 1648 to 1653, the year in which Bossuet preached his panegyric; and the Peace of the Pyrenees, the treaty signed on November 7, 1659, ended twenty-four years of warfare between France and Spain. Bossuet is not here exaggerating.

[145] As we have just seen, it would be another six years before France and Spain signed the Peace of the Pyrenees, and eight years after that Louis XIV launched the first of a series of wars that lasted until the signing of the Treaty of Utrecht in 1713. Bossuet had died in 1704, but for almost all his life, France had been at war.

8

Touching, Moving, Converting
The Unction of François Fénelon

INTRODUCTION

All that needs to be said of Fénelon's bitter controversy with Bossuet has already been said in chapter 2, and his life exemplifies the turning of Boethius's Wheel of Fortune, raising him to the heights of royal favor, and bringing him down to end his days in royal disgrace. François de Salignac de la Mothe-Fénelon was born on August 6, 1651, to an old and illustrious Gascon family, received a sound classical education, entered the seminary of Saint-Sulpice in Paris, and was ordained to the priesthood in about 1675. He then served for a while in the parish before being appointed superior of the *Nouvelles Catholiques*, an institution founded in 1634 "to strengthen the faith of newly converted females in the doctrines that they had embraced, and to instruct persons of the same sex who shewed any desire of conversion."[1] He was further involved with Protestantism after the Revocation of the Edict of Nantes in 1685, when he took part in a mission in the west of France intended to provide instruction to those Huguenots who, by the orders of Louis XIV, had been forcibly converted from Protestantism to the Catholic

---

[1] [Louis-François de Bausset], *The Life of Fenelon, Archbishop of Cambrai; compiled, from Original Manuscripts, by M. L. F. de Bausset. Translated from the French, by William Mudford* (London: Sherwood, Neely, and Jones, 1810), 1:19.

faith. His approach was humane, but he also demanded strict orthodoxy in matters of belief.

Shortly afterward he was back in Paris and was appointed tutor to Louis de France, duke of Burgundy (the grandson of Louis XIV), a difficult and refractory child on whom Fénelon had a profound and wholly positive influence. In fact, he completely transformed the boy. At the same time he became the spiritual director of a group of devout people at Court, a group that included the royal mistress Madame de Maintenon, and it was inevitable that the royal favor would result in appropriate honors. In 1693 he was admitted to the *Académie française* and two years later was named archbishop of Cambrai. But the Wheel of Fortune continued to turn, and from these heights Fénelon now began his inevitable descent.

There were two main reasons for this. The first was that in one of the works he had written for the education of the young duke of Burgundy—the celebrated *Télémaque* or *Telemachus*—there had been implicit criticism of certain ideas and policies of Louis XIV (always a dangerous thing to do), and the second, as we have seen already, was his defense of the Quietist ideas of Madame Guyon. This alienated him from the king and Madame de Maintenon and brought him into direct conflict with Bossuet; the publication, in 1697, of his *Explication des maximes des saints sur la vie intérieure*, which defended a number of the essential ideas of Madame Guyon, was the last straw. The book was immediately attacked by Bossuet and condemned by Pope Innocent XII in March 1699.

Fénelon's disgrace was now complete, and he was removed from his position as preceptor of the duke of Burgundy, banished from Court, and exiled to his archdiocese, where he spent the remaining years of his life. While at Cambrai, however, he still maintained good relations with certain of the devout party at Court as well as with his former pupil, and when that pupil's father died in 1711 and the duke of Burgundy became the dauphin, the direct heir to the throne, Fénelon had hopes of a return to the royal favor. Unhappily, this was not to be, for in February 1712 the duke's wife contracted measles and died on the twelfth of the month. The duke, who loved her dearly and had stayed with her throughout her illness, contracted the disease himself and died six days later. He was twenty-nine. There was now no hope of Fénelon's return to Court, and he spent the remaining fifteen years at Cambrai, administering his diocese with intelligence, charm, humanity, and efficiency. He died on January 7, 1715.

Fénelon's sermon for the feast day of Saint Bernard was delivered to what appears to have been a mixed congregation of Feuillants and Feuillantines in an unknown year. All the indications point to a time prior to his disastrous involvement in the Quietist controversy, and it is therefore probable that the sermon was delivered in Paris, perhaps at the church of the Feuillants on the rue Saint-Honoré. In one of the editions of the text (followed by Migne), the sermon has as its subtitle "His solitary life, and his apostolic life,"[2] which tells us that Fénelon is thinking in just the same terms as Bossuet. As the basis of his exposition, however, he chooses Luke 3:4, which applies the well-known verse from Isaiah—Isaiah 40:3—to John the Baptist: "A voice crying in the wilderness: Prepare the way of the Lord," *Vox clamantis in deserto: Parate viam Domini.* But Bernard is also a voice crying in the desert of this world, he says, filling it with the fruits of the penitence he preached and preparing us for the second coming of Christ. By his solitary life, we are told, Bernard restored the monastic state to its ancient glory; by his apostolic life, the world was reformed and the Church triumphed; and these are the two divisions of Fénelon's discourse.

For much of the first division, Fénelon's exposition runs directly parallel to that of Bossuet. We see the young Bernard hearing in his heart the call of the desert, and we see his brothers caught up in his charisma. Fénelon, like Bossuet, quotes the

---

[2] See n. 14 below.

words of Nivard, "What? You take Heaven and leave me only Earth?" (§5), and, again like Bossuet, he tells us of Bernard's entry into Cîteaux with thirty of his relatives or friends. There follows, as with Bossuet (but more briefly), an account of Bernard's novitiate and his mortification of the senses. Bernard is then appointed abbot of Clairvaux, and Fénelon presents a paraphrase of William of Saint-Thierry's description of the abbey when he first visited it in 1118/1119. We are then told of Bernard's extreme austerities and the visit of William of Châlons, and—like Bossuet and Rancé—Fénelon takes the opportunity to contrast Bernard's asceticism with the laxity of his own times and to rebuke those who take alarm at the slightest infirmity and who, always listening to "la nature lâche," are ever seeking comfort and ease. Bernard, on the contrary, would give no heed whatever to the demands of his body, even when that body was ready to fall into ruin!

Fénelon then tells us of Innocent II's visit to Clairvaux in 1131 and his admiration for what he saw there (this does not appear in Bossuet), and then moves on to laud the astonishing expansion of Clairvaux in the years following Bernard's appointment as abbot. But after this, Fénelon returns immediately to Bernard's life of prayer (which is far more important than study) and the way in which he combined a "savage and impatient zeal" against the least imperfection with a true love and tenderness for all his monks. His own profound humility was an example to them, he says, but his efforts and his austerities took their toll, and after speaking of the impact of the death of Bernard, Fénelon returns to his theme of renewal and reform. He begs, he implores, he exhorts the nuns in his congregation to live as Bernard himself had lived, and to show themselves to the world as true daughters of their saintly father.

Fénelon now turns to the second point of his panegyric and offers us a swift and summary tour of Bernard's more notable achievements in the world. We hear of the papal schism, the council of Étampes in 1130, Bernard's meeting with Henry I of England, the Holy Roman emperor Lothair III's involvement in the Investiture Controversy, the conversion of Duke William X of Aquitaine, the battles against the forces of Roger II of Sicily, Bernard's travels in Italy, the affair of Louis the Fat, Louis the Young, and Thibaut of Champagne, and—in his last days—the way in which Bernard saved the city of Metz, a matter on which Bossuet, understandably, dwells at some length. Fénelon then glances at the Second Crusade and its failure, Bernard's condemnation of Abelard, Gilbert de la Porrée, and the followers of Henry of Toulouse, and then spends some time dealing with a matter studiously avoided by most of the panegyrists we have so far considered: Bernard's miracles.

Both Rancé and Bossuet looked with disquiet, if not suspicion, on marvels and miracles. They did not and could not, of course, deny them, but Rancé was accused of refusing to acknowledge the authenticity of certain miracles accepted as genuine by the Church if they did not accord with his principles,[3] and Bossuet thought that too much interest in miracles could be decidedly dangerous. On March 4, 1694, he wrote to Madame Guyon, saying, "I include among the things you should put aside all predictions, visions, miracles, and, in a word, all things that are extraordinary, however ordinary they may appear to you in certain states; for all these things go to nourish self-love [*l'amour-propre*] unless one takes great care."[4] Thus, although Rancé and Bossuet certainly mention Bernard's miracles in their panegyrics, they mention them only in passing: there are some half-dozen lines in Rancé, a single sentence in Bossuet, and that is all.

Fénelon, however, not only summarizes Bernard's achievements in curing the sick, making the blind see, the deaf hear, and the lame walk, raising paralytics from their beds, giving health to the dying, and foretelling the future; he also offers a number of specific examples: the episode of the blessed bread at Sarlat in the Dordogne, the numerous cures at Constance, and other miracles in "a town in Germany," at Frankfurt am

---

[3] See Bell, *Understanding Rancé*, 158–59.
[4] Bossuet, *Correspondance*, 6:164 (Letter 1004).

Main, and one or two other places. Although he had the soul of a mystic, Fénelon does not venture into the perilous water of Bernard's mystical experiences, but his detailed account of his miracles reveals an interest in these matters either unshared or avoided by Bossuet and most of his contemporaries.

But he then returns to the main theme of his discourse. In some of his writings Bernard rebukes us in no uncertain terms for our lax and wicked ways, but to return to the straight path, to the "way of the Lord" proclaimed by John the Baptist, is far from easy. Our world is a world of confusion and sin, and the worst is not yet over. We see vanity and affliction of spirit, and it is easier to laud the condition of the dead than to praise the state of the living. The very Church itself is the subject of attack and blasphemy from the mouths of the Protestants—those proud and monstrous sects to which the North gave birth in the last century—and the Catholics are not much better. People no longer worship idols of gold and silver, that is true: they worship gold and silver *per se*! War rages between Christians,[5] and God, in his wrath, leaves them all to follow the desires of their own hearts. And where will that lead them? To the Abyss.

We have, in fact, returned to the times of paganism. Those who repent of their sins and battle against sensual desires are ridiculed. To fear God's omnipotent justice is regarded as weakness. To live according to faith and to hope for a blessed eternity are seen as folly. What we need, says Fénelon, is another Bernard to bring back truth and justice to the world. But if this is asking too much, then for this one day at least, let us try not to harden our hearts. One thing, he tells us, is sure: the day of God's Judgment will come, and when it does come, it will be very terrible. Yet even with this dread certainty looming, the Bernardine nuns of his congregation are not doing their part. "I have offered you blessing [*la bénédiction*]," he says, "but you have rejected it. Malediction [*la malédiction*] is

---

[5] This is of no help in dating the panegyric. Wars raged between Christians for almost the whole of Fénelon's adult life.

coming, it is coming, and you will be swept away by it!" (§33). So will we all if we do not amend our lives, and, as we might expect, in the final paragraph of his sermon, Fénelon begs for Bernard's intercession so that God may show us mercy rather than vengeance and that we, in the fullness of time, may rejoice with Bernard in paradise.

Save for the details of Bernard's miracles, this is a sermon whose content runs parallel to that of Bossuet and, indeed, parallel to a number of the other panegyrists. For both Bossuet and Fénelon the two essential features of Bernard's life are his humility and penitence on the one hand and his apostolic zeal in spreading and defending the faith on the other. Both were typical themes of the Counter-Reformation religious revival in seventeenth-century France. Like Bossuet, Fénelon's sources are limited: Scripture, naturally, and then John Chrysostom, Tertullian (if it is indeed Tertullian), and the *Vita prima*, which is Fénelon's source for the whole of Bernard's life and, I suspect, for his brief quotations from Bernard's letters, the *De consideratione*, and the sermons on the Song of Songs. And apart from the verse from Isaiah and Luke that is the text of his sermon, there is no Latin whatever.

But if the content of the panegyric is similar to that of Bossuet, the style is eminently Fénelon's own. If Bossuet's panegyric is a stately limousine, a Rolls-Royce Silver Ghost, proceeding with a sedate and secure pace down a long straight road, Fénelon's is a sports car, a two-seater Bentley, moving far faster, and carrying us along with it whether we like it or not. Nor does Fénelon tell us the tales of Bernard's exploits and then, at the end, exhort us to imitate him. His exhortations are to be found throughout his discourse and are an integral part of the text. Cardinal Maury considered him the equal of the "three immortal preachers," Bossuet, Bourdaloue, and Massillon, simply on the grounds of two great sermons alone,[6] but

---

[6] See Maury, 2:21–22.

it is the way in which Fénelon touches the heart that moves him most. In the matter of *onction*, he writes,

> there is a smooth and flowing eloquence that, without producing any startling shock, steals effortlessly into the soul and there awakens the most devout feelings of the human heart. It is a succession of natural and moving ideas poured out in abundance, and, at the very moment the listener hears them, he forgets the orator who inspires them and believes he is conversing with himself or, rather, that in a certain way he is present as a witness at a secret meeting between his judge and his conscience. The impression one receives of so tender and so telling a feeling soon shows itself outwardly: every word adds to the emotion one shares, and I cannot tell you what formidable benefits it produces. It makes all good hearts throb and moves them with a need to weep tears of sorrow or repentance, tears that never stream forth without also giving one some comfort. Such is the eloquence of Fénelon.[7]

Such indeed is the eloquence of Fénelon, and, on the whole, Tréverret agrees. In his view, Fénelon was a man of genius who could see what was lacking in the pulpit oratory of the two giants, Bossuet and Bourdaloue, and sought to address these deficiencies in his own works. He had "a lively and curious intelligence that was always seeking new projects and new ideas, or an effective return to those of antiquity,"[8] and one of the most important of these new ideas involved the way in which a panegyric should be constructed. Fénelon did not like the neoscholastic divisions and subdivisions that were

---

[7] Maury, 2:241. The entire brief chapter (240–42) bears the title "On the unction of Fénelon." Maury's esteem for Fénelon is reflected in his long 1771 "Eulogy on Fénelon" in his *Essai*, 2:291–359 (text), 361–443 (notes).

[8] Tréverret, 158.

standard at the time (Biroat is certainly the best example) and sought instead to impose on his panegyrics an essential and overall unity in which all that is said illustrates a single theme. How was this to be done? "Since the best way of praising a saint," said Fénelon, "is to give an account of his praiseworthy deeds, . . . I will content myself with weaving a cloth from the main facts . . . , and to these I will add all the moral reflections that I believe to be most appropriate."[9] The vague and exorbitant praise, he continues, that fills so many panegyrics is not particularly effective, and there is little point in simply repeating generalizations, saying that a particular saint was worthy of admiration, or that his virtues were heavenly, or that he was more angel than human, and so on. No. One should praise the saints by giving a detailed account of their thoughts and deeds, by offering to one's audience a complete picture of their character and using this as a basis for those moral exhortations and reflections that the preacher deems to be the most touching and effective.[10]

Does Fénelon succeed in this? Not quite, for in his panegyric on Bernard, the preacher does not practice what he preaches. He falls back into the old way of dividing his discourse into two parts, and each of the two parts follows essentially the same order: first the *tissu* of historical fact, then warning, exhortation, and encouragement. And there are yet further problems, says Tréverret. In his opinion, Fenelon's account is too concise and moves too quickly. This speed may have its charm—as we have said, it certainly carries one along—but it must be admitted that it sometimes leaves an incomplete image of the saint and of his century, whereas a complete image is very necessary if we are to see and appreciate what he was really like.[11] Yet Tréverret is swept away by Fénelon's eloquence, and he points

---

[9] Tréverret, 161, quoting Fénelon. See also Tréverret, 209.
[10] See Tréverret, 161–62.
[11] See Tréverret, 165–66.

out that if Fénelon's goal is simply to outline for his listeners the person of the saint, to have him loved and admired, and then to lead them by their enthusiasm to a practical conclusion, namely, to hold in contempt all those pleasures and all those excesses that Bernard condemned in his own time, then he has certainly succeeded. And that, says Tréverret (unusually for him), is enough. But, says he, the section from "In the twelfth century of the Church" to "Bernard left Rome five days after it was ended"—sections 20–23 in the translation below—is, in his opinion, "the most beautiful narration that one can find in the panegyrics of Fénelon."[12]

Albert and Court are less positive. They recognize the liveliness of his sermons and the richness of his imagination, but they cannot put them forth as models of eloquence. They admit that there are many useful observations and reflections, but Fénelon's reasoning is not always sound, and he does not always follow the rules of seventeenth- and eighteenth-century rhetoric. Nor do they care for his rejection (in theory) of the divisions and subdivisions used by virtually all the preachers of his day, pointing out that if these are properly used, they can give order and method to a discourse and help to produce a well-organized whole in which each section follows neatly and logically from that which precedes it.[13] Nowadays, when the rules of classical rhetoric are largely forgotten and the neo-scholastic principles of logical organization largely ignored, Fénelon receives a better press. But the best way to come to any judgment in the matter is to read his panegyric on Saint Bernard, and here it is.

---

[12] Tréverret, 175. Tréverret's discussion of the panegyric on Bernard is to be found primarily on pages 164–68 of his ninth chapter. The other panegyric he discusses is that on Saint Teresa of Jesus.
[13] See Albert / Court, 94–95.

THE PANEGYRIC
SERMON FOR THE FEAST DAY OF SAINT BERNARD[14]

Vox clamantis in deserto: Parate viam Domini.
(Isa 40:3; Luke 3:4)
"The voice of him who cries in the wilderness:
Prepare the way of the Lord."

1. The prophet Isaiah, lifted above himself in the spirit, had heard a mysterious voice that was already preparing the way in the desert for the people of God to return from their captivity in Babylon, though this was two hundred years before it actually happened.[15] But this return was no more than a figure of the true deliverance reserved for the Savior; and Saint John [the Baptist], as we learn from the Gospel, was the promised way who prepared humanity to be delivered by the Son of God.

---

[14] *Œuvres complètes de François de Salignac de La Mothe Fénélon, archevêque-duc de Cambrai, prince du Saint-Empire. Nouvelle édition, revue et corrigée avec soin, par [Jean-François de] La Harpe. Tome III* (Paris: Briand, 1810), 182–203; *Œuvres de Fénélon, archevêque de Cambrai, publiées d'après les manuscrits originaux et les éditions les plus correctes; avec un grand nombre de pièces inédites,* [ed. Augustin-Pierre-Paul Caron and Jean-Edme-August Gosselin,] Tome XVII (Paris: J. A. Lebel, 1823), 222–44; *Œuvres de Fénelon, archevêque de Cambrai, précédées d'études sur sa vie, par M. [Louis] Aimé-Martin.* Tome deuxième (Paris: Lefevre, 1835), 393–400; *Œuvres de Fénelon, archevêque de Cambrai, savoir: ses Lettres sur divers sujets de religion et du métaphysique; ses Sermons, Entretiens, et plans de sermons: précédés de sa Vie par le Cardinal de Bausset, suivie des pièces justificatives, publiées par M. l'abbé [Jacques-Paul] Migne* (Paris: J.-P. Migne, 1861), cols. 936–48. The Caron / Gosselin edition, followed by Migne, gives the subtitle "His solitary life, and his apostolic life."

[15] Isaiah was prophesying in the eighth century BCE; the Babylonian Captivity came to an end in about 539 BCE.

2. Today, my brothers,[16] Bernard, walking in the footsteps of John, makes the wilderness resound with his cries[17] and fills the earth with the fruits of the repentance[18] he preaches.[19] In this last age of the world, he is the voice that still cries, "Prepare the way of the Lord for the second coming of Jesus Christ." *Vox clamantis in deserto: Parate viam Domini.*

3. Through Bernard's own solitary life, the desert flourishes again and the monastic state regains its former glory. Through Bernard's apostolic life, the world is reformed and the Church triumphs. This is the voice that, issuing from the wilderness, makes itself heard to the very ends of the earth. He himself is both the patriarch of solitaries and the apostle of the nations, and it is these two ideas, my brothers, that will comprise the whole subject of my discourse.

4. Oh Savior, you who gave him [what he needed] to do your work, give me [what I need] to speak of it. May the torrents of light and grace that poured from his mouth to flood cities and provinces pass now from my own mouth, sinner though I am, deep into the hearts [of those who hear me]. Give me, Lord, give me [this strength], according to the measure of our faith; give it to me for the glory of your name and for the nourishment of your children. Mary, on whom he called with such loving trust, on you we, too, call with him: *Ave Maria*.

[FIRST POINT]

5. To what [dangers] is one not exposed, my brothers, not only through human malice and one's own frailty but also by

---

[16] Fénelon usually address *mes frères,* but since he also addresses *filles de Bernard* ("daughters of Bernard") in §15, *épouses de l'Agneau* ("brides of the Lamb") in §18, and *vierges du Seigneur* ("virgins of the Lord") in §19, he is clearly speaking to a mixed audience.

[17] Throughout his sermon, Fénelon makes great use of the Historical Present (or Dramatic Present or Narrative Present), which certainly gives a sense of immediacy.

[18] *Pénitence*: see appendix 1, s.v. *pénitence* / penitence.

[19] See Matt 3:2; Mark 1:4; and Luke 3:3.

the very gifts bestowed by God! From his earliest years Bernard has to deal with shameless people who seek to destroy his innocence, with his own good looks, which according to the wise man are a stumbling block,[20] and finally with his own spirit, which tempts him to vanity because of his success in his studies. Everywhere he turns there are traps! And us?[21] We abuse the very gifts that come from the pure hands of God so as to forget him and please ourselves. But nothing can steal from Jesus Christ what he holds in his hand, what he has chosen and sealed[22] with the seal of his everlasting love.[23] When God leads people by the hand, they walk without the least concern through the shadows of death, they tread on the asp and the basilisk, they trample underfoot the lion and the dragon; a thousand arrows on their left and ten thousand on their right fall at their feet, yet they remain unscathed.[24] Already a soft inner voice thrills Bernard to the marrow and calls him to the desert. In vain do his relatives and friends seek to stop him: he carries them with him in the speed of his flight! When the youngest of his brothers [Nivard] sees the others leaving their paternal inheritance and fleeing, stripped of everything, to carry the cross of Jesus Christ, he cries, "What's this, my brothers? You take Heaven and leave me only Earth?" And the child follows

---

[20] Sir 9:5: "Do not stare at a young woman, lest perhaps her beauty be a stumbling-block for you."

[21] Unlike the other panegyrists, who generally set out what Bernard did in the world (or the cloister), then what he did in the cloister (or the world), and then, at the end, what all this means for their congregations and why they need to clean up their act, Fénelon interweaves his criticisms into his sermon from the very beginning (though he brings them to a terrifying conclusion at the end).

[22] See 2 Cor 1:22; Eph 4:30.

[23] *Dilection éternelle*: *dilection*, which always refers to love in a good or positive sense, is a fairly rare word for love. Bossuet also speaks of God's *dilection éternelle* for his erring children, but the term is far from common. See further appendix 1, s.v. *charité* / charity.

[24] See Ps 22:4; Ps 90:7, 13.

the holy flock.[25] Thus it is that Bernard, at the age of twenty-three,[26] makes his way into the wilderness and draws after him, as in a [Roman] triumph, his defeated flesh and blood. Thirty of his relatives or friends, whose chains he shatters, are the living and honored offerings he presents to God.[27]

6. Learn from this, my friends, to hope against all hope, and never to be discouraged in working for the faith. Stephen, abbot of Cîteaux,[28] was seeking help and being ground down by the long wait. His disciples were dying, and the austerity of his house terrified those who were thinking of taking vows there. At the very moment when the whole enterprise was about to fail (for God will take things as far as they can go when testing his own), God restored everything when all human resources had been exhausted. Hurry, Bernard, hurry! Comfort this holy old man and support this tottering house of God! Among the thirty novices here is one who is the leader and model for all the others, and every day he asks himself, "What have I come here to do?"[29] He resents the time he needs for sleep, and any food, even after the longest fasts, is a cross for him. At the end of a year he still does not know how his dwelling place is constructed.[30] He makes no distinction in the foods that nourish him. All his curiosity[31] is extinguished and

---

[25] For the story of Nivard, see *Vita prima* 1.3.17 (William of Saint-Thierry); PL 185:236CD; CF 76:20–21.

[26] See chap. 7 (Bossuet), n. 63.

[27] The date was probably May 1113: see chap. 7 (Bossuet), n. 63.

[28] Stephen Harding (d. 1134), third abbot of Cîteaux from 1109 to 1133. He resigned the office in 1133 as a result of old age and infirmity and died the following year.

[29] *Vita prima* 1.4.19 (William of Saint-Thierry); PL 185:238A; CF 76:22: *Bernarde, Bernarde, ad quid venisti*, quoting Matt 26:50 and RB 60.3.

[30] The dwelling place (*la maison*) was the novitiate at Cîteaux. William of Saint-Thierry tells us that Bernard spent a full year there without ever noticing that it was vaulted (*Vita prima* 1.4.20 [William of Saint-Thierry]; PL 185:238D; CF 76:23).

[31] See appendix 1, s.v. *curiosité* / curiosity.

all his feelings suppressed. The spirit of prayer consumes everything, and even manual labor cannot distract him from it.[32]

7. In spite of his youth, he was sent off to found a new colony of solitaries in the dreadful valley of Clairvaux, where there were no signs of any other human beings save robbers.[33] Once there, the brothers were often reduced to eating grass and leaves. But the new abbot, relentless in his fight against nature, is indifferent to all its demands, and other desires set his heart ablaze. When his monks are afflicted by temptations and come to lay them before him so as to find relief and accuse themselves of still being weak, Saint Bernard, instead of giving them comfort, groans to find that those whom he already wants to see transformed into angels are still merely men.[34] Yet they suffer his harsh reproofs without complaint. This gentle and quiet humility finally opens his eyes. "It is in the furnace of temptation," he said then, "that gold is purified. A true father should be the comforter of his children and shelter them under his wings as his chicks in a storm." But nature, ever unpredictable, passed from this excess of severity to a different kind of excess, that of discouragement, and he had decided to condemn himself to silence, had not a heavenly vision[35] given him the instruction and reassurance [he needed] from that moment on. Have no fear, disciples of Bernard: grace is poured

---

[32] For his descriptions of Bernard's asceticism, Fénelon is dependent on *Vita prima* 1.4.20–22 (William of Saint-Thierry); PL 185:238B–40B; CF 76:23–26.

[33] Fénelon now follows the account in *Vita prima* 1.5.25–6.29 (William of Saint-Thierry); PL 185:241C–44C; CF 76:28–33. Clairvaux was founded in 1115; Bernard was twenty-five.

[34] Fénelon is following *Vita prima* 1.6.28 (William of Saint-Thierry); PL 185:243AC; CF 76:31–32.

[35] The vision, that is, of a boy standing in front of him, who tells him that whenever he is about to speak, he should say with confidence (*fiducialiter*) whatever comes first into his mind, for his words will be those of the Holy Spirit (*Vita prima* 1.6.29 [William of Saint-Thierry]; PL 185:244BC; CF 76:33, echoing Matt 10:20).

on his lips from on high, a law of clemency is impressed on his tongue, and from his mouth you will now hear only wisdom and sweetness.

8. How splendid it is, my brothers, to hear William of Saint-Thierry, the historian of [Bernard's] life, tell us the story of his first visit to Clairvaux![36] "I thought at first (he said) that I was seeing the deserts of Egypt peopled with solitaries: a deep and narrow valley surrounded by high mountains covered with gloomy forests, a few poor dwellings like shepherds' huts, built by the hands of the solitaries themselves, the valley filled with men continually moving about, yet everywhere there reigned order and silence: there was no other noise save that of their labor and the praises of Jesus Christ. The brothers ate bread that was so coarse as to be almost earth, which they prepared by the sweat of their brow. Their eyes were lowered, and they saw almost nothing; their faces were pale and emaciated, but they shone serenely with the love of God. Their bodies, thin and wasted, were animated only by the joy of the Holy Spirit and the hope of heaven." But it was Bernard, my brothers, who appeared to the astonished eyes of William to be the most precious ornament of this wilderness. He wore a hairshirt,[37] and underneath his cheap[38] habit there was a young man whose once delicate beauty was now almost entirely lost. He who had been naturally lively and delightful was now listless and driven by his austerities to the very gates of death.

---

[36] This was in 1118/1119, and for what follows Fénelon is dependent on *Vita prima* 1.7.34–36 (William of Saint-Thierry); PL 185:247C–48D; CF 76:39–42.

[37] See *Vita prima* 1.8.39 (William of Saint-Thierry); PL 185:250A; CF 76:44. Bernard wore the hairshirt for as long as he could keep it hidden, but as soon as he found out that others knew of it, he discarded it.

[38] The adjective is *vil*, whose main meaning is cheap or low-priced, but the implication is that Bernard's habit was in a fairly disgusting condition. Indeed, after reading William's account, one can only conclude that Bernard himself was also in a fairly disgusting condition.

But then, in obedience to the bishop of Châlons,[39] who had been given total authority over him by the Order, he rebuilt his health with the nourishment of milk and vegetables.

9. Oh you, who panic at the least infirmity and who never cease paying attention to your lax human nature, so greedy for comfort, you who do not blush to deprive your soul of its true food, which is fasting and prayer, so as to give your body only that which serves to soften and destroy it: come and see how this man of God regrets giving anything to his sinful body, even when it is ready to fall into ruin!

10. On his return from Liège [in 1131],[40] Pope Innocent II spent a few days at Clairvaux and admired what he saw. His eyes could not get enough of the spectacle of these earthly angels. He wept tears of joy, and the bishops who were with him could not stop themselves from weeping with him.[41] O sweet tears! Who will move us now to weep thus and wash away these other tears, so bitter, which are forced from us every day by so much misery and so many scandals? Oh blessed joy of the Church, when will God restore you once again to earth? Oh you unmoved people, who do not deign to open your eyes and cast even one glance on that which the universe has most revered! They are in this assembly as if they were not; the presence of God robs them both of others and of themselves!

11. While Bernard plants and waters, God brings all to bloom. Cultivated by pure hands, the desert sprouts, blossoms, and gives forth a scent that perfumes the whole Church. In this field, wild with brambles and tangled thickets, myrtle trees are growing! Where once were thornbushes, we now see lilies!

---

[39] William of Champeaux (d. 1121), bishop of Châlons-sur-Marne from 1113 to his death. See *Vita prima* 1.7.32 (William of Saint-Thierry); PL 185:246BC; CF 76:37. William had been given authority over Bernard for a period of one year.

[40] See Williams, *Saint Bernard*, 109–10.

[41] *Vita prima* 2.1.6 (Arnold of Bonneval); PL 185:272AB; CF 76:84–85; Williams, *Saint Bernard*, 110–11.

Look, my brothers, look at this great tree planted at Clairvaux! Not long ago, this was no more than a feeble plant clinging to the ground, a prey to every wind; now its branches reach the heavens and stretch to the ends of the earth. It is planted by running streams, and a river of grace bathes its deepest roots. The posterity of Bernard is blessed like that of Abraham.[42] How is it, he says to himself, that I, who am a barren trunk, have given life to all these? Where do they come from, all these children and heirs of my poverty and my solitude? From Flanders they come, from Aquitaine, from Italy, from Germany, and they come in crowds! O you winds, carry them on your wings to their father's bosom, and may people everywhere give glory to God and admire his fruitfulness!

12.[43] My brothers, do you want to see the bole of the tree that bears so much fruit? Look at Bernard! The lights that he shed on his [monks] he drew not from study but from prayer. He said himself that his instruction came less from book learning than from the silence of his desert.[44] No longer do we see a man of savage zeal, impatient with the least imperfection; on the contrary, he is now a tender mother who is everything to everyone: with one hand he gives solid food to those who are full grown; with the other he holds the little ones to his bosom so that they may suckle at his breast. He cannot look on the death of the least of his children without weeping, and despite their countless numbers, he is so fond of them that each and every one of them is aware of it. They are the apple of his eye, whom he scarcely ventures to touch. Must he correct them?

---

[42] See Gen 26:4.

[43] For the whole of this next paragraph, Fénelon is following Geoffrey of Auxerre: *Vita prima* 3.7.25–28; PL 185:317C–20A; CF 76:171–76.

[44] See *Vita prima* 1.4.23 (William of Saint-Thierry); PL 185:240D; CF 76:26–27, and compare Bernard's Ep 106.2, SBOp 7:266–67, to Henry Murdac: "Believe me, who have experience of this: you will find more in the woods than in books, and stones will teach you what you cannot hear from any master."

Straightaway his heart bleeds. Take note of the delicate touch of a charity[45] that fears everything. My dear children, he says, I am like the apostle, caught between two extremes, and I do not know which to choose.[46] Shall I be content and ease my conscience by telling you the truth, or shall I torment myself by having told you yet seen no fruit? It would not be pleasing to God if a mother were to comfort herself for the death of her child on the grounds that she had neglected nothing in trying to cure him![47] It may be said that he put up with too many who were by nature incorrigible, yet it often happened that patience produced changes in these obdurate souls, [changes] one would not have dared to hope for. Learn therefore, you whom God has raised above the heads of others to govern them, learn to abase yourself at their feet, to suffer, to hold your tongue, to await from God what you cannot obtain from any human being. Humility conquers everything! When [Bernard] saw that someone was angry with him,[48] what did he say? "I will yield to you," he said, "despite you and despite myself."[49] This is the price, my brothers, that one pays to win over hearts and sweep away all resistance. But woe, woe to

---

[45] *Charité*: see appendix 1, s.v. *charité* / charity.

[46] See Phil 1:22-23.

[47] This is what Fénelon says, but the Latin is clearer: "If a mother has a sick son and does everything she can to love and cure him, but if, at the end, she sees herself thwarted and that nothing she did had any effect, and the boy dies, is [the fact that she did all that she could] any reason for her to hold back her tears?" (*Vita prima* 3.7.26 [Geoffrey of Auxerre]; PL 185:319A; CF 76:174; Geoffrey is quoting Bernard, SC 43.3.5; SBOp 2:36). In other words, the fact that Bernard has done all that he can to lead his monks on the right path is no comfort to him if and when some of them go astray.

[48] This was Hugh, abbot of Prémontré, who had accused Bernard of stealing two of his monks and preventing him from building a nunnery: see Williams, *Saint Bernard*, 234.

[49] Fénelon is paraphrasing Geoffrey of Auxerre, *Vita prima* 3.7.27; PL 185:319C; CF 76:174–75, and Geoffrey is quoting Bernard's Ep 253.10; SBOp 8:155, to Hugh of Prémontré. What Bernard actually

us who so often find God's work impossible because we do it negligently and without faith. Woe to us when we complain of obstacles that we ourselves put there by our own arrogance, our own indiscretion, or our own laxity!

13. Does it surprise you, my brothers, that after so much labor and so much suffering, at the age of sixty-three, the victim who had been sick for so long now comes to his end? "I have received your letter," he wrote to Arnold, abbot of Bonneval, "with tender feelings, but not with pleasure. What pleasure could I have in a life that is an ocean of bitterness? Sleep itself has left me so that suffering never leaves me."[50] You see him in these tender and courageous words, you see him now, in the very grasp of death, still preserving these keen and ingenious turns of phrase.[51] You see before you this inner man who rebuilds himself day by day on the ruins of the outer man who is ready to die. At the news of his imminent departure, the silence of the desert is troubled, all are moved, all are groaning, all are weeping. The bishops and abbots flock to his side. "Here I am," Bernard says to them, "torn between my desire to go to Jesus Christ and my desire never to be separated from you. But the choice is God's alone."[52] The choice is already made, my brothers. No more was he holding to earth; he was escaping from the tender embraces of his own. Amid the sorrowful sighs from his grieving house, his soul flew into the joy of his God.

---

wrote was "I shall cling to you, even though you do not wish it; I shall cling to you, even if I do not wish it."

[50] *Vita prima* 5.1.10 (Geoffrey of Auxerre); PL 185:356D–57A; CF 76:242–43 = Ep 310; SBOp 8:230, to Arnold of Bonneval. See also Alan of Auxerre's *Vita secunda* 30.83; PL 185:520D–21A.

[51] Bernard was always a great Latinist and remained a great Latinist to his death. His last letter—if it is truly his (it has been suggested otherwise: see the discussion in SBOp 8:xiv–xv)—does indeed contain phrases that are *vifs et ingénieux*.

[52] See *Vita prima* 5.2.12 (Geoffrey of Auxerre); PL 185:358B–59A; CF 76:244–45.

14. Oh father! Oh father! they say, beating their breasts. Oh father! Oh leader of the children of Israel! Why do you abandon us? Alas! The burning lamp is extinguished in the house of God! Woe, woe to us, for we have sinned, and God strikes us!

15. Oh children, listen to the voice of your father. Oh daughters of Bernard,[53] it is not I, an unworthy sinner, whom you hear: it is Bernard himself who speaks to you from the heights of heaven where he reigns with Jesus Christ. There he reigns with him, and thence he will descend with him when the Son of Man comes to judge the earth. How will you answer him when he asks you about the divine fire that the breath of his mouth had kindled here below? Does it still burn in your hearts?

16. Oh solitude, dear refuge of virgin souls! Save these daughters of Bernard from the deceptions of the world and the fiery shafts of Satan! May they know nothing of the contagion of the world around them, and may they desire nothing more than to know nothing! May they feel in themselves how sweet it is to be forgotten by the children of men when one tastes the gifts of the consecrated Bridegroom.

17. Oh reform, oh reform, which cost Bernard so many vigils, fasts, tears, sweat, and ardent prayers! Could we ever believe that you would come to an end? No, no, may that thought never enter my head! Perish rather the evil day that would reveal such a collapse! What? Would Bernard himself, from the sanctuary where he is crowned, see his house despoiled, his work defaced, and his children a prey to worldly desires? I would rather my eyes became fountains of tears, I would rather see the whole Church groaning night and day to prevent that which makes its glory from becoming a disgrace.

18. Oh brides of the Lamb, you comfort the Church for the outrages she suffers from her children; you wipe away the tears she sheds on the flood of iniquity that covers the face of the earth. Do not take this comfort away; do not pile sorrow

---

[53] See n. 16 above.

on sorrow; do not come, with a parricide's hands, to tear open her wounds already streaming with blood, but remember that the salt of the earth is soon made tasteless and trampled underfoot.[54] If the heart opens itself but a little to the vanities and pleasures of the world, it will be intoxicated by them. At first one says this is nothing, but this nothing determines everything! A seductive amusement [creeps in] under the name of a necessary consolation; an occupation that seems innocent, but that dissipates a spirit weary of recollection[55] and bored by [spiritual] exercises; a friendship in which one pours out one's heart to no purpose and in which that heart, already softened, now becomes like mere wax; the freedom to judge for oneself, which gives rise to grumbling and which takes away the taste of happy simplicity and makes bitter whatever obedience demands; or finally, those secret and undetectable reservations that divide the heart and that anger a jealous God. Virgins, flee that old serpent[56] who slithers along among the grass and the flowers. Flee him, you virgins, for every one of his bites is venomous. Oh daughters of Bernard, show forth in yourselves your father who lives in you! In his time, he restored a monastic discipline that had almost ceased to exist. Do you want to leave it to perish in your own [time], when [that discipline] itself asks that its glory be preserved through you? Despite himself, he was dragged into the midst of the world by princes and by the needs of the Church, yet he preserved his recollection [of God], his simplicity, and his fervor: Will you do away with all these virtues in your silence and solitude?

19. But take careful note of what it was that made him a wall of bronze[57] against all the attacks of the Enemy. It is because he never spoke to anyone in his solitude save to distribute

---

[54] See Matt 5:13.

[55] *Recueillement*: see appendix 1, s.v. *recueillement* / recollection.

[56] See Rev 12:9 and 20:2.

[57] This is the *murus aereus* of Jer 1:18. Rancé and Massillon use just the same expression to describe Bernard.

the gifts of God. Virgins of the Lord, if you must meet with those from outside to offer them some enlightenment, let the occasions be brief and rare, and then, straightaway, return to your house with a greater taste for the hidden life. [Bernard] did what he did only to make people aware of Jesus Christ through his miraculous gifts, yet he feared his own miracles and dared not perform them at Clairvaux, lest his solitude be invaded by crowds of people. It was this love of the desert that led him to refuse the bishoprics of Reims and Milan.[58] Keep far away, therefore, daughters of Bernard, far away from these delightful dreams that can bewitch your senses. Keep far away from this accursed illusion that passes away,[59] this world, this glorious phantom that will fade away. For if we have seen Bernard leaving [the solitude of] Clairvaux so many times, it is on the express orders of the pope and for the most pressing needs of the Church. Thus it was that John [the Baptist] came forth from the desert to bear witness to the Savior and, with no fear, to tell kings[60] what they should do; it is now time, my brothers, to show you this in [Bernard's] apostolic work [in the world].

[SECOND POINT]

20.[61] In the twelfth century of the Church, God was angry with men and women, and with his rod of iron[62] he struck the shepherds of his people. The flock was growing ever weaker,

---

[58] See *Vita prima* 2.4.26 (Arnold of Bonneval); PL 185:283B; CF 76:106, which lists Langres, Châlons-sur-Marne, Genoa, Milan, and Reims.

[59] See 1 Cor 7:31.

[60] I.e., Herod Antipas.

[61] This paragraph is an exceedingly brief summary of Arnold of Bonneval's account in *Vita prima* 2.1.1–2.2.11; PL 185:268C–76A; CF 76:79–92. For the Councils of Étampes and Pisa, see Williams, *Saint Bernard*, 105–8 (Étampes) and 137–38 (Pisa).

[62] Ps 2:9; Rev 2:27; 19:15.

far from its pastures and at the mercy of ravening wolves. The antipope Anacletus lights a fire that spreads rapidly from kingdom to kingdom, and nothing can extinguish it. Innocent II, chosen for his virtues, succumbs and escapes to Pisa. People everywhere are undecided and do not know who is the true shepherd. The Church of France, assembled at Étampes, [in 1130,] sees that only Bernard can decide the matter and waits for God to speak through his mouth. And then, enlightened by him, it opens its arms and takes to its bosom the true fugitive pontiff. Straightaway I see Bernard instilling new life into the pope and cardinals by his invigorating counsel, [I see him] leading the king of England [Henry I] back to unity by his gentle persuasion, [I see him], by the authority of his power, putting a stop to the emperor Lothair [III of Supplinburg], who wished to profit from the troubles to renew his claim to investitures,[63] [I see him] calling on this very prince to lead Innocent to Rome in order to dethrone the proud Anacletus, [I see him] convoking a council at Pisa [in 1135] where the whole western Church, with one voice, excommunicated the antipope, and finally [I see him] vanquishing the city of Milan, which had stubbornly supported Anacletus in the schism by displaying to her, by his miracles, the whole power of the Most High. This is how the man of God speaks, this is how he acts, when he is sent by God.

21. And you, proud duke of Aquitaine,[64] who, with your strong hands, are still supporting a schism that is already on its way to ruin, you yourself, like a new Saul,[65] will be cast down and groveling in your conversion. You tremble, you

---

[63] See appendix 2, s.v. Lothair III of Supplinburg.
[64] See appendix 2, s.v. William (Guillaume) X, duke of Aquitaine. As we have mentioned, this dramatic episode (with justification) was meat and drink for the panegyrists.
[65] Not King Saul of 1 Samuel, but the Saul who became Saint Paul. Like him, William of Aquitaine will also experience a dramatic (and lasting) conversion.

breathe out against the saints only blood and carnage.[66] In vain you avoid any discussion with the man of God; in vain you persecute the shepherds; you will fall! But stop! Here is Bernard coming to you with the Eucharist in his hands! I see his face ablaze, I hear his terrible voice. Listen, my brothers, listen to what he says! "The whole Church has begged you [to change your position], and you have scorned her tears. Behold before you the Son of the Virgin, the Head of the Church that you insult. Behold your Judge before whom every knee shall bow, whether in heaven, or on earth, or in the places under the earth. Behold your Judge, who holds your soul in his hands: will you scorn him too?" At this thunderbolt, the persecutor falls at Bernard's feet, and no one can raise him up. This roaring lion becomes a lamb.

22. Make haste, my brothers, to follow our Saint Bernard, as a bolt of lightning flashes from East to West. He is already in the farthest reaches of Italy! Coming to Rome, he delivers a mortal blow to the nascent schism. The righteous are comforted, the lost sheep return home, the very foundations of this proud and confused building[67] are undermined. Roger [II], king of Sicily, who is still keeping the schism alive,[68] wants Bernard to meet with Peter of Pisa[69] at Salerno—[Peter] was a deeply learned legal expert and a great orator and belonged to the party supporting Anacletus. But arguments that come from human wisdom, however persuasive and convincing, can do nothing against the truth of God! The prince, as obdurate as Pharaoh,[70] will be vanquished in a battle, just as Bernard had

---

[66] Fénelon is echoing Acts 9:1: "Saul, still breathing out threats and slaughter."

[67] The allusion is to the Tower of Babel (Gen 11:9), which was regularly seen as a symbol of the confounding and confusing of the Church by heresies and schisms.

[68] See appendix 2, s.v. Roger II of Sicily, and *Vita prima* 2.7.43–44 (Arnold of Bonneval); PL 185:293B–94B; CF 76:126–28.

[69] See appendix 2, s.v. Anacletus II, and *Vita prima* 2.7.45–46 (Arnold of Bonneval); PL 185:294B–95C; CF 76:128–31.

[70] See Exod 7:3.

foretold,[71] and Peter of Pisa, struck down by the voice of the man of God, will come [to Rome], humble and trembling, to the feet of the true shepherd whom he had failed to recognize.

23. It is done, my brothers, it is all over. The last flickers of a flame that had swept through the whole of Europe are extinguished: there is again one shepherd and one flock. And Bernard, who had labored for seven years to bring about this reunion, leaves Rome five days after it has been achieved in order to return to his solitude.[72]

24. [But that solitude], my brothers, could not hold him for long, for he was given power over human hearts to make him an angel of peace. Join me now and see him soon announcing to Louis the Fat, with all the authority of a prophet, what will happen to his family and his crown if he does not reconcile himself with his bishops.[73] Soon after that he leaves his monks to their prayers, goes to the camp of Louis the Young, and makes him drop the sword he had already turned against Thibaut, count of Champagne.[74] Soon after that he is promising the queen that she will have a son, but only on condition that she makes peace [with Thibaut].[75] And finally [we see him] saving

---

[71] See *Vita prima* 2.7.43 (Arnold of Bonneval); PL 185:293D; CF 76:126–28. Roger is about to go to battle with Ranulf II, count of Alife and Caiazzo, and is warned by Bernard, "If you enter the conflict, you will leave it defeated and in disorder," and that is precisely what happened. The battle was the Battle of Nocera, fought on October 30, 1137.

[72] Fénelon is following the *Vita prima* 2.7.47 (Arnold of Bonneval); PL 185:296B; CF 76:131–32.

[73] Fénelon's chronology is at fault here. Louis VI the Fat had died on August 1, 1137, and Bernard left Rome for Clairvaux ten months later, on Friday, June 3, 1138. Fénelon is actually referring to Louis's opposition to the French bishops taking part in the Council of Pisa in 1135: see appendix 2, s.v. Louis VI the Fat.

[74] See appendix 2, s.v. Louis VII the Young.

[75] See appendix 2, s.v. Louis VII the Young, and *Vita prima* 4.3.18 (Geoffrey of Auxerre); PL 185:332AB (omitted in CF 76), though the queen had a daughter, Marie, not a son (*fils*). For the whole complicated story, see Williams, *Saint Bernard*, 212–16.

the city of Metz from a conflagration of a war that would have left the city in ashes.[76]

25.[77] But what shall I say of the crusade he proclaimed to help the Christians in the East, [a crusade] that, though sanctioned by the authority of the pope [Eugenius III], the desire of princes, and so many miraculous signs, came to such an unfortunate end?[78] O God, you are terrible in your counsels on the children of men [Ps 65:5]! For it is true that after you had inspired them with what they should do, you rejected them before your face.[79] Why? Perhaps because they subsequently made themselves unworthy to be the instruments of your Providence,[80] or perhaps because you yourself put the enterprise in their hearts only to have them experience a salutary embarrassment! Whatever the reason, my brothers, at the very moment that France is dismayed to learn that the crusaders have been totally defeated, Bernard says these words: "I prefer that people murmur against me rather than against God."[81] And then, taking in his arms a blind child who had been brought to him, he cries out, "Oh God, if it is true that I was inspired to preach the crusade by your Spirit, show that to be the case by restoring the sight to this blind child!" And

---

[76] See chap. 7 (Bossuet), §§48–49, for the story and the sources.

[77] For this paragraph, Fénelon follows the *Vita prima* 3.4.9–10 (Geoffrey of Auxerre); PL 185:308C–9C; CF 76:154–57.

[78] Antoine Anselme and Louis-Bénigne Bourru also deal at some length with the reasons for the failure of the Second Crusade, which was a disaster in itself and a source of considerable embarrassment to Bernard.

[79] See Jer 7:15.

[80] This echoes Bernard's own explanation for the failure of the Crusade in the second book of the *De consideratione*. On Providence, see appendix 1, s.v. *Providence* / Providence.

[81] *Vita prima* 3.4.10 (Geoffrey of Auxerre); PL 185:309B; CF 76:156 = Csi 2.1.4; SBOp 3:413: *Malo in nos murmur hominum quam in Deum esse*, which we might paraphrase as "I'd rather people criticize me than God."

scarcely had the saint uttered this prayer than the child cried out, "I can see!"[82]

26.[83] But what victory in the Church now presents itself before me? Where are those futile philosophers, so curious with regard to the secrets of a wisdom that is wholly earthly? Has he not declared this presumptuous wisdom to be folly?[84] Be silent, Abelard: your subtle thinking[85] will be confounded! Gilbert de la Porrée, you who make the whole Church groan with your profane novelties,[86] return to that sound teaching that has been proclaimed since the days of old! Oh Henry [of Toulouse],[87] through you the saints of the Lord are put to scorn and the most revered mysteries held in derision. Bernard sets out for Toulouse, where [Henry's] erroneous teaching holds sway. Why do you flee, Henry, you who promise to your followers the luminous weapons of the Gospel? The lies in which you put your hope abandon you to all your shortcomings: you cannot stand even the sight of Bernard, from whom shine out the most piercing rays of the truth!

27. Here, my brothers, miracles that are already beyond count are multiplied yet more in order to avenge that truth that has been scorned and to humble every proud head that raises itself against the knowledge of God.[88] Lord Jesus, you

---

[82] *Vita prima* 3.4.10 (Geoffrey of Auxerre); PL 185:309C; CF 76:156–57.

[83] Fénelon now follows the *Vita prima* 3.5.13–6.17 (Geoffrey of Auxerre); PL 185:310D–13C; CF 76:158–63, but his account, as usual, is much abbreviated. For Abelard, Gilbert de la Porrée, and Henry of Toulouse, see appendix 2.

[84] 1 Cor 3:19: "The wisdom of this world is foolishness with God."

[85] *Votre subtilité*: see appendix 1, s.v. *subtil, subtilité* / subtle, subtlety. Subtlety is always a pejorative term.

[86] *Profanes nouveautés*: see appendix 1, s.v. *nouveautés* / novelties. "Novelties," by definition, are always dangerous.

[87] For Henry and his teaching, see appendix 2, s.v. Henry of Toulouse.

[88] Fénelon takes from the *Vita prima* more examples of Bernard's miracles than any other of the panegyrists. We discussed the matter in the Introduction to the panegyric.

said that your disciples, in your name, would do greater works than yours:[89] but what you gave to your apostles to plant the faith, you give again in the sight of all nations so that this faith, so close to being uprooted, may flourish once more. What do I see, my brothers, what do I see? I feel I have been carried away to the Holy City [of Jerusalem]! I believe I see Palestine and the Lord visiting it once more! A blessed power came forth from Bernard, it poured out from him effortlessly as if from a spring, and it even seemed to be beyond his control. He heals everyone who is sick, fevers obey him, and every malady flees from him. The blind see, the deaf hear, the lame walk, paralytics take up their beds, those dying regain their health. He foresees the future and reads it like a book. At Sarlat,[90] to show that what he taught was the truth, he promises that the bread he has blessed will cure every sick person who eats it. "Yes," replies [Geoffrey], bishop of Chartres, who is afraid that Bernard had promised too much, "those who have faith." "No, no," says Bernard, "God's work has nothing to do with faith. Whether they believe or whether they do not believe, they will be healed all the same."[91] And indeed, the whole crowd of sick people, without one exception, feels the hand of God.

28. At Constance, in a single day, eleven people who were blind, ten cripples, and eighteen who were lame are healed.[92] At Metz, a powerful but impious lord refused to listen to him: "If you are not prepared to hear my words," he says to him, "then a deaf man shall hear them!" He puts his fingers into the ears of the deaf man and cures him![93] In a town in Germany

---

[89] See John 14:12.

[90] In the department of the Dordogne in the southwest of France. Bernard passed through Sarlat as part of his missionary journey in Languedoc to root out heresy.

[91] *Vita prima* 3.6.18 (Geoffrey of Auxerre); PL 185:313D–14A; CF 76:164; Williams, *Saint Bernard*, 341.

[92] *Vita prima* 4.5.30 (Geoffrey of Auxerre); PL 185:338B; CF 76:208–9.

[93] *Vita prima* 4.8.49 (Geoffrey of Auxerre); PL 185:349BD; CF 76:228–29.

he sees a blind woman begging: "You ask for money," he says to her, "and God gives you sight." He touched her, and she, opening her eyes, saw with amazement the grace of God by the light of day.[94] At Frankfurt [am Main], the [Holy Roman] emperor [Conrad] himself bears him away on his shoulders lest he be smothered by the crowds of people he is healing.[95] He dares not return to the places where his hand and voice did so many marvels. Now he embarks on a boat; now it is from a window that he sends forth God's power on those who are sick. As soon as he begins to speak in the public squares tears flow and sinners beat their breasts. Happy the one who can touch his garments! Happy the one who can at least kiss the prints his feet have left in the sand! God grants this man's prayers, cries the crowd, must we not listen to him?

29. I tell you, my brothers, and I tell you with joy, that I am overwhelmed by the weight of all the wonderful things I still have left to show you.[96] Oh sweet and tender writings, drawn out and woven by the Holy Spirit itself! You precious monuments with which he enriched the Church, nothing will be able to destroy you, and the course of the centuries, far from obscuring you, will draw from you only light! You will live forever, and Bernard will live in you! Through you, we have the consolation of seeing him, of hearing him, of consulting him, and of pondering what he said. And through you, oh great saint, the whole Church echoed to the sound of that mysterious trumpet that proclaimed the Gospel in the midst of Zion and announced to Judah its iniquities.[97] All are judged: princes and pastors of the people, heads of orders, monks and men of the world. He thunders forth, he strikes like lightning,

---

[94] *Vita prima* 4.8.50 (Geoffrey of Auxerre); PL 185:349D; CF 76:229–30.

[95] *Vita prima* 4.5.31 (Geoffrey of Auxerre); PL 185:338D–39C; CF 76:209–11; Williams, *Saint Bernard*, 280.

[96] Fénelon now turns from Bernard's miracles and delivers a paean of praise for his writings.

[97] See Joel 2:1 and 2:15.

and the cedars of Lebanon are cut down by the sharpness of the words that come from his mouth![98] But must you still be (alas!), to our confusion, a sentence of anathema against our own century, as well as against the one whose wickedness, like a new Jeremiah, you deplore? But in so much power, how is it that one can also detect so much gentleness? Here flows the oil of anointing, descending from the living fountains of the apostles and prophets to flood the house of God; here I sense those sweet perfumes of the bride who exudes [the scent] of ambergris and who languishes for love in the bosom of the Bridegroom, intoxicated with his delights![99]

30. Oh souls who burn with the fire of Jesus, come, make haste to learn from his commentary on the Song of Songs the consolations,[100] trials, and martyrdom of the brides whom a jealous God wishes to purify. How is it that, at the end of the ages, which seem reserved for the curse,[101] God still shows us a man who would have brought back the glory and joy of the first days? It is because the Church, according to the promise of its Bridegroom, has an everlasting beauty, and, even in its old age, it is still fruitful. So in these times of confusion and sin, should we not have seen a renewal of its light? But alas, these days when sin abounds are not over, for what do we see in ours, my brothers? What we would be more than happy never to see at all! Vanity of vanities, and yet more vanity, with toil and affliction under the sun.[102] At the sight of so much

---

[98] See Ps 28:5.

[99] See Song 1:3 and 2:5. This last sentence serves to introduce the next paragraph, which is concerned with Bernard's commentary on the Song of Songs.

[100] "Consolations," in both French and English, is a technical term of mystical theology: see appendix 1, s.v. *consolations* / consolations.

[101] I.e., the Curse of Adam, which is, in essence, sin and death. It was the consequence of eating the fruit of the forbidden tree. See also Sir 41:11-13; Dan 9:11; and n. 113 below. For all the hideous details of what happens when God's curse falls on a people, see Deut 28:15-68.

[102] See Eccl 1:2-3.

wickedness, I envy the dead and I pity the living! What are we being kept for? Outside all those proud and monstrous sects to which the North gave birth in the last century[103] are making game of the sacred text of the Scriptures so as to justify everything their hearts envision and are turning their mouths to heaven to utter blasphemies against the Church—yet the children of the Church itself tear at its bowels and cover it with shame. Indeed, we are reduced to counting as miracles of grace those few Christians who have been saved from the flood of corruption and who have not been driven mad by ambition! People everywhere adore the gods of flesh and blood, who they hope will make their fortune. Their hearts are enslaved by avarice, which, according to Saint Paul, is idolatry.[104] As Saint [John] Chrysostom put it: We no longer adore idols of gold and silver: it is gold and silver itself that we adore, and in it we place our hope![105] Far, far from selling all, adds this Father, as did the first Christians, we buy endlessly. We buy, do I say? We acquire, rather, at the expense of others, we usurp by guile or by authority. Far from easing the burden of the poor, we make them poor all over again! Creditors without number go into decline and ruin for lack of what is owed them. Do you see these Christians who gnaw at themselves, who tear at themselves, who sharpen their venomous tongues, and who arm themselves so as to wash their hands in the blood of their brothers?[106] Do you see them eating away at themselves with their black rages of envy and vengeance? Do you see them sunk without shame in their filthy pleasures and sodden with their unnatural passions? God himself draws back, and in his wrath he gives them over to the desires of their hearts. They believe everything they see, they believe everything they hear,

---

[103] I.e., the Protestants.
[104] Col 3:5: "covetousness [*avaritia*], which is the service of idols."
[105] John Chrysostom, In Rom, hom VI, on Romans 3:8.
[106] See Ps 58:10. If this is a reference to wars between Christians, it is of no help in dating the panegyric: see n. 5 above.

but they see nothing and hear nothing. They grope their way along the edge of the abyss, half asleep with the spirit of drunkenness and dizziness. They will die without ever knowing what they are or who made them.

31. Where then, my brothers, is that happy time of persecution, when Tertullian said to the persecutors, "Go into the prisons, and if you find anyone there in chains accused of any crime other than that of confessing the Lord Jesus, be assured that he is not a Christian; for the true Christian is he who walks the straight path of the Gospel and is accused only for the faith."[107] Do we have the courage now to defy the pagans in this way, and will they surpass us in sins?[108] Alas! Christians are now accused of all manner of excesses. Accused, do I say? They accuse themselves, or, rather, they boast about all the wicked things they do. They no longer know how to blush. Vice triumphs in the public squares, and any sense of shame hides its face. But it is not to avoid praise that it hides itself; rather it is to escape from insults and derision. But although this vice is coarse and shameless, I see another yet more hideous: it is the vice of hypocrisy, which seeks to make evil the rule and which adopts an air of wisdom so as to sanction folly. It calls evil good and good evil (Isa 5:20). It poses as a reformer and laughs at the simplicity of the children of God. It does not reject the Gospel, but under the pretext of avoiding too imprudent a zeal, it dilutes the Gospel and reduces the cross to nothing. This is the iniquity that is growing beyond all bounds and that will soon reach its peak. Every day I hear talk that offends my ears and breaks my heart! I hear piety[109] being mocked. Truth suffers violence.[110] Those who are weak are ashamed of

---

[107] If this is indeed Tertullian, I have not been able to trace it. It looks as if it should appear in the *Apologeticus*, but translating key terms from French into Latin and checking the standard databases has so far proved ineffective.

[108] *Crimes*: see appendix 1, s.v. *crimes* / sins.

[109] *Piété*: see appendix 1, s.v. *piété* / piety.

[110] See Matt 11:12.

the Gospel, just as they were in the days of paganism. Souls [divinely] moved[111] are insulted and are asked, as David was asked, "Where is your God?" [Ps 42:3].

32. Who are you, you ungodly people, who merely laugh when you see a sinner renewed in Jesus Christ, someone who stands firm against the tidal wave of all his passions? What then? You cannot bear it if people declare themselves openly for the God who created us! According to you, it is weakness to fear his eternal and almighty justice and not to be ungrateful for his goodness. According to you, it is foolish to live in accordance with the faith in the hope of eternal blessedness. Who are you then, you people who make fun of religion as well as of those who wish to follow its precepts? Do you belong to some other religion? Do you believe any of them? Leave our churches, go far away from our mysteries, and live without hope, without anyone to save you, without God; go where your ungodly and brutish despair will take you. But, alas! who could believe this? You are Christians, and you have promised to renounce the world and all its pomp, to carry the cross with Jesus Christ, and to hold in scorn everything seen so as to aspire to all that is unseen.[112] I say again, you have promised: you dare not deny that promise, you dare not deny your salvation, for you quake with fear when the nearness of death shows you the abyss that yawns at your feet! You wretched and foolish people! You want to be thought wise, yet you call those fools who, hoping for the good things you do not say you have renounced, strive to make themselves worthy. What a reversal of human reason! What monstrous stupidity! They are possessed by demons! It is not they who speak, but the demons who blaspheme in them. Oh my brothers, we need another Bernard to bring back truth and righteousness to men and women, yet I do not know whether this ungodliness, unknown

---

[111] *Ames touchées*: *toucher*, "to touch, move, affect," is a technical term of French pulpit oratory and is discussed in some detail in chap. 3 of this book.

[112] See Heb 11:1.

in his days, but so deeply rooted in ours, would not withstand even his words and miracles. Does he not speak to you every day through his writings and contemporary accounts, all of which bear witness to everything he did? Listen to him, my brothers.

33. At the very least, my children (for thus he calls you, and thus he is entitled to call you, he who renewed your nation in the name of the Gospel), take care these days that you do not harden your hearts. Oh my children, must I set myself up against you as God's judge? The light your fathers saw and which, from generation to generation, has been reflected on you, will it not serve to show you your iniquities? What have I not endured to present you all together as one spotless virgin to the holy Bridegroom? But what do I see in your midst, oh my children? I have offered you blessing, and you have rejected it. The curse[113] is coming, it is coming, and you will be swept away by it. It will fall on your heads drop by drop until the end. No, I will no longer be your father. I will harden my heart and reject you forever! I will not recognize you! I will be ashamed of you when Jesus Christ comes again, and my words will demand vengeance—or rather, it is his [word], so often scorned.

34. Man of God, given to France and the whole Church, may you never tire of lifting your fatherly hands to God on our behalf. What will happen to us if the very heart of our father is angered, and if the means of mercy calls down vengeance upon us? Oh father! look on our grief and despair, look upon it and hasten! Look upon it, and move our sovereign Judge to mercy so that when you come with him in glory you may lead us to the foot of his throne as your children. May you be followed by a holy company, walking with palms in their hands,[114] and may we, with you, receive the crown that never fades away. May it be so.

---

[113] See n. 101 above.
[114] See Rev 7:9.

9

Bernard in Battle

The Anti-Quietist Polemic of Charles de La Rue

INTRODUCTION

Charles de La Rue (or LaRue) was born in Paris on August 3, 1643, and, after the usual schooling, entered the Society of Jesus on September 7, 1659, when he was sixteen. For some years he taught humanities and rhetoric at Paris, composed poems, tragedies, and comedies in Latin, and, in 1675, published an annotated edition of Virgil, which was received with great acclaim and republished many times thereafter. His heart's desire was to go to Canada and work with the Jesuit missions (the first had been established in 1609), but his numerous requests were refused by his superiors, who assigned him instead to preaching. In this he achieved great success, being called to preach the Advent series at the royal Court for the first time in 1687. After that he preached a further nine *stations*, both for Advent and Lent; when Bossuet died in April 1704, La Rue delivered his funeral oration. He also spent three years preaching to Protestants in the Languedoc (we shall discuss the reasons for this below), but although his discourses were well received, they met with limited success. He was an old man of almost eighty-two when he died, ill and infirm, on May 27, 1725.[1]

Albert and Court have high, though not the highest, praise for him. We may regard him, they say, "as a model of sublime

---

[1] See DLF XVII, 711; DS 9:315–16; Albert / Court, 231–36; Hurel, 2:168–85.

eloquence that both pleases and instructs," though his sermons do not achieve the same heights as those of Bourdaloue or Massillon: one finds neither the solidity nor power of the former, nor the unction nor beauty of the latter.[2] Tréverret agrees.[3] In his view, La Rue has real difficulty in conveying "the sense of the *pathétique*,"[4] by which Tréverret does not mean "pathetic" in the modern sense, but what we have termed *onction*, the capacity to move the heart or touch the soul of the listener. La Rue's panegyrics, he says, have a dryness about them that compares unfavorably with those of, for example, Massillon. Nor do we see the sublimity of Bossuet, nor the fire of Fénelon.[5] Although he lived until 1725, by 1700 La Rue, "with his memories, his experience, and his natural talent," had developed a characteristic style that he had no intention of changing.[6] If there is sufficient historical information, says Tréverret, La Rue tends to concentrate more on this than on the moral and religious life of the saint, and his sermons in praise of the saints can read more like biographies than panegyrics. In his panegyric on Saint François de Sales, for example, he presents us with a portrait of the saint drawn against the background of his time and place, "combating heresy and purifying piety," and this was something new at the time of La Rue. But it is the approach of a historian rather than a moralist.[7] If, however, there is a dearth of historical facts, as, for example, in the case of the virgin and martyr Saint Agnes of Rome, La Rue will fill the void with moral reflections and exhortations. But for Tréverret, the

---

[2] See Albert / Court, 231–33.

[3] Tréverret devotes chap. X (185–206) to La Rue. On page 189 he mentions, in passing, the panegyric on Saint Bernard, but Tréverret did not have access to the unrevised version, which was not published until 1901 (see n. 9 below).

[4] Tréverret, 193.

[5] See Tréverret, 201. On page 206 he describes La Rue as a warmer Fléchier but a weaker Bourdaloue.

[6] Tréverret, 186.

[7] See Tréverret, 187.

end result of this is not entirely satisfactory, though if the historical facts are there, then La Rue "is the most accurate in his accounts, the most faithful, after Fénelon, to historical truth."[8]

The two versions, unrevised and revised, of his panegyric on Saint Bernard are of the greatest interest. For the first, or unrevised, version, which is less a panegyric than a harsh anti-Quietist polemic, we are indebted to Henri Chérot (also a Jesuit), who published the text for the first time in 1901.[9] His source was a manuscript copy of La Rue's sermon made by Léonard de Sainte-Catherine, an Augustinian canon, which gives every indication of being a faithful and reliable transcript.[10] The second, revised version had appeared much earlier in La Rue's *Panégyriques des saints*, published in 1740, fifteen years after his death.[11] The editor of this volume was yet another Jesuit, François Bretonneau, born in the Touraine in 1660, died at Paris in 1741, and himself a preacher. His sermons were "sound, well constructed, clear in their style, but lacking any real greatness,"[12] and he is best known, if he is known at all, for his editions of the sermons of others, including Bourdaloue. The revised version omits most of the polemical material in the unrevised version and corrects the historical inaccuracies, and we shall say more about it in the next chapter.

---

[8] Tréverret, 206. As we shall see, this is not quite the case in La Rue's unrevised panegyric on Saint Bernard.

[9] Henri Chérot, *Autour de Bossuet. Le Quiétisme en Bourgogne et à Paris en 1698 d'après des correspondances inédites. Avec le panégyrique antiquiétiste de saint Bernard de P. de La Rue* (Paris: V. Retaux, 1901), 71–114 (Appendice). This is an excellent study.

[10] See Chérot, *Autour de Bossuet*, 29–30.

[11] [Charles de La Rue], *Panégyriques des saints, Par le Père de La Ruë. De la Compagnie de Jésus. Avec quelques autres sermons du mesme Auteur, sur divers Sujets. Tome premier* (Paris: P. Gissey & M. Bordelet, 1740), 1–42; reprinted in Chérot, *Autour de Bossuet*, 77–113.

[12] DLF XVIII, 226; DHGE 10:630–31; Albert / Court, 57–59. Bretonneau himself composed an unimpressive panegyric on Bernard.

To appreciate the power and polemic of the unrevised version we need to bear in mind all that was said in chapter 2, for the sermon was delivered on August 20, 1698, at the very height of the Quietist controversy. The conference at Issy had taken place three years earlier, not long after the appearance of Madame Guyon's *Short and Easy Method of Prayer*; Madame Guyon herself had been arrested and was being held under what might be called house arrest at Vaugirard near Paris (she would be transferred to the Bastille the following year); Fénelon had published his *Explications des maximes des saints* in 1697; and Bossuet and Fénelon were now in the midst of a pamphlet war that would end with the condemnation of twenty-three articles from the *Explications* in the Apostolic Letter *Cum alias ad apostolatus*, promulgated by Innocent XII on March 12, 1699. The atmosphere in Paris in 1698 was nothing if not charged, and the battle raging between Bossuet and Fénelon is exactly the battle we see in La Rue's unrevised panegyric: Bossuet is Bernard *redivivus*, and Fénelon is Peter Abelard (and, to a lesser extent, Gilbert de la Porrée). Neither Bossuet nor Fénelon is named, but no one at the time could have missed the parallels. This was not the first time that La Rue had spoken out in public against the Quietists,[13] but it is certainly his fiercest attack.

In his sermon, La Rue refers to the Quietists as hypocrites[14] and heretics, and their ideas as phantoms, delusions, and abuses of true *dévotion*, which we must here translate as "spirituality."[15] Their unfortunate ideas are no more than vain affectations, the fanciful fabrications of oversubtle thinkers, fantastical and affected notions of the nature of perfection, fabrications used by the devil to take over one's freedom, cast one into debauchery, and expose to mockery that true spiritu-

---

[13] See Chérot, *Autour de Bossuet*, 32.

[14] La Rue had no time for hypocrisy or those he regarded as hypocrites: see Chérot, *Autour de Bossuet*, 38–39.

[15] See n. 21 below.

ality that was taught by Jesus Christ himself, and, after him, by Saint Bernard. This indeed is the essential theme that our preacher sets out at the very beginning of his discourse: the contrast between the *vraie* or *véritable dévotion*—true or genuine spirituality—of Bernard (in his seventeenth-century incarnation as Bossuet) with what he regards as the false spirituality of the Quietists, and, especially, of Fénelon. In the course of his sermon, he draws attention to four main errors of the Quietists, though Fénelon did not actually maintain all of them. They are (i) that one can achieve a state of pure love that can become habitual and in which there is no place for either fear or hope, (ii) that in the state of holy indifference one is also indifferent to the matter of one's own salvation, (iii) that the state of perfection is incompatible with devotion to the cross, the saints, or the Mother of God, and (iv) that for one who has achieved this state there is no need nor any call to practice the virtues. La Rue will demolish every one of these false and fantastic notions with the aid of Bernard's life, works, and writings, and it cannot be denied that he has a point: Bernard would have had no time for any of them. As he is swept along by the ferocity of his polemic, La Rue makes errors in dates and facts—errors that are corrected in the second and much gentler version of his sermon—but there can be no doubt of his hatred and, indeed, fear of Quietism. It was indeed a seductive system. Nor can there be any doubt, as Chérot has pointed out, that Bossuet had a hand in the composition of the panegyric,[16] though how much of a hand we cannot say. It may have been no more than the inspiration for the discourse.

La Rue divides his oration into two parts. The first, which examines Bernard's fidelity or faithfulness (*fidélité*), concentrates on the need to preserve the theological virtues of faith and hope together with charity and the need, in general, for the practice of the virtues. This reflects the Bernard who, in the

---

[16] See Chérot, *Autour de Bossuet*, 33–34.

words of Psalm 44:8, loved righteousness, and it is here that we find most of La Rue's specific arguments against the views of the Quietists. The second part, which examines Bernard's zeal, is a call to combat these fanciful notions, reject them utterly, and return to the way of the Gospel. This reflects the Bernard who, in the words of the same Psalm, hated iniquity.

La Rue begins by pointing out that Bernard, though graced by heaven and renowned on earth, never forgot the need for penance and mortification, and, despite his talents, fame, and accomplishments, his greatest virtue was his humility. Furthermore, says La Rue, "though penetrated through and through by the purest love, he never banished hope from his heart" (§8). He has already begun his attack on Quietism. The young Bernard is good-looking, intelligent, and of a sweet disposition, and although he could easily have enjoyed all the delights the world had to offer, he was unaffected by the world. And since the world held no pleasure for him, he decided to live a life of prayer and devotion in his parents' house. This, however, proved to be insufficiently rigorous for his austere temperament, and he left home for the desert of Cîteaux, taking with him thirty noble relatives and friends. La Rue then gives an account of how Bernard treated his body with "holy cruelty," subjecting it to mortifications, fasts, vigils, and so on; but when it was suggested to him that he relax these austerities somewhat, he refused, for in his view, all he was doing was imitating his Master and the way of the cross. His school was the school of Jesus Christ, not that of Hippocrates.

Of all Bernard's virtues, the greatest, as we have said, was his humility. La Rue contrasts his renown in the world, when kings and princes, popes and prelates sought his aid, with his own abject humility. He mentions his refusal of bishoprics and archbishoprics (though the list is not quite accurate and is corrected in the revised version of his panegyric), for Bernard not only renounces the world, a world to which he is utterly indifferent; he also renounces himself. We now come to the second anti-Quietist argument, in which La Rue tells us that indifference to the world and one's body does not mean that one should be indifferent to one's salvation. And when we look at those who maintain this deluded idea, what do we find? "These people say they are indifferent to the greatest good of Heaven, but are they indifferent to the goods and honors of the world?" (§18). Not in the view of La Rue, who points to their intrigues, their seeking favor at Court, and their desire for worldly esteem.

Furthermore, as much as Bernard loved righteousness and as much as he was favored by God, he never abandoned fear. On this matter, too, the Quietists are wrong. But are we not told in 1 John 4:18 that perfect love casts out fear? And does this not support the Quietist view? It does not, says La Rue, for (following Bernard) we must distinguish between servile fear and chaste fear. Servile fear is the fear of anything that may be done to us by people or worldly circumstances, and it is this fear that is cast out by love. Chaste fear, however, is the fear of God and his judgments, and that fear always remains, as it always remained with Bernard. We see it in his writings all through his life, and even on his deathbed he writes to Arnold of Bonneval asking him and his brothers to pray for him. Even after forty years of asceticism, prayer, and the practice of the virtues, he is still afraid of Judgment! This leads La Rue to his next criticism of Quietism, in which he demonstrates that achieving a state of perfection here below does not prevent one from making acts of devotion to the saints and the Mother of God, and certainly not from saying, in the Lord's Prayer, "forgive us our trespasses." These ideas, we might add, were not those of Fénelon, but of Miguel de Molinos, and they had already been condemned by Innocent XI in 1687.[17] In short, neither the apostles nor Bernard was aware of any sort of pure love that was not accompanied by chaste fear and righteousness, and the virtues of penance, humility, and hope.

---

[17] See nn. 72 and 74 below.

It is true, says La Rue, that in heaven there is neither hope nor faith, for in the celestial realm hope has been fulfilled and faith has become vision. But here on earth (as Saint Paul says) faith, hope, and charity are an inseparable part of a Christian's duty, and any idea that one can achieve, here below, a habitual state of pure love that excludes all hope is a complete and utter delusion. But does not Saint Bernard, in his eighty-third sermon on the Song of Songs, tell us that "pure love is not mercenary; it does not draw strength from hope"? And does not this support the case of the Quietists? It may seem to, says La Rue, but it does not. For when Bernard says that pure love is not mercenary, he means that pure love has no interest in anything that the world can offer, no interest in anything that is earthly and temporal. But just as a bridegroom longs to be joined to his bride and a bride to her bridegroom, so the soul, in pure love, longs to be united to the divine Bridegroom. That is her hope. And what is her fear? That she might mingle with her love something that might prevent that hope from being realized. It follows, then, that hope and fear are perfected by love, and anyone who says that pure love is devoid of hope and fear is stupid, deluded, hypocritical, sacrilegious, and just plain wrong. Thus La Rue concludes the first part of his panegyric by asserting that the perfection of spirituality consists in the pursuit and practice of all the virtues and that there is not one of them that is unworthy of God or incompatible with loving him perfectly, and not one of them that is contrary either to our eternal interest or to our salvation.

In Part One, La Rue has been concerned with Bernard's private life; in Part Two he turns his attention to Bernard's public life, and it is here that Bernard (that is to say, Bossuet) has to sally forth from his cloister to do battle with Abelard (that is to say, Fénelon). In attacking heresy and schism, Bernard was never held back by the rank, dignity, or power of his opponents, never held back by the bonds of friendship, never held back by ignorance or perplexity. La Rue's examples are Bernard's respectful rebukes to Eugenius III, Lothair III, Henry

I of England (not, as La Rue says, Henry II), Louis the Fat (he mentions the Council of Étampes), Duke William X of Aquitaine, Suger of Saint-Denis, and Peter the Venerable.

He then comes to Abelard, "the subtlest thinker of them all, who, with his overly sophisticated learning, sowed his errors on all sides" (§51), but his portrait of Abelard is not so much a portrait of Abelard as a somewhat skewed portrait of Fénelon. He speaks of Abelard's returning from high contemplation and revealing things that God has not permitted to be revealed, of his introducing into the faith pointless novelties, of his speaking of vices and virtues in a wholly different way from the moral teaching of the Gospel, and of his spouting out a multitude of nonsensical ideas about the perfect way, revelations, raptures, and intimate union. Abelard, in fact, said nothing at all about revelations, raptures, and so on, but as we have said, Abelard is no more than a mask for Fénelon and the Quietists.

La Rue then turns to Gilbert de la Porrée, who is yet another mask for Fénelon. Bernard's harsh attacks on Gilbert were criticized by many, and there are those who accused him of being haughty, arrogant, headstrong, unruly, ambitious, and jealous of Gilbert. But once again, it is not really Bernard and Gilbert of whom La Rue is speaking here, but Bossuet and Fénelon. Friends and supporters of Gilbert / Fénelon then try to arrange a compromise solution, but Bernard / Bossuet will have none of it. Gilbert, like Fénelon, must be condemned. Carried away by his polemic, La Rue makes historical and factual errors,[18] errs in his chronology, and confuses Abelard and Gilbert (this is corrected in the second, revised version of the panegyric), but the actual facts of the matter are secondary to his message. And what is that message? That there has never been a saint

---

[18] E.g., he has Bernard entering Cîteaux at twenty-five (§11), confuses Cîteaux and Clairvaux (§11), has the emperor Conrad rescuing Bernard from the crowds in the wrong place at the wrong time (§22), tells us that Bernard wrote ninety sermons on the Song of Songs (§31), and confuses Henry I with Henry II (§40).

who loved God perfectly who was not ready to do battle with his enemies, and it is our duty to do the same. And if we do not have the weapons to enter the fight directly, then let us shun these new and wrong ideas, these fantastical notions of what constitutes union with God, these heretical suggestions that the practice of the virtues is not necessary. Let us say the Lord's Prayer in faith, let us love God in fear and in hope, so that we, like Bernard, may, in the fullness of time, come to possess that God, and be possessed by him, in indescribable and everlasting bliss.

Such is Charles de La Rue's unrevised panegyric on Saint Bernard. It is unique, and we have not and will not come across any other panegyric quite like it. La Rue's sources, apart from Scripture, are entirely confined to the *Vita prima* and certain of Bernard's own works: his letters, the *De consideratione*, the *Apology*, the sermons on the Song of Songs, and the sermon on the nativity of John the Baptist. The sermon is a violent anti-Quietist and anti-Fénelon polemic and appears to have caused something of an uproar after La Rue preached it in the church of the Feuillants on the rue Saint-Honoré in Paris on August 20—Bernard's feast day—in 1689. The supporters of Fénelon were naturally outraged, but so were La Rue's Jesuit colleagues in Rome.[19] Even Bossuet, who had heard the sermon delivered, thought La Rue had gone too far.[20] Feelings ran sufficiently high for the superior general of the Jesuits, Thyrse Gonzalès, to dispatch La Rue off to the Languedoc to preach to the Protestants until things had quieted down. He left in 1700 and did not return to Paris until three years later. Whether La Rue reacted to the uproar by toning down his panegyric or whether the revised version was entirely the work of Bretonneau is a matter we shall have to discuss in our next chapter. But here, for the moment, masquerading as a

---

[19] See Chérot, *Autour de Bossuet*, 30.
[20] See Chérot, *Autour de Bossuet*, 47, 75 (quoting Léonard de Sainte-Catherine).

panegyric on Bernard of Clairvaux, is Charles La Rue's fierce and fiery attack on Fénelon and the Quietists.

THE PANEGYRIC
PANEGYRIC ON SAINT BERNARD ON THE SPIRITUALITY[21] OF THE TIMES, PREACHED ON HIS FEAST DAY, 20 AUGUST, BY THE REVEREND FATHER DE LA RUE, JESUIT, IN 1698, TO THE FEUILLANTS, IN PARIS.[22]

Dilexisti justitiam et odisti iniquitatem; propterea unxit te Deus, Deus tuus, oleo laetitiae prae consortibus tuis. (Ps 44:8)
"You have loved righteousness and you have hated iniquity; for this reason you have received from God a greater anointing of joy than all those of the last centuries."[23]

1. But gentlemen, if I am to confine my praise of a saint to the love of virtue and a horror of iniquity, is this not a poor response to your grand ideas? For you, Bernard was the marvel of his age, but what is there particularly marvelous in these two qualities that I have borrowed from the prophet [David] to write his panegyric? Yet it remains a fact that in these two qualities the prophet set forth a high idea of Jesus Christ.[24] It is

---

[21] *Dévotion*: see appendix 1, s.v. *dévotion* / devotion. In this case, and in much of this panegyric, the best translation is what we would now call spirituality, but *spiritualité* was a word treated with some caution by seventeenth-century writers, not least because of an association with Quietism. See appendix 1, s.v. *spiritualité* / spirituality. La Rue never uses the word *spiritualité* in his panegyric, and any time *spirituality* occurs in this translation, it translates *dévotion*.

[22] The sermon was preached in the church of the convent of the Feuillants on the rue Saint-Honoré: see chap. 4 (Biroat), n. 11.

[23] This is La Rue's translation. What the Latin actually says is "You have loved righteousness and hated iniquity, wherefore God, your God, has anointed you with the oil of gladness above your fellows."

[24] La Rue is here referring to Heb 1:9, in which the author of that letter takes Ps 44:7-8 and applies the two verses *ad Filium*, i.e., to Christ.

to these two degrees of perfection that he attributes the anointing by God that led to him reigning in joy and peace over all that humanity whose nature he had assumed:[25] *Dilexisti*, etc.

2. Indeed, I do not know that it is not very rash of me to apply to the servant [Bernard] words consecrated to the honor of the Master [Jesus], and at another time I might, perhaps, have been more hesitant. But the unfortunate ideas of the times in which we live leave me no choice but to confirm the examples of the Master by the examples of the servant, and to have you see the importance of what I plan to say by the importance of curbing all those abuses that have slid into true spirituality, and of proposing today, to all the faithful, Bernard as the model and doctor of what genuine spirituality ought to be.[26]

3. What century has ever aspired more than ours to this high degree of perfection and to a complete understanding of true spirituality? But yet, as we come to the end of this turbulent century, what success do we see even in the works and studies of the most subtle thinkers[27] of our times? Have we really made any advance in perfection? If we are trying to outdo our fathers in their religious way of life,[28] is it not rather through hypocrisy than by a true foundation of spirituality? Are we not suddenly bewitched by the novelty[29] of

---

[25] The reference is now to Heb 1:8, "Your throne, O God, is for ever and ever: a scepter of justice [*aequitas*] is the scepter of your kingdom."

[26] La Rue sets out clearly what he intends to do. He will contrast the true or genuine spirituality (*dévotion*) of Bernard / Bossuet with what he regards as the false spirituality of Fénelon and the Quietists.

[27] *Des plus subtils*. See appendix 1, s.v. *subtil, subtilité* / subtle, subtlety. *Subtils* or "over-subtle thinkers" are always dangerous. Fénelon, the seventeenth-century Abelard, is a *subtil*.

[28] *Religion*: see appendix 1, s.v. *religion* / religion. Here *religion* is a life lived in accordance with the general principles of the Christian religion.

[29] *Nouveauté*, which is always, by definition, perilous: see appendix 1, s.v. *nouveautés* / novelties.

certain ideas rather than recognizing them as phantoms and rejecting them as delusions? Such, again, is the malice of this age that, far from fighting against the error, it even takes pains to pursue the falsehood!

4. Dear listeners, these are not the lessons that Bernard teaches us in his doctrine and his actions. He was not content only with loving righteousness: he also hated iniquity, and never did he appear more zealous than when he discovered errors that might corrupt true spirituality. We may therefore say that his faithfulness and his zeal were the two foundations of that perfect spirituality by which God wished to single him out from so many others: *Dilexisti justitiam et odisti iniquitatem; propterea*, etc.

5. Now, therefore, we set before those Christians who seek true and genuine spirituality [two things]. First, they must cultivate all the Christian virtues:[30] this is the faithfulness of the perfection of Bernard, and it will be the first point [of my sermon]. Secondly, in order to arrive at this perfect spirituality, they must be ready to fight against all the delusions that cloud it: this is the zeal of the spirituality of Bernard and the subject of my second point.

6. It obviously follows from this that everything that is not based on these two principles is no more than hypocrisy and

---

[30] As we have seen, this was not the view of the Quietists. La Rue speaks of the Christian virtues in general (see also §7 below) but is thinking especially of the three theological virtues of faith, hope, and charity. In the Apostolic Brief *Cum alias ad apostolatus* of March 12, 1699, two of the propositions of Fénelon that were condemned were (a) that "in the state of the contemplative or unitive life, every interested motive of fear and hope is lost" (Denzinger, no. 2352), and (b) that "Holy mystics have excluded from the state of transformed souls the exercise of the virtues" (Denzinger, no. 2371). La Rue will use Bernard to demonstrate that faith, hope, and fear are lost only when the soul possesses God—or, more accurately, is possessed by God—in the Beatific Vision. Until that time, faith, hope, and love *remain* (see §29 below).

deceit. Holy Virgin, who had for Bernard a mother's heart, extend to us the honor of your protection and gain for us from Heaven the help we need to profit from his lessons and his example. Thus, prostrate at your feet, we say, *Ave Maria*.

[FIRST PART]

7. That Christians ought to strive for what is more perfect is taught to us by Saint Paul in these words: *Aemulamini charismata meliora* ["Strive for the better gifts" (1 Cor 12:31)]. But if you think that striving for the greater perfection allows us to neglect those things that are less perfect, this is a delusion wholly injurious to salvation. Among the virtues there are different degrees of nobility and eminence, that I admit, but there is not one among them that does not possess its own particular nobility and eminence and, in consequence, not one of them that should be neglected. This is what Jesus Christ long taught us by his own example when he was on earth. Wholly perfect though he was, he submitted to baptism by John and said himself that the reason for this was to fulfill all righteousness: *sic enim decet nos implere omnem justitiam* ["for so it is fitting for us to fulfil all righteousness" (Matt 3:15)]. In this example from the Son of God himself, you see a model for the most perfect Christians.

8. Saint Bernard, wholly righteous though he was, embraced mortification and penance[31] and never abandoned them. Although he was raised so high in merit and dignity, he never neglected humility. Though wholly favored by Heaven, he never cast aside fear. Though penetrated through and through by the purest love,[32] he never banished hope from his heart.

---

[31] *Pénitence*: see appendix 1, s.v. *pénitence* / penitence.

[32] *Plus pur amour*: La Rue is intentionally using the term used by the Quietists—*purus amor* or *caritas pura*—and will demonstrate that "pure love" does *not* eliminate hope or fear. According to Fénelon, *caritas pura* is a habitual state that contains no self-interest, and in

The love that he had for God never prevented him from hoping to possess God.

9. But what man could be more content with his lot and banish from his heart the hope of some good other than what he already enjoyed in the world? Intelligence, nobility, beauty, good looks, natural advantages, a gentle and sweet disposition:[33] all were to be found in Bernard in a way that made the world equally pleasant and open to him, but by a special operation of grace, he tasted[34] the world without tasting its amusements and pleasures. He knew how to be pleasing to the world, but the world was displeasing to him.

10. When, in his desire to practice virtue, he sought a shelter from the snares of the world, it was easy for him to find a suitable place. He had only to put aside the sword to protect himself from the perils of his profession,[35] and, without leaving the bosom of his family, take up a way of life that was gentler and more peaceful. He had only to arrange for himself an appropriate place of solitude in his parents' house, somewhere in which he could pursue his profound studies undisturbed. There he could pray at his leisure, do good works when he wished, and do penance as he chose. There he gave God a full account of his remorse for his past waywardness, there he poured forth at length his sighs and groans, there he reserved for himself the freedom to laugh or cry as he wished and to

---

this state there is no longer any place for either fear of punishment or desire for reward (Denzinger, no. 2351). "Pure love itself alone constitutes the whole interior life" (Denzinger, no. 2372). Both propositions were condemned by Innocent XII.

[33] See *Vita prima* 1.13 (William of Saint-Thierry); PL 185:228BC; CF 76:5–6, and 3.1.1 (Geoffrey of Auxerre); 303B–4B; CF 76:146–47.

[34] The verb is *goûter*: to taste, enjoy, relish, appreciate.

[35] Bernard came from a knightly family. His father, Tescelin, "was of the ancient stock of the Chevaliers de Châtillon, members of which held feudal lordship over a vast extent of territory both in Burgundy and in Champagne" (Williams, *Studies*, 43). And in his mother's veins "there flowed the ducal blood of Burgundy" (45).

moderate from time to time the rigor of his withdrawal by time spent with his family. Nothing is more common today, gentlemen, than these types of undemanding and comfortable retreats. That a man has spent the better part of his days in sin and self-indulgence troubles him no more: provided he loves God, that is enough! He even believes that his salvation is assured in the arms of indolence and laziness!

11. Saint Bernard has no time for such lax arrangements. Even though he had always preserved his innocence, he goes off to bury himself in a desert. But in what desert? In that which had been made most formidable and dangerous by age and the ferocity of wild beasts: the desert of Cîteaux![36] He does more! He wins over seven of his companions[37] and, while still only twenty-five years old,[38] gathers together no fewer than thirty noblemen[39] and leads them into the house of Clairvaux![40] There

---

[36] See *Exordium parvum* III; Chrysogonus Waddell, *Narrative and Legislative Texts from Early Cîteaux*, Studia et Documenta, IX (Brecht: Cîteaux—Commentarii Cistercienses, 1999), 238, 420–21. The desert (*eremus*) called Cîteaux was well off the beaten track, and few people went there: it was heavily wooded with lots of thornbushes and inhabited only by wild beasts.

[37] The "companions" (*compagnons*) were actually family members or kinsmen: Bernard's maternal uncle, his brothers, and Godfrey de la Roche and Robert de Châtillon: see Williams, *Studies*, 62–68, and the same author's *Saint Bernard*, 10–11.

[38] Twenty-five is certainly incorrect, and should be amended to either twenty-two or twenty-three, with twenty-three being more likely: see chap. 7 (Bossuet), n. 63. In the revised version of the panegyric, Bernard's age is corrected to twenty-three.

[39] *Vita prima* 1.4.19 (William of Saint-Thierry); PL 185:237C; CF 76:22, reads *cum sociis amplius quam triginta*, "with more than thirty companions." Watkin Williams suggests that there were actually thirty-one, including Bernard and Robert de Châtillon, but since Robert's novitiate was postponed, the number of those actually admitted to Cîteaux was, in fact, thirty (Williams, *Studies*, 71).

[40] La Rue says Clairvaux but means Cîteaux. This is corrected in the second version of the panegyric.

he laid the first foundations for his Order, which, since that time, has spread throughout the whole world.

12. There, with all the difficulties facing the first poor establishment of his Order, he neglected nothing in making a perfect but terrible sacrifice of his body through penance. Straightaway he pushed this formidable task to its limits, whether in his food, which he ate to destroy and ruin his body rather than sustain it, or his ceaseless prayers, or his endless fasts, or the continual subjection of his senses and his flesh. He treated himself with a holy cruelty that could not possibly be the result of the sins of his past life, and he wanted to make his body a wretched victim, despite all the reasons that obliged him to treat it gently, for there was no human reason to inflict on himself such harsh penances.[41] There were those, indeed, who gave him good reasons to the contrary as to why he should mitigate or do away with all this severity: the advice and entreaties of friends, for example, who showed him what a high position he might hope to attain in the world, or the need to preserve his health for the good of his order and its expansion, or, yet more to the point, the innocence of his way of life. All these reasons, each one so favorable to self-love,[42] were suggested to Bernard.

13. Every day a thousand voices whispered these things in his ears, but if any of his friends urged him to dispense with such harsh penance in view of the high degree of perfection he had reached, did Bernard relax for this reason? Did he let himself be persuaded that, because he had attained this intimate union of the soul with God, all the other virtues and holy

---

[41] Bernard's austerities are described in detail in the *Vita prima* 1.420–23 (William of Saint-Thierry); PL 185:238B–40D; CF 76:23–27.

[42] *Amour propre*: the overcoming of self-love or egocentricity lies at the heart of Bernard's spirituality—as, indeed, it lies at the heart of the teaching of all mystical traditions. The logic is simple: the less we love ourselves, the more we can love God, and since (following Augustine) love and will are essentially the same thing, the less we love ourselves, the more we are attuned to the will of God.

works should seem to him irrelevant?⁴³ Ah! To spare his body, did he join the ranks of the hypocrites? He who could not abide the idea that the school of Hippocrates was more important than that of Jesus Christ?⁴⁴ He who did not wish even to take care of his own health since he knew that Jesus Christ had promised part of his glory to those who would bear his cross and die for love of him? Would he who found in penance so much joy and consolation have asked Christians to abandon their own sufferings and mortification? He who justified all the sufferings he imposed upon himself by always regarding himself as a slave to sin and a sensualist?⁴⁵ And could he have tolerated the idea that a Christian would believe himself sufficiently purged of all faults with no need of penance? *Ut fortior potio necessaria sit*, ["I needed a stronger remedy," says Bernard,⁴⁶] he who based his own mortifications and austerities on the example of John the Baptist. *Quae crimina quae sacrilegia puniebat in se Joannes?* "What crimes, what sacrileges," he wrote, "could John the Baptist have committed to treat himself so harshly?"⁴⁷ Could he not have said the opposite: "What

---

⁴³ Such was the view of the Quietists (see n. 30 above), the "hypocrites" of La Rue's next sentence.

⁴⁴ La Rue plays on the words *hypocrite* and *Hypocrate* (in seventeenth-century spelling), and his source is Bernard's thirtieth sermon on the Song of Songs: "Hippocrates and his followers teach how to keep our souls well in this world; Christ and his disciples [teach us] to lose them. Which of the two do you choose to follow as your Master? . . . Hippocrates does everything he can to sustain the life of the soul in the body; the Savior tells us to lose it" (SC 30.4.10; SBOp 1:216–17, echoing Matt 16:25 and parallels).

⁴⁵ Bernard, *Apologia* 4.7; SBOp 3:87: "I was carnal, sold under sin," quoting Rom 7:14.

⁴⁶ La Rue is here paraphrasing the *Apologia* 4.7; SBOp 3:87–88, which actually reads *cui fortior esset potio necessaria* "[I realized that my soul was so weak] that it needed a stronger remedy." Different medications are prescribed for different illnesses, he continues, *et fortioribus fortiora*: more powerful remedies for more dangerous illnesses.

⁴⁷ La Rue is now misquoting Bernard's sermon in *Nativitate S. Joannis Baptistae* 8; SBOp 5:181, which actually reads *Quae enim homicidia,*

innocence, what purity, what a wealth of graces are in this holy forerunner? What need, then, for such penances, such mortifications, such austerities in the face of such virtues? Yet Jesus Christ never said anything like this. Neither the apostles nor Bernard ever did away with the penance that accompanies righteousness. They never suggested that perfection was either an obstacle to penance or a dispensation from it: *dilexisti justitiam* ["You have loved righteousness!"]. Let us now move on and see what they have to say about humility.

14. Among all Bernard's virtues, there is not one that he carried to such a high degree as his humility. No man was more honored than Bernard. The report of his virtues spread throughout the whole world. The greatest respected him; the most powerful sought his aid; the proudest revered him—so much so that one could say of him what was said of Solomon: that his name was revered by every nation on earth, *et erat nominatus in universis gentibus per circuitum* [1 Kgs 4:31],[48] that all the kings and princes of the earth came to receive the rulings of his wisdom, *et veniebant de cunctis populis ad audiendam sapientiam eius* [1 Kgs 4:34],[49] and that the whole earth desired his presence so as to hear the oracles that the wisdom of God had put in his heart, *et universa terra desiderabat vultum Salomonis, ut audiret sapientiam eius quam dederat Deus in corde eius* [1 Kgs 10:24].[50]

15. Nothing like this was ever seen again from Solomon's time to that of Bernard, who was like the wisest of all kings. His God had raised him so high over all other men that all of them, from the very least to the very greatest, had recourse to

---

quae sacrilegia, aut que flagitia sic puniebat Ioannes in seipso? "For what murders, what sacrileges, or what shameful acts led John to punish himself in this way?"

[48] Lit. "and he was renowned in all nations round about."

[49] Lit. "and they came from all peoples to hear his wisdom, [and from all the kings of the earth]."

[50] Lit. "and all the earth desired to see the face of Solomon and hear his wisdom that God had put in his heart."

him. There was no one so wise or so enlightened that he did not do him the honor of seeking his advice, no one so powerful that he did not tremble at his threats, no one so carefree that he did not listen to his voice as to the voice of God, no rebel that he did not subdue, no troublemaker that he did not appease. Popes used his authority among themselves to make peace in the Church; kings made use of his power to reign securely over their people. Whether he was protecting the small from the great or acting as mediator with the great between God and ordinary men and women, everyone felt these effects of his greatness, while in his own eyes he was only ever more humble. All that he did was done only for the glory of the Master who had made him great.

16. In truth, Lord, if he had followed his own interests in that high state to which you had raised him, which of all those [episcopal] thrones that awaited him could he not have possessed? Genoa, Vienne, Milan, Grenoble, Reims, Sens, Châlons[-sur-Marne]: all chose him and asked him to be their bishop.[51] They added entreaties to their prayers and tears to their entreaties. He resisted [them all], and never for a moment did his profound humility find itself tempted to yield to their copious tears.

17. In his humility he made no distinctions, yet we may note that when he refused such dignities and honors, he always found ways to make his refusal seem reasonable: *non jactanter respuendo, sed humiliter declinando* ["not rejecting them boastfully, but declining them humbly"].[52] In this way, he es-

---

[51] This is a slight exaggeration. In the second version of the panegyric, the list is amended in accordance with the *Vita prima* 2.4.26 (Arnold of Bonneval); PL 185:283B; CF 76:106, which lists Langres, Châlons-sur-Marne, Genoa, Milan, and Reims.

[52] *Vita prima* 1.14.69 (William of Saint-Thierry); PL 185:265A; CF 76:73. The text actually has *sed religiose et rationabiliter declinando*, which makes better sense. The whole sentence reads "Consider the highest ecclesiastical honors or the favor of secular princes, which

caped courteously from the hands of those who asked [these things] of him, but this world, which was bound to take vengeance for these refusals and which could not take vengeance on Bernard himself, took vengeance instead on his [monastic] children. People went everywhere to uproot his children from the secret of their solitude and raise them up on the thrones of the Church, for if they could not have the shepherd, they carried off his sheep! Germany, France, Spain, Italy were content to have as shepherds the children of Bernard. And he himself? He wished only to guide the simple flock of his holy fold, and when he saw the [papal] tiara or the miter on the heads of twenty or thirty of his children—may I say without jealousy? May I say without complaint?—he himself never entertained the slightest thought of accepting any one of the illustrious positions he was offered. He was so humble that he even placed himself below his children, saying to himself that they were far more worthy than he of the honors to which, on his refusal, they had been raised. Ah! What depth, what an abyss of humility! It is this, dear listeners, that comprises this famed renunciation, this perfect disinterestedness.[53] Listen, faithful souls, it is here that we find the highest point of Christian perfection, and we cannot do better, I confess, since it is here that Jesus Christ himself tells us to place it when he says

---

constantly pursued him as being most worthy of them: he did not reject them boastfully but declined them reverently and reasonably."

[53] *Désintéressement parfait.* As we saw in chap. 2, this was a most important technical term in Quietism and means much the same as "holy indifference," "detachment," or "abandonment" (*désappropriation*: see §18). "In the state of holy indifference [*sancta indifferentia*]," wrote Fénelon, "we wish nothing for ourselves, everything for God [*nihil nobis, omnia Deo*]" (Denzinger, no. 2355), a proposition that was condemned by Innocent XII. La Rue will use Bernard to show the nature of true disinterestedness in contrast to what he regards as the distorted and delusional view put forward by the Quietists in general and Fénelon in particular. See further appendix 1, s.v. *dégagement* / detachment.

that in order to be his disciple, his faithful servant, we must renounce ourselves and all the honors and comforts of this life: *Si quis vult venire post me, abneget semetipsum* ["If anyone wishes to come after me, let him deny himself" (Matt 16:24)].

18. But is there anything else that we should do to fulfill this duty imposed upon us by Jesus Christ? Does it also mean that we should have no concern for our spiritual progress? That we should have no regard for our eternal happiness, neither our salvation nor our celestial beatitude?[54] [Such ideas] are the vain affectations, the fanciful fabrications of the subtle thinkers[55] of our days. To come to these conclusions takes no more than a little pretense and hypocrisy, for if we examine the actual conduct of these people, what sort of renunciation and abandonment[56] do we find? What does it really mean for them to arrive at this happy indifference that, they tell us, comprises the state of perfection? They say they are indifferent to the greatest good of heaven—but are they [indifferent] to the goods and honors of the world? They say they are unconcerned about the terrible Judgment of God—but are they [unconcerned] about the judgment of the world?

---

[54] According to Mme Guyon, the soul that has achieved a pure disinterested love exists for God alone. Such a soul has no concern for itself at all and no concern for its own salvation, perfection, eternity, life, or death (see Pourrat, *Christian Spirituality. Later Developments. Part II*, 197). Fénelon is more subtle: in the state of holy indifference we do not wish for salvation as our own salvation (*ut salutem propriam*), but "we wish it with our whole will as the glory and good pleasure [*beneplacitum*] of God" (Denzinger, no. 2356). The proposition was condemned by Innocent XII.

[55] *Subtils*: see n. 27 above.

[56] *Désappropriation*: see n. 53 above. The word, which was not common, means to disassociate oneself from all goods or, as here, from any trace of self-interest. It is the *heureuse indifférence* of the next sentence. For La Rue, it is disassociation from all the things of this world, not disassociation from the fear of Judgment or the hope of heaven. See §20 below.

19. What good are all these intrigues, these cabals, these devious doings at Court,[57] all these ways of ingratiating themselves with those in power so as to push themselves where they are not or maintain themselves where they are? Are they doing all this for the love of God alone while they themselves play no part whatever? They sacrifice all interest in their salvation, but do they also sacrifice all interest in riches or honors?

20. When Jesus Christ spoke so many times of leaving everything, selling everything, abandoning everything to follow him—*vade, vende, relinque opus tuum, dimitte mortuos sepelire mortuos, sequere me* ["Go, sell, leave your work, let the dead bury the dead, follow me"[58]]—was he not referring to worldly interests? If this is not so, how could they explain all the counsels of perfection? When he said, "First purify yourselves inwardly," *munda prius intus*,[59] did he mean, "Do not seek me in heaven, which is removed from you even though it is promised you, but seek me in the intrigues of the court?" [Did he mean,] "Do not seek me in solitude, but in the midst of the world?" [What he said was] *Intus*! ["Within!"]: there and only there will you find me! They are wholly deluded, Christian listeners! What must be purged within is everything temporal and everything human! It is everything that is of the world and that holds to the world—[that world] from which we must disassociate[60] ourselves entirely. Other than that, there is nothing but cajolery, amusement, and hypocrisy.

---

[57] The devious doings were discussed briefly in chap. 2. The key figure was Madame de Maintenon, *maîtresse-en-titre* or official mistress (and, later, second wife, though the marriage was never formally acknowledged) of Louis XIV.

[58] This is an amalgam of partial texts from Matt 19:21; 5:24; and 8:22, but *relinque opus tuum* is not to be found. Matt 5:24 reads *relinque munus tuum*.

[59] The reference is to Matt 23:26: *Pharisaee caece, munda prius quod intus est calicis et paropsidis*, "Blind Pharisee, first clean the inside of the cup and the dish [so that the outside may become clean]."

[60] *Désapproprier*: see nn. 53 and 56 above.

21. Let us now continue and add a third trait to our portrait of Saint Bernard. As much as he loved righteousness—*dilexisti justitiam*—wholly favored as he was by heaven, wholly filled as he was with the gifts of God, he never abandoned fear. But who could possibly have banished fear from his heart more justly than this man of God? To whom could the thought of death and the judgments of God be sweeter than to Bernard? He saw himself regarded as the soul of [Church] councils, the oracle of the world, the master of the fate of popes. His wisdom was such that all came to consult him; he possessed the power of miracles to a degree that God had bestowed on none since the apostles: a sovereign empire over bodies and elements that he changed as he willed.

22. But what were the circumstances that accompanied this divine power? If he performed miracles, it was not in private, in secret, far from people, in the tomb. It was in public, in the marketplaces, in the streets, on the roads, living and walking on the earth, with popes, bishops, and kings each laying before him the ills of their countries for him to heal! They admired especially the amazing cure that [took place] one day in Milan [and that led to] the emperor Conrad [von Hohenstaufen] having to cover Bernard with his royal mantle and steal him away so that he would not be crushed by the crowds.[61] To have any doubts after this of Bernard's absolute power is to be more malicious than his cruelest enemies and to refuse to see the precious signs of the particular goodness that God had for him. Is it possible, therefore, that there was any fear of anything left

---

[61] For Bernard's reception in Milan and the Milanese miracles, see *Vita prima* 2.2.9–3.16 (Arnold of Bonneval); PL 185:273D–78A; CF 76:87–96, but La Rue has confused both the time and place. The episode of Conrad's covering Bernard with his cloak and carrying him away for his own safety took place in Frankfurt am Main, and the crowds were not there to see healing but to hear Bernard preaching the Second Crusade: see *Vita prima* 4.5.31 (Geoffrey of Auxerre); PL 185:338D–39A; CF 76:209–10, and Williams, *Saint Bernard*, 280.

in his heart? Could he have felt even its slightest twinge, he who had carved love and charity[62] so deeply in his heart? Is it possible that he who had filled his heart and memory with the holy books and sayings did not know or had forgotten these words of Saint John: *perfecta caritas foras mittit timorem* [1 John 4:18]? Perfect charity casts out fear. Certainly he knew it, and he remembered the words well, and it was because he was so well instructed in these truths that he believed that charity and fear are always inseparable.[63] Perfect charity does indeed drive out fear, but what this means, he said, is that the suffering of disquiet that comes with fear is never found with perfect charity, *poena servilis tollitur* ["servile punishment is removed"]. But chaste and filial fear is still to be found with charity: *timor autem castus manet in saeculum saeculi* ["chaste fear remains forever"[64]].

23. It is this salutary fear that he joined to his perfect charity that saw him now concerning himself with matters in the abbey in which he dwelt, now leaving it to seek the greatest works

---

[62] *Amour et charité*: see appendix 1, s.v. *charité* / charity.

[63] La Rue now turns to Bernard's Ep 11.7 to Guy / Guigo of la Grande Chartreuse; SBOp 7:57–58 = Dil 14.38; SBOp 3:152, which forms the basis for the last part of this section. What Bernard says, at its simplest, is that just as there are two sorts of love—chaste love (which is the love of God for his own sake, and of oneself and one's neighbor for the sake of God) and any other form of love—so, too, there are two sorts of fear, chaste fear and servile fear. Chaste fear is the fear of God and his judgments (as in Prov 9:10, "The fear of the Lord is the beginning of wisdom"); servile fear is the fear of anything that may be done to us by people or worldly circumstances. Bernard had no fear whatever when rebuking princes, prelates, and popes, but (as we shall see) he never lost his fear of God and his judgments. Perfect love, therefore, casts out servile fear, but chaste fear (or salutary fear) always remains.

[64] Bernard, Ep 11.7; SBOp 7:58 = Dil 14.38; SBOp 3:152, which actually reads *Poena tantum tollitur, sine qua esse non potuit, dum fuit servilis; et timor manet in saeculum saeculi castus et filialis*, "Punishment is lifted, for without it, [the law], while it demanded servitude, could not function; but chaste and filial fear remains for ever."

elsewhere, now dealing with his monks and begging them to pray for him, now leaving them to go and reap a harvest in other unprofitable lands and increase his merit by winning new souls for his God. "My brothers," he would often say, "do not believe that even the most perfect among you should be exempt from fear, for all must pass through the hands of God their judge, *perfecti quique sub stricto Dei judicio stant* ["each of the perfect stands under the strict Judgment of God"].[65] Thus would he bid them farewell when he set out on his various journeys, and even when he was dying he joined the precepts of a good shepherd to the tender advice of an affectionate father, telling his monks that they should always join the fear of God's judgments to the perfect love they had for Him.[66]

24. But was he perhaps recommending to others something that he did not think necessary for himself? Alas, [no!]. Not only had [the idea] penetrated to the very depths of his heart, but did he not go on to speak of it in his writings? Did he ever miss any opportunity of displaying his salutary fear? And, looking to the judgments of his God, did he not pour forth groans and tears? What does he not say on the matter in all his writings? How does he explain these words in his commentary: *posuerunt me custodem in vineis* ["They have made me the guardian in the vineyards" (Song 1:5)]? They have entrusted me with guarding the vineyard of the Lord, which is the souls of the faithful.[67] But alas! Woe to me, with what danger to myself? *Vae mihi, quo periculo animae meae?*[68] And speaking

---

[65] This apparent quotation is not to be found in any of Bernard's works. It appears nowhere in the Patrologia Latina nor in any of the standard Latin databases.

[66] See, for example, *Vita prima* 5.2.9 (Geoffrey of Auxerre); PL 185:356BC; CF 76:241–42.

[67] See Bernard, SC 30.3.6; SBOp 1:213.

[68] Bernard, SC 30.3.7; SBOp 1:214, which actually reads, *Vae autem mihi etiam nunc a periculo vineae meae*, "Woe to me even now because of the danger to my own vineyard" (i.e., my own soul).

to his children, he says to them, "Help me, you others, with your prayers and your tears, so that I may save my soul": *quo imbre perfundere possitis sterilitatem animae meae?* ["What rain can irrigate the sterility of my soul?"][69]

25. But perhaps he changed his mind later on? Ah! He held to these ideas until his dying day, when he again took pen in hand to write to [Arnold], abbot of Bonneval, asking him to ask his monks to pray for him and gain for him the special protection of God. "Pray for me, my brothers," he said to them in this letter, "so that your prayers may supply what is lacking in my merits. Pray for me to this great God who desires not the death of a sinner but rather that he be converted and live [Ezek 18:23]. May he take care of my soul, may he take me under his protection so that the devil, who is always watching for an opportunity, may not catch me in his snares and, in this perilous passage to eternity, prevail over me: *Orate Deum, qui non vult mortem peccatoris, sed ut convertatur et vivat, me custodiat, ut is qui insidiatur, non inveniat ubi vulnus infligat*" ["Pray to God, who desires not the death of a sinner, but that he be converted and live, to watch over me so that he who lies in wait for me may find no place to wound me"].[70]

---

[69] Bernard, SC 30.3.7; SBOp 1:214, which actually reads *Quo imbre lacrymarum perfundere sufficiam sterilitatem animae meae?* "What rain of tears will be enough to irrigate the sterility of my soul?" *Sterilitatem animae meae* is a quotation from Ps 34:12.

[70] Bernard, Ep 310 to Arnold of Chartres, abbot of Bonneval; SBOp 8:230 = *Vita prima* 5.2.10 (Geoffrey of Auxerre); PL 185:357A. This is an amended and abbreviated text of Bernard's last letter (if it is by Bernard: doubts have been expressed on the matter [see chap. 8, n. 51]), written on his deathbed. The actual text of the letter reads *Orate Salvatorem, qui non vult mortem peccatoris, ut tempestivum jam exitum non differat, sed custodiat. Curate munire votis calcaneum nudum meritis: ut is qui insidiatur, invenire non possit unde figat dentem et vulnus infligat,* "Pray to the Savior, who desires not the death of a sinner, that he will not delay my timely departure, but watch over me [in my passing]. Protect, I beg you, with your prayers a heel naked of merits [see Ps 48:6], so that [the enemy]

26. Take note, my dear listeners, that it is a man of perfection, of perfect charity, of prayer, of labor, of miracles, of vision, of contemplation who speaks in this way! Even after forty years of penance he still asks his brothers for their tears so as to expiate his sins. After forty years of weary labors for the glory of God, he still thinks of himself as a useless servant. After forty years of prayers and supplications, he still looks for others to intercede for him with the Savior. After forty years passed in the unceasing exercise of virtue, he still believes himself to have no merits. After forty years of victories over the devil, he still fears his snares and surprise attacks. Even at death he seeks weapons wielded by others to fight against the powers of hell, he who had so often provided [such weapons] to the great of the earth. This man, who had experienced an intimate union with God, still seeks special protection—and from whom? From men, from other monks less perfect than he! *Dilexisti justitiam*!

27. He wholly dismissed, therefore, [any idea] that a pennyweight of perfection[71] should lead one to turn one's eyes away from looking to God, or thinking on the cross of Jesus Christ or the holy Virgin or the saints.[72] He wholly dismissed a fear so base and servile[73] that one would not even dare to say to God the words that he himself instructed us to repeat

---

who lies in wait for me may find no place to fix his teeth and wound me." Bernard died a few days later. See further Williams, *Saint Bernard*, 360–61.

[71] *Un scrupule de perfection*.

[72] Among the Quietist errors of Miguel de Molinos condemned in 1687 by Pope Innocent XI, proposition 35 tells us that it is not fitting for "interior souls" to perform acts of love for the blessed Virgin, the saints, or the humanity of Christ, "because, since these are objects of the senses, so, too, is their love for them" (Denzinger, no. 2235). Proposition 36 states that "no creature, neither the blessed Virgin nor the saints, ought to abide in our heart, because God alone wishes to occupy it and possess it" (Denzinger, no. 2236).

[73] On servile fear, see n. 63 above.

many times a day in the Lord's Prayer: "Lord, forgive us our trespasses as we forgive those who have trespassed against us": *dimitte nobis*, etc.[74]

28. All these fantastical and affected notions of perfection have been kept for our century alone! Only in a century as depraved as ours could one hope to see such delusions as these well received—[delusions] so harmful to salvation—and as part of its corruption it hides these horrors under the cloak of pure love![75] The apostles and Bernard were not aware of any sort of pure love that was not accompanied by righteousness and the virtues of penance, humility, and hope.

29. Let us then add this last trait to Bernard's spirituality: here below, one should never lose hope of one's salvation, and one must never abandon [that hope] here on earth. Only in heaven is there no more hope, for it is only in heaven that we experience the realization of all our hopes. Nor is there faith in heaven, for there one sees its goodness face-to-face, ready to be unveiled. But while we are on earth, said Saint Paul, faith, hope, and charity continue to exist,[76] and these three things are an inseparable part of a Christian's duty. *Nunc autem manent fides, spes, caritas: tria haec* ["Now there remain faith, hope, and charity: these three" (1 Cor 13:13)]. It is true, says the apostle, that charity is the noblest of the three—*major autem horum est caritas* ["the greatest of these is charity"]—but faith and hope can never be separated from it: *nunc autem [manent fides, spes,*

---

[74] Matt 6:12. Proposition 34 of the errors of Miguel de Molinos condemned by Innocent XI (see n. 72 above) states, "To give thanks to God by words and speech is not for interior souls, which should remain in silence, placing no obstacle before God, since he works within them; and the more they give themselves up to God, the more they find that they cannot recite the Lord's Prayer or *Pater noster*" (Denzinger, no. 2234). See also n. 132 below.

[75] See n. 32 above.

[76] The verb is *subsister, subsistere* in Latin, which means to stand firm or continue to exist or remain in existence. Thus, when Saint Paul says that faith, hope, and charity *remain*, that is what he means.

caritas: tria haec;] major autem horum est caritas. Just as there is no charity so perfect that it can take the place of faith, so too, here below, there is no faith or charity that can take the place of hope. *Nunc autem manent fides, spes, caritas.*[77]

30. It is true that one can perform an act of faith without performing an act of hope, and an act of hope without performing an act of charity, and an act of charity without performing a specific act either of hope or of faith. But to suppose, as some these days wish to suppose, that this so-called charity can become habitual,[78] that it can become a [continual] state that excludes all hope, and that in this imagined state one claims to have attained the highest degree of the perfection of piety on the part of the faithful, and [the highest degree] of devotion to God, is a complete delusion. It is a fabrication used by the devil to take over one's freedom, cast the flesh into debauchery,[79] and expose to the critics' mockery that true spirituality that we were taught by Jesus Christ himself and, after him, by Saint Bernard.

31. Keep us, Lord, from ever thinking that there was the least trace of these delusions in the spirituality of your servant Bernard: we cannot accuse him of not having spoken of the

---

[77] The two important words here are *nunc* "now" and *manent* "they remain": here and now, in this world, all three theological virtues continue to exist, and they will continue to exist until we pass from this world to the next. Thus, when the Quietists maintain that in the state of holy indifference there is no place for hope, they are wrong, and Saint Paul's words prove them wrong.

[78] The very first of the propositions of Fénelon condemned by Innocent XII in March 1699 states, "There is a habitual state of the love of God [*habitualis status amoris Dei*], which is pure charity, unmixed with any motive of self-interest" (Denzinger, no. 2351). Similarly, proposition 16 tells us that "there is a state of contemplation so sublime and so perfect that it becomes habitual" (Denzinger, no. 2366). As far as La Rue is concerned, this is arrant nonsense.

[79] Because practicing the virtues or leading a virtuous life is not necessary: see n. 30 above and §7.

contemplative life and [not having] described its nature. He has left us a clear idea of his own behavior and his own views in what he says on the subject of the bride [of Christ] in the letter he wrote to the general of the Carthusian Order[80] and in the ninety[81] sermons he composed on the Song of Songs. These are the crown of his writings and the glorious end of his life, and [in them] he sets forth all that took place within his heart. *Magna res est amare Deum* ["It is a great thing to love God (but there are degrees in this love)"].[82] A bride, says this Father, stands at the highest degree of charity, then comes a son. A son may sometimes love tenderly, that is true, but not in the way that a bride loves her bridegroom. In loving his father, a son does not stop thinking of the inheritance that is due to him, and it is this that makes his love a selfish[83] love. But perfect love, says Saint Bernard, is never mercenary, and it does not feed on hope or return to it: *purus amor mercenarius non est; de spe vires non sumit* ["pure love is not mercenary; it does not draw strength from hope"].[84]

32. What could you ask that is more explicit or that strengthens your case more, you who do not wish to introduce into your pure love any [personal] interests[85] or idea of hope? It

---

[80] I.e., Ep 11 to Guy / Guigo, fifth prior (not general) of La Grande Chartreuse; SBOp 7:52–60.

[81] This is what La Rue says, but it is four too many.

[82] Bernard, SC 83.2.5; SBOp 2:301, which actually begins not with *Magna res est amare Deum* but with *Magna res amor; sed sunt in eo gradus*, "Love is a great thing, but there are degrees in it." The two degrees here are, first, the love of the bride for the bridegroom, which is a pure love, a love for love's sake; and, second, the love of children for their father, which is a mercenary love, since they are thinking of their inheritance.

[83] *Intéressé*, or self-interested.

[84] Bernard, SC 83.2.5; SBOp 2:301, which repeats *purus amor* in the second phrase (*Purus amor de spe vires non sumit*).

[85] The goal of the Quietists was "disinterested love": see nn. 53–54 above.

seems here that Bernard is completely on your side! Take it in this way, by all means, but distinguish carefully what he means by interests and what he is really saying. What exactly is this interest that should be excluded from pure love? It is everything that is of no interest to this pure love! And what is this interest that one can sacrifice without hesitation for the love of God? It is every interest that is worldly and temporal! It is pleasures, honors, comforts, inward joy, even the joys of heaven considered apart from heaven and without the essential possession of heaven. All this can be separated from the perfect love of God because pure love has no interest in it. But does this love have an interest? It is the return of the bridegroom to the bride and of the bride to the bridegroom. The bridegroom puts all his hope in the return of his bride, and the bride puts all hers in the return of the bridegroom:[86] *solam amoris vicem requirit sponsus* ["the bridegroom requires in return only love"].[87]

33. Open your eyes, you subtle deceivers, you who surrender yourself to your fine flashes of insight that lead you only into delusion and error! Remember well these names of bride and bridegroom, which Bernard and other Fathers have chosen to use so as to lead you straight to God and show you how the soul is united with him. There you will find the key to your futile subtleties[88] and the solution to all the fantastical objections you have put forward. For a bride waits for the return of her bridegroom because she loves him, but to imagine a bride who loves her bridegroom on condition that she agree never to be loved by him and always to be separated from him

---

[86] Bernard says specifically that *sponsae res et spes unus est amor*, "Love is the being *and hope* of a bride" (SC 83.2.5; SBOp 2:301).

[87] Bernard, SC 83.2.5; SBOp 2:301. The text actually reads *sponsi amor, immo sponsus amor, solam amoris vicem requirit et fidem*, "the love of the bridegroom, or rather the bridegroom who is himself love, requires in return only love and trust."

[88] See n. 27 above.

is an absurd and stupid idea with regard to the world, and sacrilegious with regard to God, who commands us to love him not only as God but as *our* God. *Ego sum Dominus Deus tuus* ["I am the Lord your God" (Exod 20:2)]. The bride loves her God in a unique way because she hopes that one day she will see him. That is her hope. And because she hopes to see him, she is afraid to mingle with [her love] anything that will prevent that. That is her fear. But fear and hope are perfected by love, which is why Bernard knew that he should put in the mouth of the bride these words of David, words that served as a solemn contract of her love for her bridegroom. [The same words] express the true contract that the soul who perfectly loves his God makes with him, and they set it out in precise terms and without equivocation: *Mihi adhaerere Deo bonum est, ponere in Deo spem meam* ["It is good for me to cleave to God, to put my hope in God" (Ps 72:28)]. Lord, this is the whole of my happiness: to be united inseparably to you and to place in you all my hope, *mihi adhaerere*. This is why [Bernard] said in another place that, in this life, he cannot have charity that is not followed by hope: *nunquam est caritas sine cupiditate, sed ordinata* ["charity is never without self-interest, but (it will be) ordered"].[89] As for me, he adds, if you ask me what I think, I would say to you that it seems to me impossible that there should be perfect charity without some hope. *Mihi impossibile*

---

[89] Ep 11.7; SBOp 7:58 = Dil 14.38; SBOp 3:152: *Numquam erit caritas sine timore, sed casto; numquam sine cupiditate, sed ordinata;* "Charity will never be without fear, but it is chaste fear; never without self-interest, but an ordered [self-interest]." On "chaste fear," see n. 63 above. Ordered charity must necessarily start with some self-interest. As Bernard said to Bruno, archbishop-elect of Cologne, "Right order requires that you learn first to take care of yourself, and after that [you can take care of] others" (Ep 8.1; SBOp 7:48). The four stages of love in *De diligendo Deo* represent ordered charity, but they begin with the love of self for self. The essence of true order is that the body and the senses should be subject to reason, and that reason should be subject to God.

videtur ["it seems to me impossible"], etc.[90] But if it seems impossible to Bernard, to which of those who, in our days, [claim to be] perfect will pure love without hope be possible?

34. We will pause here, Christian listeners, and conclude with Saint Bernard that the perfection of spirituality consists in the pursuit and practice of all the virtues and of everything that depends upon them,[91] that there is not one of them that is unworthy of God or incompatible with loving him perfectly, and, as a consequence, still less unworthy of ourselves, and that none of them is contrary either to our eternal interest or to our salvation. This is just how Saint Bernard acted and thought in his love of righteousness: *dilexisti justitiam*. But it is not enough to be, like him, faithful to the duties incumbent on true spirituality. We must also be zealous, as he was, against all the erroneous interpretations of true spirituality, and that will be the subject of the second part [of my sermon].

[SECOND PART]

35. We have seen Saint Bernard in his private life, faithful to all these duties of devotion and spirituality:[92] this is the true miracle of God. Let us see him now in his public life, animated by his zeal for the glory of God: this is the true miracle of man.

36. In the past, the Lord chose the prophet Ezekiel to tame a rebellious people and spoke to him in these words: *fili hominis, speculatorem dedi te domui Israel* ["Son of man, I have made you

---

[90] There is confusion here. Ep 11.8; SBOp 7:59 = Dil 15.39; SBOp 3:153, reads *Asserant hoc si qui experti sunt; mihi, fateor, impossibile videtur*, "Let those who have experienced it say so: I confess that, for me, it seems impossible." But what seems to Bernard to be impossible here is not the absence of any hope from charity, but the attainment of the fourth degree of love, when we love ourselves only for the sake of God. He doubts (he says) whether anyone has ever reached this stage perfectly in this life.

[91] *qu'elles [les vertus] y gardent toutes leurs subordinations*.

[92] *Piété et dévotion*: see n. 21 above.

a watchman over the house of Israel" (Ezek 33:7)], "Son of man, I have commissioned you to watch over and govern the house of Israel." Bernard was charged with the same commission. The whole Christian world was put in his care: it was placed under his watchful gaze and exposed to his censure. There was no heresy, no discord, no war, no disorder, no error that escaped his knowledge and that he did not fight with zeal. He was never dazzled by the rank and dignity of those with whom he had to deal, which is the first obstacle that usually douses the zeal of even the most dedicated. He was never shaken by the violence of the powers against whom he had to fight, which is the second obstacle that can hold one back. He was never moved to pity for reasons of the most tender kindness and friendship, which is the third obstacle. And finally, he was not perplexed by any empty subtleties,[93] either of knowledge or of error, which is the fourth and last obstacle. He gloriously overcame all these obstacles that hold back so many people and that hinder them from fighting against vice. Let us try to summarize what he did in a few words.

37. First of all, he was never dazzled by the brilliance of anyone's rank or dignity, and when he set out to conquer vice he was in no way deterred by any claim to greatness. He himself was a gentle solitary who loved peace, but when he set about uprooting sin,[94] there was nothing that could soften him: in his ardent zeal he took his fight even as far as the throne. For him, the courts and kings and palaces of nobles were no refuge for iniquity, and, with wise discernment, he respected rank while everywhere pursuing vice.

38. When he writes to Pope Eugenius what does he say to him? "You are the first of the bishops, the successor of the apostles, Peter in dignity, Jesus Christ by anointing."[95] You see

---

[93] See n. 27 above.

[94] *Crime*: see appendix 1, s.v. *crimes* / sins.

[95] Bernard, Csi 2.8.15; SBOp 3:423, which is very slightly different: "You are the prince of the bishops, you are the successor of the apostles, . . . Peter in power, Christ by anointing."

his respect for rank. "But what can one say when we see you walking in state through the city of Rome with a retinue of servants and an ostentatious train, all covered with gold and silver? Was it thus that Peter drew simple people to himself? Was it thus that Paul hurried from city to city? *Sic jactitabat Petrus? sic jactitabat Paulus?*" ["Did Peter show off in this way? Did Paul show off in this way?"][96] You see how he pursues iniquity.

39. What did he say to the emperor [Lothair III] when he spoke to him? "It is God who has placed you over his people to guide them: you stand in his place on earth. You are invested with the government of a great empire, and you are master of your people's fate." You see his respect for rank. "But think how you should respond to these gifts, how you should carry out your duties, and put an end to this cruelty, this harshness toward your subjects! You will only bring down on yourself the stored-up anger and wrath of God if you treat badly those who serve you well. [If you wish] to be well received by God, you must treat well those whom he has entrusted to your governance. Moreover, do not think that I am imposing these things on you, I am simply telling you the truth, and if I am harassing you, it is only because I am being loyal to you."[97] *Odisti iniquitatem.* You see how he pursues iniquity.

40. What did he say to Henry II,[98] king of England, to persuade him to join the party that supported Innocent II, the true pope, and leave that of Anacletus, the false pontiff? "Sire, I

---

[96] These last four sentences are based on Csi 14.3.6; SBOp 3:453–54, but *Sic jactitabat Petrus? sic jactitabat Paulus?* occurs nowhere in Bernard and is not recorded in either the Patrologia Latina or any of the standard databases. See also Ep 238.2; SBOp 8:116–17.

[97] This whole paragraph is a brief summary of Bernard's Ep 139; SBOp 7:335–36, to the Holy Roman emperor Lothair III of Supplinburg (listed in appendix 2).

[98] La Rue confuses the Henrys: for La Rue's *Henry II* read Henry I (see appendix 2).

have no wish to draw to your attention the laws of honor or the duties of the dignity to which you have been raised: that would be not to know you and an insult to your lofty position."[99] You see his respect for rank. "But knowing that it is your custom to bestow favors on those who have raised you [to where you are] and to grant nothing to those who constrain you, beware of committing one [more] sin in supporting these unjust interests, and consider how you can deal with all your other sins!"[100] Is this not the pursuit of iniquity? *Odisti iniquitatem.*

41. What did he say to Louis the Fat? "This same God who has placed you on this throne is ready to give you a higher and more honorable throne—provided you are faithful in following what he has ordained for you."[101] You see his respect for rank. But when Bernard saw that [Louis] had insulted the priests of the Lord, he threatened this same king with the anger and wrath of God and predicted the death of his son, and the fact followed swiftly on the threat.[102] And as this has happened to so many others who paid no heed to Bernard's rod, it shows us that God has not failed to bear witness to his servant's zeal. *Odisti iniquitatem.*

42. Was he any more peaceable when it came to upholding the interests of the Church? What did he not take on in this cause? He was but a simple monk, without support, without protection, without power when the antipope Anacletus, having usurped

---

[99] Based on Bernard's Ep 138; SBOp 7:334, to Henry I.

[100] Based on *Vita prima* 2.1.4 (Arnold of Bonneval); PL 185:271AB; CF 76:82–83.

[101] Bernard, Ep 45.1; SBOp 7:133. The letter is addressed to Louis from Stephen Harding and "the whole assembly of the abbots and brothers of Cîteaux" but was almost certainly the work of Bernard.

[102] See *Vita prima* 4.2.11 (Geoffrey of Auxerre); PL 185:327D–28A (omitted in CF 76). Louis's elder son, Philip, died on October 13, 1131. He was riding with some friends when a black pig tripped up his horse. Philip was thrown over the horse's head, suffered severe injuries, and died the next day without regaining consciousness. He was fifteen.

the throne of Saint Peter, had already made himself master of all the surrounding lands. And when Innocent II, the true pope, was chased out of Rome and forced to seek refuge in France, [Bernard] was no more than a simple solitary, sunk in a corner of his solitude. Yet for the peace of the Church, with what zeal did he undertake to reestablish Innocent and dethrone Anacletus? On the orders of the king of France [Louis VI] the Council of Étampes is convened [in 1130], and the Council agrees to follow Bernard's opinion in the choice of the legitimate pope. You see before you Bernard, the arbiter of the [papal] tiara and of the most glorious throne in the universe! His vote was for Innocent, and the whole world accepted his opinion.

43. From there he journeys in England, Germany, and Spain,[103] passes through Italy, and spends some time in Pavia and Milan, seeking support for the just cause of the legitimate pontiff and persuading [the cities] to abandon the party of the usurper.[104] All the kings and rulers of these foreign kingdoms paid homage to the minister of Jesus Christ in the way they all deferred to his voice. He then came back to France to put an end to what remained of the schism of the antipope in Guyenne.

44. William, duke of Aquitaine, was the leader in this war, and also the most stubborn [of Bernard's opponents].[105] Bernard confronted him, but with what band of supporters and with what weapons against someone so powerful and obstinate? [He came] attired in his priestly vestments, at the entrance of the church [of Notre-Dame-de-la-Couldre], with the

---

[103] La Rue is here misreading Arnold of Bonneval, *Vita prima* 2.7.45; PL 185:294D (omitted in CF 76), who tells us that Bernard traveled through France and Germany, and that Spaniards, English, and others in more remote places were overwhelmed (by his arguments). Arnold does not say that Bernard visited either Spain or England, which is just as well since he never set foot in either country.

[104] See Williams, *Saint Bernard*, chaps. V–VII.

[105] See appendix 2, s.v. William (Guillaume) X, duke of Aquitaine. The panegyrists can rarely resist telling the story of his dramatic conversion.

holy Host in his hand, and said to him these words: "Behold your Judge, before whom all greatness bows, before whom every knee bends, and into whose hands your soul will one day fall! Do you still wish to persecute him and make war on him?" At these words the duke, in utter confusion, fell to the ground, on the pavement, frozen with fear, and lost both his wits and his power of speech.[106] He recovered his voice only to confess his fault. But was it a hero [who did this]? Was it a conqueror? A captain famed everywhere for his brilliant successes and victories over the proudest powers of the world? No, dear listeners, it was a simple man, a poor monk, who was incapable of tolerating iniquity. *Odisti iniquitatem*.

45. But was it perhaps the case that this man, hitherto so indifferent to the glory of high rank or dignity, was softened when it came to friendship? No, no, Christians, if neither rank nor dignity could hold him back in his pursuit of vice, he could no more be held back by the kind feelings that accompany friendship. He had friends in many places, but he had especially close ties with an abbot of Saint-Denis[107] and an abbot of Cluny, who was well known and venerated by the Church through his writings and even more by the holiness of his life.[108] Wholly amenable though he was to his friends, [Bernard] did not hesitate to take both of them to task. His friendship was not so great that he preferred its pleasures to the interests of Jesus Christ. What a stir he made when he set out to fight against vice! He had no fear of reproaching Suger for his haughty bearing, the magnificence of his train, the pomp of his retinue.[109] He admonishes him publicly; he shows him that

---

[106] Arnold of Bonneval tells us that it looked as if the duke had suffered an epileptic seizure (PL 185:290C), which is indeed quite possible.

[107] Suger of Saint-Denis: see appendix 2.

[108] Peter the Venerable: see appendix 2.

[109] See Bernard's Ep 78 to Suger; SBOp 7:201–10, especially §3 and §10.

he cannot support his overbearing conduct, that he should change his way of life, and the zeal with which he delivered his reproaches was soon followed by success.

46. Was he any less amenable with his friend the venerable Peter of Cluny? Did his kindly feelings, his submissiveness, his friendship hold him back from tenderly reproving him? The monastery of this pious abbot was sliding into disorder, and when Bernard learned of it, he warned [Peter] of what was going on. But when he saw that the cure did not keep pace with his zeal, he redoubled his protests and made his threats more resounding, and, notwithstanding the tender bonds that linked [the two friends], he pushed them to their limits when Peter of Cluny did not profit from his advice.

47. And how did the wicked world react to all this? What was the common talk? "What's this?" people said. "If two friends have both made profession of virtue and charity, how can one treat a dear friend in this way? What a business! What injustice!" But Bernard did not hold back his zeal in the face of these empty criticisms from a blind world. Ah! he wrote to the holy servant of God, [Suger,] "there is no friendship without truth!"[110]

48. Learn from this example, you worldly men and women, you false friends who base your friendships on the bonds of flattery, dissimulation, hypocrisy, falsehoods, and self-satisfaction! These are the brittle bonds, the feeble bonds, the shameful bonds of a carnal friendship! But the unique and legitimate bonds of friendship are truth, sincerity, and doing the right thing. May they be found in you! For if, like Bernard, you speak the truth sincerely to your friends and it results in a scandal in the wicked world, you must rather suffer that than abandon

---

[110] Bernard, Ep 78.13; SBOp 7:210: *Tunc demum verae erunt amicitiae, si veritatis fuerint foederatae consortio*, "Then, finally, there will be true friendship between you if it is bound by a common love of truth." In La Rue's panegyric, the two friends of §§47–48 are, or course, Bossuet and Fénelon. See also §53 below.

the party of truth: *melius est, ut oriatur scandalum quam ut veritas relinquatur* ["it is better that scandal should arise than that truth be abandoned"].[111]

49. You see how Bernard's zeal against the enemies of truth stands out? *Odisti iniquitatem*. Do you have the same spirit, you worldly people who are listening to me?

50. But was his zeal any less forceful when he was dealing with the subtleties of knowledge? He was never intimidated! The fact that there were so few scholars increased their authority, and what they tried to do was to bind the Gospel too closely to the world. But in their desire for too great a refinement of their learning, they ended up by changing the true doctrine of Jesus Christ.

51. Abelard was the subtlest thinker of them all, and, with his overly sophisticated learning,[112] sowed his errors on all sides. He spread his novel ideas[113] on the mystery of the Most Holy Trinity[114] in all directions, and the number of his disciples increased from day to day. Bernard was much concerned about this discord and believed that he should no longer remain silent on the matter of these novelties. He therefore contacted [Abelard] and tried to lead him back to the right path by giving him loving advice and remonstrating with him in a helpful way. The innovator promised that he would leave it there until the matter was cleared up, but before long [the

---

[111] Bernard, Ep 78.10; SBOp 7:208, which actually reads *melius est ut scandalum oriatur quam veritas relinquatur*, but the differences are insignificant. This, in turn, is based on Gregory the Great, In Ezech lib. I, hom 7.5; PL 76:842C, which reads *Si autem de veritate scandalum sumitur, utilius permittitur nasci scandalum quam veritas relinquatur*, "If scandal should come into being through truth, it is better that scandal be allowed to arise than that truth be abandoned."

[112] "His overly sophisticated learning" renders the French *ses raffinements*.

[113] *Ses nouveautés*: see n. 29 above.

[114] See appendix 2, s.v. Abelard, Peter, and Bell, *Many Mansions*, 141–46, for a summary of Abelard's Trinitarian teaching.

seeds of his ideas] were being sown again, and it was claimed that Bernard had exaggerated what Abelard had actually proposed or that he had even drawn conclusions that had been specifically denied by their author. But, said Saint Bernard, what point is there in denying the conclusions if one accepts the bases from which they derive? What man, he said, would wish to reveal to us the secrets of God? These are Bernard's own words.[115] Is he bent on coming to us only to tell us that, having ascended into heaven in intimate union with God, one[116] has more right [to say these things]? And that having returned from that high contemplation to reveal to us, in obscure and ambiguous words, ineffable things that it is not permitted for any human to reveal: *scrutabitur et rediens ad nos loquitur ineffabilia verba, quae non licet homini loqui* ["I shall look, and, returning to us, speak ineffable words that no human being is permitted to speak"]?[117] Is there anything more vain, then, anything more proud, anything more hypocritical than these types of novelties when they concern the things of the faith? [That faith] is wholly simple and wholly pure, yet here these simple things are ridiculed, and questions that God himself has answered and confirmed are mocked. In their place one seeks to introduce into Christianity other [questions] that are so rarefied and lofty that no one can possibly understand them,

---

[115] The title of chapter 7 of Bernard's Ep 190 to Pope Innocent II reads *Abaelardum perstringit, impie ac temere Dei secreta scrutantem et extenuantem*, "He rebukes Abelard for impiously and rashly examining and depreciating the secrets of God."

[116] La Rue here changes to the impersonal *on*, "Is one bent," for although he is, in theory, speaking of Abelard, his real target is Fénelon.

[117] Bernard, Ep 190.1; SBOp 8:18, to Innocent II, reading *et scrutatur alta Dei, rediensque ad nos refert verba ineffabilia, quae non licet homini loqui* (2 Cor 12:4), "He searches out the deep things of God, and then, returning to us, he brings back unspeakable words that it is not lawful for a man to utter." Once again, the quotation is from Bernard's letter against Abelard, but what La Rue is really attacking is the Quietist view of the nature of contemplation.

and so obscure and ambiguous that no one can grasp them. In short, what one is trying to do by means of these pointless novelties is to give to the perfection of religion a foundation different from that laid down by Jesus Christ. One speaks of vices and virtues in a wholly different way from the moral teaching of the Gospel, and then goes on to spout all these [ideas] about the perfect way, about revelations, about raptures, about intimate union.[118] Delusions! Phantoms! But it is not just that these things are merely useless, nor that they are the results of vanity alone. No. There is something here that is worse than all that.

52. In a few words, when Abelard saw that Bernard spoke in this way about his false subtleties, he had the gall to appeal his case to a Council convoked at Sens [in 1141]. Bernard went there, argued against his ideas in the strongest terms, and straightaway confounded him. So [Abelard] appeals to the pope [Innocent II], but the pope confirmed the opinion of Bernard and condemned Abelard. This condemnation, however, did not put an end to the complaints and false zeal of other subtle thinkers, and one of them, [Gilbert de la Porrée,[119]] distinguished by his rank and the subtlety of his thought, comes to Bernard and proposes a battle. He wants to dispute[120] with him, but finding Bernard, as always, perfectly ready to fight for the truth, he tempered his fire.

53. What was the judgment of worldly people with regard to all this? It is a scandal, they said, to see good people so divided in their opinions. How can one have so little consideration for the person and rank of the other? [Bernard] pushes things too

---

[118] The reference is clearly to the Quietists, since Abelard says nothing about the perfect way, revelations, raptures, and intimate union.

[119] See appendix 2, s.v. Gilbert de la Porrée.

[120] "[Il] veut disputer contre lui"; that is, he wants a disputation / *disputatio* in the medieval sense of a formal debate following fixed rules with references to recognized established authorities (*auctoritates*).

far and, furthermore, attacks a great and learned man [Gilbert] on the basis of trifling details and a few equivocal terms! Some went much further [in their attacks] on Bernard's zeal. It was said that Bernard had a proud spirit, that he was haughty, arrogant, headstrong, unruly, and ambitious, and that if he had not been jealous [of Gilbert] he would not have begun the dispute.

54. It was these [complaints] that were sent to Rome from every direction, and it was in this way that he was attacked with writings and defamatory pamphlets that we may still see in books of his time. But ah! the man of God was not discouraged, and his zeal did not cool down! The Church of France assembled at a Council at Reims [in 1148]. Gilbert, bishop of Poitiers, appeared there since he was suspected of teaching false doctrine on the question of the divine essence.[121] Bernard attacked him on the matter of his faith. They disputed with each other. The disputation heated up and lasted two full days. What a disputation!

55. Gilbert's friends could not bear the idea that their friend had been openly condemned by the Council,[122] and they tried to reach a compromise arrangement or, at least, a delay in condemning [Gilbert's] errors. The whole Council was ready to conclude its business without making any decision on the bishop's doctrines. But Bernard, on his own, destroyed every attempt at resorting to influence or politics; on his own he prevailed over all the intrigues of these powerful friends and finally brought about the condemnation of Gilbert.[123] But what

[121] See Bell, *Many Mansions*, 146–48, for a summary of Gilbert's Realist views on the Trinity.

[122] He had not, in fact, been openly condemned, but La Rue's account of the case of Gilbert, like the similar accounts of all the other panegyrists, is quite unreliable historically. Their business was to show how Bernard triumphed over Gilbert (which he did not). In any case, in La Rue's panegyric, the friend who had been condemned was Fénelon.

[123] This also was not the case. Gilbert was not condemned for heresy, though it was agreed that the book that began the contro-

we must also note here is that after Bishop Gilbert had been condemned, Abelard, concerned for his own safety, hated his own errors from that time on and submitted himself entirely to the judgment of the Holy See.[124] He edified everyone and, by this submission, made amends for all the hurt and ruin that his wicked doctrines had brought upon the Church. Thus Bernard had the holy pleasure of seeing his victory complete, for if he had the honor of conquering Gilbert on his own, he then had the consolation of seeing Abelard conquer himself and, in taming his own spirit, achieve the most notable of all victories.[125]

56. What crowns, Lord, do we see placed on the head of this zealous servant; yet they are still no more than tender flowers placed by human hands on Bernard's head. The crown of righteousness has already been bestowed upon him, but your crown, Lord, the crown of eternal glory, which no one can say he does not deserve, when will that come? Is it not time that he possessed that for which he has waited so long? The joyous reward for which he has worked so much and suffered so much? Here it is, Christians, it is ready for him! Bernard leaves this world and his soul flies to heaven: freed from this body, it enters in! And now Bernard is in heaven, where he had always longed to be, always hoped to be, always labored to be, and there he has no more fear, no more hope. There he loves

---

versy—Gilbert's commentary on Boethius's *De Trinitate*—was not to be disseminated in any form.

[124] La Rue's chronology is at fault here: Gilbert was examined at Paris in 1147 and Reims in 1148. Abelard had died in 1142. But almost all of what La Rue says in §55 is wrong.

[125] La Rue here confuses Gilbert and Abelard. It was not Abelard but Gilbert who submitted himself to the judgment of the Holy See—at the Council of Reims he repeatedly stated that he was ready to retract any errors that might be found in his works—and if Abelard could be said to have been conquered by Bernard, it was Gilbert who conquered himself. All this is corrected in the second version of La Rue's panegyric, primarily by omitting any reference to Abelard.

without fear and without hope, for he now possesses all that he feared to lose and all that he hoped to possess.

57. And you, dear listeners, are you prepared to be saints? Perhaps you wish to be a saint like Teresa [of Ávila] or Francis de Sales?[126] Be one! I agree to it! But know that they were not more holy than Bernard. Since it is said in the Gospel that we are saints,[127] let us be as saintly as were the saints, and, in order to be like them, let us love God as the saints [loved him], and not like these subtle thinkers and scholars. But let us add to our love for God a hatred of the evil that opposes him, let us join to our love of righteousness the zeal to fight against error and falsehood. If you love someone tenderly, you cannot bear to be false to him. There has never been a saint who loved God perfectly and who was not ready to do battle with his enemies. Bernard, who was human like us, sets us an example. *Dilexisti justitiam et odisti iniquitatem* ["He loved righteousness and hated iniquity"].

58. Let us respect, then, the knowledge of the learned, the integrity of the good, and the piety of the devout—but let us pay no heed to those subtle novelties[128] that lead only to error. Let us avoid the company of those of our brothers and sisters who give credence to these errors, of those shameful hypocrites who want to make themselves conspicuous and in this way achieve their goals in the world. Let us rather join with those

---

[126] La Rue wrote panegyrics on both of them: La Rue, *Panégyriques des saints*, 1:43–86 (Saint François de Sales), 307–48 (Saint Teresa). In that on Saint Teresa, he makes it clear that, in his view, mystical rapture is not a habitual state that can be achieved by any short and easy way (as Madame Guyon would have us believe), but a rare and extraordinary grace given by God to very few.

[127] Nowhere in the gospels does it say that we are saints, but there are numerous instances in Paul's letters where Christians are referred to as *sancti*. La Rue, however, might have been thinking of John 10:34, where Jesus says to the Jews, "Is it not written in your law: 'I said, You are gods [*Dii estis*]'?" quoting Ps 81:6.

[128] *Subtiles nouveautés*: here La Rue combines both pejorative terms.

who are closest to the saints, from whom these [hypocrites] distance themselves by a fantastical idea of intimate union with God.[129] Let us not mingle with the heretics but join with those closest to the faith, never doubting the charity and rectitude of their heart. But let us also try to make those [who have these wrong ideas] amend their words, while we ourselves remain opposed to those basic principles that can produce such pernicious results. For if we give any latitude to these erroneous expressions on account of the good intentions of their authors we are betraying the cause of God to preserve the interests of human beings. We would be ignoring the straightforwardness and simplicity of the faith, for the more undetectable the evil that one teaches, the more contrary and dangerous it is to the faith. Where would the faith be today if our Fathers [in the Church] had deferred to the empty inventions of the heretics? Where would we be if our past teachers[130] had tolerated the false principles of so many ambitious innovators who wished to rise up and lure to themselves all the sheep of the fold of Jesus Christ? [Where would we be] if they had slackened their watch? All the heretics condemned and proscribed by the Church—the Ariuses, Nestoriuses, Eutycheses—would now, among us, have taken the place of the Jeromes, the Ambroses, the Augustines, the Chrysostoms, and would perhaps be as revered as the Athanasiuses, the Cyrils, and the Leos. Their errors with regard to the consubstantiality of the Word, the distinction of the Persons, the two wills of Jesus Christ might have been no more than the products of too subtle thinking, but what confusion did they not produce in the Church, what havoc did they not wreak in Christianity? Their novel ideas on the procession of the Holy Spirit and its consubstantiality with the Son may have seemed almost nothing—one syllable

---

[129] The "shameful hypocrites" are, of course, the Quietists. La Rue regularly refers to them as hypocrites.
[130] *Nos anciens docteurs.*

or a single letter[131] making all the difference between scholars who were true to the faith and those who were not—but what heresies were more damaging to the Church of Jesus Christ?

59. But [what we face] today is not just a matter of one word, but every one of the virtues; not just a matter of a single letter, but charity itself! How can we be indifferent to the peril that this brings? What? Are we to have no concern for the honor of so many virtues consecrated by the cross and example of Jesus Christ? Ah! If we are less passionate about this, less energetic, less resourceful than our fathers, it is because we have less zeal, less wisdom, and—if I may venture to say so—less faith and less religion than they. Let us stir ourselves, then, at least by means of [the Lord's] prayer,[132] to come to the assistance of truth, the prayer that was taught and recommended to us by Jesus Christ himself. Let us stir ourselves to come to the help of charity by defending that hope without which we cannot be saved. Let us stir ourselves to hope by the fear of the terrible judgments of our God. Let us stir ourselves to the hope of our own particular bliss by means of the words of God himself, who has charged us to love him not only as God but as *our* God: *Diliges dominum Deus tuum*, etc.[133]

60. You above all, Reverend Fathers, worthy children of Bernard, heirs of his discipline as well as his profound wisdom, you who, from his time to ours, have always given new life to the spirit of his virtues: his profound humility, his rigorous penance, etc.—it is for you, today, to again give new life to

---

[131] La Rue may be thinking of the difference between *homoousios* "of the same substance" and *homoiousios* "of similar substance" (there is a single additional iota), though the matter pertained to the relationship of Father and Son, not the relationship of the Son and the Holy Spirit. Our author, however, is speaking rhetorically, not theologically. He is condemning Quietist heretics, not giving a lecture on early Christian doctrine.

[132] See n. 74 above.

[133] Deut 6:5; Matt 22:37; Mark 12:30; Luke 10:27; and see §33 above.

the vigor of his zeal by taking up arms in defense of a firmly grounded spirituality[134] that he sanctioned so well by his own teaching and example. Our hope that this will be so comes from your enlightened actions and from the holy burning love you have for a God whom you hope one day to possess and whom we wish to possess with you forever and ever. Amen.

---

[134] *Une dévotion solide*: i.e., a solidly based spirituality in contrast to the airy-fairy speculations of the Quietists. *Une dévotion solide* or *une vraie dévotion* stood in contrast to *une fausse dévotion*. See Lucy Tinsley, *The French Expressions for Spirituality and Devotion: a Semantic Study* (Washington, DC: Catholic University of America Press, 1953), 234, 237.

10

The Flames Die Down

The Revised Panegyric of Charles de La Rue

INTRODUCTION

Two essential questions need to be answered with regard to this second version of La Rue's panegyric on Bernard: first, just what changes have been made to the earlier, unrevised version, and second, who was responsible for these changes? The changes are considerable and include omissions, corrections, additions, and a good deal of rewriting. The most significant omissions are almost all the direct attacks on Fénelon and the Quietists,[1] and what is left has been toned down. In the unrevised version of the discourse, these attacks are to be found almost from the beginning to the end; in the second version they are essentially confined to a single section, §§21–25,[2] in which La Rue summarizes his own view of the nature of pure and disinterested love and shows that hope (and hope in one's own salvation in particular) always remains and that the Quietists' idea of a permanent and habitual state of disinterestedness is nonsense.

Saint Bernard had achieved a state of continual recollection of God, a state in which he was totally unaware of his own

---

[1] This is easy to see in Chérot's text, since he prints the two versions on facing pages and italicizes all the sections in the unrevised version that do not appear in the revised.

[2] There are some further fairly general allusions in the final paragraphs.

physical surroundings, but he never lost either his hope of salvation or his fear of God's judgments. We might add that in this revised version, La Rue bolsters his case by adding further material from Bernard's eighty-third and twenty-third sermons on the Song of Songs and *De diligendo Deo* and presents a rather better argument.

As to corrections, most of the inaccuracies in the unrevised version have been amended: Bernard's age at leaving home for Cîteaux (not Clairvaux), for example, or the list of episcopal sees he was offered (and refused), or the chronological and historical mess that appears in §55 of the unrevised version. Some Latin quotations also appear more accurately. A couple of errors still remain—La Rue still has the wrong circumstances when Conrad von Hohenstaufen had to shelter Bernard in his arms (§16), and he still confuses Henry I of England with Henry II (§32)—but these are minor. As to additions, La Rue adds Bernard's description of himself as the chimera of his age (§17), he provides more quotations from Bernard's own works, he introduces Roger II of Sicily (§33), and he augments his account of the dramatic conversion of Duke William X of Aquitaine (§34). He also completely revises the section on Abelard (§39), adds to it more material from Bernard himself, and makes Abelard sound more like Abelard and less like Fénelon. In other words, the revised version of the panegyric has been the subject of major rewriting, and we must now ask who was responsible.

Henri Chérot was in no doubt. It was François Bretonneau, and he is harsh in his condemnation of this "ruthless corrector."[3] In his hands, he says, "this panegyric on Saint Bernard, stripped of everything that set it in its living frame, is now one of those dead works of the religious literature of the time, which, uselessly and ponderously, shed their dusty rays on the burial-places of books."[4] I cannot agree, though there is no

---

[3] Chérot, *Autour de Bossuet*, 36.
[4] Chérot, *Autour de Bossuet*, 29.

doubt that the fire of the first version is but a warm glow in the second. To my mind, the rewriting has been far too extensive to be laid at the door of any editor, and it is surely far more likely that La Rue himself made the additions, corrections, changes, and so on that we see in Bretonneau's text. This is not to deny that Bretonneau might have made some minor editorial revisions, but I cannot believe that he rewrote the sermon. Nor is it difficult to find a reason that La Rue might have modified his text. As we saw in the last chapter, when the panegyric was delivered in August 1698 it caused something of a commotion, and the superior general of the Jesuits found it expedient to dispatch Father La Rue to the Languedoc on a missionary journey until the dust had settled. But that was in 1700, and La Rue still had a quarter of a century to live. It seems to me quite possible, therefore, that he toned down the ferocity and corrected the errors of the first version in order to preach the panegyric on some other occasion. Unlike the unrevised version, Bretonneau's text has no date, and what I suspect came into Bretonneau's hands was La Rue's own revision of his earlier fierce attack on Fénelon and the Quietists. It is even possible that the revisions were made after Fénelon's death in 1715. What is certain is that, if the first version was more polemic than panegyric, the revised version is more panegyric than polemic, and here it is.

THE PANEGYRIC
PANEGYRIC ON SAINT BERNARD[5]

Dilexisti justitiam et odisti iniquitatem; propterea unxit te Deus, Deus tuus, oleo laetitiae. (Ps 44:8)

---

[5] See chap. 9 (La Rue 1), n. 11, for the edition. In the following notes, a note number or section number preceded by an asterisk—thus: *n. 23 or *§4—refers to the notes or sections in the first, unrevised, version of La Rue's panegyric.

"You have loved righteousness and hated iniquity. For this reason you have received from the Lord your God the anointing of joy."[6]

1. It was to the Messiah that the prophet [David] addressed these words, anticipating what was to happen in the future, because in the days of his mortal life, this unique Son of the Father, sent down to earth, loved righteousness: that is to say, he practiced all the virtues and taught them to humankind: *Dilexisti justitiam* ["He loved righteousness"], and equally because he hated iniquity and came here to combat the vices and banish them, *Et odisti iniquitatem* ["And he hated iniquity"]. You see why he deserved to receive the heavenly anointing of the Spirit of grace and, as a result, to taste its most delicious sweetness: *Propterea unxit te Deus, Deus tuus, oleo laetitiae* ["Wherefore God, your God, has anointed you with the oil of gladness"].[7]

2. Bear with me, Christians, if I apply to the servant [Bernard] what is said of the Master [Jesus], but I could not draw from the sacred books a more appropriate or a more suitable text to set forth the true character of the glorious Patriarch whose feast we celebrate [today]. The divine anointing that flooded his soul so abundantly made him, of all the saints, one who was especially marked out by a loving and tender spirituality:[8] *Unxit te Deus oleo laetitiae*. But how did he come to be favored with this precious gift if not because his heart was ready to follow every one of God's wishes and to fulfill every one of the duties of his profession: and, in addition, [because of] an untiring and burning desire to defend the interests of God and his Church against all errors and mistaken ideas?

3. There were some saints who, through their own particular inclination, lived a life in which they were wholly devoted to God and tightly bound to him, but in which they neither

---

[6] See *n. 23.
[7] For the relationship of Ps 44:7-8 to Heb 1:8-9, see *nn. 24–25.
[8] *Dévotion*: see *n. 21.

spoke out against his enemies nor attacked them. Such were the contemplatives and solitaries. Others, however, learned and zealous, spent their lives making war on heretics and sinners, whether by word of mouth or by their soundly argued works, but they found that this continual tension, this superfluity of disputes and writings troubled somewhat the peace of their pious devotion[9] and dried up its essence. In the case of Saint Bernard, however (and here, in a few words, you will see how this discourse will be divided), he had the privilege and singular advantage of uniting in his own person, and uniting to the highest degree, [both these qualities]. On the one hand, he had an inviolable determination to practice righteousness and all the perfection of his [monastic] state, *Dilexisti justitiam*. That will be the first part [of my sermon]. And on the other, he had an inexhaustible zeal to pursue iniquity and confound falsehood, *Et odisti iniquitatem*. That will be the second part.

4. Holy Virgin, you whom Bernard ever regarded as a mother and an advocate, and on whom he called on every occasion, seeing you as his mediator[10] with the Great Mediator, be our mediator with the Holy Spirit, so that we may obtain the enlightenment we need and that we seek through your intercession, as we say with the angel: *Ave [Maria]*.

[FIRST PART]

5. Penance[11] and mortification of the flesh, contempt for oneself and humility of spirit, devotion of the heart and love of God [are] essential virtues, and they contain within themselves Christian righteousness—above all, the righteousness and holiness pertaining to a religious way of life. This is what

---

[9] *Piété*: see appendix 1, s.v. *piété* / piety.

[10] *Médiatrice* or "mediatrix," but the word, though it exists in English, is not common. For the doctrine, see Bell, *Many Mansions*, 248–53.

[11] *Pénitence*: see appendix 1, s.v. *pénitence* / penitence.

we were told by the Savior of humankind; this is what we were taught by the apostles and, after them, by all the masters of the interior and spiritual life.[12] Without mortification of the flesh, the senses rebel and shake off the yoke of the Lord; without humility of spirit, pride mingles with even the best works and corrupts them; without the love of God, the heart attaches itself to frivolous objects and all one's piety dies away. This is what Bernard understood early in his life. He had no need to await the maturity of age, for wisdom anticipated years. By means of the heavenly light that illumined him, he knew from the start which ways were straightest and determined to follow them.

6. He therefore took this plan of perfection as the pattern for his whole life. Even though he was wholly chaste and wholly righteous from his earliest youth, he condemned himself to all the rigors of mortification and wished to live as a penitent. Even though he had received the gift of miracles and other signs of heaven's favor, in his own estimation he placed himself at the very lowest rank and, so far as was possible for him, he wanted to live in obscurity, withdrawn [from the world]. Finally, even though he was so dearly loved by those who, coming from all sides, had recourse to him and sought him out, he was never parted from the most intimate union with God, and not one of his affections was ever directed anywhere else. Listen carefully now to all that I have to say, and let us draw out for ourselves from this salutary material [the meaning of] *Dilexisti justitiam*.

7. Nobility, intelligence, a distinguished appearance, a happy and engaging disposition—all were united in Bernard in a way that made the world equally pleasant and perilous to him. But by a singular grace, he recognized the perils without

---

[12] *La vie spirituelle*: in the seventeenth century, *spiritual*, as an adjective, did not have nearly the same negative connotation as *spirituality*, and, Tinsley says, "while retaining its rather general meanings, becomes more vitally expressive of affective relationships of the soul to God" (Tinsley, *French Expressions*, 226).

tasting the pleasures. He pleased the world, and the world displeased him. His wish, even when he was still almost a child, was to seek out a refuge in which he would be able to preserve his innocence.

8. If we were to consider this plan as we might consider it today, then nothing was easier for him than to find such a refuge in the bosom of his family. He had a father who had grown old in the profession of arms, an honest and upright man of the old school. He had a mother who was careful to keep the house in order. He had five brothers and one sister, all as intelligent as could be. To devote himself to God he had only to put aside the sword, and, with the sword, all those occasions when it imperiled one's salvation. He had only to pass his days in quietness, simplicity, and modesty. In this way he was able to taste the peace of the solitude he loved, and he was also able to share in the pleasure of his parents' company without having to involve himself in their business. He was able to decide what he would do without anything standing in his way, [he could choose] what he would study without any concerns, [he could do] good works to his heart's content, and, in a word, [he could live his life according to] rules of which he was the master.

9. Nothing is so common these days as to suppose that one can save oneself in this way while in the arms of laziness. Though a man has spent long years in pleasures and shameful excess, he believes that he can satisfy God's justice by means of this domestic indolence, and, by allowing himself to be called spiritual,[13] he takes credit for being truly penitent.

10. Bernard's ideas were the complete opposite of this. He had preserved his moral purity from the abominations of the world, but to guard himself against the future, he withdrew into the desert. For this purpose, he chose a religious order whose austerity at that time made it most worthy of commendation: this was the Order of Cîteaux. He does more!

---

[13] *Dévot.*

He takes with him his brothers and thirty of his relatives or friends! What talk there was in Burgundy! A young man of twenty-three[14] burying himself and his whole family in the shadows of a cloister! But how false is human judgment! What lights, Lord, have you brought forth from these dark places!

11. Once there, Bernard neglected nothing in making his whole body a sacrifice to penance, and it took but little time for him to succeed: continual fasting, food designed to destroy his health rather than preserve it, the coarsest bread, vegetables that were raw or poorly prepared, water to quench his thirst, hard and unremitting manual labor, little sleep—should I say a few hours or a few moments?—ceaseless prayers, and an overall subjection of all his senses so that by the end of a whole year he had still not noticed how his cell was arranged.[15] You see what soon reduced him to a state of chronic infirmity and devastating weakness. But does he look for any relief? Does he ask for it? Does he have recourse to the art [of medicine] to restore his failed strength? Does he complain about the weight of the yoke he has imposed on himself and think how it might be lightened? Ah! If the flesh is weak, the spirit is always prepared, always firm and steadfast. He was his own implacable enemy, and he paid attention only to the holy hatred he directed against himself. Let [human] nature groan![16] Let it speak out! He pays no attention to its cries. And if it has to be overcome, he agrees to die on the cross, a victim of the mortification of Jesus Christ!

---

[14] La Rue corrects the inaccurate twenty-five to be found in the earlier version of the panegyric: see *n. 38. Nor does he have Bernard leading his thirty companions to Clairvaux rather than Cîteaux: see *n. 40. That, too, is corrected.

[15] See *Vita prima* 1.4.20 (William of Saint-Thierry); PL 185:238D; CF 76:23: Bernard spent a full year in the novitiate—*in cella Novitiorum*, not an individual cell—without ever noticing that it was vaulted, and an even longer period in and out of the church while thinking that there was but one window in the apse when there were actually three.

[16] See Rom 8:22: "We know that every creature groans."

12. Think of all the reasons that might have led him to take more care of himself and stop treating himself with so little restraint. But the Gospel is above reason and has no regard whatever for our narrow and limited views. Perhaps it might seem that his superiors should not have let him go to these extremities and, in contrast, used their authority to restrain him. But God's control over this noble penitent was so marked that they may have been afraid to oppose it, and, moreover, what they may have seen as the real value of his example was the way in which it edified his fellow-monks and inspired them to greater fervor. Whatever the reason, he would never hear of sparing himself, and, as he himself explained, he could not tolerate the idea that, in the house of God, the School of Medicine should take precedence over the School of the Son of God. Let Hippocrates, he said, and let his followers teach how to look after the body and keep it alive. We have another Master, one who has come to us from heaven, and it is this divine Master with his disciples who teaches us that we must lose the life of the body in order to save it.[17] This is the maxim that he followed religiously until he breathed his last and that he made an inviolable rule. But it is a maxim to which he joined a virtue still more essential and yet more excellent: that is, humility of spirit.

13. We may justly say that, of all the saints, there was not one who, in the course of his life, encountered more obstacles to humility than did Saint Bernard. In the midst of a series of extraordinary achievements and plaudits fit to seduce his heart, what victories did he not have to achieve over himself, and what efforts did he not have to make to protect himself against the attacks of vainglory? I do not think I am overdoing things when I apply to him what Scripture says of Solomon: that he was renowned by all nations: *Nominatus in universis gentibus*; that kings came to consult the oracles of his wisdom:

---

[17] See *n. 44.

Et veniebant ab universis regibus qui audiebant sapientiam ejus; that the whole world desired to see his face: *Et universa terra desiderabat vultum.*[18]

14. Was there ever any monarch who did not accept his advice, who did not grant him all that he asked, who did not pay heed to his warnings, who did not tremble at his threats, and who did not hear his voice as that of a prophet inspired by God? Popes sought his influence with kings; kings made use of his authority over their people; and the people had recourse to him in their needs. Protector of the weak, mediator between the great, intercessor with God—all acknowledged his authority, and his authority had as its end only complete submission in all things to the authority of the Lord.

15. Given that peoples and princes so appreciated his discretion and his holy intentions, to what dignities did they not wish to raise him? Genoa, Milan, Langres, Reims, and Châlons chose him as their bishop.[19] They accompanied their choice with prayers and entreaties, but they could not sway his humility. So these people, in spite of his determined refusals to do what they pressed him to do (at least by the mouths of those subject to his discipline) transferred to his children the honors they had intended for the Father. They came and tore his disciples from his bosom and entrusted them with the government of the most important churches. Thus, since Germany, France, Italy, and the rest of the Christian world could not have Bernard to govern them, they took for their shepherds the sheep of his flock. But he saw the miters on the heads of his monks, and even the tiara of the sovereign pontificate [of Eugenius III], not only without envy, but with joy, convinced that they were all more worthy than he.

16. Yet to have acquired this ascendancy over men and women would have been a small thing had not God upheld

---

[18] See *nn. 48–50.

[19] See *n. 51: La Rue has amended the slightly exaggerated list provided in the first version of his panegyric.

him with an abundance of other more precious gifts, such as the understanding of Holy Scriptures, the knowledge of future events, a lively and effective eloquence, a power of miracles beyond anything that had been seen since the apostles, and a sovereign empire over all sickness as well as over the elements. And look at the circumstances that confirmed these prodigies: prodigies that were done on the highways, in public places, in the sight of great crowds! How many times did prelates and kings themselves bring the sick to him? Indeed, [on one occasion] the crowds were so great that the emperor Conrad [von Hohenstaufen] himself had to shelter him in his arms so that he could escape from the press of people.[20] To doubt these marvels, which were witnessed by whole towns, is to be more unjust to him than his own enemies, for even they, wounded though they were by the severity of his zeal against their errors, could not, in their writings, refuse him the title of a man of miracles.[21]

17. But given all these sure signs of God's special Providence,[22] what might he have thought of himself if his heart had been as vain as ours? Dazzled by such splendor, how self-satisfied he would have been when he conversed with himself! And if he had had this secret regard for himself, would it not have been reflected outwardly in what he said and what he did? But how did he actually speak and how did he act? What language he used, Christian listeners! And did humility ever show itself to be more profoundly humble? This man, heaped with honors, this man, who was one of the greatest ornaments of the Church, regarded himself as the vilest and most contemptible of individuals! If anyone tried to put a stop to his

---

[20] See *n. 61. La Rue has removed the incorrect reference to Milan but still has the circumstances wrong. The crowds were there to hear Bernard preaching the Second Crusade, not for miracles of healing.

[21] Cf. Joseph Meglinger, *Epistola familiaris de itinere ad Comitia Generalia S. Ordinis Cisterciensis*, 68; PL 185:1608D.

[22] See appendix 1, s.v. *Providence*/Providence.

excessive penances by pointing out to him that he was going too far, that he was ruining his health, that he was murdering himself, his only response was that he knew what he was and they did not. The most severe [penitential] practices, [he would say,] were never too much for a sensualist like him, a slave to sin. He knew what he deserved, and the sicknesses of his soul required the strongest remedies.[23] If he happened to think of the repute he had among great and small and of his reputation in the world, he straightaway countered this with the idea he had formed of what he really was: the chimera of his age. This is none other than what he called himself: *chimaera saeculi*![24] He saw himself as neither secular nor religious! Since he has renounced the world and devoted himself to God, he is no longer a true secular; but on the other hand, since he is so often obliged to come out into the world and leave his solitude, it seems to him that he is no longer a religious! So what is he? A monster he holds in horror! You see here the reasoning by which he is confused in himself while from far and wide he is canonized: *chimaera saeculi*!

18. People everywhere call attention to the value of what he does and exalt his merits before God, yet he himself closes his ears to all their praises, and, withdrawing into himself, spends his time only in weeping for his poor and miserable showing. He wished to pour out floods of tears on the sterile earth of his soul and make up for what he lacked by the bitterness of his regrets: *Quo imbre lacrymarum perfundere sufficiam sterilitatem animae meae?* ["What rain of tears will be enough to irrigate the sterility of my soul?"][25] This is a view he never relinquished,

---

[23] See *nn. 45–46.

[24] Bernard, Ep 250:4 to the Carthusian prior of Portes; SBOp 8:147: *Ego enim quaedam chimaera mei saeculi, nec clericum gero nec laicum,* "I am a sort of modern chimera: what you see is neither cleric nor layman!" La Rue does not quote this description in the first version of his panegyric.

[25] See *n. 69. Here La Rue quotes Bernard's text more accurately.

and it was one that filled him with fear when he remembered the judgments of God. The last time in his life he took pen in hand was to write to his friend [Arnold], the abbot of Bonneval, and to all those in the centuries that followed, and tell him how the thought of death terrified him, and how, at that terrible moment, he needed the help of the faithful and their prayers to sustain him against the attacks of the Tempter who would come to attack him, to bring down upon him the mercies of the Lord, who had no desire for the loss of a sinner, and to have him find favor with his Judge, to whom he had nothing to offer: *Orate Salvatorem, qui non vult mortem peccatoris. Curate munire votis calcaneum nudum meritis* ["Pray to the Savior, who desires not the death of a sinner. Protect, I beg you, with your prayers a heel naked of merits"].[26]

19. Think about this, my brothers. After forty years of watchfulness, of works, and unceasing vigilance to perfect himself in and according to his [monastic] state, Bernard reproaches himself for the things in which he has been remiss and is afraid that God will impute them to him. After forty years of complete renunciation of self and the harshest penances, Bernard still thinks he is loaded down with debts in the face of divine Justice and is afraid to appear at his tribunal. After forty years of the most laborious service and the most demanding exercises, Bernard persuades himself that he has accomplished nothing and fears to be rejected as a useless servant. After forty years of progress in all the virtues, Bernard found in himself no virtue at all: all he saw were imperfections and transgressions for which he feared he would be unable to render account or avoid punishment. After forty years of winning victories over the Enemy of his salvation, Bernard is still afraid, and in his fear of being overthrown in his final hour he seeks supporters to uphold him and asks for their help by their prayers.

---

[26] See *n. 70. Again, La Rue quotes Bernard more accurately.

20. Oh vain souls, humble yourselves! Because you are free from some of the worst vices that are all too common in the world, because you are not thieves, nor unjust, nor adulterers, any more than was the Pharisee [in the gospel[27]], because you even devote yourselves to some practices of piety, charity, and prayer, you flatter yourselves that you belong to the number of those who are perfect! You separate yourselves from the multitude as if you stood apart from it,[28] you are untroubled about your eternal destiny and hardly ever give any thought to that fearful Judgment by which it will be decided, you think yourselves beyond reproach in all that you do, and you see nothing that needs to be changed. The apostle says, "I have nothing on my conscience," but he goes on to add, "I am not for that reason justified" [1 Cor 4:4]. In saving others, he is afraid that he himself will be rejected. He chastised his body and reduced it to servitude lest the flesh should corrupt the spirit within him, yet, seized with fear, he wrote, "How deep are God's intentions!"[29] Who knows whether one deserves his love or hatred? Let us therefore return to our saint and follow his example. Let us be as humble as he, for humility will open our eyes and prevent us from being deceived. And besides that, to whom does God impart himself with a greater outpouring of his love if not to those who are humble? He loves them, and they love God. This is the divine love in which Bernard excelled and which is the acme of true righteousness: *Dilexisti justitiam*.

---

[27] Luke 18:11, where the Pharisee, praying in the temple, gives thanks to God that he is not like other men, who are "thieves, unjust, adulterers," just like the tax collector who is also praying in the temple.

[28] The root of the word *Pharisee* is the Hebrew verb *parash*, "to separate from" or "to set apart."

[29] Echoing Rom 11:33: "Oh the depth of the riches of the wisdom and knowledge of God! How incomprehensible are his judgments, how unsearchable his ways!"

21. It is from the abundance of the heart that his mouth speaks and his hand writes. Is there anything we read in these wonderful treatises in which the holy solitary pours out his soul in the presence of God, and which he has left to posterity, that is not the living expression of what he felt in his heart? It is there that he teaches us to love [God] as he loved him. He is not satisfied with a superficial love, a love that is casual, timid, lukewarm, fickle, lightweight, venal, shared between the Creator and the creature. No. He wants a love that is solidly grounded,[30] a love that is noble, constant, effective, ardent, and tender: a love purged of all worldly affections, unshared and disinterested.[31]

22. Disinterested? What am I saying here? Does he mean that once the soul has renounced all human interests for the sake of God, it also renounces, with one final effort, any interest in its own salvation? God forbid! Just as charity never destroys faith, so too it never destroys hope. It is true that in heaven hope and faith will be no more: faith will be no more since we will have a direct vision of God and will see him no longer only in likeness;[32] hope will be no more because all our hopes and all our desires will be completely fulfilled in the joy of possessing God and there will be nothing left to desire. But for us in this world it is not the same. There are three gifts of God, faith, hope, and charity, and [all three] must be united in us and continue to exist[33] together, for it is only through these three virtues that one is Christian. Each one can be practiced separately, but none of them can be omitted because of one's complete renunciation of [any interest in] possessing God. Much less can one bring about in oneself a permanent and

---

[30] *Un amour solide*: see *n. 134.

[31] *Sans partage, sans intérêt*: in sharp contrast to the first version of his panegyric, it is only here, in §§21–25, that La Rue launches a direct attack on Fénelon and the Quietists.

[32] See 1 Cor 13:12.

[33] *Subsister*: see *n. 76.

habitual state of this alleged sacrifice[34] and establish there the height of perfection: *Nunc autem manent fides, spes, caritas, tria haec* ["But now, faith, hope, charity remain: these three" (1 Cor 13:13)].[35]

23. So what is the true nature of that pure and disinterested love that Bernard experienced and that he knew how to express so well? One never loves God without being rewarded, he tells us, but perfect love never looks to this reward: it deserves it without seeking it. *Praemium non quaerit, sed meretur* ["It does not seek reward, but deserves it"].[36] It never loses either desire or hope, but it does not draw its power from this desire or from this hope because it is neither this desire nor this hope that binds it to God. I love God for himself, not for me.[37] I love him because he is good in himself, not because he is good for me. I love him as a faithful bride loves her bridegroom.[38] A servant loves his master, but only because he is waiting for his wages. A child loves his father, but he does not stop thinking of the inheritance due to him. A bride, however, is at a higher level: she loves only her bridegroom independently of all the good things she may receive from him, but which are not him. This is why they can properly be called bridegroom and bride. *Hinc ille sponsus, et illa sponsa* ["He therefore is the bridegroom, she the bride"].[39] And if you go on to ask Bernard how he loves, this is his reply: "My love is sufficient for itself; its value lies in itself, and it looks for nothing beyond that. Love itself is its

---

[34] See *n. 78.

[35] This paragraph summarizes *§§29–30 in the earlier version of the panegyric.

[36] Bernard, Dil 7.17; SBOp 3:134, reading *Verus amor praemium non requirit, sed meretur*, "Pure love does not look for reward, but deserves it." This does not appear in the first version of the panegyric.

[37] In *De diligendo Deo*, this is the third degree of love, in which God is loved *propter seipsum* (Dil 9.26; SBOp 3:140–41).

[38] La Rue now turns to Bernard's eighty-third sermon on the Song of Songs as in *§§31–33 of the first version of the panegyric.

[39] Bernard, SC 83.2.5; SBOp 2:301: *Hinc ille sponsus, et sponsa illa est.*

own beginning and its own end. I love because I love, *Amo quia amo*; I love in order to love, *amo ut amem*.⁴⁰ This movement of love that sweeps me away is my whole treasure and all the sweetness of my life." This is a language that many people do not understand, but anyone who does not understand it has never known what it really means to love a God.⁴¹

24. Bernard certainly understood it! The noble and sublime ideas he had of the greatness and perfection of God descended from his spirit to his heart and ravished⁴² and transported him. From then on he never lost sight of the continual presence of God—he saw him everywhere as Moses (if we may quote Saint Paul) saw the invisible⁴³—everywhere conversing with him, listening to him, and speaking to him. From then on he was so recollected⁴⁴ in God (a recollection from which nothing could distract him), so absorbed in the memory of this First Being and this Supreme Majesty, that he did not notice the most obvious objects, things that were right there before his eyes.⁴⁵ From then on this firm and inflexible determination to do everything and

---

⁴⁰ Bernard, SC 83.2.4; SBOp 2:300: *Amo, quia amo; amo, ut amem*. Neither this text nor that in n. 39 above appears in the first version of La Rue's panegyric.

⁴¹ *D'aimer un Dieu*: "to love *a* God," not "to love God."

⁴² The verb is *ravir* (*rapere* in Latin), which means to ravish, carry off, steal, enrapture, snatch away, ravage, or carry off by force. It is a technical term in the Christian mystical tradition: see the useful discussion by Dyan Elliott in *The Cambridge Companion to Christian Mysticism*, ed. Amy Hollywood and Patricia Z. Beckman (Cambridge: Cambridge University Press, 2012), 189–99 (though Elliott limits herself to the Middle Ages). At its heart lies the principle that we cannot command mystical union but only prepare for it. Then, if he wills and only if he wills, God snatches away the soul and plunges it into his own being.

⁴³ See Heb 11:27.

⁴⁴ *Recueillement* or recollection is also a technical term: see appendix 1, s.v. *recueillement* / recollection.

⁴⁵ The reference is to the well-known episodes of the windows in the church, the vaulting in the novitiate, the day's journey by Lake

suffer everything for God [led him] to hesitate at nothing and refuse nothing, however hard and humiliating it might be. From then on this resolve to please God in all things did not allow him to omit the least of his [monastic] observances nor to miss the slightest opportunity of making some progress and of moving forward. From then on his devotion was so tenderhearted that, when praying, he would burst out in a thousand sighs and his eyes would be filled with tears.

25. Who could say what happened then in the depths of his soul? [Who could describe] the fires that consumed him, the consolations[46] with which he was flooded? He himself tells us something about them, but only in general terms and without entering into detail about these mysterious and indescribable effects of grace. "Happy moments," he wrote, "and what sweet repose in the arms of my God! But alas! Moments rare and brief! *Rara hora et parva mora* ["How rare the occasions, how short the stay!"].[47] "Suddenly," he adds, "I found myself filled with such confidence and ravished by such joy that it seemed to me that I was one of those elect whose happiness I had just described; Oh, if only these holy feelings lasted longer! *O si durasset!* ["Oh, if only it lasted!"][48] In short, from then on [he was possessed by] this taste and desire to withdraw so as to concern himself with God alone and taste him better. It was only necessity that ever drew him forth from [this retreat], though it was always by inclination that he returned to it.

Geneva, and the harness of his horse: see chap. 6 (Rancé), §§20–25. See also n. 15 above.

[46] *Consolations* is another technical term: see appendix 1, s.v. *consolations* / consolations.

[47] Bernard, SC 23.6.15; SBOp 1:148.

[48] Bernard, SC 23.6.15; SBOp 1:149. La Rue does not cite this remarkable sermon in the first version of his panegyric. La Rue's point is that although a rapturous mystical union with God may certainly occur (as Bernard himself testifies), it is a rare and fleeting experience and not, emphatically not, the continual or habitual state envisaged by Fénelon and the Quietists. See *n. 78.

And why? Because in the silence of the woods, released from all cares, the exchanges he had with the God of his heart were more open and more serene. It was there that he contemplated when he wished, and [it was there], in the fervor of prayer, that he ceaselessly renewed and ever more enflamed the fire of his love.

26. But when do we enflame this sacred fire in our hearts? When do we, like Bernard, fulfill all righteousness?[49] He sacrificed his body to God through penance, he sacrificed his heart through love, and he sacrificed his spirit through humility. But what of us, my brothers? What do we sacrifice to this Master to whom we belong and to whom, without reservation, we owe all that we are? As sinners who deserve the harshest punishment, what penances do we practice? What do we ever refuse to this sinful[50] flesh that we worship as an idol? Is there anything we do not give it to gratify it or that we can procure for it? What a strange turnabout we see here! Those who are most guilty conduct themselves as if they were entirely innocent and as if nothing in their whole lives deserved punishment, while those who are most innocent inflict on themselves holy cruelties and treat themselves as if they deserved the entire vengeance of heaven and were loaded down with sins. At the very least we should recognize our slackness and our failings and make a humble confession at the feet of the Lord; but as much as we are averse to mortifying ourselves, by that much and more are we averse to humbling ourselves! Is it surprising, then, that we are so cold and indifferent with regard to God? We are far from loving him with this pure love,[51] stripped of everything that might involve ourselves, as the saints love him, but do we yet love him with this love of hope and recognition

---

[49] Matt 3:15: see *§7 of the first version of the panegyric.

[50] *Criminelle*: see appendix 1, s.v. *crimes* / sins.

[51] I.e., the *amour pur* of Bernard, Bossuet, and La Rue, not that of the Quietists. It is a love that has been stripped of all self-love (*amour propre*), but not of hope and fear.

that is due to him not only by right but for all the good things [he has done for us]? I leave you to think about it. But now, after making clear to you Bernard's faithfulness in practicing righteousness and perfecting his [monastic] state, *Dilexisti justitiam*, I must now show you his zeal in pursuing iniquity. *Et odisti iniquitatem*. This is the second part [of my sermon].

[SECOND PART]

27. We have seen Bernard in the obscurity of the cloister, attentive and faithful to all the duties of the religious life. Let us see him now in the full light of day, instructing the people of God and defending the Church and its honor. God says to the prophet Ezekiel, *Fili hominis, speculatorem dedi te domui Israel* [Ezek 33:7]. "Son of man, I have set you up to watch over the house of Israel." Does he not seem to have charged Bernard with the same commission? The whole Christian world was exposed to his sight and, in consequence, to his censure. In his time there was no heresy, no schism, no error, no scandal—in a word, no iniquity—that escaped his penetrating eye, or his ardor, or his zeal. Where did his gaze not reach and on whom did it not rest, irrespective of person? In four words: he was never dazzled by the splendor of high rank, he was never intimidated by power or threats, he was never weakened by flattery or friendship, and he was never caught off his guard by subtlety[52] or guile. He overcame each one of these four obstacles with just the same courage: *Odisti iniquitatem*. So now, if you please, give me twice your attention: what I am going to say requires it.

28. He himself was a simple monk, but there was none so great on earth whose luster bewitched his eyes, much less caused him any fear. Vice disguised itself in vain: his zeal sought it out even in palaces and on thrones. And by means of a wise combination of strength and gentleness, he knew how

---

[52] See *n. 27.

to condemn what seemed to him to be in need of condemnation without offending the dignity [of the person involved] and without failing to show proper respect.

29. Eugenius III was a great pope, but Bernard did not let him forget that he had been [Bernard's] disciple.[53] He wrote to him five books detailing his duties, all with the greatest respect, but also with the most unrestricted freedom. "You are the first among the bishops," he tells him, "you are the successor of the apostles: a second Peter in your authority, a second Christ by anointing."[54] Nevertheless, adds the saint, "dispense the gifts of the Lord, give food to his people, preside but do not reign": *Des illis escam in tempore: dispensa et non imperes* ["Give them food in due season; administer and do not rule"].[55] You are the successor of Peter, continues Bernard, and you sit on his throne, but did he go out in public glittering with gold and diamonds as you do? To appear in such finery is to be the successor of Constantine,[56] not the successor of Peter! *In his successisti non Petro, sed Constantino* ["In this you are the successor not of Peter, but of Constantine!"].[57]

30. How did he act with regard to emperors? He heaped blessings on Lothair II[58] and praised God for having chosen this prince to restore the imperial majesty.[59] But when it came to protecting those towns and states that upheld the rights of

---

[53] See appendix 2, s.v. Eugenius III.

[54] See *n. 95.

[55] Bernard, Csi 3.1.2; SBOp 3:432, reading *Ut des illis escam in tempore: hoc est, ut dispenses, non imperes*. The differences are insignificant.

[56] I.e., Constantine the Great, Roman emperor, in one way or another, from 306 to 337.

[57] Bernard, Csi 4.3.6; SBOp 3:453. The quotations from *De consideratione* that appear in nn. 55 and 57 do not appear in the earlier version of the panegyric.

[58] La Rue has *Lothaire second*, but Lothair appears as both Lothair II and Lothair III (more commonly the latter), depending on whether one includes the Lothair who was the son of Lothair I in the list of German kings. See appendix 2, s.v. Lothair III of Supplinburg.

[59] See Bernard, Ep 139.1; SBOp 7:335.

the Church and the empire, he could not bear to see Lothair so indifferent. "I am only a poor recluse," he wrote to him, "but if I become importunate, it is only because I cannot do other and still remain loyal to you." *Pauper sum, fidelis tamen vester* ["I am a person of no significance, but I am your loyal friend"].[60]

31. How did he honor Louis [VII] the Young, king of France? How did he speak to him? Theobald [II], count of Champagne, was one of the greatest lords of the realm, but he had so angered the king that the latter had launched an all-out attack on him and put the country to fire and sword. He captured Vitry[-le-François] and even went so far as to burn alive more than five hundred people who had taken refuge before the altars [of the town church].[61] What a dreadful and bloody deed! When Louis came to himself, he was tormented with remorse, and at Bernard's earnest request, he and the Count were reconciled. But the truce lasted only a short time, for Louis soon became just as suspicious [of Theobald] as he had been at first. He told Saint Bernard of this, and in what terms did Bernard express himself in his reply to the king? What resolve! What severity! "What is this, Sire? Would you pile sin on sin? Do you wish to be overwhelmed by the wrath of God? What has Count Theobald done to warrant this recurrence of your anger? In the name of the eternal God, do not resist the King of Kings! Do not dispute with him the possession of his wholly lawful rights! Do not raise your hand, as you are doing so often, with these renewed blows against 'the Terrible One, against Him who takes away the spirit of princes' [Ps 75:12-13]": *Nolite manum extendere adversus terribilem, et eum qui aufert spiritum principum.*[62] I speak sharply because I fear sharp things for you; I would fear

---

[60] Bernard, Ep 139.2; SBOp 7:336.
[61] See appendix 2, s.v. Louis VII the Young.
[62] Bernard, Ep 220.2; SBOp 8:83, to Louis the Young: *Nolite . . . manum extendere tam frequenti et temerario ausu adversum Terribilem, et eum qui aufert spiritum principum, terribilem apud reges terrae*, "Do not raise your hand with such frequent and rash audacity 'against the

less if I loved you less: *Acriter loquor quia acriter vobis timeo. Non ita vehementer timerem, nisi vos vehementer diligerem.*[63] Happy the kings to whom God gives such ministers and counselors. It is a heavenly gift all the more precious as it is so uncommon.

32. And he was just the same with all the other great powers. He urged the king of England, Henry II,[64] to support Pope Innocent, but after [Henry's] first audience [with the pope at Chartres[65]] the king's meaningless scruples had returned, and he had cooled. "Sire," wrote[66] Bernard, "do penance for the other sins you may have committed. As to this one, if there is anything [to answer for], I will take the whole thing on myself."[67] And straightaway they both went off for a meeting with the vicar of Jesus Christ.

33. Roger, king of Sicily, was the avowed enemy of the same pope [Innocent] and was about to give battle in favor of the antipope Anacletus. Bernard sought him out [near Salerno] at the head of his army, urged him to recognize the true pontiff, and predicted his defeat if he persisted in his intention to fight. Roger scorned both the entreaty and the threat: he risked battle, and lost.[68] Let us move on.

Terrible One, against him who takes away the spirit of princes, who is terrible with the kings of the earth' [Ps 75:12-13]."

[63] Bernard, Ep 220.2; SBOp 8:83: *Acriter loquor, quia acriora vobis formido: quod non ita vehementer timerem, nisi vos vehementer diligerem,* "I speak sharply because I fear sharper things for you: I would not fear them so much if I did not love you so much." Neither this quotation nor that in n. 62 above appears in the first version of the panegyric.

[64] As in *§40 of the first version of the panegyric, La Rue confuses Henry II with Henry I.

[65] See appendix 2, s.v. Henry I, king of England.

[66] For "wrote," one should read "said." Arnold of Bonneval records the exchange.

[67] *Vita prima* 2.1.4 (Arnold of Bonneval); PL 185:271AB; CF 76:82–83. See also *n. 100.

[68] See appendix 2, s.v. Roger II of Sicily, and *Vita prima* 2.7.43-44 (Arnold of Bonneval); PL 185:293B–94B; CF 76:126–28. This is the

34. If high rank never dazzled Saint Bernard, neither did any display of power intimidate him. He was convinced that Innocent was in the right against Anacletus, and he stirred up the whole of Europe in order to put an end to the schism there and restore unity. The antipope held Rome by armed force, and, as master of Italy, he had forced Innocent to seek refuge in France. A solitary [Bernard] undertook the task of restoring everyone's spirits and placing them all under the authority of the fugitive. He had him proclaimed [as the legitimate pope] by the king of France and by the prelates at the Council of Étampes [in 1130]. From there he hurries to the king of England [at Chartres] and enrolls him in his party.[69] He then goes to Germany, where he wins over the emperor. He makes his way to Italy, and the whole of Lombardy yields to his voice. He then returns to France and finds there no opposition save from William [X], duke of Aquitaine.[70] [Bernard] appears before him, but with what weapons? On what battlefield? At the door of the church [of Notre-Dame-de-la-Couldre], where this prince had already been excommunicated, Bernard held him at arm's length and prevented him from entering during the celebration of the Holy Mysteries. When the sacrifice [of the Mass] had ended, Bernard, attired in his priestly vestments and carrying the body of Jesus Christ, returned to the prince and, in tones that seized him [with fear], addressed to him these daunting words: "Behold your Judge! Behold the Judge before whom all must bow, whether in heaven, or on earth, or in the places under the earth! You will appear before him: Will you scorn him then? Will you still make war on him?" And then an amazing thing! At these words the duke fell to the

---

Battle of Rignano, fought on October 30, 1137. Roger does not appear in the earlier version of the panegyric.

[69] See §32 above.

[70] La Rue here presents a somewhat augmented account of the dramatic conversion of Duke William of Aquitaine, which appears in *§44 of the first version of the panegyric. See also *nn. 104–6.

floor, frozen with fear. His limbs stiffened, he dragged himself along the ground, he uttered loud groans, he could not speak, and his eyes rolled in his head. After violent convulsions he recovered sufficiently to confess his sins,[71] but when he [was well enough to] resume his duties he did so in a way wholly contrary to his scandalous conduct in the past: a prince given over to pleasure, a slave to his animal passions as well as to error, became (so we are told by the writers of his time) a prince filled with pious devotion. It was not that there were no new occasions when he strayed, but he made an end by being sincerely repentant and by making a pilgrimage, [to Santiago de Compostela,] where he died.

35. What name shall we give to the minister whom God uses to work such great marvels? Is he a prophet? Is he an angel? No, he is man, just a man, but one who was incapable of tolerating iniquity or of yielding to what it tried to do: *Odisti iniquitatem* ["He hated iniquity"].

36. But if he could not be overcome by force, perhaps he would let himself be swayed by friendship? No, Christians, his zeal here is no less resolute! Given his character, it is easy to understand that he had many illustrious friends. Two of them were particularly distinguished: one was Suger, abbot of Saint-Denis and regent of the kingdom while Louis the Young was away on Crusade;[72] the other was Peter, abbot of Cluny, called the Venerable for his teaching and his piety.[73] We know from their writings the esteem and cordial friendship they had for one another, but Bernard sees a certain laxity creeping into the monasteries of his two friends. He sees the abbey of Saint-Denis full of courtiers and men-at-arms, echoing to the din of worldly affairs and the clash of weapons.[74] He sees

---

[71] *Crimes*: see appendix 1, s.v. *crimes* / sins.

[72] See *n. 107. See appendix 2, s.v. Suger, abbot of Saint-Denis. Suger was regent from 1147 to 1149.

[73] See *n. 108.

[74] See Bernard, Ep 78.4; SBOp 7:203, to Suger.

Suger appearing in public with a showy following of horses and footmen, something that the dignified position he had held for so long seemed to justify in the eyes of the people, but not in the eyes of Bernard: he was utterly convinced that a monk whom a king's trust had loaded with worldly honors never lost the obligation to maintain the essential duties of his [monastic] state. This was not a maxim to be questioned, and it was a maxim that had a profound effect on the great man to whom it was addressed. Suger was touched to the heart with the remorse that his holy friend had tried to inspire in him, and the edifying reform of the abbot and his monks proceeded so swiftly that nothing remained for Bernard but to congratulate him in terms that revealed an unfeigned joy. This joy and their accord grew only deeper for the remaining twenty-five years of Suger's life.[75] A few days before his death he received letters from Bernard that showed the heartfelt tenderness he had for him and that comforted him by foretelling the happiness they would both enjoy, inseparably, for all eternity. "I have loved[76] you," wrote the saint, "from when I first knew you; I will love you to the end. I am not losing you; I only see you leaving [this world] before me. Remember me when you arrive whither you are going, so that I may not have to wait too long to be reunited with you." *Memento mei cum veneris, quo nos praevenis* ["Remember me when you come to where you precede us both"].[77]

---

[75] Bernard's letter to Suger dates from 1127, and Suger died a quarter of a century later on January 13, 1151. Bernard died about two and a half years after his friend. Suger's reform of Saint-Denis was remarkably successful.

[76] La Rue uses the verb *chérir* to translate the Latin *diligere*—*dilexi a principio, diligam sine fide* (Ep 266.2; SBOp 8:176)—which is a perfect translation. English lacks subtlety when it comes to verbs for loving.

[77] Bernard, Ep 266.2; SBOp 8:176, to Suger, reading *Tantum memento nostri cum perveneris quo nos praevenis*, "So remember us when you arrive at where you precede us." The quotation does not appear in the first version of the panegyric.

37. With regard to Peter the Venerable, there was more work to be done, and success came more slowly. A long series of abbots recognized as saints[78] had not prevented Cluny from falling into disorder. So obvious a change could not escape Bernard's knowledge, and he felt he had no choice but to stir up his friend's vigilance by expressing his opinion as quickly as possible. The outcome, after various attempts at defending [the Cluniac position], was a general chapter of all the superiors of the Order—more than twelve hundred of them[79]—where the Rule [of Saint Benedict] was reestablished. The whole business was the subject of much discussion among those who made an idol out of friendship and sacrificed everything to it. No one, they said, who has made an open profession of virtue, should treat a friend in this way! "No!" replied Bernard, "There is no true friendship that is not joined with truth!" *Verae sunt amicitiae, si veritatis fuerint consortio foederatae* ["There is true friendship when it is bound together by a common love of truth"].[80] What are the bonds of friendship between worldly people? Self-interest, pleasure, flattery, passion: feeble bonds! Truth is the bond of solid friendships: either we cease to be friends or our friendship is based on truth: *Da operam, quomodo et ipse amicus sis[81] veritatis* ["Do what you can to make him, too, a friend of truth"].[82]

---

[78] Almost all the abbots of Cluny who preceded Peter were canonized.

[79] This was the general chapter that began on Sunday, March 20, 1132. According to Orderic Vitalis, *Historia Ecclesiastica* 13.13, who must ultimately be La Rue's source here, it was attended by 200 priors of the Order and 1,212 *fratres* (*Orderici Vitalis Historiae Ecclesiasticae Libri Tredecim*, ed. Augustus Le Prevost [Paris: J. Renouard, 1855], 5:26).

[80] Bernard, Ep 78.13; SBOp 7:210, to Suger: *Tunc demum verae erunt amicitiae, si veritatis fuerint foederatae consortio*, "Then at last there will be true friendship if it is bound together by a common love of truth."

[81] *Sic*, for *sit*.

[82] Bernard, Ep 78.13; SBOp 7:210, to Suger.

38. It is time now, my dear listeners, to put in the crown of our saint the last splendid jewel: it is that he never let himself be caught out by the guile or subtlety of those whose errors he undertook to combat. In his time the world was beginning to emerge from the darkness of ignorance into which it had long been plunged. But the fact that there were so few new scholars increased their authority and, as a result, their audacity, for they wanted to make faith dependent on reason and make too easy a marriage between the Gospel and philosophy. And then, in their attempt to provide our most formidable mysteries with a clarity they do not possess,[83] they took away their simplicity and almost their truth.

39. Bernard's century was plentiful with these subtle thinkers, and one of the most famous was Abelard. I say famous as much for his corrupt morals as for his wrong ideas. We know his story: and who can not know it after he took so much pleasure in publishing it?[84] Yet from day to day his name attracted an ever-greater crowd of disciples, and Bernard believed he could not possibly remain silent. He tried to put a stop to the evil with warnings so grave that the innovator promised to reform his principles. But since, instead, he continued to expound them, this led to disputes and justifications. The doctor and his friends claimed that the abbot of Clairvaux had poisoned an innocent teaching. "All that has been imputed to me is detestable and diabolic," Abelard explained; "It is only through pure malice that I can be accused [of these things]": *Tanquam diabolica quaedam abhorreo et detestor* ["I abhor and

---

[83] "Our theologian [Abelard]," writes Bernard, "says 'What's the use of speaking of doctrine if we cannot explain what we want to teach so that it can be understood?'" (Ep 190.1.2; SBOp 8:18, to Innocent II). See further appendix 2, s.v. Abelard, Peter.

[84] The reference is to Abelard's *Historia calamitatum*, of which a French translation had been published in 1695 as *Histoire des infortunes d'Abailard* (Amsterdam: Pierre Chayer). A second edition appeared in 1697.

detest these things as coming from the devil"].[85] But Bernard was not satisfied with these words: he penetrated beneath the surface and discovered only error. "He is making game of the well-established faith of the [simple] faithful," he said: *Irridetur simplicium fides* ["The faith of the simple is held to scorn"].[86] He stirs things up with new and reckless questions: *Quaestiones temerarie ventilantur* ["Questions are aired recklessly"].[87] He builds so-called truths on foundations hitherto unknown: *Fundamentum aliud ponitur, quam id quod positum est* ["A foundation is being laid different from that which has been laid"].[88] And what he says of vices and virtues is contrary to the principles of Christian morality: *De virtutibus et vitiis non moraliter disputatur* ["Virtues and vices are being discussed immorally"].[89] Abelard summoned[90] Bernard to the Council of Sens and then, seeing himself condemned, appealed to the pope. But when the pope had been told of what had taken place at the Council, he confirmed its decision.

---

[85] See note 177 to Bernard's Ep 190.1.2 in PL 182:1055C–56C.

[86] Bernard, Ep 188.1; SBOp 8:11, to the bishops and cardinals of the Curia.

[87] Bernard, Ep 188.1; SBOp 8:11, reading *Quaestiones de altissimis rebus temerarie ventilantur*, "Questions concerning the highest matters are recklessly aired."

[88] Bernard, Ep 189.2; SBOp 8:13, to Innocent II, reading *praeter* for *quam*. Precisely the same sentence appears in his Ep 330; SBOp 8:267, also to Innocent, with *nobis* after *ponitur*.

[89] Bernard, Ep 330; SBOp 8:267, to Innocent II. None of the quotations in nn. 86–89 appears in the first version of the panegyric.

[90] *Abaillard appela Bernard*, which was not quite the case. Bernard had asked Abelard privately to correct his errors but had told others that they were "full of poison." Abelard, understandably angry, then demanded that the bishops call a public meeting at Sens when he could confront Bernard and defend himself publicly. Bernard was most unhappy about this and did not wish to go but was eventually persuaded to do so by his friends. See A. Victor Murray, *Abelard and St Bernard. A Study in Twelfth Century "Modernism"* (Manchester: Manchester University Press, 1967), 37–38.

40. The condemnation of Abelard did not bring an end to the abuses of the innovators. Gilbert, bishop of Poitiers, had been raised to this rank through his reputation for virtue and knowledge, but after a few years in this position he himself walked the paths of error in what he taught about the essence and attributes of God.[91] A new field for Bernard, and new battles: but, at the same time, a new opportunity to criticize him on the part of those who were unconcerned about the difficulties faced by the Church. "What a scandal!" they say, "Not to spare so worthy a prelate! Not to respect his character! He goes too far!" They go yet further in their attacks on Bernard. They call him bad-tempered, an unsettled and carping critic, haughty and jealous, who wants to get the better of everyone in everything! We can see that this is what they thought, and even what they wrote, from a number of authors who have told us of it.

41. But did the man of God let any of this slacken his zeal? Did he stop what he was doing? With his ringing voice he silenced the slanders, and the world woke up! The Church assembled at Reims; Pope Eugenius himself presided; the bishop of Poitiers appeared before the Council; Bernard examined him on his ideas and expressions; the disputation lasted two days. What doings there were in the two opposing parties! Gilbert's friends, and they were many, could not bear to see him shamed and condemned. They did all they could to gain time, to delay the judgment, and to have the Assembly dissolved without making any pronouncement at all. But truth triumphs over politics and error. The writings in question are censured and proscribed![92]

42. What was most remarkable about all this, and what the Church praised most (think about this, my brothers), was

---

[91] See *n. 121.

[92] This is a somewhat more accurate account than appears in *§55 of the earlier version of the panegyric. Gilbert's commentary on Boethius's *De Trinitate* was indeed censured; Gilbert himself was not. See *n. 123.

the way in which the bishop of Poitiers, who had undertaken to continue with his teaching only if it were approved by a decision of the Council, had the courage to accept what the Council decided. There can be little doubt that this example of humility was an unusual and unexpected way of atoning for the harm that his subtle thinking, which he had carried too far, had caused among the faithful. But [Gilbert] did not hesitate; he did not quibble; he did not limit himself to changing his language while not changing his ideas. We can only applaud his return [to the fold], and Bernard had the great comfort of seeing his adversary share with him the gains brought about by his victory. For if Bernard conquered the error, Gilbert conquered himself, and overcoming one's own brilliant self is far more difficult than overcoming the errors of others.[93]

43. Such submission, if I may be so bold as to point it out, is vitally necessary for maintaining order, union, and peace in the kingdom of God, which is his Church! If we go back to the first centuries, or to the later centuries that followed them, or even to our own days, what do we see, at all times and with great sadness, but the most shameful upsets and schisms?[94] And why? Because there are some intractable individuals who do not know how to surrender or lay aside their prejudices.[95] Full of themselves, and ardent admirers of their own thoughts, they are never able—we say rather that they are never willing—to admit that they have lost their way. Such an admission would have humbled them, but in humbling them, it would also raise them up. What they lack is a humble submissiveness, and that is what has led them astray. Sinning in this one thing, they have sinned in all the others! The weapons they should have used

---

[93] La Rue here corrects the chronological and historical mess that appears in *§55 of the earlier version of the panegyric. See *nn. 124–25.

[94] La Rue omits the specific references to heretics—Arius, Nestorius, and so on—and heresies that appear in *§58 of the first version of the panegyric.

[95] La Rue is referring, of course, to the Quietists.

in defense of true doctrine are the weapons they have turned in favor of falsehood. Flocks of followers whom they have seduced have joined with them, and these disciples, the inheritors of their masters' ideas, have also inherited their obstinacy and stubbornness. The evil is communicated from the leaders to the followers, it is passed down, as it were, from generation to generation, and its pernicious effects are all too evident. A submissive spirit would have prevented this: they could still have stopped its course. When will heaven hear our prayers?

44. But let us return to our saint, with whom I shall bring my eulogy to an end. What merits there were in the hands of this faithful servant! What laurels he won with so many works! Is it not now time for him to place all these at the feet of the Lamb and receive the crown of righteousness? For so many of the years he served you, Lord, he was weighed down with sickness, and what he had of ardor and strength [was directed] only to you. All this has gone now, and all that remains to him, deep in his heart, is to beg of you this last grace, for which we can hope only with some fear, since we can never strictly deserve it. His [monastic] children, ever attentive to his lessons, see him [leave them], and, in leaving them, confirm the examples he never ceased to give them throughout his whole life. He breathes his last. His blessed soul begins to enjoy eternal rest. It is only now that he has no more fear and even no more hope, for he possesses that which he loves, and all the virtues[96] are absorbed in the love and enjoyment of this Sovereign Good.

45. What a beautiful model for us, servants of Jesus Christ! Think of what this zeal can do for the honor of God, the advancement of the Church, the sanctification and reformation of all our human conditions. What can it not do? A zeal that goes far beyond any deference to human opinion, a zeal that is assured and unswerving, sustained by a holy confidence, a

---

[96] Especially the virtues of faith, hope, and the fear of God. This is La Rue's last attack on Fénelon and the Quietists.

zeal that is pure and disinterested,[97] that cannot be shackled or held back by any intimacy or affection, a zeal, finally, that is enlightened in order to discover error and eager to pursue it. Such is the zeal of the Gospel; such was the zeal of Bernard! Is it also ours? Is the [battle]field now smaller than it was then? Has vice made less progress in our days? Has it infected fewer hearts? Is faith suffering any less from heresy? Is it subjected to fewer attacks? The Son of God said to his disciples, "The harvest is plentiful: ask the Master to send forth laborers" (Matt 9:37-38). And I myself can say to you: *Levate oculos vestros et videte regiones* ["Open your eyes and look around you" (John 4:35)]. Open your eyes, my brothers, and see all that is happening! Iniquity is spread abroad on all sides, and what has it not corrupted? It reigns in the houses of both small and great; the cloister is not free from its contagion; and how many tares have grown up among the good grain,[98] even in the Church of the living God?

46. What would Saint Bernard have thought of this spectacle? What would he have said? What would he have done? It is what we would have thought, what we would have said, what we would have done, had we been inspired by the same spirit as he. Entrusted with the same ministry, let us remember that we must carry out the same duties! Perhaps we find it sufficient to be regarded as the ministers of the Lord and dispensers of the mysteries of God,[99] and perhaps we are happy to say with Saint Paul, even in a situation so different from that of the apostle, *Sic nos existimet homo* ["Let people so regard us" (1 Cor 4:1)]. But in Saint Paul's day it was not enough just to have the name and occupation of dispenser: they also had to be found faithful. *Hic jam quaeritur inter dispensatores, ut fidelis quis inveniatur* ["Here, moreover, it is required among the dispensers that they be found faithful" (1 Cor 4:2)]. What this means

---

[97] *Un zéle pur et désintérressé.*
[98] See Matt 13:24-30.
[99] See 1 Cor 4:1.

is that for the cause of the Lord, for cutting out abuses, for the strengthening of religion, they should not be impeded by fear nor entangled by self-interest nor affected by any special attachment, and that no spineless sense of toleration should close their mouths or bind their hands: that is what it means to be faithful, *Ut fidelis quis inveniatur* ["that they be found faithful"]. So what more can I do, my brothers? The model I have set before you of this glorious zealot whose memory we honor [today] tells us enough. Let us hold to it! We have seen it, not only in the way he manifested his zeal, but in the practice of Christian righteousness in which, whatever our calling, we can imitate him. Let us all, therefore, work with the same virtues so that we may arrive at the same happiness, which I wish for you, etc.[100]

---

[100] The "etc." represents the usual closing doxology and appears in almost all of Bretonneau's editions of La Rue's panegyrics. Many of them, in fact, end in precisely the same way as that of Bernard: *que je vous souhaite, etc.*

11

Bernard the Mystic
Henri-Marie Boudon

INTRODUCTION

In this chapter, for the first time, we enter realms hitherto studiously avoided. We will see, standing before us, Bernard the mystic, the Bernard of the fourth degree of love in the *De diligendo Deo*, the Bernard so beloved of most modern writers. Charles de La Rue had used Bernard to destroy what he regarded as the absurd mystical pretensions of the Quietists; Henri-Marie Boudon will introduce Bernard as a true mystic in his own right, inhabiting, by God's extraordinary grace, the innermost mansions of the Interior Castle of Saint Teresa of Jesus. Who, then, was Henri-Marie Boudon?

His is an interesting story.[1] He was born at La Fère, about twelve miles northwest of Laon in Picardy, on January 14, 1624, and studied at Rouen and Paris, where he was known for his intellectual ardor, his piety, and his life of extreme poverty. In 1654 he was appointed grand archdeacon of Évreux, twenty-

---

[1] Five biographies of Boudon were published between 1705 and 1863 (see DS 1:1894), of which the best is that by Pierre Collet (1693–1770), of the Congregation of the Mission and principal of the *Collège des Bons-Enfants* at Paris: *La vie de M. Henri-Marie Boudon, grand archidiacre d'Évreux* (Paris: J.-T. Hérissant, 1753, 1762 [revised and enlarged ed.]). For a convenient and concise biography, see DS 1:1887–89, which forms the basis for my own brief account.

eight miles south of Rouen, and once installed, and without relinquishing anything of his pious and austere lifestyle, he devoted himself to reforming the diocese of Évreux, which, at that time, was in a sorry state. He required regular church services, he demanded that priests teach the catechism, and he did his utmost to lure new recruits to the depleted ranks of the clergy. He was also staunchly anti-Jansenist, and when Jansenism began to make decided headway in the diocese of Évreux, Boudon immediately went on the attack. The result was a prolonged and bitter conflict, and this—together with his high ethical demands (and refusal to bestow benefices on candidates he considered unworthy)—led to a large number of complaints being made to the bishop of Évreux, Monseigneur Henri de Maupas du Tour.

The situation was exacerbated when Boudon was accused (quite unjustly) of having illicit relationships with two women—or, more precisely, with one woman and a transvestite. The woman was Madame de Fourneaux, a widow and the mother of a family, who had cared for Boudon when he was taken seriously ill while preaching at Neufbourg in 1665. But Boudon's prolonged convalescence in the house of Madame de Fourneaux gave rise to scandal (though there was no truth in the accusations), and the situation was made worse by the curious story of "frère Claude," who was not a "frère" at all, but a "sœur." She was, in fact, a young girl from Rouen who, in order to protect her virtue from certain seducers, had taken to wearing male attire and calling herself Claude Petit. Her way of life was so devout and her conduct so pious that she became known as Brother Claude. Sometime later she—the supposed he—left Rouen and made her way to Évreux, where, on rare occasions, she went to Boudon for confession and attended his Mass. There in Évreux she died in an odor of sanctity. But when the body was being prepared for burial, her true sex was, of course, revealed, and the story was put about that this holy transvestite had been Boudon's servant, and that the relationship between them had not always been entirely chaste. The result was a *cause célèbre* with bawdy songs being sung in the streets of Paris, and Boudon (who, we might add, was entirely innocent of all the charges) was deposed from his archidiaconate. He accepted his deposition with uncomplaining humility until 1675, when his principal accuser, conquered by conscience, retracted the accusations. Boudon immediately found himself back in favor with Bishop Maupas du Tour and restored to his diocesan position. His later years were marked by a great deal of travel and a great deal of publication, and he died, aged seventy-nine, on August 31, 1702.

Boudon's spirituality is dominated by two themes: the love of God and the Providence of God,[2] and it is easy to see how some of his comments led him to be suspected of Quietism. There is no doubt, too, that he was of a strongly mystical bent, more similar to Fénelon and quite unlike either Rancé or Bossuet, and two of his favorite authors were Teresa of Ávila and John of the Cross. For Boudon, the sole object of "divine and pure love" (*divin et pur amour*) is God alone.[3] Thus we should desire not so much Paradise as the God of Paradise. We should seek not so much salvation as the God of salvation. And we should hope not so much to avoid the pains of purgatory as to gain the goal of Paradise. And why? Because it is in Paradise that God may be loved and glorified more perfectly. Even our love for our neighbors is really our love for God, for by loving our neighbors as best we can, we draw them away from sin and set them on the path that leads to God alone. *Dieu seul*, in fact, is Boudon's watchword,[4] and it is an easy step from this principle to the idea of total abandonment (*abandon*) to the Providence of a loving God: "God alone, God alone in three Persons, and always God alone in the union of

---

[2] See appendix 1, s.v. *Providence* / Providence.

[3] See DS 1:1892.

[4] See DS 1:1891–92. Jean-François-Frédéric Darche's biography of Boudon, published in two volumes at Paris in 1863, was entitled *L'homme de Dieu seul, ou le célèbre Boudon*.

our good Savior Jesus Christ. Entrust yourselves to his loving Providence. I have said this to you before, and I say it to you always: [Providence] is the best and most faithful of mothers. As it is all that I wait for, so it is all that I hope for you."[5]

It is easy to see how these ideas of *pur amour* and *abandon* could lead to the suspicion that Boudon was a crypto-Quietist, and two of his works were indeed censured by the church, though not for the same reasons. His *Dévotion à l'esclavage de l'admirable Mère de Dieu* (1674) was condemned for its incipient Mariolatry (and there is no doubt that some of Boudon's expressions are extreme), and his *Dieu seul, ou l'association pour l'interêt de Dieu seul* (1662) was placed on the Index on September 9, 1688, twenty-six years after its first publication, because of its Quietist tendencies. What we have here, however, is a case of the church being wise after the event. *Dieu seul* appeared in 1662, and the Quietist controversy did not begin in France until about 1685. When *Dieu seul* was first published, even Bossuet gave it his approval,[6] for although there are expressions that, when taken out of their overall context, could give rise to suspicion, the essential feature of Quietism condemned by Bossuet—the abnegation of the human will in the pursuit of virtue—is nowhere to be found. Had Boudon been writing a quarter of a century later, he might indeed have rephrased certain passages, but he cannot be blamed for providing ammunition to a party that, in 1662, did not yet exist, or for a quarrel that was far in the future.

---

[5] Boudon, Letter 58, in [Henri-Marie Boudon], *Œuvres complètes de Boudon, grand archidiacre d'Évreux* (Paris: J.-P. Migne, 1856), 3:866.

[6] Bossuet, *Correspondance*, 1:502–3, Approbation no. 6 (November 18, 1662). The book deserved to be given to the faithful "to rekindle and purify their zeal by carefully reading and pondering deeply the truths it contains" (503). Bossuet and Boudon had actually met two or three times, and Boudon had been of assistance to Bossuet in the matter of indulgenced prayers and confession (see Bossuet, *Correspondance*, 7:320, §10; and 325, §20).

It remains true, however, that Boudon was far more interested in mysticism and mystical experiences than most of the writers we have met hitherto, and this is clearly apparent in his panegyric on Saint Bernard. When the sermon was delivered is unknown,[7] but the internal evidence makes it quite clear that, whatever the year, it was delivered on the feast day of the saint to a congregation of Feuillants.[8] Which congregation is also unknown. The nearest Feuillant house to Évreux was about thirty miles away at Rouen, and the main house at Paris about twice this distance. Let us therefore turn to the content of Boudon's panegyric.

Although, as we might expect, the standard themes of mortification and apostolic zeal both appear, the way in which Boudon approaches them is quite different from anything we have seen so far, and his sources are far more extensive. Apart from Scripture and the *Vita prima*, he introduces the names of no fewer than twenty-one authorities: *ps.*-Albertus Magnus, Ambrose of Milan, Augustine and *ps.*-Augustine, Cardinal Baronius, Bede, Bonaventure and *ps.*-Bonaventure, *ps.*-Dionysius, Francis de Sales, Gilbert of Hoyland, Gregory the Great, Jerome, Richard of Saint-Victor, Rupert of Deutz, Teresa of Ávila, Tertullian, Theodoret of Cyrrhus, Thomas Aquinas, William of Saint-Thierry (referred to, as usual, as "the historian of [Bernard's] life"), and Zeno of Verona. Of Bernard's own works he quotes from his letters, *De diligendo Deo*, *De consideratione*, and two sermons.

The exordium of Boudon's panegyric is also quite different from anything we have yet seen. It is wholly Marian (we have

---

[7] If the *est-il saint* at n. 142 below is to be taken literally—i.e., as "he is a saint," rather than "he is holy"—then the sermon must have been delivered after the canonization of Francis de Sales by Pope Alexander VII on April 19, 1665. But the words could be taken either way. On the other hand, the evidence from Claude Lion's panegyric on Bernard, discussed in the next chapter, might indicate a date after 1683.

[8] See §§1, 27, and especially 33 of the panegyric.

already mentioned that Boudon's devotion to the Mother of God could get a little out of hand), and if Bernard is to be praised for anything at all, it is only through the grace of "the admirable Virgin." If Bernard is the *homo Dei*, "man of God" (Boudon's text from 1 Tim 6:11), it is only because he has been enlightened by Mary. If Bernard is full of grace, it is because he has been nourished by the Mother of Grace. If his thoughts are angelic, it is because he has been favored by the Princess of the Angels. If his sermons are sweeter than honey, it is because he has been suckled by her virginal milk. If his actions are heavenly, it is because they are guided by the Queen of Paradise, and so on. All is due to Mary.

When Boudon returns to earth from his Marian exuberance, he tells us that Bernard's life may be divided into three periods: in the first, he was clothed only to be unclothed or stripped; in the second, he lived only for death; in the third, he existed only to achieve nonexistence.[9] And it is on these three truths, says Boudon, that he intends to base his discourse. To illustrate the first, he will use the Epistle to the Ephesians; to illustrate the second, the Epistle to the Romans; to illustrate the third, the Epistle to the Corinthians. Thus, it will not be Boudon the sinner who preaches, but the apostle Paul, "the marvel among the saints" (§5). And with these three truths we are straightaway plunged into those realms of mystical teaching and mystical experience assiduously avoided by everyone we have met so far.

Corresponding to these three truths, says Saint Bonaventure (more accurately, *ps.*-Bonaventure, who is almost certainly Rudolf von Biberach), are three degrees of the spirit: the spirit of or in the spirit, the spirit on the spirit, and the spirit without the spirit. And according to "le saint abbé Gilles," who is actually Gilbert of Hoyland, these are the three beds on which the soul takes its rest: the bed of the bride, the bed of the bride

---

[9] Boudon will explain the meaning of the technical terms *dépouillement* and *néant*, "stripping" and "nonexistence," in due course.

and God, and the bed of God alone—*Dieu seul*. So what are these three degrees, these three beds?

The first is illustrated by Ephesians 4:22, which tells us to put off or strip away (the Latin verb is *deponere*, which Boudon accurately renders as *dépouiller*) the *vetus homo* (the "old man," or what we might call the lower self). We may then attire ourselves in the *novus homo secundum Deum*, and this "new man" is that of which we speak when we use the expression "man of God." And what is this "unclothing," this *dépouillement*? It involves (says the apostle) renouncing all worldly desires and detaching oneself from all *temporalia*, both natural and sensual. It is the first rung on the ladder that leads to Paradise, and it is the call of the Holy Spirit (who dwells within the human spirit) for the latter to raise itself above itself, to strip itself of all attachment to exterior things in order to devote itself to those that are interior. Boudon here cites *ps.*-Dionysius and Jerome to support his case and sets before us Saint Bernard, in whom this "stripping off" can so clearly be seen.

Boudon now turns to Bernard's life as recounted by William of Saint-Thierry, and, for a while, rejoins the straightforward course already charted by the preachers we have already discussed. We hear of the unsuccessful attempts of Bernard's relatives to dissuade him from entering Cîteaux and of his own dedication to the unquestionable will of God. His detachment from worldly things was so great, says Boudon, that he would not even receive his own sister, Hombeline, since she was dressed in a worldly way, and this leads our author into a violent denunciation (not altogether unjustified) of women's bosom-baring fashions in *le grand siècle* (§11). But I must return to my theme, says Boudon (calming down a little), and with that he cites, once again, Gilbert of Hoyland to support his contention that a soul destined for God must enter the dark night of the senses.[10] According to Saint Albert the Great

---

[10] Boudon is, of course, echoing Saint John of the Cross, one of his favorite mystical writers.

(though the work cited is not from his pen), such a soul must be utterly disinterested in all external things, just as if its bodily eyes were closed and all its senses sealed. This is just what we see in Bernard, and Boudon repeats the familiar stories of Bernard's failure to notice his immediate surroundings. We have heard them all before. To these he adds equally familiar tales of his mortification of the palate, when he ate grease instead of butter, drank oil instead of water, and subsisted on a meager and tasteless diet.

God, however, rewarded our saint with extraordinary graces, and Boudon here recounts in some detail (almost a full column in the *abbé* Migne's edition) the miracle-story of the *Amplexus*, when the crucified Christ detached himself from the cross to embrace his beloved servant. The crucifixion, the death of Christ, and the blood of the cross naturally lead Boudon to his second point: that Bernard lived only for death. His proof text comes from the Epistle to the Romans: *Existimate vos mortuos*, "Regard yourselves as dead bodies" (Rom 6:11). And just as we must die with Christ, so too must we be buried with Christ. Boudon's authority is here Saint Augustine, and the principle corresponds to the second degree of the spirit, which we mentioned above: "the spirit on the spirit." What does this mean? It means that the spirit now undergoes a complete spiritual death and so is at one and the same time "outside itself and above itself." This, says *ps.*-Dionysius, is far more difficult to achieve than stripping oneself of worldly desires. Dying, after all, is always much harder and much more troublesome than taking off one's clothes! What we are concerned with here, in fact, is nothing less than the abolition of self-will (*notre propre volonté*), our own inherent egocentricity, which (as we are told by "the angelic doctor," Saint Thomas Aquinas) was what led Lucifer from the joys of heaven to the torments of hell.

For a start, therefore, Bernard buried himself in the obscure tomb of his monastery, and if his body was forced to come forth into the world, his spirit remained true to its vocation. Thus he utterly refused all the high ecclesiastical offices the church wished to bestow upon him, for he was dead to all honors and lived only for death. And just as high office could not tempt him, insults and injuries could not harm him. How can one injure a corpse? But having joined Jesus on the cross, Bernard was reborn, like a divine phoenix, to new life and new vigor. He gave up his life only to preserve it (here Boudon supports his argument by quoting Tertullian and Zeno of Verona), and he was so dead to the world and his own body that he could truly be said to exist in nonexistence.

This is Boudon's third point, and it is illustrated by Saint Paul, who tells us that God should be all in all: *Ut sit Deus omnia in omnibus* (2 Cor 15:28). This is the last of the three beds on which the bride reposes, and on this bed there is only God, *Dieu seul*. Boudon explains the matter further in a passage of considerable mystical importance; as we have said above, our author had a deep interest in mysticism and mystical experience. It is not (he says) that the soul loses its "natural state," what it is by nature. The soul does not cease to be the soul. What it loses is its normal, natural way of acting—something it preserves in the two previous states (i.e., the spirit in the spirit, and the spirit on the spirit)—but here it is united with Christ as two flaming torches giving forth one light, as a drop of water falling into a river and merging with the sea, as a great light entering a room through two separate windows, and then becoming only one. And Boudon's source here? The seventh mansion of Saint Teresa's *Interior Castle*.[11]

This, says Boudon, is exactly the thought of Saint Bernard, and he goes on to quote *in extenso* the well-known passage from the *De diligendo Deo* in which Bernard is describing the fourth degree of love, the love of self for God's sake. Here, says the

---

[11] It cannot be denied that these analogies are dangerous: see David N. Bell, "A Doctrine of Ignorance: The Annihilation of Individuality in Christian and Muslim Mysticism," in *Benedictus: Studies in Honor of St. Benedict of Nursia*, ed. E. Rozanne Elder, CS 67 (Kalamazoo, MI: Cistercian Publications, 1981), 30–52 (especially 32–33).

saint, the soul is truly united with God, and that union is similar to a drop of water being mixed with a quantity of wine: the water seems (*seems* is a crucial word here[12]) to lose itself in the color and taste of the wine. Otherwise, we may take the analogies of red-hot iron, which seems to have renounced its natural form and become one with fire, or air so flooded with sunlight that it seems to be not so much lit as light itself. Boudon then continues in this vein, effortlessly supporting his case with quotations from *ps.*-Albert the Great and Richard of Saint-Victor, both of whom speak of the soul appearing to lose itself in God, so that God alone remains. Yet now Boudon introduces a note of caution. We must not think that in this state of "annihilation" the virtues too have been annihilated. On the contrary. Both Saint Thomas and Saint Bonaventure make it perfectly clear that the virtues are not lost, but transformed. They become the "virtues of a soul that has been purged," which are the virtues of the blessed in heaven. These, indeed, are the virtues we see in Bernard. For him, God has become *omnia in omnibus*, "all in all," and he can say with Saint Paul, "I live—but no, *I* live no longer. There is only Jesus who lives in me" (§24).

Nothingness, therefore—*néant*—is a precious thing. It is far from being "nothing" in the normal sense of the term, for it is really full of everything. "From the nothingness of nature," says Boudon, "God drew forth the whole of this great universe, and from the nothingness of sin the whole world of grace and of glory" (§24). Thus it is that, in Bernard, who was so totally lost and dissolved in God, so wholly engulfed by him, God could draw forth from his nothingness all the miracles and marvels that graced his life. He could truly say with Saint Paul, "I can do all things in him who strengthens me" (Phil 4:13).

---

[12] Boudon is never so heretical as to assert that the human soul actually becomes God. The two may *seem* to be one, may *appear* to be one, but the human person continues to subsist (see n. 28) in the divine nature: the creature can never become the Creator.

Our author now leaves these high mysteries and returns to earth—more precisely, to the creation. According to Scripture, immediately after he had created heaven and earth, God created light. But then, on the fourth day, he created the sun. What is the reason for this? ask Saint Augustine, the Venerable Bede, and Rupert, abbot of Deutz. What need was there for a sun in the world when there was already light? The usual answer, says Boudon, is that the first light was an angelic light, too subtle for our mortal eyes, and that God had to gather it up and unite it with the body of the sun. We may see this echoed in Bernard. In the body of this divine doctor, the light and spirit of the early fathers were gathered together and united, and we may say of him what was said of Saint Benedict: "He was filled with the spirit of all the righteous" (§26).

Boudon now returns to familiar territory: Bernard's apostolic life and his achievements in the world, though his account is brief. He preached penitence like a Saint Ambrose; he loved the church like a Saint Jerome; he was the scourge of heretics like a Saint Augustine, and in the moral interpretation of the Gospel, he was another Saint Gregory. We then meet the figures, so familiar to us now, of Louis the Young, Peter of Pisa, Henry of England, Roger of Sicily, Pope Eugenius III, and Gilbert de la Porrée.

And so we come to the final section of the panegyric, in which Boudon first repeats what he had said earlier. Bernard was truly the man of God, *homo Dei*, who was clothed only to be stripped of everything, who lived only for death, and who existed only in nonexistence. But what does this say to those who love the world? What does it say to those who value riches and comfort and ease and honor? What it says is that the only way to achieve true blessedness is to strip off the world and take up the crosses of mortification. It is these that will adorn you (Boudon now addresses his congregation directly), it is these that will enrich your souls with heavenly graces. But alas! there are all too few of whom this can be said, all too few who have felt in their souls "the sweet anointing of the Holy Spirit" (§33). One who did feel it was Saint Francis de Sales, who, while assisting at the celebration of Mass in a Feuillant congregation, felt impelled to bear witness to it in public. And here, alas, the manuscript breaks off. There then follow a further twenty lines that the editor found to be illegible. It is possible to decipher only three or four words at the beginning of each line, and, as he himself says, "We prefer to leave the panegyric incomplete, rather than substituting our own thoughts for those of Boudon."

Such is Boudon's panegyric on Saint Bernard. It is, as we have said, dramatically different from those we have examined so far, not only in its impressive display of learning, but especially in its extraordinary interest in the highest level of mystical experience as it is described by Bernard, Teresa of Ávila, *ps.*-Albertus Magnus, Richard of Saint-Victor, *ps.*-Bonaventure, and Thomas Aquinas. On the other hand, his descriptions of Bernard's work in the world are very brief, and there is no mention at all of Abelard or Henry of Toulouse. That is certainly unusual, though not unique. There are, however, curious similarities between Boudon's panegyric and that of a far more obscure figure, the Oratorian Claude Lion, who was Boudon's almost exact contemporary. Boudon lived from 1624 to 1702, Lion from 1625 to 1704. But the relationship between the two panegyrics, and question of whether Boudon had read Lion, or Lion had read Boudon, must be left for discussion until our next chapter. For the moment we will content ourselves by presenting a complete translation of Boudon's paean of praise for Bernard the True Mystic.

THE PANEGYRIC
PANEGYRIC ON SAINT BERNARD[13]

Homo Dei. (1 Tim 6:11)[14]

"The man of God."

1. By the mouth of the Royal Prophet [David], the Holy Spirit declares to us the greatness and excellence of her who was called to be the mother of the Messiah, the admirable Virgin.[15] Among the many things he tells us of this holy City of God, he teaches us that "a man and a man is born in her": *homo et homo natus est in ea* (Ps 86:5), [which means] that she will be the mother of the God of the man and [the mother] of the man of God. She is the mother of the God of the man since she is the mother of Jesus; but she is the mother of the man of God since she gives birth to him for salvation, for the spiritual life, and for God. The same dazzling truth [is to be seen] in the person of the illustrious Saint Bernard, whose glorious memory we honor on this solemn [feast] today.[16] Saint Bernard is a man of God. Neither nature nor human nature, with all their strength and skill, can give to the world someone who is so little of the world, who is in it only to abandon it, who sees it only to de-

---

[13] [Henry-Marie Boudon], *Œuvres complètes de Boudon, Grand Archdiacre d'Évreux, réunies, pour la première fois, dans un ordre logique et analogique, Renfermant ses divers opuscules ascétiques, et un très-grand nombre de lettres et d'exhortations jusqu'ici inédites . . . publiés par M. l'abbé [Jacques-Paul] Migne. Tome troisième et dernier* (Paris: J.-P. Migne, 1856), 1393–1408. The panegyric, and a number of other works, are noted as being "éditées pour la première fois d'après les manuscrits autographes" (cols. 1393–94).

[14] The expression is indeed to be found in the letter to Timothy but was a standard appellation of saints. There are numerous occasions in the *Vita prima* when Bernard is referred to in this way, though *vir Dei* is more common.

[15] Boudon's enthusiastic veneration of the Virgin is discussed in the Introduction. The church found it a little too enthusiastic.

[16] August 20. A solemnity is one of the highest ranking feast days in the liturgical calendar of the Roman Catholic Church.

spise it, who knows it only to hold it in contempt. But it is the divine Mary who illumines this wholly divine man. If Bernard is indeed a man full of grace, there is nothing surprising about that, for he calls himself a nursling of the Mother of Grace.[17] If his thoughts are wholly angelic, it is because he is the favorite of the adorable Princess of the Angels. If his sermons are more pleasant to the taste than honey itself—*mel et lac sub lingua tua* ["honey and milk are under your tongue" (Song 5:11)]—it is because he is suckled by her virginal milk.[18] If his actions are wholly heavenly, it is because they are carried out under the guidance of the august and most worthy Queen of Paradise. If Bernard is a great marvel, if he is a patriarch filled with miracles, if he is the Thaumaturge of the West,[19] it is because Jesus has entrusted him to the care of her whom he uses to work his greatest wonders.

2. What should we not hope for, what should we not expect from such a holy and glorious nurturing? It must surely be said that the eternal Father has great plans for a person whom he nourished with the same milk as Jesus, [a person] to whom he gives as a teacher[20] her whom he gave to the uncreated Word, his beloved Son. Blessed[21] be the child who has as a mother the Mother of God. Blessed be the mouth that has sucked the milk from her virginal breasts. Blessed be the soul that has

---

[17] See Bernard, *In labore messis,* S 3.3; SBOp 5:223 (lines 25–27).

[18] As is clear from the next paragraph, this is a specific reference to the legend of the Lactation of Saint Bernard, on which see chap. 5 (Senault, et al.), n. 37.

[19] *Le Thaumaturge de l'Occident.* The title has almost certainly been taken from the penultimate page of the unpaginated preface "to the Reader" of Le Maistre's *Vie*: "quelques Auteurs Catholiques ont eu raison de l'appeler *le Thaumaturge de l'Occident."* Cf. also Horstius at PL 185:367. The Thaumaturge of the East was Saint Gregory Thaumaturgus (ca. 213–ca. 270). The same expression is used of Bernard by Claude Lion and Louis-Bénigne Bourru.

[20] *Gouvernante,* but "governess" gives entirely the wrong impression.

[21] Or happy (*bienheureux*), or, indeed, both blessed and happy.

been brought up by hands so beautiful and so divine. Happy is the heart that receives from that [upbringing] such pure dispositions and such Christian inclinations. How beautiful are the feet—*quam speciosi pedes* (Rom 10:15)—that walk in these pleasing paths, enriched with the most precious gifts of the Empress of the Empyrean. Blessed, therefore, be the great Saint Bernard, the favored recipient of all these graces. Admirable Virgin! Let those who now hear me know of this happiness: *Clarifica, o Maria! filium tuum* ["Oh Mary, glorify your son!"].[22] If the honor of the child is the honor of the mother, then you, in a holy way, are directly affected by this. This is the grace for which I hope from your merciful goodness. It is also the favor I await from Jesus through the loving solicitude of your charitable heart.[23]

3. The apostle, writing to the Corinthians, tells them that he knows no one according to the flesh: *Itaque nos ex hoc neminem novimus secundum carnem* ["From now on, therefore, we know no one according to the flesh" (2 Cor 5:16)]. When the divine Spirit fully possesses a [human] spirit, it can no longer see anything or value anything save God alone.[24] The earth, and whatever great and beautiful things are to be found there—if there are any at all—all vanish away before its eyes. For this reason we must walk in the footsteps of the apostle and see our saint only in the light of God and of God alone.

4. It is not that I am unaware that one can praise great men in different ways. Some [authors], in order to present the person they wish to praise in the best light, write books with

---

[22] John 17:1 reads *Pater, venit hora, clarifica Filium tuum*, "[Jesus said], Father, the hour is come, glorify your son." Boudon addresses the words to Mary.

[23] This is obviously the end of the exordium, but, unlike the other panegyrists, Boudon does not divide his sermon into the usual sections. He sets out the three truths (*vérités*) he is going to discuss in §5.

[24] *Dieu seul*. As we saw in the Introduction, this was Boudon's motto. The expression occurs a number of times in the panegyric.

the title *The Statesman*, but since states are so unstable and always subject to so many revolutions, and, finally, pass away with the world, which itself will come to an end, the men who govern them cannot be regarded as suitable subjects for great praise. If we want to celebrate the achievements of a man of letters, we say that he is a learned man, an erudite man; but since God thinks so little of these fine natural sciences that he has left them to the demons,[25] and since, in consequence, not only do these learned men have something in common with the demons but have even surpassed them, this is hardly something to be esteemed. In the case of a victorious prince or some conqueror, the world says that he is a great man, but since this whole universe is no more than a tiny speck in the eyes of heaven, no more than a nothingness[26] in the presence of God, someone who gains a small part of this tiny speck, a fragment of this nothingness, cannot possess any true glory in the presence of God and his angels. *Itaque neminem novimus secundum carnem* ["Therefore we will know no one according to the flesh" (2 Cor 5:16)]. We must therefore agree with the divine Paul and declare to you that we do not know anyone according to the flesh, according to what the world thinks of them, and we will concern ourselves only with the spirit of God.

5. That is why we have taken as the text of our eulogy of the great Saint Bernard *Homo Dei*, "the man of God." It is the same praiseworthy title that Saint Paul gives to his dear Timothy, one of the most illustrious saints of the Church, and it is the title that we give to Saint Bernard, one of her most glorious defenders: *Homo Dei*, "the man of God." He is the man of God at the beginning of the ways[27] [that lead to] salvation, the man of God in making progress in a holy life, the man of God in reaching the final goal of holiness achieved. In the first of these

---

[25] See John 12:31; 2 Cor 4:4.

[26] *Un néant*, a term we discussed in the Introduction. Only God has true being.

[27] See Job 40:14; Prov 8:22.

three states he is the man of God who is clothed only in things to be stripped off; in the second he lives only for death; in the third he subsists[28] only on nothingness. These are the three truths that will be the subject of this discourse. I take the first from the Epistle to the Ephesians, the second from the Epistle to the Romans, the third from the Epistle to the Corinthians, so that it will not be this sinner, but the apostle himself, the marvel among the saints, who will preach to you of a saint who is the glory of the faithful, the honor of the Church, and the ornament of the religious life.

6. These are the three truths that gave to Saint Augustine and Richard of Saint-Victor (as we are told by Saint Bonaventure in his little work *On the Seven Ways of Eternity*) the idea of distinguishing three different degrees of the spirit.[29] They call the first the spirit of the spirit, the second the spirit on the

---

[28] [*Il*] *ne subsiste que sur le néant*. The use of *subsister*, "to continue to exist, to remain in existence," is important here. The soul does not exist in its own right—it is itself a nothingness, just as the universe is a nothingness—and its existence is entirely derivative, being given to it by God. Putting it another way, the soul *is* only because it participates in the being, the "isness," of God. But when it achieves union with God (something that Boudon will discuss in detail later), it does not cease to exist: that is to say, it retains its own derivative being in a world that has only derivative being, and never becomes God. That would be heresy. Boudon's description is therefore precisely accurate: when the soul lives for God alone (who alone has true existence)—*Dieu seul*—it subsists on nothingness.

[29] The *Des sept chemins de l'éternité* is the *De septem itineribus aeternitatis* commonly attributed to Bonaventure, but not from his pen. It was almost certainly the work of the Franciscan Rudolfus de Biberaco / Rudolph von Biberach (ca. 1270–ca. 1329), but Boudon could not have known that. The treatise was regularly included among the works of Bonaventure. Neither is Saint Augustine Saint Augustine. Rudolph refers not to Saint Augustine, but to "the author of the *De spiritu et anima*," who remains unknown. The work is often attributed, on no good grounds whatever, to Alcher of Clairvaux, but since it was commonly, if erroneously, attributed to Augustine, that is what

spirit, and the third the spirit without the spirit.[30] These are the three beds on which the soul rests, as we may see from the holy abbot Giles's[31] explanation of this verse from the Song of Songs: *In lectulo meo* ["On my bed" (Song 3:1)]: the first bed is that of the bride, the second that of the bride and God, the third that of God alone.[32] It is in this rest that the bride becomes wholly beautiful and uniquely pleasing to the eyes of her chaste and divine spouse, beautiful in the flesh, beautiful in the soul, beautiful in the spirit.

7. Of the first truth, therefore, I read these words in the Epistle to the Ephesians: *In ipso edocti estis deponere vos, secundum pristinam conversationem, veterem hominem*: "You have been taught in Jesus Christ to strip yourself of the old man"; *qui corrumpitur secundum desideria erroris*, "who is in the corruption carried by deceiving desires"; *et induite novum hominem secundum Deum*, "but clothe yourselves in the new man according to

---

is reflected by Boudon. Richard of Saint-Victor, however, is indeed Richard of Saint-Victor. See n. 30 immediately below.

[30] *Ps.*-Bonaventure [Rudolph von Biberach], *De septem itineribus aeternitatis*, 1.3; *Des sept chemins de l'éternité. Œuvres spirituelles de S. Bonaventure, traduites par M. l'abbé [Louis] Berthaumier. Tome troisième* (Paris: J. Vivès, 1854), 213 (§1.2.3). Rudolf is following *ps.*-Augustine, *De spiritu et anima*, 34; PL 40:804, and Richard of Saint-Victor, *Benjamin Major*, 5.12; PL 196:181D–82B.

[31] The text refers to the *saint abbé Gilles*, but this is clearly an error for the *saint abbé Gilbert*, the "holy abbot Gilbert [of Hoyland]." Giles of Rome did indeed write a commentary on the Song of Songs, but it does not contain this exegesis of *In lectulo meo*, which does appear in Gilbert (see n. 32 below). For Giles, the little bed is our conscience, and the bed is so narrow that only one person can lie on it. Who is that person? Christ or the Devil: the choice is ours (see Giles of Rome, ed. John E. Rotelle, *Commentary on the Song of Songs and Other Writings*, The Augustinian Series, 10 [Villanova: Augustinian Press, 1998], 96). And although Giles of Rome was a holy prior general of the Augustinian Order and the holy archbishop of Bourges, he was never a holy abbot. The case is not in doubt.

[32] Gilbert of Hoyland, SC 2.4; PL 184:19BD.

God" (Eph 4:21-22, 24).[33] It is this new man whom we call *homo Dei*, "the man of God." But apart from assuring us that to be the "man of God" demands that we strip ourselves and then reclothe ourselves, he also indicates to us what this involves. This he does in his letter to Titus where he says these divine words: *Apparuit gratia Dei Salvatoris nostri omnibus hominibus erudiens nos*, "The grace and goodness of God has indeed appeared in us instructing us" (Titus 2:11-12),[34] instructing us, that is, by his own mouth, not by that of someone else: *Ut abnegantes impietates et saecularia desideria*, "so that in renouncing impiety and all worldly things," [*sobrie et*[35]] *juste et pie vivamus in hoc saeculo*, "we may live in sobriety, righteousness, and piety" (Titus 2:12).[36] So according to the apostle, stripping off [the old self] consists of renouncing worldly desires, that is to say, in detaching oneself from temporal, natural, and sensual things, in avoiding the riches of position, office, or marriage, and in forgoing all the pleasures that can satisfy the senses. These are the first steps that should be taken by the soul that truly yearns for God. It is the first bed of the bride, it is that first stage when grace raises up a spirit called by the Holy Spirit in the spirit—that is to say, the spirit within itself, outside the flesh, the spirit wholly recollected[37] inwardly by a perfect stripping off of all exterior things. For according to Saint Denis

---

[33] Lit. "You have been taught in him [Jesus] to strip off, according to your former way of life, the old man, who is corrupted according to the desire of error, and put on the new man according to God." Nowadays we would normally speak of the "old self" rather than the "old man," but "old man" is necessary for Boudon's exegesis.

[34] Lit. "The grace of God our Savior has appeared to all of us, instructing us." Boudon changes the "to us" of the biblical text to "in us" (*en nous*).

[35] *Sobrie et* has been omitted from the printed text by accident, since Boudon translates it.

[36] Lit. "so that, denying ungodliness and worldly desires, we should live in this world soberly, righteously, and in a godly manner."

[37] *Tout recueilli*: see appendix 1, s.v. *recueillement* / recollection.

[the Areopagite], the soul that aspires to divine union must remove from itself two deformities: the first being that which comes from the great variety of outward things, insofar as they cause it to leave what is inward; the second being that which comes from what is inward. Once these two things have been attended to, the soul finds itself like the angels, in that it has left aside all things and is now wholly for God alone.[38] But it has to begin by strictly detaching itself from everything external.

8. When God commanded Moses to come to the mountain and speak with him, he ordered him to climb up alone, leaving behind him the children of Israel. He even forbade them to pasture their beasts within sight of the mountain.[39] In this we have an excellent figure of the state of the soul that directs itself unswervingly to God. It must leave behind the children of Israel, which is every attachment it may have to the good opinion and friendship of creatures; and it must be sure that the beasts, that is to say, its sensual appetites, no longer appear in sight of the mountain, [and this it does] by strict and perfect mortification. The man of God must see himself as no more than a pilgrim, no more than a stranger in this world. He must strip himself of it without any regret, says the learned Saint Jerome, just as [he would take off] his clothes.[40]

9. So let us admire the way Saint Bernard, the man of God, practiced these Christian truths. God called him to a holy life; his brothers [tried to] dissuade him from it.[41] But he was not

---

[38] Boudon or his editor here refers to *ps.*-Dionysius, *De divinis nominibus* chap. 9, but I cannot see how this is so, though the chapter does contain a discussion of likeness to God (9.6; PG 3:913C–16A). The passage may be a reflection of *De divinis nominibus* 7.2; PG 3:868B–69C, but I am not certain of that.

[39] See Exod 19, *passim*.

[40] If this is indeed Jerome, I have not been able to trace it. Searching the standard databases for *denudare, exuere, sine dolore*, and so on, does not identify it.

[41] See *Vita prima* 1.3.9 (William of Saint-Thierry); PL 185:231D–32A; CF 76:11–12.

deaf to the voice of his God, says the historian of his life,[42] for he had heard these words of the gospel: "If anyone comes to me and does not hate his father and his mother, his wife, his children, his goods and possessions, and, finally, himself, he cannot be my disciple" (Luke 14:26).[43] He vows that God will be his master, that Jesus will be his favorite, and, closing his ears to anything the world might have to say, that he will no longer hear any voice but that of his Savior. The prudence of the flesh[44] is naturally opposed to this, but Bernard knows that the wisdom of the wise of this world is no more than pure foolishness in the eyes of God and his angels.[45]

10. His relatives persist. There is not one plausible reason they omit to turn him from his intention or, should that be impossible, at least to persuade him to postpone it for a while, proving to him by all sorts of apparently good reasons that this is what his own conscience demanded of him. And indeed, they took things so far that they almost overcame Bernard's resolve.[46] But he remembers that, according to the teaching of him who cannot lie, the soul's enemies are its nearest and dearest: he remembers these words of his Master, written in Saint Matthew: "I have not come to bring peace, but the sword, for I have come to separate a man from his father and a daughter from her mother" (Matt 10:34-35). He bears in mind the story Saint Luke tells of the man who wanted to follow the Savior,

---

[42] See *Vita prima* 1.3.8 (William of Saint-Thierry); PL 185:231C; CF 76:10–11.

[43] What the gospel actually says is, "If anyone comes to me and does not hate his father and mother, his wife and children, and brothers and sisters, and even himself, he cannot be my disciple."

[44] See Rom 8:6: *Prudentia carnis, mors est*, "The prudence of the flesh is death." Nowadays, we would translate it as something like "The mind ruled by the flesh is death," but Boudon is quoting the Vulgate.

[45] See 1 Cor 3:19.

[46] The last three sentences echo *Vita prima* 1.3.9 (William of Saint-Thierry); PL 185:231D; CF 76:11–12. What follows in this paragraph is Boudon.

but first asked him, very humbly, if he might have his permission to go and bury his father. And what was Jesus' reply? "Let the dead bury the dead; go, and proclaim the Kingdom of God" (Luke 9:57-60). So let us go, says Bernard, let us indeed go and proclaim the Kingdom of God! By doing what he tells us, let us show the whole world that he is truly the Sovereign, and that there is no creature on earth, whoever it may be, whether a close relative or a distant, whether friend or enemy, who can hinder us [from doing this]!

11. He therefore leaves his family, detaching[47] himself from it to such a degree that when his own sister came to see him after he had become a monk, he did not wish to see her since she was dressed in too worldly a fashion. He did not know[48] her in this condition, for she, not knowing God, was too well known to the world. Great saint, what would you do if you were to look at our century? If your chaste eyes were to see the vile nakedness of these worldly women who bedeck their bosoms, their wretched flesh that, in a little while, will be eaten by worms, or who reveal [all their charms], or who veil them with no more than something transparent? They come up to our altars to make war on God. They open their mouths for prayer and bare their bosoms for immodesty. They approach God to arrange their salvation, ignoring the fact that they may have bestowed death on a great number of souls. They come to hear

---

[47] Lit. "He therefore leaves his family *avec un tel dégagement* . . .": *dégagement*, "detachment," is a technical term in seventeenth-century French spirituality. See appendix 1, s.v. *dégagement* / detachment.

[48] *Il ne la connaissait pas*. Bernard obviously knew his sister, and we would normally translate this as "he did not acknowledge her." But to translate the sentence effectively, with its play on *connaissait, trop connue du monde*, and *ne connaît pas Dieu*, demands the verb "know." See also §12 below. Boudon is here following *Vita prima* 1.6.30 (William of Saint-Thierry): PL 185:244CD; CF 76:34, which is far more vicious: Bernard curses and reviles his sister (*detestans et exsecrans*). Boudon now erupts in a fiery denunciation of contemporary women's fashions. Tertullian (whom he quotes later) would have heartily approved.

sermons in support of the party of the flesh and the devil,[49] while the very word of God fights against them. They belong to the party of hell, they are the wretched tools of demons, and, adding impiety and effrontery to their abominable practices, they still have the nerve to come to Holy Communion, to the virgin body of the Son of God, often appearing in our confessionals without feeling the least guilt for their exposed breasts and without finding this in any way disgusting, which should be the case with every Christian soul.[50]

12. But I return [to my subject]. Our saint does not know his sister because he could say with the apostle, "We no longer know anyone according to the flesh." He now yearns only for the knowledge of his Beloved, for whom he searches with the Bride "during the night" (Song 3:1), that is to say, says abbot Gilbert [of Hoyland] in a treatise he wrote on the Song of Songs, in the shadow and mortification of all things external. For the Bride does not say that she searches for the Bridegroom in the midst of shadows, because shadows do not hide things entirely: she says "during the night," which entirely conceals from us the knowledge of [things]: *Dilectio ipsa hanc noctem inducit, qua reliqua omnia nec respicit, nec notare putat, dum ad illum quem diligit intenta suspirat,* ["Love itself entices this night, for it does not notice and cannot pay any heed to anything else, so long as it sighs only for him whom it loves"].[51] It is love that brings about so dark yet so holy a night, which links the soul to the God of its heart so strongly that it no longer sees

---

[49] On the various reasons for attending sermons in seventeenth-century France, see chap. 3.

[50] Boudon is not exaggerating. By the end of the sixteenth century, an extremely low neckline was *de rigueur* for ladies of fashion, "but in the early seventeenth century the new interest in the bosom demanded more exposure than compression, and the bosom began to look as if it might escape. The exposure of the nipple, although not formally permitted, did occur" (Anne Hollander, *Seeing Through Clothes* [Berkeley: University of California Press, 1993], 205–6).

[51] Gilbert of Hoyland, SC 1.5; PL 184:15D.

or thinks about anything else. As Saint Albert the Great says in his book *On Cleaving to God*,[52] [the soul] must not concern itself with anything [external], just as if its eyes and senses were all blocked off.[53] *Oh! quis mihi dabit sic advesperascere?* ["Oh, who will grant that I might walk thus into the dusk of evening?"][54] Who will do us the favor of leading us into this divine obscurity?

13. Our saint was completely immersed in this dark and mystic night: *Induxit illum in nubem*, ["He led him into a cloud" (Sir 45:5)]. He had eyes, yet saw nothing; ears, yet heard nothing; hands, yet touched nothing. For after spending much time in the church of his monastery, where the windows contained many panes of glass, he did not know whether there was one or more.[55] Having spent a whole day in the sun, he had never noticed it. And here is a strange tale! One day, he had gone to visit the prior of a Carthusian house far distant from his own monastery [of Clairvaux] and had ridden there on a horse that had been lent to him, [a horse] that had a very ornate saddle. When the good Carthusian father saw this, he was astonished at such trappings, for they seemed to him unworthy of those servants of God whose lives were lived in poverty. Bernard then begins to open his eyes and he, like the good Carthusian father, is equally astonished at the trappings, and assures

---

[52] *De adhaerendo Deo*, commonly attributed to Albert and included in the 1898 edition of his *Opera Omnia* (see n. 53 below), but not written by him.

[53] Ps.-Albertus Magnus, *De adhaerendo Deo* 2; *B. Alberti Magni, Ratisbonensis Episcopi, Ordinis Prædicatorum, Opera Omnia, cura ac labore Augusti et Æmilii Borgnet. Volumen tricesimum septimum* [37] (Paris: L. Vivès, 1898), 524.

[54] Gilbert of Hoyland, SC 1.5; PL 184:15D.

[55] *Vita prima* 1.4.20 (William of Saint-Thierry); PL 185:238D; CF 76:23. Boudon has not got the story quite right. According to William, despite Bernard's regular attendance at church, he thought there was only one window in the sanctuary when there were actually three.

him that he had never noticed them.[56] [On another occasion], he walked for a whole day along the shore of the great lake of Geneva, and that evening, when [his companions] were speaking of it, he did not know what they were talking about, for he had seen neither water nor lake.[57] He had seen only God.

14. Jesus Christ is the unique gate of the eternal way, but the gate is narrow: not one will pass through who has not stripped himself. "I am the gate," says our Savior, "if anyone passes through, he shall be saved," *ingredietur et egredietur*, "but he will go in and go out" (John 10:9). "What is the meaning of these words?" asks the learned Theodoret.[58] "To go in in Jesus Christ," replies this great man, "is to take care of what is interior; to go out through Jesus Christ is to mortify our bodies and our sensual appetites."[59] Saint Bernard did indeed mortify them, for he ate fat in place of butter, and drank oil, believing it to be water.[60] His ordinary nourishment was only bread and water and a little soup.[61] I leave you to imagine what sort of soup this might be, since it was made from beech leaves.[62] Given that his senses were so mortified and his detachment from exterior things so complete, it does not surprise me that heaven was so liberal in bestowing its favors on our saint. The gospel parable that tells us that a man asked his friend for three

---

[56] *Vita prima* 3.2.4 (Geoffrey of Auxerre); PL 185:305BD; CF 76:149–50.

[57] *Vita prima* 3.2.4 (Geoffrey of Auxerre); PL 185:305D–306A; CF 76:150.

[58] Theodoret of Cyrrhus (ca. 393–ca. 460). His collected works, edited by the Jesuit Jacques Sirmond, were published at Paris in 1642.

[59] I have not been able to trace this quotation in Theodoret.

[60] *Vita prima* 1.7.33 (William of Saint-Thierry); PL 185:247AB; CF 76:39.

[61] *Vita prima* 1.8.39 (William of Saint-Thierry); PL 185:250A; CF 76:44.

[62] The beech leaves come from the *Vita prima* 1.5.25 (William of Saint-Thierry); PL 185:241D; CF 76:29, describing the monks' diet in the early days of Clairvaux.

loaves of bread—that is to say, the three theological virtues of faith, hope, and charity—also tells us at the same time that this happened at midnight,[63] which draws our attention to the fact that the soul must deprive itself of all the things of earth if it seeks the favors of heaven. But just as our saint deprives himself in such a special way, so the gifts, graces, and favors that heaven bestows upon him were wholly extraordinary.

15. That this is true may be seen from the lives of all men of God, but [in Bernard's case] it is especially evident in the vision of the crucified Jesus, who detaches himself from the cross to come down to this great saint[64]—a truly marvelous spectacle and one that certainly deserves our attention. The Son of God leaves Paradise, the blessed abode of all imaginable delights, to make his way down to our earth, the place of misery, weeping, and tears. It is the love of the cross that makes him do this, and, in the sight of Bernard, Jesus detaches himself from his cross, which he sought with so much joy and so much ardor. We must say that Bernard's charms must have been utterly delightful and his attraction particularly powerful to have Jesus leave that which was most beloved by Jesus. I raise my eyes to heaven, I fix them on the cross, and I see a God who takes the cross and leaves heaven, and then this same God leaves both heaven and the cross to come to Bernard! Does it not seem, does it not appear that Bernard, in some way, has something more than both heaven and the cross? What is this, oh my Lord? During those days when you were flesh, was not the cross the object of your most tender love, the subject of your most tender yearnings? You made this sufficiently clear when you said these loving words: *Desiderio desideravi*, ["With desire I have desired" (Luke 22:15),] [which means] that you desired it with the greatest desire. What has happened to these yearnings, this love, and

---

[63] See Luke 11:5.
[64] This is the celebrated *Amplexus Bernardi*: see chap. 5 (Senault et al.), n. 38.

these desires? Can it be that the heart of Bernard has won the day and that he now has the upper hand?

16. When Saint Peter, the unique Head of our Church, Saint Peter, that most loving apostle, tried, because of his love for you, to dissuade you from this dear subject to which you were so lovingly attached, your dear cross, you called him a Satan![65] Oh meek[66] Savior! This is how you treat an apostle who is so dear to you, you who are meekness itself, and who, like a meek lamb, remained silent in the face of all the insults and injuries done to you by your enemies.[67] I can see, however, that this is the result of your love for the cross, which is the cause of this love; yet although this love exceeds all bounds, it yields to your love for Saint Bernard. Furthermore, I know that your thirst for the cross cannot be quenched either by the tears of your divine Mother or by the blood that streams down on all sides from your sacred body in the garden [on the Mount] of Olives;[68] and, in the sight of Bernard alone, this love leaves you as you leave the cross. You detach yourself from it to embrace this great saint, to unite yourself with him and attach[69] yourself to him. It is thus, thus, that those who surrender themselves to the service of my Master will be honored. Oh, how good it is to serve such a Lord! How good, yet how sweet, to strip oneself of the world so as to be reclothed and adorned in this way with such precious favors! It is this that makes the man of God, [the man] who is reclothed only after being stripped!

17. But he lives only for death. I learn this second truth, as I did the first, from the great apostle, who, writing to the Romans, says to them, *Existimate vos mortuos*, "Consider yourselves to be dead bodies" (Rom 6:11[70]). And if he speaks of life,

---

[65] See Matt 16:23.
[66] *Débonnaire*: see chap. 4 (Biroat), n. 26.
[67] See Isa 53:7; Acts 8:32.
[68] See Luke 22:44.
[69] Boudon contrasts *détacher* and *attacher*.
[70] The text actually says *Existimate vos mortuos quidem esse peccato*, "Consider yourselves to be dead to sin," but as we have seen, the panegyrists will commonly adapt a text to suit their purposes.

he places it only in death: *Vita vestra abscondita est cum Christo in Deo*, "Your life is hidden with Jesus[71] in God" (Col 3:3). But he tells them this only after he has told them that they are dead: *Mortui estis*, "You are dead" (Col 3:3). Those who live with Jesus die with Jesus, and that is why Saint Augustine, in his letter to Volusianus, says that the apostle introduces this truth of death by teaching us that those who belong to Jesus are those who have been crucified, for one must be crucified in order to die.[72] Jesus is dead because he was crucified. He teaches that we must be buried: *Consepulti estis* ["you are buried" (Rom 6:4)[73]]. We must follow our Savior into the tomb in order to take on a new life with him: *Ita et nos in novitate vitae ambulemus*, ["so that we too may walk in newness of life" (Rom 6:4)]. This truth is also justly prefigured in the Old Testament, when God commands Joshua, who is to take possession of the Promised Land, to destroy completely the town of Jericho and to leave no creature there alive: neither men, nor women, nor children, nor animals, nor the old, nor the young.[74] [In just the same way], everything must be killed in a Christian soul, both the great and the small, the few and the many: nothing may be excluded. Such is the second degree of the spirit. According to the division made by Saint Augustine, the first [degree] is the spirit in the spirit, the second is the spirit on the spirit.[75] In the first, by stripping off all exterior things, [the spirit] is outside the flesh, but in itself. Here, as a consequence of its total death, it is both outside itself and above itself. According to Saint Denis [the Areopagite],[76] this is achieved by the removal of

---

[71] Boudon substitutes "Jesus" for "Christ" in the biblical text.

[72] *Pace* Boudon, this is not to be found in Augustine's letters to Volusianus (Epp 132 and 137). It appears to reflect the ideas in his letter 55 to Januarius: *Ad inquisitiones Januarii* (Ep 55) 2.2.3; PL 33:205–6.

[73] The text actually reads *Consepulti enim sumus cum illo*, "*we* are buried with him."

[74] See Josh 6:5, 20-21.

[75] Augustine is here *ps.*-Augustine, the author of the *De spiritu et anima*, mediated via *ps.*-Bonaventure: see n. 30 above.

[76] See n. 38 above.

the second deformity, which comes from within, and which is much rarer and much more difficult [to achieve] than the first.

18. Also, it is much harder and more trying to die than to strip oneself, which is why our saint says, *Citius et lenius relinquitur facultas quam voluntas* ["it is quicker and easier to give up the means than the will"[77]]. We do indeed leave aside external things more quickly and more easily than our desire for them, which is our self-will. This is the difficult task that he undertook and over which he gloriously triumphed. This is why he stayed [for six months] at Châtillon[-sur-Seine], to live there unknown to the world;[78] this is why he stayed in Cîteaux, to die to human memory in the hope of being forgotten like a broken dish: *Factus sum tanquam vas perditum* ["I have become a vessel that is destroyed" (Ps 30:13)]. His friends pointed out to him that even his intention to serve God did not mean that he should bury himself so soon in these tombs: he needed time for study, [they said,] and it was only right that he should be acquainted with good literature.[79] Bernard listened to all these things and was unmoved: and why? Because he is dead. Do what they may, say what they may, they will gain nothing: talking to a corpse is a waste of time. And then again, he was not unaware that it was too great a desire for knowledge that brought about the fall of the first of the angels. In his discussion of this, the angelic doctor [Thomas Aquinas] notes that in Ezekiel, Lucifer, who was the first of the seraphim, is [now] called a cherubim: *Tu Cherub protegens* ["You, a cherub, protecting" (Ezek 28:14)]. This, says the great doctor, is the [lower]

---

[77] With all due respect to Boudon, our saint never said anything like this, nor does anyone else as far as I can see. Neither the sentence nor any like it appears in the Patrologia Latina or any of the standard databases. I have no idea where Boudon found it.

[78] *Vita prima* 1.3.13–16 (William of Saint-Thierry); PL 185:234C–36C; CF 76:16–20; Williams, *Saint Bernard*, 11–12.

[79] See *Vita prima* 1.3.9 (William of Saint-Thierry); PL 185:231D; CF 76:11–12.

rank he was given because of his crime: *scelus nomen imposuit* ["the crime imposed the name"].[80] The love of God had given him the first place among the seraphim; his curiosity,[81] filled with ambition, now gives him the name of cherubim, and he is lost forever in misery. This is why our saint says that this apostate angel is infinitely unhappy, for he had been *Lucifer* [the Light-Bearer], a spirit filled with light. He will learn, he says, through all eternity, that he should have been *Ignifer* [the Fire-Bearer], uniquely ablaze with the fires and flames of the love of God alone.[82]

19. Saint Bernard was convinced of these truths and wished only to live as one dead, in the gloom of the sepulcher, and if God calls him forth from the tomb, he will never lose its spirit. It is for this reason that he refuses all the great and illustrious dignities that the Church offered him. Milan asked him to be its archbishop, Reims, too, desired it, Geneva wanted him as its prelate, Châlons[-sur-Marne] chose him, Langres wanted him.[83] He resisted all their entreaties, he rejected all their pleas, he was unmoved by all their requests. He considered all these

---

[80] See Thomas Aquinas, *Super Sent*, lib. 2, div. 6, qu. 1, art. 1, arg. 1, and *Summa theologiae*, I, qu. 63, art. 7, arg. 1. Cherubim rank below seraphim in the celestial hierarchy.

[81] On the vice of *curiositas*, see appendix 1, s.v. *curiosité* / curiosity.

[82] The last two sentences are not readily intelligible without reading that section of the sermon they summarize: Bernard, *Dominica in Kalendis Novembris* S 3.1; SBOp 5:311–12. The name *seraph*, says Bernard, means something burning, but although Lucifer had an abundance of light, he had no warmth or heat. Perhaps, then, he was not really a seraph at all. As the Light-Bearer, he desired too much to shine, and his ambition brought him down. He should have been like John the Baptist, who not only shone but burned with love for his Lord. Lucifer, therefore, will himself be burned up, annihilated, by the blasting beams of the Sun of Justice. The contrast is between the cold light of ambitious pride (or proud ambition) and the fiery heat of that love that finds its joy in service: Lucifer versus Ignifer.

[83] See *Vita prima* 1.14.69 (William of Saint-Thierry); PL 185:265B; CF 76:73, n. 81, and 2.4.26 (Arnold of Bonneval); PL 185:283B; CF 76:106.

efforts, all these attempts, only to reject them utterly and refuse them all. He was dead to all honors and could say with the divine Paul that the only answer he could give was the answer of death.[84] This he showed very clearly on one occasion when the dead (as sometimes happens) came to life, for we cannot emphasize enough how sensitive people are about what is done to them. Yet this is not the case with a man of God, [a man] such as Saint Bernard, who lived only for death. [One day], he meets a canon who tells him that if he possessed any of his books, he would tear them to pieces, and at the same time he adds injuries to insults by giving [Bernard] a hard slap across the face. Those who were present are roused and angered at this insolent affront to the man of God and run after the wretched ecclesiastic, but the man of God shouts out that they must take care not to do him any harm.[85] Every time anything like this happened, he would recount the wrongs done to him or his monasteries with a smile on his face, and never judge them. It seemed, in fact, that when he spoke of the insults or injuries he had received, he was speaking about somebody else. The spirit of death that he carried within him meant that he, Bernard, was no longer Bernard.[86]

20. But just as Jesus, when he ascended the cross—which Saint Augustine calls "the child-bed of the Savior," *Thalamus parturientis* ["the marriage bed of child-birth"][87]—gave life to us by ending his own, so too Bernard, his servant, lives in death. Like a divine phoenix, he builds himself a sepulcher or bed,

---

[84] See 2 Cor 1:9 (*responsum mortis*).

[85] *Vita prima* 3.7.25 (Geoffrey of Auxerre); PL 185:317C–18A; CF 76:171–72. Boudon is the only one of the panegyrists to recount this story.

[86] Lit. "he was no longer himself because of the spirit of death he bore [within him]."

[87] *Pace* Boudon, this expression occurs in no work by or attributed to Augustine, and there is no record of it in the Patrologia Latina nor in any of the standard databases. Searching for *parturientis* alone is of no help.

and there he dies and is reborn. This funeral pyre is made from the perfumed logs of his virtues, and when he has set it on fire, he buries himself in its flames and then, reborn from the ashes, takes on a new life and new strength. The man of God comes into being by dying: *Ut custodiat perdit* ["In order to preserve (life), he loses it], says the learned Tertullian: he loses his life only to keep it.[88] It is for this reason, says Saint Zeno, that he comes, he runs, he flies to the tomb like the sun, boldly and fearlessly: *Sol intrepidus ad sepulcrum contendit* ["the fearless sun speeds to his tomb"],[89] for he finds in his end a beginning that will have no end, and in his death a birth that will last forever. The man of God lives only for death, just as he is clothed only to be stripped. In a word, he subsists only on nothingness.[90]

21. This [third] truth, like the two that precede it,[91] is taken from the same great apostle who, when writing to the Corinthians, tells them that God should be all in all: *Ut sit Deus omnia in omnibus* (1 Cor 15:28). For if he is all, then there is no longer anything else, and this admirably indicates Christian annihilation.[92] It is the last bed on which the bride takes her rest, and here there is nothing but God alone.[93] According to Saint Denis [the Areopagite], this is the state in which we are

---

[88] Tertullian, De resurr carnis 12; PL 2:810B. This is part of a long passage in which Tertullian uses the cycle of the seasons as an analogy for resurrection: the earth is stripped in winter in order to bloom again in the spring. Boudon adapts it to the spiritual life of the *homo Dei*.

[89] Zeno of Verona, *Tractatus. XVI de resurrectione* 8; PL 11:380AB. Zeno also introduces the analogy of the phoenix.

[90] See n. 28 above. The words are exactly the same.

[91] Boudon's discussion of the first truth (stripping off the old self) began at §7; the second (living only for death) at §17.

[92] *L'anéantissement chrétien*: *anéantissement*, "annihilation, becoming nothing, being reduced to nothing," is a technical term of seventeenth-century French spirituality: see appendix 1, s.v. *anéantissement* / annihilation. As we saw in the Introduction, Boudon is sailing into perilous waters in this and the following paragraphs.

[93] *Dieu seul*: see n. 24 above.

conformed to the angels and become like them;[94] it is the final degree of the spirit, which the Fathers call "the spirit without the spirit,"[95] and from this we can see the difference between the state of death and of annihilation. According to abbot Gilbert [of Hoyland], in the state of death the bed of the soul is the bed of both the bride and God, but in that of annihilation it is the bed of God alone.[96] In the state of death, the spirit is above the spirit; in the state of annihilation, the spirit is without the spirit. It is not that the soul loses its natural state: what it loses is its natural way of acting, which it retains in the [two] previous states, for here it is totally transformed into God. In the state of death, as Saint Teresa [of Ávila] tells us, the soul is betrothed to its divine spouse; in the state of annihilation, they are [joined] in marriage. In the state of death, the soul and Jesus are united like two lighted candles joined together: they produce only a single light, but then again, it is easy to separate them. In the state of annihilation, the union is like rain falling into a stream whose waters flow into the sea, like bright sunlight coming into a room through two windows, but then becoming only one [light].[97]

22. This is also the thought of Saint Bernard, whom we honor today and who instructs us by his example as well as by his teaching. Here is what he says in the treatise he wrote *On the Love of God*: "As a drop of water mixed with a quantity of wine appears to lose itself and take on the taste and color of the wine, or as red-hot iron seems to lose its own nature and becomes fire itself, or as air radiant with sunbeams is trans-

---

[94] See n. 38 above.
[95] See n. 30 above.
[96] Gilbert of Hoyland, SC 2.4; PL 184:19BD.
[97] See Teresa of Ávila (Teresa of Jesus), *Las Moradas del Castillo interior (The Interior Castle)*, 7.2; *Saint Teresa of Jesus: The Complete Works*, trans./ed. E. Allison Peers, New Ark Library (London and New York: Sheed and Ward, 1963), 2:334–35. *The Interior Castle* had been available in French since at least 1671.

formed into the brightness of light itself, so, in the saints, in some indescribable way, every human affection becomes, melts into, is transformed into the will of God. Otherwise how could [God] be all in all if something still remained in man?"[98] "The soul," said Saint Albert the Great in chapters 7 and 8 of [his work] *On Cleaving to God*, "must exist as if there was nothing there but God."[99] And Richard of Saint-Victor says that "The soul seems to give up what is human to the divine, so that it is no longer what it was: *Ab humano in divinum videtur deficere, ita ut ipse jam non sit ipse*.[100]

23. But let us listen to the voices of those two great lights of theology, Saint Thomas and Saint Bonaventure, who will teach us only those truths that have a solid foundation. In the first part of the Second [book of the *Summa theologica*], quaest. 59, art. 5, q. 61, art. 6, Saint Thomas is speaking about the virtues of these states that he calls *virtutes animi purgati*, "the virtues of the purified spirit."[101] He says that in these states prudence looks only to divine things, temperance no longer knows any earthly desires, fortitude is ignorant of the passions, and justice is perpetually linked to the divine Spirit and imitates it in all things. He then goes on to say that these virtues are the virtues of the blessed in heaven, but also of some people of great perfection here on earth and in this present life.[102]

---

[98] Bernard, Dil 10.28; SBOp 3:143. As we saw in the Introduction, the key term here is *seems*. The human soul does not become God.

[99] *Ps*.-Albertus Magnus, *De adhaerendo Deo* 7–8; *B. Alberti Magni . . . Opera Omnia*, 37:529–32 (especially §8, col. 2, p. 531).

[100] Richard of Saint-Victor, *Benjamin Major* 5.12; PL 196:182C: "[The soul] seems to abandon the human for the divine, so that itself is now not itself."

[101] These are the four cardinal virtues: prudence, temperance, fortitude, and justice.

[102] Thomas Aquinas, *Summa theologiae* I/II, q. 61 art. 5 co.: *Quaedam vero sunt virtutes iam assequentium divinam similitudinem, quae vocantur virtutes iam purgati animi. Ita scilicet quod prudentia sola divina intueatur; temperantia terrenas cupiditates nesciat; fortitudo passiones ignoret; iustitia*

24. Saint Bonaventure says the same thing in his first sermon on the Luminaries of the Church. "Prudence," says the Seraphic Doctor, "not only prefers divine things, but knows only them: it does not even look at other things, regarding them as nothing. Temperance does not so much suppress earthly desires as forget them entirely. Fortitude, in a certain way, is unaffected by any earthly feelings or passions.[103] And justice is perpetually united to the divine spirit, *ut sit Deus omnia in omnibus*, 'so that God may be all in all'" (1 Cor 4:28).[104] In this way, the man of God can exclaim with the divine Paul, "I live, but no, I live no longer: there is only Jesus who lives in me!" [Gal 2:20].[105] It is God who, so to speak, sees through the eyes of the man of God, speaks through his words, and acts through his actions. Oh annihilation, what a precious thing you are! Oh Christian nothingness, which is better than any sort of somethingness![106] It is in you that my God works all his great marvels! And indeed, it is from the nothingness of nature that God draws out this great universe, and from the nothingness of sin the whole world of grace and glory, in such a way that heaven and earth, Paradise and the world, all the

---

cum divina mente perpetuo foedere societur, eam scilicet imitando. "Besides these there are the virtues of those who have already achieved the divine likeness: these are called the 'virtues of the purified soul.' Thus, prudence sees nothing other than the things of God; temperance knows no earthly desires; fortitude knows nothing of the passions; and justice, by imitating the Divine Mind, is united to it by an everlasting covenant."

[103] Lit. "Fortitude, in a certain way, possesses a certain sort of impassibility."

[104] Bonaventure, *Illuminationes ecclesiae in Hexaemeron*, S I; *S.R.E. Cardinalis S. Bonaventurae . . . Opera Omnia*, ed. Adolphe C. Peltier (Paris: L. Vivès, 1867), 9:24–25 (an extensive discussion summarized very briefly by Boudon).

[105] Lit. "I live, now not I, but Christ lives in me."

[106] This is the best I can do for *O néant chrétien, qui vaut mieux que tout l'état des choses!*

marvels of nature, grace, and glory are drawn forth from this precious nothingness!

25. Saint Bernard, being completely lost, melted, engulfed (if I may use these terms) in this [nothingness], no longer esteems, is no longer surprised at all the great things the All Powerful[107] does in and through him: for what is not possible for a heart that is in the hands of God and that, unresisting, goes along with everything he plans? Is it not this that makes Saint Paul say *Omnia possum in eo qui me confortat*, "Yes, I am all powerful in the strength of God"? (Phil 4:13[108]). We see just the same thing in our saint.

26. Scripture says that God created light at the very beginning of creation, and then adds that on the fourth day he gave to the world the sun.[109] This caused some surprise to Saint Augustine, the Venerable Bede, and abbot Rupert [of Deutz], for why, they asked, did the world need a sun if it already had its light? This led them to understand that what was meant by this [first] light was the angels,[110] though the common opinion is that it referred to a corporeal light that was so subtle that it was not suited to our eyes. For that reason, God gathered it together and united it in the body of the sun. But since the adorable Jesus, my brothers, has never left his Church without a head, it seems (says a historian[111]) that in the old age of the world, when he brought about the birth of Bernard, he gathered together in him the light and spirit of the early fathers so that this divine doctor appeared as a wonderful sight to the

---

[107] *Tout-Puissant*, which we would normally translate as "the Almighty." Here, however, Boudon's exegesis demands "All Powerful," echoed in the verse from Philippians.

[108] Lit. "I can do all things in him who gives me the strength."

[109] See Gen 1:3, 16.

[110] See Augustine, De Gen ad litt 2.8.16–18; PL 34:269–70; Bede, *Hexaemeron* I; PL 91:16C–17B; Rupert of Deutz, In Gen 1.10–11; PL 167:206C–9A.

[111] This sentence appears to echo *Vita prima* 1.7.34 (William of Saint-Thierry); PL 185:247C; CF 76:39–40.

eyes of all the faithful who would come after him. Indeed, we may say of him what was said of Saint Benedict, *Spiritu omnium justorum plenus fuit*,[112] that he was filled with the spirit of all the righteous.

27. Like a Saint Ambrose, he preached penitence[113] to ordinary people and kings, to both great and small. Like a Saint Jerome, he loved the Church and especially the Apostolic See. Like a Saint Augustine, he was the flail of heretics. And like another Saint Gregory [the Great], he was incomparable in the moral exposition of the Gospel.[114] He preached penitence, which is the second pool in which one is cleansed from one's sins,[115] and since God had destined our saint for this apostolic office and had set him on the candlestand of his Church, there to enlighten all the faithful and open the eyes of sinners, it was not without Providence that he had him born at Fontaines, a little village at the gates of Dijon, a château that has now become the home of his children, the Reverend Fathers of the Feuillants.[116] The house is so full of the Lord's blessings that one cannot enter without feeling completely set on fire, completely consumed by the flames of divine love, just as I myself experienced when I had the good fortune to celebrate our awesome mysteries [of the Mass] there. So you will find a wonderful relationship between fountains and light, for foun-

---

[112] Rupert of Deutz, De div offic, VIII.iii; PL 170:212AB.

[113] See appendix 1, s.v. *pénitence* / penitence.

[114] Boudon is here following the unpaginated preface "to the Reader" in Le Maistre's *Vie de S. Bernard*.

[115] The first cleansing pool is the pool of Bethesda, with its moving waters and five porches: see John 5:2-7.

[116] The Feuillants took possession of the property on September 24, 1613. See further, Louis Chomton, *Saint-Bernard et le Château de Fontaines-lès-Dijon. Étude historique et archéologique. Volume 3* (Dijon: Union typographique, 1895); and Sigrid Pavèse, *Les Feuilllants et le Monastère royal de Fontaine-lès-Dijon: Exposition, Bibliothèque municipale de Fontaine-lès-Dijon, 12 septembre–3 octobre 1998* (Fontaine-lès-Dijon: Bibliothèque municipale, 1998).

tains are, so to speak, the eyes of the fields and the earth, just as the sun is [the eye] of the whole universe. And just as tears flow from one's eyes, so fountains are springs of living waters. Furthermore, the Hebrews used the same word, *naha*, for both fountains and light.[117]

28. Fontaines[-lès-Dijon], then, is the fortunate birthplace of our saint, because his task will be to enlighten sinners, to wash away the filth and stain of their sins, and to bring forth from their hearts the tears of genuine repentance. And indeed, everywhere he went, on all sides one saw only wonderful conversions: kings, those in power in the world, the whole earth was shaken by the voice of Bernard. He imposed heavy penances on monarchs as well as on the common people, as we may easily see in the case of Louis the Young, whom he ordered to undertake a great and arduous penance.[118] He preached penitence everywhere, to both great and small, just like a Saint Ambrose. He upheld the Church like a Saint Jerome and, like this learned Father, was regarded as its oracle and its light.

29. The Church is one, true, and holy, and to preserve its unity, Jesus, who has a physical body and a mystical body, suffers his side to be pierced and his physical body divided so as to bring about the unity of the mystical [body]. Take careful note of this, my brothers, for schism, [which divides the mystical body,] is a greater evil than if one were to strike Jesus' [physical body]. It was this that roused the zeal of the great Saint Bernard and that led him to say, when replying to Peter of Pisa (a most eloquent man who supported the schism[119]), "As for us, we are more used to plowing and tilling than to

---

[117] Boudon is almost, but not quite, correct. *Nahar*, not *naha*, means a river, stream, or current, and *naharah* (again, not *naha*), means light or daylight. Both words derive from the root NHR, "to flow or run."

[118] For the complicated background to this, see Williams, *Saint Bernard*, 204–16. Louis's "great and arduous penance" was to go on the Second Crusade: see appendix 2, s.v. Louis VII the Young.

[119] See appendix 2, s.v. Anacletus II.

speeches and oratory. Indeed, we would keep silence, as befits our profession, if we had not been engaged to defend the cause of the faith.[120] But now that the robe of Jesus Christ is rent, that robe that neither the Jews nor even the pagans dared tear in two at the time of the Passion, it is time to speak."[121] And he spoke with such force and such blessing that he made the whole of France, which had relied on the saint's [judgment] in this matter, subject and obedient to Innocent, the Sovereign Pontiff. He did the same in the case of [Henry I,] the king of England.[122] He went to Sicily to find Roger [II], its king, and from being the rebel that he was, made him a wholly obedient child of the Holy See.[123] "There is but one faith," he said to him,[124] "one Lord, and one baptism; and we recognize neither two lords nor two baptisms. There was but one ark at the time of the Flood; the eight people who took refuge therein were saved, all the rest were lost."[125]

30. You may say that it was as if he led the pope by the hand, establishing his authority everywhere, which is why the great Cardinal Baronius, after having called him a genuinely apostolic man, a true apostle sent by God, powerful in words and deeds, in no way inferior to the great apostles, adds that he ought to be called the buttress[126] of the Roman Church and the

---

[120] This is legal language: one engages a lawyer to defend a case.

[121] *Vita prima* 2.7.45 (Arnold of Bonneval); PL 185:294BD; CF 76:129.

[122] See appendix 2, s.v. Henry I, king of England, and *Vita prima* 2.1.4 (Arnold of Bonneval); PL 185:271AB; CF 76:82–83.

[123] This is an exceedingly brief summary of a long and complex story: see appendix 2, s.v. Roger II of Sicily, and Williams, *Saint Bernard*, 151–57.

[124] In the text of the *Vita prima* (see n. 125 immediately below), Bernard is still addressing Peter of Pisa, not Roger.

[125] *Vita prima* 2.7.45 (Arnold of Bonneval); PL 185:294CD; CF 76:128–30.

[126] *Appui*, which translates Baronius's *fulcimentum*, a prop, stay, support, or pillar. I think buttress is better.

Holy See.[127] That is why the Hohenstaufens at Magdeburg[128] described him as the most powerful and zealous defender of the See of Antichrist, which is how heretics speak[129] of the Apostolic See and the Sovereign Pontiff: *Acerrimus propugnator fuit sedis Antichristi*, ["he was the most determined defender of the See of Antichrist"].[130] This is because they had read in Letter 242, addressed to Pope Eugenius, that there was no Christian in the world who should not glory in being united to the Roman Church, which is the head of all the others.[131] And in Book II of *On Consideration* (chap. 8, n. 15), "Each of the other [shepherds] has his own flock, but all the sheep in general have been placed in your care, and as one single flock they belong to you, and you are not only the shepherd of the sheep but also [the shepherd] of the shepherds."[132]

31. He knew that [Geoffrey,] the count of Anjou, had rebelled against the orders of the Sovereign Pontiff. Bernard went to see him and, in his holy zeal, swore that it was impossible that God would not take memorable vengeance. And that is what happened, for he died after fifteen days.[133] Thus did [Bernard] uphold the unity of the Church like another Saint Jerome, but

---

[127] *Caesaris S. R. E. Cardinalis Baronii Annales Ecclesiastici, denuo et accurate excusi* (Paris and Fribourg: Consociatio S. Pauli, 1880), vol. 19 (1147–1198), 69 (§14).

[128] I presume the reference is to events associated with the siege and sack of Magdeburg in 1631 during the Wars of Religion.

[129] Boudon uses the present tense: this is how Protestants in his day referred to the see of Rome. Its origins lie with Luther.

[130] I have not been able to trace this quotation, and none of the standard databases is of any help.

[131] In the editions of Horstius and Mabillon, Bernard's Letter 242 is addressed not to Eugenius, but to the people of Toulouse, and although I have read all the letters addressed to Eugenius, I have not found this exact sentence.

[132] Bernard, Csi 2.8.15; SBOp 3:423. Boudon's (or his editor's) citation is here absolutely accurate. For Eugenius III, see appendix 2.

[133] *Vita prima* 4.3.13 (Geoffrey of Auxerre); PL 185:329AD (omitted in CF 76). Geoffrey Plantagenet, Geoffrey V the Handsome, Count

he also fought against heresy like Saint Augustine. This he did with such determination and with so great a horror of [any heresy] that when, at the Council held at Reims in the time of Pope Eugenius III [in 1148], he saw that a number of prelates wanted to condemn the opinions of Gilbert de la Porrée, bishop of Poitiers, without condemning Gilbert, he stirred up his zeal, united himself with the French bishops on this matter, and brought it about that the bishop himself rejected what he had written.[134]

32. Finally, he was as incomparable as was Saint Gregory [the Great] in his moral exposition of the Gospel. So tellingly did he preach that contempt for the world that the Gospel teaches us, that [when he entered Cîteaux] he took with him thirty gentlemen who would renounce the world.[135] Others came in crowds from all parts and from far distant countries to embrace the religious life. Professors of all branches of knowledge leave everything to study only the knowledge of Jesus crucified; ecclesiastics leave their benefices. No fewer than a hundred novices made their profession.[136] Clairvaux was filled with great lords—indeed, there were even two brothers of kings.[137]

33. *Homo Dei*: he was truly the man of God, who is clothed only to be stripped, who lives only for death, who subsists

---

of Anjou, Touraine, and Maine, died suddenly on September 7, 1151, apparently from some sort of fever (see Williams, *Saint Bernard*, 217).

[134] See *Vita prima* 3.5.15 (Geoffrey of Auxerre); PL 185:312AD; CF 76:160–62.

[135] See chap. 9 (La Rue 1), n. 39.

[136] See *Vita prima* 7.12.16 and 7.29.62 (*Exordium Magnum Cisterciense*); PL 185:422CD and 450B.

[137] They were Henry, brother of Louis VII the Young (see *Vita prima* 4.3.15 [Geoffrey of Auxerre]; PL 185:330B–31B; CF 76:193–95), who went on to become archbishop of Reims, and Peter (Pedro), brother of Alphonsus (Afonso) I of Portugal (see Bernard's Ep 308; SBOp 8:228). Boudon's source is undoubtedly the marginal note on page 16 of the unpaginated preface to Le Maistre's *Vie*.

only on nothingness. So let us conclude by reviewing these [three] truths. My brothers, the manna from heaven was given to the children of Israel only when they had run out of the flour they had brought with them from Egypt.[138] If you wish to be clothed in the livery of grace, you must strip yourself of any attachment to the world. "Ah! How narrow is the gate!" cried our Master (Matt 7:14), speaking of our entry into eternal life, that is to say, the self is much bigger than you think it to be! *Populi meus, qui te beatum dicunt te seducunt* ["My people, those who call you blessed deceive you" (Isa 3:12)]. Yes, all those, whoever they may be, who say, "Happy are the rich, the great, those comfortably off, those held in honor or esteem," yes, those who say these things are deceived by the world! Yes, you are deceived, you who say these things! The man of God is clothed only to be stripped. It is this that will make you happy, my brothers, for the crosses you bear of the life of mortification, [the crosses] that strip you of the world, adorn you and, in your souls, enrich you with the holiest graces of heaven, these are the crosses that, as we can say with your blessed Father [Bernard], are blessed in so many ways.[139] But the sweet anointing of the Holy Spirit that you feel inwardly is felt by very few: *Multi vident cruces, pauci unctiones* ["Many see crosses, few are anointed"].[140] The great bishop of Geneva[141]

---

[138] See Exod 16:1-36 and Num 11:1-9.

[139] If this is a quotation from Bernard, I have not found it.

[140] I have not been able to trace this sentence. It is not to be found in the Patrologia Latina and is not recorded in any of the standard databases.

[141] Saint Francis de Sales, who died in 1622, two years before Boudon's birth. The bishop had a close and cordial relationship with the Feuillants, and in May 1622, when the Feuillants could not agree over the election of a general, had been commissioned by Pope Gregory XV to preside over their chapter. Shortly afterward, he went to Turin, where, on being invited to a splendid reception in his honor, he declined to attend and said he would prefer to spend time with the Feuillants.

had seen them and felt them. He, too, is a saint[142] and belongs to that small number, and in one of your Congregations, when he was assisting [at Mass] on behalf of the Sovereign Pontiff, he felt he had to bear witness to that in public. Your holy Congregation, whiter than the habits you wear,[143] demands that you live a wholly heavenly life, for it knew it must be filled with the spirit of Saint Bernard. It is this spirit that transforms the Feuillant into an angel.

34. Finally, the man of God lives only for death: our whole life consists in dying, dying to all that is not God, so as to live in that perfect nothingness where God works whatever he wills and whatever to him seems good.[144]

---

[142] Or "he, too, is holy": see n. 7 above. If "he, too, is a saint" is correct, the panegyric must have been composed after Francis de Sales's canonization in 1665.

[143] The Feuillants retained the white Cistercian habit, but, unlike their confrères, went about in their convents with bare head and bare feet.

[144] Here the panegyric breaks off, with the editor adding this note at the foot of cols. 1407–8: "There remain another twenty lines in the autograph manuscript from which we have edited this panegyric, but they are indecipherable, partly because of the tiny writing and partly because three or four words have been torn off at the beginning of each line. We prefer to leave the panegyric incomplete, rather than substituting our own thoughts for those of Boudon."

12

Panegyrical Plagiarism?

Claude Lion, François Ogier, and Esprit Fléchier

In this chapter we shall deal with the panegyrics of three preachers, one of whom, Esprit Fléchier, enjoyed in his day a far greater renown than either of the other two. All three, however, composed panegyrics on Saint Bernard that are linked to other panegyrics by other preachers. In the case of Claude Lion, the link is with Henri-Marie Boudon, the subject of our last chapter and Lion's contemporary, and while the evidence seems to point to some interdependence, we cannot be quite certain as to who was dependent on whom, though it seems more probable that Boudon was dependent on Lion. The case of François Ogier and Esprit Fléchier is far more obvious. Ogier lived from 1597 to 1670, and Fléchier, a preacher of the next generation, from 1632 to 1710. Ogier preached his panegyric on Saint Bernard in 1638; Fléchier preached his forty-five years later in 1683. Fléchier unashamedly borrows from Ogier's earlier discourse, sometimes quoting passages almost word for word, and although he presents what he has to say in his own inimitable style, the voice is the voice of Jacob, though the hands are the hands of Esau. But let us begin with Claude Lion.

Claude Lion

Claude Lion was a priest of the Oratory of Jesus, the congregation founded in 1611 by Pierre de Bérulle.[1] He was born in Marseille in 1625 and entered the Oratory at the age of seventeen, but it seems that he had too high an opinion of his own abilities.[2] His superiors did not think that he had a real aptitude for teaching and therefore allocated to him the task of looking after the young confrères of the congregation. Lion, however, disagreed, considered himself perfectly qualified to teach, and spent his unsought leisure in composing works that, in his opinion, would immortalize him. They did not. But when it was pointed out to him that these writings were deficient in both style and eloquence, he took these criticisms not as friendly advice but as a result of either envy or the fact that his critics simply did not know any better. He himself had made a deep study of both the classical and the French orators, and his works were permeated by their language and expressions.

After he was ordained to the priesthood, he turned immediately to the composition of panegyrics, and—unlike so many of the other panegyrists—made sure that they were published to his own credit during his own lifetime. He also turned his hand to poetry, composing a certain number of verses each day. But though he was a competent versifier, "he lacked the

---

[1] Bérulle died on October 2, 1629, and Lion preached his panegyric: see [Claude Lion], *Panégyriques des saints, preschez par le R. P. Claude Lion, Prestre de l'Oratoire de Jésus. Tome quatrième* (Lyon: Jean Certe, 1690), 346–86. He also preached a panegyric on Bérulle's successor as superior-general of the Oratory, Charles de Condren, who died on January 17, 1641: see *Panégyriques des saints . . . Tome troisième* (1690), 81–116.

[2] For what follows I am dependent on the account from the *Athenaeum Massiliense* reproduced in the *Dictionnaire de la Provence et du Comté-Venaissin, dédié a Monseigneur le Maréchal Prince de Beauveau. Par une Société de Gens de Lettres. Tome troisième* (Marseille: Jean Mossy, 1786), 454.

taste that characterizes true poets."[3] In 1690 he published a collection of his poetry, which (as he said) would have been more extensive had he not mislaid a number of poems. But as one of his critics observed, "those who know the work do not regret the loss."[4] For all that, Lion seems to have had a real talent for administration and was appointed superior of the Oratorian house at Condom, in the southwest of France, which he governed well and effectively for many years. He spent more than sixty years in the Congregation of the Oratory and died in 1704 at the age of seventy-nine.

Lion composed a great number of panegyrics—five volumes of them were published between 1683 and 1694, and a further collection of *Nouveaux panégyriques des saints* in 1704—but he is not counted among the great orators of the seventeenth century. According to Albert and Court, at the beginning of the *Nouveaux panégyriques* there is a letter to Abel-Louis de Sainte-Marthe, the fifth superior-general of the Oratory, "in which it appears that Father Lion was a very aged preacher and that he had composed a number of his pieces in his old age. We must not therefore seek the polished style and apt language that we see in the panegyrics of our own century."[5] When he composed his panegyric on Saint Bernard[6] is unknown (I can find no clue within the text), nor do we know where or to whom he preached it, except that it was to *Messieurs* who were not monks. It is not a great work, but as we have already said, it bears a number of interesting similarities to Henri-Marie Boudon's panegyric on Bernard, and, in general, is more remarkable for its sources than for its doctrine.

---

[3] *Dictionnaire de la Provence*, 454.
[4] *Dictionnaire de la Provence*, 454.
[5] Albert / Court, 153.
[6] [Claude Lion], *Panégyriques des saints, preschez par le R. P. Claude Lion, Prestre de l'Oratoire de Jésus. Tome premier* (Lyon: Jean Certe, 1683), 430–60, cited below as Lion.

Lion takes as his text 1 Timothy 4:16, which he translates as "Pay heed to yourself and to the instruction of others; remain steadfast in these exercises."[7] He then tells us that since we cannot comprehend the infinite greatness of God, we can attempt to see a reflection of it in his saints, and he proves his point by quoting Saint Augustine: "We do not take away from the praise of God when we praise the works of God."[8] And "Saint Bernard was one of his most straightforward copies and one of his most perfect images. . . . He was the disciple of Jesus Christ before becoming the master of men, and he drew from Scripture the truths he taught to them. And the instructions he gave them were only the lessons he had received from this divine school."[9] *Attendite tibi et doctrinae*, therefore, "Pay heed to yourself and to doctrine," which brings Lion back to the text of his sermon, and, as was customary, he begs the help of Mary in delivering his eulogy, by saying with the angel *Ave Maria*.

His panegyric will contain the usual three divisions: he will present Bernard "as a Christian who is holy, as a teacher (*docteur*[10]) who is enlightened, and as a religious who is penitent. As a Christian he pleases God, as a teacher he serves the Church, as a religious he masters his passions."[11] The whole of Lion's first point is a rather long-winded paean in praise of virginity (*virginité*), by which he means not so much physical virginity as chastity, innocence, and purity. In fact, the entire eleven pages can be summed up in a single sentence: "Be pure and chaste in thought, word, and deed, as true Christians are required to be." But if we find this difficult, and if there is a

---

[7] This is Lion's extended paraphrase of *Attende tibi et doctrinae, insta in illis*, "Pay heed to yourself and to doctrine; persevere in them." But as we have already seen, and as we shall see again, the panegyrists frequently translate the biblical text to suit their own purposes.

[8] Lion, 430–31, quoting Augustine, S 313.2.2 *in natali Cypriani martyris* 5; PL 38:1423.

[9] Lion, 431.

[10] See chap. 4 (Biroat), n. 55.

[11] Lion, 433.

continual battle to be fought against temptations and all the wiles of the devil, we can take heart from Bernard. Even as a young boy he was tempted and overcame temptations, and Lion, unusually, recounts all three of the youthful episodes that appear in William of Saint-Thierry's section of the *Vita prima*. We hear not only the famous story of the icy pool, but also the tales of how Bernard overcame one temptress by doing nothing whatever (he just lay there), and another by shouting out "Robbers! Robbers!" whenever she tried to approach him, thereby rousing the entire household and driving her back to her own bed. Mind you, we have to give the woman credit for her persistence: she tried three times.[12]

But Bernard had already been led to the path of chastity by a vision and confirmed in it by a miracle. The vision was that of the infant Jesus on Christmas night in the old chapel of Saint-Vorles at Châtillon-sur-Seine[13]—a vision also recounted by Fléchier and Louis-Bénigne Bourru—and the impact of the vision, says Lion, was that from that moment on the young Bernard could say to Jesus, with the prophet Jeremiah, "*Pater meus, dux virginitatis meae*. You are my Father, the initiator and guide of my virginity."[14] As to the miracle, that was the celebrated Lactation of Saint Bernard,[15] which also appears in the panegyrics of Planchette, Boudon, Bourru, and (vaguely) Fléchier. For when the Holy Virgin (who had a great tenderness for Bernard) saw how ardently he loved virginity, she nourished him with milk from her own breast. Lion, however, goes one step further and compares this marvel to the mother of Cato the Elder suckling other children of her household with the

---

[12] Lion, 438–42. For the three episodes, see *Vita prima* 1.3.6–7 (William of Saint-Thierry); PL 185:231B–32B; CF 76:9–10, or Le Maistre, *Vie*, 16–19.

[13] See *Vita prima* 1.2.4 (William of Saint-Thierry); PL 185:228D–29B; CF 76:6–7, and Williams, *Saint Bernard*, 6.

[14] Lion, 442–43, quoting Jer 3:4.

[15] See chap. 5 (Senault et al.), n. 37.

same milk as her own son, so that having received the same nourishment, they would have for her son the same love.[16]

And so Lion concludes the first part of his panegyric with an exhortation to his listeners to take Bernard as their example of chastity, purity, and innocence, and moves on to consider what he did for the Church: "May the purity of Bernard be an example for you. Imitate this saint, who was so pleasing to God through his virginity and the innocence of his life as a Christian, and who was so useful to his own and to the whole Church by his zeal and his knowledge as a teacher. *Utilis suis* ["useful to others"[17]]. And that is the second point of my sermon."[18]

What is zeal? asks Lion at the beginning of this second part. It is an intense and one-pointed love, he says, "which thrusts aside everything opposed to its plans and which, like a flaming fire, consumes and annihilates, so far as it can, everything that is not in agreement with its intentions."[19] But Bernard's love for God and his Church was not a selfish love: he wished to have as many others as possible join him in his love. And so Lion tells us the story of Bernard's brothers (not least young Nivard), his father, relatives, and friends who followed him to Cîteaux. His zeal and eloquence then attract crowds of others, so that during his life he founded no fewer than a hundred and sixty monasteries[20] and saw no fewer than seven hundred and seventy (*sic*) religious at Clairvaux.[21] His zeal for the truth was supported by his knowledge, though it was not a knowl-

---

[16] The *histoire prophane* (Lion, 443) in which this story is to be found is Plutarch, *Parallel Lives*, *Cato major* 20.3. Lion, as we know, had immersed himself in the classics.

[17] Bernard, SC 57.4.11; SBOp 2:126.

[18] Lion, 445.

[19] Lion, 445.

[20] See chap. 4 (Biroat), n. 97.

[21] Lion, 447, has here misread his source. For *sept cent septante* (770), read *sept cent* (700): see *Vita prima* 5.3.20 (Geoffrey of Auxerre); PL 185:363AB (*septingenta*); CF 76:253.

edge learned from books. Bernard's masters were the trees and woods, for "it was not by men that he was instructed, but by God himself."[22] And reiterating what Lion said at the beginning of his panegyric (and, incidentally, foreshadowing Massillon[23]), he tells us that it was in the Holy Scriptures that Bernard found all that he needed:

> He knew them so perfectly and had mastered them so completely that in his writings and books he spoke only through Scripture, and it seemed to be his natural language. . . . The Holy Scriptures were the treasure of his heart, and from them he drew all those rich thoughts that embellish his writings, which are no more than a holy compilation and unbroken weaving of the truths of the Gospel, the teachings of the apostles, and the oracles of the prophets.[24]

But—alas!—there were those who were not satisfied with this, who found God's own word insufficient, and who set up their own teachings in opposition to those of Holy Church. And so, predictably, Lion tells us of Bernard's zeal in the overthrow of Abelard, Gilbert de la Porrée (he mentions the Council of Reims), and Henry of Toulouse. But Bernard's goal in this matter was not only to cast down—though there were times when that had to be done—but to build up, and in a charming classical analogy, Lion compares him to a Christian Archimedes: "Archimedes asked one thing only: some point outside the world where he could set up his lever, and he swore he would shift the earth from its place.[25] Here is Bernard who,

---

[22] Lion, 448, echoing *Vita prima* 1.4.23 (William of Saint-Thierry); PL 185:240D; CF 76:26–27.

[23] See chap. 14 (Massillon), §47.

[24] Lion, 449.

[25] The ultimate source for this is Pappus of Alexandria, *Synagoge*, Bk. VIII, who reports Archimedes as saying, "Give me the place to stand, and I will move the earth."

like a Christian Archimedes, has set up his heart outside the world (having set it up in God) and who levers everyone into the heart of God, detaching them from the earth, and giving them no other love but a love for Heaven."[26]

Nor did his achievement end with his death, for he continues his levering each and every day in the books and writings he has bequeathed to us.

How do we know that his teachings are true? Because God confirmed them by his many miracles:

> How many of those possessed did he deliver [from their demons]? To how many blind did he restore sight? How many dead did he bring back to life? It is enough to say that he was the Thaumaturge of the West. Indeed, he did so many miracles during his life and even after his death that, after his death, the abbot of Cîteaux had to command him, as his Superior, to do no more! In light of so many marvels, the learned Baronius called our saint an apostle sent from God, powerful in works and words: *Verus Apostolus missus a Deo potens opera et sermone.*[27]

Here our author echoes Henri-Marie Boudon and anticipates Louis-Bénigne Bourru, who also call Bernard the Thaumaturge of the West[28] and who quote precisely the same passage from Cardinal Baronius.[29]

Thus Dom Lion arrives at his third, final, and fairly brief point. The true prudence[30] of a Christian, he tells us (and again

---

[26] Lion, 453.

[27] Lion, 453–54.

[28] See chap. 11 (Boudon), n. 19.

[29] *Caesaris S. R. E. Cardinalis Baronii Annales Ecclesiastici, denuo et accurate excusi* (Paris and Fribourg: Consociatio S. Pauli, 1880), vol. 19 (1147–1198), 69 (§14). The passage appears in the unpaginated preface to Le Maistre's *Vie*. See also chap. 11 (Boudon), §30, and chap. 13 (Anselme and Bourru), nn. 74–75.

[30] Prudence / *prudentia* is one of the Four Cardinal Virtues.

we are reminded of Boudon[31]), is to think often of his or her salvation; and since a perfect religious is, or should be, a perfect Christian, "he is also a man of great prudence, since he flees the world, which is no more than corruption, to withdraw into the solitude where one breathes only the air of holiness."[32] Lion then goes on to praise the virtues of solitude, especially that of Clairvaux, "a savage place, full of horror,"[33] for it was there that Bernard, in forgetting himself, thought only of God, spoke only of God, and found it happily impossible to love anything other than God. True, he often had to leave this solitude to attend to important matters of church and state, but if charity compelled him to leave his desert, he preserved his solitude in his heart. As "the historian of his life"—William of Saint-Thierry—says, "he provided for himself his own solitude of heart, and carrying this solitude with him, he was everywhere alone."[34]

So fixed was he on God, so strongly recollected[35] in himself, that he often failed to notice his surroundings, and Lion tells us the familiar tales of the magnificent harness of his borrowed horse, of his day by Lake Geneva, and of his drinking oil when he thought he was drinking water.[36] This leads to a brief discussion of the need for penance and mortification, and in his own penance and mortification Bernard was imitating his divine Master. He could justly say with Saint Paul, "I am nailed to the cross with Christ" (Gal 2:19), "and he could say this with truth because one day, when he was praying before the image of Jesus crucified, the image detached itself from the

---

[31] See chap. 11 (Boudon), §§23–24.
[32] Lion, 454.
[33] Lion, 455.
[34] *Vita prima* 1.4.24 (William of Saint-Thierry); PL 185:241A; CF 76:27. Senault quotes the same passage: see chap. 5 (Senault et al.), n. 13.
[35] See appendix 1, s.v. *recueillement* / recollection.
[36] Once again Lion parallels Boudon (chap. 11, §§13–14). Rancé tells the same tales: chap. 6, §§23, 25, 28.

wood and came down to him to embrace him."[37] The reference, of course, is to the famous story of the *Amplexus Bernardi*,[38] which also appears in Boudon and Bernard Planchette,[39] and which (according to Lion) led to Bernard's utter and complete devotion to the cross of his Savior. This is not, obviously, something we should expect for ourselves, and Lion's descriptions of Bernard's absolute chastity, purity, and innocence, and the severity of his penances and mortifications, may be beyond our own limited capabilities. Our author is well aware of this, and his final advice to his congregation is therefore down to earth, straightforward, and practical: "If you can only admire the virginity of Bernard and his great penitence, at least imitate his profound humility."[40] You do not have to be celibate to be saved, and you do not need to withdraw into the solitude of a monastery, "but you cannot be saved if you are not humble."[41]

It cannot be said, I think, that Lion's panegyric possesses *onction*, that it touches the heart, though it certainly has some points of interest. The first is the numerous parallels to Boudon's panegyric, though the essential difference between them is that whereas Boudon dwells at length on Bernard's mysticism and mystical experiences, Lion says nothing whatsoever about them. And he mentions Bernard's miracles only because they confirm his teaching. Nor does he say anything about Bernard's role in bringing an end to the papal schism, and that is unusual.

His sources, however, like those of Boudon, are unusually wide. Tertullian, Ambrose, Augustine, Jerome, Gregory the Great, and John Chrysostom may cause us no surprise, and the *Orationes* of Gregory of Nazianzus are not uncommon. Hildebert of Lavardin/Le Mans/Tours has undoubtedly been

---

[37] Lion, 458.

[38] See chap. 5 (Senault et al.), n. 38.

[39] See chap. 11 (Boudon), §15, and chap. 5 (Senault et al.), n. 38.

[40] Lion, 459, adapting Bernard, Miss Hom 1.6; SBOp 4:18: Lion substitutes *in Bernardo* for Bernard's *in Maria*.

[41] Lion, 460.

borrowed from the unpaginated preface *Au Lecteur* of Le Maistre's *Vie de Saint Bernard*, but Peter Chrysologus is certainly more unusual, and Basil of Seleucia and Thalassius of Syria are rare indeed. We may also be justly surprised at a quotation from the *Panegyricus de quarto consulatu Honorii Augusti* of the court poet Claudian. Together with Boudon, Lion quotes from Thomas Aquinas and the *Annales* of Cardinal Baronius, and his source for Bernard's life is, naturally, the *Vita prima*, Le Maistre's *Vie*, or both. William of Saint-Thierry never appears by name, however, but always anonymously as "the author of [Bernard's] life" or "the historian of his life," a common designation among the panegyrists. Of Bernard's own works, we find quotations and allusions to his letters, the sermons on the Song of Songs, and a number of other sermons. From Lion's own times, we find a reference to the founder of the Oratory, Cardinal Pierre de Bérulle (we may remember that Lion preached his panegyric on his death), but as he himself said, "Monsignor the Cardinal de Bérulle has furnished me with many ideas that I have adapted for my own use. He is our most honored Father and Founder, and his works are our heritage."[42] The work he cites in his panegyric on Bernard is Bérulle's *Traité des énergumènes*.[43]

There cannot, I think, be much doubt that the panegyrics of Lion and Boudon are related, though by no means to the same extent as those of Ogier and Fléchier. But if borrowing has indeed occurred, who has borrowed from whom? Lion died, an old man, in 1704, and the venerable archdeacon of Évreux died, almost equally old, just two years earlier in 1702. But Lion's panegyric on Bernard was published in 1683 and Boudon's not until 1856, long after his death, when the *abbé* Migne edited it

---

[42] Lion, page 2 of the unnumbered pages of the Preface to this volume.

[43] Lion, 432–33, referring to chaps. 1.5–6 of the *Traité des énergumènes, par l'Illustrissîme & Révérendissime Cardinal de Bérulle* (Paris: Fiacre Dehors, 1631), 13–18.

"for the first time after the autograph manuscripts."[44] Boudon might have read Lion, therefore, but Lion could not have read Boudon. Whether there was correspondence between them we do not know—no letter survives—and Claude Lion is not mentioned in any life of Boudon. Nor is there any evidence that either of them ever heard the other preach. The implication, then, is that Boudon had read Lion's panegyric and had borrowed some of the material for his own unique discourse. If this was so, Boudon must have delivered his panegyric sometime between 1683 and his death in 1702. The name of Saint Bernard appears three times in Pierre Collet's Life of Boudon[45] but offers no clue as to the date of the sermon. Whatever the relationship, there is no doubt that Boudon's panegyric is of far greater interest than that of Lion, and those interested may read a complete translation in the last chapter.

The situation with regard to the panegyrics of François Ogier and Esprit Fléchier is, as we have said, very different. There can be no doubt whatever that Fléchier has pilfered a great deal of material from Ogier's earlier discourse, and to the evidence for that we shall now turn.

François Ogier

Ogier was born in Paris in 1597, the younger son of a legal counselor to the *Parlement* of Paris, the most important legislative and judicial institution in the country. His elder brother was Charles Ogier, who would become a respected diplomat, Latin poet, and man of letters. François also had a great love of literature, and after taking holy orders and realizing his natural talents as a preacher, took this love of literature with him into the pulpit. His prowess caught the attention of the king, who made him *prédicateur du roi* and rewarded him with a number of rich benefices. Like his brother, he was and remained

---

[44] See chap. 11 (Boudon), n. 13.
[45] Pierre Collet, *La Vie de M. Henri-Marie Boudon, Grand Archidiacre d'Évreux. Nouvelle édition* (Paris: J.-T. Hérissant, 1762), 369, 378, 490.

a man of letters, and we may see this in his spirited defense of Honoré de Balzac when the latter was attacked by Jean de Saint-François Goulu, superior general of the Feuillants. Ogier's *Apologie* for Balzac was published in 1627 and ran to some three hundred pages. In time Ogier would relinquish the pulpit and devote himself entirely to literature, and he died in his seventies on June 28, 1670.[46]

His panegyrics were highly esteemed in his day, and Albert and Court praise him for being circumspect in his display of profane learning and for banishing from his sermons "those ridiculous witticisms that were formerly thought necessary to gain the attention of the audience."[47] Problems, however, remained. Ogier, they say, is still somewhat too lavish in his citations of the Greek and Latin poets and philosophers, and "he still draws too much of a parallel between pagan morality and that of the Gospel."[48] They also accuse him of not being sufficiently natural or unaffected in his discourses, and, in his quest for high style, of using long (and sometimes meaningless) words and of relying too much on bombast and fustian.[49] Tréverret concurs. He describes Ogier's eloquence as "verbose, empty, and overblown, though not quite so absurd as one might fear."[50] He does not provide his panegyrics with a firm historical foundation, and he does not know how to give to his work a strong and effective unity. The truth of the matter, says Tréverret, is that Ogier is only a *rhéteur*, a rhetor, a flowery talker, a wordsmith, a speechmaker.[51]

---

[46] On Charles and François Ogier, see *Biographie universelle, ancienne et moderne . . . Ouvrage entièrement neuf, rédigé par une Société de Gens de Lettres et de Savants. Tome trente-unième* (Paris: L. G. Michaud, 1822), 529–30.
[47] Albert / Court, 198.
[48] Albert / Court, 198.
[49] Albert / Court, 197–98.
[50] Tréverret, 22.
[51] Tréverret, 22.

Ogier's panegyric on Bernard is to be found in the first volume of his collected sermons, panegyrics, and funeral orations, published in Paris in 1652 under the title (the "vague and somewhat profane title," according to Paul Jacquinet[52]) of *Actions publiques*,[53] and some of the criticisms levied against him may certainly be seen in this discourse. There is sometimes an affected tone; the poets and philosophers of Greece and Rome do make their appearance (they usually manifest as *les anciens*); there are passages in which pagan and Christian morality appear side by side. And if truth be told, the classical allusions are not always really necessary. The story of Baucis and Philemon, for example, does nothing for Ogier's sermon and could happily have been left with Ovid, and although Brutus and Cassius are revealed as true friends with different philosophies, it cannot be said that they are an essential part of the preacher's exegesis. He certainly does not provide a solid historical framework—Tréverret is right in this, though perhaps too severe in his other criticisms—nor does he tell us in his exordium what he will speak of in his discourse and how it will be divided. In fact, it falls into two parts, each with some slight overlap.[54] The first part deals with Bernard's life within the cloister; the second with his life outside it. This, as we have seen, may almost be called standard.

But for all that, Ogier's panegyric is, to my mind, a panegyric worth reading—or, more accurately, some parts of it are worth reading. There are some quite charming passages, and some that reveal considerable psychological insight. There is a most interesting section on preaching and preachers (which

---

[52] Paul Jacquinet, *Des Prédicateurs du XVIIe siècle avant Bossuet*, 2nd ed. (Paris: E. Bélin et fils, 1885), 288, n. 2.

[53] [François Ogier], *Actions publiques de M. François Ogier, Prestre et Prédicateur* (Paris: Louis de Villac, 1652), 157–97, cited below as Ogier. The book has a long and interesting preface on the difficulty of composing panegyrics.

[54] The unmarked division occurs at page 174 of the *Actions publiques*, just about halfway through Ogier's sermon.

Fléchier steals)—what an audience expects, and what it should; why a preacher preaches, and why he should—which gives us an illuminating glimpse into the filled pews of a Parisian church in the first half of the seventeenth century. There is a delightful passage that describes Philosophy trying to inveigle her way into the Christian Church, and a most unusual one in which Ogier favorably compares Bernard and Abelard and actually admits that, in Abelard, there were traits worthy of admiration. This is most unusual in a seventeenth-century French panegyric on Saint Bernard, where Abelard is usually depicted in wholly negative terms, a fox in the vineyard of the Lord. These more intriguing passages are all translated below. His sermon is long, even by the standards of his time—I estimate a delivery time of at least an hour and a half—so whatever he was going to say, he had plenty of time in which to say it.

Ogier preached his panegyric to a congregation of Feuillants in their church on the rue Saint-Honoré in Paris on Bernard's feast day, August 20, 1638—the date appears in the printed text[55]—and in 1638 (as is clear from the last paragraphs of Ogier's panegyric with their pleas for peace) France was at war. She was, in fact, involved in two wars, the Thirty Years' War (1618–1648) and the Franco-Spanish War (1635–1659), the latter being a result of her involvement in the former. Just two days after Ogier delivered his panegyric a French fleet attacked and destroyed a Spanish fleet at the battle of Getaria in northern Spain, but most French military ventures at this time met with disaster. On September 5 of the same year, the future Louis XIV was born at the Château of Saint-Germain-en-Laye to the west of Paris.

Ogier chooses as his text for his discourse Psalm 138:6, which he quotes only in Latin: *Mirabilis facta est scientia tua ex me*. It is, in fact, a tricky text to translate, for the *ex me* is a decidedly odd construction. The Douai-Reims version renders it as "Your knowledge has become wonderful to me," and the Hebrew

---

[55] Ogier, 157.

original reads something like "Such wonderful knowledge is far above me." In Ogier's sermon, however, it is clear that *ex me* is to be taken quite literally as "through me," not as "to me" or "above me," for God's knowledge is transmitted and made wonderful through Bernard and, ideally, through the mouth of the preacher. We must therefore translate the verse as "Your knowledge has been made wonderful through me." He then begins his panegyric in an interesting and unusual way—by asking whether he should be delivering it at all:

> If praise were as distasteful to the saints who now reign in heaven as it was odious to them when they were on earth, it would be in vain, Gentlemen, that we should take it upon ourselves to celebrate their feasts and compose their panegyrics. Instead of accepting them with pleasure, they would treat them only with contempt, knowing how easily praise can become flattery, and we would be suspected of being people who would lay traps for their virtue and wish to see them lose their humility. But now that they have been raised to such a high degree of glory, now that they are confirmed in grace and deserve to be praised from the mouth of God himself, it is not unreasonable for us, with the Church, to offer up incense. By this I mean that precious perfume that is made up of the esteem and high opinion we have of their sanctity, a perfume that gives forth an odor all the more delightful when it is burned on the altar of love and charity, which joins us anew to them in the communion of the saints. Indeed, it is of little consequence to praise them if we do not love them, and of little consequence to love them if we do not imitate them—and that is the principal goal and intention of both God and the Church in celebrating their feasts and in singing their praises.[56]

---

[56] Ogier, 157–58.

Ogier, therefore, will indeed praise Saint Bernard, for he is "our brother, our compatriot, of our blood," and because what he did so splendidly he did for France, "our common homeland."[57] He therefore invokes the Holy Spirit to assist him in his task, although, as we pointed out above, he does not tell us what that task is. Instead, he launches immediately into a discussion of the nature of God's knowledge, which must be, by definition, incomprehensible and infinite. Why? Because this divine knowledge is the knowledge by which God knows himself, and since God is incomprehensible and infinite, so too is his knowledge. We, however, are finite, and our minds are incapable of this knowledge. If they were capable, we would be able to understand God, which is *a priori* impossible. Witness Saint Paul in his letter to the Romans, "Oh the depths of the riches of the wisdom and knowledge of God! How incomprehensible are his judgments, and how unsearchable his ways! For who has known the mind of the Lord?" (Rom 11:33-34). And those who strain their brains to explain, by means of their subtle thinking,[58] divine things would do well to remember this.

But although we cannot comprehend God's infinite knowledge, we may yet understand it to some extent by its effects and how it is reflected in his creation. It is like the sun, says Ogier: we cannot look at it directly, but its light is all around us. The whole variety of creation, therefore, from the tiniest gnat to the biggest elephant, from the vilest of men to the greatest angel of the celestial hierarchy, bears witness to the workings of this divine knowledge, or, more accurately, of this divine wisdom. But of all the glories of creation (and Ogier gives a series of examples) the greatest is the human being, "this universe-in-miniature, this collection of the miracles of nature,

---

[57] Ogier, 159. Later in his panegyric Ogier again emphasizes Bernard's Frenchness and his love for his country: see n. 93 below.

[58] *Nostre subtilité* (Ogier, 160), which is always pernicious: see appendix 1, s.v. *subtil, subtilité*/subtle, subtlety.

this masterpiece of the hands of God."[59] There is nothing in the whole of nature, says our preacher, that makes God's knowledge more worthy of admiration than the structure of his—Ogier's—own being. Consider the symmetry and proportion of the human body, think of how the outer parts correspond to the inner, look at how the bodily organs facilitate the use of the senses, see what powers the body has and what it can do! It is indeed the most admirable of all the works of creation, and Ogier quotes Saint Augustine to prove his case.[60]

But if this is true of the body, what can we say of the soul, the most wonderful part of our being? It animates the body and gives it life (something it has in common with trees and plants), it provides it with sense-perception and movement (something it has in common with the animals), and—most important—it gives it reason, which makes it capable of knowledge, and this it has in common only with creatures who are divine and angelic.[61] Ogier then distinguishes between human knowledge and angelic knowledge by pointing out that, whereas angels possess the fullness of angelic knowledge from the moment of their creation (they are, by definition, celestial intelligences), human knowledge develops little by little over the course of time. There then follows a paragraph in which Ogier traces this development from the first movements of the rational soul in organizing the bodily functions to the desire of the mind to know the principles, causes, and secrets of nature. It wants to enter nature's back room (*arrière-boutique*) and study the very sources of things, but this it cannot do unless it pushes at the

---

[59] Ogier, 162.

[60] Ogier, 163, quoting Augustine, S 226.3.4; PL 38:699–700: "Man admires other things: let him admire himself as the greatest miracle!"

[61] Ogier is referring to the Aristotelian-Augustinian-Aquinian Great Chain of Being. All things are dependent on God, who alone has true existence: stones participate in being; plants in being and living; animals in being, living, and sensing; and human beings in being, living, sensing, and rationality.

door for a long, long time: "I mean by this with much sweat, work, toil, and study":

> You know this well, you learned minds, you who are possessed by this noble passion for knowing! It costs you your time, your health, and your sleep. You deprive yourselves of life's enjoyments, you rid yourselves of any interest in the mad pursuit of wealth in order to acquire this excellent quality that God has offered us as a reward for our stubborn labors, so that we may marvel at his knowledge by means of our own, since [his knowledge] is the source of ours and [our knowledge] is a marvellous emanation from his: *Mirabilis scientia tua ex me* ["Your knowledge is wonderful through me"].[62]

But beyond this there is a knowledge that comes from God, which is not based on first principles, which does not proceed in stages, which is not subject to error, and which can have a profound impact on other minds. Anyone who has this knowledge may truly say, "Surely, Lord, your knowledge has become wonderful in me!" "Such, Gentlemen, was the knowledge of the great Saint Bernard: a knowledge that, when put into practice, was the source of all his fine deeds and whose exercise occupied the entire course of his life."[63]

We have finally arrived. It has taken Ogier nine pages—just about a quarter of his panegyric—but we have now arrived at Saint Bernard himself. God, we are told, raised him up to influence the mind of the whole church, especially the minds of its pastors and principal ministers, and to renew its apostolic spirit, whose first concern had been to proclaim the doctrine

---

[62] Ogier, 164. Human beings are not rational in their own right, but only because they participate in the rationality of God. In other words, human knowledge is a participation in (or emanation of) God's knowledge.

[63] Ogier, 165.

of salvation. The knowledge possessed by the apostles was not acquired through work and study, it was not the result of sleepless nights and long deliberation. Just as something is lit up at the very moment the sun's rays fall upon it, so their understanding was enlightened by the knowledge of things divine and human, to the extent that God judged it necessary for establishing the Faith. He provided them with all that they needed to stand before emperors and judges, to dispute with philosophers, and to teach all nations the mysteries of the Christian religion. They had no need to think about what to say, for the Lord himself had told them that, in the hour they needed it, he would inspire them with what they should say and how they should respond.[64]

Such had been the school in which Bernard, too, had received his instruction: "He did not owe his divine eloquence to the Masters of Rhetoric, nor his philosophy to the books of Aristotle, nor his deep understanding of the Scriptures to the ancient Fathers and exegetes."[65] It came, rather, from the source of Truth itself, the treasury of knowledge, the abyss of wisdom, and Ogier distinguishes between acquired knowledge, which is gained through using the human mind aided by study, and inspired knowledge, which comes directly from God. The former does not have the same "secret influence" on us as does the latter, especially when it comes to the question of persuasion, or of "moving" or "touching" the human will.[66] And by acquired knowledge, Ogier also means (alas!) the divine knowledge acquired in theological schools and preached in the pulpit. It, too, has little effect. It is a miracle, he says, if,

---

[64] See Matt 10:19.

[65] Ogier, 166. We must treat this statement as panegyrical license. Bernard might not have learned much from Aristotle, but he had immersed himself in the writings of the Fathers. Antoine Anselme's panegyric on Bernard as the Last of the Fathers provides a much more accurate picture.

[66] Ogier, 167.

among all those thousands—*plusieurs milliers*—who listen to a sermon, even one goes home better persuaded of the truth of the Faith or more disposed to act in accordance with its principles. This distinction between the two sorts of knowledge is stolen by Fléchier and appears, almost word for word, in his own panegyric.

But the knowledge infused by God is totally different. It has real power. Think of Saint Peter after the Holy Spirit has descended on him and his colleagues as tongues of fire! Did he not bring three thousand souls into the Christian church in one day?[67] That indeed is impressive! But consider now Saint Bernard! Peter's achievements were the achievements of a mature man, but Bernard, while still young, converted every member of a large family, a family that included his closest relations! His brothers, his uncles, his sisters[68] were the first to esteem him, hear him, and follow him, and "persuaded by him, they renounced their possessions, their fortune, their nobility, to follow this young man in practising what the gospels counseled."[69] This is the first actual historical fact that Ogier mentions (and that not very accurately). We will see whether he adds any more.

Ogier now contrasts the way in which all Bernard's family renounced everything they had with the members of his audience, who rejoice in their servitude to the things of this world, and who are thereby in possession of far more effective ways of destroying themselves. Not so were those who divorced themselves forever from worldly things to withdraw with the saint into the solitude. This leads him to introduce a story from Greek/Roman mythology—something for which he has been criticized by Albert and Court—and bring us to the poor and rustic cottage of Baucis and Philemon. Ogier attributes the story

---

[67] See Acts 2:41.
[68] Brothers, uncles, and sisters all appear in the plural, which, except for the brothers, is something of an exaggeration.
[69] Ogier, 169.

to "the poets," but it was, in fact, the work of only one poet, Ovid, in Book 8 of his *Metamorphoses*. Baucis and Philemon are an old married couple living in a small town in Phrygia when Zeus/Jupiter and Hermes/Mercury descend to earth, disguised as peasants, and seek a night's lodging in the town. All the doors are slammed in their faces until they come to the humble cottage of Baucis and Philemon, who welcome them, make them comfortable, and offer them in hospitality everything they have. Jupiter rewards them by telling them to accompany him to the top of the mountain just outside the town since he intends to destroy the place for its gross lack of hospitality. This he does, and when they reach the summit, Baucis and Philemon see that the entire town has been swept away by a flood, and that the only surviving structure is their own house, which has now been transformed into a splendid temple. The old couple ask Jupiter if they might be guardians of the temple until their deaths, and that when one of them dies, the other might die at the same time. Both wishes were granted, and upon their deaths, Baucis and Philemon were changed into two intertwined trees, one an oak, the other a linden.

So what does Ogier draw from this? Not very much, as a matter of fact, and to be honest, the story does not have much point. But if this tale is astonishing, he says, here is something every bit as astonishing (and much more credible): a whole family—Bernard's family—is transformed from being worldly to being religious, and a household that, though it could not be called profane, was composed of people of the world was suddenly converted to holiness and virtue. "And what brought about this marvel? The preaching, the discourse, of a young lad. And who put into his mouth such persuasive words and such effective teaching? The inspiration of God."[70]

So who were his teachers in these matters? The woods and the trees, the oaks and the beeches—Ogier quotes the *Vita*

[70] Ogier, 171.

prima[71]—and it was among these that he was instructed by "a secret Master" for the salvation of all men and women. Fléchier says just the same thing. The ancient writers, continues Ogier, tell us that the most excellent effect of speech and eloquence was to lead human beings out of their forests and caves, where they had lived almost as savage beasts, and unite them together as states and republics where they might live in societal harmony under a body of common laws. We, however, will say just the opposite. The most notable effect of the inspired knowledge and preaching of Saint Bernard was to take men and women away from the towns, away from the business of worldly affairs, away from the courts of princes, and lead them into the solitude—not to make them savages, but to make them angels, not to have them hate human society, but to join them more closely to God. And come they did, all sorts and conditions of men and women from all walks of life. Indeed, everyone might have come to his cloister if God had not sent him forth to teach everyone, for it was not God's will, says Ogier, that Bernard's inspired abilities and competence should be employed only in directing a monastic family. No. His talent was too universal to be confined within such strict limits and was owed to the whole church and the entire Christian world.[72] But he adapted his guidance to those he guided. He taught the common people with a superior and paternal authority, but when he had to reprove prelates and high ecclesiastics, he did so with humility and filial, not servile, obedience. There is no better example of this than his five books, *De consideratione*, addressed to Pope Eugenius III, and Ogier (like many of the

---

[71] Ogier, 171, quoting a slightly amended version of *Vita prima* 1.4.23 (William of Saint-Thierry); PL 185:240D; CF 76:26–27. It is rare that the panegyrists do not mention the woods and trees as Bernard's teachers.

[72] If Ogier's panegyric had had divisions, this is where the second division would have begun, with Bernard's achievements outside the cloister (Ogier, 174): see n. 54 above.

panegyrists) spends some time in contrasting the honorific titles with which Bernard praises the pope with the reproofs he is obliged to address to him.

At this time, too, the unity of the church and the purity of its doctrine were being threatened by schism and heresy, and there was no doctor more opposed to these enemies of the Faith than Bernard, and no doctor who fought against these monsters more firmly, more courageously, and more effectively, both with voice and pen. The heretics were men such as Peter of Bruys (Ogier is the only one of the panegyrists we deal with to mention him[73]), Arnold of Brescia, Henry of Toulouse, and Peter Abelard (whom we shall meet again), but far more dangerous to the unity of the church was the papal schism. We are on familiar ground here, but Ogier's account is very brief. He makes a fairly obvious pun on the name of "the famous Antipope Leon"—he becomes the rapacious Lion seeking to invade the Apostolic See—and we meet, but only in passing, two of his most influential supporters, Peter of Pisa, "the greatest canonist of his day,"[74] and Roger, king of Sicily. Bernard then takes center stage, Bernard the Shield of the Faith and the Oracle of the Holy Spirit, who, with his inspired knowledge, defeats the imposter, destroys all the machinations of those seeking to support him in the schism, and "reunites the faithful in the same flock under the same shepherd."[75] Ogier, however, provides no detail as to how exactly this was achieved and moves on to Bernard's victories in the secular world. He brokers peace between contending armies, and "it is he who throws the caduceus into the midst of the combatants, calms their fury, and reconciles them together."[76] Here again we see Ogier the Classicist, for the caduceus, the short staff with its entwined serpents carried by Hermes/Mercury, was

[73] See appendix 2, s.v. Peter of Bruys.
[74] Ogier, 178.
[75] Ogier, 180.
[76] Ogier, 180.

also carried by human heralds and when brought into battle signified a desire and need for negotiation and mediation.

Ogier then moves on to the most significant involvement of Bernard in the world outside the cloister, namely, the disaster of the Second Crusade: "It is Bernard who joins together the Christian princes in such a holy undertaking, and if it did not succeed as it had begun, it was because they did not follow his wise counsels."[77] That is all Ogier has to say (and Fléchier steals it word for word), and from a historical point of view, it is, of course, nonsense, but Ogier is preaching a panegyric, not writing history. Fénelon, Antoine Anselme, and Louis-Bénigne Bourru provide much longer explanations for the failure of the Crusade, based on Bernard's own *apologiae* for the fiasco in his letter to Pope Eugenius and in Book II of the *De consideratione*.

We now move on to a further consideration of the nature and demands of Christian unity, and Ogier begins by telling us that "the whole of Christian perfection is contained in two articles: to be faithful, and to be a good person; in a word, to believe rightly and to act rightly."[78] But the understanding and union by which God joins us to himself through the Christian religion, and by which Christians are themselves joined to one another, is quite different from the sort of unity that we may see in a well-run state, or even between good friends. In human friendships it is enough to give our will and affection to the other person, while retaining our own ideas and judgment. Consider, says our classical preacher, the deep friendship of Brutus and Cassius,[79] one an Epicurean, the other a Stoic, whose beliefs were directly opposed and irreconcilable, yet whose friendship was firm and unshakeable. But this is not the same as that Christian charity that unites us with each other and with God. That unity is based not just on shared affection

---

[77] Ogier, 180.
[78] Ogier, 182: *en un mot, à bien croire, & à bien faire*.
[79] I.e., the two most important coconspirators in the plot to assassinate Julius Caesar.

but on shared belief. Brutus and Cassius were true friends who were happy to disagree, but this cannot be the case with us and God. Nor indeed can it be the case among Christians, who are united not just by mutual affection but by an unwavering acceptance of the truths of the Faith. We can appreciate, therefore, Bernard's overwhelming concern for the purity of Catholic doctrine, and we can understand his determination that human knowledge should never go beyond the limits set by the Fathers. And he was right to be concerned.

> For it was in his time, Gentlemen, that Philosophy, that had long been banned from the Christian school, battered on the door to be let in; and to make her entry easier, she put forth certain proposals that well merited consideration. "Long ago," she said, "you chased me out of your school as if I were a Mistress of Deception who, by the subtlety of my sophisms—or, rather, by my deceptive illusions—wished to stifle the truth of the Gospel at its birth. Your teachers and your apostles denounced me as the voice of deceit, the instrument of doubt, the imposter laying traps for Christian simplicity. Your great Saint Paul is careful to warn you to be on your guard against my surprise attacks, and your learned Tertullian, my sworn enemy, paints me in such dark colors that he makes me appear as a monster and accuses me of doing much wrong—as if I were only good for providing heretics and unbelievers with their ideas.[80] But now that I wish to be Christian, I endure these [attacks] with patience."[81]

In other words, Philosophy now promises to do away with her reliance on the natural world and the axioms of Aristotle and to use all her power, arguments, and syllogisms to defend the principles of the Gospel and grace. She declares herself now to

---

[80] See Tertullian, *De praescriptionibus adversus haereticos* 7; PL 2:19A–21A. Tertullian was always a favorite with the panegyrists.

[81] Ogier, 184–85.

be *in obsequium fidei*, "in the service of the Faith,"[82] and wishes to enter the church not as its head but as its servant, and to do all that she can to help the truths of the Gospel to flourish.

These proposals, says Ogier, did indeed deserve consideration, and it might have been possible for Philosophy and the church to come to terms. But alas! she was welcomed too avidly by certain "subtle minds," she was brought into the church too quickly and not yet cleansed from views that were too irreverent and too liberal. "She spoke about the mysteries of religion with too much freedom and explained them in terms unfamiliar to the Christian school. In short, she would pass over into heresy and create sects in the Church, just as she did long ago in the family of the philosophers."[83]

The worst of these new heretics was, of course, Peter Abelard, though Ogier (most unusually) also recognizes his more admirable qualities, not least his penitential life and his holy death. This leads him to compare Abelard and Bernard, and the paragraph in which he does so deserves translation:

> In both these men we may see a great similarity in birth, age, eloquence, and studies. Both enjoyed a great reputation in the mouths and esteem of others, but this they achieved in very different ways. The one excelled in divine knowledge, which, as we have said, he had acquired by inspiration; the other triumphed in human knowledge, which he acquired by means of a good brain and unstinting labor. The innocence of the one made him worthy of respect; the penitence of the other made him worthy of admiration. Saint Bernard's vocation is more perfect, for he was called from his earliest childhood, before the contagion of the world could have any effect on his spirit or corrupt the purity of his habits. Abelard's vocation is admirable: he was a man

---

[82] Ogier refers to 2 Cor 10:5, which actually reads *in obsequium Christi*. *Obsequium fidei* occurs in Phil 2:17.

[83] Ogier, 185–86.

involved in the most violent of youthful passions, in loving, in hating, and in vengeance; [but then,] struck, touched by God, both in his body by a wound and in his soul by the inspiration of God's grace, he goes to weep for his sins in a desert.[84]

This is a remarkable passage, and stands in sharp contrast to the picture of Abelard drawn by virtually all the other panegyrists. I cannot recall any one of them ever saying that Abelard was worthy of admiration. Yet Ogier obviously cannot stop here and must go on to lead both men before the bishops assembled at Sens (Ogier does not mention the name, referring only to a *conférence publique*). Here the similarities give way to differences: "On the one side I see holiness; on the other, doctrine. Here I see religion, piety, the faith of our Fathers; there I see innovation, philosophy, human reasoning, and—in a word—error, armed with arguments and syllogisms."[85] Yet Abelard is defeated and vanquished, for he could not oppose the Spirit of God, who spoke through the mouth of his saint.

On the other hand, what is so remarkable about Bernard's victory is that Abelard was not only vanquished but persuaded of his errors. That this is not historically the case is neither here nor there: the panegyrists, as we have said, were not writing history. "They can be conquered," says an ancient writer with regard to certain heretics; "they cannot be persuaded."[86] Such a conversion, therefore, was no small triumph for the church and leads us yet again to admire the effectiveness of God's knowledge in the mouth of Saint Bernard: *Mirabilis facta est scientia tua ex me*, "Your knowledge is made wonderful through me."

---

[84] Ogier, 187. The wound in his body refers to Abelard's castration as a result of his love affair with Héloïse. Abelard then entered the abbey of Saint-Denis near Paris.

[85] Ogier, 187. As we know well, innovation—the *novitates* of 1 Tim 6:20—are always suspect. See appendix 1, s.v. *nouveautés* / novelties.

[86] Ogier, 188. The ancient writer is Jerome, *Contra Luciferianos* 28; PL 23:182B, reading *facilius eos vinci posse, quam persuaderi*.

Conversion, however, is not just for individuals like Abelard, not just for the conversion of heretics, but for the conversion of all Christians. Such, indeed, is the purpose of preaching, but is it really effective?

> We preach, we speak, we orate. The pulpits resound with invectives against vice. We thunder against extravagance, immodesty, usury, graft, breach of faith, inhumanity, injustice—but do we see people being any more modest, any more frugal at their banquets, any more chaste in their marriages? Do we observe fewer money-lenders at the Exchange, fewer thieves in the financial world, less infidelity in civil society, less favoritism, iniquity, and underhand dealings in judgments? No, Gentlemen. Ah! How comes it that so many good sermons are delivered in vain?[87]

Ogier will tell us, and what he says offers us a little vignette—a decidedly critical vignette—of preachers and preaching in seventeenth-century France. Much of the blame, he says, is to be laid at the door of the preacher's audience. Why do they come to church?

> They come to hear the sermon simply as a public monologue, where they are not so much listeners as judges. They do not come with the intention of correcting their own faults, but to criticize the faults of the preacher. They do not come to put their own lives in order, but to see whether the preacher's periods are properly proportioned and delivered with a well-measured cadence. [They do not come] to be appropriately moved, but to see whether the preacher's movements are appropriate.[88] [They do not come] to color themselves with virtue, but to see whether the colors of rhetoric have been properly applied.[89]

---

[87] Ogier, 188–89.
[88] On the bodily gestures expected of a preacher at this period, see chap. 3.
[89] Ogier, 189.

And the preachers themselves are no better:

> What they preach is themselves! All they have in view for themselves are vanity, plaudits, and miters! What they do has nothing in common with what they say. They give far too much weight to their own ingenuity. They woo their listeners to gain their applause. The only reason they compose the panegyrics of the saints with so much study and display is that people may sing panegyrics of them when they have left the pulpit![90]

How different was Saint Bernard! He preached only Jesus Christ, not himself, and he proclaimed the truth without any trace of self-interest. He had no concern at all with the approbation of the crowd, and in him there was not the least vestige of pride and no desire for rank or status. He saw his own disciples elevated to the highest positions in the church—even to the very throne of Saint Peter—without the least trace of envy and would have been content simply to remain in his cell if he had not been called forth to proclaim the way of salvation to all men and women and to preach penitence. And forth he came, preaching in towns, castles, and villages in France, Germany, and Italy (this will also appear in Fléchier) and gaining a great reputation not only for his words but also for his deeds—especially his miracles. Ogier, however, provides no details of these, but summarizes them as so many paralytics being restored to health, so many blind people having their sight restored, and so many who were desperately sick being cured. But the real power of the miracles, he tells us, was that they paved the way for the power and impact of Bernard's words, words that (as Saint Paul says in the epistle to the Hebrews) penetrated to the joints, to the marrow, to the most secret places of the heart.[91]

---

[90] Ogier, 189–90.
[91] Ogier, 191, quoting Heb 4:12.

If you do not believe this, says our preacher, if you think this is exaggeration and hyperbole, then read his words for yourselves! Open his books and read what he has to say! Ogier himself was certainly moved and impressed, but, in a charming passage, he asks himself why:

> As for me, Christians, I do not know whether it was because I was nourished from my youth by the reading of his divine works, or whether my love of my country makes me take more kindly to books written by a Frenchman than by a foreigner, or (which is rather more credible) that there is some secret power of persuasion that dominates the discourses of this divine man; but it happened that I could never cast my eyes on them without receiving in my soul a certain stimulus,[92] which, in truth, does not force you, but which urges and goads you unceasingly until you have no choice but to transform your good intentions into specific plans formed by piety and virtue.[93]

The problem for us, of course, is that we no longer have Bernard with us. His words and discourses are now bereft of his physical presence, his modest mien, his mortified countenance. It is the same sword that strikes the blow, says Ogier, but it is not wielded by the same arm nor with the same strength. All is lost. Or is it?

"No, Gentlemen, I am wrong! Just as Saint Bernard has left us the traces of his divine eloquence in his writings, he has also left us the living and breathing image of his life in the persons of his disciples!"[94] And we must remember that Ogier is

---

[92] *Éguillon*, which is a most unusual word, and perhaps a little affected. It comes from the Latin *aculeus*, a prick or sting, and is related to the modern French *aiguille*, a needle. An *éguillon* is a sort of goading stimulus that, in this case, never lets up.
[93] Ogier, 192–93.
[94] Ogier, 194.

preaching to a congregation of Feuillants. Bernard lived again in them, not only in the way in which they follow his example in proclaiming the word of God from the pulpit, "but even more because their life, reformed on the model of their great Patriarch, is a perpetual preaching and a public censure of the vices and degenerate morals of the world."[95] This then leads Ogier to contrast their simple, holy, and ordered way of life with the extravagance, disorder, and so on of those who live in the world, and this, in turn, leads him to his final exhortation. He bewails our hardness of heart, our stupidity, our unparalleled blindness. How can we expect Bernard's words to penetrate this armor? How can we expect this stubborn obduracy to give way to conversion? "Who is there now who can truly say what we have said to God in his name with such good cause: *Mirabilis facta est scientia tua ex me*? ["Your knowledge is made wonderful through me.] O personage divine! May your knowledge be made wonderful *ex me, ex me* ["through me, through me"]! By my conversion, by the change in my own life, by the practice of your virtues, and by fulfilling your beneficent counsels!"[96]

This indeed is the best way to praise the saint—by imitating him! Ogier returns to the very first paragraph of his panegyric. The best way we can honor him is by walking in his steps and by reforming our life and morals on his model. No, we do not need to be monks or nuns. We do not all need to follow the strict and austere rule that his faithful disciples—the Feuillants—observe so assiduously. But all Christians are obliged to keep the commandments of God and the precepts of divine love, and happy are we that, in these matters, Bernard has left us such admirable lessons.

> O great saint, who reigns in Heaven with Jesus Christ, even though you are a member of God's own

---

[95] Ogier, 194.
[96] Ogier, 196.

household and a fellow citizen of the saints in the heavenly Jerusalem; even though your zeal extends universally over the whole Church, you have not laid aside the special love[97] you had for your homeland. Look upon her with pity, and consider how she is afflicted as much by her vices as by her miseries.

As we ask grace and pardon from God for our sins through your intercession, so through the same [intercession] we ask for an end to our sorrows. Long ago you brokered a peace between the most antagonistic of princes through your wise negotiations; inspire them now with the same [desire for peace] through your fervent prayers. You have been the successful mediator; be now the indulgent intercessor, so that we, having [found] Christian and spiritual peace through our pardoned sins, and civil peace through an end to the war, may enjoy a day of eternal peace in Paradise with you. Amen.[98]

Such is François Ogier's eulogy of Saint Bernard. As we said at the beginning of this chapter, it is certainly not without its faults, and the criticisms levied against it by Albert, Court, and Tréverret are not without foundation. But it has a number of interesting and sometimes delightful passages, and Valentin-Esprit Fléchier found it sufficiently engaging to steal most of it for his own panegyric on the saint. Ogier makes no great display of his sources. The only names that appear in the text are those of Aristotle and Tertullian; Jerome appears as *un Ancien*; Ovid is "the poets"; and there are marginal references to Augustine, Accursius,[99] and the *Vita prima*. Of Bernard's own works, he cites only a few letters and the *De consideratione*.

---

[97] *Charité*, but, for once, the word is better translated simply as "love."

[98] Ogier, 196–97.

[99] Ogier refers to a gloss in Accursius's *De quinque pedum praescriptione*, in which Abelard is reported as having said "I do not know"

His classical learning appears more as an atmosphere than as specific citations. Bernard the miracle worker is dismissed in a single sentence, and of Bernard the mystic, the Bernard of the fourth degree of love in the *De diligendo Deo*, there is no trace. Let us see, then, how Esprit Fléchier adopts and adapts (or, if one prefers, steals and changes) his predecessor's panegyric.

Valentin-Esprit Fléchier

Esprit Fléchier was a preacher far better known than either Claude Lion or François Ogier. He was born on June 10, 1632, in the little village of Pernes (since 1936, Pernes-les-Fontaines[100]) in the south of France, but was brought up by his uncle, superior of the *Congrégation des Doctrinaires* (or *Prêtres de la doctrine chrétienne*), at Tarascon, just thirty miles to the southwest. The congregation had been founded in 1592 with the purpose of providing catechetical instruction to the French countryside and by the time of Fléchier's childhood owned numerous houses, schools, colleges, and seminaries. Fléchier himself entered the congregation at the age of fifteen but found its regulations too restrictive, and, when his uncle died, he left and went to Paris, where he devoted himself to writing poetry. His poems in Latin were more highly esteemed than those in French. Once in Paris, he was appointed tutor to Louis-Urbain de Caumartin, councilor of state and intendant of finance under Louis XIV, and then (with others, including Bossuet) tutor to the dauphin. He was also made almoner-in-ordinary (effectively a chaplain) to the dauphine. Meanwhile he was becoming known for his sermons, especially his panegyrics and funeral orations, and his preaching caught the attention and gained the favor of the king, who rewarded him first by

---

(*Nescio*) for the one and only time in his life: see François and Élisabeth C. P. Guizot, *Abailard et Héloïse: Essai historique* (Paris: Didier, 1856), 346.

[100] With some justice: there are more than forty fountains in the village, most installed in the second half of the eighteenth century.

making him commendatory abbot of Saint-Séverin in the diocese of Poitiers, then, in 1685, bishop of Lavaur, and finally bishop of Nîmes. The year 1685 was also that in which Louis XIV revoked the Edict of Nantes, but there remained a strong contingent of Calvinists in Nîmes. Fléchier's approach to them was lenient and charitable, and although he succeeded in converting only a few, he was highly respected by the Protestants both during his episcopacy and after his death at Montpellier, aged seventy-seven, on February 16, 1710.

Fléchier enjoyed a great reputation as a preacher in his own day—Louis XIV certainly liked him—but not everyone agrees that that reputation was entirely justified. There is no doubt about the beauty of his language and the balanced harmony of his discourses, though his use of antithesis is sometimes (indeed, more than sometimes) overdone. Albert and Court praise the skill, refinement, eloquence, and nobility of his sermons, especially the funeral orations and panegyrics, but (they say) his delivery in the pulpit had something of a mournful (*lugubre*) quality that poured cold water on the fire of his expressions.[101] The *abbé* Trublet agreed.[102] Fléchier, he says, never lacked grace or power, but the grace sometimes became affectation, and the power sometimes became a harangue. There was little unction and warmth in his discourses. Moreover, his careful study of the sermons of older preachers and the way in which he had assimilated their ideas gave to his own sermons an old-fashioned quality, more appropriate to the beginning of his century. "He preached," said Trublet, "with old taste and modern style."[103] As we shall see, there is not the slightest

---

[101] Albert / Court, 96–101.

[102] See Nicolas-Charles-Joseph Trublet, *Panégyriques des Saints, précédés de réflexions sur l'éloquence en général, et sur celle de la Chaire en particulier* (Paris: Briasson, 1755), 74–75. Trublet, archdeacon and canon of Saint-Malo, lived from 1697 to 1770.

[103] Trublet, *Panégyriques*, 75: "Il prêchoit avec un vieux goût & un style moderne."

doubt that his panegyric on Bernard is based on a panegyric preached forty-five years earlier.

Cardinal Maury, writing in the second half of the eighteenth century, noted that Fléchier's panegyrics, once studied in colleges as masterpieces of rhetoric, have how fallen from the position they once enjoyed (he uses the term *usurped*),[104] and he speaks of Fléchier's being "seduced by dazzling antitheses, or confined by the demands of a measured delivery, high-flown and harmonious."[105] Tréverret is even more severe.[106] He agrees with Albert and Court that Fléchier's panegyrics are superior to his sermons, but he strongly disagrees with those who speak of Fléchier as "the master of the genre," *le maître du genre*. On the contrary. Though his panegyrics are almost always a pleasure to hear, Tréverret also finds them *faible*: weak or shallow or lacking in substance.[107] Fléchier, he says, studies and analyzes the character of the saints he celebrates, but rather than telling us their story, he presents us with a "moral portrait" (*portrait moral*)—he *paints* their life rather than recounting it.[108] He sets before us the principles of their conduct and the nature of their virtues, but he does not know how to communicate to us the true fervor or fire of the saints. No, says Tréverret, there is no doubt that Fléchier is an able artist, but only of the second or perhaps even the third rank. When, at the end of his panegyrics, he exhorts us to imitate the virtues of the saint, his exhortations are cold and lacking in color (*froides et monotones*),[109] and when you have read one you have read them all. This is not to say that there are not

---

[104] Maury, 1:175: "Les panégyriques de Fléchier . . . sont étrangement déchus aujourd'hui de la gloire qu'ils avoient usurpée."

[105] Maury, 1:199: "séduit par des antithèses éblouissantes, ou resserré dans l'alignement d'une diction cadencée, nombreuse et sonore."

[106] See Tréverret, chap. VIII (122–57), for his estimate of Fléchier.

[107] Tréverret, 134.

[108] Tréverret, 137.

[109] Tréverret, 144.

occasional passages in which Fléchier charms and surprises his listeners, but they are unfortunately rare. Tréverret agrees with the *abbé* Trublet that Fléchier's sermons tend to be rather old-fashioned—he looks backward to Senault and Ogier rather than forward to Bossuet and Bourdaloue—and although he is a most competent writer and a fine observer, he has certainly been overrated. His eloquent panegyrics deserve to be mentioned with honor, but Fléchier is not the great preacher some have maintained him to be.

Most of these criticisms may be seen in Fléchier's panegyric on Bernard.[110] He does not recount the life of the saint—he follows Ogier in providing a minimum of historical fact—and he does indeed paint a *portrait moral* in broad and sweeping strokes. His discourse is rather old-fashioned in style (which is hardly surprising given that it is based on a panegyric delivered when Fléchier was six), and I think one must admit that the exhortation at the end is unimpressive. On the other hand, the language (with its many antitheses) is delightful, and rarely affected. If it were delivered in the "lugubrious tone" mentioned by Albert and Court, it might indeed lack unction and warmth, but, reading it myself, I found some parts of it extremely effective.

Like Ogier, Fléchier, too, preached his panegyric to a congregation of Feuillants in their church on the rue Saint-Honoré in Paris. The date was August 20, 1683.[111] Louis XIV had been forty years on the throne, and less than a month after Fléchier had delivered his discourse, the Ottoman Turks were defeated

---

[110] *Panégyriques et autres sermons, Prêchés par Messire Esprit Fléchier Evêque de Nîmes, ci-devant Aumônier Ordinaire de Madame La Dauphine. Tome second* (Paris: G. Martin, J.-B. Coignard, et les Frères Guerin, 1741), 45–85; *Œuvres complètes de Fléchier, Évêque de Nîmes, et membre de l'Académie française, publiées par M. L'Abbé Migne. Tome premier* (Paris: J.-P. Migne, 1836), cols. 719–33 (Sermon 11). All citations below are to the 1741 edition, cited simply as Fléchier.

[111] The date and place are given at the beginning of the panegyric (Fléchier, 45).

before the gates of Vienna. Fléchier chose as his text the same verse from the book of Wisdom—Wisdom 10:10—that Bourru would use for his second panegyric on Bernard and translates it thus: "[God] gave him the knowledge of the saints,[112] he made him glorious in his works, and he heaped blessing upon him."[113] But Fléchier begins his panegyric by reminding us not of Bernard's greatness, but of his humility. However great he was before God and human beings, he was always insignificant in his own eyes. Whatever praise he deserved, he would accept none. He believed his faults to be all too true, and his virtues all too flawed. And he was the only one who did not believe that he was indeed a saint. In his eyes, all the good that was said of him was either a trap to undermine what he regarded as his insecure humility or an act of charity at the expense of truth and justice.

But despite Bernard's view of himself, Fléchier is about to praise him. The fact of his undoubted humility cannot conceal his consummate virtues, and it is the business of a preacher to preach the word of God so as to encourage the faithful by the example of those who have put that word into practice with wisdom and constancy. Fléchier then beseeches the Mother of God to help him in his task:

> Holy Virgin, you regarded him as your son,[114] and he honored you as his Mother. You were the object of his

---

[112] *Scientia sanctorum*, which the Douai-Reims version translates, correctly, as "knowledge of holy things." Fléchier's exegesis, however, demands "the knowledge of the saints."

[113] Wis 10:10, which should be translated literally as "[Wisdom] gave him the knowledge of holy things, honored him in his labors, and completed his labors." There is no mention of heaping him with blessings. But as we have seen many times, the panegyrists have no hesitation in adapting a scriptural text to their own needs.

[114] This is probably a vague allusion to the miracle of the Lactation, but Fléchier says no more about it. For a much fuller account, see chap. 11 (Boudon), §§1–2.

tender and pious devotion and the most moving subject of his praises. If his heartfelt exhortations drew to you so many vows and so much respect, and if through your potent intercession you obtained for him so much illumination and so many graces, we now implore your help and hope for it, and we say to you with the angel: *Ave Maria*.[115]

When the Church is afflicted with troubles and error, God sends to its assistance those who can preserve its truth and reestablish its discipline. These are the saints. To assist them in this, he enlightens them with his light, so that they, in turn, might enlighten others; he gives them the authority they need to reaffirm the demands of morality and destroy the stumbling blocks of error, and he rewards them by the success he gives to all that they do and the blessings he showers on their words and their works. But if we may see these graces in all the saints, we may see them even more clearly and more wonderfully in Saint Bernard. And thus, says Fléchier, for the instruction and edification of his congregation, he will speak of three things: (1) how Saint Bernard was filled with the knowledge of God, (2) how Saint Bernard was clothed in the glory and power of God, and (3) how Saint Bernard was accompanied by the grace of God in everything he did.[116] But there is nothing in what he will say that will be new to us.

When we speak of Bernard's knowledge, we are not speaking of "a pretentious accumulation of sterile and empty learning, acquired by work and study, and fed by curiosity[117] and

---

[115] Fléchier, 47–48.

[116] The numbers appear in the text. It seems from this that there will be three parts to Fléchier's sermon, but this is not the case. Following Ogier, it has but two parts (with some trifling overlap): the first, as usual, deals with Bernard's life within the cloister; the second with his life outside it.

[117] *Curiosité*, as always, is a pejorative term, and curiosity is to be avoided at all costs. See appendix 1, s.v. *curiosité* / curiosity.

pride, which often falls into error and inconsistency."[118] No indeed. "I speak of a knowledge that has its source in God's knowledge, which is formed more in the heart than in the head, which is maintained by humility and prayer, and which produces justice and charity."[119] Such is the knowledge of the saints, the *scientia sanctorum*, with which Bernard was gifted from his infancy. The child Jesus himself appeared to him on the night of Christmas in the old chapel of Saint-Vorles at Châtillon-sur-Seine and revealed to him there the mystery of his holy nativity,[120] something that remained with Bernard for the whole of his life. As a consequence, he determined that all that he did should be for the sake of Jesus Christ alone, and this led him to an utter contempt for the world with all its dangers and temptations. Fléchier then tells us in fairly general terms (save for the famous episode of the icy pool) how Bernard overcame all these temptations, and contrasts Bernard's achievements with ours, we who walk "without fear and without precautions"[121] in a world that subtly seduces our hearts and minds.

From these early experiences, Bernard realizes that the only effective way to conquer the world and all its perils is to flee it, and this he does—but does so in an unusual way. Those whom God calls to the religious life, says Fléchier, usually keep quiet about their intention until the moment they actually put it into practice. They are all too aware of the obstacles that might be placed in their path by parents, relatives, friends—even by themselves—and they confide their plans to God alone. Not so Bernard! He tells all his friends and all his family, and, not being content just to inform them of his plans, he wants to lead them, too, in a general withdrawal from the world. But where shall he go? He has no interest in easygoing abbeys where

---

[118] Fléchier, 49–50.
[119] Fléchier, 50.
[120] Fléchier, 50–51. See n. 13 above.
[121] Fléchier, 52.

monks may hide under their habits inclinations and desires that are still far too worldly: "If they plan to be solitaries, their desire, at the least, is to make for themselves a solitude to their liking. They renounce worldly dignities, but they still wish to be honored for their piety, and to comfort themselves for having withdrawn from men, they are quite happy that men, in their turn, should come to them."[122] Bernard will have none of this, and Fléchier quotes a slightly variant form of a saying that appears in the letter to the Carthusian brethren of Mont-Dieu, the Golden Letter: *Si vis incipere, perfecte incipe*: "If you want to begin, begin perfectly."[123] So when Bernard speaks of withdrawal from the world, he means withdrawal from the world, and "he sought for himself a retreat where he could forget the world, where he himself could be forgotten, and where he could practise virtue without having the reputation of being virtuous."[124]

Fléchier then tell us of the origins of Cîteaux fifteen years earlier, and how the severity of its strict discipline, its stringent poverty, and its wholly penitential way of life had reduced its numbers to almost nothing. But it was to this poor house that Bernard came, and it was here that he hid himself, dying to himself and to others: "This solitude was for him a sort of school of knowledge and holiness where his spirit, purifying itself and separating itself in a certain way from his body, was more susceptible to the impressions of grace."[125] Like Ogier and many of the other panegyrists, Fléchier refers to the oaks and beeches as Bernard's masters and asks them, "How many

---

[122] Fléchier, 55.

[123] Fléchier, 55. In Fléchier's day, the Golden Letter of William of Saint-Thierry circulated under the name of Bernard. What William actually says is *Si incipis, incipe perfecte* (*ps.*-Bernard / William of Saint-Thierry, *Ep ad fratres de Monte Dei* 4.11; PL 184:315B; SCh 223:174 [§39]).

[124] Fléchier, 55.

[125] Fléchier, 57.

times did he wander among your shady ways, or sit motionless in contemplation of a mystery that occupied him, or a passage of Scripture whose sense and meaning he sought with humility?"[126] How different, alas, are we, in our concern with outward things, with the vanities of the world, and we devote ourselves so much to them that we are neither worthy nor capable of understanding the things of God. Bernard, however, had no time for or interest in anything else but God. He was perfectly recollected,[127] and so dead to himself that he saw without seeing, heard without hearing, and ate without tasting. The natural world had become invisible to him, and his curiosity—that vice for which Bernard had no time at all—was not only mortified but well and truly dead. Is it surprising, then, that in this total preoccupation with God, God would reveal to him his secrets?

There is a difference, says Fléchier (who here follows Ogier almost word for word), between knowledge acquired through study and knowledge inspired by God. The former does not possess that secret power that can touch the heart and change the mind, and what it produces is empty admiration, not effective conversion. The latter, however, demands that it be heard, penetrates the spirit, and produces that conversion that every preacher seeks, and such, of course, was the wholly divine knowledge of Saint Bernard. Fléchier then reminds us of all those who came to the saint to receive his instruction, and how Bernard himself, in his zeal for the salvation of souls, came forth from his cloister "to proclaim the truth, to preach penitence, and to inform us—you and me—of our obligations."[128] We then have a lengthy passage in which Fléchier, following his model, Ogier, sets out just what preaching is and what it is supposed to achieve, and, in so doing, condemns the sermon-tasters (like Madame de Sévigné) of his own day. We

---

[126] Fléchier, 57–58.
[127] See appendix 1, s.v. *recueillement* / recollection.
[128] Fléchier, 60.

have seen what Ogier has to say on this matter; let us now translate Fléchier's account. Those who came to hear Bernard, he tells us,

> did not come to swell the crowd, but to be touched and instructed; not to honor the minister of the word, but to profit from his ministry. They saw the sermon as an exhortation to which they should listen with respect, not as a simple declamation that they should judge. Their intention was not to note down the faults in the preacher's delivery, but to correct their own faults. They did not turn these devout, modest, and silent assemblies into a tumultuous meeting-place of vanity, curiosity, and adulation. They did not seek titillating pictures of the vices of their day, where everyone thinks they see someone else's portrait instead of their own, where they even make a pleasure out of their own sin by cunningly applying what they themselves do to the sin of others, and where they turn the wise reproofs of the preacher into secret slanders and satires against their neighbor. They came meekly, they went home contrite and humbled, and the tears they shed were the true praise of the sermon they had just heard.[129]

And then Fléchier, that celebrated preacher, turns his attention to the preachers themselves. What of them? Bernard, obviously, is his ideal, but what he says of Bernard applies to all those who have been called to the pulpit and the ministry of the word:

> The preacher, for his part, was worthy of his task. He did not involve himself with the gospel ministry before he had purified himself in his retreat [from the world], and he did not dare to speak of God before he had long listened to him in secrecy and silence. Whatever

---

[129] Fléchier, 61.

talents he had that would lead to his being esteemed, he preached Jesus Christ and did not preach himself. He did not see preaching as a means of distinguishing oneself, nor as a way of achieving high position in the Church. He was never seen to solicit the plaudits of his audience, nor was he concerned about bolstering up a shaky reputation by plots and intrigue. His way of life did not detract from the sanctity of what he said, and he was always ready to practise in the gloom of his [monastic] cell what he would come forth to teach in the light and in the pulpits of the Church. He sought for what would touch sinners and convince them, not in what he made up himself, but in the pure source of the Scriptures.[130]

In Bernard's time, Fléchier continues, all this was vitally necessary, since the church was being threatened "by vain and subtle minds, who wished to amalgamate human reason with the Gospel and the mysteries of Jesus Christ with the rules of Plato and Aristotle, thus transgressing those sacred bounds that had been set by our Fathers, and confusing Philosophy with Religion."[131] They were introducing into the simplicity of the faith those profane novelties condemned by Paul in his first letter to Timothy,[132] and one of the worst of these innovators was, of course, Peter Abelard. We are now back on home ground with the Council of Sens and the defeat and discomfiture of this "philosopher-theologian,"[133] but Abelard does not receive the positive press that he receives from Ogier. Fléchier then mentions, but only in passing, Gilbert de la Porrée, Arnold of Brescia, and Henry of Toulouse (he omits Peter of Bruys),

---

[130] Fléchier, 62–63.
[131] Fléchier, 63. Fléchier is again following Ogier but omits the latter's charming description of Philosophy tying to inveigle her way into the Christian Church.
[132] 1 Tim 6:20. See appendix 1, s.v. *nouveautés* / novelties.
[133] Fléchier, 64.

likens Bernard to a second Augustine, and brings to an end the first part of his sermon. We have seen what Bernard was like in his sublime knowledge; let us now see what he was like in his glorious deeds.

Apart from the beauty of Fléchier's language, there is less in this second section to interest us. As with Ogier, we have the usual contrast between Bernard the solitary and Bernard the public figure, Bernard the simple monk and Bernard the oracle of the Holy Spirit in church councils, Bernard the contemplative, who preferred the silence of his cell to the plaudits of princes; and this contrast leads, naturally, to an account of "the bloody and universal schism that devastated the kingdom of God by dividing it."[134] Fléchier spends some considerable time on this, much more than Ogier, but offers us hardly anything in the way of historical detail. Not one familiar face makes an appearance: not Henry I, not Lothair III, not Louis VI, not Roger of Sicily, not even Duke William X of Aquitaine, whose dramatic conversion is mentioned by almost everyone. Tréverret, as we have seen above, criticized him for this.

So rather than telling us how the schism originated or the course it took, our preacher tells us that there are two unities in the church, an interior unity, which is a communion of spirit that links together all the faithful in the principles of the faith and a common charity, and an exterior unity, which links all the members of the Body of Christ to their visible and invisible Heads—the pope and Jesus Christ himself. Both these unities were shattered by the schism, but the end of the schism was heralded by the Council of Étampes (which Fléchier does mention), when Bernard stood forth as the voice of the entire church, and where, in accordance with his prudent judgment, the church recognized her true Pastor and rejected "the mercenary."[135] Fléchier then glances at Bernard's efforts and

---

[134] Fléchier, 68.
[135] I.e., Anacletus, whom Fléchier never mentions by name. See appendix 2, s.v. Anacletus II.

achievements in putting an end to the schism in other places (but provides no details) and quotes his reluctant recognition of himself as "the monster and prodigy of my age."[136]

As a consequence of all this, it was inevitable that Bernard would be admired and esteemed. If he had sought rank and position, they were open to him. But he himself remained a humble monk. Indeed, the more he was praised, the more he abased himself; and the more he was seen by the world as great, the more he saw himself as a sinner and penitent. As a telling example of this, Fléchier describes, again in general terms (no names are mentioned), the visit of Innocent II to Clairvaux in 1131.[137] Bernard is then offered various episcopates[138] but refuses them all: he is content to see his own disciples elevated to these dignities, but he himself was happier to remain in the silence of his cloister. This, however, was not to be, for his deep concern for the conversion of ordinary men and women demanded more. As he passed through France, Germany, and Italy (Fléchier has now rejoined Ogier), "he drew them to him by his gentleness, edified them by his penitence, amazed them by his marvels, and touched them by his discourses."[139] In his own person he was, at one and the same time, an apostle, a prophet, a doctor,[140] who combined "miracles, predictions, teachings, and—what is no less useful for souls—examples of a life that was beyond reproach, edifying, and completely holy."[141] But this is all that Fléchier has to say about miracles and predictions, and the only examples he

---

[136] Fléchier, 72, paraphrasing Bernard, Ep 250.4; SBOp 8:147, to the Carthusian prior of Portes: *Ego enim quaedam chimaera mei saeculi*. Not surprisingly, the description is cited by a number of the other panegyrists.

[137] Fléchier, 74–76. See chap. 8 (Fénelon), §10.

[138] Fléchier, typically, names none, but refers to them simply as "the most honorable sees in France and Italy" (76).

[139] Fléchier, 78.

[140] See chap. 4 (Biroat), n. 55.

[141] Fléchier, 79.

offers are the somewhat vague allusions to the Lactation and Bernard's childhood vision at Saint-Vorles at the beginning of his panegyric.

Bernard did not, however, confine his attention to ordinary men and women. Such was his love for the church and for perfection on the part of its pastors and ministers that he had no hesitation, when necessary, of reproving those who had fallen short and reminding them of where their duties lay. Nor did he confine his reproofs to those in the church. Indeed not. He had no fear in intervening in the affairs of kings and princes if their actions, in his eyes, were contrary to the principles of the Christian faith. He brokered peace between warring parties (again, like Ogier, Fléchier provides no historical details), calmed the fury of combatants, and "undertook a holy war to deliver the homeland of Jesus Christ from its enslavement by the infidels."[142] But Fléchier devotes only a single unpersuasive sentence to this disastrous failure, and that single sentence is taken directly from Ogier: "He urged the Christian princes to this holy enterprise, which might, perhaps, have had a happy outcome if they had followed the sound advice of this holy man."[143]

Bernard's reproofs, however, were always balanced. Though he spoke with the freedom of the Gospel, his approach was never lacking in modesty, and his advice and reproaches never degenerated into blame and abuse. He was never too harsh, yet never too accommodating. He knew how to put forth the truth without being unduly severe, and how to instruct without being offensive. Led by the Spirit of God, he was able to combine the freedom of the Gospel with Christian humility, and we may see this clearly in his five books, *On Consideration*, addressed to Pope Eugenius III, though Fléchier, unlike Ogier, whom he is here following closely, never mentions its title. "One cannot be too careful," he says, "when addressing

---

[142] Fléchier, 81.
[143] Fléchier, 81.

the common Father and general Pastor of souls."[144] Thus, on the one hand, Bernard praises the pope, using some of the most laudatory titles from both the Old and New Testaments; on the other, he recognizes his inevitable failings as a human being. He distinguishes in him the fullness of power from the fullness of justice—what he can do as distinct from what he should do—and reminds him that he should rule himself not by his will, but by his reason and his conscience.

And so Fléchier draws his panegyric to a close by asking, as we would expect him to ask, what his listeners can learn from all this. As with other panegyrists, he tells them that he obviously does not expect them to do all that Bernard did, but that certain things are incumbent upon all Christians, and not just on great saints. It belongs to everyone, he says, not to judge too quickly, to moderate one's passions, to mortify oneself in one's way of life, to be humble in one's opinions, and to be gentle and charitable in one's dealings with other people. All this we may learn from Bernard. We should therefore work to model ourselves on his instructions and his example, so that by imitating his actions in this world, we may deserve his reward in the next. And Fléchier ends his discourse with the usual doxology.

As we said earlier, Fléchier's panegyric presents us not with a historical account of Bernard's life and works, but with a *portrait moral* based on a sermon delivered more than four decades earlier. Bourru's first panegyric on Bernard, delivered some years later, is very similar, providing even less in the way of historical detail. Fléchier's sources are limited to Scripture, Saint Augustine, John Chrysostom, and the *Vita prima*, and, as with Ogier, there is no untoward display of erudition, but Fléchier delicately removes the clouds of classicism that hover over (and sometimes obnubilate) Ogier's discourse. He cites no work of Bernard by title, though he quotes his famous descrip-

---

[144] Fléchier, 83.

tion of himself from his letter 250 (as Ogier does not), and he is obviously referring to the *De consideratione* toward the end of his sermon. As with Ogier (and so many others), Bernard the mystic makes no appearance. That Fléchier's panegyric is based on that of Ogier cannot be doubted. He follows him in the path he takes, he follows him in dividing his sermon into Bernard's life and achievements inside and outside the cloister, though without specifically marking the division, he follows him in what he has to say of acquired and infused knowledge, he follows him in his brief discussion of the Second Crusade, and so on. Sometimes, as we have said, the borrowings are almost word for word. This is not to say that Fléchier does not add material of his own—he does—and there is equally no doubt that his pulpit eloquence is of a higher order than that of Ogier. But many of the delightful and interesting passages that we find in Ogier do not appear in Fléchier, and I must admit that, despite the latter's greater reputation, I found Ogier's panegyric a greater pleasure to read.

13

Last of the Fathers and the Angel of the Lord

Antoine Anselme and Louis-Bénigne Bourru

Fléchier died in 1710, and with the two panegyrists who will be the subject of this chapter we move on a generation. Antoine Anselme died in 1737 and Louis-Bénigne Bourru a year later. The Sun King himself had died in 1715, but the panegyrics of Anselme and Bourru are too interesting to be omitted from this survey. Their names are not well known today, if indeed they are known at all, but in their own time both of them, especially Anselme, enjoyed a certain celebrity. Anselme's panegyric on Bernard as *ultimus Patrum*, the Last of the Fathers, is an impressive tightly knit panegyric on a single overarching theme; Bourru's two panegyrics on the saint are rather more conventional, but nevertheless of interest, though not always for what they have to say about Bernard. Let us begin with Antoine Anselme, a preacher esteemed in his day by no less a judge than Madame de Sévigné, who thought him intelligent, eloquent, charming, and devout.[1]

Antoine Anselme

He was born at L'Isle-Jourdain, just over twenty miles west of Toulouse, on January 13, 1652, and was a prodigious infant

---

[1] Madame de Sévigné, letter of April 8, 1689, quoted in Hurel, 2:121. "There's hardly anyone I'd rather hear than him," she says.

who, from an early age, could repeat word for word, with appropriate gestures, sermons he had heard but once. He was known as "the Little Prophet" (*le Petit Prophète*). He studied in Toulouse and, after his ordination, preached in Toulouse, where his admirable sermons caught the attention of Louis-Henri de Pardaillan de Gondrin, marquis de Montespan. He was married to the beautiful, cultured, and witty Françoise-Athénaïs de Rocheouart de Mortemart, who, as Madame de Montespan, would become the most celebrated of Louis XIV's official mistresses. In due course, she would bear the king seven children, but before that she had borne to the marquis a daughter, Marie-Christine, and a son, Louis-Antoine, the marquis d'Antin and later the duc d'Antin. To this son, the marquis appointed Antoine Anselme tutor and brought him to Paris. Here he met with great success as a preacher and, in 1681, the *Académie française* chose him to preach the annual panegyric on Saint Louis—a signal honor. Soon afterward he was called to Court and became *prédicateur ordinaire du roi*. Louis was so impressed with his preaching that he rewarded him with the rich commendatory abbacy of Saint-Sever, which lies about a hundred miles west of his birthplace, and it was there that he died on August 8, 1737. He was eighty-six.[2]

Albert and Court praise his discourses for their soundness, elegance, purity of language, and piety, but although they find them most gratifying to read, they would have liked to have seen "a little more of that warmth and power that one needs to take the truth deep into the soul and to touch the heart."[3] Anselme's three volumes of panegyrics and funeral orations (he preached the oration for Queen Marie-Thérèse in 1683) were published at Paris in 1718, and Albert and Court,

---

[2] For Anselme's life and works, see Jean-Baptiste Ladvocat (*l'abbé* Vosgien), *Dictionnaire historique-portatif, contenant l'histoire des Patriarches* . . . (Paris: la veuve Didot, 1760 [revised and enlarged ed.]), 69–70; Albert / Court, 6–8; Hurel, 2:120–29; DHGE 1:497–98.

[3] Albert / Court, 7.

once again, are happy to take the panegyrics as models and place them on the same rank as those of Fléchier, Bourdaloue, and La Rue, for they contribute (they say) to the glory of the saints as much as they serve for the edification of the faithful.[4] The panegyric on Bernard is to be found in the second of the three volumes.[5] When Anselme preached it is unknown, and I can find no clue within the text. It was delivered on August 20, Saint Bernard's feast day, in the church of the Feuillants, presumably on the rue Saint-Honoré in Paris, but no year is mentioned. The *abbé* Hurel (who esteemed his discourses) tells us that he preached a great deal between 1693 and 1709,[6] but whether this period included his panegyric on Saint Bernard we do not know.

Anselme's text is Ecclesiasticus / Sirach 33:16, which he translates as "I came last of all, as one who gathers up the grapes left by the grape-pickers,"[7] and this verse encapsulates his whole panegyric. Bernard is the Last of the Fathers, *ultimus Patrum*, "the name now given him by the whole Church,"[8] and Anselme will show exactly how Bernard is the Last of the

---

[4] Albert / Court, 7.

[5] *Panégyriques des saints, prononcez par Messire Antoine Anselme, Abbé de Saint Sever Cap de Gascogné, Prédicateur ordinaire du Roi, de l'Académie Royale des Belles Lettres. Tome II* (Paris: P.-F. Giffart, 1718), 197–242; reprinted in *Collection intégrale et universelle des Orateurs Sacrés du premier ordre . . . , publiée, selon l'ordre chronologique par M. l'abbé [Jacques-Paul] Migne. Tome vingtième* (Paris: J.-P. Migne, 1845), cols. 1220–38. All citations below are to the 1718 edition.

[6] Hurel, 2:128.

[7] As usual, Anselme had adapted the text to his own use. A literal translation would be something like "I was the last to keep vigil [*ego novissimus evigilavi*], as one who gathers grapes after the grape-gatherers." The Douai-Reims version translates *evigilavi* as "I awoke."

[8] Anselme, 198. On the title *ultimus Patrum* or *ultimus inter Patres*, see the essential discussion by Mabillon in the *Praefatio generalis* to his edition of Bernard's works: *Praef. gen* 2.23–29; PL 182:26–29 (English translation in *Life and Works of Saint Bernard, Abbot of Clairvaux*, trans./ed. Samuel J. Eales, 2nd ed. [London: Burns & Oates Ltd.,

Fathers, how in him both the Latin and the Greek Fathers live again, how he casts additional light on what they taught, and how he completes what they left incomplete. There is nothing new in the factual content of his panegyric—what Bernard said and what Bernard did (we have seen it all before)—but his presentation is novel and refreshing.

Jesus Christ himself, says Anselme, was the first and the last,[9] and as the last "he renews all, perfects all, and brings all to a close. So what could be of greater honor for Saint Bernard than to be in some way with regard to the Fathers what Jesus Christ is with regard to all things?"[10] "He is the last of the Fathers, and as such he is the resurrection of the Fathers, the perfection of the Fathers, and the end of the Fathers. He is their renewal and resurrection because all the Fathers live again in him. He is their adornment and perfection because what is lacking in the other Fathers is found in him. He is their end and termination because there are no more Fathers after him. He renews their spirit. He completes their works. He brings to an end their presence."[11] But if Bernard was the last of the fathers of the church, he was first among those devoted to the Mother of God, and, as we would expect, Anselme invokes the aid of Mary in the delivery of his panegyric by saying with the angel, *Ave Maria*. We shall meet Mary again a little later.

What makes a father of the church? There are two essential features. The first is preeminence in doctrine, infused rather than acquired (we are reminded of Ogier and Fléchier), and gained in the School of Heaven rather than the Academies of Earth. The second is preeminence in virtue, by which one's actions reflect the truth one preaches. Someone who possesses one of these two features but not the other may be called by

---

1889], 1:20–29). See also Icard, "Saint Bernard, effigie du catholicisme classique," 333–36.

[9] Rev 1:8, 17; 21:6; 22:13.
[10] Anselme, 199.
[11] Anselme, 199.

many names—Doctor, Theologian, Master, or even Saint—but not a father of the church. Bernard, however, possessed both, uniting knowledge with piety in accordance with the words of Saint Augustine: *scienter pius, et pie sciens* ["learnedly pious and piously learned"].[12] In him, therefore, we see resurrected the knowledge and piety, the doctrine and the virtues, of the ancient Fathers. How, exactly, is this so?

Anselme begins with the Fathers—more accurately, the Four Great Doctors—of the Latin Church: Jerome, Ambrose, Augustine, and Gregory the Great, and demonstrates how each of them lives again in Bernard.[13] For this section he is largely dependent on the unpaginated preface to Antoine Le Maistre's *Vie de Saint Bernard*.[14] Thus, when Bernard corrects those who have abandoned the religious life, when he upholds the cause of the unfortunate, when he defends the liberties of the church, when he rebukes monks, bishops, and popes for their conduct and tells them how it may be amended, do we not recognize here the character of Saint Jerome? When he praises so eloquently the virtue of virginity, when he exhorts those who have chosen this path to guard the integrity of their bodies, when he exhorts them to love this virtue that the Son of God gave to the world and that makes them the equal of the angels, do we not take him for the interpreter of Saint Ambrose?[15] When he raises himself up to contemplate the truth in God himself, when he unveils the meaning of Holy Scripture, when he leaves us in no doubt of the absolute necessity of God's grace, is it not Saint Augustine who speaks? And when he describes the sorry road

[12] Augustine, Ep 194.4.18; PL 33:880.

[13] The same comparison from the same source appears in Texier and Boudon: see chap. 5 (Senault et al.), n. 87, and chap. 11 (Boudon), §27.

[14] That Anselme was much influenced by this very popular work is not in doubt: he refers to it directly on page 204.

[15] Anselme is thinking especially of Ambrose's treatises *De virginibus* and *De virginitate*, and his *Exhortatio virginitatis*.

taken by sinners, when he speaks so profoundly of the duties and discipline of the Christian life, when he shows so clearly how Christians should observe the Law of God in accordance with the moral principles set forth in the Gospel, is he not repeating the injunctions of Saint Gregory the Great?

What, then, of the Greek Fathers? Here Anselme compares Bernard with Athanasius, Gregory of Nazianzus, John Chrysostom, and Basil the Great. The most obvious comparison with Athanasius is to be found in the latter's battles with heresy. In the case of Athanasius, the battle was with the Arians (and a hard-fought battle it was); in Bernard's case it was with Peter Abelard (who "substituted the inventions of Plato for the doctrine of the Fathers of the Church"[16] and was defeated at the Council of Sens), with Gilbert de la Porrée (who mingled with what he taught "a hidden poison and a suspect teaching"[17] and who was defeated at the Council of Reims), and with Henry of Toulouse (who "declared war on the sacraments of the Church and on its ministers"[18]). But Anselme himself makes it easy for us here and offers us his own summary of this section of his work. As Athanasius defended the faith at the Council of Nicaea,[19] so Bernard defended it at the Council of Sens. As Gregory of Nazianzus heroically renounced the patriarchate of Constantinople,[20] so Bernard refused the archbishopric of Milan. As John Chrysostom fought

---

[16] Anselme, 204.
[17] Anselme, 205.
[18] Anselme, 206.
[19] Anselme is here guilty of what we might call historic license. Athanasius was only a deacon at the time of Nicaea and attended the Council as personal secretary to his bishop, Alexander of Alexandria. He therefore had no official voice at the Council, though there is no doubt that he acted as advisor to Alexander. Athanasius's triumph came after the Council, but Anselme is not here giving a lecture on early Christian history.
[20] Gregory was bishop of Constantinople for just a few months, from November 380 to June 381, when he resigned.

against the corruption that had infected the whole of the Eastern church, so Bernard fought against it in the whole of the Western church. And as God had kindled in the heart of Basil the Great such a profound love of solitude, so he also kindled it in the heart of Bernard, for whom the monastic cell was another heaven. Sometimes, as we know, Bernard (like Basil) had no choice but to come out of his solitude to attend to affairs of the church. Here Anselme tells us, very briefly, of Bernard's role in putting an end to the papal schism (he mentions the Council of Étampes in 1130) and quotes his complaint that he is neither lay nor ecclesiastic, that he has kept a monk's habit but has abandoned the monk's life, and that he is the chimera of his age.[21]

Anselme now comes to the second point of his sermon: How does Bernard shed new light on what the Fathers have said, and how does he complete what they have left incomplete? What Bernard will do is what has already been done by his Lord and Master with regard to the law of Moses, for Jesus Christ was the end of the Law inasmuch as he perfected the Law. And how did Jesus Christ perfect the Law?

> First of all, he changed the ground on which it was established,[22] replacing fear with love. Then he changed its end, promising an eternal reward to those who observed the Law of the Gospel, whereas the Jews had kept the Law only in hope of gaining temporal goods. He revealed the true spirit of the Law, which, until his coming, had been known only to a few righteous people of the Old Testament, and in this way he shed a light on this Law that it had not received from Moses. But because this same Law had not said everything, Jesus Christ, its perfecter, supplied what was lacking

---

[21] Bernard, Ep 250.4; SBOp 8:147, to Bernard, Carthusian prior of Portes. See chap. 5 (Senault et al.), n. 78. The description, understandably, was popular.

[22] Lit. "he changed the *motif.*"

by adding to it those precepts and counsels that provide men and women with the means to make themselves perfect.[23]

For we must remember, says Anselme, that although not all people are born to be fathers of the church, all people are born to be saints.[24]

Thus, what Jesus Christ did with regard to the world and the Law, Bernard did with regard to the Fathers. He shed new light on the truths he found in their writings and added to their teachings those ideas that their time and place necessarily precluded from discussion. The new light he shed came from God's own word in Holy Scriptures, and (as we have seen) he had so immersed himself in the sacred writings that their ideas and language were a natural part of his life and speech. But he also read the fathers with deep humility ("never was there a saint who consulted the saints more," says Anselme[25]), and while further illuminating what they wrote he never challenged their decisions.[26] Indeed, even so celebrated a biblical scholar as Hugh of Saint-Victor had no hesitation in consulting him, and always found that, in his replies, he was in complete accord with the tradition of the church. Bernard himself wrote to Hugh saying that he himself followed Paul's advice to Timothy, to avoid questions and wars of words about new and dangerous ideas,[27] but "I put forward only the opinions and words of the fathers, not my own, for we are not wiser than

---

[23] Anselme, 216.

[24] Anselme, 214. We may compare chap. 4 (Biroat), §36, and especially chap. 9 (La Rue 1), §57.

[25] Anselme, 217.

[26] We may compare Mabillon's comments in his Praef gen 2.25; PL 182:27–28 (English translation in *Life and Works of Saint Bernard*, trans./ed. Eales, 1:23–26).

[27] See 1 Tim 6:4-5.

our fathers."[28] And which fathers in particular? Augustine and Ambrose, those two pillars of the faith.[29] "We see here, gentlemen," Anselme continues,

> the true character of a Doctor of the Church, for whom there is nothing more dear than the sacred deposit[30] of the teachings of his Fathers. The last of them has respect for what was said by his predecessors. He ponders their maxims, he approves them, he sheds further light upon them, he practises them. What a great example to so many presumptuous spirits who prefer their own opinions to the ideas of those who alone have the right to make decisions on religious matters, and who corrupt the morals of Christians by substituting their own pernicious novelties[31] for the best truths founded on the doctrines of antiquity![32]

But we will not stop here, says our preacher. We must move on to speak of those things that Bernard added to the teaching of the Fathers, for we must remember that although the only goal of the Fathers was to offer to the faithful a perfect knowledge of Jesus Christ, it was a knowledge of the whole of Jesus Christ. And what does that mean? It means the body of the church united to its Head, "what Saint Augustine calls *Christus totus*, because he considers Jesus Christ and the Church to be but one single person, *unus homo Christus et Ecclesia*."[33]

---

[28] Bernard, Ep 77, *praefatio*; SBOp 7:184, to Hugh of Saint-Victor (*Tractatus de baptismo aliisque quaestionibus*).

[29] See Bernard, Ep 77.2; SBOp 7:189–90.

[30] See 2 Tim 1:14.

[31] *Nouveautez pernicieuses*: see appendix 1, s.v. *nouveautés* / novelties. "Novelties" are always pernicious.

[32] Anselme, 219.

[33] Anselme, 220, citing Augustine, Tract in Ioh 28:1; PL 35:1622: *Non enim Christus in capite et non in corpore, sed Christus totus in capite et in corpore*, "For it is not the case that Christ is in the head and not in the body, but the whole Christ is in the head and the body"; and En

But the Fathers did not give a great deal of attention to the mother of this single person,[34] and that is the first of three things that Bernard will add to their teachings. Who is this mother? "It is Mary, who is not only the Mother of the Head of the Church, but also the most perfect image of the Church; for just as Jesus Christ was born physically from the womb of a virgin, he is united spiritually with holy Church, who is his bride and who is also virgin."[35]

To this Mother, says Anselme, to this perfect image of the church, Bernard consecrated his heart and his tongue. Of all the Fathers, he says most about her, and he is "the interpreter of her mysteries, the herald of her privileges, the repository of her secrets, and, to put it all in one word, Mary's devoted servant."[36] He also makes it clear in his teaching that true devotion to Mary—indeed, the only devotion pleasing to her—is the imitation of her virtues. That is sufficient in itself, and without this, any other form of devotion, even though it may be good from the point of view of faith, is useless. On this matter, it is interesting to note Anselme's last sentence on Mary: "For a Virgin," he says, "who, by her divine maternity, is raised to the rank of Queen of Humans and Angels, has no need of being

---

in Ps 18.2.10; PL 36:161: *unus homo caput et corpus, unus homo Christus et Ecclesia, vir perfectus, ille sponsus, illa sponsa*, "Head and body, one person; Christ and the Church, one person, the perfect man, the former is the bridegroom, the latter the bride."

[34] This is not, of course, correct, but in a eulogy such as this, Anselme may be forgiven for saying so. In his panegyric on Mary for the feast of the Assumption he cites Ambrose, Augustine, Origen, Epiphanius, Andrew of Crete, and John of Damascus (*Panégyriques des saints, prononcez par Messire Antoine Anselme, Abbé de Saint Sever Cap de Gascogné, Prédicateur ordinaire du Roi, de l'Académie Royale des Belles Lettres. Tome I* [Paris: P.-F. Giffart, 1718], 44–83). But there is no doubt that Bernard's devotion to Mary did take the veneration of the Virgin to a new level.

[35] Anselme, 220–21.

[36] Anselme, 221. Bernard is *le dévot de Marie*.

offered any false honors, she who is filled with genuine ones: *Virgo Regina falso non indiget honore, veris cumulate honorum titulis* ["The Virgin Queen does not need false honor, since she has an abundance of true titles to her honor"[37]].

This last quotation comes from Bernard's letter to the canons of Lyon in which he chastises them for introducing into the churches of Lyon a feast celebrating Mary's conception—a letter that was regularly cited by those who opposed the doctrine of the immaculate conception. Such a feast, says Bernard, "is a new festival, a rite of which the Church knows nothing, which reason does not prove, nor ancient tradition hand down. Surely we are not more learned or more devoted than the fathers?"[38] In Bernard's view, Mary was conceived with original sin but cleansed from it before her birth, and the same remarkable blessing preserved her free from sin for the whole of her life. He is more than happy, therefore, to celebrate a feast of her nativity, but not a feast for her conception.[39] Of all those born on earth, he says, only one was ever conceived without sin, and that was he who cleansed all sinners, namely, the Son of God. What the Psalmist says of himself, that he was conceived in sin (Ps 50:7), is true of all men and women, and given this fact, "what reason can there be for a Feast of the Conception?"[40] It is "a presumptuous novelty, a mother of thoughtlessness, a sister of superstition, a daughter of frivolity."[41] And, in any case, if the canons had wished to introduce such a foolish festival, they should have consulted the Apostolic See, which they had not.

Père Anselme is not, however, introducing into a panegyric on Bernard a veiled attack on the doctrine of the immaculate

---

[37] Anselme, 222, quoting Bernard, Ep 174.2; SBOp 7:388, to the canons of Lyon. Anselme's text reads *Virgo Regina* for Bernard's *Virgo regia* ("royal Virgin"), and *non indiget* for Bernard's *non eget*. Anselme echoes the same passage in his panegyric for the assumption of Mary (see n. 34 above), p. 81.

[38] Bernard, Ep 174.1; SBOp 7:388.

[39] See Ep 174.5; SBOp 7:390.

[40] Ep 174.9; SBOp 7:392.

[41] Ep 174.9; SBOp 7:392.

conception, though controversy on the question was still alive and well in the France of his times. The Jansenists, in general, had no time for the doctrine, but those who supported it formed the decided majority. In Anselme's view, Mary had anticipated—the verb is *prévenir*—God's grace from the first moment of her existence,[42] and although our preacher leaned heavily on Antoine Le Maistre's *Vie de Saint Bernard*, he did not share its author's Jansenist sympathies. In any case, although such devotions may well be *bon en foi*, "good from the viewpoint of faith," if you really wish to show your devotion to the Mother of God, then (like Bernard) imitate her virtues! And as a final note on these Marian matters, we may observe in passing that, unlike Boudon, Planchette, and Lion, Anselme does not introduce the miracle of the Lactation.

The second addition that, according to Anselme, Bernard makes to the teachings of the Fathers is what he calls the question of "subordination in the Church,"[43] by which he means the question of authority, particularly episcopal authority and papal authority. There was no occasion for the early fathers to speak out on this matter, but times had changed by the century of Bernard, and he found it necessary to say a considerable amount on the question, especially in two of his writings: the last chapter of his letter-treatise *de moribus et officio episcoporum* addressed to Henry of Sens[44] and part of Book Three of the *De consideratione* addressed to his erstwhile disciple, Pope Eugenius III.[45] The essence of what Bernard says here is that every single member of the Body of Christ must know his place and keep it; otherwise that body will be deformed and

---

[42] *la grace dont elle avoit été prévenuë dés le premier instant de son être* (Panegyric on Mary for the feast of the Assumption [see n. 34 above], p. 56).

[43] Anselme, 222.

[44] Bernard, Ep 42 / *De moribus et officio episcoporum* 1.10.33–37; SBOp 7:127–31.

[45] Csi 3.4.14–18; SBOp 3:441–46. Anselme offers more than two dozen lines of an abridged translation of these sections (Anselme, 223–34).

disordered. So just as seraphim, cherubim, and all the other angelic ranks are arranged in due order under God, so here on earth primates, patriarchs, bishops, priests, abbots, and all the rest are arranged under one supreme pontiff. Nor is this order a merely human invention: its author is God, and its foundation lies in heaven.

The third thing that the early Fathers did not do, and could not possibly have done, was to speak of the recovery of the Holy Land. But Bernard, "prompted by the orders of the pope, by the earnest request of the king of France, and still more by the ardor of his own zeal, preached to all the Christians of the world a wholly Christian war."[46] Which means that Anselme is going to have to explain just why the Second Crusade was such a disastrous failure. The only one of the panegyrists we have discussed thus far who deals with this at any length is Fénelon, who, following the account by Geoffrey of Auxerre,[47] suggests that the reason the Crusade failed was either that the Crusaders, having been chosen by God, then made themselves unworthy to be his instruments, or that God put the idea of the enterprise in their hearts only to have them experience a salutary embarrassment.[48] The total failure of the Crusade certainly proved a problem and embarrassment for Bernard, who had to call on God for a miracle in order to prove that he had been right to preach it.[49] His *apologia* for the débacle at the beginning of Book Two of his *De consideratione* cannot be called especially effective.

Anselme discusses the question at somewhat greater length, invokes the names of the Englishman William of Newburgh, "one of the most renowned historians of the times,"[50] and John,

---

[46] Anselme, 225.

[47] *Vita prima* 3.4.9–10 (Geoffrey of Auxerre); PL 185:308C–9C; CF 76:154–57.

[48] See chap. 8 (Fénelon), §25.

[49] See chap. 8 (Fénelon), §25. Fénelon is again following Geoffrey of Auxerre.

[50] Anselme, 225.

abbot of Casamari, to explain the failure and give the whole unfortunate affair a positive slant. It was not the zeal of Saint Bernard that was at fault, he tells us, but the dissolute conduct of the Christians. The army was so blackened with sin that it was violating not only all Christian discipline but military discipline as well. Its leaders placed all their confidence in their numbers and armed might and forgot the God who, through Eugenius III and Bernard, had inspired the Crusade. But God is a jealous God, who casts down the proud and raises up the lowly, and the more the Crusaders trusted in themselves, the more they were doomed. But all was not lost, and Anselme explains how all was not lost by borrowing directly from John of Casamari's letter to Bernard, in which he tries to comfort him for what appeared to be a total disaster.[51] "Do not think, my brothers, that Providence[52] had been cheated in the outcome of its plans! God found an enterprise that he himself had inspired to be extremely fruitful, though not in a way that any of the men involved had imagined."[53] How was this so? Because God made the wickedness of the Crusaders serve his mercy by sending them afflictions to purify them. If the church in the East had not been delivered by the war, the church in heaven had been filled with souls; and if there were dissolute soldiers who had abandoned the way of the Lord, there were also noble soldiers who had had the happiness of expiating their sins by a holy death. And why does God fulfill his own designs in so surprising a way? That is a question we cannot answer, for he knows, and we do not. "Our business in this is to humble ourselves and learn from the illustrious saint whose memory we honor that although God never does other than his will, we are never dispensed from doing all that we ought."[54] This last

---

[51] John of Casamari, Ep 386.2–3; PL 182:590C–91A. The marginal reference on page 226 to Ep 333 is to Horstius's edition (1679), vol. 1, pt. 2, p. 134.

[52] See appendix 1, s.v. *Providence* / Providence.

[53] Anselme, 226.

[54] Anselme, 227.

sentence is Anselme's paraphrase of Bernard's own words in his letter to Pope Eugenius urging (unwisely) the pope to come to the help of the church in the East and not to be discouraged by the "sad and grievous news" of the fall of Edessa.[55]

Thus does Bernard complete what is lacking in the writings of the Fathers, and Anselme moves on to the third and final section of his panegyric. Here we are back in more familiar territory, though Anselme still has a surprise in store. We find in this last division, as indeed we would expect to find, a contrast between Bernard's zealous humility and the ministers of Anselme's own times, lax and proud ministers who shame Jesus Christ and his Gospel, slaves of chance and self-love, flatterers who never speak of suffering lest they be constrained to suffer themselves. But none of this diminishes the glory of Saint Bernard himself, who, as the Last of the Fathers, remains as great a Father as any of his predecessors, and Anselme demonstrates this by offering the analogy of the Trinity itself:

> Far, then, from being afraid to say it—I am afraid *not* to say that the last of the Fathers is equal to the others, and that just as in the order of the Divine Persons the Father and Son have only a priority of origin over the Holy Spirit, which does not make them greater or older than [the Spirit],[56] so in the order of the Fathers,

---

[55] Bernard, Ep 256.2; SBOp 8:164, to Eugenius III: *Numquid ideo non debet facere homo quod debet, quia Deus facit quod vult?* "Are we not therefore duty bound to do our duty, because God does what he wills?" Edessa fell to Imad-ad-Din Zengi on December 24, 1144. Eugenius issued the bull *Quantum praedecessores*, calling for the Second Crusade, on December 1 of the following year.

[56] The eternal Father eternally begets the Son, who, therefore, has no beginning. And since the Holy Spirit proceeds eternally from the eternal Father and the eternal Son, the Spirit, too, has no beginning. Thus, the Father and Son have a *logical* priority over the Spirit, but not a *temporal* priority, and the three Persons of the Trinity are consubstantial, coequal, and coeternal.

the Ambroses and the Augustines, the Basils and the Chrysostoms have only a priority of origin over Saint Bernard, which does indeed make them older than he, but not any greater.[57]

Those who are well grounded in the faith, he continues, will not find this a rash suggestion if they bear in mind that the Son of God brought to the church two remarkable gifts: the fire of charity[58] and the light of teaching. The latter he entrusted to the fathers of the church, the former to the children of the church. But the children have let the fire die, and centuries of iniquity have caused charity to grow cold. Among the children, therefore, the last have much to do if they are to equal the first, for the fire of charity grows dimmer day by day. "But among the Fathers of the Church the last do equal the first, for the light of their teaching has never experienced a similar decay and, in consequence, has never been clouded."[59] And what is this teaching? It is the teaching of the Truth, the Truth that Jesus Christ taught his apostles and that they taught to the fathers who came after them. And since that Truth is indivisible, it matters not whether it be taught "by Gregory or Bernard, by Bernard or Leo."[60] But if the light shed on the church by the first fathers was like the dawn, the Last of the Fathers, who united in himself all the earlier teachings and completed what they lacked, has transformed that dawn into the full light of day, *crescit usque ad perfectam diem*.[61]

Yet all this was done in the spirit of true humility, for Bernard's own view was not that he was the Last of the Fathers,

---

[57] Anselme, 233.
[58] See appendix 1, s.v. *charité* / charity.
[59] Anselme, 234–35.
[60] Anselme, 235. Gregory and Leo are Gregory the Great and Leo the Great.
[61] Anselme, 236, quoting Prov 4:18, "But the path of the righteous, like a shining light, goes forth and increases even to perfect day."

but that he was, effectively, last in all things. It is for us to imitate this true humility. And how? By recognizing what we are and what we do! We are condemned before we see the light of day.[62] We reject the regeneration of our baptism by a life of sin. Though God still calls us, we are deaf to his voice. We follow the leanings of our own corrupt nature, not the Spirit of God. And if we would only acknowledge these things, we would have no choice but to put ourselves in the last place and be profoundly afraid to be called to be first. In this, since Saint Bernard is our example, "let us have sufficient control over ourselves to suppress the unruly movements of our proud heart and fix all its desires on submission and self-abasement; for having been struck by the example of the person of Saint Bernard, who, being the Last of the Fathers, renews them all, perfects them all, ends them all, we have no choice but to admit that it belongs to humility to bring about such great gifts, for it makes those who are most humble on earth the greatest saints of Heaven."[63]

Thus does Anselme conclude his panegyric. His discourse may not have the oratorical power of Bossuet or the psychological insight of Massillon, but Anselme presents us with a tightly knit discourse that never loses sight of its principal theme of Bernard as the Last of the Fathers. It may appeal more to the head than to the heart, and it may, as Albert and Court suggest, lack the power and *onction* "to take the truth deep into the soul and touch the heart," but it is a fine sermon for all that.

What are Anselme's sources? In this panegyric, they are by no means copious. Apart from the Old and New Testaments (the New much more than the Old), we find citations from Tertullian, Augustine, and the *Carmen de ingratis* of Prosper of

---

[62] Anselme, of course, is a good, sound, Augustinian Westerner who accepted without question the Augustinian doctrine of the total corruption of the human race—*una massa peccati*, "one lump of sin"—as a consequence of Adam's fall. The child in the womb is 100 percent corrupt.

[63] Anselme, 241–42.

Aquitaine. For his reference to Prosper, as also for his reference to the *Gesta Friderici imperatoris* of Otto of Freising, Anselme is undoubtedly dependent on Antoine Le Maistre. In his *apologia* for the failure of the Second Crusade, he refers, as we have seen, to William of Newburgh and John of Casamari's letter of consolation to Bernard. There is also reference to one of Peter the Venerable's letters to Bernard, and, of Bernard's own works, we find allusions to or quotations from the letters (these comprise the great majority of the quotations), the letter-treatise on the errors of Abelard, the letter-treatise to Henry of Sens on the duties of bishops, the *De consideratione*, the *De gratia et libero arbitrio*, and a few sermons, including those on the Song of Songs. There is no mention at all of any of Bernard's miracles, little of his spiritual teaching, and no allusion whatever to his mysticism or mystical experiences. It is, however, a well-constructed discourse and is unique in the way in which it binds itself unerringly to its single theme. I estimate the time of delivery to have been about an hour and twenty minutes—more or less average—and I admit that, had I been sitting in the church of the Feuillants listening to Anselme's panegyric, the time would have passed quickly. But we must now leave the earthly Fathers and raise our eyes to heaven, there to see the serried ranks of angels and understand our saint as one of their celestial company, a true *angelus Domini*. Let us introduce Louis-Bénigne Bourru.

Louis-Bénigne Bourru

Of Bourru's life we know hardly anything. The *Dictionnaire universel* of Louis-Mayeul Chaudon and his colleagues tells us only that he entered the Congregation of the Oratory, that he became parish priest of Grury in Burgundy, and that he died at Paris in 1738.[64] Grury is a little village in the *département* of Saône-et-Loire, more or less in the center of France, and at

---

[64] *Dictionnaire universel, historique, critique, et bibliographique* . . . *Tome III*, ed. Louis-Mayeul Chaudon, et al., 9th ed. (Paris: Mame

the present day has only about 550 inhabitants. Bourru, as we shall see, tells us a little more about himself in the preface to his only published work, the *Recueil de panégyriques et autres discours de piété*, which appeared in 1726.[65] It is dedicated to no less a personage than Her Serene Highness Louise Adelaide d'Orléans, abbess of Chelles, who was a figure of major importance in the religious history of France during the Regency of Louis XV (1715–1723). She was born at the palace of Versailles on August 13, 1698 (her mother was Françoise-Marie de Bourbon, a legitimized daughter of Louis XIV and Madame de Montespan), and grew up to be not only intelligent but very, very beautiful. She and her younger sister were educated in the abbey of Chelles, a famous house on the eastern fringe of modern Paris, and it was there, in 1717, that she took the veil. Two years later she was appointed abbess, and she administered the abbey with great skill and success until her death from smallpox on February 10, 1743. She was forty-four.

In his preface, Bourru tells us that his style is simple, and that one should not seek in his panegyrics those empty and eloquent meanderings that so many preachers strive to achieve. That sort of eloquence may captivate its audience, but it will not make them Christian.[66] It may please the heart, but it will not correct it. The word of God is not a banquet offered to the refined palates of sinners, but a remedy for their infirmities. Do not seek, therefore, to find here those puerilities of the College or the amusements of the Academy so cherished by

---

Frères, 1810), 225. There is no entry for Bourru in the DTC, DS, DHGE, or DBF.

[65] *Recueil de panégyriques et autres discours de piété. Par M. Louis-Bénigne Bourru, Curé de Grury en Bourgogne* (Paris: Chez Paulus-du-Mesnil, 1726). It is a volume of 420 pages, with an unpaginated dedicatory letter, preface, and (at the end) a useful table of contents. It is cited below as Bourru.

[66] Bourru, p. 4 of the unpaginated preface. The French is neater: "cette eloquence qui fait des curieux & non pas des Chrétiens."

young orators. He himself, he tells us, has had much experience in these matters, for he has preached in many cathedrals of the kingdom for more than twenty years,[67] and he knows what he is talking about! He also disparages the complicated divisions and subdivisions that were standard in the sermons of his time and warns his readers that they will not find them in his simple style. And if they find that style to be less rulebound than what they are used to, that does not trouble him at all, for "the Fathers of the Church with their simple homilies captured their listeners' attention and reduced them to torrents of tears. But all these rules to which the discourses of our present day are subject, far from touching [*toucher*] those that hear them, serve only to tickle their ears or often, happily, send them to sleep."[68] The purpose of preaching (as we know) is to touch or move the heart and bring about a true conversion, and that is what Bourru hopes to accomplish with his simple but effective style.

It was not, however, entirely to the liking of Albert and Court, whose ever-critical eyes found Bourru's simplicity somewhat over simplified. His divisions, they say, are indeed simple, but the points he makes are not always presented as logically or as solidly as they might be, "and it seems that the author too often neglects using those subdivisions that contribute not a little to making a discourse clear, accurate, and easier to remember."[69] I cannot say that I agree—if you want a sermon with a plethora of divisions, subdivisions, and subsubdivisions, go to Biroat—and I enjoy the flow of Bourru's work. Alone of all the preachers we have considered, he offers us two panegyrics on Bernard,[70] both preached on his feast

---

[67] Bourru, p. 7 of the unpaginated preface: "l'expérience que je dois m'être acquise depuis plus de vingt ans que j'ai l'honneur de prêcher dans plusieurs Cathédrales du Royaume."

[68] Bourru, p. 12 of the unpaginated preface.

[69] Albert / Court, 422–23.

[70] Bourru, 42–78 (Panegyric I), 79–116 (Panegyric II).

day, August 20, and both apparently to a mixed audience, but there is no clue as to the year.

For his first panegyric, Bourru takes as his text the description of the ideal Jewish priest as we find it in Malachi 2:7. This we would now translate as "The lips of the priest should guard knowledge, and people should seek instruction from his mouth, for he is the messenger of the Lord of Hosts." The Hebrew word for *messenger*, however, is *mal'ak*, which has exactly the same root as the Greek word *angelos*, namely, "to bring or bear a message" or "to announce"; *angelos* became *angelus* in Latin and *angel* in English. In other words, an angel is simply one of God's messengers.[71] Thus, in the Vulgate, the priest is the *angelus Domini exercituum*, the "angel" of the Lord of Hosts, and to understand Bourru's panegyric, we must think of angels not just as human messengers but also as heavenly beings—celestial Intelligences—with wings. He himself translates his text as "They take the Law from him as from an angel of the Lord."[72] The *him*, obviously, is now going to be Bernard of Clairvaux, not a Jewish priest.

Bourru, of course, is well aware of this double meaning and explains it at the beginning of his panegyric. The term *angel*, he says, may indeed refer to the heavenly powers, but it may also refer to "apostolic men and those who are truly zealous for the glory of God."[73] The Patriarchs, for example, from whom the people received God's law,

> and it is in this sense, Gentlemen, that, in order to give the eulogy of the devout Saint Bernard who has been praised with such eloquence by so many mouths and pens, and having found on earth nothing sufficiently great to provide me with ideas commensurate with

---

[71] The name Malachi itself means "my messenger."

[72] Bourru, 42. As we have seen many times, the preachers of the period regularly translated their texts to suit their own purposes.

[73] Bourru, 43.

my zeal and the veneration I have for him, I think that I should take my attempt to heaven itself, and seek among the blessed Intelligences some traits that may set out the character of this great saint and, from the life of the angels, give us some idea of the whole extraordinary life of this great patriarch, whom, it seems, God has made a visible angel in order to make him a doctor of his Church and an interpreter of his will.

And so, Gentlemen, when I call him the unshakeable buttress and the foundation stone of the Church, the destroyer of schisms and heresies, I will be using only the words of the historians of his life, those who have given him these high-sounding and splendid titles. If I call him the apostle of his age, God's agent on earth, the thaumaturge of his time, I shall be putting forth only the ideas of an illustrious and learned cardinal [Baronius[74]] who tells us that this saint performed more miracles than any other mentioned in his Ecclesiastical Annals. If I call him the oracle of the councils, the voice of the Holy Spirit, the mouth of truth, I will be uttering but a faint echo of what has been said by holy pontiffs, by the most powerful monarchs, and the most learned men—all of whom have presented us with these views of this man of God. It is this that gives me the right to call him an angel, whom God used to announce a law of love and grace.[75]

And since it was through the intercession of the Virgin that Bernard received "that sweet and holy unction without which no preacher can touch his audience,"[76] Bourru, too, pleads for the help of the Queen of the Angels—*Ave Maria*—in delivering a eulogy worthy of one who was so devoted and so dear to her.

---

[74] Baronius also appears as an authority in the panegyrics of Fromentières, Lion, and Boudon.

[75] Bourru, 43–45.

[76] In these few words we have a neat summary of the purpose of the seventeenth- (and eighteenth-) century sermon. See further chap. 3.

There then follows a discussion of the nature of angels—what they are, what they do, how they bear "the character of Divinity,"[77] their relationship to God and to humans (a matter that includes the nature and duties of guardian angels[78]), how they may sin, and the effects of that sin—which is of the greatest interest to those interested in seventeenth-century French angelology. That, however, is not here our concern, and after these preliminary observations, Bourru brings us back to earth by telling us that Bernard was an angel in visible form simply "by the penances he performed from his youth, which is the subject of my first point, and by the innocence he preserved in all the great matters which were entrusted to him, which is the subject of my second point."[79]

Just as angels are perfect from the very moment of their creation, and receive from God all the fullness of grace and perfection that they are capable of possessing in eternity, so Bernard, "this angel on earth," was also perfect from his human birth in his practice of virtue. Here we are back on familiar ground. The young, we are told, are generally corrupted by two major faults: an inordinate love of pleasure, which serves only to inflame their passions, and a lack of piety, which leads them to have a distaste for the practice of virtue. In Bernard (as we might expect) neither of these shortcomings was to be found. He preserved his angelic purity throughout all temptations, and since he knew that angels are wholly spirit and have nothing to do with physical bodies, "he believed that he should choose a retreat where his heart could be ever open to God and closed to the world."[80]

This, in due course, would lead him to Cîteaux, but first it led him to the old chapel of Saint-Vorles at Châtillon-sur-Seine,

---

[77] Bourru, 46.

[78] There was much interest in guardian angels in the seventeenth and eighteenth centuries: see chap. 4 (Biroat), n. 40.

[79] Bourru, 47–48.

[80] Bourru, 53.

where, on the night of Christmas, he was vouchsafed a vision of the child Jesus, who revealed to him the mystery of his holy nativity.[81] Claude Lion and Fléchier also record this vision, but it is by no means common among the panegyrists. Our preacher then likens Bernard to Benjamin, who is described in Psalm 67:28 as *adolescentulus in mentis excessu*, "a very young man in ecstasy of spirit." Does this mean that Bourru will actually describe Bernard's own mystical experiences? We shall see. For the moment, he continues by telling us that his vision was a result of Bernard's overwhelming love of God, and he laments his own inability to express its depths and profundity in suitable words. But one thing is certain: "there is but one thing by which we can worthily come to know God, and that sole thing is the love we bear him. For until then, continues the great saint, the language of love is unknown and barbarous to one who does not love."[82]

But how can I tell you what went on in his heart? asks Bourru. How can I describe the heights to which his love bore him? These are unknown to me, he says, but if "the preludes of his devotion" were the ecstasies of his infancy, how much greater will be their consummation, when the Bridegroom leads the loving soul into the holy wine cellars, "where he lovingly inebriates them with torrents of heavenly pleasures and everlasting delights."[83] Bernard's devotion to God in his childhood might have been remarkable, but it was only a foretaste of what was to come. Bourru then plays on the fountain of Fontaine-lès-Dijon, where Bernard was born, by paraphrasing Mordecai's dream in the book of Esther when he saw "a little fountain that grew into a river, and was turned into light, and then into the sun."[84] For Mordecai, this was Esther; for Bourru,

---

[81] See *Vita prima*, 1.2.4 (William of Saint-Thierry); PL 185:228D–29B; CF 76:6–7. See also Williams, *Saint Bernard*, 6.

[82] Bourru, 54–55, quoting Bernard, SC 79.1.1; SBOp 2:273.

[83] Bourru, 55, quoting Ps 35:9, which Bernard himself also quotes numerous times.

[84] Esth 10:6.

of course, it is Bernard: "Yes, Saint Bernard, from little Fontaine and Châtillon, would become a dazzling light for the whole of France, and as a sun to the whole Christian world. But just as penance made him an angel from his youth, let us see now how it preserved his innocence in all the great things for which Heaven had destined him. This is the second part [of my discourse]."[85]

Bourru begins his second part by returning to the nature of angels. Angels, he says (on the authority of Saint Thomas Aquinas "and other theologians") have a totally simple and spiritual substance in which flesh and blood play no part, but on occasion they may take visible form. This is what the archangel Raphael did when he appeared to Tobit as a handsome young man, properly attired, and apparently ready to accompany him on his road.[86] He even appeared to eat, though he did not need to,

> for being indivisible in his being (as the theologians tell us), he did not need to keep up his strength nor add anything to his substance. The life of this angel was therefore a life without life, tangible and earthly in appearance through the body he borrowed, while spiritual and heavenly in his own nature.
>
> Such, Gentlemen, was the life of that earthly angel Saint Bernard. He was, so to speak, an intelligence united to a body: he animated his [physical] material but without being there, save in the manner of a pure spirit. And I do not think I exaggerate when I say that he lived without living, insofar as he was dead to his senses and his passions.[87]

---

[85] Bourru, 56–57.

[86] See Tobit 5:5. Bourru has two interesting pages on just how angels, whose substance, as we have seen, is wholly simple and spiritual, can take on human form, which is neither simple nor spiritual.

[87] Bourru, 59.

Bourru then tells us the well-known tales of Bernard not knowing whether the dormitory was vaulted with stone or paneled with wood, of his day's journey by Lake Geneva without noticing it, of the rich harness of his borrowed horse when he visited the Carthusians, of his drinking oil instead of wine, and of reducing his food almost to nothing since eating was a torment for him.[88] Indeed, he had no taste for anything, save what was given to him by the spirit of penance and the love of God. He lived in the flesh, but not according to the flesh, and Bourru quotes, in the margin, a well-known saying that he attributes, incorrectly, to Bernard: *In carne praeter carnem vivere, non humana sed angelica vita est,* "To live in the flesh but apart from the flesh is not the human but the angelic life."[89] Saint Paul says much the same thing.[90]

Bernard, then, was oblivious to anything the world might have to offer. Pleasures, honors, riches meant nothing to him. His eyes and his heart were fixed on God alone, "a God before whom all created things are nothing but deformities, all greatness nothing but meanness, all riches nothing but poverty; a God whose goodness and beauty make all things good and perfect, with whom nothing is everything, and without whom everything is nothing."[91]

Thus it was that Bernard lived without living, for he lived only for the spirit, finding sweetness only in loving God and wholly renouncing all the things of earth. And now, for the last dozen or so pages of his first panegyric, Bourru contrasts Bernard's angelic way of life with ours—what he says here is only what we would expect, but he says it very well and lays

---

[88] We have read all these stories in the other panegyrics.

[89] Bourru, 62. This does not appear anywhere in Bernard, but in this or similar form it appears in a considerable number of other writers.

[90] See Rom 8:13: "If you live according to the flesh, you shall die; but if, by the Spirit, you mortify the deeds of the flesh, you shall live." Bourru quotes the text in Latin with a French paraphrase on page 62.

[91] Bourru, 63.

out the contrasts in compelling detail. It is clear, too, that he is speaking to a mixed congregation, for he rebukes the ladies in his audience in just the same way as the gentlemen. He condemns their concern with empty adornment, their love of luxury and finery. They spend more time with their pet dogs and birds than in seeking God, to say nothing of the hours they waste in foolish games, in showing themselves off in public, and in even more perilous pursuits. The time and leisure God has given them were not meant for such frivolities, but for seeking the God who gave them! Their unruly hearts lead them into useless conversations, into scandalmongering, into idleness and vice. They do not take the time to reflect on what they are really like, on the fact that they are wicked sinners, and that their conduct is so often so wayward and sinful in the eyes of God. "In short, you worldly people, whatever your sex, whatever your state, whatever your condition in life, take note, I beg you, that no human act is ever neutral. Every one of them is either good or bad, according to the end to which it is directed, for in matters of morality, it is the end that determines the act. Do you take the time always to direct your efforts to a good end? An end in which cupidity, ambition, greed, and carnal pleasure play no part?"[92] Obviously they—and we—do not, and the passage that follows deserves to be quoted in full:

> Every morning, you say, we give our hearts to God and offer up to him all that we do in the course of the day. That's all good, that's all Christian—but here's what's bad. When you wake up, you give your hearts to God, but you don't notice that two hours later you take it away from him! You offer up your actions to God in the morning, and the rest of the day you give them over to the Devil! In the morning you say, "My God, my wish is that all my thoughts, my words, my actions may be to your glory," and the rest of the day you devote

---

[92] Bourru, 74.

them to sensual pleasures and created things. What this means is that in the morning you chant a song or prayer to God that you have been taught in school or in the convent, and the rest of the day what you say and what you do are for yourselves, for the world, for your own self-love![93]

Only by following in the glorious footsteps of the great saint will we achieve salvation; only by imitating his sublime virtues will we share in his victories and come, one day, to share the crown that he already possesses in heaven.

Such, in essence, is Père Bourru's first panegyric on Saint Bernard, but interesting though it is for the study of angels, it is singularly lacking in those historical facts that, for Armand-Germain de Tréverret, were so important. We do not meet Peter Abelard or Gilbert de la Porrée or Henry of Toulouse. We hear nothing about the papal schism. The names of Innocent and Anacletus are never mentioned. We do not meet any of the usual *dramatis personae* associated with that schism (not even our favorite duke, William X of Aquitaine). There is no mention of any church council. And we hear nothing of Bernard's miracles.

All this, however, will be rectified in our preacher's second panegyric, preached on a text from the book of Wisdom that Bourru paraphrases thus: "The Lord guided this just man by right paths; he made him glorious in his works and heaped blessings upon him."[94] In this panegyric, the angels are left where they belong, in heaven, and we now witness Bernard's labors on earth. We begin, therefore, not with Bernard the earthly angel, but with Bernard the just abbot of Clairvaux, whom God would lead *per vias rectas*, "by right paths," who would see him highly honored for what he accomplished, and

---

[93] Bourru, 75.
[94] Wisdom 10:10, abbreviated and amended. Esprit Fléchier used essentially the text in his panegyric of 1683 (see chap. 12).

who would crown his career with success in all that he undertook. Bourru will therefore divide his discourse into three parts. In the first he will show the impact that the voice of the saints can have on the most insensitive beings in the natural world. In the second he will show the impact that the wisdom of the saints can have on the proudest and most rebellious minds in the moral[95] and political world. In the third he will show the impact that the goodness of heart of the saints can have on God's own heart in the celestial and divine world. And to help him achieve all this, he begs for the illumination of the Holy Spirit through the intercession of the Holy Virgin: *Ave Maria*.

In the natural world, says Bourru, we see a marvelous harmony between heaven and earth, bodies simple and composite, bodies animate and inanimate, days and nights, months and years, and so on. This is how it has been since creation (which took place six thousand and more years ago[96]), and creation (as Tertullian says) is truly a work worthy of God.[97] And just as it was the voice of God that brought all things into being, so it is God who sustains them and moves them in their appointed courses, and in a similar way, it is God who gives to the voice of his saints (feeble though it may appear to us) such an astonishing power that it seems that the whole of nature is subservient to them. And in whom can this best be seen but in the great Saint Bernard? What man, since the apostles, has ever worked more miracles, performed more marvels, and changed the order of things? Nor did these wonders take place now and then, here and there, with just a few witnesses. Indeed

---

[95] The *monde moral*, which is the world of right and wrong, is also the world of true and false doctrine. This, therefore, is where we shall hear of Bernard's battles with heresy and heretics.

[96] Bourru, 85: "depuis six mil ans & plus." In Bourru's day, suggested dates for the first day of creation varied from 4004 BCE (James Ussher) to 3949 BCE (Joseph Scaliger) BCE.

[97] Bourru, 85, quoting Tertullian, *Adversus Marcionem* 1.13; PL 2:260A.

they did not. They took place in the sight of entire kingdoms, in the presence of people of every age, both sexes, and every state and condition of life, of those who believed and those who did not believe, in the towns and cities as well as in the countryside. And Bourru goes on to narrate at some length the miracle of the blessed bread at Sarlat and then tells the story of the ten cripples, eleven blind men, and eighteen lame healed in a single day at Constance.[98] What he did in Cologne is no less worthy of our admiration, says Bourru, and although he does not say so, he is undoubtedly referring to the occasion when Bernard was in the city preaching the Second Crusade and performed so many remarkable cures that the streets were thronged with people, all crying out "Christ, uns gnade! Kyrie eleison! Die Heiligen alle helffen uns!"[99] Even demons were subject to his will, as may be seen from the many demoniacs he delivered from their afflictions in Milan and Padua. He was indeed the Thaumaturge of the West—Bourru echoes Boudon and Claude Lion[100]—but the greatest miracle was the way in which he was not in the least dazzled by the glory that his miracles brought him, and that he still saw himself as nothing while the whole world applauded his deeds.

How different are we! We are consumed by pride (and it was through his pride that Adam fell) and all the effects of self-love and self-will. But it is God, not we, who must be the master of our heart, and we can only lose our self-will by losing it in the will of God. We may then say with the apostle, "I live, yet not I: Christ lives in me."[101] But what do we see when we examine

---

[98] Both miracles are also recounted by Fénelon: see chap. 8 (Fénelon), §§27–28, for the sources. Senault also records the miracle at Sarlat.

[99] See *Vita prima* 6.8.28 (Gerard of Clairvaux); PL 185:391CD; Williams, *Saint Bernard*, 275.

[100] Bourru, 90. See chap. 11 (Boudon), n. 19, and chap. 12 (Lion et al.), nn. 27–29.

[101] Bourru, 92, quoting Gal 2:20 in Latin.

ourselves? A weak and feeble spirit and a heart that tends too easily to wickedness. Before the strength and perfection of God, we are as nothing. And this is something Bernard never forgot. In the midst of all his great deeds he never forgot that he came from dust, and he was ever aware of human frailty when compared with the power of God. Such, indeed, is the effect of true Christian humility: we always recognize our lowliness, we are always aware of our weakness, we are always pierced by the knowledge of our own sinfulness, "and we always grovel before God and human beings."[102]

This is just what we see in Bernard. Despite his fame, despite his renown, despite the power he wielded, despite his wisdom, despite his marvels and miracles, he remained truly humble. But the more he humbled himself, the more he was sought out by kings and those in authority, and the more he abased himself, the more they called on his wisdom to solve the problems and difficulties in the moral and political world.

So what is this *monde moral et politique*? Bourru leaves us in no doubt:

> By the moral and political world, Gentlemen, I mean this grandiose assemblage of towns, provinces, states, and sovereignties, empires and monarchies that unite the small with the great, the weak with the strong, servants with their masters, citizens with magistrates, subjects with their princes, the children of the Church with their common Father [the pope], who is the Vicar of Jesus Christ on earth, under those laws and ordinances that Eternal Wisdom has dictated to each according to his or her condition in life.[103]

---

[102] Bourru, 93. The verb is *ramper*, "to grovel, creep, crawl": a powerful word.

[103] Bourru, 93–94. Bourru naturally agrees with Cecil F. Alexander: "The rich man in his castle, / The poor man at his gate, / He made them, high or lowly, / And ordered their estate." Nowadays, for obvious reasons, this verse is usually omitted from the hymn.

Last of the Fathers and the Angel of the Lord 477

And what is the secret of preserving this unity, this harmony? It is to observe these laws and ordinances with faithfulness, sincerity, and perseverance. But do we see this in those around us? Indeed we do not!

> Oh deadly blindness of the human spirit! Into what dark places do we not see people falling every day? Into what aberrations, what grave dangers, what confused ideas, and, in a word, what rejections of these wonderful laws of Eternal Wisdom? [We see it with] kings on their thrones, the strong and valiant in the armed forces, Ministers of State at the courts of their princes, pastors of the people in the Church, scholars in their disputations, monks and nuns in their cloisters, and freethinkers and the ungodly in the corruption of the world.[104]

And since it was just this sort of disorder, rebellion, darkness, and confusion that Bernard found around him in his own century, Bourru can now tell us what he did, and how, in his God-given wisdom, prudence, and judgment, he was able to restore order to disorder and replace falsehood with truth. We are now, so to speak, on home territory, as Bourru tells us of parts of the country ravaged by fire and blood, of the papal schism, and of the curse of heresy. He takes us to the Council of Sens, called to examine the ideas of Abelard, "the most famous teacher and most subtle mind of his day,"[105] to the Council of Reims, called to decide on the dangerous ideas on the mystery of the Trinity put forth by Gilbert de la Porrée, bishop of Poitiers, and to the Council of Étampes, where Bernard declared the election of "Peter de Leon, surnamed Anacletus" to be null and void and that the whole church should recognize Innocent II as the true pontiff. We hear of

---

[104] Bourru, 94–95.
[105] Bourru, 97. *Subtle*, as usual, is here a pejorative term: see appendix 1, s.v. *subtil, subtilité* / subtle, subtlety.

his meeting with Henry I of England at Chartres, we hear (of course we hear!) of the astonishing conversion of Duke William X of Aquitaine, we hear of Bernard's achievements in ending the schism in Milan and Pisa, we hear the stories of Roger, king of Sicily, and the Holy Roman emperor Lothair III, and of the eventual ending of the schism with the death of Anacletus.

But hardly had the schism been healed than Bernard was faced with new challenges. Bourru now tells us of his battle with Arnold of Brescia, a man whose way of life was sweet as honey but whose teachings were pure poison, a man with the head of a dove and a tail of a dragon (Bourru is quoting Bernard's own description[106]). He then makes a brief return to the iniquities of Abelard before moving on to Henry of Toulouse and the problems in the Languedoc. Gilbert de la Porrée puts in a last fleeting appearance before our preacher summarizes Bernard's achievements: by the power of his hand, pen, or voice, by his letters, sermons, or discourses, the heretics, whoever they were and wherever they might have been, either withdrew in shame or embraced Bernard as the master, the conqueror, the destroyer of all the false ideas to which their proud reasoning had given rise.

But the power that Bernard had over other minds might also be seen in other ways, not only in his victories over heresy and false doctrine. Did he not persuade his maternal uncle, Gaudry of Touillon, to join him "in the horror of his frightful desert" at Cîteaux?[107] Did he not do the same with his brothers, his father, and thirty young friends? And before his death, did he not have the consolation of seeing a hundred and sixty houses of his Order as so many notable trophies to the power of his wis-

---

[106] Bourru, 102, quoting Bernard, Ep 196.1; SBOp 8:51, to Guy, cardinal legate in Bohemia. Bourru has *tail of a dragon* for Bernard's *tail of a scorpion*.

[107] Bourru, 104. See *Vita prima* 1.3.10 (William of Saint-Thierry); PL 185:232B; CF 76:12–14. Bourru calls Gaudry Ulderic, but that is no more than a typographical error for Galdericus or Galdricus.

dom over the most rebellious minds in the moral and Christian world? He did indeed, and with this last demonstration of the remarkable impact of Bernard's wisdom on *le monde moral et politique*, Bourru turns to his third and last point, namely, "to have you see the effect of the goodness and innocence of his heart on the heart of God himself."[108]

It is only natural, says Bourru, that if Bernard did so much for the glory of God and his church, that God would do great things for him. And so he did. He showered him with graces and favors in three ways: first, with regard to his body; second, with regard to his spirit; and third with regard to his heart. With regard to his body, God gave him a remarkable charm and beauty, but this was combined with so great an angelic chastity and modesty that the Queen of the Angels herself did not disdain to adopt him as her son. Bourru is referring, of course, to the miracle of the Lactation, mentioned also by Boudon, Planchette, and Lion, when Bernard was nourished with the same milk that nourished the body of Jesus Christ himself. But after that, what taste could he have for earthly food? As "the historian of his life"—William of Saint-Thierry—tells us, the very idea of eating with his brethren was a torment to him.[109] But why did the Mother of God accord him this astonishing grace, asks Bourru (somewhat impertinently)? Perhaps for two reasons: the first to show Bernard that she had truly adopted him as her son, and the second to make him understand that her wish was that he should work earnestly to make himself similar to her and to Jesus Christ in his absolute purity. He has now become the foster-brother of his Lord and Savior.

The second of the three graces that Bernard received was that which pertained to his spirit. Like a second Samuel, God

---

[108] Bourru, 105. It will be remembered that the first two points were (1) Bernard's impact on the natural world, and (2) his impact on the moral and political world.

[109] See *Vita prima* 1.4.22 (William of Saint-Thierry); PL 185:239CD; CF 76:25–26.

had revealed to him his will and his mysteries from his infancy, and he had had no other masters but the Holy Spirit. It was the Spirit who taught him in the woods and forests[110] and revealed to him the perfection of God through created things, the power of God in their creation and preservation, the wisdom of God in the beauty of their order, the providence of God in their government, the immensity of God in their far-reaching compass, the eternity of God in their continuance, and the justice of God in their punishments and rewards. It was just the same master who explained to him inwardly all the divine mysteries and all the senses of Scripture—he himself said that in his meditations or prayers, the true meaning of all the Holy Books was laid before him[111]—but what Bourru finds so remarkable in all this is the way in which Bernard continued his prayers and meditations while embroiled in all that he was called to do in the world. "Let me explain," he says:

> In other men, it is rare if action does not succeed the contemplation of divine things in a sort of continual interchange. Something that Saint Denis [the Areopagite] calls a miracle and a circle,[112] now Martha, now Mary, one after the other. But in our saint, says his historian, by the privilege of a special grace, he is at one and the same time both in action and in contemplation.[113] It has

---

[110] Bourru here follows a number of the other panegyrists in echoing *Vita prima* 1.4.23 (William of Saint-Thierry); PL 185:240CD; CF 76:27, and Bernard's own statement in his Ep 106.2; SBOp 7:266–67, to Henry Murdac: "Believe me, who have experience of this: you will find more in the woods than in books, and stones will teach you what you cannot hear from any master."

[111] See *Vita prima* 3.3.7 (Geoffrey of Auxerre); PL 185:307BC; CF 76:152–53.

[112] See ps.-Dionysius, De div nom 4.9; *Dionysius the Areopagite. The Divine Names and the Mystical Theology*, trans. Clarence E. Rolt (London: SPCK, 1940), 98–99.

[113] See *Vita prima* 1.4.23 (William of Saint-Thierry); PL 185:240CD; CF 76:26–27.

been said that while he was completely occupied with what he had to do externally, inwardly he was totally occupied with God.[114]

Yet all this had not the least effect on how Bernard viewed himself. However great he was before God and man, in his own eyes he was always utterly insignificant; and whatever praise he justly deserved, he would accept not one word of it. He saw himself only as the monster and the prodigy of his time,[115] and if he knew that his course had been directed by God, no rebuke, no censure, no denunciation, no ridicule could affect him. Consider, says Bourru, his preaching of the Second Crusade.

Bernard preached the Crusade in obedience to Pope Eugenius III, but after it had failed, and failed so disastrously, he found himself the butt of jokes, insults, and even curses. "How do you think his great heart was affected by all this? Far from being troubled by them, he accepted these jokes, insults, and curses with more joy than he had ever accepted compliments!" He wrote to the Holy Father himself, saying, "We said 'Peace,' and there is no peace. We promised good news, and behold! disaster!"[116] What I said and what I did was at your command, "but who can fathom the secrets of God and the incomprehensible ways of his wisdom?"[117] Bourru then goes on to offer more of Bernard's *apologia* for the failure of the Crusade, telling us that, far from being grieved by the insults and the ridicule, he gloried in them! My glory, he says

---

[114] Bourru, 111, quoting *Vita prima* 1.4.23 (William of Saint-Thierry); PL 185:240C; CF 76:26: *simul et totus quodammodo exterius laborabat, et totus interius Deo vacabat*.

[115] Bourru, 112, quotes Bernard's famous description of himself—*chimaera mei saeculi*—from his Ep 250:4; SBOp 8:147, to the Carthusian Prior of Portes. Texier, Rancé, La Rue, and Anselme also cite the passage.

[116] Bourru, 113, quoting Bernard, Csi 2.1.1; SBOp 3:411.

[117] Bourru, 114, echoing (but not quoting) Bernard.

(quoting Psalm 68), "is to become the companion of Christ, who himself said 'The reproaches of those who reproach you have fallen on me.'"[118]

This indeed is the Christian way, for the whole of Christian perfection is to be found in doing all that one can to receive from heaven a truly noble heart, a heart that is raised above all the pleasures, riches, and honors that the world might offer, a heart that believes itself wholly unworthy of its own nobility and greatness,[119] a heart that lives only for humiliation, scorn, and abasement, and a heart that finds its true happiness only in its esteem and love for the way of the cross. And thus Bourru concludes his panegyric with a fervent prayer that this might be so. "Great God,"[120] he says,

> I do not ask you today for the power you gave to Saint Bernard over the most unfeeling of creatures, or the victories that the wisdom of his spirit achieved over the most rebellious of other spirits, but only that you grant me, as you did him, to win over your divine heart, [to gain] a purity that will shelter me from all the attacks and temptations of the flesh, a spirit of wisdom to conduct myself appropriately in conformity with my state in life, and finally, a heart filled with your holy love so that I might deserve your grace in this life and the possession of your glory in the next. May it be so![121]

We cannot, perhaps, call Bourru's two panegyrics psychologically profound—they do not have the penetrating power of Massillon—but they are certainly interesting, as much for

---

[118] Bourru, 114, quoting (in the margin) Csi 2.1.4; SBOp 3:413; and Ps 68:10.

[119] I.e., because we are created in the image and likeness of God (Gen 1:26-27), crowned with glory and honor, and, in rank, just a little lower than the angels (Ps 8:6; Heb 2:7).

[120] *Grand Dieu* is one of Bourru's favorite expressions.

[121] Bourru, 116.

what their author says about angels as for what he says about Bernard. He is also fairly comprehensive in what he covers, and, unlike so many others, he is not afraid to spend some time on Bernard's many miracles, including the Lactation. He does not, however, give any real consideration to his mystical experiences, preferring to draw the picture only in broad and general strokes. He mentions Bernard's early vision of the infant Jesus at Saint-Vorles, likens him to Benjamin *in excessu mentis*, and refers briefly to the wine cellar—the *cella vinaria*—of Song of Songs 2:4, where the loving soul is inebriated by the Bridegroom with torrents of heavenly delight, but he comes nowhere near the lengthy discussion we find in Henri-Marie Boudon. In the second panegyric, *ps.*-Dionysius makes a brief appearance, but only to point out that, whereas in virtually all people action and contemplation succeed each other in a circular motion, Bernard acted while in contemplation and contemplated while in action. But after saying that, Bourru passes on swiftly to the matter of the failure of the Second Crusade. He does much the same in his panegyric on Teresa of Ávila, calling her "the infallible guide for spiritual seekers, the heavenly torch of contemplatives, the oracle of the most hidden mysteries of the mystical life, the prodigy of her sex, the miracle of her time, the dear Bride, the preferred and well-beloved Bride of Jesus Christ,"[122] but devoting his panegyric to her organizing abilities, her penitence and sufferings, and her love of God. He tells us, more than once, of her vision of the seraph with the golden spear, driving it again and again into her heart, but Teresa's descriptions of the inner rooms of the Interior Castle are discreetly avoided. On one hand, this should not surprise us.

Bourru's sources are much as we might expect, save for the fleeting glimpse of *ps.*-Dionysius: Tertullian, Ambrose, Augustine, Jerome, John Chrysostom, Thomas Aquinas (on the matter of

---

[122] Bourru, 242.

angels), and Cardinal Baronius. We have met them all before. For Bernard's life he is dependent, ultimately, on the *Vita prima*, and if he mentions, in passing, Pierre Gassendi and René Descartes,[123] it is only because a study of their ideas is a waste of time. Of Bernard's own writings, the *De consideratione* makes its usual appearance, together with some of the letters, and a couple of sermons from his commentary on the Song of Songs.

We said above that neither of Bourru's panegyrics has the penetrating power of Massillon, and neither does that of Anselme, impressive though it is. We have also had occasion to praise the psychological insight of Massillon in other chapters, and it is now time to go to the preacher himself. He is the last we shall consider in this book, and it was he who, having preached the Advent and Lenten series more than once before Louis XIV, preached that monarch's funeral oration on September 1, 1715. Louis had often been called Louis the Great, but Massillon began his eulogy with the famous words "Dieu seul est grand," "God alone is great," to the great consternation of the congregation that packed the basilica of Saint-Denis near Paris.

---

[123] See Bourru, 72.

14

Bernard the Second Samuel

The Psychological Acuity of Jean-Baptiste Massillon

INTRODUCTION

In 1851 the Reverend Edward Peach published an edited translation of Massillon's sermons for Sundays and feast days[1] and left his readers in no doubt of his admiration for his subject:

> Never, perhaps, was there a Christian orator who possessed a more perfect knowledge of the heart of man. He insinuates himself into its inmost recesses: he explores and lays open every avenue to public inspection. He delineates the affections, describes the first causes of the corruption, and displays the inward workings of the mind, with such precision and clearness that every individual who has departed from the ways of virtue beholds as exact a delineation of his own features as if the picture had been designed for him alone.[2]

If there is some Victorian hyperbole here, there is not much. Massillon was indeed an acute psychologist, and he could

---

[1] *Massillon's Sermons for All the Sundays and Festivals throughout the Year*, translated from the French by the Rev. Edward Peach (Dublin: J. Duffy, 1851). The collection does not include the panegyric on Bernard.

[2] *Massillon's Sermons*, viii.

indeed penetrate to the depths of the human heart. There is a famous story of Louis XIV, a king not especially known for his virtue, who, after hearing Massillon's Advent *station* at Versailles in 1699, said to him, "My father, I have heard many great orators in my chapel, and I have been much pleased with them. But with you, every time I have heard you, I have been very displeased with myself."[3] Louis's displeasure with himself might not have lasted overlong, but in that emotional and lachrymose age Massillon clearly made an impression. So who was this remarkable preacher who could so move—*toucher*—the heart of the Sun King?

He was born at Hyères in Provence on June 24, 1663, the son of a notary, and, having been educated by the Oratorians, joined the Congregation of the Oratory at the age of eighteen. He taught for a time in a number of colleges of the congregation—Pèzenas, Marseille, Montbrison, and Vienne—but the beginning of his fame as a preacher came in 1693 when he delivered the funeral orations for Camille de Neufville de Villeroy, archbishop of Lyon, and, six months later, for Henri de Villars, archbishop of Vienne. From July to November in 1696 he withdrew to the Cistercian abbey of Sept-Fons, an abbey of the Strict Observance then under the charismatic leadership of Dom Eustache de Beaufort. Here he developed a high esteem for the monks and an appreciation of manual labor, and years later, when he was bishop of Clermont, he looked back on his time there with nostalgic regret: "How I would love to find myself once again back in my little cell. It would be much better for me, and much more to my taste, to

---

[3] "Mon Père, j'ai entendu plusieurs grands orateurs dans ma chapelle; j'en ai été fort content: pour vous, toutes les fois que je vous ai entendu, j'ai été très-mécontent de moi-même" (*Œuvres de Massillon, évêque de Clermont. Tome premier* [Paris: Lefèvre, 1833], viii). Louis Dussieux, *Le Château de Versailles. Histoire et description*, 2 vols. (Versailles: L. Bernard, 1881), 2:110, offers a slight variation: "My Father, when I have heard the other preachers, I have been much pleased. But with you, when I hear you, I am very displeased with myself."

wear the cowl rather than the miter."[4] Apart from Bossuet and, obviously, Rancé, he is the only panegyrist of Saint Bernard to have had firsthand experience of the Cistercian tradition, and his respect for the Strict Observance is reflected in his comments in §14, §16, §18, and especially §26 of his panegyric.

His retreat at the abbey ended when, at the instigation of the archbishop of Paris, Louis-Antoine de Noailles, he was called by his superior in the Oratory to take over the direction of the Oratorian house of Saint-Magloire in Paris, and, once there, he rapidly became known for his oratorical skills. In 1699 he was chosen to preach the Advent *station* before the king and Court at Versailles, and in 1701 and 1704 he preached the Lenten *stations* with great success. Then, for reasons that are not entirely clear, he fell from the royal favor and, during Louis's lifetime, was never summoned to Court again. Nor was he offered a bishopric, the usual reward for those "prédicateurs épiscopants"[5] who had caught the attention of the king. When Louis died, however, it was Massillon, as we have seen, who preached his funeral oration, and after the king's death he returned to favor at Court, and, in 1717, the Regent, the Duke of Orléans, nominated him bishop of Clermont, a large and wealthy diocese in central France. The following year he preached the *Petit Carême*—a Lenten series of just ten sermons—before the young Louis XV, and a few months later he was elected to the *Académie française*.

After his appointment to Clermont he devoted himself to work in his diocese, and from 1718 preached no more at Court or in Paris. His labors as bishop are not here our concern,[6] but he was a devoted pastor to his flock, and when he died, on

---

[4] *Sept-Fons. Étude historique sur l'abbaye de N.-D. de Saint-Lieu Sept-Fons, depuis sa fondation jusqu'à ce jour, par un Religieux de ce monastère* (Moulins: A. Ducroux et G. Dulac, 1873), 85.

[5] See chap. 3, n. 4.

[6] The best account of Massillon's years as bishop remains Émile-Auguste Blampignon, *L'Épiscopat de Massillon d'après des documents inédits suivi de sa correspondance* (Paris: E. Plon, 1884).

September 28, 1742, he was much lamented. According to the critic and literary historian Ferdinand Brunetière, Massillon was "one of the best, the most amiable, and the most virtuous of all those who could hold an honored place in the history of our literature and of the French episcopate."[7]

In his sermons, he was known for his probing of the heart and the passions and his psychological insight,[8] and in the opinion of Albert and Court he opened up a completely new direction in the ministry of preaching.[9] The vast majority of the preachers of his day concentrated on what might be called the outward aspects of morality, drawing attention to the all-too-varied vices of their audience, reminding them forcefully of truths they already knew and exhorting them to follow general principles with which everyone was familiar. Massillon emphasized the inward aspect, seeking the motives that led to these errors and investigating the innumerable subtle ways in which self-love could lead one astray. As Edwin Dargan has said, he "sought to awaken and guide the purest and noblest sentiments,"[10] and he appealed more to the feelings than to reason or the imagination. His method was not, in general, that of vigorous denunciation (as may be seen in Bourdaloue and so many others), but of gentle and subtle persuasion and remarkably acute psychological analysis. This is not to say that he could not be severe. There are some sermons in which Massillon sounds positively Jansenist. Yet there are others in which his listeners thought they could detect a Jesuitical laxity.

It is understandable, therefore, that Massillon normally avoids any discussion of Christian doctrine and confines himself almost entirely to ethics and morals. It is equally understandable that that would not go down too well with Tréverret, who has no problem with the idea that Massillon wishes to

---

[7] See DLF 18.857.
[8] See Van Eijnatten, "Reaching Audiences," 142.
[9] Albert / Court, 167.
[10] Dargan, *History of Preaching*, 2:89.

instruct his audience, but (says Tréverret) what Massillon fails to recognize is that a detailed precise account of the actions of a saint is itself a means of instruction.[11] In his view, Massillon's panegyrics are not sufficiently specific in historical terms, and he does better in his sermons.[12] The *abbé* Trublet, too, considered Massillon to be a preacher only of the second rank, and he much preferred the solidity (*solidité*), inexorable logic, and appeal to human reason of Bourdaloue.[13] In Trublet's view, Massillon's sermons certainly possessed *onction*, there is no doubt about that, but unless that unction were restrained by logic, his sermons could be a little too unctuous. Cardinal Maury tends to agree. While lavishing high praise on Massillon's captivating style—*son style enchanteur*—he also suggests that his reasoning was not always as sound as it might have been, and that this sometimes detracts from the impact and weight that his sermons should have had.[14] What, then, of his panegyric on Bernard?

Massillon's text is the eulogy on Samuel that appears in chapter 46 of Ecclesiasticus/Sirach, and just as Samuel spent his first years in the peace of the sanctuary, then came forth to become "the lawgiver of the tribes," and, finally, was inspired by God to be a true prophet in defense of the faith, so Bernard, "the Samuel of his century," would spend years in the cloister as the perfect monk, come forth to solve problems of church and state as the apostolic man, and, as the undefeatable doctor, utterly demolish the dragons of heresy. These are the three parts of Massillon's discourse—Bernard in the cloister, Bernard in the world, Bernard confounding heresy and schism—and in the course of his sermon Massillon compares him to no less than eight figures: six from the Old Testament (Samuel,

---

[11] Tréverret, 208.
[12] See Tréverret, 210.
[13] Trublet, *Panégyriques des Saints*, 70–71.
[14] Maury, 2:20. His whole chapter on Massillon (2:1–21) is well worth reading.

Daniel, Elijah, Jonah, Joseph, and Moses), one from the New Testament (John the Baptist), and one church father (Ambrose). The exordium ends with a cursory invocation to the Virgin, but that is not uncommon in Massillon.[15]

For the story of Bernard's life, Massillon is entirely dependent on the *Vita prima*, and he introduces nothing that we have not already seen. On the other hand, there is more in the way of specific historical information than we might expect from reading Tréverret, though Massillon himself (like Bernard Planchette before him) distinguishes eulogy from history.[16] We are told of Bernard's early years in a pious household, we hear of the episode of the icy pool, we see him leading a host of friends and relatives to Cîteaux, we learn of Stephen Harding's joy at receiving him, and we are told of Bernard's asceticism and mortification at Cîteaux and Clairvaux. And what was the reason for this? His love of penance and the cross of Christ!

Then, in Part Two of the panegyric, we move on to Bernard's work in the world. He comes forth from his beloved cloister to heal the papal schism and to see his own monks appointed to the highest positions in the church. He rebukes those who would challenge the church or contravene the essential principles of Christian morality: he mentions Louis VI the Fat's "usurping the rights of the Church," the massacre at Vitry instigated by Louis VII the Young, Suger's reform of Saint-Denis, Eleanor of Aquitaine's conflict with Bernard, the five books *On Consideration* addressed to Pope Eugenius III, Bernard's rejection of his sister when she came to visit him at Clairvaux, and the reasons for the failure of the Second Crusade.

Part Three begins with an account of Bernard's passion for the Holy Scriptures, for it was his knowledge of the Holy Books that made him such a formidable opponent. Massillon now offers a short history of the papal schism and its resolution

---

[15] See n. 36 below.
[16] See §56: "a eulogy is not a history, and we cannot include everything." For Planchette, see chap. 5 (Senault et al.), n. 55.

at the Council of Étampes (he mentions, though very briefly, the dramatic conversion of William X of Aquitaine) and then passes on, as we might expect, to the heresies of Peter Abelard, Gilbert de la Porrée, and Henry of Toulouse. And then, finally, he returns to the theme of Bernard's humility, citing his refusal of bishoprics and archbishoprics, telling the story of Innocent II's visit to Clairvaux, and quoting Bernard's description of himself as the chimera of his age.

There is, as we have said, nothing here that we have not seen before: the difference lies in Massillon's unique style. The historical information is not presented as a lump, to be followed by a second lump of criticism and encouragement. It is rather woven seamlessly into the whole, and Massillon's admonitions and exhortations to his audience appear throughout. There can be no doubt, too, of his psychological insight (witness the subtlety of §61, where Massillon shows how holy charity itself can sometimes lead us astray[17]), and Albert and Court are right when they tell us that Massillon has turned the ministry of preaching in an entirely new direction. Like so many of his confrères, he makes no mention at all of Bernard's mysticism or mystical experiences, and although he refers to his miracles, there is no detailed account of any of them. His sources are limited, but that is usual with Massillon. He is not a Claude Lion or a Henri-Marie Boudon with their notable displays of erudition. He cites the Old and New Testaments in almost equal proportion (there is slightly more Old than New), he quotes a passage from Augustine's *Confessions*, and there are passing allusions to Benedict and Ambrose. His source for Bernard's life and works is the *Vita prima* in either Latin or French, which is quoted more than a dozen times, though only once with the attribution to "a historian," who is, as usual, William of Saint-Thierry. Of Bernard's own works, he cites three of his letters and refers to, but does not quote from, the *De consideratione*, and that is all.

---

[17] See also his subtle analyses in §17 and §43.

Where, when, and to whom the panegyric was delivered is unknown. It was certainly preached on Bernard's feast day, August 20, but I can find no indication in the text as to place or year. There may be an oblique allusion to the Revocation of the Edict of Nantes (1685) in §56, and the reference to the "ever-fortunate monarch" (*monarque toujours heureux*) in the same section seems to me to imply that Louis XIV is now dead. In that case the panegyric was preached sometimes between 1715 and 1742, which is not a great deal of help. Nor is it clear to whom Massillon was preaching. Fourteen times he addresses his audience as "my brothers," which could mean almost anything; once he addresses them as "Christians" (§11), which tells us nothing, and once he speaks to *femmes du siècle*, "you worldly women" (§40), but they were not necessarily there in the congregation. Whoever his audience, they would have been listening to Massillon for about an hour and a half, and it is to be hoped they had an intimate knowledge of Scripture, especially the Old Testament. Massillon's panegyric is replete with biblical allusions and references (hence the large number of footnotes), and to most modern readers, many of them will be far from obvious.

Massillon's sermons were first edited and published three years after his death by his nephew, Joseph Massillon, also an Oratorian, but the best edition is that of the *abbé* Émile-Auguste Blampignon, published at Bar-le-Duc between 1865 and 1867. That is the edition I have used here. This was one of the most difficult panegyrics to translate, not so much because of grammar or vocabulary, but because of Massillon's inimitable style. He could produce a veritable torrent of words, and, in French, his style could certainly captivate a congregation and, like a tsunami, sweep them away. I cannot hope to achieve the same impact in English, but, if I may quote Pilate, what I have written, I have written.

THE PANEGYRIC
SERMON FOR THE [FEAST] DAY OF SAINT BERNARD.[18]

Dilectus a Domino Deo suo, renovavit imperium, et unxit principes in gente suo: in lege Domini congregationem judicavit, et in fide sua probatus est propheta. (Sir 46:16-17)

"He was loved by the Lord his God; he gave to the whole government a new face, poured out a holy unction on the princes of his people, presided over the assemblies of Israel, judged according to the law of the Lord, and appeared as a true prophet in his faith." (This is the Holy Spirit's eulogy on Samuel in chapter 46 of Ecclesiasticus, 16-17.)[19]

1. Israel, unfaithful to the God who had brought her out of Egypt, had long been the prey of the nations and regarded by her neighbors with contempt. Morality was sadly corrupted, the holiness of the Law had been perverted, the worship of the Lord neglected, and the sacrifices and offerings polluted, either by the ungodliness of the priests or the superstition of the faithful. The sons of Eli, who ministered in the sanctuary, made the very functions of their ministry the occasion for their disorderly behavior,[20] and the Holy Ark no longer gave forth its oracles at Shiloh.[21] It had been captured by the Philistines and placed in the temple of Dagon,[22] and after that it wandered

---

[18] [Jean-Baptiste Massillon], *Œuvres complètes de Massillon, évêque de Clermont . . . par l'abbé É[mile]-A[uguste] Blampignon. Tome deuxième* (Bar-le-Duc: L. Guerin, 1866), 582–93. Blampignon provides a detailed summary of the panegyric on pages 580–82.

[19] This is Massillon's translation. A more literal version is "He was loved by the Lord his God, he renewed the government and anointed princes over his people; by the law of the Lord he judged the congregation [of Israel], and by his faith he was shown to be a prophet." As we have so often seen, the panegyrists have no hesitation in adapting the biblical text to their own purposes.

[20] See 1 Sam 2:12-22.
[21] See 1 Sam 4:3-11.
[22] See 1 Sam 5:2.

hither and thither in the Judean countryside.[23] In a word, all the brilliance of the daughter of Zion[24] was darkened, her solemn ceremonies and Sabbaths had become dismal spectacles; no comforter came to her, her prophets no longer upbraided her for her iniquity so as to rouse her to repentance,[25] and the Lord, in his wrath, had caused the abundance of Israel to wither and had not spared the beauties of Jacob.[26]

2. Such was the state of the synagogue[27] when God, moved by the groans and calamities of his people, raised up for them Samuel, this cherished prophet from heaven, who renewed the government, poured out a holy unction on the princes of his nation, and judged the assembly of Israel according to [God's] law. This was the prophet who first called on the Lord under the eyes of the High Priest Eli in the peace and quiet of the sanctuary and who was then consulted by all Israel at Shiloh, the place he had chosen for his solitude.[28] He appeared at the head of the people of God and was known from Dan to Beersheba.[29] He settled disputes between the various tribes; he reestablished the worship of the Lord and kept a watchful eye[30] on the kings and princes of the people. To him was entrusted the truth of [God's] law, and he was known to be faithful in his words because he had seen the God of light.[31] He confounded Amalek and crushed the insolence of the princes of Tyre and all the lords of the Philistines.[32]

---

[23] See 1 Sam 5-7 for the wanderings of the ark.
[24] See Ps 9:15 and many other places.
[25] *Pénitence*: see appendix 1, s.v. *pénitence* / penitence.
[26] Ps 46:5.
[27] There were, of course, no synagogues in the time of Samuel. Massillon, like many others of his generation, is simply using it as a synonym for the Temple cult.
[28] See 1 Sam 3:18-21.
[29] 1 Sam 3:20.
[30] Lit. "He was the *censeur* of the kings and princes."
[31] Sir 46:18.
[32] Sir 46:21.

3. Is this a prophecy, my brothers? Is this a history? And how could it have come about that the century of Samuel was so similar to that of Bernard? And that this prophet, so famous and so often praised in the holy books, [is so similar] to him whose eulogy I undertake today?

4. Never had the bride of Jesus Christ been covered with more blemishes and wrinkles than in those dark and dissolute times when Providence,[33] in its eternal counsels, took note of the birth of this great man. Among the faithful, faith had been extinguished, religion had been perverted and flooded with superstition, the clergy and priestly princes were plunged in ignorance and vice, the vigor of monastic discipline had been enfeebled, and even the elect (if I may be so bold as to say so) were on the point of yielding to the flood and letting themselves be swept away by erroneous ideas. But you, Lord, did not close your eyes or harden your heart to all these hideous and affecting calamities and wounds; instead, you took from the treasury of your mercy one of those remarkable resources you never refuse to your Church when she is in dire need.

5. Bernard, the Samuel of his century,[34] is born. He spends the first years of his life in the peace and quiet of the sanctuary, and it is there that you bestow upon him the secret and ineffable marks of your love: *Dilectus a Domino Deo suo* ["He was loved by the Lord his God" (Sir 46:16)]. Soon afterward, his name is noised abroad, and people come from all parts to consult the visionary. He leaves his solitude and becomes the lawgiver of the tribes. He renews the face of the government, and princes are moved by the unction and grace of his words: *Renovavit imperium, et unxit principes in gente suo* ["he renewed the government, and anointed princes over his people" (Sir 46:16)]. Finally, instructed by the God of light[35] himself, he

---

[33] See appendix 1, s.v. *Providence* / Providence.
[34] Massillon also calls Bernard a second Ambrose, a second Daniel, a second Elijah, a second Jonah, a second Joseph, a second John the Baptist, and a second Moses.
[35] Sir 46:18.

confounds heresy and schism, adjudicates at [Church] councils, and presides over the assemblies of Israel. And, despite senseless opposition, he is recognized as a true prophet by the greatness of his faith: *In lege Domini congregationem judicavit, et in fide sua probatus est propheta* ["by the law of the Lord he judged the congregation [of Israel], and by his faith he was shown to be a prophet" (Sir 46:17)]. And you see all these things represented in the three main circumstances of his life: the perfect monk, the apostolic man, and the doctor who can never be defeated. This is the most natural way of presenting his eulogy, and this is the path I shall take. We implore [the aid of the Mother of God, saying:], *Ave Maria*.[36]

[FIRST PART]

6. When Providence destines a creature for glorious ventures and wishes to make him an instrument for its most noble projects, it arranges things early on in countless different ways that would seem to be the result of chance alone. It pours into his soul gifts and graces that are like the sacred seeds of all the marvelous things it intends to do through its intervention, and, since it is always heedful of the dangers that surround him, it surrounds his heart from the start with a wall of bronze[37] to safeguard his innocence with a shield of salvation.[38] It leads

---

[36] Massillon is customarily terse in his invocation of Mary, and sometimes the printed text records no invocation at all, though Massillon would undoubtedly have added one. The most we get is a single sentence in the sermon for the feast of a Holy Martyr: "We have need of the illumination of the Holy Spirit: let us invoke it through the intercession of Mary. *Ave Maria*" (*Œuvres complètes de Massillon*, 2:637). In the panegyric on Bernard, Blampignon's text reads *Implorons . . .* (with three dots). In other words, Massillon added whatever was necessary before reciting the *Ave Maria*. We may contrast the remarkable Marian exordium of Boudon's panegyric (chap. 11, §§1–2).

[37] This is the *murus aereus* of Jer 1:18.

[38] 2 Sam 22:36; Ps 18:35.

by the hand all his passions from the moment they come into being and when they are still in need of controlling. With infinite care it cultivates the seed of the Gospel it has sown there, the seed that it wants to raise up above all other plants and whose holy branches are destined one day to be a refuge for all the birds of heaven.

7. This is what grace did with Bernard. From his birth he received this goodness in his soul and a disposition that was without guile, as a portent and first glimpse of piety and devotion.[39] [He received, too,] a charitable temperament, a sweet and serene spirit, a tranquil and innocent heart, and, deep within him, a hatred of excess and vice. His careful upbringing would be of help in realizing these happy expectations, and, for him, the examples he found at home were lessons in virtue. His father [Tescelin] was just and upright, and had always walked faithfully before the Lord. [He had] a devout and tender mother, [Aleth,] whose heart had been shared only between Jesus Christ and her husband and who, distanced from the world and enclosed within the wall of her duties, sought to sanctify herself (as Saint Paul says[40]) in the midst of her children by encouraging them to persevere in faith, charity, and holiness, and to lead a disciplined life worthy of the saints.

8. These were the first blessings that heaven provided for our vessel of election,[41] who was destined one day to carry the word of truth before princes and kings, the nations, and the children of Israel. Happy was he, in an age when the heart was so easily withered, not to have breathed in, like so many others with whom he lived, the baleful smell of death and not to have found in their way of life rocks on which his own innocence might have foundered. For alas! where have most of us studied iniquity, if not in the examples set by our fathers?

---

[39] See appendix 1, s.v. *piété* / piety.
[40] See 1 Cor 7:14.
[41] Acts 9:15, translating *vas electionis*.

Where have we seen the man of sin,[42] which we carry deep inside us, given form—or, rather, grow and be strengthened—if not under the very eyes of those who should have given form there to Jesus Christ? Whence do they come, these first impressions so deadly to the heart, if not from the indiscretions and profligacy of those closest to us? And where, finally, have we learned to worship idols, as Rachel did, if not in the very house of Laban?[43]

9. Such were the promising tendencies with which Bernard comes into the world. But what effect can a most correct and careful upbringing have on an age when the heart, which cannot yet take the necessary precautions and is still wide open, feels on all sides the dawning of the passions! What can someone happy and successful do against the examples all around him, and the allurements that iniquity offers at every one of his steps? Aaron adored the golden calf with the [Israelite] host,[44] and Jonathan could not help tasting at least a morsel of the deadly honey he found on the ground.[45]

10. Ideas like these are rarely to be found in the thoughtless days of youth, yet they are already present in the mind of Bernard. Hardly had he cast his first glance on the world than he discovered there an infinity of stumbling blocks that one rarely notices save afterward, and to which our eyes are opened only by our falls. Even now the sight of an attractive young woman[46] had tried to strew in his heart some sparks of sin, for violating the pact he had made with his eyes,[47] he

---

[42] 2 Thess 2:3, translating *homo peccati*.

[43] I.e., in her own house: Laban was Rachel's father. See Gen 31:19, 33.

[44] See Exod 32:4-6.

[45] See 1 Sam 14:24-29.

[46] *Une beauté mortelle*: *beauté* can mean either beauty or a beautiful woman, and *mortelle* can mean mortal (as in a mortal woman), fatal (as in a mortal wound), or deadly (as in a mortal sin). Massillon is implying all these possibilities.

[47] See Job 31:1, "I made a pact with my eyes, that I would not even think about a young woman [*virgo*]."

had let his wandering gaze light on a dangerous object.[48] But you will come thus far, powers of darkness, and no further, for you will now see something that will shatter your passion and your expectations! Bernard, like a mysterious lion, is never stronger than when he is lightly wounded. He throws himself into an icy pond, and it straightaway punishes his frailty:[49] in this new bath of repentance[50] he extinguishes the burning shafts of Satan, and like a second Jonah, by throwing himself into the waters, he calms the nascent tempest that his infidelity has aroused in his heart.[51]

11. What fastidious innocence, which cannot bear even for a moment the weight of the lightest transgression! But, Christians, when it comes to perils, the past is a poor guarantee for the future: even the most righteous cannot be held answerable either for grace or for themselves! There are twelve hours in the day, and every one of them brings something new. Virtue is worn down, so to speak, and weakened by its own victories. Our successes are often merely a pretense of the Enemy, who lets us win the first battles to divert us and lure us [into sinning] more often. Bernard is not unaware of this, and since he believed that there was no such thing as taking too many precautions in the matter of one's salvation, he seeks in the wilderness a peace that the world cannot give[52] and believes that avoiding the Enemy is the surest way to vanquish him.

12. What were the glorious circumstances of this withdrawal [from the world]? We do not have here a humbled penitent fleeing from the Enemy like someone conquered, cut, and beaten. What we have here is a Moses who goes forth from Egypt to seek the solitude of the desert only after he has

---

[48] See *Vita prima* 1.3.6 (William of Saint-Thierry); PL 185:230C; CF 76:9. William quotes the verse from Job.
[49] *Vita prima* 1.3.6 (William of Saint-Thierry); PL 185:230C; CF 76:9.
[50] Or of penance or penitence (*pénitence*). The first bath is the water of baptism.
[51] See Jonah 1:4-15.
[52] See John 14:27.

vanquished Pharaoh and who, in his very withdrawal, retains all the appearance of a conqueror! But to shake off the yoke of the prince of this world[53] from himself alone counts for nothing, unless he also delivers his brothers. He cannot bring himself to leave his friends and relatives wandering sorrowfully in a strange land[54] while he himself goes forth into the desert to taste there the sweetness of the Lord.[55]

13. "What do we need?" he asks them, just as the courtier [asked] so long ago, as Saint Augustine tells us: "On what end, finally, do we set our sights and our hopes? The favor of the prince is the highest goal to which we may aspire, but how many dangers must we face to arrive at the greatest danger of all? And besides, how long will it take? *Quamdiu istud erit?* ["How long will it be?"] Whereas if I wish to be a friend of my God, I become so immediately: *Ecce nunc fio!* ["See? I have now become one!"].[56] And that is the treasure that fears neither worms nor rust nor devouring time nor human greed.[57] And so, followed by his brothers and most of his friends,[58] like so many noble captives whom he comes to deliver from the prince of the world,[59] he leaves the world loaded down with these glorious spoils, and like his divine Master, in rescuing them from the empire of death,[60] he draws after him principalities and powers and leads them openly in triumph in full view of the world: *Traduxit confidenter, palam triumphans* ["He has led them with confidence, triumphing publicly" (Col 2:15)].

---

[53] John 12:31; 14:30; 16:11.

[54] I.e., Egypt.

[55] See Ps 15:25; 30:20; 33:9; and elsewhere.

[56] Augustine, Conf 8.6.15; PL 32:756.

[57] See Matt 6:19-20.

[58] Massillon is paralleling Moses leading the Israelites out of Egypt at the Exodus with Bernard leading his brothers and companions out of the world into Cîteaux.

[59] Massillon now changes the metaphor to a Roman triumph.

[60] Heb 2:14.

14. Ah! if the angels in heaven, in the very abode of glory, are able to rejoice anew at the conversion of a single sinner,[61] what should be the joy of those angels of the desert, those devout solitaries who, some time ago, had withdrawn to Cîteaux,[62] when they saw Bernard arriving at the head of a flourishing flock! The silence, the vigils, the fasts, and all the rigor of monastic discipline, which elsewhere had been relaxed or completely extinguished, were observed without any mitigation at Cîteaux, so that those worldly people who wished to give up the world found it a fearful thing to approach this solitude.[63] This holy land was seen as a land peopled by extraordinary men, [a land] that devoured those who dwelt there: few there were who had the courage to go there and take on a way of life that was all the more demanding as it was so little accessible to a world where laxity had become the dominant taste. This chaste Zion was deserted and barren, whereas the other brides, who were less faithful, gloried in the number of their children. Indeed, it was feared that this devout foundation would ultimately collapse through lack of numbers.

15. Stephen [Harding], the abbot of the monastery, a man venerated for his great age[64] and his consummate piety, saw with sorrow that the fruit of all his labors was on the point of perishing. Countless times he had raised his pure hands to heaven to ask God to multiply his people,[65] and he was confidently waiting for his prayers to be granted when Bernard,

---

[61] See Luke 15:7, 10.

[62] Massillon is referring to the first monks who came to the New Monastery with Robert of Molesme in 1098. Bernard arrived fifteen years later (see chap. 7 [Bossuet], n. 63).

[63] See *Vita prima* 1.3.8 (William of Saint-Thierry); PL 185:231BC; CF 76:10–11.

[64] He was probably about sixty at the time of Bernard's arrival (see Claudio Stercal, *Stephen Harding: A Biographical Sketch and Texts*, trans. Martha F. Krieg, CS 226 [Collegeville, MN: Cistercian Publications, 2008], 9).

[65] Gen 28:3; 48:4.

followed by his companions, came to throw himself at his feet. What tears of joy and love streamed then from the eyes of this holy old man! How many times does he say to the Lord what Simeon said, that he could now die in peace since his eyes, at last, had seen the salvation of God and him whom he had prepared to be the light of the nations and the glory of Israel![66]

16. Nor were the holy abbot's hopes disappointed by what followed. Our new solitary seems to have stripped off his shameful worldly garments and, with them, whatever was left of the inclinations of the old self,[67] and he no longer places any bounds on the fervor of his faith. Ridding himself of everything that binds him [to the world], he takes wing toward heaven and is almost out of sight even to the most advanced [of his fellow monks]. Every day he says to himself, "Bernard, what have you come to seek in this solitude? Have you left the world only to drag its chains behind you? Do you, like so many others, want to hide under an austere religious habit a profane and unmortified[68] heart? *Ad quid venisti?*"[69] Ah! if you could have been assured of your salvation by being virtuous in an easy and pleasant sort of way, why did you leave the world, which regularly errs in sanctioning this, and come to this place of penance[70] where purer lights and holier examples condemn it?

17. Behold your model, you who begin with a dramatic conversion and the sudden adoption of an outward and austere piety but who then, little by little, fall off from this first fervor and finally come to that state of questionable virtue,

---

[66] See Luke 2:29-32.

[67] Rom 6:6; Eph 4:22; Col 3:9 (*vetus homo*, "old man").

[68] *Immortifié*: the word is as rare in French as "unmortified" in English. It is used by Bossuet and Fénelon, though not in their panegyrics on Bernard.

[69] *Vita prima* 1.4.19 (William of Saint-Thierry); PL 185:238AB; CF 76:22.

[70] See n. 50 above.

lukewarm and untroubling, which does indeed serve to restrain the grossest of the passions but which places no check on most pleasures and does away with integrity and vigilance. *Ad quid venisti?* Apply this question to yourselves! What are my intentions in proposing for myself a lukewarm and faithless life? If I still have any concern for my salvation, why do I follow a road that is both uncertain and perilous? But if I want to destroy my first faith completely, eh! what good does it do me to hold myself back from certain pleasures and still preserve a remnant of useless virtue? The life I lead is [ruled] too much by the senses if my plan is to save myself; but if I want to destroy myself, it is still too hard a task!

18. With the help of such pious reflections, Bernard nourished his faith and ceaselessly revitalized in himself the grace of his vocation. Nevertheless, O my God, from the foundation of your sanctuary you had already poured out on this young Samuel those infinite blessings he needed to make him the prophet and lawgiver of your people. Since the time of Benedict himself, the cloister had not seen more consummate virtue, and this was already a happy portent of the reestablishment of the rule of that great patriarch, which, by this time, was not being properly kept in most monasteries in the West. For it is the way of human things to change for the worse the further they are from their source, and to fall from the high point of their fervor and austerity, visible to all, into mitigations, accommodations, and privileges.

19. Bernard's body was frail and his constitution far from strong, yet there were no mortifications that could satisfy him in his love for the crosses[71] and for penance. And what mortifications, my brothers? Eternal silence, strict solitude, continual vigils, unceasing fasts, nourishment that, far from profiting the body, was repulsive to it in its tastelessness, the hardest manual labor, and a countless series of arduous exercises that

---

[71] *Les croix* in the plural: see chap. 11 (Boudon), §33.

gave self-love no time to breathe and that, in changing the object, themselves changed only in the torture they inflicted. Surrounded by these instruments of penance,[72] he still found his cross too easy and believed himself to be, like the bridegroom, in the midst of roses and lilies.[73] The saints tremble with fear because of a single fault expiated by a lifetime of penance, and we put our hope in a single act of penance, reduced to nothing in a lifetime of sin!

20. The entry of Bernard and his companions into Cîteaux, together with its austerity and their innocent way of life, already spread abroad an odor of life;[74] many were attracted by such noteworthy examples and hastened there from all parts. In fact, the number of disciples grew [so quickly] that the enclosure of Cîteaux was found to be too cramped to contain them, and it was necessary to find a new land: this holy people was to be split up.[75] So Bernard, at the head of a chosen tribe, regretfully left a place in which everything called to mind the sweet memory of those first favors he had received from his divine Master and established a foundation at Clairvaux.[76] This, at the time, was an unknown wilderness but afterward became more celebrated than all the great cities of Judah by the presence of him who would one day govern Israel.[77]

21. Elevated to the dignity of abbot of this monastery, what spectacles of virtue does he not offer in his new rank! Far from affecting those odious distinctions and empty marks of authority that leave so huge a gap between children and a father, he was never more eager to abase himself. Far from regarding his

---

[72] Massillon is referring to a torture chamber and the instruments of torture.

[73] See Song 2:16; 6:2.

[74] 2 Cor 2:16 (*odor vitae*).

[75] Massillon returns to the metaphor of the Exodus.

[76] The date was 1115.

[77] Massillon is now back with Bernard as the second Samuel, and Israel is presumably the Cistercian abbeys.

dignity as a reasonable pretext for mitigations and ease, he was never more severe with himself. Who here, my brothers, could give a detailed account of the effects of grace on his soul: this spirit of prayer and recollection,[78] these indescribable consolations[79] of the Holy Spirit, this total death to himself and to all created things, the use of the senses almost extinguished! But alas! he mortified his taste to such an extent that he did not even know what he was eating, and unlike the Israelites, who found in the same manna different tastes,[80] for him, the most diverse dishes all tasted the same.[81] He did not remember seeing things that had been right there before his eyes:[82] he was so wholly a citizen of heaven[83] that every deed that arose from his soul was fixed on that [end], and it may be said of him (though in a different way) what the prophet [David] says of idols: that they had eyes, but did not see, noses, but no sense of smell, and a mouth and hands that served no purpose.[84]

22. It was then that God granted [Bernard's] wishes: his father [Tescelin] was called by God to enter Clairvaux and withdraw completely from the world. This man, so happy in the midst of his family, and whose children, like those of Jacob, would one day be so many patriarchs, finally leaves the land of Canaan and comes to join Joseph, his beloved son.[85] He bows

---

[78] See appendix 1, s.v. *recueillement* / recollection.

[79] See appendix 1, s.v. *consolations* / consolations.

[80] See Exod 16:31; Num 11:8.

[81] See *Vita prima* 1.7.33 (William of Saint-Thierry); PL 185:247AB; CF 76:39.

[82] Such as the vaulting in the novitiate, the windows in the church, the trappings of his borrowed horse, or Lake Geneva: see *Vita prima* 1.4.20 (William of Saint-Thierry); PL 185:238B; CF 76:23, and *Vita prima* 3.2.4 (Geoffrey of Auxerre); 305B–6A; CF 76:149–50. We have seen the stories before.

[83] *Sa conversation toute dans le ciel*, quoting Phil 3:20: *Nostra autem conversatio in caelis est*.

[84] Ps 113:13-15.

[85] See Gen 45:28; 46:28-30.

before his pastoral staff, the sacred symbol of his authority, and shortly thereafter, full of days, he falls asleep in the Lord in this land of Goshen[86] under the eyes of a son who had given him birth in faith and charity.[87]

23. This, my brothers, is how the saints are found pleasing to God. All those whom the Church honors as such, it honors as penitents. The Spirit of God does not offer a variety of paths to this end, and we cannot say that it works in any different way. Do we delude ourselves in thinking that there might be a special way, just for us? Will we be treated more favorably because we are more guilty? If those beloved by the heavenly Father have drunk from the bitter cup,[88] do we think that the dregs and bitterness will not be for us? But if the kingdom of heaven is not the prize of violence alone,[89] can it then be [the prize] of depravity? And if one can be holy without penance, can one then be [holy] after [indulging in] pleasures?

24. Such was our new Samuel in the enclosure of the sanctuary. He was dear to the Lord his God: *Dilectus a Domino Deo* (Sir 46:16). Let us set the widest possible bounds to his zeal: he comes to give to the government a new face and to pour out unction on the princes and the people: *Renovavit imperium, et unxit principes in gente sua* ["he renewed the government and anointed princes over his people" (Sir 46:16)]: and after faith has made him a perfect monk, charity is about to make him an apostolic man.[90] That is the second point [of my sermon].

---

[86] See Gen 47:27-29.

[87] According to the *Vita prima* 1.6.30; PL 185:244C; CF 76:34, Tescelin, "who had remained at home alone, went to his sons and joined them. After remaining with them for some time [*aliquantum tempus*] he died in goodly old age." Williams, *Saint Bernard*, 29, suggests that the *aliquantum tempus* was two or three years. "In goodly old age" (*in senectute bona*) is a quotation from 1 Chr 29:28.

[88] See Matt 20:22-23; Mark 10:38-39.

[89] See Matt 11:12: "From the days of John the Baptist until now, the kingdom of heaven suffers violence, and the violent carry it off."

[90] See §5 above.

[SECOND PART]

25. There are different gifts in the church, says Saint Paul,[91] and, in accordance with the secret plans of the Spirit, which blows where it wills,[92] these gifts are shared by the various members who make up [the church]. All are not apostles, prophets, or teachers[93] at one and the same time: to each is given a particular grace, according to the measure of the gift of Jesus Christ.[94] One, in the stillness of his withdrawal, keeps his soul pure and stainless, but if taken from there into the world, he may see his innocence lost and his faith wholly extinguished. Another, whose business is the ministry of the word and the other duties of the apostolate, shines like a star in the midst of a corrupt and perverse people and forms Jesus Christ in their hearts but once in the desert [of the cloister] finds himself yearning for [the comforts of] Egypt[95] and becomes lukewarm and despondent. Yet another is sent to preach the Gospel to the simple and ignorant but fears to carry the name of the Lord before the princes and kings of the earth. Another will set himself up like a wall of bronze[96] on behalf of the house of Israel but dares not touch the Lord's anointed[97] or contradict legal pundits. And there are those, finally, who have the gift of interpreting the Scriptures but do not have [the gift] of miracles to serve as a sign to those who do not believe. But although you

---

[91] See Rom 12:6; 1 Cor 12:4-10.

[92] John 3:8.

[93] 1 Cor 12:28. Massillon's *docteurs*, "teachers," are the *doctores* of the Latin text.

[94] Eph 4:7: *secundum mensuram donationis Christi*. In other words, most people receive these gifts with certain limitations—they can do so much but then come up against psychological, social, or political obstacles that prevent them from doing more—but there are a few (like Bernard) who receive the gifts in their entirety and without measure. Such as these are not held back by anything.

[95] See Exod 16:3.

[96] See n. 37 above.

[97] See Ps 104:15.

have established this pattern yourself, O my God, you are not bound to it as by law: there are certain souls on whom, when it pleases you, you pour out handfuls of your various gifts and to whom you do not measure out your Spirit.

26. In Bernard's day there was need for such a soul. Discord at home, foreign wars, and the ignorance that is always their unfortunate fruit had infected the whole country with a license and barbarity I cannot describe, and these are always fatal to that holiness, cultured morality,[98] and lack of guile that are part of the Christian way of life. Ambition, ostentation, and vices yet more shameful had insinuated their way into the sanctuary and had turned the house of God into a place of scheming, self-indulgence,[99] and scandals. Cloisters were no longer refuges from the contagion of the world, and the people of God who dwelt in this holy land cared little for the covenant their fathers had made and had allied themselves with the nations and had adopted their manners and customs.[100] The wise laws of the founders were no longer written, save on the stone tablets,[101] and their spirit had been destroyed by the admixture of human traditions. These arid and dismal deserts had become lands flowing with milk and honey.[102] No longer were they lonely places where, weary of the world, one could go from time to time to breathe the air of piety. Once famous for the

---

[98] *Politesse*. One would normally translate this as *politeness, good manners, civility,* or *courtesy*, but in Massillon's time the word had a much stronger moral content than it does today.

[99] *Mollesse*: literally "softness," but self-indulgence and laxity is what Massillon implies. The word can also mean effeminacy.

[100] Massillon is back in the Old Testament and is referring to the problems that all the prophets had with the Israelites after the Exodus. They did not keep their part of the covenant, they followed after false gods, and they adopted the manners and morals of the pagan peoples.

[101] See Exod 24:12 and thereafter.

[102] See Exod 3:8 and thereafter, but Massillon is using the expression in a pejorative sense: a land of opulence, wealth, and superfluity.

saints who dwelt there, these solitudes were now renowned only for splendid buildings, stately temples, vast riches, and lavish donations—so much so that the pious gifts of the faithful and their holy reduction (to quote the apostle[103]) had become the excess of this people once so simple and so isolated.

27. From then on, my brothers, what a flood of iniquity has inundated the world! For we must say here that although the lamps of Israel cannot go out,[104] they give forth a thick smoke that spreads far and wide and dims all the glory and gold of the tabernacle, and the pillars of the temple will never collapse unless they take with them the rest of the building. But to speak frankly, not figuratively, the vices of the clergy and those persons consecrated to God are always like the pernicious standards of disorder raised in the midst of the people: *Signum in nationibus* ["a sign to the nations" (Isa 5:26)].

28. To deal with these needs, so dire and diverse, you, Lord, set up a new Moses whom you brought out of the desert of Midian,[105] and between your hands, Bernard strikes out at kings and kingdoms, reforms the tabernacle on the model you had shown him on the mountain,[106] confounds the murmuring ministers, restores the high priesthood to the pontiff you had established,[107] casts down the idol that the children of Israel had made for themselves,[108] destroys the enemies of your name,

---

[103] Rom 11:12: "If their offence be the riches of this world, and the reduction (*diminutio*) of them the riches of the Gentiles, how much more the fullness of them!" The sentence is as odd in Latin as it is in French. What it means is that "If Israel's transgression means riches for the world, and if Israel's failure means riches for the Gentiles, what greater riches there will be when they are fully included with us."

[104] See Lev 24:2.

[105] See Exod 3:1.

[106] See Exod 25-27.

[107] I.e., Innocent II: see further Massillon's more detailed account of the papal schism in §§49–52 below, and appendix 2, s.v. Anacletus II.

[108] I take this to be a somewhat oblique allusion to the defeat of Anacletus.

and would have led your tribes to conquer Jerusalem had not their ingratitude and excesses made you withdraw from their midst your strength and your arm.[109]

29. How ardent, how determined, how far-reaching he was in his zeal! Nature had bestowed on him those advantages of body and mind that seemed to predestine those who had been provided with them for the ministry of the word, but who, lacking the grace and calling of heaven, are never more than a sounding brass or a tinkling cymbal.[110] [But in his case, he had] a great mind that had been nourished by reading the Holy Scriptures, a tender heart with which, it seems, had been born mercy and the ability to touch the souls of others,[111] a gentle and mortified outward appearance that prepared hearts for grace and the very sight of which straightaway gave to the soul an indescribable taste of the heavenly gift[112] and the good things of the world to come.

30. So picture to yourselves, my brothers, this new forerunner[113] coming out of the desert, poorly garbed, penitence painted on his face, seeking in what he says not to make himself pleasing to sinners but to make sinners displeasing to themselves, laboring not for his own glory but to prepare the ways of the Lord,[114] smoothing out not the roughness of the path of the Gospel but [the roughness] of rebellious hearts, and preaching not easy ablutions and outward ceremonies that cleanse only the outside[115] but laying the axe to the root[116]

---

[109] This last section is a reference to the failure of the Second Crusade and the reason for its failure: Massillon deals with the matter in some detail in §42.

[110] 1 Cor 13:1.

[111] "the ability to touch the souls of others" renders the technical term *l'onction*: see the discussion in chap. 3.

[112] Heb 6:4.

[113] Bernard now becomes a second John the Baptist.

[114] See Matt 3:3; Mark 1:3; Luke 3:4.

[115] See Matt 23:25-26.

[116] See Matt 3:10; Luke 3:9.

of the passions and proclaiming a baptism of repentance.[117] One takes him for Elijah or one of the prophets: the whole of France hastens to hear this new teaching, and, moved[118] by the words of grace and power that came from his mouth, crowds of people come to him to learn whether the wrath of the Lord, like his gifts, cannot be turned back, and whether there is no longer any way for them to move him to pity.

31. Eh! What could one expect from a minister of Jesus Christ who, far removed from the world, had long meditated on God's law[119] in silence and prayer, and whose heart, emptied of all created things, was filled only with the Spirit who spoke in him, and who could say to the faithful with all the confidence of the apostle, "Be imitators of me, as I am of Jesus Christ" (1 Cor 4:16; 11:1). What could one expect, I say, but the renewing of his world and the rebirth of faith and piety? If our own ministry does not enjoy the same success, it is not because the world is more corrupt, but because the motives for what we do are not the same. Is it [only] the Spirit of God that opens our mouths? And does no human weakness mitigate our zeal?

32. Then, my brothers, [with Bernard's arrival,] the darkness over the abyss[120] began to dissipate: France, like another chaos, gradually took shape, and cloisters saw a revival of their original spirit, that precious inheritance they had once received from their fathers. New flocks of solitaries coming from Clairvaux spread throughout Europe, filling the deserts once again with people. The greatest men of the age competed with each other in retiring there, even princes preferred the reproach of Jesus Christ to the pomp of the Egyptians,[121] and

---

[117] Mark 1:4; Luke 3:3.

[118] *Touchés*: like *onction* (see n. 111) this, too, is a technical term of seventeenth-century preaching. The matter was discussed in chap. 3.

[119] See Ps 1:2.

[120] See Gen 1:2.

[121] Heb 11:26. There were indeed two royal princes at Clairvaux: see chap. 11 (Boudon), n. 137.

those who dwelt in the palaces of kings no longer desired to indulge themselves with fine garments. Thereafter, as though from a new Upper Room,[122] crowds of renowned shepherds came forth and appeared at the heads of our churches, and the children of Bernard became the fathers of the faithful. But what men these bishops were, my brothers! What zeal! What simplicity! What innocence! What austerity in their way of life! For them the episcopate was no more than honorable servitude: they shone, like Moses,[123] only with light from heaven and did not think there was need for an empty affectation of ostentatious ease to make a ministry of tender care and humility respected by the people. But let us not confine ourselves to being envious of this happy century: let us remember, my brothers, that faithful pastors rarely agree about anything except [the need for] the prayers of the people, and that the failings of holy ministers, which we sometimes complain about, far from someday excusing us, will perhaps be a sin for which we have been responsible.[124]

33. To the fervor of his charity, Bernard joins strength. Do not imagine that we have here one of those timid ministers who, under the pretext of honoring the great, think that they should also respect their vices and who, dazzled by the brilliance that surrounds them, dare not face up to what they actually do. They willingly put a veil before their eyes lest they should see this, and they justify their weakness by saying,

---

[122] This is the Upper Room (*cénacle* = *coenaculum*) of Acts 1:13, where the eleven disciples, "the women" (unnamed), and Jesus' mother and brothers were all gathered together immediately after the ascension. From there the disciples (with Matthias taking the place of Judas) went forth to preach the Christian message.

[123] See Exod 34:29-35.

[124] This is what Massillon appears to be saying in this difficult sentence. If we do nothing to correct the failings of holy ministers, then we are ultimately responsible for what they do: their sin is laid at our door. Massillon uses the word *crime* for sin: see appendix 1, s.v. *crimes* / sins.

fallaciously, that they are being considerate or prudent. There are few Samuels who dare say to those who reign over them, "Prince, is it not the Lord who has made you king over Israel? Why, then, have you not listened to his voice? He has no need of your sacrificial victims and the pride of your offerings: the sacrifice most pleasing to him is submission and obedience."[125] Bernard, however, leaves the following example to posterity.

34. Louis the Fat usurps the rights of the Church. Certain noble prelates oppose this new measure. He takes strong measures against them.[126] Our saint is called upon for help.[127] "Prince," he says to [Louis], "the Church raises its voice against you before its Bridegroom and complains that he whom she received as her defender has himself become her persecutor. Eh! Why do you reign on earth if not to have justice and piety reign there?"[128]

35. What public demonstrations of penitence did he not get from Louis the Young because of the massacre at Vitry?[129] Like a new Ambrose, he boldly tells him that the voice of the blood he has shed cries out to the Lord and demands vengeance against him, and by these open reproofs he gives again to the

---

[125] This is a paraphrased summary of 1 Sam 15:17-22. Samuel is speaking to King Saul.

[126] *Il les proscrit*. The verb has a fairly wide meaning.

[127] For the details of this matter, which was a great deal more complicated than would appear from Massillon's brief summary, see Williams, *Saint Bernard*, 197–202. See also appendix 2, s.v. Louis VI the Fat.

[128] Massillon is paraphrasing Bernard's Ep 45.1; SBOp 7:133. The letter is addressed to Louis from Stephen Harding and "the whole assembly of the abbots and brothers of Cîteaux," but was almost certainly the work of Bernard. Mabillon, followed by Eales, dated it to 1127; Williams, *Saint Bernard*, 198, suggested, with greater likelihood, 1129.

[129] For the massacre at Vitry, which (rightly) haunted Louis, see appendix 2, s.v. Louis VII the Young. Louis's penance was to take the cross in the Second Crusade.

Church the consoling spectacle of a humbled king, covered in ashes, prostrate at the door of her temples, and thus he renews the examples, so rare, set by David[130] and Theodosius.[131]

36. But how can I recount here all the different ways in which he acted firmly? There was abbot Suger,[132] that minister so wise and renowned in our history books, whose worldly pomp (which, little by little, had been brought into [Saint-Denis] by the atmosphere of the royal Court) was the subject of his warnings and correction,[133] or Queen Eleanor herself, a proud and worldly princess, who was thwarted in her plans on a most delicate matter[134] and who finally had no choice but to

---

[130] See 2 Sam 12:13-17, recounting David's penitence for arranging the death of Uriah the Hittite in his lust for Bathsheba.

[131] Massillon is referring to the penitence of the emperor Theodosius I imposed on him by Saint Ambrose after the Massacre of Thessalonica in 390. Theodoret places the number of dead at about seven thousand (Theodoret, *Historia ecclesiastica* 5.17). See Ambrose, Ep 51. It was eight months before Ambrose readmitted the emperor to the church. Massillon is here following the unpaginated preface to Le Maistre's *Vie*.

[132] See appendix 2, s.v. Suger, abbot of Saint-Denis.

[133] See Bernard's Ep 78 to Suger (SBOp 7:201–10), especially §3 and §10. See further chap. 10 (La Rue 2), §36, who provides rather more detail.

[134] The *point assez délicat* was Eleanor's encouragement of her younger sister Petronilla (the two were very close) in pursuing an adulterous relationship with Raoul I, count of Vermandois. Eleanor pressured her husband, Louis VII, into allowing Raoul to repudiate his wife in favor of Petronilla, and they married in 1140. The marriage was regarded as illegitimate, and both Raoul and Petronilla were excommunicated by Innocent II. Bernard had rebuked Eleanor so strongly for abusing her influence that she came to him and begged his prayers to help her conceive. Bernard agreed, but only on condition she mend her ways. She did indeed conceive, and her first child, Marie, was born the following year (1145). See *Vita prima* 4.3.18 (Geoffrey of Auxerre); PL 185:332AB (omitted in CF 76). Eleanor's repentance, we might add, seems to have lasted just long enough for her to get pregnant. See further appendix 2, s.v. Louis VII the Young,

fall in with Bernard's views. This was rare indeed in a young princess,[135] still intoxicated by pleasure and prestige, who loved to dominate both minds and hearts, who took offense at any opposition, and who did not value virtue sufficiently to tolerate any challenge to her wishes. We read that Elijah was able, on occasion, to make even the impious Ahab have a respect for the truth,[136] but we do not read that Jezebel ever forgave him for what he said on the one occasion he spoke of her,[137] nor for his opposition to her in what she wanted to do so unjustly to Naboth.[138]

37. People of all centuries will admire the effective and moving instructions, and the noble style and frankness of expression that reign throughout his book *On Consideration* to Pope Eugenius. It is true that it was under the eyes and discipline of our saint that this pontiff had seen the growth of those great qualities that would afterward raise him to the pontificate,[139] but it might be thought that the reverent submission owed to everything that issues forth from the August Throne and the unending respect with which the pontiff is surrounded would make him little acquainted with Christian frankness and addresses not designed to praise him. But charity dares anything! And Bernard, ever like Samuel, naturally honors the Lord's Anointed before the people but does not hesitate then to tell him what heaven requires of him.

38. [In Bernard's day], princes and sovereign pontiffs had respect for the frank outspokenness of the Spirit of God in his

---

and Williams, *Saint Bernard*, 215–16. The only other panegyrist to mention Eleanor—and then not by name—is Fénelon (§24).

[135] She was probably about twenty-two when Bernard met her. She died in her early eighties. She was a formidable woman, but I am not sure that she deserves to be likened to Jezebel.

[136] See 1 Kgs 21:27-29.

[137] See 1 Kgs 21:23.

[138] See 1 Kgs 21:1-16.

[139] See appendix 2, s.v. Eugenius III.

servant. But in the world of today, my brothers, if we happen to be born into a distinguished family, we expect from the ministers of Jesus Christ a respect and consideration unworthy of their character. We are offended by their zeal. We think ourselves defamed if they tell us the truth as they tell it to ordinary people. We say that the holy severity of the Gospel applies only to common souls and that the vices of the great are born as noble as they themselves, and that we should respect [their vices] just as [we respect] their persons!

39. Ah! When it came to sin, no part of it could be hidden from the zeal of our saint! He hunted it down to the highest seats of power,[140] and the ties of flesh and blood, so perilous to our ministry, did not lure him from his unswerving path. Moved, but in vain, by the reports of his miracles and reputation, or perhaps from idle curiosity to see him, his sister comes to Clairvaux. Her proud attire and the worldly pomp that surrounds her straightaway reveal to the saint how far removed she is from the kingdom of God. When her ostentatious visit is reported to him, he groans; he withdraws into the monastic enclosure; and despite the tender feelings he has for his sister and the touching sight of her grief and tears, he refuses to see her, unless, in place of the worldly finery she displays, she covers herself with modesty and decency.[141] This is another Moses, who, heedful only of the interests of the glory of his Master, has no hesitation in keeping his sister out of the camp of the Lord and forbidding her to enter the tabernacle until she was cleansed from the leprosy that covered her body, and from these shameful marks of her pride and lack of faith.[142]

40. If today, you worldly women, you find ministers who are more accommodating, that is no excuse for your errors, for the weakness of the priest does not weaken the law of God. It

---

[140] Lit. "to the throne."

[141] See *Vita prima* 1.6.30 (William of Saint-Thierry); PL 185:244CD; CF 76:34–35.

[142] See Num 12:10-15.

is the punishment for your sins, and a just judgment of God's anger upon you, that condemns the false reasoning you use (against your own lights) to justify your indolent and worldly lives by means of ministers who give it their sanction.

41. In a word, my brothers, [Bernard's] voice shattered the cedars of Lebanon, shook the deserts, and thundered in the midst of the waters,[143] by which I mean among the people. Never before him was seen prophecy that had such authority to reprove vice: it seemed, in fact, that heaven had set him up as the censor[144] of the morals of his century. What disputes among princes were appeased by his wisdom! What letters were written to reestablish discipline and piety! We still see in those that have come down to us, set out in immense detail, the care and provisions that stemmed from his charity. What style! What expression! What forceful constructions of divine eloquence! France, Italy, Germany saw him spread abroad the divine fire that Jesus Christ came to bring upon earth[145] and that blazed in his heart. He alone could do all that was necessary for the infinite and varied needs of the Church, and, like the bronze serpent [Moses] raised up in the desert,[146] there was no affliction that was proof against his presence.

42. The only thing lacking in all he did was the reward of the saints—by which I mean persecution and slander—but [now] he had the consolation of sharing in them. He heard the fatuous complaints made against him as a result of the wretched ending of the venture of the French in the Holy Land. The miracles with which God had accompanied his preaching to inflame Christians [with a desire to join] this consecrated army were downplayed and regarded with credulity. His powerful sermons, which almost emptied France and Germany by inspiring the people with the desire to take the cross, passed

---

[143] Ps 28:3, 5-7.
[144] *Censeur*: see n. 30 above.
[145] Luke 12:49.
[146] See Num 21:8-9.

for indiscretion and misdirected zeal. But he, worshiping in the secret depths of his heart the inscrutable designs of Providence,[147] remembered the Israelites, who, though called by God to the conquest of a holy land, perished in the desert because of their infidelities.[148] He recalled the story of the tribes who were specifically ordered by Heaven to go into battle against the Benjamites yet who suffered the disgrace of a double defeat.[149] But [Bernard], groaning over the excesses of the Christians who had brought upon themselves these calamities from heaven, was more affected by what the infidels, proud of having had the best of the conflict, were asking in their insolence, "Where now is the God of the Christians?" and blaspheming his name, than by the outrageous things his brothers [were saying] in an attempt to blacken his own [name].

43. But the world is always ready to find fault with the conduct of the saints. It looks on what they do only with animosity and malice. It wants them to answer for every venture in which they have played a part that has come to an unfortunate end, and if their zeal does not meet with success, it is [regarded as] irresponsible. In fact, just to lead an upright life is almost enough [to ensure] that one will not be treated with any indulgence here on earth. I do not know whether it comes from a hatred of virtue or a love of ourselves, but we never fail to take note of any human weakness in the saints: it may be that because we believe them to be righteous, we also come close to requiring them not to be human, or it may be that since we cannot succeed in being like them we can at least try to persuade ourselves that they are like us!

---

[147] See n. 33 above.

[148] See Num 11 and elsewhere. For this sentence and the remainder of this paragraph, Massillon is dependent on Bernard, Csi 2.1–3; SBOp 3:410–13.

[149] See Judg 20:1-26. In the first battle, the tribes lost 22,000 men and in the second 18,000. In the third battle the tide turned, and the Benjamites were almost entirely annihilated. The tide did not turn for the Crusaders, and the whole venture was an unmitigated disaster.

44. We have now seen all that our saint did to reestablish morality and piety; let us now show in a few words what he did to reestablish faith and doctrine. And in this apostolic man we shall see again the most brilliant and yet the most humble teacher[150] of his times: *In lege Domini congregationem judicavit, et in fide sua probatus est propheta* ["By the law of the Lord he judged the congregation (of Israel), and by his faith he was shown to be a prophet" (Sir 46:17)]. I shall finish very shortly.[151]

[THIRD PART]

45. The Church, this new Jerusalem, is indeed founded on holy mountains; winds and storms hurl themselves in vain against its sacred walls, and her Bride has promised her that the gates of hell shall never prevail against her.[152] Nevertheless, although she is wholly invincible, she is not at peace. Those who persecute her may not know how to destroy her, but they can certainly cause her grief. She has no fear of those conquerors who would force her, like a slave, to adopt their gods and their sacrifices, but she can have enemies who threaten her peace or who defile the purity of her worship. There have been few centuries when she has not seen someone or other rise up against her. Born in conflict and persecution, it seems that her destiny is never to escape them; yet heresies and schisms do have their usefulness. We owe the glory of the martyrs to the rage of tyrants, and to whom are we indebted for the precious works of those who, in the days of old, defended the truth, if not those who, at various times, taught error?

46. God, who had destined Bernard to restore his law, had revealed ineffable secrets to him in the desert [of the monastery].

---

[150] *Docteur*: see chap. 4 (Biroat), n. 55.

[151] *Je finis dans un moment*. It will be a fairly long moment. By my estimation, Massillon will not finish for about another twenty minutes.

[152] See Matt 16:18.

Without having been a disciple of anything but the oak trees and forests, says a historian,[153] and without having had any other master but grace, we see him pass all at once from his solitude into the world, from the shadow of the woods into the light of day. His knowledge did not consist of a mass of empty learning acquired through hard work and spouted forth fruitlessly and ineffectively.[154] He did not seek to dazzle people's minds with new discoveries, nor to gain honor for himself by uttering profundities entrancing in their singularity. [What he sought was] to reform hearts and to rebuild the faith of his fathers on the ruins of profane novelties.[155] In short, he was not among those who treat knowledge as shameful trade and who make this gift, intended to preserve the worship of the Lord and the honor of his sacrifices, a means of gain and an excuse for their greed.

47. The study of the holy Scriptures was dearest to his heart, and there was nothing that seemed to him more worthy of the greatness of the human mind than the story of God's wonders in the books of Moses, the beauty of his law, the divine raptures of his prophets, and the touching words[156] of the other inspired authors. Furthermore, so eagerly had he devoured this sacred volume, and so much had he made it part of his own being, that he knew no other language to speak in his own writings: scriptural expressions are sown there by the handful, and seem to be his own natural style. Oh holy and pious monuments of his love for the Scriptures, precious fruits of his enlightenment

---

[153] *Vita prima* 1.4.23 (William of Saint-Thierry); PL 185:240CD; CF 76:26–27. This is a common *topos* with the panegyrists: see chap. 13 (Anselme and Bourru), n. 110.

[154] *Sans fruit et sans onction*: see n. 111 above.

[155] These are the *profanas novitates* of 1 Tim 6:20, and for the Catholic writers of Massillon's generation (and, indeed, long after) all profane novelties are, without exception, dangerous. See appendix 1, s.v. *nouveautés* / novelties.

[156] "Touching words" here renders Massillon's *onction*: see n. 111.

and piety, you are still in our hands, and that in itself is sufficient for your eulogy!

48. But the reading of the divine Scriptures that, in times past, was the great delight of the first faithful has given way among the Christians of our own day to sinful works filled with falsehood, destructive to the mind, which they fill with countless profane ideas, and deadly to the heart, where they sow those seeds of sin[157] that always, in course of time, produce the fruits of death![158] Alas! Do we not already bear in our depths tendencies well suited to iniquity without adding to them from outside? Is the leaven of corruption[159] that grows within our heart not enough to threaten our innocence without [adding other things] to help it in its malice? And do the passions, in which we come into this world too well instructed, need to be helped by our own ingenuity?

49. It was this knowledge of the holy books that made Bernard so formidable to the enemies of the Church. The throne of Peter had become the prey of a usurper [Anacletus II]; Dagon had taken the place of the Ark [of the Covenant];[160] an intruder, filled with malice and guile, had appeared in the sanctuary and had been paid homage by the people of God. The faith of the churches hung in abeyance at the novel sight of two pontiffs, each claiming to be the Lord's Anointed, and waited, as in the days of old, for God himself to make known him whom he had chosen. One no longer knew whether one should go to Jerusalem to worship or to Mount Gerizim.[161] In Rome, Peter

---

[157] *Crime*: see n. 124.
[158] See Rom 7:5.
[159] See 1 Cor 5:6; Gal 5:9.
[160] See 1 Sam 5:2.
[161] At about the time of the prophet Nehemiah (mid-fifth century BCE), the Samaritans built their own temple on Mount Gerizim, about thirty miles north of Jerusalem, and the question of which was the true Temple of the Lord—that on Mount Gerizim or that on Mount Zion in Jerusalem—became the main point of divergence between the Samaritans and the Jews.

de Léon[162] enjoyed the fruits of his iniquity, and surrounded by his worshipers, this man of sin[163] was seated in the temple of God while the true pontiff, Innocent II, was forced from his see. He wandered from place to place like the Ark of Israel,[164] with a retinue little suited to his dignity, until at last he came to France, where he found a more honorable refuge under the pious protection of our kings.[165] Such indeed had always been the destiny of France: to open her arms to pontiffs and sovereigns who had lost their thrones and to see these monarchs [re]armed against usurpers and rebels.

50. Well, my brothers, the Church is in a sorry state when she is torn apart in this way from within. See how the standard of rebellion and discord is raised even in the sanctuary of peace and unity! Some are for Cephas, some are for Paul, none is for Jesus Christ.[166] Her high offices are either the prize or the place of rebellion; her graces, far from being administered majestically, are offered meanly; her thunderbolts are no longer the punishment of vice, but the instruments of [human] passion, and on both sides one seeks to make friends not by means of the riches of iniquity, but with the very treasures of the sanctuary!

51. What scandal was more worthy of the zeal and acumen of Bernard than this? He appears in the midst of the prelates of the kingdom assembled at Étampes [in 1130] to adjudicate their differences. He presides, like a second Daniel, at the assembly of the elders:[167] the princes, if I may use the words of Job, cease to speak before him and are attentive to his judgments.[168] All the fathers at the Council respect Bernard's authority—an

---

[162] Massillon calls him Pierre de Léon (see appendix 2, s.v. Anacletus II) and never uses his [anti]papal title Anacletus.
[163] 2 Thess 2:3.
[164] See n. 23 above.
[165] Louis VI (primarily) and his son Louis VII.
[166] See 1 Cor 1:12.
[167] See Dan 13:45-62 = Sus 1:45-62 (the end of the story of Susanna).
[168] Job 29:9.

authority I cannot describe that came from his outstanding virtue—and they unanimously accept his decision. The eyes of the whole illustrious assembly are fixed on this man of miracles; he alone is the interpreter of the Holy Spirit; he alone guides an entire Council, and the whole of France accepts from his hand Innocent II as the lawful pope. He is ever the Samuel of his century who, in the midst of the assembled tribes, shows how the die had been cast in favor of him whom the Lord had anointed and destined to rule over his people.

52. What courses of action were needful in Sicily, Italy, and Germany to extinguish the last sparks of the schism and gather the eagles together round the body![169] We see [Bernard] strike down a prince whose influence was keeping the discord alive: he meets him in a temple armed with the body of Jesus Christ, and, on behalf of the terrible God whom he holds in his hands, orders him to trouble the Church no longer. At this astonishing sight, the Duke of Guyenne is perturbed: all his pride is changed into dread, and cast down, like Paul, by the presence of the God whose majesty he [now] perceives, he is transformed, like him, from being an instrument of the fury of a false pontiff into a vessel of election.[170]

53. But there was much more to be done to reestablish peace within the Church. After [Bernard], like Moses, had ensured the high priesthood of Aaron against those who opposed it,[171]

---

[169] See Matt 24:28; Luke 17:37. Massillon says nothing of what happened in Sicily, Italy, and Germany and confines himself to alluding to the now familiar story of the conversion of Duke William X of Aquitaine, whom Massillon refers to as the duke of Guyenne. It effectively brought the schism in France to an end. See appendix 2, s.v. William (Guillaume) X, duke of Aquitaine.

[170] Acts 9:15 (*vas electionis*). William proceeds to die in an odor of sanctity on the way to Compostela. Massillon now concludes the third part of his panegyric with Bernard's victories over Gilbert de la Porrée, Peter Abelard, and Henry of Toulouse. It is familiar territory, and all will be found listed in appendix 2.

[171] Massillon is referring to the ill-fated rebellion of Korah, narrated in Num 16.

he had to protect the people of God from being led astray by Balaam.[172] The Councils of Sens [in 1141] and Reims [in 1148] respected him for his abundant insights and the power of his genius and saw him make a glorious defense of the antiquity and simplicity of the faith against the dangerous and preposterous ideas of a bishop of Poitiers, [Gilbert de la Porrée,] and the profane novelties[173] of Abelard.

54. This man was puffed up with empty learning and gifted with natural talents well suited to leading minds astray and giving to falsehood the air of truth. Eloquent, polished, ingenious in his discourses, vain with countless curious facets of learning, he undertook to make the mysteries of the faith subject to human reason, and in place of this lamp that shines in darkness,[174] he sought to bring in a light that will appear only after we have been transformed from glory to glory.[175] The faithful had already been attracted by the charm of his eloquence and the appeal of his novel ideas—something that inevitably happens to people's minds in matters of religion— and they began to transgress those boundaries that had been so wisely established by our fathers. This mystery of iniquity[176] hardly bothered now to work in secret, and Abelard, proud of his success, haughtily challenged the people of God, as did the giant of the Philistines [Goliath],[177] to bring forth a worthy opponent to fight him. But the insolence of this heresiarch led to new glory for Bernard.

[172] See Num 22–24.

[173] See n. 155 above.

[174] See John 1:4. Massillon is referring to the lamp of the Gospel.

[175] See 2 Cor 3:18. In other words, according to Massillon, what Abelard was trying to do was to bring into this life the knowledge and certainty that are reserved for the next. Massillon's view is that of Saint Paul in 1 Cor 13:12: "We now see through a glass in a dark manner, and then face to face. I now know in part, but then I shall know even as I am known."

[176] 2 Thess 2:7: "the mystery of iniquity is already at work."

[177] See 1 Sam 17:8-10.

55. Both made their way to the Council of Sens, and there, before the high priests of the Lord,[178] the learning that puffs up yields to the simplicity that enlightens, the crafty words of human wisdom [yield] to the power of the cross and the [Holy] Spirit, and the proudest philosopher of his time [yields] to a scribe educated in the kingdom of heaven.

56. From this victory he hastens to Toulouse, where the apostate monk Henry was preaching a new doctrine.[179] He had set himself up against the holy institution of the sacraments and the tradition of the Church and had already prepared the way for the birth of those monsters that error begot during the last century[180] and that an ever-fortunate king was first to stifle in a kingdom that was almost the first to have seen them born.[181] But we must stop here: a eulogy is not a history, and we cannot include everything.

57. In any case, my brothers, it is not this that is most instructive for us in the life of our saint. It is true that these astonishing events embellish the life of the saint we are praising, but they do not offer us sinners who are listening to it anything to imitate.[182] They certainly reveal great deeds, but they do not provide us with examples [to follow]. Bernard's humility in the midst of all his glory is something far more fitting to move [our hearts].[183] Alas! A flimsy reputation, where human error is more important than our good qualities, magnifies mightily the idea

---

[178] Massillon continues with his Old Testament allusions.

[179] See appendix 2, s.v. Henry of Toulouse.

[180] The monsters (*monstres*) are the sects or the ideas of Protestantism, especially Calvinism, and the "last century" is the sixteenth. Massillon, with some justice, sees Henry as a sort of proto-Protestant, a forerunner of Luther and Calvin.

[181] I presume that the *monarque toujours heureux* is Louis XIV, and the "stifling" (the verb is *étouffer*) may well refer to the Revocation of the Edict of Nantes in 1685. This is a difficult sentence to translate.

[182] In other words, we are not expected to work miracles or single-handedly put an end to schisms and heresies.

[183] *A nous toucher*: see the discussion in chap. 3.

we have of ourselves, but Bernard, having achieved the greatest glory that France had ever seen in one man, always had his eyes fixed on his own wretchedness and never turned them from it to see all that shone about him or to take note of the regard of men eager to make him the subject of their admiration.

58. He now refused [the requests] of those illustrious churches that begged him to be their pastor,[184] and regarded the episcopal throne as a sort of holy [burning] bush he was not allowed to approach.[185] Though now clothed by the popes with the character of universal legate to the Christian world, all he saw in this new title was the sovereign pontiff above him, and he paid worthy and respectful homage to bishops, acting only on their orders and refusing to circumvent this authority established by God. He would not even allow his own [disciples] to evade the laws binding on all and accept those prerogatives and exemptions that are, indeed, useful in their institution and holy in their outcome but that never fail to be remedies that are almost as trying as the sickness. The need for such is always a result of lukewarmness and laxity in the Church, for they draw attention either to an abuse of authority on the part of pastors or to a love of independence on the part of ministers subject to them.

59. He was now honored at Clairvaux by the visit of a sovereign pontiff [Innocent II] followed by a magnificent and numerous retinue. He himself appeared at the head of his monks, all of them with their eyes cast down and keeping absolute silence. On their faces, in the midst of this extraordinary and awesome occasion, there appeared only the expression of penitence and recollection[186] that the pontiff then saw.[187] And

---

[184] See *Vita prima* 1.14.69 (William of Saint-Thierry); PL 185:265B; CF 76:73, n. 81, and 2.4.26 (Arnold of Bonneval); PL 185:283B; CF 76:106, listing Milan, Reims, Genoa, Châlons-sur-Marne, and Langres.

[185] See Exod 3:5.

[186] *Recueillement*: see n. 78 above.

[187] See *Vita prima* 2.1.6 (Arnold of Bonneval); PL 185:272AB; CF 76:84–85. The visit took place in 1131.

the holy abbot, still and calm in his bearing and seeming hardly to notice this newest of honors, calls to mind the prophet of Israel [Elisha] who, visited in his solitude by Naaman, a prince surrounded by glory and splendor, was so little affected by this novelty that he did not deign to see him. So occupied was he with the misfortunes of Israel and his attempt to appease the wrath of God that his people had aroused that he seemed to pay hardly any attention to the rank of this prince or the splendor that surrounded him.[188]

60. Finally, when he speaks with anyone it is only to make them citizens of heaven,[189] and he ceaselessly bewails to himself and his friends the dissipation of his own life and regards what he does for the people as infractions of his real duties. "I no longer see myself," he said, "either as cleric or layman. Long ago I ceased to follow the path of the monk whose habit I wear. What am I then? I am no more than a sort of weird marvel and the monster of my age."[190] And how many times, moved by the kings of the earth who came to consult him in his wilderness and disturb him in his [monastic] tomb,[191] did he give them the reply that Samuel gave to Saul: "Ah! Why do you wish to resurrect for the sake of the world a man buried among the dead?" *Quare inquietasti me ut suscitare?* ["Why have you disturbed my rest that I should arise?" (1 Sam 28:15)].

61. There you see, my brothers, the feelings of fear and humility that have always accompanied the most heroic deeds of

---

[188] See 2 Kgs 5:1-14.

[189] Phil 3:20: *Nostra autem conversatio in caelis est*, which is best rendered as "For our citizenship is in heaven."

[190] Bernard, Ep 250.4; SBOp 8:147, to the Carthusian prior of Portes. This is the famous passage in which Bernard describes himself as *quaedam chimaera mei saeculi*, "a sort of modern chimaera." The description also appears in Texier, La Rue, and Anselme.

[191] The idea of the monastery as a monk's tomb is an ancient one, and monks were, effectively, dead men walking. Rancé often said that he regarded La Trappe as his tomb, and he advised nuns to look on their cells as their graves (see Bell, *Understanding Rancé*, 107).

the saints. Charity, like self-love, has its own pious errors and innocent enticements. Grace and desire are almost equal in the wrong idea they give us of ourselves. And just as most of our vices find a safe place for themselves only by the false ideas we form of them, so the virtues of the saints are often concealed only by the misleading impressions they give of themselves.

62. Such is life in the world, with all the dangers of human intercourse and interaction, the sinful diversions of plays and entertainments,[192] the emptiness and uselessness of all that we do, and the unending quest for new pleasures. But you see all this only as innocent amusements and the unavoidable ways of relaxation that human frailty needs, and your works of charity, the outward works of mercy, are, in the eyes of the saints you call upon, no more than dangerous disturbances to the soul's recollection[193] and obstacles to the secret consolations[194] of grace. And so Bernard misjudged himself so far as to think his life had been monstrous, because the needs of the Church and the call of heaven involved him in tempestuous affairs little suited to the silence and withdrawal of a solitary. Yet every day, O my God, your ministers delude themselves

---

[192] The French Church of the seventeenth century generally condemned the theater, which it regarded as a far too popular rival to itself, especially since theatrical performances took place on Sundays. It saw the theater as enacting and encouraging those very vices that it, the church, was seeking to extirpate, and what one saw on the stage was an exaltation of the creature, not the Creator. As Massillon says, plays were no more than "sinful diversions." In many dioceses bishops included actors with witches and prostitutes and denied them the sacraments unless they renounced their profession. But despite its continuing efforts, the church never succeeded in persuading the civil authorities to close the theaters: they were just too popular. The matter is a complex one, and the best account in English (there is a great deal in French) is J. Henry Phillips, *The Theatre and its Critics in Seventeenth Century France* (Oxford: Oxford University Press, 1980).

[193] See n. 78 above.

[194] See n. 79 above.

in thinking that they can live a wholly worldly and ungodly life and yet fulfill the holiness of their [clerical] estate and the demanding obligations of the priesthood. Alas! The errors of humility you see in your saints are treated almost as their weakness, but the errors of our own passions we regard as the proper reward of our prudence! Break, Lord, this deadly spell, and enlighten the eyes of our hearts,[195] that we may no more stray from your ways but follow the paths that your saints have laid down for us and arrive, like them, at a blessed eternity. May it be so.

---

[195] See Eph 1:18.

Conclusion

The Saint in the Sun

You have now made the acquaintance of the Bernard who was preached from the pulpits, especially the pulpits of Paris, in the France of the Sun King. As we have said many times, he is not Bernard the mystic, and the reasons for that have been explained in some detail in chapter 2. Indeed, studies of Bernard's mysticism would not appear for another two centuries, though Elphège Vacandard spent some time on the question in his classic *Vie de Saint Bernard*, first published in 1895.[1] It is interesting to note, however, that even at the very end of the nineteenth century the ghosts of Madame Guyon and Fénelon had not yet been completely exorcised. After describing the nature and importance of chaste love in Bernard's mysticism, Vacandard goes on to say that "It seems that such a doctrine is very close to that of Fénelon and Madame de Guyon. But one important fact separates them. Bernard does not believe in a state, properly speaking, of pure love. In his eyes, ecstasy is something transitory," and so on.[2] Bossuet and Pope Innocent XII would have heartily agreed.

The first studies of any consequence of Bernard's mysticism did not appear until the 1930s: Watkin Williams's *The Mysticism of S. Bernard of Clairvaux*, which appeared in 1931,[3] and Étienne

---

[1] Elphège Vacandard, *Vie de Saint Bernard, abbé de Clairvaux* (Paris: V. Lecoffre, 1895), with a number of later editions.

[2] Vacandard, *Vie de Saint Bernard*, 3rd ed. (Paris: V. Lecoffre, 1902), 1:491.

[3] Watkin W. Williams, *The Mysticism of S. Bernard of Clairvaux, with an Approbation by the Abbot General of the Cistercians, S. O.* (London: Burns, Oates & Washbourne, 1931).

Gilson's *La théologie mystique de saint Bernard*, first published in 1934.[4] With the single exception of Henri-Marie Boudon, the Bernard of the panegyrists is the Bernard of Jacques Biroat. He is the model of humility, *pénitence* (as penance, penitence, and repentance), a model of asceticism and austerity, who, in following the way of the cross, has died to himself, to the world, and to all worldly things. He is a man whose love for God and the Gospel, for God incarnate and the Mother of God, is manifested in his deeds, and a man whose life was, quite simply, an *imitatio Christi*, an imitation of his Lord and Savior, Jesus Christ. As we have seen in chapter 1, for the seventeenth-century *spirituels*, Jesus Christ was the Great Penitent. He was a man who had no fear in reproving and rebuking, when necessary, the great and mighty—princes and kings, prelates and popes—and he was equally fearless in going to battle with heretics and schismatics when his beloved church was threatened or torn asunder by her enemies.

The panegyrists invariably begin with an account of Bernard's life in the cloister and an account, longer or shorter, of his triumphs over youthful temptations. The episode of the icy pool appears a number of times, though only Claude Lion takes from the *Vita prima* all three stories. We hear of Bernard's austerities at Cîteaux and Clairvaux, his love of silence and solitude (especially in Bernard Planchette), his failure to notice his physical surroundings or the food he ate, his dedication to what Claude Lion calls *virginité*—chastity, innocence, and purity of body and soul—and his total and unswerving love of God. Our saint, says Jean-François Senault, "died to the world when he entered the religious life; he died to all his friends when he left them; he died to his hopes when he renounced

---

[4] Étienne Gilson, *La théologie mystique de saint Bernard* (Paris: J. Vrin, 1934). A fourth edition appeared in 1980. English translation by A. H. C. Downes: *The Mystical Theology of Saint Bernard* (London and New York: Sheed & Ward, 1940; repr. Kalamazoo, MI: Cistercian Publications, 1990).

them; and he died to himself when he buried himself in the cloister."[5] His teachers were not mortal men, but the Spirit of God himself, speaking to Bernard through the woods and trees, and his knowledge, which was not acquired but infused (this is François Ogier, whose ideas were stolen by Esprit Fléchier), rendered him invincible in his defense of the teachings of the church.

And so the panegyrists turn to Bernard's work in the world beyond the cloister, speaking, in more or less detail, of his deep involvement in the papal schism and his defeat of those who would imperil the unity of the church and its teachings. Virtually all the preachers mention Abelard, Gilbert de la Porrée, and Henry of Toulouse; four of them—Texier, Ogier, Fléchier, and Bourru—mention Arnold of Brescia; and one alone, François Ogier, mentions Peter of Bruys. Their accounts are usually taken from the *Vita prima*, and all, naturally, are biased. The business of the panegyrists, after all, is to celebrate their hero, not to present a balanced historical account. Abelard, therefore, always appears as the villain of the piece, and only François Ogier has anything good to say about him. Gilbert de la Porrée is defeated by Bernard (which he was not) at the Council of Reims, and Henry of Toulouse is a convenient predecessor of those Protestants, especially Calvinists, so disliked by Bossuet, Rancé, Fénelon, and Massillon.

The *dramatis personae* of the papal schism all come from the pages of the *Vita prima* (nothing good, therefore, will be said of the wicked usurper Anacletus), and some appear more frequently than others. The panegyrists are especially fond, with good reason, of the splendid story of the conversion of Duke William X of Aquitaine, though some tell it better than others. We then have examples of the way in which Bernard rebuked prelates and princes, and most, though not all, of the preachers mention or cite the five books *De consideratione* addressed to

---

[5] See chap. 5, n. 14.

Bernard's former disciple at Clairvaux, Eugenius III. Rancé, understandably, reverses the usual order, and first deals with Bernard's work in the world so that he can concentrate on the real meat of his conference, Bernard as the ideal monk, the true successor of Saint Benedict. But Rancé is not preaching a sermon in a church; he is delivering a conference to the Strict Observance monks of La Trappe.

Bernard the mystic, as we have said, is avoided, save by Henri-Marie Boudon and a very brief mention by Bourru, and Bernard the worker of miracles does not fare a great deal better. Modern scholarship is finally coming to realize the real importance of the miracle stories in Bernard's life,[6] but except perhaps for Fénelon, the *spirituels* of *le grand siècle* do not dwell on the matter. His youthful vision in the old chapel of Saint-Vorles is mentioned by Lion, Fléchier, and Bourru; the Lactation appears in the panegyrics of Planchette, Boudon, Lion, Bourru, and (vaguely) Esprit Fléchier; and the *Amplexus* in those of Planchette, Boudon, and Claude Lion. Of Bernard's own miracles, Fénelon offers the most complete account, summarizing the saint's achievements in curing the sick, giving sight to the blind and hearing to the deaf, restoring to the lame the use of their legs, raising paralytics from their beds, giving health to the dying, and foretelling the future. He also introduces some specific examples, such as the miracle of the blessed bread at Sarlat, the numerous cures at Constance, and other miracles at Frankfurt am Main and one or two other places.

---

[6] See, for example, André Picard and Pierre Boglioni, "Miracle et thaumaturgie dans la vie de saint Bernard," in *Vies et légendes de saint Bernard de Clairvaux, création, diffusion, réception (XIIe–XXe Siècles)*, ed. Patrick Arabeyre, et al. (Brecht and Cîteaux: *Cîteaux: Commentarii Cistercienses*, 1993), 36–59, and Christopher J. Holdsworth, "Reading the Signs, Bernard of Clairvaux and His Miracles," in *Writing Medieval Biography 750–1250: Essays in Honour of Professor Frank Barlow*, ed. David Bates, Julia Crick, and Sarah Hamilton (Woodbridge: Boydell Press, 2006), 161–72.

For Antoine Anselme above all, Bernard is the Last of the Fathers, *ultimus Patrum*. He sees him as continuing the work not only of the four great Doctors of the Latin Church (in which he is following Antoine Le Maistre)—Augustine, Ambrose, Gregory the Great, and Jerome—but also four great teachers of the Greek Church: Athanasius the Great, Gregory of Nazianzus, John Chrysostom, and Basil the Great. But in three areas, he tells us, Bernard added to what they had taught. The first was in his devotion to the Virgin (but the only devotion truly pleasing to her is the imitation of her virtues). This was also something dear to the heart of Henri-Marie Boudon, who begins his panegyric with a long paean of praise to the Mother of God. Second, in what Bernard has to say on "subordination in the Church," by which Anselme means the question of authority, particularly episcopal authority and papal authority and their interrelationship. And third, in his preaching the recovery of the Holy Land in the Second Crusade, something that Anselme refers to as "a wholly Christian war."[7] This, of course, was something of an embarrassment to the panegyrists (as it was also something of an embarrassment to Bernard himself), since the Crusade was an unmitigated disaster. Only Fénelon, Anselme, and Bourru deal with the reasons for the failure at any length, and all three, naturally, exonerate Bernard from any miscalculation and the pope from any error.

The panegyrists do not always stay quite on track. In their efforts to praise their subject they may find it necessary, like Bossuet, to present their audience with a preliminary intensive course in the theology of the incarnation, beginning with God as pure reason and intelligence, moving through the doctrines of eternal generation and the hypostatic union, and ending with a discussion of Jesus' "theandric activities." Boudon and Anselme have much to say on Mariology and the way

---

[7] Chap. 13, n. 46.

in which all Bernard's achievements, however remarkable, were possible only through the grace of the Mother of God. Ogier and Bourru, on the other hand, tell us much about seventeenth-century French angelology, while Bernard Planchette dwells at length on the importance of the desert in spiritual development, making mention of the sages of India and Egypt, the centaur Chiron, Aesculapius, Hercules, many worthies of the Old Testament, Paul the First Hermit, Antony the Great, Hilarion, and Moses, and finally proving his point with a quotation from Guerric of Igny. Others, such as François Ogier and Claude Lion, introduce classical analogies, which, it must be admitted, are neither particularly apt nor especially helpful.

In almost all cases, Bernard is likened to earlier figures, some from the Old Testament, some from the New, some from the classics, some from late Antiquity and the Patristic period. He is a second Abraham, a second Joseph, a second Moses, a second Samuel, a second Daniel, a second Ezra, a second Elijah, a second Jonah, a second Jeremiah, a second Solomon, a second Judas Maccabeus, a second John the Baptist, a second Augustine, a second Ambrose, a second Gregory the Great, a second Jerome, a second Benedict, a second Athanasius, a second Gregory of Nazianzus, a second John Chrysostom, a second Basil the Great, and, remarkably, a second Osiris in Bernard Planchette and a second Archimedes in Claude Lion. In the anti-Quietist polemic of Charles de La Rue, however, it is Bossuet who is a second Bernard.

Most of the panegyrists tell the various stories of Bernard's life and then, at the end of the major divisions of their orations, apply them to their wayward and worldly congregations. This is the old and well-tested approach that we may see stretching from Biroat to Bourru, though it is not invariable. In Fénelon's eloquent and flowing panegyric, for example, the reproaches and exhortations are an integral part of the text, and the same is true of the splendid panegyric of Massillon. But if Biroat's early discourse looks back to the divisions, subdivisions, and sub-subdivisions of later scholasticism, Massillon, as Albert and Court have said, opened up a completely new direction in the ministry of preaching.[8]

As to sources, all the preachers, without exception, root their discourses in Scripture and the *Vita prima S. Bernardi*, either in the Latin editions of Horstius or Mabillon, depending on date, and/or the *Vie de S. Bernard* of Antoine Le Maistre. William of Saint-Thierry hardly ever appears by name (only in Bossuet and Fénelon), but almost always as "the historian of Bernard's life." As to Scripture, some, such as Massillon, cite the Old Testament more than the New, some, such as Biroat and Bossuet, cite the New more than the Old (with a preponderance of references to the letters by or attributed to Saint Paul), and in some, such as Rancé, the proportions are more or less equal.

Classical citations are not common, though in preachers such as Ogier or Claude Lion there is an aura, an atmosphere, of classicism—sometimes too much, in the opinion of Albert and Court. Planchette quotes a well-known saying from Persius, Senault has a line from Seneca the Younger, and Lion quotes Claudian. Ogier mentions Aristotle by name and is dependent on Ovid, whom he refers to as "the Ancients" (in the plural), for the story of Baucis and Philemon. But that is all. There is a much richer variety of patristic sources, with Augustine or *ps.*-Augustine leading the field. He is cited by a dozen of the panegyrists. Then comes Tertullian, always a favorite not only for the purity of his Latin but also for the forcefulness of his opinions. He appears in nine panegyrics. Following Tertullian we have Gregory the Great in six sermons, Ambrose, Jerome, and John Chrysostom in five, Philo of Alexandria in three, and Gregory of Nazianzus and *ps.*-Dionysius in two. After these come a dozen writers who are cited by only one of the preachers: Basil of Seleucia (Lion), Bede (Boudon), the Rule of Saint Benedict (Rancé, with a passing allusion

---

[8] See chap. 14, n. 9.

in Massillon), Cassiodorus (Texier), Eusebius of Caesarea (Planchette), Gregory of Nyssa (Texier), Maximus of Turin (Biroat), Peter Chrysologus (Lion), Prosper of Aquitaine (Anselme), Thalassius of Syria (Lion), Theodoret of Cyrrhus (Boudon), and Zeno of Verona (Boudon).

Of the writers of the Middle Ages, Thomas Aquinas is cited by Boudon, Lion, and Bourru, and then a number of authors are mentioned in but one panegyric: *ps.*-Albertus Magnus, *ps.*-Bonaventure, Richard of Saint-Victor and Rupert of Deutz by Boudon (a different *ps.*-Bonaventure appears in Biroat), Otto of Freising, William of Newburgh, and Peter the Venerable by Anselme, Accursius by Ogier, and Hildebert of Lavardin by Claude Lion. Cistercian writers, apart from the authors of the *Vita prima*, are limited to three: Fastred of Clairvaux in Rancé, Gilbert of Hoyland in Boudon, and Guerric of Igny in Planchette. Of the postmedieval writers, the *Annales ecclesiastici* of Cardinal Caesar Baronius appear in four panegyrics, and then we have Francis de Sales and Teresa of Ávila in Boudon, and Pierre de Bérulle in Claude Lion. The panegyrists are not always accurate in their quotations and sometimes attribute them to the wrong authors. They cannot always be blamed for this, since they could not have known (for example) that the *Golden Letter—the Letter to the Brethren of Mont-Dieu*—was not written by Bernard but by William of Saint-Thierry, or that the *De septem itineribus aeternitatis* was not from the pen of Bonaventure but almost certainly a work of Rudolf von Biberach. In a number of cases, the citations have undoubtedly been borrowed directly from the preface "to the Reader" in Le Maistre's *Vie de S. Bernard*. Such is the case with Baronius, Hildebert of Lavardin, Otto of Freising, Peter the Venerable, and Prosper of Aquitaine.

Except for the letters and the *De consideratione* (both of which appear in about a dozen panegyrics), quotations from or allusions to Bernard's own works are by no means numerous. The sermons on the Song of Songs are cited in eight discourses, but not those sections dealing with ecstatic rapture or mystical experience. There is a scattering of other sermons, and the *De diligendo Deo* appears in two panegyrics, as does the letter-treatise on the errors of Abelard. Antoine Anselme cites the letter-treatise to Henry of Sens on the duties of bishops and the *De gratia et libero arbitrio*, while Bernard Planchette and Charles de La Rue are alone in quoting from the *De gradibus humilitatis et superbiae* and the *Apology* to William of Saint-Thierry, respectively. Many of these citations, especially those from the letters and *De consideratione*, have been taken directly from the *Vita prima* in either Latin or French.

Such is the Bernard of the seventeenth and early eighteenth centuries. He is, in fact six Bernards, though only two appear in all the panegyrics. First, he is Bernard the model of humility, *pénitence*, mortification, and contempt for the world. Second, he is Bernard the defender of the church and its teachings, the Bernard of the Counter-Reformation. Third, in Armand-Jean de Rancé, he is Bernard the Ideal Monk. Fourth, in Louis-Bénigne Bourru, he is Bernard the Angel. Fifth, in Antoine Anselme, he is Bernard the Last of the Fathers. And sixth, in Henri-Marie Boudon alone, he is the Bernard we know so well today, Bernard the Mystic. All six Bernards were part of the one Bernard, and if the panegyrists present their hero as someone rather more perfect than he actually was, they cannot be blamed for that. That, after all, was their business. But in their lengthy discourses, some more eloquent than others, some possessing more of that *onction* that was so important to preachers in the age of the Sun King, we may see a Bernard who was indeed, as he himself said, the chimera of his age.

Appendix 1

Technical Terms

Anéantissement / **annihilation**. This is obviously a dangerous idea, and we must distinguish carefully between ontological annihilation, which is the total loss of self in God, and the annihilation of the human will in the will of God. The former implies that the creature has become the Creator, which, in Christian terms, is heresy; the latter is the goal of the spiritual path, when all one's egocentricity, self-love, and self-will has been reduced to nothing. One is now an instrument on which God plays. The problem is that when mystics such as Bernard of Clairvaux or Teresa of Jesus describe this highest of all states, they do so in terms that are often ambiguous, and if, with Teresa, we experience this state as a drop of water falling into a river and merging with the sea, it is difficult to see how there can be any sense of self left. See further David N. Bell, "A Doctrine of Ignorance: the Annihilation of Individuality in Christian and Muslim Mysticism," in *Benedictus: Studies in Honor of St Benedict of Nursia*, ed. E. Rozanne Elder, Studies in Medieval Cistercian History, VIII (Kalamazoo, MI: Cistercian Publications, 1981), 30–52. The matter was not helped by Madame Guyon's telling us that "We can honor the All of God only by our own annihilation [*anéantissement*], and we are no sooner annihilated than God, who never suffers a void without filling it, fills us with himself" (chap. 2, n. 39). We can understand, therefore, the caution with which the panegyrists approached this term, and of all of them, only Henri-Marie Boudon is prepared to discuss it at any length (chap. 11, §§21–25).

Charité / **charity**. Generally speaking, *amour* (*amor* in Latin) is the generic term for love and may refer to all forms of love, good or bad, properly directed or misdirected, spiritual or carnal alike. *Charité* (*caritas* in Latin) always refers to love that is properly directed. Augustine provides an exact definition: "I call charity a movement of the soul towards the enjoyment of God [*ad fruendum Deo*] for his own sake, and of oneself and one's neighbor for the sake of God" (*De doctrina Christiana* 3.16; PL 34:72). Such is Bernard's usage. Charity is one of the three Theological Virtues (the other two being Faith and Hope), and Saint Paul provides a precise description of its nature in 1 Cor 13:4-8. In English, charity normally implies some sort of alms-giving, but that is never the usage here. In these translations, therefore, I translate *charité* and *caritas* as charity, even if it sometimes looks a little odd in English. It is important to keep the terms distinct. A much rarer word for love in a good or positive sense is *dilection* (*dilectio* in Latin), but of the panegyrists represented here only Fénelon uses it (chap. 8, §6, n. 23). It is a less specific and more all-embracing term than *charity*. Fénelon is referring to God's everlasting *dilection* for erring humanity.

Consolations / **consolations**. *Consolations*, in both French and English, is a technical term. They are "God's warm, peaceful, joyful, encouraging visitations, which effect tears of love, repentant sorrow, a desire for heavenly things, prompter service of God, and affectively intensify faith, hope and love" (*A Dictionary of Christian Spirituality*, ed. Gordon S. Wakefield [London: SCM Press, 1983], 94). For a full discussion, see DS 2:1617–34, "Consolation spirituelle," but one can hardly do better than to read chapters 1 and 2 of the Fourth Mansions of *The Interior Castle* of Saint Teresa of Jesus. In the third of his Rules for the Discernment of Spirits, Saint Ignatius Loyola distinguishes three types of consolations. The first is when the soul experiences an inward movement that enflames it with the love of God and when, in consequence, no created thing is loved in itself, but only in God. The second is when one weeps in remorse for one's sins or for the passion of Christ and these tears lead to an ever-greater love for God. And the third is when the soul experiences any increase in faith, hope, or love or any inward happiness that calls one to heavenly things and one's soul's salvation and leaves the soul quiet and at peace in God. Some consolations are transitory, such as the tears that lead to a greater love of God. Some produce a permanent change of state, such as the continual experience of an indescribable inner joy that is never lost even in the midst of adversity. This is what happened to Bernard, for having achieved a unity of spirit with God, God was always present to him, and he was always recollected in God. See further s.v. *recueillement* / recollection.

Contemplation / **contemplation**. In his *Scala claustralium*, a work well known to seventeenth-century theologians (who attributed it to Bernard or Augustine), Guigo II of La Grande Chartreuse distinguishes clearly between contemplation and meditation. "Meditation [*meditatio*] is the studious action of the mind, seeking out the understanding of a hidden truth under the direction of one's own reason. Contemplation (*contemplatio*) is when the mind is in some way lifted up to God and suspended above itself, tasting the joys of everlasting sweetness" (Guigo II of La Chartreuse, *Scala claustralium* 2; SCh 163:84). In other words, meditation is active and discursive and makes use of the intellect and the imagination; contemplation is passive and experiential and is entirely dependent on God. As we saw in chapter 2, this is the usage of Molinos. But it was precisely because of the association of passive infused contemplation with Quietism that the seventeenth-century preachers tended to avoid the term. This is clear from the first version of the panegyric of Charles de La Rue. Both the noun and the verb (*contempler*) occur, certainly, but "to contemplate" usually means no more than to reflect on, muse on, think about, ruminate, or ponder. In Fléchier's panegyric, it is the equivalent of Bernard's "consideration" (*consideratio*).

***Crimes* / sins**. In the preachers represented here, *crimes* does not mean "crimes" but sins. It is a common usage among seventeenth-century French spiritual writers. Much nonsense has been written about Rancé saying that "religious congregations are gangs of criminals" (*De la sainteté et des devoirs de la vie monastique* [1683], 1:392): he simply means that they are collections of sinners, not that they are wanted by the French police.

***Curiosité* / curiosity**. *Curieux* does not mean "curious" in the usual modern sense, but refers to writings that titillate and pander to our human curiosity, and *curiosité* (*curiositas* in Latin) was roundly condemned by a multitude of monastic writers, including Bernard, as being both useless and dangerous. In all the preachers who appear in this volume, the terms *curiosity* and *curious* are always pejorative. See Richard Newhauser, "The Sin of Curiosity and the Cistercians," in *Erudition at God's Service: Studies in Medieval Cistercian History, XI*, ed. John R. Sommerfeldt (Kalamazoo, MI: Cistercian Publications, 1987), 71–95. *Curiosity* goes hand in hand with *novelties*, which are equally dangerous. See s.v. *nouveautés* / novelties.

***Dégagement* / detachment**. *Dégagement* is one of four words that all mean much the same thing, the others being *dépouillement* "stripping," *désappropriation* "dispossession," and *désintéressement* "disinterestedness." Detachment or nonattachment does not necessarily involve the removal of physical objects or the elimination of relationships, but rather their taking second place to one's love for God and for the things that pertain to God. The principle is set forth in Colossians 3:9-10 and Ephesians 4:22-24, both of which speak of stripping off the old self and its deeds and putting on the new self, which is a recognition of our creation in the image of God. It does not involve the rejection of created things, which are, by definition, good (see Genesis 1:31), but rather a rejection of our desiring them, seeking them out, and binding ourselves to them. According to Henri-Marie Boudon, stripping off the old self "consists of renouncing worldly desires, that is to say, in detaching oneself from temporal, natural, and sensual things, in avoiding the riches of position, office, or marriage, and in forgoing all the pleasures that can satisfy the senses. These are the first steps that should be taken by the soul that truly yearns for God" (chap. 11, §7). "Disinterestedness" may mean much the same thing—namely, a lack of any interest in the things of this world—but when the Quietists take the term and mean by "perfect disinterestedness" (*désintéressement parfait*) a lack of any interest in our own salvation or damnation, this, as we have seen, was not a view that the church was prepared to countenance. It is understandable, therefore, that the panegyrists tend to avoid the term. For *dégagement spirituel*, the *Dictionnaire de spiritualité* directs the reader to *dépouillement* (DS 3:455–504 [for Bernard, see cols. 468–69]) and *désappropriation* (DS 3:518–29).

Dévotion / **devotion**. This is one of those tricky words that, in the seventeenth century, enjoyed a wider range of meanings than it commonly does today. For an excellent selection of texts, see Lucy Tinsley, *The French Expressions for Spirituality and Devotion: A Semantic Study* (Washington, DC: Catholic University of America Press, 1953), 186–205. It can mean devotion or devotional exercises or an attachment to religious practices, and it can mean devotion in the sense of being devoted to someone or something. It may also be almost or exactly a synonym for *piété* (q.v.), which is another tricky word (see Tinsley, *French Expressions*, 205–10). In Charles de La Rue's unrevised panegyric on Bernard (chap. 9), the best translation is what we would now call spirituality, but *spiritualité* (q.v.) was a word treated with some caution by seventeenth-century writers, not least because of an association with Quietism. See Tinsley, *French Expressions*, 226–38, especially 234–35.

Méditation / **meditation**. See s.v. *contemplation* / **contemplation**.

Nouveautés / **novelties**. Novelties or new ideas are always perilous and pernicious, and the basis for their general condemnation lies in Paul's advice to Timothy in 1 Timothy 6:20:

"O Timothy, guard what has been committed to you [*depositum custodi*], avoiding the profane novelties of words [*profanes vocum novitates*] and the oppositions of knowledge falsely so called." The contrast is between the *depositum*, which is the traditional teaching of the church, handed down from Christ to his apostles, and from the apostles to the members of the Post-Apostolic College, who are the bishops of the church, and the new and profane ideas put forth (in Bernard's time) by heretics such as Abelard or Gilbert de la Porrée or Henry of Toulouse or (in the days of Louis XIV) by Madame Guyon, Fénelon, and others. "Are we not suddenly bewitched by the novelty of certain ideas," asks Charles de La Rue, "rather than recognizing them as phantoms and rejecting them as delusions?" (chap. 9, §3), and he goes on to castigate Abelard's "pointless novelties" and "over-subtle novelties," where Abelard is no more than a mask for Fénelon.

Pénitence / **penitence**. There is always a problem of translation with *pénitence*, for the French word can mean either penitence or repentance (which are inward) or penance (which is outward). Sometimes, as, for example, in the expression *faire pénitence*, "do penance," there is no doubt what is meant; in other cases, the translation must be adapted to the context. It is sometimes said that in seventeenth-century France penitence without penance was inconceivable, but while that is true it is also misleading. A penance given by a Jesuit (whom a Jansenist would regard as Laxist) would be quite different from a penance given by a Jansenist (whom a Jesuit would regard as Rigorist). See further Bell, *Understanding Rancé*, chap. 4, *passim*. All the panegyrists (and, anachronistically, Bernard) were more Jansenist than Jesuit in their approach to *pénitence* (though Fénelon could exhibit both approaches), and both the interior change of heart and its outward expression were matters of the utmost seriousness. In the translations presented here, penance always involves penitence and repentance, and repentance and penitence usually involve penance. In other words, whenever one of the terms appears, the other two are usually implied.

Piété / **piety**. The word can mean "piety" in the English sense but is often better translated as "pious devotion," though in seventeenth-century French *dévotion* (q.v.) is stronger than *piété*. *Piété* can be no more than a proper respect for anything to do with the church or the Christian religion, or it may be an indefinable mixture of dutiful reverence, dedicated faithfulness, godliness, and what we would call spirituality. A "pious" person may exhibit all of these things. I have usually translated *piété* as "pious devotion," but sometimes "piety" is better.

Providence / **Providence**. The power of Providence was of first importance for all seventeenth-century theologians, Catholic and Protestant alike. Providence is, essentially, God's will in action, the Creator's total and beneficent control over all that happens in his creation. This does not mean, however, that human beings are no more than puppets in God's hands, or that human beings may sit back and let Providence do all the work, though Calvinism undoubtedly tends in this direction. God's Providence provided manna in the wilderness, but the Israelites still had to gather it up, bake it, and eat it. Our business is to collaborate—literally to be colaborers or coworkers—with God's Providence, though in this cooperation, God's work is always primary and ours always secondary. In other words, human beings may share or participate in the providential activity of God. As Augustine said, in the matter of our justification "we ourselves work, but we are fellow-workers with him who does the work" (Augustine, De nat et grat 31.35; PL 44:264). Human beings are, by definition, human, which means that we have a human will, albeit a will stained or corrupted by Original Sin. Thus, in cooperation with grace, and only in cooperation with grace, we may use that will to cooperate (or not) with God's Providence, although, in the end, as Thomas à Kempis has said, *Homo proponit, sed Deus disponit*, "The human being proposes, but God disposes" (Thomas à Kempis, *The Imitation of Christ*, bk. I, chap. 19, based on Prov 16:9).

Recueillement / **recollection**. This is an important technical term in seventeenth-century French spirituality. It involves the deliberate withdrawal of the mind and intellect from outward earthly things in order to focus them on the inward presence of God in the soul. The term itself first appears in Spanish in the mid-fifteenth century, and Spanish writers, especially Francisco de Osuna (who regarded recollection as a way of life) and Teresa of Ávila, have much to say on the matter. For Teresa, the Prayer of Recollection leads to the Prayer of Quiet, and the Prayer of Quiet leads to the Prayer of Union, but the writers represented here are not so precise. Recollection may be active or passive. With the help of grace (and only with the help of grace) active recollection is within our own power: it is the one-pointed fixing of the will and the attention on God and things divine and, as a technique, may be found in many spiritual traditions. Passive recollection, on the other hand, is entirely a gift from God, an extraordinary grace infused by God, in which there is a direct, if momentary, experiential union between creature and Creator. Active recollection is normally a prelude to passive recollection, but the former does not guarantee the latter, and the latter is not dependent on the former. For the panegyrists represented here, recollection is invariably active—passivity in any form is too reminiscent of Quietism—and the term may be used for almost any sort of interior or spiritual exercise. Such is the case with Fénelon, where recollection and spiritual exercises appear virtually as synonyms (chap. 8, §18), or with Massillon, who speaks of "the spirit of prayer and recollection" (chap. 14, §21). See further DS 13:247–67.

***Religion* / religion**. In seventeenth-century France *religion* was a word of wide meaning. It could mean religion in general, the Christian religion in particular, religious belief, religious sentiment, religious faith, or the religious way of life, i.e., monasticism—just as *religious* are monks and nuns, and *entrer en religion* is "to become a religious." It might also be translated by "piety" or "godliness." The translation, therefore, depends entirely on the context.

Spiritualité / **spirituality**. As we use the term today, *spirituality* is a word of recent coinage. In its sense of "attachment to or regard for things of the spirit as opposed to material or worldly interests" (*Oxford English Dictionary* [Oxford: Oxford University Press, 1986], 16:259) it dates in English from the first decades of the sixteenth century. Its association with interiority, infused grace, and experiential knowledge came later—from the seventeenth century in France and the nineteenth in England—although in both countries the main diffusion of the term dates from the second decade of the twentieth century. In *le grand siècle*, the term *spiritualité* was closely identified with Quietism, and Bossuet described the ideas of Madame Guyon and Fénelon as *la nouvelle spiritualité*. As Sister Lucy Tinsley has said, "in an age which claimed so many genuine mystics, but in which mystical phenomena were widely discussed and misunderstood in devout circles, there were bound to be extravagances and illusions. Thus the majority of texts attach some pejorative shade to the terms *spiritualité* and *mystique*, which became associated—and publicized, especially through the disputes of Bossuet and Fénelon—with all of these abuses. The shades range from mere caution to violent contempt" (Tinsley, *French Expressions*, 235). It is understandable, therefore, that all the panegyrists avoid the term, and when Charles de La Rue discusses what we would now call "spirituality," the word he uses is *dévotion* (q.v.). See further Aimé Solignac, "Spiritualité," in DS 14:1146–50, and Tinsley, *French Expressions*, 301, s.v. *spiritualité*.

Subtil, subtilité / **subtle, subtlety**. In all the writers here represented, the terms *subtilité* and *subtil* are invariably pejorative, and the *subtils* or "subtle thinkers" always dangerous. *Subtil* can mean subtle, rarefied, intelligent, acute, discerning (in a positive sense), elusive, or refined, but for all the panegyrists, it means too refined, too subtle, too intelligent, dangerously devious, or just plain misleading. Abelard was a *subtil*, and so (according to Charles de La Rue) was his seventeenth-century reincarnation, Fénelon.

Vertu / virtue. *Vertu*, like *virtus* in Latin and *virtue* in English, can mean virtue in the sense of virtue versus vice, or the power, quality, or capacity to do something (as in "some plants have healing virtues"). It may also mean moral strength, courage, valor, bravery, manliness, worth, or excellence. The translation therefore depends entirely on the context.

Appendix 2

Personalities

ABELARD, PETER (1079–1142/43). It is understandable that most of the panegyrists mention Bernard's victory over the most famous of his adversaries, though their accounts are based on the *Vita prima* and naturally biased. Abelard does not appear in the panegyrics of Senault, Bossuet, or Boudon. It was not, of course, in the interests of the preachers to present a balanced view of the conflict with Bernard, and François Ogier is alone in presenting an Abelard in whom could be seen traits worthy of admiration. Yet this is not to say that Abelard was right. Indeed not. In Bernard, Ogier sees "religion, piety, the faith of our Fathers"; in Abelard he sees "innovation, philosophy, human reasoning, and—in a word—error, armed with arguments and syllogisms" (chap. 12, n. 85). The other panegyrists are in agreement. Antoine Anselme condemns Abelard for substituting "the inventions of Plato for the doctrine of the Fathers of the Church" (chap. 13, n. 16), and Bernard Planchette calls him "a Philosopher who preferred his own novelties to the teaching of the holy Fathers and did his utmost to destroy that teaching by the empty subterfuges of his learning and the supposed sublimity of his reasoning" (chap. 5, n. 70). Fénelon speaks of his "over-subtle thinking," which will be confounded by Bernard (chap. 8, §26), and Massillon describes him as a man "puffed up with empty learning and gifted with natural talents well suited to leading minds astray and giving to falsehood the air of truth. Eloquent, polished, ingenious in his discourses, vain with countless curious facets of learning, he undertook to make the mysteries of the faith subject to human reason" (chap. 14, §54).

In the first unrevised version of the panegyric by Charles de La Rue, Abelard appears as "the subtlest thinker of them all, who, with his overly sophisticated learning, sowed his errors on all sides" (chap. 9, §51), but La Rue's Abelard is really Fénelon, and conflict between Abelard and Bernard is actually the conflict between Fénelon and Bossuet. In this first version, La Rue also confuses Abelard and Gilbert de la Porrée. In the second, revised version of his panegyric, La Rue corrects his errors, and the new and revised Abelard is much more like Abelard and less like Fénelon. Bernard's victory over Abelard is, of course, assured, and the panegyrists' descriptions of what happened at the Council of Sens in 1141 are quite untrustworthy. Jacques Biroat's account is representative: Abelard, "who had one of the most acute and intelligent minds of his century, and who had never lacked a response to any question put to him, states that he had felt such an indescribable sense of astonishment that he had been brought to tears" (chap. 4, §27).

For those who wish to meet the real Abelard, Matthew T. Clanchy's *Abelard: A Medieval Life* (Oxford: Blackwell, 1999) may be recommended. For the conflict between Abelard and Bernard, A. Victor Murray's *Abelard and St Bernard: A Study in Twelfth Century "Modernism"* (Manchester: Manchester University Press, 1967) retains its value, and the recent survey by Constant J. Mews, "Bernard of Clairvaux and Peter Abelard," in *A Companion to Bernard of Clairvaux*, ed. Brian P. McGuire (Leiden and Boston: Brill, 2011), 133–68, is excellent. For the date of the Council of Sens—1141 rather than 1140—see Constant J. Mews, "The Council of Sens (1141): Abelard, Bernard, and the Fear of Social Upheaval," *Speculum* 77 (2002): 345–54.

ANACLETUS II, antipope from February 14, 1130, to January 25, 1138. On the death of Honorius II on February 13, 1130, Cardinal Pietro of Santa Maria in Trastevere, a scion of the noble, wealthy, and influential house of the Pierleoni, was hastily elected by a majority of the cardinals meeting in the basilica of San Marco. Earlier in the day, a minority of cardinals had already (and clandestinely) elected Gregorio Papareschi as Innocent II and had enthroned him in the Lateran at daybreak. Both elections were, in fact, irregular, but the two opposing parties did not, for once, reflect the political rivalry of powerful Roman families, but disagreements among the cardinals as to the way in which the church should be reformed. This was the beginning of the papal schism that lasted eight years until Anacletus's death in 1138. There is not the least doubt that Bernard, who supported Innocent II, played a major role in the downfall of Anacletus and the legitimization of Innocent, though he was not alone in this. Norbert of Xanten also played an important part, though his name appears in none of the panegyrics.

A key event in bringing about the recognition of Innocent as the lawful pontiff was the Council of Étampes, convoked by Louis VI the Fat in late August or early September 1130. Bernard had been invited by the king himself as well as by the leading French prelates, and according to Arnold of Bonneval, once Bernard had taken his seat, the whole assembly expressed its unanimous desire that God's servant should speak on God's business and that the final decision should be his alone (see *Vita prima* 2.1.3; PL 185:270D; CF 76:81–82). Bernard, as we know, decided in favor of Innocent, and his judgment (says Arnold) was received by all as the oracle of the Holy Spirit. Following the Council, most of Europe came out in favor of Innocent, with the exception of Scotland, Aquitaine (see below, s.v. William X of Aquitaine), certain Italian cities (including Milan), and Sicily and southern Italy. The last sovereign to continue in his support for Anacletus was Roger II of Sicily, but the end came late in 1137 when delegates from both parties presented their respective arguments before Roger at Salerno. Bernard himself was there, and each side had four days to present its case. The most important spokesman for Anacletus was Peter of Pisa (Peter Pisanus), cardinal-priest of Saint Susanna and a fine canon lawyer. Bernard addressed him eloquently and, it seems, persuasively (his speech is preserved in the *Vita prima* 2.7.45; PL 185:294B–95A; CF 76:120–30), for Peter and his colleagues yielded to his arguments and abandoned the cause of Anacletus. Roger alone remained defiant. Anacletus himself held out in Rome for another few weeks until death claimed him, still in possession of the Lateran, on January 25, 1138.

Whether Bernard was wise in choosing Innocent has been debated, and not a few scholars have suggested that Anacletus would have been a more effective pontiff. He was probably more intelligent than Innocent, if that counts for anything, but Innocent was a more wily politician (though his political skills failed him in his last years) and appears to have lacked the intense personal ambition of Anacletus. The panegyrists, naturally, have no time for Anacletus at all. He is the antipope, the proud usurper of the papal throne, a notorious sinner, a monster who raised himself to the highest dignity by a series of unjust measures, a wicked man, filled with malice and guile, but since they are praising Bernard, who can do no wrong, that is what we would expect.

ARNOLD OF BRESCIA (ca. 1090–1155). Arnold was born in Brescia but studied in France before returning to Italy, where he became an Augustinian canon. Here his criticisms of the church's involvement in a contentious land struggle in Brescia, and his condemnatory preaching against the worldliness of the church in general led to his own condemnation by the Second Lateran Council in 1139, and he was forced to leave Italy. He then returned to France, where he became a supporter of Peter Abelard, and, at the instigation of Bernard at the Council of Sens in 1141, he was again condemned along with Abelard. He then made his way to Paris, where he continued to support Abelard and criticize Bernard; this led to his being silenced by Bernard's protégé, Innocent II. He was again forced into exile, but in his preaching he continued his call for reform in the church and a return to the ideals of evangelical purity and apostolic poverty. Sometime later he managed to make a short-lived peace with Eugenius III, but when he came to Rome he found the city in the hands of the Commune of Rome and threw in his lot with them.

The Commune had been established by the brother of the antipope Anacletus, and while its members recognized the spiritual authority of the papacy, they utterly rejected its temporal authority. They accordingly seized Rome from the papal forces, established a vaguely democratic republic, and forced Eugenius (whom Arnold referred to as a "man of blood") into exile. This led to Arnold's excommunication by Eugenius on July 15, 1148. When the pope died in July 1153, his successor, Adrian IV, made an alliance with the emperor Frederick I Barbarossa, and Frederick took Rome from the republican Commune in 1155. Arnold was captured by the imperial forces and handed over to the Roman Curia to be tried for rebellion, not for heresy. The outcome was never in doubt, and in June 1155 Arnold was duly convicted and hanged. His body was burned and his ashes cast into the Tiber to prevent his burial place from becoming a place of pilgrimage, for Arnold had been a popular leader in the city and was regarded as a hero by much of the Roman populace.

Arnold's essential teachings, as we have said, were a return to the ideals of the Gospel, especially evangelical poverty, and in his view, any cleric who owned property was not worthy to celebrate the sacraments. Arnold is mentioned, but only briefly, by four of the panegyrists—Texier, Ogier, Fléchier, and Bourru—and Bourru quotes Bernard's own description of the man as someone whose way of life was sweet as honey, but whose teachings were pure poison, a man with the head of a dove and a tail of a dragon (Bernard, Ep 196.1; SBOp 8:51, to Guy, cardinal legate in Bohemia). Le Maistre mentions him once, but only in passing (*Vie,* 623). See further Williams, *Saint Bernard,* 320–45. The only biography of Arnold in English appeared in 1931: George W. Greenaway, *Arnold of Brescia* (Cambridge: Cambridge University Press, 1931).

ELEANOR OF AQUITAINE (ca. 1122–1204): see s.v. Louis VII the Young (le Jeune).

EUGENIUS III, pope from February 20, 1145, to July 8, 1153. Bernardo da Pisa was born at Pisa at an uncertain date and by 1138 had risen to occupy an important administrative position in the Pisan archdiocese. Sometime around this date he had met Bernard of Clairvaux and fallen under his spell; he entered Clairvaux as a monk in 1138. A year later he returned to Italy, and in autumn 1140 Innocent II appointed him abbot of the Cistercian abbey of Sts. Vincenzo and Anastasio at Tre Fontane, just outside Rome. The monastery had been Cluniac, but since the Cluniacs had supported Anacletus in the papal schism (Anacletus himself being a Cluniac), Innocent II, after securing the papacy, took it from them and gave it to the Cistercians. Bernardo was abbot when he was elected pope on February 15, 1145.

Bernard was not happy with the election, fearing that the papacy, at a difficult time, was being placed in the hands of an inexperienced, cloistered monk, but Eugenius proved remarkably capable, though deeply under Bernard's influence. It was Eugenius who commissioned Bernard to preach the Second Crusade, and its ultimate failure was a grave disappointment to him. It was he, too, who excommunicated Arnold of Brescia (q.v.), who would be executed by Eugenius's successor, Adrian IV, in 1155. Eugenius himself died at Tivoli on July 8, 1153. He was, of course, the pope to whom Bernard addressed his *De consideratione*—something mentioned by virtually all the panegyrists—and there is no doubt that Bernard's influence may be seen in Eugenius's determined, if unsuccessful, efforts to reform the church. During his pontificate he continued to live as a Cistercian monk, and after his death his tomb soon became renowned for miraculous cures. He was beatified by Pius IX on December 28, 1872.

GILBERT DE LA PORRÉE, GILBERT OF POITIERS (ca. 1080–1154). Most of the panegyrists mention Gilbert (Bossuet and Senault do not), but the only one who deals with his case at any length is Charles de La Rue. Antoine Anselme simply accuses him of mingling with what he taught "a hidden poison and a suspect teaching" (chap. 13, n. 17), Fénelon tells us that he made the whole church groan with his "profane novelties" (chap. 8, §26), and Bourru adds that these novelties concerned the mystery of the Trinity (which is true). The affair came to a head at the Council of Reims in 1148, presided over by Pope Eugenius III, and according to Biroat it was here that Bernard compelled Gilbert "to submit himself to the judgment of the Church" (chap. 4, §28). Henri-Marie Boudon adds the further detail that when Bernard saw that a number of the prelates present at the Council wished to condemn Gilbert's opinions without condemning Gilbert, "he stirred up his zeal, united himself with the French bishops on this matter, and brought it about that the bishop himself rejected what he had written" (chap. 11, §31). All this is based on Geoffrey of Auxerre's brief account in *Vita prima* 3.5.15; PL 185:312AD; CF 76:160–62.

Charles de La Rue tells us more (chap. 10, §§4–42). Gilbert, he says, had been raised to the episcopate "through his reputation for virtue and knowledge, but after a few years in this position he himself walked the paths of error in what he taught of the essence and attributes of God." Bernard then came forth to defend the church, but his involvement in the affair drew considerable criticism. He was criticized for attacking so worthy a prelate and was accused of being "bad-tempered, an unsettled and carping critic, haughty and jealous, who wants to get the better of everyone in everything!" Such charges, however, had no effect on our hero, whose zeal for the church and its traditional teaching could not be quenched.

Both parties, those for and those against Gilbert, then appeared at the Council of Reims, and the dispute lasted two whole days; La Rue draws attention to the lobbying and political maneuvering that went on behind the scenes: "What doings there were in the two opposing parties! Gilbert's friends, and they were many, could not bear to see him shamed and condemned. They did all they could to gain time, to delay the judgment, and have the Assembly dissolved without making any pronouncement at all. But truth triumphs over politics and error. The writings in question are censured and proscribed!"

(chap. 10, §41). He then goes on to praise Gilbert for his humility in accepting the decision of the Council and for submitting himself to the judgment of the church: "[Gilbert] did not hesitate; he did not quibble; he did not limit himself to changing his language while not changing his ideas. We can only applaud his return [to the fold], and Bernard had the great comfort of seeing his adversary share with him the gains brought about by his victory. For if Bernard conquered the error, Gilbert conquered himself, and overcoming one's own brilliant self is far more difficult than overcoming the errors of others" (chap. 10, §42).

Such is La Rue's account in the revised version of his panegyric, and it is more or less correct. The case at issue was indeed Gilbert's views on the essence and attributes of God, though the inquiry (technically a consistory), which did take two days, was held in the chambers of the archbishop of Reims after the Council was over. Despite strong pressure from Bernard (which offended some members of the consistory), Gilbert himself was not condemned, though it was agreed that the book that began the controversy—Gilbert's commentary on Boethius's *De Trinitate*—was not to be disseminated in any form. Gilbert accepted the decision of the consistory, returned to Poitiers as its bishop, and died as its bishop on September 4, 1154. The whole affair was one of Bernard's few failures. See further H. C. van Elswijk, *Gilbert Porreta. Sa vie, son œuvre, sa pensée* (Leuven: Spicilegium sacrum Lovaniense, 1966), and John Marenbon, "Gilbert of Poitiers" and "A Note on the Porretani," in *A History of Twelfth-Century Western Philosophy*, ed. Peter Dronke (Cambridge: Cambridge University Press, 1988), 328–52, 353–57.

HENRY I, KING OF ENGLAND (1068–1135), king from 1100 until his death in Normandy on December 1, 1135. Henry was originally a supporter of Anacletus in the saga of the papal schism, and his meeting with Bernard took place at Chartres in November 1130. This was after the Council of Étampes, when

Bernard had spoken out in favor of Innocent II, and when virtually all the French bishops had accepted his judgment. The English bishops were also supportive. As Pietro Pierleoni, Anacletus had been apostolic legate in England and had enjoyed wide approval, and the English bishops were putting strong pressure on Henry to support him. It is understandable, therefore, that Henry was somewhat hesitant about making submission to Innocent. When Bernard met him he was aware of Henry's scruples and the pressures placed on him by the English bishops, and (according to Arnold of Bonneval) addressed him thus: "What are you afraid of?" he asked. "Are you afraid of sinning if you obey Innocent? Think (he said) of all the other sins for which you will have to answer to God, and leave this one to me. I will take this sin on myself." At these words, which were so effective, the king was persuaded (*Vita prima* 2.1.4; PL 185:271AB; CF 76:82–83). And Henry duly made his submission to Innocent. The only panegyrists who do not mention the incident are Bossuet, Fléchier, and Massillon, but the only one who reports it in any detail (though he confuses Henry I and Henry II) is Charles de La Rue, who bases himself both on Arnold's account in the *Vita prima* and on Bernard's letter 138 to Henry (chap. 9, §40; chap. 10, §32). See further Williams, *Saint Bernard*, 105, 109.

HENRY SANGLIER, ARCHBISHOP OF SENS from 1122 to his death in 1142. Of a noble family, Henry was elected to the archbishopric of Sens in 1122 at the request of Louis VI the Fat, and, as archbishop for twenty years, was much involved in the ecclesiastical issues and politics of his day. He was at the Council of Étampes in 1130 (see s.v. Anacletus II), where he fully supported the cause of Innocent II, and he presided over the Council of Sens in 1141 when Abelard and Arnold of Brescia were condemned. He was a powerful prelate who knew his own mind, and this inevitably brought him into conflict with other powerful men, including kings and popes. His interest for the panegyrists—Biroat, Senault, and Antoine Anselme—

lies in the letters from Bernard to Henry mixing courteous praise with justified rebuke. Thus, says Jacques Biroat, at the beginning of his letter 182, "there is nothing but sweetness, but he then goes on to express his outspoken opinions on the abuses and disorders that were being committed at the time" (chap. 4 [Biroat], §17).

The most important of these letters is letter 42, the letter-treatise *de moribus et officio episcoporum*, "on the conduct and office of bishops" (SBOp 7:100–31), which Anselme uses in his discussion of the relationship between papal and episcopal authority. According to Bernard, it had been requested by Henry himself (see Ep 42, *ep praef*; SBOp 7:100), but it does not seem to have done a great deal of good. Henry became more and more willful and obdurate the older he became, but the letter itself remains a lucid presentation of Bernard's own views on the nature of authority, clerical reform, the dangers of worldliness, and the essential importance of charity and, above all, humility. See further *Bernard of Clairvaux: On Baptism and the Office of Bishops*, translated by Pauline Matarasso with introductions by Martha G. Newman and Emero Stiegman, CF 67 (Kalamazoo, MI: Cistercian Publications, 2004), 11–82. See also Williams, *Saint Bernard*, 200–201.

HENRY OF TOULOUSE (d. ca. 1148), otherwise known as Henry of Lausanne or Henry of Le Mans. Little is known of his early life. He was probably a Benedictine monk who began his preaching around 1116 and died in prison in about 1148. His precise teachings are still a matter of scholarly dispute. He seems to have been a sort of proto-Protestant who preached evangelical poverty, rejected the disciplinary and doctrinal authority of the church, and looked to Scripture alone as the only rule of faith. What is not in dispute is that he was the leader of a widespread and popular heresy that swept swiftly through the south of France and that caused the church grave disquiet. The best account (in English, with translated sources) is to be found in Walter L. Wakefield and Austin P. Evans, *Heresies of the High Middle Ages* (New York: Columbia University Press,

1991), 107–38. See also Elphège Vacandard, "Les origines de l'hérésie albigeoise," *Revue des questions historiques* 55 (1894): 50–83, and Williams, *Saint Bernard*, 337–43.

It is quite true that the restoration of Roman (and papal) orthodoxy owed much to Bernard's eloquence and reported miracles. Most, though not all, of the panegyrists mention Henry, but their accounts are all brief. He does not appear at all in the discourses of Boudon, Bossuet, Fromentières, La Rue, Planchette, or Senault. Fénelon tells us that through him "the saints of the Lord are put to scorn and the most revered mysteries held in derision" (chap. 8, §26), and Anselme states that he "declared war on the sacraments of the Church and on its ministers" (chap. 13, n. 18). According to Massillon, who tells us most, Henry was preaching a new doctrine and had "set himself up against the holy institution of the sacraments and the tradition of the Church, and had already prepared the way for the birth of those monsters that error begot during the last century" (chap. 14, §56). The monsters, of course, were the Protestant sects, Lutheranism and (especially) Calvinism. Henry was a disciple of Peter of Bruys (q.v.).

LOTHAIR III OF SUPPLINBURG (1075–1137), duke of Saxony, king of Germany, and (from 1133) Holy Roman emperor. He also appears as Lothair II. His interest for the panegyrists lies in the role he played in the papal schism and in the Investiture Controversy. In the two papal elections of 1130, both parties had sought Lothair's support, and he might have profited from the situation had he not had his own problems in his own territories. Anacletus had promised him the imperial crown in exchange for his support, but Lothair seems to have seen the way the wind was blowing in Europe, and came out in favor of Innocent. In 1131 Innocent and his retinue made their way to Liège, where they were received with honor by Lothair; his queen, Richenza of Northeim; and a host of German princes and prelates. A council was held on April 1, attended by the whole of this distinguished company and more than fifty abbots, including Bernard of Clairvaux, but it was initially overshadowed by the Investiture Controversy. This controversy, which lasted from 1076 to 1122, was essentially a dispute between popes and Holy Roman emperors as to who had the right to invest bishops and abbots with the ring and the crozier, the symbols of their office.

The Controversy was officially ended by the Concordat of Worms in 1122, but Lothair tried, perhaps not very seriously, to resurrect it and reclaim the right of lay investiture as a condition of his support for Innocent. He could not have chosen a worse moment. Bernard would have none of it, and (says Arnold of Bonneval) "the holy abbot imposed himself like a wall. Boldly resisting the king, he rebuked him for his wicked suggestion with amazing freedom, and, by his astonishing authority, restrained him" (*Vita prima* 2.1.5; PL 185:271D–72A; CF 76:83–84). The conflict over investitures is mentioned by just three of the panegyrists: Fénelon, Bernard Planchette, and Rancé.

Lothair duly made submission to Innocent and agreed to assist him against Roger II of Sicily (q.v.), a staunch ally of Anacletus. In return, Innocent crowned Lothair as *Rex Romanorum*, "King of the Romans," on March 29, 1131. This title was normally seen as a claim to become Holy Roman emperor, and Lothair was crowned as such by Innocent two years later on June 4, 1133. Since Rome at that time was mostly controlled by Anacletus, Saint Peter's Basilica was closed to them, so the coronation took place at the Lateran. The campaign against Roger began in 1136 but was only partially successful, and Lothair died crossing the Alps on his way home on December 4, 1137.

LOUIS VI THE FAT (LE GROS), KING OF FRANCE (1081–1137), king from 1108 to his death on August 1, 1137. He was the son and successor of Philip I and spent much of his reign subduing the robber barons who preyed on the environs of Paris. For some twenty years he was at war with Henry I of England (q.v.) and with Henry's son-in-law, the Holy Roman emperor Henry V. He appears in the panegyrics as the monarch who convoked the Council of Étampes in 1130 (see s.v. Anacletus II), when Bernard declared in favor of Innocent II, in the matter of his opposition to the French bishops taking part in the Council of Pisa in 1135. This was a council convoked by Innocent II, which, predictably, confirmed his own authority and condemned Anacletus. Louis's opposition to the Council drew forth Bernard's Ep 255, SBOp 8:161–62, in which he warns Louis that the royal wrath is directed not against strangers, but against himself and his own family (*non plane in extraneos, sed in semetipsam et suos*). See further Williams, *Saint Bernard*, 135–38, and Robert Somerville, "The Council of Pisa, 1135: A Re-examination of the Evidence for the Canons," *Speculum* 45 (1970): 98–114.

LOUIS VII THE YOUNG (LE JEUNE), KING OF FRANCE (1120/21–1180), king from 1137 until his death on September 18, 1180. He was the son of Louis VI the Fat, and in the first year of his reign married Eleanor of Aquitaine, the oldest of the three children of William X of Aquitaine (q.v.). The marriage would later be annulled, and Eleanor would then marry Henry of Anjou, who, in 1154, became Henry II of England. Eleanor's conflict with Bernard is mentioned by Fénelon (§24) and Massillon (§36). See further Williams, *Saint Bernard*, 212–16.

Louis generally appears in the panegyrics in connection with his role in the massacre at Vitry as part of his two-year war with Theobald / Thibault, count of Champagne. Late in 1142 Louis invaded Theobald's territory and ravaged wide stretches of the countryside, and his depredations culminated in the attack on the small town of Vitry, about twenty miles from Châlons-sur-Marne. When Louis's soldiers seized the place, they utterly destroyed it, and when several hundred of the inhabitants took refuge in the church, the church and all those within it were burned to the ground. The town became known as Vitry-le-Brûlé, "Vitry-the-Burned" (now Vitry-en-Perthois), and the deed haunted Louis, who had witnessed the atrocity. Overwhelmed with guilt (and castigated by Bernard), he withdrew his forces from Champagne, returned the territories to Theobald, and, at Bourges on Christmas Day 1145 declared his intention to take the cross and go on Crusade to atone for his sins. This he did in 1147—it was the unsuccessful Second Crusade that Bernard had preached at Vézelay at Easter 1146—and he remained away from France for two years. The story of the destruction of Vitry appears in Le Maistre's *Vie de S. Bernard*, 460–61 (which gives the number of those who died in the church as thirteen hundred); the most detailed account among the panegyrists is to be found in the revised version of the discourse of Charles de La Rue (§31). See further Williams, *Saint Bernard*, 209–10.

PETER OF BRUYS (d. ca. 1131). He was born at an unknown date in Bruis, in the southeast of France, was ordained a priest, but was deprived of his faculties for his unorthodox preaching, which appears to have begun between 1117 and 1120. Exactly what he himself taught is still not entirely clear, but according to Peter the Venerable (*Adversus Petrobrusianos*; PL 189:719–850), his followers, the Petrobrusians, maintained (1) that baptism of children before the age of understanding was invalid, (2) that church buildings were useless since the Church of God consisted not of assembled stones, but of assembled believers, (3) that since the cross was an instrument of torture, it was not worthy of veneration, and crosses should be broken and burned, (4) that since Christ did not have a true human body—in technical terms, the Petrobrusians were docetists—he did not truly suffer and die, and that the idea of the Real Presence in the Eucharist is therefore nonsense, and (5) that prayers, alms-giving, and other good works on behalf of the dead have no effect whatever. Peter's iconoclasm with regard to crosses led to his death: an angry mob threw him into one of his own bonfires in about 1131 (the precise date is uncertain). Henry of Toulouse (q.v.) was one of his disciples. Only one of the panegyrists—François Ogier—mentions his name, and he appears but once, as "Pierre de Bruis Heresiarque," in Le

Maistre's *Vie* (430). Bernard never met Peter and was never in contact with him.

PETER OF PISA: see s.v. Anacletus II.

PETER THE VENERABLE (1092 or 1094–1156), eighth abbot of Cluny. Peter was an oblate at the Cluniac priory of Sauxillanges and, after serving as prior at Vézelay and Domène, was elected abbot of Cluny in 1122. He would administer the abbey for more than thirty years, and in the earlier part of his abbacy he was the instigator of a number of important and necessary reforms—reforms that aroused strong opposition. These reforms are the concern of those few panegyrists who mention Peter—Antoine Anselme, Biroat, and Charles de La Rue—and of these Anselme and Biroat make but passing reference. The longest account appears in the second, revised panegyric of La Rue (§37). Peter and Bernard shared a deep friendship and an equally deep love for the monastic life, and the conflict between them, with misunderstandings on both sides, is a sad story.

See further M. David Knowles, *Cistercians and Cluniacs: the Controversy between St. Bernard and Peter the Venerable*, Friends of Dr. Williams's Library, Ninth Lecture, 1955 (Oxford: Oxford University Press, 1955), and Gillian R. Knight, *The Correspondence between Peter the Venerable and Bernard of Clairvaux: A Semantic and Structural Analysis* (Aldershot and Burlington: Ashgate, 2002). For a more detailed account of the controversy, see Adriaan H. Bredero, *Cluny et Cîteaux au douzième siècle: l'histoire d'une controverse monastique* (Amsterdam and Maarssen: APA-Holland University Press, 1985). Despite its age, Knowles's lecture offers a judicious and balanced account in thirty-two pages from which neither party emerges unscathed.

ROGER II OF SICILY (1095–1154). Roger became count of Sicily in 1105, duke of Apulia and Calabria in 1127, and king of Sicily in 1130. The royal crown was Roger's reward for having chosen to support Anacletus (q.v.) in the papal schism, and his coronation took place in Palermo on Christmas Day 1130. It would be followed by a decade of intermittent war. The details of the war need not concern us, though the Battle of Nocera on July 25, 1132 (in which Roger was defeated), is mentioned by Fénelon (§22) and the Battle of Rignano on October 30, 1137, by Rancé and Charles de La Rue. Before this last battle, says La Rue, Bernard sought out Roger "at the head of his army, urged him to recognize the true pontiff, and predicted his defeat if he persisted in his intention to fight. Roger scorned both the entreaty and the threat: he risked battle, and lost" (chap. 10, §33). Bernard followed the defeated Roger to Salerno, and it was then that the eight-day conference took place in which the supporters of Anacletus and Innocent presented their respective cases (see s.v. Anacletus II).

The supporters of Innocent, led by Bernard, won the day, and Roger alone remained defiant. But Anacletus himself died not long afterward on January 25, 1138, and Roger was then forced to seek confirmation of his royal title from Innocent. Innocent agreed, but only if Roger would agree to the establishment of an independent principality of Capua, which would act as a buffer state between Roger's kingdom of Sicily and Innocent's own Papal States. One can understand the pope's caution. Roger, however, would not agree to this, and in the summer of 1139 Innocent and his army invaded Roger's territory. It was an unwise move, for on July 22 the papal army was ambushed at Galluccio, about thirty-seven miles northwest of Naples, and the pope was captured. If he wished to be released, he now had no choice but to recognize Roger's kingship; this he did three days later, on July 25, by the Treaty of Mignano. The kingdom thus established would last for seven hundred years.

In later life, Roger became one of Europe's greatest and most cultured kings. He created a state in which Italians, Greeks, Arabs, and Jews coexisted in harmony and in which the arts and letters flourished. He died at Palermo on February 26, 1154, and is buried in the cathedral. The panegyrists, as we might expect, are not interested in Roger's greatness. For them, he is simply a hated adversary of Bernard and a despised supporter of the antipope Anacletus. See further Williams, *Saint Bernard*, chap. 7 (134–58).

SUGER (ca. 1081–1151), abbot of Saint-Denis, near Paris. A man of great talent, he administered his abbey's lands efficiently and well and for much of his life was an influential advisor to the French monarchy. When Louis VII the Young (q.v.) was absent on the Second Crusade, Suger was one of the regents of the kingdom and fulfilled the role so well that on his return Louis rewarded him with the title "Father of the Country." He is mentioned by only three of the panegyrists—La Rue, Massillon, and Senault—and then only in connection with Bernard's role in his reform from a haughty prelate to a humble monk and the reform of his abbey from a cloister "full of courtiers and men-at-arms, echoing to the din of worldly affairs and the clash of weapons" (chap. 10, §36), to a true house of God. The same is true of Peter the Venerable (q.v.).

WILLIAM (GUILLAUME) X (1099–1137), duke of Aquitaine, duke of Gascony, and (as William VIII) count of Poitou, was one of the staunchest supporters in France of Anacletus. He was "a difficult personality, elusive in his movements, evasive in his engagements; a man of feeble will yet obstinate in unexpressed reservations; who lived loosely and thought muddle-headedly; just the wrong sort of ruler; a ready tool for the hand of an accomplished schemer" (Williams, *Saint Bernard*, 131). The story of his dramatic conversion was (understandably) a favorite among the panegyrists, and all follow Arnold of Bonneval's account in *Vita prima* 2.6.38; PL 185:290AD; CF 76:120–21, or that of Antoine Le Maistre in his *Vie de S. Bernard* 87–90. The events took place toward the end of 1134 when the apostolic legate, Geoffrey of Chartres, called on Bernard to visit Aquitaine, where the papal schism remained unresolved. William was at the château of Parthenay, about thirty miles west of Poitiers, and adjoining the château was the church of

Notre-Dame-de-la-Couldre, which served as its chapel. Bernard, followed by a huge crowd, went into the church to celebrate Mass, but William (who had also followed) remained at the entrance.

After the *pax* (the Kiss of Peace) Bernard placed the consecrated Host on the paten and, "with burning face and eyes aflame," bore it reverently to the door of the church, where William stood. "We have petitioned you, he said, and you have spurned us. Many servants of God who were at the assembly at which you were present have added their supplications to ours, yet you have treated them with contempt. Behold, there comes to you the Virgin's Son, the Head and Lord of the Church, which you persecute! Your Judge is here present, at whose name every knee shall bow, whether in Heaven, on earth, or beneath the earth. Do you also spurn him? Do you also treat him with the same contempt with which you treat his servants?" (*Vita prima* 2.6.38; PL 185:290AB; CF 76:120). At these words the duke trembled, grew rigid, and fell to the ground. His soldiers picked him up, but he fell again, unable to speak, foaming into his beard, and uttering deep groans, as if (says Arnold) he were suffering an epileptic seizure. Bernard came up to him, touched him with his foot, commanded him to rise and then to make reparation to the bishop of Poitiers, whom William had driven from his church, and to submit to Innocent as the legitimate pontiff.

From this moment William was a changed man. He was reconciled with the bishop; he acknowledged the authority of Innocent; he founded the Cistercian abbey of La Grâce-Dieu (twenty miles east of La Rochelle) and determined to make the pilgrimage to the great shrine of Santiago de Compostela. This he did, garbed as a pilgrim and attended only by a small retinue, but when he reached Compostela he was seriously ill either from food poisoning or from drinking contaminated water. He was carried into the cathedral and died the same day—it was Good Friday, April 9, 1137—shortly after receiving Holy Communion. He was buried before the High Altar next to the shrine of Saint James himself. It is hardly surprising that almost all the panegyrists mention this splendid story (a few do not: Antoine Anselme, Boudon, and Fléchier, for example), and the longest accounts appear in the discourses of Charles de La Rue and Bernard Planchette, who tells the tale very well. See further Williams, *Saint Bernard*, 131–33.

Bibliography

As the primary sources for this book—the volumes in which the panegyrics are to be found—are all listed in the relevant chapters, they are not repeated here.

Albert, Antoine, and Jean-François de Court. *Dictionnaire portatif des prédicateurs françois*. Lyon: Pierre Bruyset Ponthus, 1757; repr. Geneva: Slatkine Reprints, 1970.

Arabeyre, Patrick, Jacques Berlioz, and Philippe Poirier, eds. *Vies et légendes de saint Bernard de Clairvaux. Création, diffusion, réception. (XIIe–XXe siècles). Actes des Rencontres de Dijon, 7–8 juin 1991*. Brecht and Saint-Nicolas-lès-Cîteaux: "Présence cistercienne"; Cîteaux – Commentarii cistercienses, 1993.

Bayley, Peter. *French Pulpit Oratory 1598–1650. A Study in Themes and Styles, with a Descriptive Catalogue of Printed Texts*. Cambridge: Cambridge University Press, 1980.

Bergin, Joseph. *Crown, Church and Episcopate under Louis XIV*. New Haven and London: Yale University Press, 2004.

Bredero, Adriaan H. *Bernard of Clairvaux. Between Cult and History*. Grand Rapids: W. B. Eerdmans, 1996.

———. "Études sur la *Vita prima* de saint Bernard." *Analecta Cisterciensia* 17 (1961): 3–72, 215–60, and 18 (1962): 3–59.

———. "St. Bernard and the Historians." In *Saint Bernard of Clairvaux: Studies Commemorating the Eighth Centenary of His Canonization*, edited by M. Basil Pennington. CS 28. Kalamazoo: Cistercian Publications, 1977. 27–62.

Bremond, Henri. *Histoire du sentiment religieux en France depuis les guerres de religion jusqu'à nos jours*. 11 vols. Paris: Bloud and Gay, 1916–1933.

———. *A Literary History of Religious Thought in France from the Wars of Religion down to Our Own Times*. English translation of first 3 volumes of French version: translated by K. L. Montgomery. London: SPCK, 1928–1936.

Bruun, Mette B., ed. *The Cambridge Companion to the Cistercian Order*. Cambridge: Cambridge University Press, 2013.

Candel, Jules. *Les Prédicateurs français dans la première moitié du XVIIIe siècle*. Paris: A. Picard, 1904.

Chérot, Henri. *Autour de Bossuet. Le Quiétisme en Bourgogne et à Paris en 1698 d'après des correspondances inédites. Avec le panégyrique antiquiétiste de saint Bernard de P. de La Rue*. Paris: V. Retaux, 1901.

Cognet, Louis. *Post-Reformation Spirituality*. Translated by P. Hepburne Scott. New York: Hawthorne Books, 1959.

[Cousin d'Avallon, Charles-Yves]. *Dictionnaire biographique et bibliographique des prédicateurs et sermonnaires français, par l'abbé de La P*****. Paris: Persan; Lyon: Périsses Frères, 1824.

Cragg, Gerald R. *The Church and the Age of Reason 1648–1789*. The Pelican History of the Church, 4. Harmondsworth: Penguin Books, 1970.

Dargan, Edwin C. *A History of Preaching, Volume II: From the Close of the Reformation Period to the End of the Nineteenth Century 1572–1900*. New York: Armstrong, 1912; repr. New York: B. Franklin, 1968.

Denzinger, Heinrich. *Enchiridion symbolorum definitionum et declarationum de rebus fidei et morum. Compendium of Creeds, Definitions and Declarations on Matters of Faith and Morals. Latin-English*. Edited by Peter Hünermann. 43rd ed. San Francisco: Ignatius Press, 2012.

Dewez, Léon, and van Iterson, Albert. "La Lactation de saint Bernard: légende et iconographie." *Cîteaux in der Nederlanden* 7 (1956): 165–89.

Dictionnaire de biographie française. Paris: Letouzey et Ané, 1933–.

Dictionnaire des lettres françaises. Le XVIIe siècle. Edited by Patrick Dandrey. Paris: Fayard, 1951; repr. with revisions, 1996.

Dictionnaire des lettres françaises. Le XVIIIe siècle. Edited by François Moureau. Paris: Fayard, 1960; repr. with revisions, 1995.

Dictionnaire de spiritualité. Paris: G. Beauchesne, 1937–1995.

Dictionnaire de théologie catholique. Paris: Letouzey et Ané, 1903–1972.

Dictionnaire d'histoire et de géographie ecclésiastiques. Paris: Letouzey et Ané, 1912–.

Dunlop, Ian. *Louis XIV.* London: Chatto and Windus, 1999.

François, Jean. *Bibliothèque générale des écrivains de l'Ordre de Saint Benoît.* Bouillon: Aux dépens de la Société Typographique, 1777–1778; repr. Louvain-Héverlé: Éditions de la Bibliothèque S.J., 1961.

Gastaldelli, Ferruccio. "I primi vent'anni di San Bernardo: Problemi e Interpretazioni." *Analecta Cisterciensia* 43 (1987): 111–48.

Goodrich, W. Eugene. "The Reliability of the *Vita Prima S. Bernardi*. The Image of Bernard in Book I of the *Vita Prima* and His Own Letters: A Comparison." *Analecta Cisterciensia* 43 (1987): 153–80.

Henneau, Marie-Élisabeth. "Bernard de Clairvaux: Du Classicisme aux lumières: destin d'une œuvre, image d'un homme." In *Vies et légendes de saint Bernard de Clairvaux*, edited by Patrick Arabeyre, et al. 291–305.

Holdsworth, Christopher. "Bernard of Clairvaux: His First and Greatest Miracle was Himself." In *The Cambridge Companion to the Cistercian Order,* edited by Mette B. Bruun. 173–85.

———. "Reading the Signs, Bernard of Clairvaux and His Miracles." In *Writing Medieval Biography 750–1250: Essays in Honour of Professor Frank Barlow,* edited by David Bates, Julia Crick, and Sarah Hamilton. Woodbridge: Boydell Press, 2006. 161–72.

Hsia, R. Po-Chia. *The World of Catholic Renewal 1540–1770.* 2nd ed. Cambridge: Cambridge University Press, 2005.

Hurel, Augustin-Jean. *Les orateurs sacrés à la cour de Louis XIV.* 2nd ed. Paris: Didier et Cie, 1872.

Icard, Simon. "Saint Bernard, effigie du catholicisme classique, Étude du frontispiece de *La Vie de saint Bernard* d'Antoine Le Maistre (1648) d'après Philippe de Champaigne." *Cîteaux – Commentarii cistercienses* 62 (2011): 321–37.

Jacoebee, W. Pierre. "The Classical Sermon and the French Literary Tradition." *Australian Journal of French Studies* 19 (1982): 227–42.

Jacquinet, Paul. *Des Prédicateurs du XVIIe siècle avant Bossuet*. 2nd ed. Paris: E. Bélin et fils, 1885.

James, Nancy C. *The Conflict Over the Heresy of "Pure Love" in Seventeenth-Century France. The Tumult over the Mysticism of Madame Guyon*. Lewiston: Edwin Mellen Press, 2008.

Janauschek, Leopold. *Bibliographia Bernardina*. Vienna: A. Hölder, 1891; repr. Hildesheim: G. Olms, 1959.

Jervis, W. Henley. *A History of the Church of France from the Concordat of Bologna, A.D. 1516, to the Revolution*. London: J. Murray, 1872.

Knox, Ronald A. *Enthusiasm. A Chapter in the History of Religion, with Special Reference to the XVII and XVIII Centuries*. Oxford: Clarendon Press, 1950.

Lough, John. *France Observed in the Seventeenth Century by British Travellers*. Stocksfield, UK, and Boston: Oriel Press, 1985.

Martin, Henri-Jean, *Print, Power, and People in 17th-Century France*. Translated by David Gerard. Metuchen, NJ, and London: Scarecrow Press, 1993.

Maury, Jean Sifrein. *Essai sur l'éloquence de la chaire, par le cardinal Jean Sifrein Maury. Édition publiée sur les manuscrits autographes de l'auteur*. Paris: A. Pigoreau, [1810].

———. *The Principles of Eloquence Adapted to the Pulpit and the Bar by the Abbé Maury. To Which are added Mr. Wesley's Directions concerning Pronunciation and Gesture*. Abridged translation by John N. Lake. New York: B. Waugh and T. Mason, 1833.

McGuire, Brian P., ed. *A Companion to Bernard of Clairvaux*. Leiden and Boston: Brill, 2011.

McManners, John. *Church and Society in Eighteenth-Century France*. Oxford: Clarendon Press, 1998.

Phillips, Henry. *Church and Culture in Seventeenth-Century France*. Cambridge: Cambridge University Press, 1997.

———. *The Theatre and its Critics in Seventeenth Century France*. Oxford: Oxford University Press, 1980.

Picard, André, and Boglioni, Pierre. "Miracle et thaumaturgie dans la vie de saint Bernard." In *Vies et légendes de saint Bernard de Clairvaux*, edited by Patrick Arabeyre, et al. 36–59.

Plongeron, Bernard. "Lumières contre épopée mystique: les 'lectures' de saint Bernard du XVIIe au XIXe siècles." In *Vies et légendes de saint Bernard de Clairvaux*, edited by Patrick Arabeyre, et al. 306–27.

Posset, Franz. "*Amplexus Bernardi*: The Dissemination of a Cistercian Motif in the Later Middle Ages." *Cîteaux—Commentarii cistercienses* 54 (2003): 251–400.

———. "The Crucified Embraces Saint Bernard: The Beginnings of the *Amplexus Bernardi*." *Cistercian Studies Quarterly* 33 (1998): 289–314.

Pourrat, Pierre. *Christian Spirituality. Later Developments. Part II: from Jansenism to Modern Times*. Translated by Donald Attwater. Westminster, MD: Newman Press, 1955.

Pranger, M. B. "Bernard of Clairvaux: Work and Self." In *The Cambridge Companion to the Cistercian Order*, edited by Mette B. Bruun. 186–98.

Tinsley, Lucy. *The French Expressions for Spirituality and Devotion: A Semantic Study*. Washington, DC: Catholic University of America Press, 1953.

Tréverret, Armand-Germain de. *Du Panégyrique des Saints au XVIIe siècle*. Paris: Ernest Thorin, 1868.

Trublet, Nicolas-Charles-Joseph. *Panégyriques des Saints, précédés de réflexions sur l'éloquence en général, et sur celle de la Chaire en particulier*. Paris: Briasson, 1755.

Vacandard, Elphège. *Vie de Saint Bernard, abbé de Clairvaux*. Paris: V. Lecoffre, 1895, with a number of later editions.

Van Eijnatten, Joris. "Reaching Audiences: Sermons and Oratory in Europe, 1660–1800." In *The Cambridge History of Christianity, Volume VII: Enlightenment, Reawakening and*

Revolution 1660–1815, edited by Stewart J. Brown and Timothy Tackett. Cambridge: Cambridge University Press, 2006. 128–46.

Williams, Watkin W. *Saint Bernard of Clairvaux*. Manchester: Manchester University Press, 1935; repr. 1953.

———. *Studies in St. Bernard of Clairvaux*. London: SPCK; New York and Toronto: Macmillan, 1927.

Index of Names and Places

This index is confined to names and places that appear in the text of the volume. It does not include names and places that appear in the numerous notes.

Abbreviations: abb. = abbot; abp. = archbishop; bp. = bishop; card. = cardinal; emp. = emperor.

Aaron, 139, 199, 498, 523
Abelard, Peter. *See* Peter Abelard
Abraham, 253, 535
Accursius, 429, 537
Adam, 475
Adrian IV, pope, 553, 554
Aesculapius, 120, 128, 535
Agen, Lycée d', 69
Agnes, Saint, 71, 272
Ahab, 515
Albert, Antoine, and Court, Jean-François, 73, 74, 110, 129, 245, 271–72, 399, 409, 417, 429, 431, 432, 433, 447–48, 462, 465, 488, 491, 536
Albertus Magnus, *ps.-*, 57, 358, 360–61, 363, 365, 377, 387, 537
Aleth, Bernard's mother, 211, 497
Alex, Jean d'Arenthon d', bp. of Geneva, 31–32
Alexander III, pope, 21
Alexander VII, pope, 8
Amalek, 494

Ambrose of Milan, xiii, 57, 116, 123, 131, 132, 143, 317, 358, 364, 390, 391, 406, 450, 454, 461, 483, 490, 491, 513, 534, 535, 536
Amplexus, miracle of the, 118, 146, 361, 379–80, 405–6, 533
Anacletus II, antipope, 77, 93–95, 153, 195, 227, 259–60, 306, 307, 342, 343, 420, 477–78, 521–22, 532, 550–52, 553, 554, 556, 557, 559, 560, 561, 563, 564, 565
Angoulême (Charente), 94
Anne of Austria, queen consort of France, 1, 136–37, 143, 189
Annonciades, convent, Paris, 148
Anselm of Canterbury, 47
Anselme, Antoine, abb. of Saint-Sever, 24, 72, 75, 421, 446–63, 484, 534, 537, 538, 549, 554, 557, 558, 559, 563, 567

Antin, Louis-Antoine, marquis d', 447
Antony of Egypt/Antony the Great, 120, 535
Antwerp, 109
Aquinas, Thomas. *See* Thomas Aquinas
Aquitaine, 129, 253, 551, 565
Archimedes, 403–4, 535
Ardutio, bp. of Geneva, 114
Aristotle, 56, 196, 416, 422, 429, 440, 536
Arius of Alexandria, 317, 451
Ark of the Covenant, 493, 521, 522
Arnauld, Catherine, 24
Arnold of Bonneval, 20–21, 140, 196, 255, 277, 297, 332, 551, 557, 560, 565–66
Arnold of Brescia, 16, 132, 145, 420, 440, 478, 532, 552–53, 554, 557
Athanasius of Alexandria, 317, 451, 534, 535
Athens, 131
Aubignac (Haute-Loire), 117
Augsburg, 18
Augustine of Hippo, xiii, 9–10, 11–12, 18, 38, 43, 47, 53, 57, 76, 95–96, 98, 116, 124–25, 127, 131, 132, 145, 187, 196, 209, 317, 358, 361, 364, 370, 381, 384, 389, 390, 394, 400, 406, 414, 429, 440, 444, 450, 454, 461, 462, 483, 491, 500, 534, 535, 536, 540, 541, 545
Augustinians, 273
Austria, 22
Avignon (Vaucluse), 64

Babylon, 246
Balzac, Honoré de, 409
Bar-le-Duc (Meuse), 492
Baronius, Caesar (Cesare Baronio), card., 57, 137, 141, 144, 145, 358, 392, 404, 407, 467, 484, 537
Basil the Great, 131, 451, 452, 461, 534, 535
Basil of Seleucia, 407, 536
Bastille, La, Paris, 45, 274
Baucis and Philemon, 410, 417–18, 536
Bausset, Louis-François de, card., 191
Beaufort, Eustache de, abb. of Sept-Fons, 486
Beauvilliers, Paul de, duke of Saint-Aignan, 47
Bede, the Venerable, 57, 358, 364, 389, 536
Beersheba, 494
Bell, David N., 539, 544
Benedict of Nursia and the Benedictine Rule, 101, 102, 103, 117, 151, 152, 154–55, 158–59, 166, 174, 181, 346, 364, 390, 491, 503, 533, 535, 536–37
Benjamin, 469, 483
Benjamites, 518
Berger, David, 16
Bernard of Clairvaux, *passim*
Bernardus Silvestris, 18
Bertran, Edmund, 66
Bérulle, Pierre de, Oratorian, card., 398, 407, 537
Beussan, priory, 73
Biroat, Jacques, Cluniac, xii, 10, 24, 57, 60, 71, 72, chap. 4

passim, 109, 113, 126, 133, 152, 153, 244, 465, 531, 535, 536, 537, 550, 555, 557–58, 563
Blair, Hugh, 65–66
Blampignon, Émile-Auguste, 492
Blampignon, Nicolas, 74–75
Blois (Loir-et-Cher), 45
Boethius, 556
Bona, Giovanni, card., 47
Bonaventure and ps.-Bonaventure, 57, 76, 358, 359, 363, 365, 370, 387–88, 537
Bordeaux (Gironde), 69, 73, 129
Bossuet, Jacques-Bénigne, bp. of Meaux, xi, xii, xiv, 4, 6, 15, 16, 34–35, 41, 45–48, 50, 54, 55, 57, 58, 60, 61, 63, 67, 69–70, 72, chap. 7 passim, 236, 237, 238, 239, 240, 241, 242, 243, 271, 272, 274, 275, 278, 279, 280, 356, 357, 430, 433, 462, 487, 530, 532, 535, 536, 547, 549, 550, 554, 557, 559
Boudon, Henri-Marie, archdeacon of Évreux, xi, 25, 50, 57, 72, 118, 127, 131, chap. 11 passim, 397, 399, 401, 404, 405, 406, 407–8, 457, 475, 479, 483, 491, 531, 533, 534, 536, 537, 538, 539, 542–43, 549, 555, 559, 567
Bourbon, Françoise-Marie de, 464
Bourdaloue, Louis, Jesuit, xiv, 53–54, 55, 58, 60, 63, 67–68, 70–71, 149, 185, 242, 243, 272, 273, 433, 448, 488, 489
Bourges (Cher), 562

Bourru, Louis-Bénigne, Oratorian, 72, 401, 404, 421, 434, 444, 446, 463–84, 532, 533, 534, 535, 537, 538, 553, 555
Brabant, Marie, duchess of, 143
Bredero, Adriaan, 19, 21–22, 563
Bretonneau, François, 273, 280, 321–22
Brunetière, Ferdinand, 488
Brutus, 410, 421–22, 422
Burgundy, Louis de France, duke of, 47, 237–38
Burnet, Gilbert, bp. of Salisbury, 67
Bussy-Rabutin, Roger de, 60

Calvin, John and Calvinism, 12–13, 136, 532, 545, 559; see also Protestants and Protestantism
Cambrai (Nord), 237
Canaan, 505
Canada, 271
Carcassonne (Aude), 58
Carthage, 131
Carthusians, 22, 301, 377, 437, 471
Casey, Michael, 25
Cassiodorus, 134, 537
Cassius, 410, 421–22
Castel Sant'Angelo, Rome, 31, 65
Cato the Elder, 401–2
Caumartin, Louis-Urbain Lefebvre de, 430
Cephas, 522
Châlons-sur-Marne (Marne), 290, 329, 383, 561
Champvallon, François de Harlay de, abp. of Paris, 149

Champagne, 562
Chantelou, Claude, Maurist, 19
Charenton, Paris, 33
Charpentier, Marc-Antoine, 2
Chartres (Eure-et-Loir), 142, 342, 343, 478, 556
Chartreuse, la Grande, abbey, 169
Châtillon-sur-Seine (Côte-d'Or), 382, 401, 436, 468, 470
Chaudon, Louis-Mayeul, Cluniac, 117, 128, 463
Chelles, abbey, 464
Chérot, Henri, xiii, 273, 275, 321
Chiron, 120, 128, 535
Cîteaux, abbey, 102–3, 112, 138, 155, 194, 214, 223, 239, 249, 276, 286, 321, 326 (Order of), 360, 382, 394, 402, 404, 437, 468, 478, 490, 501, 504, 531
Clairvaux, abbey, 21, 81, 88, 100, 121, 130, 139, 155, 186, 195, 225, 226, 231, 239, 250–51, 252–53, 258, 286, 321, 348, 377, 394, 402, 405, 442, 473, 490, 491, 504, 505, 511, 516, 526, 531, 533, 554
Clanchy, Matthew T., 550
Claudian, 407, 536
Clement XI, pope, 13
Clement of Alexandria, 47
Cleopas, 137
Clermont (Puy-de-Dôme), 487
Cluny and Cluniacs, 103, 194, 309, 346, 554, 563
Coincy, Cluniac priory, 73
Collet, Pierre, 408
Cologne, 18, 22, 475
Condom (Gers), 189, 399

Congrégation des Doctrinaires, 430
Constance, 132, 240, 264, 475, 533
Constantine I/Constantine the Great, 340
Constantinople, 451
Conrad, duke of Burgundy, 90
Conrad III of Hohenstaufen, king of Germany, 114, 265, 294, 321, 330
Costello, Hilary, 23
Couperin, François and Louis, 2
Court, Jean-François. *See* Albert, Antoine, and Court, Jean-François
Cousin d'Avallon, Charles-Yves, 134
Cragg, Gerald, 51–52
Crawford, Henry, 66–67
Crusade, Second (1147–1149), 240, 262–63, 344, 421, 445, 458–60, 463, 475, 481–82, 483, 490, 517–18, 534, 554, 562, 565
Cyprian of Carthage, 43
Cyril of Alexandria, 317

Dagon, 493, 521
Dan, 494
Daniel, 490, 522, 535
Dargan, Edwin, 56, 63, 488
David, king, 115, 169, 178, 269, 281, 303, 323, 366, 505, 514
Descartes, René, 484
Demosthenes, 185
Dijon (Côte-d'Or), 186, 188
Dionysius the Areopagite, *ps.*-, 57, 358, 360, 361, 372–73, 381–82, 385, 480, 483, 536

Discalced Carmelites, Paris, 148
Domène, Cluniac priory, 563

Edessa, fall of (1141), 460
Egypt, 120, 121–22, 126, 134, 251, 395, 493, 499, 507, 511, 535
Elba, 65
Eleanor of Aquitaine, queen consort of France and England, 490, 514–15, 561
Eli, 493, 494
Elijah, 179, 490, 511, 515, 535
Elisha, 527
Elizabeth I, queen of England, 14
Emmaus, 137
England, 45, 53, 58, 94, 141, 143, 308, 547, 557; *see also* Henry I, king of England
Esther, 469
Étampes, council of (1139), 77, 94, 114, 125, 140, 239, 259, 279, 308, 343, 441, 452, 477, 491, 522, 551, 556–57, 561
Eugenius III, pope, 90, 100, 114, 135, 262, 278, 305–6, 329, 340, 349, 364, 393, 394, 419–20, 421, 443–44, 457, 459–60, 481, 490, 515, 533, 552, 553–54, 555
Eusebius of Caesarea, 127, 537
Eutyches, 317
Évreux (Eure), 354–55, 358
Ezekiel, 304–5, 339, 382
Ezra, 125, 535

Falmagne, Hilin/Hillin de, abp. of Trèves, 186, 231
Fastred of Clairvaux, 57, 155, 537
Favier, Jean, 148
Félibien des Avaux, André, 150–61
Fénelon, François de Salignac de la Mothe-, abp. of Cambrai, xi, xiii, 16, 33–36, 45–49, 50, 57, 62–63, 67, 68, 71, 72, 115, chap. 8 *passim*, 272, 273, 274, 275, 277, 278, 279, 280, 320, 321, 322, 356, 411, 421, 458, 530, 532, 533, 534, 535, 536, 540, 544, 546, 547, 549, 550, 554–55, 559, 560, 561, 564
Feuillants and Feuillantines, 17, 75–76, 111, 118, 133–34, 238, 280, 281, 358, 365, 390, 396, 409, 411, 428, 433, 448, 463
Flameng, Guillaume, monk of Clairvaux, 23
Flanders, 253
Fléchier, Valentin-Esprit, bp. of Nîmes, 56, 60, 68, 71, 72, 75, 186, 397, 401, 407–8, 417, 419, 421, 426, 429, 430–45, 445, 448, 449, 469, 532, 533, 541, 553, 557, 567
Fontainebleau, Edict of (1685), 15, 236, 492
Fontaines-lès-Dijon (Côte-d'Or), 390–91, 469, 470
Foucarmont, abbey, 152
Fourneaux, Madame de, 355
France, *passim*
Francis/François de Sales, 34, 43, 44, 47, 57, 69, 272, 316, 358, 365, 395–96, 537
Francisco de Osuna, 546
François, Jean, Benedictine, 73

Franco-Spanish War (1635–1659), 411
Frankfurt am Main, 240–41, 265, 533
Frederick I Barbarossa, emp., 553
Fromentières, Jean-Louis de, bp. of Aire, 72, 109, 135–46, 559
Fronde, civil war of the, 2, 24, 195
Furetière, Antoine, 53

Galen, 175
Galluccio, battle of (1139), 564
Gassendi, Pierre, 484
Gaudry of Touillon, Bernard's uncle, 222, 478
Geoffrey V the Handsome, count of Anjou, 393
Geoffrey of Auxerre, 20–21, 139, 196, 458, 555
Geneva, 90–91 (count of), 140, 168 (lake), 378 (lake), 383, 405 (lake), 471 (lake)
Genoa, 290, 329
Geoffrey, bp. of Chartres, 115, 264, 565
Gerizim, Mount, 521
Germany, 22, 45, 94, 115, 187, 240, 253, 264, 291, 308, 329, 343, 426, 442, 517, 523
Gervaise, François-Armand, abb. of La Trappe, 149, 150
Getaria/Guetaria, battle of (1638), 411
Gex (Ain), 32
Gilbert of Hoyland, 57, 358, 359–60, 371, 376, 386, 537

Gilbert of Poitiers. *See* Gilbert de la Porrée
Gilbert de la Porrée, 77, 96, 97, 116, 127, 132, 140, 145, 153, 163, 240, 263, 274, 279, 313–15, 349–50, 364, 394, 403, 440, 451, 473, 477, 478, 491, 524, 532, 544, 550, 554–56
Gilson, Étienne, 25, 530–31
Godet des Marais, Paul, bp. of Chartres, 34
Goliath, 524
Gonzalès, Thyrse, Jesuit, 280
Goshen, 506
Goulu, Jean de Saint-François, Feuillant, 409
Greenaway, George W., 553
Gregory I/Gregory the Great, pope, xiii, 57, 76, 80, 112, 116, 123, 132, 138, 145, 196, 198, 358, 364, 390, 394, 406, 450, 451, 461, 534, 535, 536
Gregory of Nazianzus, 47, 76, 101, 131, 406, 451, 534, 535, 536
Gregory of Nyssa, 131, 134, 537
Grenoble (Isère), 290
Grury (Saône-et-Loire), 463
Guerric of Igny, 120, 127, 535, 537
Guigo II of La Chartreuse, 27–28, 541
Guy, Bernard's brother, 222
Guyenne, 94, 308
Guyon, Jacques, sieur du Chesnoy, 31
Guyon, Madame, and Quietism, xi, xiii, 17, chap. 3 *passim*, 71, 154–55, 187, 237, 238, 240,

chap. 9 *passim*, 320–21, 322, 354, 356, 357, 530, 535, 539, 541, 543, 544, 546, 547

Harding, Stephen. *See* Stephen Harding
Hebrew language, 391, 411, 466
Henrietta Maria, queen consort of England, Scotland, and Ireland, 188
Henry I, king of England, 77, 142, 162, 239, 259, 278–79, 306–7, 321, 342, 343, 364, 392, 441, 478, 556–57, 560
Henry II, king of England, 561
Henry III, king of France, 13, 187
Henry IV, king of France, 13–14
Henry V, king of Germany and Holy Roman Emperor, 560
Henry of Lausanne. *See* Henry of Toulouse
Henry Sanglier, abp. of Sens, 90, 114, 457, 463, 538, 557–58
Henry of Toulouse, 16, 77, 96, 116, 127, 132, 140, 145, 153, 163, 240, 263, 365, 403, 420, 440, 451, 473, 478, 491, 525, 532, 544, 558–59, 562
Hercules, 120, 128, 535
Hermes. *See* Mercury
Hilarion, 120, 535
Hildebert of Lavardin, 406–7, 537
Hippocrates, 175, 276, 288, 328
Hombeline, Bernard's sister, 224–25, 360, 516
Honorius II, pope, 83, 550
Horstius, Jacob Merlo, xii, 18–19, 20, 22–23, 25, 135, 155, 196, 536
Hosea, 118

Hugh of Saint-Victor, 453
Hurel, Augustin-Jean, 68, 128, 135, 136, 448
Hyères (Var), 486

Icard, Simon, 17
Immaculate Conception, feast of the, 456–57
India, 120, 535
Innocent II, pope, 77, 93–95, 96, 114, 125, 130, 140, 146, 153, 161, 162–63, 239, 252, 259, 308, 313, 342, 343, 392, 442, 473, 477, 491, 522, 523, 526, 551–52, 552, 554, 557, 559, 560, 561, 564
Innocent X, pope, 13
Innocent XI, pope, 8, 31, 33, 277
Innocent XII, pope, 48, 237, 274, 530
Investiture Controversy, 124, 240, 259, 559–60
Isaiah, 180, 238, 242, 246
Isis, 121, 127, 128
Israel, 493, 494, 496, 497, 502, 504, 507, 509, 513, 527
Issy, conference of, 35–36, 41, 45, 46, 274
Italy, 21, 32, 49, 94, 162, 240, 253, 260, 291, 308, 329, 343, 426, 517, 523, 551, 552, 554

Jacob, 397, 494, 505
Jacquinet, Paul, 410
Jael, 99
James, Saint, 567
Jansen, Cornelius, bp. of Ypres, and Jansenism, 11–13, 18, 24, 60, 355, 457, 488, 544
Jeremiah, 100, 266, 401, 535

Jerome, xiii, 57, 131, 132, 134, 317, 358, 360, 364, 373, 390, 391, 393, 406, 429, 450, 483, 534, 535, 536
Jerusalem, 143 (queen of), 264, 429, 519, 521
Jesuits, 5, 11, 13, 58, 60, 67, 70, 72, 73, 109, 128, 129, 146, 186, 271, 273, 280, 322, 488, 544
Jesus Christ, *passim*
Jews, 392, 452
Jezebel, 515
Job, 175, 522
John, Saint, 96, 201, 295
John the Baptist, 82, 120, 127, 241, 246–47, 258, 280, 284, 288, 490, 510, 535
John, abb. of Casamari, 459, 463
John Cassian, 47
John Chrysostom, 47, 57, 123, 131, 134–35, 217, 242, 267, 317, 406, 444, 451–52, 461, 483, 534, 535, 536
John of the Cross, 34, 47, 356
Johnson, Samuel, 134
Jonah, 490, 499, 535
Jonathan, 498
Joseph, 490, 505, 535
Joshua, 381
Judah, 504
Judas Maccabeus, 126, 535
Jupiter (Zeus), 418

Knight, Gillian R., 563
Knowles, M. David, 563
Knox, Ronald, 48
Koblenz, 65

Laban, 498
Lacombe, François, Barnabite, 31–33
La Bruyère, Jean de, 59
La Cour, Jacques de, abb. of La Trappe, 192
La Fère (Aisne), 354
La Font, Jean de, abb. of Grosbot, xiv
La Grâce-Dieu, abbey, 566
La Mothe, Jeanne-Marie Bouvier de. *See* Guyon, Madame, and Quietism
La Rochelle (Charente-Maritime), 129, 566
La Rue, Charles de, Jesuit, xi, xiii, 27, 50, 71, 72, 75, chaps. 9–10 *passim*, 354, 448, 535, 538, 541, 543, 544, 547, 550, 554–56, 557, 559, 562, 563, 564, 565, 567
La Trappe, abbey, 6, 147, 148, 150, 152, 155, 156, 189–90, 191, 533
La Vallière, Louis de, 6
Lactation, miracle of the, 118, 146, 367, 401–2, 443, 457, 479, 483, 533
Langres (Haute-Marne), 329, 383
Languedoc, 271, 280, 322, 478
Lateran Council, Second (1139), 552
Latvia, 65
Lauder, Sir John, 58
Lavaur (Tarn), 431
Le Camus, Étienne, bp. of Grenoble, 32
Le Maistre, Antoine, xii, 22–25, 116, 135, 145, 196, 407, 450, 457, 463, 534, 536, 537, 553, 562–63, 565
Le Maistre, Isaac, 24
Le Mans (Sarthe), 135

Le Nain, Pierre, 148–49
Lebanon, 266, 517
Ledieu, François, 187, 191
Leo I/Leo the Great, pope, 317, 461
Leoni, Simone and Antonio Maria, 49
Liège, 252, 559
Ligny, Dominique de, bp. of Meaux, 190
Limoges (Haute-Vienne), 129
Lion, Claude, Oratorian, 72, 118, 127, 365, 397, 398–408, 430, 457, 469, 475, 479, 481, 531, 533, 535, 536, 537
L'Isle-Jourdain (Gers), 446
Lister, Martin, 58, 59
Locke, John, 58
Lord's Prayer, 30, 277, 280, 299, 318
Lorraine, 143 (duchess of), 186, 195
Lothair III of Supplinburg, emp., 124, 142, 162, 239–40, 259, 278, 306, 340–41, 441, 478, 559–60
Louis II, prince de Condé, 67, 70, 185
Louis VI the Fat, king of France, 77, 94, 114, 124, 133, 142, 240, 261, 279, 307, 308, 441, 490, 513, 551, 557, 560–61
Louis VII the Younger, king of France, 124, 133, 142, 143, 240, 261, 341–42, 344, 364, 391, 490, 513, 561–62, 565
Louis IX, Saint, 53, 64, 69, 447, 561–62
Louis XIII, king of France, 1, 14, 136
Louis XIV, king of France, xi, 1–3, 15–16, 18, 26, 33, 48, 51, 63–64, 72, 128, 136, 185, 186, 188, 189, 237, 411, 430–31, 433, 446, 447, 464, 484, 485, 487, 492, 530, 538, 544
Louis XV, king of France, 464, 487
Louis XVIII, king of France, 65
Louvre, the, Paris, 110, 188
Loyola, Ignatius, 540
Lucifer. *See* Satan
Luke, Saint, 242, 374
Lully, Jean-Baptiste, 2–3
Lyon, 456

Mabillon, Jean, Maurist, xii, 19–20, 22–23, 25, 155, 196, 536
Magdeburg, 393
Maintenon, Françoise d'Aubigné, marquise de, 33–35, 45, 237
Marenbon, John, 556
Marie-Thérèse, queen of France, 188, 447
Marseille (Bouches-du-Rhône), 398, 486
Martha, 480
Martin, Henri-Jean, 4–5
Mary, sister of Lazarus, 480
Mary, the Virgin, 5, 54, 79, 117, 119, 130, 138, 146, 193, 197–98, 201, 211, 247, 260, 277, 284, 298, 324, 357, 358–59, 367–68, 380, 400, 401–2, 434–35, 449, 455–57, 467, 474, 479, 496, 531, 534–35, 566
Mascaron, Jules, Oratorian, 68
Massillon, Jean-Baptiste, Oratorian, xii, xiii, 16, 55, 56,

Index of Names and Places 583

60, 68, 71–72, 120, 133, 143, 185, 242, 272, 403, 462, 482, 484, chap. 14 *passim*, 532, 535–36, 537, 546, 549, 557, 559, 561, 565
Massillon, Joseph, Oratorian, 492
Matarasso, Pauline, 558
Matthew, Saint, 374
Matthew, duke of Lorraine, 186, 195
Maupas du Tour, Henri de, bp. of Évreux, 355, 356
Maury, Jean-Sifrein, card., 64–66, 185, 242–43, 432, 489
Maximus of Turin, 57, 76, 81, 537
Mazarin, Jules Raymond, card., 1–2
McManners, John, 7
Meaux (Seine-et-Marne), 190–92
Mercury (Hermes), 418, 420
Metz (Moselle), 186–88, 195, 231–32, 235, 240, 262, 264
Mews, Constant J., 550
Midian, 509
Mignano, treaty of (1139), 564
Milan, 21, 31, 87, 94, 258, 259, 290, 294, 308, 329, 383, 451, 475, 478, 551
Molière, Jean-Baptiste Poquelin, known as, 3
Molinos, Miguel de, xiii, 27–31, 32, 33, 49, 50, 277, 541
Mombrizio, Bonino, 21
Montargis (Loiret), 31
Montbazon, Marie d'Avaugour de Bretagne, duchesse de, 147
Montbrison (Loire), 486

Montespan, Françoise-Athénaïs de Rochechouart, marquise de, 64, 447, 464
Montespan, Louis-Henri de Pardaillan de Gondrin, marquis de, 447
Montesquieu-Volvestre (Haute-Garonne), 76
Montpellier (Hérault), 431
Mordecai, 469
Moselle, river, 186
Moses, 97, 114, 120, 121, 131, 139, 142, 161, 336, 373, 451, 490, 499, 509, 512, 516, 517, 520, 523, 535
Murray, A. Victor, 550

Naaman, 527
Naboth, 515
Nantes, Edict of (1598), 14–15, 236
Nantes, Revocation of the Edict of. *See* Fontainebleau, Edict of (1685)
Napoleon Bonaparte, 65
Nestorius, 317
Neufbourg, Le (Manche), 355
Neufville de Villeroy, Camille de, abp. of Lyon, 486
Newhauser, Richard, 542
Newman, Martha G., 558
Nicaea, council of (325), 451
Nîmes (Gard), 431
Nivard, Bernard's brother, 194, 223, 239, 248–49, 402
Noailles, Louis-Antoine de, bp. of Charenton-sur-Marne, abp. of Paris, 35, 47, 487
Nocera, battle of (1132), 564
Norbert of Xanten, 551

Notre-Dame-de-la-Couldre, Parthenay, 308, 343, 566
Notre-Dame de Paris, 136–37
Notre-Dame-des-Victoires, Paris, 3

Ogier, Charles, 408
Ogier, François, 72, 75, 186, 397, 407, 408–30, 433, 438, 439, 440, 441, 442, 443, 444, 445, 449, 532, 535, 536, 537, 549, 553, 562
Oléron, château of, 33
Olier, Jean-Jacques, Sulpician, 10
Olives, Mount of, 380
O'Mahony, Denis, 55
Oratory of Jesus and Mary Immaculate, Congregation of the, 109–10, 135, 398–99, 407, 463, 486, 487
Orléans, 110, 487 (duke of)
Orléans, Louise Adelaide d', abbess of Chelles, 464
Osiris, 109, 121–22, 127, 128, 535
Osuna, Francisco de. *See* Francisco de Osuna
Otto of Freising, 463, 537
Ovid, 410, 418, 429, 536

Padua, 47
Palermo, 564
Papareschi, Gregorio. *See* Innocent II, pope
Paphnutius of Thebes, 155, 170
Paris, *passim*
Paris, Julien, abb. of Foucarmont, 152
Parthenay, château of, 565
Pasquet, François, prior of Grosbot, xiv

Paul, Saint, 42, 43, 48, 70, 76, 78, 83, 92, 95, 98, 111, 113, 125, 126, 130, 145, 161–62, 167, 170, 181, 189, 192, 196, 198, 202, 203, 205, 206, 207, 211, 217, 228, 229, 233–34, 267, 278, 284, 299, 306, 336, 352, 359, 362, 363, 369, 384, 388, 389, 405, 440, 453, 471, 497, 507, 522, 523, 536, 540, 543
Paul the First Hermit, 120, 155, 413, 535
Paulinus of Nola, 76, 90
Pavia, 308
Peach, Edward, 485
Pernes-les-Fontaines, 430
Perseigne, abbey, 148
Persius, 122, 127, 536
Peter, Saint, 93, 100, 106, 212, 214, 306, 308, 340, 380, 417, 426, 521
Peter Abelard, 77, 96, 97, 116, 121, 127–28, 132, 140, 145, 153, 163, 195, 240, 263, 274, 278, 279, 311–13, 315, 321, 347–49, 365, 403, 411, 420, 423–24, 425, 440, 451, 463, 473, 477, 478, 491, 524–25, 532, 538, 544, 547, 549–50, 552, 557
Peter of Bruys, 16, 420, 440, 532, 559, 562–63
Peter Chrysologus, 407, 537
Peter Leon (Pietro Pierleoni). *See* Anacletus II
Peter of Pisa, card., 260–61, 364, 391–92, 420, 551–52
Peter the Venerable, abb. of Cluny, 103, 177, 279, 309–10, 344, 346, 463, 537, 562, 563, 565

Index of Names and Places

Petit, Claude, 355
Petrobrusians. *See* Peter of
    Bruys
Petrucci, Pier Matteo, card., 49
Pézenas (Hérault), 486
Phidias, 185
Philemon. *See* Baucis and
    Philemon
Philip I, king of France, 560
Philistines, 493, 494, 524
Philo of Alexandria, 121, 127,
    131, 134, 145, 536
Phrygia, 418
Pisa, 553–54
Pisa, council of (1135), 259, 478,
    561
Pius VI, pope, 65
Pius VII, pope, 65
Pius IX, pope, 554
Planchette, Bernard, Maurist,
    72, 109, 117–28, 131, 145, 146,
    401, 406, 457, 479, 490, 531,
    533, 535, 536, 537, 538, 549,
    559, 560, 567
Plato, 56, 440, 451, 549
Poitiers (Vienne), 129
Pontas, Jean, 8
Port-Royal, abbey, 17, 24
Pourrat, Pierre, 49
Prosper of Aquitaine, 462, 537
Protestants and Protestantism,
    13–16, 32, 45, 61, 67, 188,
    195, 230, 236–37, 241, 267,
    271, 280, 431, 532, 545, 558,
    559; *see also* Calvin, John and
    Calvinism

Quesnel, Pasquier, Jansenist, 13
Quietism. *See* Guyon, Madame,
    and Quietism

Quintilian, 185

Rabi'a al'Adawiyya, 46
Rachel, 498
Rainald of Foigny, 20–21
Rambouillet, Catherine de
    Vivonne, marquise de, 4
Rameau, Jean-Philippe, 2
Rancé, Armand-Jean de, abb. of
    La Trappe, xi, 6, 9, 15, 54, 57,
    72, 146, chap. 6 *passim*, 186,
    189–92, 240, 356, 487, 532,
    533, 536, 537, 538, 542, 560,
    564
Raphael, 470
Ravaillac, François, 14
Reims, 19, 87, 117, 258, 290, 329,
    383
Reims, council of (1148), 77, 97,
    139, 314, 349–50, 394, 403,
    451, 477, 524, 532, 555–56
Reynolds, E. E., 34–35
Richard of Saint-Victor, 57, 358,
    363, 365, 370, 387, 537
Richelieu, Armand-Jean du
    Plessis, card. de, 1
Richenza of Northeim, queen of
    Lothair III, 559
Rignano, battle of (1137), 564
Roger II, king of Sicily, 77,
    94–95, 163, 240, 260, 321,
    342, 364, 392, 420, 441, 478,
    551–52, 560, 563–64
Rome, 27, 48, 65, 93, 95, 100,
    114, 245, 260–61, 306,
    308, 314, 343, 521, 552–53
    (Commune of)
Rouen (Seine-Maritime), 354,
    355, 358
Rudolf von Biberach, 359, 537

Rule of Saint Benedict. *See* Benedict of Nursia and the Benedictine Rule
Rupert of Deutz, 57, 358, 364, 389, 537

Saint-Cyr (Yvelines), 33–34, 35
Saint-Cyran, Jean du Vergier de Hauranne, *abbé* de, 24
Saint-Denis, Paris, 484, 514; *see also* Suger of Saint-Denis
Saint-Denis-des-Gastines (Mayenne), 135
Saint-Germain-des-Prés, Paris, 19, 22
Saint-Germain-en-Laye, Paris, 1, 411
Saint-Magloire, Paris, 110, 135, 138, 487
Saint-Maur, Congregation of, 117, 128
Saint-Merry, Paris, 74
Saint Paul-Saint Louis, Paris, 67
Saint Petersburg, 65
Saint-Pierre-sur-Dives (Calvados), 117
Saint-Pierremont (Ardennes), 19
Saint-Remi, Reims, 19, 117
Saint-Sever, abbey, 447
Saint-Séverin, abbey, 431
Saint-Simon, Claude-Henri de Rouvroy, comte de, 3, 51
Saint-Sulpice, Paris, 10, 35, 236
Saint-Vorles, Châtillon-sur-Seine, 401, 436, 443, 468, 483, 533
Sainte-Catherine, Léonard de, Augustinian, 273
Sainte-Marthe, Abel-Louis de, Oratorian, 399

Salerno, 260, 342, 551, 564
Sales, Francis/François. *See* Francis/François de Sales
Samuel, 479, 489, 493, 494, 495, 503, 506, 513, 515, 523, 527, 535
Sanders, Ella, 4
Santiago de Compostela, 344, 566
Sarlat (Dordogne), 115, 140, 146, 240, 264, 475, 533
Satan, 256–57, 332, 361, 376, 380, 382–83, 472, 499
Sauer, Lorenz, Carthusian, 22
Saul, 527
Sauxillanges, priory, 563
Scotland, 551
Seille, river, 186
Senault, Jean-François, Oratorian, 69, 72, 109–17, 118, 127, 128, 133, 135, 138, 146, 433, 531–32, 536, 549, 554, 557, 559, 565
Seneca the Younger, 116, 536
Sens (Yonne), 290
Sens, council of (1141), 77, 97, 132, 139, 313, 348, 424, 440, 451, 477, 524, 525, 550, 552, 557
Sept-Fons, abbey, 486
Sévigné, Marie de Rabutin-Chantal, marquise de, xiv, 60, 64, 67, 185, 438, 446
Shiloh, 493, 494
Sicily, 392, 523, 551; *see also* Roger II, king of Sicily
Soissons (Aisne), 103
Solignac, Aimé, 547
Solomon, king, 125, 288, 328, 535
Somerville, Robert, 561
Spain, 1, 27, 143, 291, 308, 411

Stephen, bp. of Metz, 186, 195
Stephen Harding, abb. of Cîteaux, 194, 214, 249, 490, 501–2
Stiegmann, Emero, 558
Suger of Saint-Denis, 114, 279, 309–10, 344–45, 490, 514, 565
Surius, Laurentius. *See* Sauer, Lorenz

Tarascon (Bouches-du-Rhône), 430
Teresa of Ávila/Teresa of Jesus, 34, 57, 69, 155, 316, 354, 356, 358, 362, 365, 386, 483, 537, 539, 540, 546
Tertullian, 57, 116, 127, 134, 242, 268, 358, 362, 385, 406, 422, 429, 462, 474, 483, 536
Tescelin, Bernard's father, 225, 497, 505
Texier, Claude, Jesuit, 72, 109, 128–35, 146, 532, 537, 553
Thalassius of Syria, 407, 537
Thaumaturge of the West, the, 367, 404, 467, 475
Theodoret of Cyrrhus, 57, 358, 378, 537
Theodosius I, emp., 143, 514
Thibault, count of Champagne, 124, 240, 261, 341, 561, 562
Thirty Years' War (1618–1648), 1, 188, 411
Thomas Aquinas, 6, 10, 47, 55, 57, 358, 361, 363, 365, 382–83, 387, 407, 470, 483, 537
Thomas à Kempis, 545
Tiber, river, 553
Tinsley, Lucy, 543, 547
Tivoli, 554
Toul (Meurthe-et-Moselle), 187

Toulouse (Haute-Garonne), 76, 129, 139, 446, 447, 525
Touraine, 273
Tours (Indre-et-Loire), 21
Tre Fontane, abbey, 554
Trent, council of (1545–1563), 53
Tréverret, Armand-Germain de, 68–71, 77, 110–11, 192–93, 243–45, 272–73, 409, 410, 429, 432–33, 441, 473, 488–89, 490
Tronson, Louis, Sulpician, 35
Troyes (Aube), 23
Trublet, Nicolas-Charles-Joseph, *abbé*, 431, 433, 489
Turks, Ottoman, 433
Tyre, 494

Vacandard, Elphège, 530, 559
Val-de-Grâce, Paris, 136
Valencia, 27
Van Eijnatten, Joris, 55, 63
Van Elswijk, H. C., 556
Vassy/Wassy, massacre of (1562), 14
Vaugirard, convent, Paris, 45, 274
Velat, Bernard, xiii
Vendôme (Loir-et-Cher), 117
Venice, 65
Verdun (Meuse), 187
Versailles, palace of, 3, 52, 63, 72, 464, 486, 487
Vézelay (Yonne), 562, 563 (Cluniac priory)
Vienna, 433
Vienne (Isère), 290, 486
Villeneuve-sur-Lot (Lot-et-Garonne), 195
Villers, Henri de, abp. of Vienne, 486
Vincennes, château of, 33, 45

Vincent of Lérins, 60–61
Virgil, 271
Visitation, convent of the, Meaux, 45
Visitation, convent of the, Paris, 33
Vitry-en-Perthois (Marne), 124, 142, 341, 490, 513, 561–62
Voltaire, François-Marie Arouet, known as, 52
Volusianus, 381

Wakefield, Walter L., and Evans, Austin P., 558–59
Wesley, John, 58–59
Westphalia, treaty of (1648), 1, 188
William X, duke of Aquitaine, 77, 94, 114, 123–24, 128, 132, 143, 153, 161, 195, 229, 240, 259–60, 279, 308–9, 321, 343–44, 441, 473, 478, 491, 523, 532, 551, 565–67
William of Champeaux, bp. of Châlons-sur-Marne, 239, 252
William of Newburgh, 458, 463, 537
William of Saint-Thierry, 18, 20–21, 57, 138, 195, 196, 226, 239, 251, 358, 360, 374, 401, 405, 407, 479, 491, 536, 537, 538
Williams, Watkin, 25, 530, 553, 558, 559, 561, 562, 565, 567
Worms, concordat of (1122), 560

Zainer, Günther, 18
Zeno of Verona, 58, 358, 362, 385, 537

www.ingramcontent.com/pod-product-compliance
Lightning Source LLC
Chambersburg PA
CBHW020630300426
44112CB00007B/74